SmartBRICS

Luca Belli • Larissa Galdino de Magalhães Santos
Editors

SmartBRICS

How the BRICS Countries are Regulating their Digital Transformation

Springer

Editors
Luca Belli
Center for Technology & Society
FGV Rio Law School
Rio de Janeiro, Brazil

Larissa Galdino de Magalhães Santos
Electronic Governance Unit (UNU-EGOV)
United Nations University
Guimarães, Portugal

ISBN 978-3-031-98203-3 ISBN 978-3-031-98204-0 (eBook)
https://doi.org/10.1007/978-3-031-98204-0

This Springer imprint is published by the registered company Springer Nature Switzerland AG
The registered company address is: Gewerbestrasse 11, 6330 Cham, Switzerland

Preface

It is with great satisfaction that we present the book "SmartBRICS: How the BRICS Countries Are Regulating Their Digital Transformation" as one of the research outcomes of an exceptional collaboration between CTS-FGV, the Center for Technology and Society at Fundação Getúlio Vargas Law School, Rio de Janeiro, and UNU-EGOV, the United Nations University Operating Unit on Policy-Driven Electronic Governance. This work emerges from the Memorandum of Understanding recently established between the two institutions, reflecting their joint commitment to promoting and improving digital governance and digital transformation practices within the public sector.

The partnership between CTS-FGV and UNU-EGOV reinforces the vital role of international cooperation in promoting knowledge, innovation and effective governance in the public sector and society. This research output was developed in the context of the CyberBRICS/SmartBRICS project with the goal of exploring how leading emerging economies are shaping their digital transformation. We hope that this book will support the improvement of data governance strategies in the public sector, inspiring future initiatives and research in the area.

This book reflects the institutions' ongoing commitment to academic excellence and joint experience in the search for effective and innovative solutions in the field of digital governance. The topics covered highlight the best practices and challenges faced in data governance in the contemporary scenario.

Enjoy the reading!

Rio de Janeiro, Brazil — Luca Belli
Guimarães, Portugal
September 16, 2025 — Larissa Galdino de Magalhães Santos

About CTS-FGV and UNU-EGOV

The Center for Technology and Society at FGV Law School, Rio de Janeiro, was founded in 2003, becoming the first research center to have been established in Brazil to analyze the impact of technology on society. The mission of CTS-FGV is to study the legal, social, and cultural implications arising from the advancement of information and communication technologies. Over the past 20 years, CTS-FGV has played a key role, shaping the Brazilian, Latin American, and global digital policy ecosystem, conducting research, and stimulating dialogue with a wide range of stakeholders, including governments and regulators, international organizations, businesses, research centers, and civil society organizations.

CTS-FGV has organized more than 100 international events and published more than 300 research outcomes on a variety of digital governance issues, including Internet access, platform regulation, data protection, AI governance, cybersecurity, online content moderation, digital transformation, and smart city governance. More than 100 researchers from 30+ nationalities have worked at CTS-FGV, and most of the CTS-FGV publications can be accessed in open access in the FGV Digital Library as well as at www.cts.fgv.br

Since 2018, the CyberBRICS Project has been hosted by CTS-FGV. CyberBRICS is the only existing research project dedicated to the analysis of digital policies in the BRICS (Brazil, Russia, India, China, and South Africa) countries. The purpose of the CyberBRICS project is to map existing regulations, identify good practices, and suggest policy solutions in the areas of cybersecurity, data governance, digital transformation, and artificial intelligence regulation. Particularly, the project aims at exploring the conditions and reasons that have led to "success stories" in terms of digital transformation in the BRICS countries. The project has organized a large number of international events, elaborated numerous research outcomes, and built a solid international network and academic credibility. All outcomes are available on www.cyberbrics.info

The United Nations University Operating Unit on Policy-Driven Electronic Governance (UNU-EGOV) is a global think tank based in Portugal (Guimarães) since 2014, focused on research, advice, and training in the area of digital governance, bridging the gap between research and public policy in this field. An integral part of the United Nations University, UNU-EGOV's mission is to support the United Nations (UN) and its Member States in transforming the mechanisms of governance and building effective governance capabilities through the strategic application of digital technologies. As such, UNU-EGOV contributes to inclusive social and economic development, environmental sustainability, and peace and security.

Considered as an international reference in the field of digital governance and a solid partner in the UN system, UNU-EGOV brings together a multidisciplinary and multicultural team of more than 30 researchers from 18 nationalities working on complex problems and emerging challenges. Since its establishment, UNU-EGOV has developed more than 60 digital governance projects in more than 18 countries, collaborated with 19 international organizations, organized more than 90 events, and produced more than 300 publications. UNU-EGOV coordinates and organizes the annual ICEGOV Conference, bringing together a community of more than 6,500 authors, academics, researchers, and professionals working in the field of digital governance.

UNU-EGOV coordinates and organizes the annual ICEGOV Conference, a significant and structured source of rich research, policy insights, and networking, reaching a global community of more than 6500 academics, researchers, and professionals from at least 96 countries. More information about UNU-EGOV's operations and publications is available at www.egov.unu.edu/.

FGV DIREITO RIO
CENTRO DE TECNOLOGIA
E SOCIEDADE

cyberBRICS

UNU

Contents

About the Editors and Contributors

About the Editors

Luca Belli, Ph.D., is Professor of Digital Governance and Regulation at the Fundação Getulio Vargas (FGV) Law School, Rio de Janeiro, where he directs the Center for Technology and Society (CTS-FGV) and the CyberBRICS project. Luca is also the editor of the International Data Privacy Law (IDPL) Journal, published by Oxford University Press, and Director of the Computers Privacy and Data Protection conference Latin-America (CPDP LatAm). He is currently a member of the Brazilian Presidency's National Cybersecurity Committee, a board member of the Global Digital Inclusion Partnership, and a member of the Steering Committee of the Forum for Information & Democracy. He is the author of more than 80 publications on law and technology, exploring data governance, cybersecurity, AI regulation, Internet access, and digital transformation. He has been consulted by several intergovernmental organizations and national regulators, including the Council of Europe, the International Telecommunications Union, the French Telecoms Regulator, etc. and his works have been quoted by numerous media outlets, including The Economist, Financial Times, Forbes, Le Monde, BBC, China Today, The Beijing Review, The Hill, O Globo, and Folha de São Paulo.

Larissa Galdino de Magalhães Santos is a Yufe4Postdoc, Marie Sklodowska-Curie at the Universität Bremen. Before, she was an Associate Researcher at the United Nations University, Electronic Governance Unit (UNU-EGOV). Larissa has been a CyberBRICS (FGV-CTS) scholarship recipient since 2020. Her research is located between digital governance, government technologies, open data, and responsible AI. She has collaborated with organizations such as the Global Center for AI Governance, the Latin American Open Data Initiative, and the Open Data Charter. She is also a Professional Fellow at Fundação Getúlio Vargas for Europe and a Ph.D. in Political Science from the State University of Campinas.

Contributors

Luca Belli Center for Technology & Society, FGV Rio Law School, Rio de Janeiro, Brazil

Senka Hadzic Research ICT Africa, Cape Town, South Africa

CyberBRICS, Law School, Fundação Getúlio Vargas, Rio de Janeiro, Brazil

Ikeng Lin NTPU Program on International Trade Negotiation, Taipei, Taiwan

Ministry of Foreign Affairs, Republic of China (Taiwan) and Taiwan Shilin District Court, Taipei, Taiwan

Larissa Galdino de Magalhães Santos Electronic Governance Unit (UNU-EGOV), United Nations University, Guimarães, Portugal

Anna Orlova São Paulo State University (UNESP), São Paulo, Brazil

Smriti Parsheera National Institute of Public Finance and Policy, New Delhi, India

Law School at Fundação Getúlio Vargas, Rio de Janeiro, Brazil

Andrey A. Shcherbovich Faculty of Law, Department of Constitutional and Municipal Law, National Research University Higher School of Economics, Moscow, Russia

Wayne Wei Wang University of Hong Kong, Pokfulam Road, Hong Kong SAR

CyberBRICS Project, FGV Rio Law School, Fundação Getúlio Vargas, Rio de Janeiro, Brazil

Untangling Digital Transformations in the BRICS Countries

Luca Belli and Larissa Galdino de Magalhães Santos

Abstract This chapter introduces the digital transformation agendas of the BRICS grouping, which are explored in this volume. We stress that digital transformation is a unique opportunity to achieve the United Nations Sustainable Development Goals (SDGs), triggering a structural change in existing economies, societies, and governance models, in synergy with technological projects. Therefore, we argue that digital transformation offers Global South countries in general and BRICS countries—namely, Brazil, Russia, India, China, and South Africa—in particular a unique opportunity of leapfrogging years of underinvestment in development to become global leaders in technology production, adoption and governance. In this context, this chapter provides an initial understanding of how the BRICS countries are planning and implementing their digital transformation processes, with particular regard to how they are evolving into "smart countries", reorganizing their digital public services and providing digital public goods. In offering this overview, we adopt a critical approach towards what constitutes the intelligence of a supposedly "smart country." Indeed, digital transformation processes are not exempt from criticism and, while mapping the digital transformation policies of the BRICS countries, this introductory chapter emphasizes that the grouping offers an ample range of success stories but also of telling tales revealing the challenges that emerging economies may face when shaping and implementing their digital transformation processes.

L. Belli (✉)
Center for Technology & Society, FGV Rio Law School, Rio de Janeiro, Brazil
e-mail: luca.belli@fgv.br

L. Galdino de Magalhães Santos
Electronic Governance Unit (UNU-EGOV), United Nations University, Guimarães, Portugal
e-mail: larissagms@yahoo.com.br

L. Belli, L. Galdino de Magalhães Santos (eds.), *SmartBRICS*,
https://doi.org/10.1007/978-3-031-98204-0_1

1 Introduction

The digital transformation agenda signals the search for solutions to economic, social, and environmental imbalances through the increasing adoption and use of digital technologies. Such transformation is a unique opportunity to achieve the United Nations Sustainable Development Goals (SDGs) (United Nations Department of Economic and Social Affairs, 2023), triggering a structural change in existing economies, societies, and governance models, in synergy with technological projects. Therefore, digital transformation has become a necessary condition to meet the challenges of the twenty-first century and offers Global South countries in general and BRICS countries—namely, Brazil, Russia, India, China, and South Africa and their increasing number of partners—in particular a unique opportunity of leapfrogging years of underinvestment in development to become global leaders.

In this context, this book aims to provide an understanding of how the BRICS countries are planning and implementing their digital transformation processes and how they are regulating such processes, with particular regard to how they are crafting their digital public services aimed at providing digital public goods. We map policies, regulations, and initiatives adopted by the BRICS to achieve the ambitious goal of becoming "smart" countries, in which the functioning of the economy, society, and democratic governance is supported and enhanced by technology, thus unleashing a remarkable evolution. In providing this overview, we adopt a critical approach towards the intelligence of a supposedly smart country. Indeed, digital transformation processes are not exempt from criticism, and, from this perspective, this book also provides useful insight not only regarding success stories but also regarding the limits of the approaches adopted by the BRICS countries.

Like most large economies, BRICS countries have adopted successive strategies to strengthen their industrial and technological capabilities through technology, building their "digital sovereignty."[1] In this publication, we adopt the definition of digital sovereignty as "the capacity to understand, develop and effectively regulate digital technologies, to retain agency, self-determination, and control over digital infrastructure, data, services, and protocols"[2] and we argue that digital transformation processes have a fundamental role in constructing digital sovereignty. In this perspective, this book needs to be read in conjunction with two other studies

[1] For an analysis of the concept of Digital Sovereignty, see: Jiang and Belli (2024), p. 21; Luca Belli et al. (2023), p. 52; Pohle and Thiel (2020), p. 3. For a digression on why emerging economies might be keen on building digital sovereignty narratives, see. Belli (2021), p. 273. For an introduction to the concept of Good Digital Sovereignty, the capacity to understand, develop, and regulate digital technologies and data, Belli (2023). For an analysis of AI sovereignty discussions and its connection with AI transparency and accountability, see Belli and Gaspar (2023).

[2] This definition is based on the previous works on digital sovereignty published in the context of the CyberBRICS project. See supra n 1. For an analysis of how such a concept applies to AI systems, see Belli (2023).

elaborated by the CyberBRICS Project,[3] which are dedicated respectively to "Digital Sovereignty in the BRICS: How the Global South and Emerging Power Alliances Are Reshaping Digital Governance"[4] and to "Digital Transformation in the BRICS."[5]

Over the past decade, the development of the digital economy has been a priority for BRICS countries, resulting in the adoption of multiple national strategies and policies to promote development. This book focuses particularly on two essentials yet much-neglected aspects of digital transformation, which should be seen as instrumental to trigger a sustainable digital transformation: the expansion of connectivity and the digitalization of public services. Indeed, we argue that connectivity and digitized public services, together with cybersecurity[6] represent key pillars of the sustainable transformation of states that will become truly smart countries.

The continuous expansion of digital products and services leveraged by technologies has been accompanied by improved Internet connectivity infrastructure, disrupting traditional sectors, social and political governance, and public administration. Hence, over the past two decades the scope of digital transformation has been increasingly expanded to the radical upgrade of the state structure. This transformation has been largely advocated for by the private sector, although we are witnessing a strong governmental push towards the digitization of the public sector for the provision of public services and public goods.

While the early 2000s already witnessed numerous calls for the promotion of "e-government," which nowadays sounds like a remarkably vintage concept, over the past years, governments have found themselves under the obligation to redefine the modus operandi of the public sector, turbocharging their digitalization process, especially under the enormous pressure brought by the COVID-19 pandemic. The implementation of digital transformation strategies resulted in new commitments related to using digital technologies to revolutionize public services, policy-making, and public governance. From automating government operations to improving processes and enabling conditions for citizens, businesses, and other entities, each strategy is sensitive to government capabilities to support digital transformation.

Over the past decade, the label "digital transformation" has been increasingly used as a buzzword, driving ambitious agendas toward the promotion of a digital

[3] Established in 2018, the CyberBRICS project has been supported by the Open Society Foundations (OSF), the Getulio Vargas Foundation (FGV), and the Ford Foundation in its different phases. The authors would like to express deep gratitude and praise the foresightedness of the founders, who have believed in the CyberBRICS project's potential to develop innovative research, exploring some extremely relevant areas of digital policy and regulation, from Global South perspectives. Detailed information about the CyberBRICS team, publications, and events are available at www.cyberbrics.info

[4] See supra n 1.

[5] Belli, L, Magalhães, L. (eds) (2024) Digital Transformation in the BRICS Countries. Computer Law & Security Review. https://www.sciencedirect.com/special-issue/10VRL9GGMQG

[6] The authors are mindful that cybersecurity is an essential dimension of digital transformation. However, the multiple facets of cybersecurity in the BRICS will not be analysed in this volume as the CyberBRICS project has already dedicated a previous publication to the issue. See: Belli L (eds) (2021) CyberBRICS: Cybersecurity Regulations in the BRICS Countries. Springer International Publishing AG, Cham.

economy. Importantly, digital transformation should be seen as a process, rather than as an end. Approaches to digital transformation have been driven by government reactions to expectations for a sustainable and digitized society in response to different political, economic, and social pressures.

As a result, governments have adopted digital transformation strategies and increased both their elaboration of digital policies and use of ICTs to support policymaking. Recent years have witnessed the emergence of data-driven policy modelling initiatives, regulatory sandboxes, and, after several years of austerity, also investments in research and development of tools to design and scale cutting-edge technologies such as cloud computing, Artificial Intelligence, 5G networks, and blockchain.

Consequently, these evolutions have triggered reflections and even controversies about digital sovereignty and technological innovation as a tool for dominance, as some countries become mere consumers of technologies, dependent on foreign suppliers, while (very few) others emerge as global technological winners.

To understand the impact of such radical updates in the functioning of national economies, societies, and democratic processes, we first need to introduce the BRICS countries. Such a preliminary introduction, presented in the section below, is also instrumental in understanding why the BRICS countries, due to their economic and geopolitical heft, as well as their ambitions, are likely to play an increasingly relevant role in shaping regional and international digital policies.

Subsequently, we will discuss why the analysis of the digital transformation of the BRICS countries is particularly relevant, especially for the Global South, whose members share many more similarities with the BRICS grouping rather than with the usual case studies of digital transformation in the developed world. Lastly, this chapter provides an overview of how the BRICS are structuring their evolutions into smart countries by transforming the provision of digital public services and, consequently, digital public goods.

1.1 What Are the BRICS, and How Have Their Interests in Digital Policies Evolved?

Few people know that the original BRICs[7] nations are the only existing countries—just five, together with the US—that are at the same time amongst the ten largest countries in the world by territory, by population, and by GDP. This peculiar situation confers enormous relevance to their policy choices and their politics, not only as regards their vast domestic environments but also—and perhaps more interestingly for our study—at the regional and global level.

[7] Here, BRICs is spelled with a small "s" because South Africa—which is the capital S in BRICS—presents considerable differences from the other BRICs countries and, indeed, was not contemplated in the original grouping and joined only at a later stage, with the first expansion of the group at the 2011 BRICS Summit in Sanya, after being formally invited at the 2010 Summit, in Brasilia.

It is useful to note that the five BRICS countries account for over 40% of the global population, or 3.2 billion people, and they account for 26% of global GDP and over 16% of global trade.[8] It is also useful to note that the increasing connectivity of these countries means that their population also represents 44% of the global Internet population,[9] as at 3.2 billion people can also be seen as up to 3.2 billion of personal data producers or "data subjects."[10]

The countries play significant leadership roles in their own regional systems as well as, to a lesser but growingly important extent, globally. In this perspective, we need to examine and understand their strategies, joint governance mechanisms, and policy choices to comprehend the significance of this alliance of emerging powers and why the BRICS' policy decisions are likely to have a significant impact, particularly on the Global South, as the grouping exercises increasing attraction of Global Majority countries.

In this regard, it is important to emphasize that the BRICS grouping is in a new expansion phase, discussed for almost a decade and finally implemented in 2023, when the grouping agreed to invite six new members: Argentina, Egypt, Ethiopia, Iran, Saudi Arabia, and the United Arab Emirates,[11] which were chosen amongst the 23 countries that have formally applied to join the grouping.[12] While Argentina's new President, Javier Milei, has later declined the invitation, the grouping has kept receiving expressions of interest from Global South countries, including some who have already joined the BRICS-led New Development Bank, which admitted Bangladesh, Egypt, the United Arab Emirates, and Uruguay as new members in 2021.[13]

It is also important to remind the readers that the initial goal of the BRICS acronym was not to imply the potential of political or normative collaboration, but rather to simply designate some of the main developing countries with some similar economic traits. Yet, a few years after Jim O'Neill, a Goldman Sachs economist,[14] coined the acronym, nations began to recognize the possibilities offered by a new

---

[8] See the official website of the Indian 2021 Presidency BRICS INDIA (2021) Ministry of External Affairs. https://brics2021.gov.in/about-brics. Accessed on 10 March 2025.

[9] Even though some BRICS countries such as China's aging population and declining birth rate pose considerable challenges to its long-term sustainable development Bai C, Lei X (2020) New trends in population aging and challenges for China's sustainable development. China Economic Journal 13:3–23. doi: https://doi.org/10.1080/17538963.2019.1700608

[10] This term is commonly utilised by data protection legal frameworks globally. For an overview of the data protection frameworks of the BRICS countries, see Belli L, Doneda D (2023) Data protection in the BRICS countries: legal interoperability through innovative practices and convergence. International Data Privacy Law 13:1–24. doi: https://doi.org/10.1093/idpl/ipac019

[11] See supra n (16). https://brics2023.gov.za/wp-content/uploads/2023/08/Jhb-II-Declaration-24-August-2023-1.pdf

[12] Tim Cocks. More than 40 nations interested in joining BRICS, South Africa says. Reuters. (July 20, 2023). https://www.reuters.com/world/more-than-40-nations-interested-joining-brics-south-africa 2023-07-20/

[13] New Development Bank (NDB) (s.d.). NDB'S member countries. New Development Bank. https://www.ndb.int/about-us/organisation/members/

[14] See (n. 1).

"post-Western" (Stuenkel, 2016) system of global governance. In this sense, the grouping has been created to foster a multipolar order where global governance and development do not depend on traditional Western driven institutions but can be led by the Global Majority, increasing relevance and benefits of developing countries.

Since the inception of the grouping, BRICS countries have developed into some of the most connected nations in the world, recognizing that the future of their economies and societies depends on digital transformation. At the same time, they have also been among the first countries to realize that such transformation, if not mustered, can easily become a considerable vulnerability and even a vector of "digital colonialism"[15] perpetrated by foreign tech giants, typically on behalf of foreign interests.

In this regard, one may contend that the disclosures made by former National Security Agency (NSA) contractor Edward Snowden were a significant catalyst for the BRICS countries' increasing interest in digital policies. In fact, since 2013, the BRICS have developed and put into effect a wide range of digital policies, laws, and regulations, specially aimed at strengthening cybersecurity and data regulation, reasserting their national sovereignty online, while fostering a digital transformation driven by local innovation.

Before even becoming BRICS with a capital S, the BRICs presidents gathered for the first time in 2009, and their inaugural Joint Declaration did not once use the words "digital" or "cyber." The XIV BRICS Summit Beijing Declaration, which was adopted on June 23, 2022, contains these terms 23 times. Following the Snowden revelations, BRICS leaders for the first time explicitly stated in their annual summit declaration the "paramount importance" of "security in the use of Information and Communication Technologies (ICTs)" (BRICS, 2013, p. 34). The BRICS ministers for science, technology, and innovation have been working together continuously since the 2013 Summit; they met for the first time in 2014 to strengthen their ties and develop new alliances.

Through an increasing number of shared documents on ICT cooperation (Kiselev & Nechaeva, 2018), beginning with the Memorandum of Understanding on Cooperation in Science, Technology, and Innovation (BRICS, 2015), the grouping structured the construction of the legislative frameworks within which intra-BRICS relationships and synergies might be formed. This progression culminated with the recent proposal for "legal frameworks of collaboration among BRICS States [and] a BRICS intergovernmental agreement on cooperation," as we will emphasize in the following section (BRICS, 2021, p. 27). The process aimed at creating partnerships, promoting joint research projects, and fostering policy synergies may be considered an example of what in Internet Governance vernacular is commonly referred to as "enhanced cooperation."[16]

---

[15] The concept of "data colonialism" is eloquently discussed in Couldry and Mejias (2019a), pp. 336–349.

[16] The concept of "enhanced cooperation" is introduced by paragraph 69 and 71 of the Tunis Agenda for the Information Society. See (n. 4). Importantly, the United Nations Economic and Social Council has acknowledged that "the Tunis Agenda underlines the need for enhanced coop-

Following the 8th Summit, the Goa Declaration took a more proactive stance towards BRICS-led policymaking initiatives, highlighting the BRICS countries' potential for cooperation that could "work together for the adoption of the rules, norms and principles of responsible behaviour of States including through the process of the United Nations Group of Governmental Experts (UNGGE)" (Belli & Doneda, 2023). The BRICS leaders crossed the Rubicon by stating the cooperative development of rules, standards, and principles publicly, clearly demonstrating their determination to further collaboration in the formulation of global digital policy. The BRICS Leaders 2021 Declaration marked yet another significant turning point because the countries have begun to express their stated interest in greater collaboration on these challenges.

In fact, the 2021 Declaration includes the BRICS Heads of State's explicit commitment to the "respect of the right to privacy of individuals" additionally promoting cybersecurity, "**advance[ing] practical intra-BRICS cooperation in this domain**, including through the implementation of the BRICS Roadmap of Practical Cooperation on ensuring Security in the Use of ICTs and the activities of the BRICS Working Group on Security in the use of ICTs, and underscore[ing] also the importance of **establishing legal frameworks of cooperation among BRICS States on this matter** and acknowledge[ing] the work towards consideration and elaboration of proposals, including on **a BRICS intergovernmental agreement on cooperation** on ensuring security in the use of ICTs and on **bilateral agreements among BRICS countries**" (BRICS, 2021) [emphasis added].

1.2 Why Is the Analysis of the Digital Transformations in the BRICS Necessary?

Despite its typically low profile, BRICS is a great learning laboratory for the world economy and global governance. Particularly, the analysis of BRICS countries' experiments with digital policy, digital cooperation, and digital transformation provides valuable lessons for the Global South. Indeed, digital policymaking, implementation of policies and strategies, and the various phases of digital transformation processes follow remarkably different dynamics and need to consider radically different contexts when they are designed and tailored to the specificities of the emerging economies of the developing world.

States' digital strategies and capabilities have been turbocharged and increasingly tested since the recent COVID-19 pandemic. During this urgent scenario, we have witnessed the development and adaptation of solutions for digitizing national economies, societies, and democracies, with mixed levels of success. While public

---

eration to enable Governments to carry out their roles and responsibilities in international public policy issues pertaining to the Internet [but does] not specify how the process of enhanced cooperation should be designed, the means by which enhanced cooperation could be achieved or how the desired results should manifest themselves in practice" (United Nations, 2011).

sector organizations started working with large datasets, embedding technologies to state functions and digitizing public services as fast as possible, the private sector consolidated the domain in development and provision of digital technologies and automatization, increasingly adopting Artificial Intelligence applications.

The ongoing platformization of the state is providing new capabilities and opportunities for governments and creating new risks, due to the massive use of data, the implementation of algorithmic tools as part of public management, and the need for proactive cybersecurity, open ecosystems and technologies, and the maintenance of inclusive policies and sustainable access to the Internet.

This movement highlights the need to define sound guidelines to orientate the path of digital transformation towards sustainability and avoid dystopian scenarios. Well-designed strategies, policies, executive agencies, and regulatory authorities are essential for the successful transition from the twentieth century analogue state to the twenty-first century smart state.

However, historically unsolved issues, such as socioeconomic inequalities, access to a stable electricity supply, connectivity gap in remote and rural areas, limited investments in public services, and concerns about security and the rule of law, result in structural obstacles that weaken the digital transformation capacity. Although the BRICS countries can take advantage of the opportunities of digital transformation, there are challenges that arise through the technological leap that must be considered in an agenda aimed at triggering sustainable changes.

On the one hand, there is a lack of an ecosystem approach capable of understanding the complexity of emerging technologies—such as Artificial Intelligence, Internet of Things, Big Data analytics, to name a few—and integrating them in a holistic vision capable of dealing with the abovementioned historically unsolved issues.

It is not just a question of reinvigorating the role of open and democratic governance and effective (crisis) management, but also of paying attention to conditions of power inequalities, digital colonialism, digital illiteracy, language barriers, and gender or racial discrimination. Such systemic vision is essential to achieve the SDGs and needs to be used to constantly test how the relative success or failure in the adoption of specific technologies fits into a larger vision of digital transformation towards sustainability.

Poorly designed dynamics of digital transformation generate processes that certainly contribute to perpetuating power imbalances, expanding the history of inequalities, technological dependence, concentration of control, and foreign exploitation of resources (including data) that generate profit elsewhere, paving the terrain for the perpetuation of violations and digital colonization (Couldry & Mejias, 2019b).

In this perspective, technological innovation must be seen in conjunction with the consolidation of governance structures, as well as the maintenance and financial sustainability of critical resources. It is important to understand that digital transformation relies not only on the performance of digital infrastructures but also on the dynamic capacity of public administrations to provide services that are essential for a sustainable technological development. Both the technological and governance dimensions are essential, and a sustainable digital transformation needs to rely on both to be successful.

The fundamental question that drives the elaboration of this volume is, therefore, how are BRICS countries reacting and building the complex digital public infrastructures and governance mechanisms that are needed to unleash sustainable digital transformations? In this book, we map, identify, and discuss critically the initiatives and processes that can be categorized—and frequently presented—as "digital transformation" to understand to what extent these actions potentially correspond to a systemic, inclusive, sustainable, fair, and sovereign digital transformation.

2 Digital Transformations, Digital Public Goods, and Public Digital Infrastructures in the BRICS

As noted, an important premise of this book is that a sustainable digital transformation needs to carefully combine technological and governance elements. In this perspective it is essential to explore how the BRICS countries are using digital transformation as a tool to expand access to digital technologies and provide digital public services and digital public goods in a more efficient, just, and inclusive fashion.

Importantly, several public services, such as education, police, justice, etc., are examples of public goods. Hence, both the new digital public infrastructures built to provide such services and the digitized version of such services can be seen as examples of digital public goods themselves. In this perspective, this volume investigates how these two relevant dimensions play out in the BRICS.

To map the state of BRICS digital infrastructures, with a particular focus on Internet access, we analyzed the context, international commitments, institutions, regulations, spectrum access, and financial resources that each of the BRICS is dedicating to connectivity. These complex architectures form the basis of digital public infrastructures of the BRICS countries.

Furthermore, this book analyses the digitization of BRICS public services, as an essential complement of the national digital public infrastructures. The analysis is structured exploring national strategies and priorities, regulations, institutions, and critical sectors, such as digital identity, Smart Cities and digitization of local administrations, digital money and payments, and other relevant examples.

3 Towards BRICS Digital Public Infrastructures

"Infrastructures are the systems that support more visible systems; infrastructures are often invisible until they break." Zuckerman (2020) warns that, although the shift from physical infrastructures towards digital public spaces seems like a natural movement, there is much more to our lives about the effect of these spaces, providing excellent reasons to be concerned.

From the same perspective, the recent pandemic has highlighted how complex the shift from offline to online spaces is and how many problems may arise when such a shift is not carefully planned and implemented. Such careful planning and implementation are, in the view of the authors, precisely the essence of the process that we can define as digital transformation.

While infrastructures are the systems that keep society functioning, the Digital Public Infrastructures (DPIs) are those that facilitate the operation of digital services for both the public and private sectors. The DPIs include Internet connectivity networks, cloud servers, digital transaction systems, data sharing and exchange systems allowing various public policy sectors to function, several forms of identification, and digital identity verification, among others. They are infrastructures that allow both the digitalization of public services and public goods, but also our participation in public and civic life through digital spaces.

Therefore, the analysis of DPIs is instrumental to allow us to understand the digital transformation in a holistic way, the systemic interaction of the elements of the digitalization of the state structures, and the technical elements related to the specific technologies used to support and regulate the transformation in given areas.

Importantly, the technological and policy choices behind the design and adoption of every DPI generate relevant positive and negative externalities. DPIs' benefits are distributed to all. However, collateral damage might be difficult to predict and propagate in remarkably complex ways, thus needing sound governance mechanisms and well-defined regulatory frameworks that consider the potential risks.

DPIs are particularly complex and not always scalable, as they are bulky infrastructures that cannot lack economic contributions for construction and maintenance, to be successful. Importantly, public institutions also play a role as essential infrastructures that operate as public goods and are instrumental in delivering public services. Due to their essential feature, public interest, and non-profitability, they are provided by governments rather than markets.

It is also important to stress the hardware and software dimensions of DPIs that are made up of technological tools and systems, from microchips to Internet cables, servers, software applications, Artificial Intelligence systems, etc., that are needed to maintain DPIs operational. Finally, the DPIs have a relevant regulatory function, shaping the flows of data, the functioning of online markets, and the availability of open resources—including databases, software, AI, etc.—in accessible and secure spaces.

3.1 Governance Focused on Public Value

The first chapter of this volume is dedicated to Brazil and explores the governance of the country's Digital Transformation Strategy through the lens of the New Public Management, stressing how the current system contributes to the scarce debate on what governance models are best suited to achieve democratic and sustainable digital transformation.

The study argues that efforts to promote the digital transformation strategy must be attentive to the composition of governance instances and, mainly, to the inclusion of multiple and heterogeneous stakeholders. Ideally, such diverse make-up should include actors with access to decision-making power; representatives of historically under-represented groups; organizations and networks articulating between local and global levels, private and public actors, under the scope of formal coordination; and specialists able to provide meaningful contributions and help leading and coordinating networks that are essential to implement a solid digital transformation strategy.

Lastly, the overall preoccupation of the governance of digital transformations should be a constant effort to develop solutions that lead to the creation or enhancement of public value and public interest. In this format, the elaboration and implementation of DPIs should aim at consensus solutions (if this is feasible), sharing and considering diverse experiences, empowerment with multiple actors, and the definition of safeguards against risks and accountability mechanisms.

3.2 The Importance of Digital Sovereignty Considerations

Data is an essential asset for digital transformation, and increasingly aware of the economic and strategic value of data, all BRICS countries are expanding their data protection, data security, and cybersecurity regulations. These regulatory systems are essential pillars of digital sovereignty and must be seriously considered for their long-term impact. The second part of this book, dedicated to Russia, investigates how state policies influence the development of the digital transformation strategy in a context challenged by the pandemic restrictions and the war with Ukraine.

On the one hand, the country made considerable efforts to facilitate the digitalization of the public administration and turbocharged resulting in investments in cloud technologies and remote work. On the other hand, the trend towards Internet isolation in Russia following the provisions of the Internet Sovereignty Act and aiming at the establishment of a Russian sovereign segment of the Internet, frequently dubbed "Runet," has shown that digital sovereignty discourse may have radical consequences on the prospect of a country.

From the perspective of the Internet Sovereign Law, digitalization programs must prioritize the use of national providers, local equipment, and national data centers. While these concerns are understandable to avoid foreign meddling, especially in a context of war, the prohibition of foreign software and hardware makes it extraordinarily challenging to guarantee the smooth operation of critical information infrastructures.

Furthermore, while digital sovereignty concerns may have a positive impact in stimulating local digital economy, innovation, and development, they can also be used to justify heavy state regulation and introduce surveillance and control measures in the digital environment.

3.3 Ability to Offer Public and Digital Services

The need for digital transformation is typically supported using democratic ideals, providing evidence of an increase in quality and accountability of public governance, and overall improvement of public administration organizational processes are often associated with. The combination of these elements usually increases the likelihood of providing good-quality public services. When it comes to the ability to deliver digital public services, it is essential to ensure easy access by design, especially for marginalized groups, and plan carefully how to support the digitalization of traditional public services through digital public infrastructures.

The third part of this book is dedicated to India and analyses the different facets of the many initiatives the country has developed at the national level as well as in the 28 states and 9 territories that compose it, paying attention to the influence played by the country's digital divides. As usually happens in very large and heterogeneous countries, the experience of connected users in less developed regions is considerably worse than in areas with higher income. Inter- and intra-state differences in digital access, skills, and infrastructure have corresponded to different levels of digital readiness and have an enormous impact on how the national plans for digital transformation need to be planned and executed.

As an instance, telecommunications licensing and right-of-way policies are divided into service areas in demarcations close to state lines, thus creating considerable complexity that needs to be dealt with to implement digital transformation strategies. To do so, the Indian government has launched digital portals, serving as a collaborative platform amongst stakeholders. While not digital portals can be deemed as a successful experience, some examples explored in this part can allow the reader to understand what factors are critical to deal with the complexity of digital transformation while also supporting inclusion.

3.4 Exploring All Financial Options

Digital transformation entails costs. To meet such relevant financial needs, the government needs to explore alternative options to finance the development and organization of DPIs. Some interesting perspectives are provided by the article opening the fourth part of this book, discussing the imperative of Chinese-style modernization, highlighting the Chinese government's normative entrepreneurship, and the constant yearning for public-private partnership measures able to guarantee the sustainability of the various digital transformation efforts.

The Chinese government has undertaken a radical digitalization program, adopting popular e-commerce platforms to facilitate the delivery of public services, or even shaping digital public services based on the experience of successful private digital platforms, and supporting the development of cloud servers and other digital infrastructures that are essential for the provision of all other services. Importantly, the Chinese experience offers several alternatives for financing and experimenting with business models supporting the digitization of public and private services.

3.5 *From Connectivity to Emerging Technologies*

With the increasing adoption of Information and Telecommunication Technologies, public sector organizations are targeting digital infrastructures that combine new generation hardware and software, AI systems, etc., in a way that facilitates data processing at scale for both public and private sectors. The Presidential Commission on the Fourth Industrial Revolution has been leading South Africa's digital transformation strategy, recognizing the essential value of the above-mentioned technologies for the proper functioning and performance of the connectivity infrastructure.

However, the current state of Internet access in the country is still one of the main obstacles to the achievement of a sustainable Fourth Industrial Revolution agenda. The last part of this book, dedicated to South Africa, discusses the value of connectivity as a fundamental pillar of a digital transformation that can be beneficial also for small and medium-sized players, acting as a key enabler of the SDGs.

4 Conclusion: What Is the Aim of This Book?

This book is one of the results of the CyberBRICS project and of its complementary phase called SmartBRICS, whose priority was to map how the BRICS countries are structuring their digital transformations, regarding Internet connectivity and telecommunications policy, and the digitization of public administrations.

To foster such understanding, the project has brought together research fellows representing each BRICS country, with very different backgrounds such as law, engineering, political sciences, and sociology. All modules of the research have been discussed with and peer reviewed by the entire team, starting from the methodology and thematic questions, until the data collection and processing, and review of the research findings.

Importantly, to provide a trustworthy picture of the digital transformation of the BRICS, this publication reviewed documents and the specialized bibliography discussing what are the main components of digital transformation, including the strategies, policies, regulations, and initiatives shaping the digital transformation of the various sectors.

Through these analyses, this publication offers a detailed view of the existing frameworks and processes, as well as critical suggestions on how such processes could be enhanced, which might be useful for both BRICS and non-BRICS countries alike. Indeed, the findings of this volume can be relevant to all policymakers and stakeholders interested in how digital transformation plays out in large developing countries in general.

Ultimately, this book aims at inspiring reflections on digital transformations—among the BRICS countries and beyond—analyzing how these emerging giants are shaping their digital public infrastructures and the consequent public goods, dealing with shared challenges, exploring good (or sometimes bad) practices, dealing with various types of asymmetries, and fostering their own conceptions of digital development.

In this sense, we believe this volume offers valuable considerations on governance, financing, structuring of digital infrastructures, deployment of connectivity strategies, increase in capacity of public services, and leadership on how to make use of digital assets. We hope that this work will stimulate a more critical debate on digital transformation, offering diverse examples of how such a process can be shaped from the perspective of the New Digital Locomotives of the Global South (Belli, 2023).

References

Bai, C., & Lei, X. (2020). New trends in population aging and challenges for China's sustainable development. *China Economic Journal, 13*, 3–23. https://doi.org/10.1080/17538963.2019.1700608

Belli, L. (2021). BRICS countries to build digital sovereignty. In L. Belli (Ed.), *CyberBRICS: Cybersecurity regulations in the BRICS countries* (1st ed.). Springer.

Belli, L. (2023). *Building good digital sovereignty through digital public infrastructures and digital commons in India and Brazil. G20's Think20 (T20)*. Retrieved January 2025, from https://t20ind.org/research/building-good-digital-sovereignty-through-digital-public-infrastructures/.

Belli, L., & Doneda, D. (2023). Data protection in the BRICS countries: Legal interoperability through innovative practices and convergence. *International Data Privacy Law, 13*, 1–24. https://doi.org/10.1093/idpl/ipac019

Belli, L., & Gaspar, W. B. (2023). Exploring the key AI sovereignty enablers (KASE) of Brazil, to build an AI sovereignty stack. In L. Belli & W. B. Gaspar (Eds.), *The quest for AI sovereignty, transparency and accountability. Official outcome of the UN IGF data and artificial intelligence governance coalition*. FGV.

Belli, L., & Magalhães, L. (2024). *Digital transformation in the BRICS countries. Special issue of the Computer Law & Security Review*. Retrieved January 2025, from https://www.sciencedirect.com/special-issue/10VRL9GGMQG.

Belli, L., et al. (2023). *Cibersegurança: uma visão sistêmica rumo a uma proposta de Marco Regulatório para um Brasil digitalmente soberano*. FGV.

BRICS. (2013). *Durban 2013: EThekwini Declaration*. http://brics.utoronto.ca/docs/130327-statement.html

BRICS. (2015). *BRICS memorandum of understanding on cooperation in science, technology and innovation*. https://www.gov.br/mre/pt-br/canais_atendimento/imprensa/notas-a-imprensa/ii-reuniao-de-ministros-de-ciencia-tecnologia-e-inovacao-do-brics-documentos-aprovados-brasilia-18-de-marco-de-2015

BRICS. (2021). *XIII BRICS Summit: New Delhi Declaration*. http://www.brics.utoronto.ca/docs/210909-New-Delhi-Declaration.html

Couldry, N., & Mejias, U. A. (2019a). Data colonialism: Rethinking big data's relation to the contemporary subject. *Television & New Media, 20*(4), 336–349. https://doi.org/10.1177/1527476418796632

Couldry, N., & Mejias, U. A. (2019b). *The costs of connection: How data is colonizing human life and appropriating it for capitalism*. https://doi.org/10.1515/9781503609754

Jiang, M., & Belli, L. (Eds.). (2024). *Digital sovereignty from the BRICS countries: How the global south and emerging power alliances are reshaping digital governance*. Cambridge University Press.

Kiselev, V., & Nechaeva, E. (2018). Priorities and possible risks of the BRICS countries: Cooperation in science, technology and innovation. *BRICS Law Journal, 5*(4). https://doi.org/10.21684/2412-2343-2018-5-4-33-60

New Development Bank. (n.d.). *NDB's member countries*. Retrieved January 2025, from https://www.ndb.int/about-us/organisation/members/.

Pohle, J., & Thiel, T. (2020). Digital sovereignty. *Internet Policy Review, 9*(4). https://doi.org/10.14763/2020.4.1532

Stuenkel, O. (2016). *Post-Western world: How emerging powers are remaking global order*. Polity Press.

Tim, C. (2023). More than 40 nations interested in joining BRICS, South Africa says. *Reuters*. https://www.reuters.com/world/more-than-40-nations-interested-joining-brics-south-africa-2023-07-20/.

United Nations. (2011). *Enhanced cooperation and internet public policy roles*. https://documents.un.org/doc/undoc/gen/n11/322/49/pdf/n1132249.pdf

United Nations Department of Economic and Social Affairs. (2023). *THE 17 GOALS | Sustainable Development*. United Nations. https://sdgs.un.org/goals

Zuckerman, E. (2020, November 17). What is digital public infrastructure? *Center for Journalism & Liberty*. https://www.journalismliberty.org/publications/what-is-digital-public-infrastructure

Luca Belli, Ph.D., is Professor of Digital Governance and Regulation at the Fundação Getulio Vargas (FGV) Law School, Rio de Janeiro, where he directs the Center for Technology and Society (CTS-FGV) and the CyberBRICS project. Luca is also editor of the International Data Privacy Law (IDPL) Journal, published by Oxford University Press, and Director of the Computers Privacy and Data Protection conference Latin-America (CPDP LatAm). He is currently member of the Brazilian Presidency's National Cybersecurity Committee, and of the the Advisory Council of the Brazilian Interministerial Committee for Digital Transformation. He is also board member of the Global Digital Inclusion Partnership and member of the Steering Committee of the Forum for Information & Democracy. He is author of more than 80 publications on law and technology, exploring data governance, cybersecurity, AI regulation, Internet access, and digital transformation. He has been consulted by several intergovernmental organisations and national regulators, including the Council of Europe, the International Telecommunications Union, the French Telecoms Regulator, etc. and his works have been quoted by numerous media outlets, including The Economist, Financial Times, Forbes, Le Monde, BBC, China Today, The Beijing Review, The Hill, O Globo and Folha de São Paulo.

Larissa Galdino de Magalhães Santos is a Yufe4Postdoc, Marie Sklodowska-Curie at the Universität Bremen. Before, she was an associate researcher at the United Nations University, Electronic Governance Unit (UNU-EGOV). Larissa also is a Researcher at the Center for Technology and Society at FGV and CyberBRICS, Law School at Fundação Getúlio Vargas. Her research is located between government technology and innovation, with a special focus on open data, smart cities, and digital transformation strategies. Co-chair of the Open Data Charter Implementation Group, she is also a Professional Fellow at Fundação Getúlio Vargas for Europe and a Ph.D. in Political Science from the State University of Campinas.

Brazil's Over-Centralised Governance of Digital Transformation

Larissa Galdino de Magalhães Santos

Abstract This chapter analyses Brazil's Digital Transformation Strategy (E-Digital) through a new public governance lens. Based on the analysis, the author finds that the governance of E-Digital is too centralised, with too much decision-making power resting with state actors at the federal level, led by the Presidency. This analysis of the Brazilian experience aims to contribute to understanding the necessary modalities for a more democratic, sustainable digital transformation governance in Global Southern contexts.

1 Introduction

While Brazil scores well in terms of digitisation of government services, occupying a seventh position among the 198 countries of the World Bank's GovTech Maturity Index 2020 (Dener et al., 2021), its progress towards digital transformation across all sectors of the economy and society is uneven. Internet access in the country is still unequal, with about 90% of the low-income population connected exclusively by cell phones (CETIC, 2021).

The Brazilian Digital Transformation Strategy (E-Digital) was launched in 2018.[1] Coordinated by the Ministry of Science, Technology, and Innovation (MCTI), E-Digital has the ambitious purpose of coordinating public policies capable of guaranteeing the adoption of technology for an economically developed, fair, and solidarity-based society. In all, about 100 initiatives have been established by E-Digital. As it is the central public policy strategy in the context of Brazilian digital transformation, it would be important to understand and evaluate E-Digital's governance model.

[1] See Decree No. 9.319 (2018). E-Digital was updated on 17 November 2022 by the Ministry of Science, Technology, and Innovation (MCTI) (2022), after the finalisation of this study.

L. Galdino de Magalhães Santos (✉)
Electronic Governance Unit (UNU-EGOV), United Nations University, Guimarães, Portugal
e-mail: larissagms@yahoo.com.br

L. Belli, L. Galdino de Magalhães Santos (eds.), *SmartBRICS*,
https://doi.org/10.1007/978-3-031-98204-0_2

There is insufficient knowledge regarding the governance modalities that best support digital transformation (Chantillon, 2021). Most research in this area covers countries with high technological performance, such as Australia, the Republic of Korea, or Denmark (see Nielsen & Jordanoski, 2020). This chapter aims, among other things, to encourage a better examination of digital transformation policy and implementation in Global Southern contexts.

I analyse Brazil's digital transformation governance through a new public governance (NPG) lens in this study. According to Pereira and Ckagnazaroff (2021), NPG is characterised as:

> type of governmental, institutional arrangement which, in articulating economic-financial, institutional-administrative and socio-political dimensions, establishes partnerships with civil society and the market through deliberative processes, and seeks innovative solutions to social problems (Pereira & Ckagnazaroff, 2021, p. 112).

As Pereira and Ckagnazaroff (2021) point out, NPG is associated with democratic inclusion that allows civil society and private sector actors to contribute to public policies in a partnership process in the search for solutions to social problems. The ideal NPG approach is one in which multiple actors contribute and influence the public policy decision-making system, consequently contributing to the delivery of public services.

In this chapter, the governance structure is understood to be the set of mechanisms used to direct, evaluate, and monitor the management and conduct of public policies and services, considering the interests of society and stakeholders. Governance structures are organised by rules, roles, and forms of articulation between decision instances, forming a multifaceted system of inter-organisational and intersectoral relationships (Jessop, 1993).

Section 2 provides more detail on the NPG framework, Sect. 3 describes the governance structure of Brazil's E-Digital strategy, Sect. 4 evaluates the patterns of governance of E-Digital, and Sect. 5 provides conclusions.

2 New Public Governance

The transition from the hierarchical and bureaucratic approach of public management[2] to the systemic approach of the NPG demands a new form of organisation from the state: an institutional arrangement based on relationships within and outside the government that configure structures according to national contexts. According to Pereira and Ckagnazaroff (2021), public governance can be analysed in terms of the following dimensions: (1) main values related to governance, such as integrity, transparency, and efficiency; (2) the structure of the institutional system that is responsible for promoting interaction to obtain results, through networks,

[2] See Osborne (2010), for a discussion of evolution from new public management (NPM) to NPG.

power, and coordination; and (3) processes of evaluating and monitoring the results of public policies.

In terms of the NPG framework, a country's governance of digital transformation can be evaluated in terms of the degree to which the institutional arrangement allows: the power of the state to shift to other actors; networks of actors to form and articulate toward a goal; and knowledge and information to be coordinated in the search for solutions (Pereira & Ckagnazaroff, 2021).

According to Nielsen and Jordanoski (2020, p. 288), governance models of cooperation and intergovernmental coordination tend to be neglected as a success factor for national digital transformation strategies. Strong governance models, with clear roles and responsibilities of all institutions and with formal intersectoral decision-making bodies, can foster intergovernmental coordination and cooperation. Likewise, high levels of inclusion of all sectors of society at all levels of government, including civil society and private actors, can increase the chances for success in implementing digital transformation strategies.

In recent years, Brazil has been promoting notions of public governance to establish mechanisms for evaluating the degree to which government policy implementation and service delivery generate public value. Article 2 of Brazil's Decree No. 9.203 of 2017 on Public Governance specifies that public value constitutes the products and results generated by public-interest state responses to societal demands.

In the same way, the updating of government ecosystem strategies for digital transformation signals the unbalanced appropriation of governance models, in most cases disconnected from the guidelines of the Public Governance Policy of the Brazilian government and rigid principles of solid public governance, such as openness and transparency, inclusion, participation, gender equality, and diversity (OECD, 2020b).

It can be argued that, in addition to government efforts to promote digital transformation strategies, a governance structure capable of contributing to the good performance of public policies must have the following attributes: (1) inclusion of multiple actors in positions with access to power; (2) forums and collegial settings that guarantee the discussion of the problems and challenges of under-represented groups; (3) networks between the local and global, private and public actors, under formal coordination; and (4) training of transformational leaders to coordinate networks for a solid digital transformation strategy.

3 Governance Structure of Brazil's E-Digital

In terms of the March 2018 Decree that established Brazil's E-Digital framework, E-Digital is the core component of the country's National System for Digital Transformation (SinDigital), with SinDigital composed of E-Digital and "its thematic axes and its governance structure" (Decree No. 9319, 2018). This chapter focuses on the "governance structure" set out in the Decree.

The Civil House of the Presidency of the Republic coordinates the governance of and decision-making structure for E-Digital. The Civil House is the coordinator of E-Digital and holds the presidency of the Interministerial Committee for Digital Transformation (CITDigital), a powerful committee that monitors, evaluates, and directs E-Digital. The Civil House of the Presidency also has the power to choose many of the Interministerial Committee's members, who come from the following bodies:

- Civil House of the Presidency
- Ministry of Foreign Affairs
- Ministry of Economy
- Ministry of Education
- Ministry of Communications
- Ministry of Science, Technology, and Innovation (MCTI)
- General Secretariat of the Presidency
- Office of Institutional Security of the Presidency

E-Digital's core ministry leads the Executive Secretariat of the Interministerial Committee, the MCTI, which means that the MCTI has a leading role in implementing, monitoring, and updating the strategy.[3]

The Interministerial Committee is responsible for establishing the priority actions of E-Digital; maintaining the coherence of the initiatives of different bodies; sharing information on the impact of sectoral initiatives; monitoring and evaluating the results of E-Digital; articulating and monitoring government, state, and municipal programmes; and issuing recommendations, updates, reviews, and deliberations on E-Digital.

The 2018 Decree establishing E-Digital also provides for the Advisory Council for Digital Transformation, mandated to ensure "permanent dialogue" between the state and non-state actors (i.e., actors in the private sector, the scientific community, and civil society). This Advisory Council is intended to be a multisectoral technical entity that provides institutionalised participation by non-state actors in terms of evaluating, implementing, and updating E-Digital. The council's role is to review E-Digital's evaluation and implementation reports, make proposals on the actions envisaged in E-Digital, and recommend periodic updating measures. The council is chaired by a member of the Civil House of the Presidency, who also serves on the Interministerial Committee. It includes representatives of the private sector and civil society, non-governmental organisations (NGOs), and academia. In addition, the Interministerial Committee has the prerogative to decide on the composition of the Advisory Council.

Arrangements have been modified since 2018 by several amendment decrees.[4] Civil society, the scientific community, and the private sector are now represented

[3] See MCTI (2022) for the MCTI's E-Digital update on 17 November 2022, which occurred after the drafting of this article.

[4] Decree No. 10.332 of 2020 instituted the Digital Government Strategy for 2020 to 2022. Decrees No. 9.804 of 2019 and No. 10.782 of 2021 changed the discipline of the governance structure and

by a council with only an advisory role concerning the Interministerial Committee of E-Digital. The overall impact of the amendment decrees has been to further centralise control of E-Digital in the Interministerial Committee.

Thus, E-Digital's governance at the strategic level is centralised in the Civil House, linked to the Presidency of the Republic. Despite the existence of decision-making bodies to facilitate cooperation and coordination, the Presidency must consider all decisions and documents. The head of the Interministerial Committee, the main body of power and information, is appointed by the Civil House.

Given the cross-cutting nature of E-Digital's activity axes, the Interministerial Committee can institute technical support activities through specific committees or technical chambers that will monitor and follow E-Digital axes. According to the Committee's Monitoring Reports,[5] there are committees to discuss the regulatory environment for start-ups, e-commerce and exports, and the Internet of Things (IoT).

The Interministerial Committee is mandated to ensure dialogue among its Executive Secretariat, its other members, and the other bodies involved in digital transformation initiatives. The Interministerial Committee determines the composition of the non-state advisory council (comprising civil society, the scientific community, and the private sector). Therefore, although information circulates between the Interministerial Committee and the non-state representatives comprising the advisory council, the implementation power lies clearly with the federal government and related state bodies.

Among the state actors, while the responsibilities are shared between different actors in the implementation of E-Digital, there is a clear imbalance of power between those actors positioned close to the apex of power in the Presidency and those farther from the apex who are at the forefront of execution. Since 2018, decision-making power and relevant information have been concentrated in the Interministerial Committee. Altogether, seven meetings[6] of the Interministerial Committee were held between May 2018 and March 2020 to discuss and deliberate on the creation of committees and subcommittees; to update or reassess the composition of the Advisory Board; to update E-Digital; and to establish the Digital Government Strategy 2022–2026. Work Plans were prepared for 2018–2019 and 2021–2022, and there were three reports, in 2018, 2019, and 2020, on the implementation of E-Digital.

The question then arises: How is the E-Digital governance structure impacting the performance of Brazil's ecosystem for digital transformation?

---

the implementation definitions of E-Digital, altered the recreation of the Ministry of Communications, and altered the powers of the MCTI.

[5] See, for example, Comitê Interministerial para a Transformação Digital (2020).

[6] The reports from all Interministerial Committee meetings between May 2018 and March 2022 can be found in the E-Digital repository (MCTI, n.d.). The repository also makes available all government degrees and resolutions by advisory structures linked to E-Digital.

4 Over-Centralisation of Digital Transformation Governance

The governance structure of Brazil's E-Digital strategy is, as we have seen above, highly centralised by a few actors at the federal level. Multiple actors can provide technical support and monitor the strategy, but for the most part, their roles are only advisory. There are, for example, no formal incentives for cross-cutting or decentralised policy initiatives, such as for smart cities, technology in agriculture, or IoT, to be adopted at the non-federal level by municipalities or states.

Overall, E-Digital's governance can be said to yield only an adequate performance level. In 2021, it was found that of the 100 actions stipulated by E-Digital, 23 actions had been completed, 60 actions were in progress, and 17 had not yet started (CGEE, 2021, pp. 97–110). Many profound digital inclusion challenges persist—challenges which are generally tied to the country's socio-digital inequalities. On E-Digital's Infrastructure and Quality of Access Networks axis, there is still a pronounced imbalance between the regions of the country, especially between the North and Northeast, concerning fibre optic coverage, access networks in schools, and extension of the mobile network. In E-Digital's Research, Development, and Innovation axis, there are persistent challenges regarding Internet access in public schools, the effectiveness of digital literacy projects, and technical training to enable a transition to the digital economy (CGEE, 2021).

Some analyses have found that although E-Digital's structure has the necessary strategic, operational, and implementation scope, its decision-making power and circulation of information are concentrated too narrowly in the hands of government representatives. This diagnosis is reflected in recent assessments (see CGEE, 2021; OECD, 2018, 2020a) of the governance of Brazilian digital transformation, including E-Digital and the Digital Government Strategy.[7]

The governance framework should help the government to achieve its digital transformation goals. According to Chantillon (2021), public administration can create public value when carrying out its governmental activities as long as governance of the activities includes all stakeholders. The public sector is one of many initiators of value-creation processes, but it is not the only one. From this perspective, there is a relative flaw in the traditional view of creating public value in the Brazilian governance structure concerning digital transformation.

Although governments are touted as the main entrepreneurs of innovation and explorers in pursuing public value for society, the public sector must be cognisant of citizens' and customers' desire for organisations to adjust their business models. The reconfiguration of the public sector business model requires incorporating knowledge and experience of all potential partners—citizens, companies, and other non-state entities (Wirtz et al., 2021).

In other words, true digital transformation is an accumulated process using emerging technologies and dynamic stakeholder interactions. This results in the

---

[7] See Decree No. 10.332 of 2020, which instituted the Digital Government Strategy for 2020 to 2022.

systematic reconfiguration of organisations and the most flexible and interactive business model, unlike the centralised model currently driving the Brazilian E-Digital strategy. The inevitable tensions generated by centralised governance and the inability to include stakeholders in decision-making can negatively influence the implementation of strategic actions. However, radical decentralisation is not the answer to the paradoxes of governance. Digital transformation efforts require centralised management capabilities, grounded in a blend of hierarchy and unity, and decentralised capabilities grounded in diversity.

Although centralisation and decentralisation may seem to represent opposing approaches to the structure of public organisations, the two can (and must) exist simultaneously—in a necessary coexistence that will sometimes be comfortable and, at other times, be characterised by paradox and tension. Reform of a public institution may, depending on the stage the institution is at in its evolution, require increasing its centralising forces (via hierarchy, unification, and centralised governance), or it may require increased decentralising forces (via devolution, diversification, and sub-national governance) (Witesman, 2020). Centralised and decentralised structures can coexist based on the pursuit of public values.

5 Conclusions

To advance knowledge about the governance factors that can influence the performance of national digital transformation strategies, this chapter has analysed the governance of the E-Digital framework in Brazil. The study seeks to contribute to the literature on public management and governance in the Global South (see, for example, Hoque & Zakaria, 2014). Based on my analysis of E-Digital's governance modalities to date, I have argued above that E-Digital's governance is over-centralised in the hands of state actors, particularly federal state actors, and even more particularly in the Presidency.

What is the model for a governance structure that supports sustainable digital transformation? The answer to this question depends on the status of the actors who engage in the strategising, operational organisation, and implementation of public policies for digital transformation. We know that a strong model includes the participation of multiple actors in decision-making and the circulation of information and power to influence the ecosystem of actors involved with the strategies. A governance structure with well-defined rules and decision-making structures does not guarantee effective digital transformation. It is necessary to go further and consider the roles of non-state actors such as private sector representatives, citizens, scientists, and academics, who will often have different perspectives and priorities from those of the government—and to allow these actors to serve as resources for optimal decision-making and implementation by public managers. Pereira and Ckagnazaroff (2021) point out in their discussion of the new public governance (NPG) model that institutional governance arrangements must foster networks of interdependencies between public and non-state actors grounded in the need to solve complex problems.

References

Centre for Management and Strategic Studies (CGEE). (2021). *Diagnóstico da E-Digital: Atualização da Estratégia Brasileira para a Transformação Digital [E-Digital diagnostics. Update of the Brazilian Strategy for Digital Transformation]*. https://www.cgee.org.br/documents/10195/734063/Diagnostico+E-digital.pdf/8c028cc0-4dae-4ff2-abf7-220acf40779a?version=1.2

Centro Regional de Estudos para o Desenvolvimento da Sociedade da Informação (CETIC). (2021). *Executive summary – Survey on the use of information and communication technologies in Brazilian households –ICT households 2020*. https://www.cetic.br/pt/publicacao/executive-summary-survey-on-the-use-of-information-and-communication-technologies-in-brazilian-households-ict-households-2020/

Chantillon, M. (2021). *A governance framework facilitating a digital transformation of the public administration*. PhD thesis. Instituut voor de Overheid, KU Leuven. https://lirias.kuleuven.be/retrieve/637247

Comitê Interministerial para a Transformação Digital. (2020). *Relatório de acompanhamento: E-Digital*. https://www.gov.br/mcti/pt-br/acompanhe-o-mcti/transformacaodigital/arquivosestrategiadigital/citdigital_relatorio-de-acompanhamento-2020-rev-12-2020.pdf

Decreto n. 9.319, de 21 de março de 2018. (2018). Institui o Sistema Nacional para a Transformação Digital e estabelece a estrutura de governança para a implantação da Estratégia Brasileira para a Transformação Digital. Brasília, DF. Recuperado de http://www.planalto.gov.br/ccivil_03/_ato2015-2018/2018/decreto/D9319.htm

Decreto n. 9.804, de 23 de maio de 2019. (2019). Institui o Sistema Nacional para a Transformação Digital e estabelece a estrutura de governança para a implantação da Estratégia Brasileira para a Transformação Digital.Brasília, DF.

Decreto n. 10.332, de 28 de abril de 2020. (2020). Institui a Estratégia de Governo Digital para o período de 2020 a 2022, no âmbito dos órgãos e das entidades da administração pública federal direta, autárquica e fundacional e dá outras providências. Brasília, DF.

Dener, C., Nii-Amponsah, H., Ghunney, L. E., & Johns, K. D. (2021). *GovTech maturity index: The state of public sector digital transformation*. World Bank. https://doi.org/10.1596/978-1-4648-1765-6

Hoque, M. J., & Zakaria, A. F. M. (2014). Challenges of public management in the Global South. *Southern Conjuncture, 5*(21–22), 23–38. https://doi.org/10.22456/2178-8839.45448

Jessop, B. (1993). Towards a Schumpeterian workfare state? Preliminary remarks on post-Fordist political economy. *Studies in Political Economy, 40*, 7–40. https://doi.org/10.1080/19187033.1993.11675409

Ministério da Ciência, Tecnologia e Inovações [MCTI]. (2022). Estratégia Brasileira para a Transformação Digital (E-Digital). Recuperado de https://www.gov.br/mcti/pt-br/acompanhe-o-mcti/transformacaodigital

Ministério da Ciência, Tecnologia e Inovações [MCTI]. (n.d.). Estratégia Brasileira para a Transformação Digital – Repositório. Recuperado de https://www.gov.br/mcti/pt-br/acompanhe-o-mcti/transformacaodigital/estrategia-digital-repositorio

Nielsen, M., & Jordanoski, Z. (2020). Digital transformation, governance and coordination models: A comparative study of Australia, Denmark and the Republic of Korea. In *Proceedings of the 21st Annual International Conference on Digital Government Research (dg.o '20)* (pp. 285–293). Association for Computing Machinery. https://doi.org/10.1145/3396956.3396987

Organisation for Economic Co-operation and Development (OECD). (2018). *Digital government review of Brazil: Towards the digital transformation of the public sector*. https://doi.org/10.1787/9789264307636-en

OECD. (2020a). *Going digital in Brazil*. https://doi.org/10.1787/e9bf7f8a-en

OECD. (2020b). *Policy framework on sound public governance: Baseline features of governments that work well*. https://doi.org/10.1787/c03e01b3-en

Osborne, S. P. (2010). Introduction: The (new) public governance: A suitable case for treatment? In S. P. Osborne (Ed.), *The new public governance? Emerging perspectives on the theory and practice of public governance*. Routledge. https://doi.org/10.4324/9780203861684

Pereira, B. A. D., & Ckagnazaroff, I. B. (2021). Contributions to consolidate the new public governance. *Cadernos EBAPE.BR, 19*(1). https://doi.org/10.1590/1679-395120200104x

Wirtz, B., Langer, P., & Schmidt, F. (2021). Digital government: Business model development for public value creation – A dynamic capabilities based framework. *Public Administration Quarterly, 45*(3), 232–255. https://doi.org/10.37808/paq.45.3.2

Witesman, E. M. (2020). Centralization and decentralization: Compatible governance concepts and practices. *Oxford Research Encyclopedia of Politics*. https://doi.org/10.1093/acrefore/9780190228637.013.1390

Larissa Galdino de Magalhães Santos is a Yufe4Postdoc, Marie Sklodowska-Curie at the Universität Bremen. Before, she was an associate researcher at the United Nations University, Electronic Governance Unit (UNU-EGOV). Larissa also is a Researcher at the Center for Technology and Society at FGV and CyberBRICS, Law School at Fundação Getúlio Vargas. Her research is located between government technology and innovation, with a special focus on open data, smart cities, and digital transformation strategies. Co-chair of the Open Data Charter Implementation Group, she is also a Professional Fellow at Fundação Getúlio Vargas for Europe and a Ph.D. in Political Science from the State University of Campinas.

Brazil: An Overview of the Telecoms and Internet Access Sector

Larissa Galdino de Magalhães Santos

Abstract This chapter develops an overview of the Brazilian situation regarding access to Internet through the following matters: number of subscribers across different categories; affordability of services; type of technology being used; gender gap; urban-rural gap, international commitments; strategy for expanding the Internet access; participation in institutions; telecommunications regulations in the country; access to the spectrum for data transmission; and financial resources.

1 Context

What is the state of Internet access in the country, in terms of:
According to the Survey on the Use of Technologies of Information and Communication in Brazilian Households (Cetic.br, 2022) of the Regional Center for Studies for the Development of the Information Society (2020), in 2020, Internet access reached 83%, representing around 61.8 million households with some type of connection.

The database on Internet access in the country, referring to the year 2020, indicates that 69% of households have fixed broadband. However, the cost of the connection continues to be a barrier to home access, as 28% of residents consider the connection expensive, and 20% do not know how to use the Internet. Furthermore, despite the recorded increase in access to the network, the concentration is in 50% of urban households and 100% of the richest classes.

Regarding the regional distribution of households of Internet users, access is greater than 80% in all regions. In the Southeast region, the proportion of access is 82%, in the Northeast it is 80%, in the Midwest it is 87%.

Therefore, the use of ICTs in the Brazilian territory is quite heterogeneous, whose greatest disparities are between macro-regions and rural and urban areas. At the same

L. Galdino de Magalhães Santos (✉)
Electronic Governance Unit (UNU-EGOV), United Nations University, Guimarães, Portugal
e-mail: larissagms@yahoo.com.br

L. Belli, L. Galdino de Magalhães Santos (eds.), *SmartBRICS*,
https://doi.org/10.1007/978-3-031-98204-0_3

time, the rapid urbanisation of the population poses enormous challenges, especially with regard to network access infrastructure, regulations, resources and institutions in the context of climate change, the struggle for housing and a lack of basic public services.[1] This context impacts the use of networks and information technologies (ICT) and the ways of accessing services, types of technology, skills and use.

(a) Number of subscribers across different categories

According to data from the 2020 survey (Cetic.br, 2022), there was diversification between the technologies used to access the network.

The proportion of households with fixed broadband increased to 695, making it the main type of connection. At the same time, there has been a reduction in mobile broadband between 2019 and 2020 to 22%. Probable reflection of social distancing and isolation policies due to the COVID-19 pandemic.

In general terms, regarding the type of broadband connection technology in households, around 56% have a cable or fibre optic connection, DSL connections correspond to 5%, satellite 5% and radio 3%. This convergence scenario reflects that 91% of Internet provider companies in the country offer fibre optics.

Despite the trend of access inequalities in Brazil, differences in access in households with broadband have reduced among households with lower income, with the observed growth of 70% for households with income between four minimum wages and 52% for households with up to two minimum wages.

Considering the Brazilian regions, there was also a reduction in the difference in the proportions of home access to the network, mainly between the Northeast and Southeast. The proportion of households connected in the Northeast region is 79% and in the Southeast region is 86%.

(b) Affordability of services

Regarding the characteristics of Internet access in households, there is a high proportion of households with Wi-Fi, reaching 85%. Among mobile Internet users, 75% used the mobile network (3G and 4G), 90% used Wi-Fi and 66% used both technologies. However, the relational pattern between areas and classes remains, with 70% of low-income households having Wi-Fi, while 100% of high-income households use the technology. Comparing urban and rural areas, only 69% of rural areas have Wi-Fi, while 87% of households in urban areas are covered.

The presence of Wi-Fi is lower in households whose main connection is mobile. This finding is associated with the value of data packets. Approximately 51% of households pay more than R$80 reais for the connection. This value is also symbolic for the most vulnerable households in terms of income 68% and location, with 66% being in rural areas.

(c) Type of technology being used

The type of device used to access the Internet is related to economy class in the first place. It is also related to infrastructure in the territorial organisation of the country.

[1]The United Nations 2030 Agenda encourages countries to invest in inclusive and sustainable cities, reinforcing interventions by digital technologies.

The 2020 household survey indicates that 58% of users exclusively use their cell phones to access the network. Being that 40 million people and 38 million people are from classes C and DE. This classification is related to the number of minimum flights, that is, family income, so class E corresponds to the range of up to 2 minimum flights, class D corresponds to the range between 2 and 4 minimum flights, and class C corresponds to the range between 4 and 10 minimum flights. At the same time, 41% of users use both cell phones and computers.

In addition to the devices used to access the Internet, approximately 97% of users access the Internet at home. Regarding access devices, there was a significant increase in the use of a television set to access the Internet, among approximately 44% of network users. This growth is linked to the pandemic period, when the level of access can be compared to access via computer, including desktop, notebook or tablet. Among other devices, approximately 30% of users access via notebook, 26% via desktop computer, and 8% access via tablet, while 10% of users use video games to connect to the Internet.

(d) Gender gap

According to the proportion of women Internet users, there has been a growth of 12% from 2019 to 2020, with 85% accessing the Internet, while 77% of users are men. However, other issues related to structuring and sociocultural factors impact on the way women access.

(e) Urban-rural gap

Although the permanence of historically structured inequalities between rural and urban areas has been observed, between 2019 and 2020, the proportion of users increased from 53% to 70% in rural areas. While in urban areas, the growth went from 77% to 83%.

What is the country's ranking in the global ICT indices, such as ITU's ICT Development Index (IDI), WEF's Network Readiness Index (NRI), A4AI's Affordability Drivers Index, GSMA's Mobile Connectivity Index (MCI)?

(a) Classification on the ITU ICT Development Index

After the release of the 2017 index (International Telecommunication Union [ITU], 2017), there were some recommendations for modifying the indicators to increase the accuracy of the assessment of the development of information and communication technologies in the countries.

However, the quality of the data for evaluation in 2018, with the recommended changes, already pointed out significant flaws in the set of indicators, so the index was not released. The most recent indicator (ITU, 2019) was also based on the original methodology, since the data obtained from the changes contained problems, even after the orientation workshops.

Therefore, the International Telecommunication Union maintained the indicators and published the 2019 index. Brazil is classified as a developing country.

(b) The classification in the WEF Network Preparation Index

The Network Readiness Index 2022 (Dutta & Lanvin, 2022) assessed a total of 131 economies and the multifaceted impact of information and communication technologies on society and the development of countries. Considering the overall scores, there are no major differences between the top-ranked countries. Brazil occupies the 44th place. On the pillars, in technology, the ranking is 43, people is 40, governance is 44, and impact is in position 61.

(c) A4AI Accessibility Driver Index classification

The index assesses the political, regulatory and supply environment for Internet access, with the aim of providing more accessible broadband. The index classifies countries according to the expansion capacity of the technology infrastructure deployed, the local political structure for equitable access and the adoption of broadband.

According to the 2022 ranking (Alliance for Affordable Internet [A4AI], 2022), Brazil occupies the 15th position, with a score of 72.89 for access and 59.09 for infrastructure. However, Brazil dropped some positions in the ranking because of delays in the implementation of rules of law and permission on tower zoning.

(d) The classification in the GSMA Mobile Connectivity Index

The most recent connectivity index is from 2022. Brazil has a score of 62.51. There are more specific relevant scores: 99% have 3G coverage, mobile connection has 106% penetration, and mobile broadband connections have 102% penetration. The infrastructure score is 74.8, with an emphasis on network coverage of 89.5, however, with a performance of 76.4. The affordability index is 59.4, the inequality is 10, handset price 62.3, taxation 73.6, and the mobile tariffs of 80. Regarding the consumer profile, readiness is 80, basic skills 67.6, mobile ownership 78.8, and gender equality 93.2. Finally, the content and service index is 87.3, with an emphasis on the low online security index of 57.5.

The connectivity index confirms the gaps in Internet access in Brazil, accentuated by the low accessibility and quality of the infrastructure, mainly due to the high cost and lack of digital skills, and low investment in local exchange points.

Does the country have a strategy for the expansion of Internet access, such as a national broadband plan or similar?

The National Telecommunications Agency (Anatel) updated the Structural Tactical Plan for Telecommunications Networks (PERT). The 2019–2020 Plan was designed with the objective of expanding access to broadband in Brazil, with adequate quality and prices, through the coordination of efforts and investments, between the public and private sectors, therefore it is a regulatory and formulation input of public policies that establish infrastructure goals for the implementation of networks essential to public services.[2]

The Structural Plan for Telecommunications Networks (PERT) focuses on structural deficiencies in the transport and access networks that support the provision of broadband services. In addition to diagnosing the telecommunications infrastructure, the document focuses on deficiencies in the access and transport network that

[2] PERT is part of Anatel's Tactical Plan 2019–2024, established through Ordinance No. 2,382/2019 (Agência Nacional de Telecomunicações [ANATEL], 2020b).

support broadband services.[3] With the diagnosis of broadband, the agency establishes priorities, guiding and coordinating the telecommunications sector. PERT is also linked to the 2015–2024 Strategic Plan, which seeks to promote consumer satisfaction, competence and sustainability in the sector, dissemination of data and information from the sector, emphasising access, use, quality and performance of services as the main commitment. Among the tactical guidelines of the agency's strategy, the following stand out: expansion of transport and access infrastructure; satisfaction, quality and price by improving consumer relations; stimulating sustainability and competition among service providers; promoting the efficient use of the spectrum and regulatory performance for a responsive model; institutional strengthening.

Among the programmes of the agency's strategic plan and the Union's 2020–2023 Pluriannual Plan, the "Conecta Brasil" programme aims to promote access by expanding broadband from 74.68% to 91.00% through regionalised targets.[4] Decree n° 9.612 of 201 established the promotion of access to telecommunications considering the economic conditions of services such as expanding broadband access in underserved, rural or remote urban areas; and digital inclusion to guarantee access to technologies in areas characterised by social inequalities.

Other specific measures are part of the 2025 Program, Communications for Development, Inclusion and Democracy—under the responsibility of the Ministry of Science, Technology, Innovations and Communications (MCTIC). The programme's goals are: to increase the average speed of fixed broadband, to increase the proportion of access to mobile broadband to 90%, to make mobile broadband available in all municipalities, and to expand the coverage with an optical transport network (backhaul).[5]

2 International Commitments

Is the country a member of the ITU?

The ITU is the United Nations System Agency dedicated to topics related to Telecommunications and Information and Communication Technologies. The entity supports the shared global use of the radio frequency spectrum, through the international cooperation of orbital satellites, the improvement of the telecommunications

[3] Telecommunications networks are divided into: core, transport and access. The access network is the local network that connects the user to the operator's network. The transport network (backhaul) is the intermediate section of the network, which connects this local network to the central network (backbone) of the provider, from which interconnection with other national and international providers takes place, enabling access to the Internet.

[4] Information about *Conecta Brasil* and the Pluriannual Plan available at the Ministry of Communication's official website (2021b).

[5] For more information about the 2025 Program, see the document released by the Ministry of Planning, Development and Management (2020).

infrastructure, establishes standards for interconnection between various communication systems, and is committed to topics such as climate change, accessibility and strengthening security cybernetics. The agency operates in three sectors: standardisation of telecommunications, radiocommunications and the development of telecommunications. Brazil has been a signatory of international technical cooperation projects with the ITU since August 1877. The headquarters of the Americas regional office is in Brasilia.

Is the country a signatory of the 1988 or 2012 version of the ITRs?
Yes. The International Telecommunication Regulations (ITRs) are global treaties applied to establish the principles of supply and operation of international telecommunications, facilitating interconnection and interoperability through networks and services. In 1988, the World Conference on International Telecommunications updated the regulations; in 2012, the rules on international tariffs were prioritised.

Does the country have a policy of following ITU recommendations and/or technical standards?
The ITU has played a crucial role in Brazil since the privatisation and modernisation of telecommunications, following the Anatel, which is the regulatory body and the Ministry of Science, Technology, Innovation and Communications. ITU and Brazil have cooperation projects aimed at the development of telecommunications, such as support and integration of indigenous communities, children and young people in the information society.

What is the composition of the country's delegations at ITU meetings, including official reunions and study groups (e.g., government only, or multistakeholder including private sector, academia and civil society representatives)?
The Brazilian composition is multi-sectorial and made up of governmental bodies and entities, private entities and the academic sector. The National Telecommunications Agency is the administrative and regulatory body and is supported by the Ministry of Science, Technology, Innovation and Communications. The delegation of associated consultants is represented by Advisia OC&C, and telecommunications operator Claro SA, as an SIO, Idea Eletronic System, Multiedgers, and SBA Communication. The academic sector is represented by the CPqD Foundation—Center for Research and Development in Telecommunications and the Federal University of Pará, in addition to the Regional Office of the ITU in Brasília.

Is the country a member of the WTO? If so, is the country a signatory of the General Agreement on Trade in Services?
In 2016, Brazil implemented its commitment to the WTO through the acceptance of the protocol on financial services. The country has acceded to the Fifth Protocol to the General Agreement on Trade in Services of the WTO (GATS) (World Trade Organization, 2016).

Is the country a signatory of any regional framework for regulation of telecommunications or a member of any regional organisation for telecommunications regulation?

Anatel has the competence to represent Brazil in international telecommunications organisations, such as: *União Internacional de Telecomunicações* (ITU), a specialised UN agency; the Inter-American Telecommunication Commission (Citel), an organisation of the Organization of American States; the International Telecommunications Satellite Organization (ITSO); and the International Mobile Satellite Organization (IMSO); Corporation for Assigning Names and Numbers on the Internet (Icann), the World Trade Organization (WTO), the Latin American Forum of Regulatory Entities (Regulatel) and the Association of Communications and Telecommunications Regulators of CPLP (Arctel-CPLP), as well and for the Communications Administrations of the States Parties to the Southern Common Market—MERCOSUR (ANATEL, 2022c).

3 Institutions

Does the country have a Telecommunications Regulatory Authority? If so, is it an independent body, and what are its attributes?

The National Telecommunications Agency (Anatel) is responsible for the policy implementation of telecommunications services, inspection, regulation and performance of activities related to service providers.

The regulatory agency was created in 1997 as part of a process of privatisation of Brazilian telecommunications, and responds to the Ministry of Science, Technology and Innovation, and the Ministry of Telecommunications. With the General Telecommunications Law, the agency became an entity that is part of the indirect Federal Public Administration, subject to a special autocratic regime that performs functions of public interest, autonomous and specialised.

The authority of the National Telecommunications Agency involves: concession and licensing the service offer; supervision and control of the spectrum and orbital slots; issuing guidelines to regulate the provision of telecommunications services, interconnection and sharing of infrastructure; integrated maintenance of network compatibility and operations; supervision and control over consumer rights; homologation of equipment to ensure electronic compatibility; quality and safety requirements for services, and supervision of network neutrality rules.

In a recent Provisional Measure, n° 980, 2020, the President of the Republic created the Ministry of Science, Technology and Innovations and the Ministry of Communications. National telecommunications policy, national broadcasting policy became the Ministry of Communications' duties until December 2021.

What is the allocation of regulatory responsibilities between the appropriate government department(s) and the Telecommunications Regulatory Authority?

Anatel was the first regulatory agency in Brazil, created in 1997, by the General Telecommunications Law n° 9.472. The agency is an entity that integrates the indirect Federal Public Administration and is subject to an autonomous regime, linked to the Ministry of Science, Technology, Innovation and Communication. Administration and budget are independent and autonomous.

The agency must adopt measures to serve the public interest and develop telecommunications, with independence, impartiality, legality, impersonality and publicity. In the list of attributes, the following stand out: implementing the national telecommunications policy; representing the country in international telecommunications organisations; radio spectrum management, use of orbits and respective standards; product certification; managing conflicts of interest between telecommunications service providers; exercising the legal powers to control, prevent and suppress infractions of the economic order, with the reservations of the Administrative Council for Economic Defense (Cade); and protect users' rights.

The provision of telecommunications services requires a series of regulatory activities by Anatel, such as specific licenses. Anatel is responsible for defining the type of service according to the purpose for users, and establishes the requirements for obtaining each license, varying by type of service. The main services covered by the regulations are: fixed telephony, mobile telephony, multimedia communication service and pay television.

There are exceptions for small broadband servers that are exempt from licensing by Anatel. Pay-TV is under the authority of Anatel, but broadcasting over the air is not under the agency. The broadcasting sector is under the competence of the Ministry of Science, Technology, Innovation and Communication. With regard to television, there are two separate legislative frameworks for broadcasting outdoors. The film and audiovisual industries are also subject to regulation by the National Film Agency (ANCINE).

If the country follows a federal structure, is there an allocation of responsibilities relating to the telecommunications sector between the central/federal government and the states?

Anatel carries out inspection activities in the telecommunication services sector and maintains Regional Managements and Operational Units in all Brazilian states. According to the General Telecommunications Law n° 13.879 of 2019, its main task is to implement the telecommunications policy at the national level.

The new General Telecommunications Law mainly changed the permission for the migration of concessions to authorisations, under the guarantee of investment in the expansion of broadband, the transfer of radio frequency authorisation to another company, as a secondary use, and the transfer of reversible assets to providers of telecommunication services. Although the changes allow services of collective and essential interest to be operated exclusively by the private sector, the responsibilities in the federal structure have not changed.

Is there a competition department within the Telecommunications Regulatory Authority?

There is no competition department, but competition matters are the competence of the Competition Superintendence that was instituted by Anatel's bylaws in April 2013. The Competition Superintendent analyses the case and submits the approval to the agency's Board of Directors.

There are caveats to the infrastructure sharing conflicts that involve the electricity, telecommunications and oil sectors, and it is supported by the joint Resolution n° 2 of 2001, between the municipalities—Anatel, the National Petroleum Agency and the National Electric Energy Agency.

Does the country have a Competition Authority? If so, is it an independent body, and what are its attributes?

The country has the Administrative Council for Economic Defense (Cade), which is a Brazilian federal autarchy, linked to the Ministry of Justice and Public Security. Component to Cade is the activities of the Brazilian Competition Defense System and the Secretariat for Economic Monitoring (SEAE).

Cade is responsible for guiding, inspecting, preventing and investigating abuses of economic power, acting on prevention and repression. The most recent regulation, Law n° 12.529 of 2011, reorganised the body into the Administrative Tribunal for Economic Defense, the General Superintendence and the Department of Economic Studies. The Administrative Court has the function of judging competitive matters, preventing, reprimanding and educating the Brazilian market; the Superintendence, on the other hand, instructs processes in the control of conduct, concentrations and market monitoring; and the Department prepares economic studies to assist other agencies.[6]

Does the country have a Data Protection Authority? If so, is it an independent body, and what are its attributes? If not, which body of the government takes care of personal data-related issues?

The data protection framework is based on the General Law for the Protection of Personal Data (LGPD) n.13.709 of August 2018. The legislation came into force in August 2020. In July 2019, Law n° 13953 amended the LGPD and created the National Authority for the Protection of Personal Data. The created body must implement, supervise and ensure compliance with the law in the national territory. The LGPD was inspired by the General Data Protection Regulation (European Union). The law regulates the processing of personal data on digital media, either by a natural person or by a legal person under public or private law. The aim is to protect the fundamental rights of freedom and privacy. The law defines data categories; determines the possibilities of collection, processing of data, purpose, and need for requesting and using personal data; establishes the rights of data subjects, including for special conditions of sensitive data and segments of the population;

[6] Information on the Brazilian Consumer Protection System is described in Law n° 12.529 of the Presidency of the Republic (2011).

establishes the obligations towards companies, a differentiated regime for the Public Power; determines the creation of a national authority to establish sanctions in case of violations, guidelines, alerts and any type of penalties; citizen guarantee system to request that data be deleted or revoked at any time. The law institutes three important figures: the Controller, the Operator, and the Supervisor. Organisations must have agents responsible for the processing of data with functions determined according to the size and volume of data processed. Therefore, Brazilian law guarantees the choice and consent, access and correction to the data, demands responsibility from data holders, and rights of reparation.

It is important to emphasise that the defence of values of privacy, data protection, intimacy, and inviolability of communications already had a relative guarantee through the following laws: Marco Civil da Internet, which developed human rights in digital media, consumer protection law, etc.

After the LGPD was in force, it was approved from the structure of regulations of the National Authority through Decree n° 10,474 of 2020. The decree created the board of directors with a mandate period and attributions of the directors. The National Authority for the Protection of Personal Data has technical and decision-making autonomy to supervise and develop guidelines and norms related to the protection, collection, use, storage, and distribution of personal data of Brazilian citizens. In January 2021, the Authority's Ordinance 11 of 2021 established a Regulatory Agenda, determined the creation of the Internal Regulation and the Strategic Planning for the 2021–2023 triennium.

Does the country have a specific public body dealing with open data? If so, is it an independent body, and what are its attributes?

There is the Federal Executive's Open Data Policy that defines rules and resources for making open government data available. The initiative was built on a series of documents, regulations and rules.

The Federal Comptroller General (CGU)[7] is the main body responsible for the management and monitoring of the Policy—Decree n° 9.903 of 2019, through the National Open Data Infrastructure (INDA) (Office of Logistics and Information Technology, 2012). A Management Committee composed of several stakeholders supports INDA. The main resource for organising data is the Brazilian Open Data Portal, which functions as a catalogue for research and use of data published by government agencies.

The planning of actions to implement and promote the opening of data by the agencies is operationalised by the Open Data Plan (Federal Government, n.d.). To execute the plan, there is a Manual for preparing open data plans. The Office of the Comptroller General of the Union has created an Open Data Policy Monitoring Panel, which allows the population to check whether the administrative bodies are

[7] The Office of the Comptroller General of the Union is a body that reports directly to the Federal Executive Branch in matters related to the defense of public assets and to the increase of management transparency, through the activities of internal control, public audit, correction, prevention and fight against corruption and ombudsman.

complying with the transparency provisions and the fulfilment of the respective plan. The execution of open data plans has a timetable for making the data available.

Does the country have a body/an authority for managing cybersecurity incidents such as CERTs/CSIRTs? If so, what are its attributes and what is the nature of such an entity (e.g., governmental, multistakeholder, private)?
The Center for Studies, Response, and Treatment of Security Incidents in Brazil (CERT.br) is a service of the NIC.br (Ponto BR Information and Coordination Center), which was created in 1997, at the initiative of the Internet Steering Committee in Brazil (CGI.br). The committee is a multi-stakeholder organisation that coordinates all Internet-related activities in Brazil. The centre is responsible for handling security incidents on computers involving the networks connected to the Internet in the country (Center for Studies, Response and Treatment of Security Incidents in Brazil, 2022).

The centre coordinates incidents for any network that uses Internet Resources allocated by NIC.br, that is, IP addresses or Autonomous Systems allocated to Brazil, and domains under the ccTLD.br.

The centre also works to raise awareness of security-related issues, such as trends and events on the Brazilian Internet, to establish Brazilian Security and Incident Response Groups (CSIRTs). CSIRTs are recognised for their strategic role in increasing the levels of security and incident handling of connected networks. The centre is supported by boards, centres, advisors, and the World Wide Web Consortium office.

Does the country have a coordination system involving the aforementioned institutions? If so, what is the nature of such an entity (e.g., governmental, multistakeholder, private)?
In 1995, Brazil created the Internet Steering Committee. In 2003, a Presidential Decree modified the committee and created institutions that consolidated the Internet governance model. The Committee is a non-state and multisectoral organisation, in which members participate in the deliberation of Internet policies and the management of technical resources.

The committee's decisions aggregate opinions from different sectors of the Internet ecosystem in Brazil. The entities, together with the committee, suggest rules and procedures, recommend standards, and promote studies, indicators and statistics for the development of the Internet in Brazil. The Ponto BR Information and Coordination Center was created to implement the decisions and projects of the Steering Committee, thus it is a legal institution under private law, non-state, non-profit association, charged with implementing decisions and projects through the following entities: Registro.br with the assignment of domain names and Internet Protocols in Brazil; CERT.br, which is part of the IT emergency response group; the Center for Studies and Research in Networks and Operations Technology that takes care of the technical quality of the Internet; the Center for Studies on Information and Communication Technologies, which is responsible for producing indicators and statistics on availability and use.

4 Regulations

Are the telecommunication regulations and standards openly and publicly accessible?

Under Article 37, item 3 of the Internal Resolution of the National Telecommunications Agency, the rights and duties observed by federal legislation with regard to access to information, agency decisions and other documents must be disclosed on the Internet. The agency has an Open Data Plan (2019–2020)[8] that guides the implementation and opening of data. The Plan is organised according to the Agency's Strategic Planning, whose objective is the dissemination of open data and sectorial information. In addition, the Plan follows the guidance of the Access to Information Law and the National Open Data Policy of the Federal Executive Branch.

The Plan is in line with the Agency's Strategic Planning, which establishes among its objectives the promotion of the dissemination of sectorial data and information. In addition, the preparation of the PDA is in line with the provisions of the "Access to Information Law," and also Decree n° 8.777 of 2016, which instituted the Federal Executive Branch's Open Data Policy.

Is there a specific general telecommunications legislation?

Law n° 13.879 of 2019 changed the telecommunications legislation in Brazil. The new framework provides for a new way of operating fixed telephony services through authorisation, and the application of balances in broadband investments. The regulation concedes more powers to companies in the telecommunications sector and the exclusive use of bands in the radio frequency spectrum.

With the change, companies acquire the right to exploit the network infrastructure of the old system, by means of authorisation, without the direct control of the public regime, which maintains the goals of universalisation, continuity and tariff control. Regarding the exploitation of radio frequency bands, companies will be able to sell part of the radio, TV, telephone, mobile and satellite Internet transmission bands, through a secondary spectrum market. In other words, the company pays for the exploration and can make a second use of this space.

According to the regulation, the value associated with the adaptation of the concession should guarantee the investment and implementation of data transmission infrastructure in accordance with the guidelines stipulated by the Government. Investment commitments must be integrated with the authorisation terms entered into with the telecoms that choose to change the regime, guaranteeing the offer of technologies that prioritise the reduction of regional inequalities, access to networks for people with disabilities and the offer of consumption plans.

Especially on universalisation, the new framework defines those services of collective interest that are operated exclusively in a private regime, maintaining universalisation duties. On the other hand, the presentation of technical projects that are compatible with the applicable rules is released.

[8] The agency's Open Data Plan was approved by Ordinance No. 1838 of 2018 and amended by Ordinance No. 1935 of 2019.

Are there any instruments other than legislations and regulations, such as license agreements, that govern the provision of telecommunication services in the country?

The Anatel has a Regulatory Agenda to publicise the entire regulatory process of the Agency. The agenda has norms conducted for a period of 2 years. The norms are constantly monitored by the Planning and Regulation Superintendence, and guided according to the manual of good regulatory practices (ANATEL, 2018).

The main regulatory instruments for the provision of telecommunications services are: resolutions, overviews, ordinances, laws, decrees, inspection instructions, inspection procedures and standards of the Ministry of Science, Technology and Innovations and Communications. According to the agency's Internal Resolution n° 612 of 2013, the Regulatory Management is responsible for drafting normative acts that the concession, permission and authorisation for the dispatch of telecommunications services, the right to use radio frequencies and the right to use satellite, and proposals for legislative adequacy and for the consistency of the regulatory model of the telecommunications sector. The Station Licensing and Licensing Management performs the processes of bidding, issuing concessions, permissions and authorisations for the exploitation of telecommunications services and authorisation for the use of radio frequency, as well as the licensing of stations. The Certification and Numbering Management oversees and controls the use of numbering resources, the certification and approval of communication products and telecommunications systems. The Spectrum, Orbit and Radio Broadcast Management oversees and controls the use of the radio frequency spectrum, proposing the allocation, destination and conditions of use of radio frequency bands, carries out the coordination and notification procedures for satellite networks and establishes their conditions of use. The Inspection Department must oversee the activities of the co-necessary companies, the telecommunications resources provided, the control of the obligations of the concessionaires and the relationship of service providers with consumers.

Is there any obligation to provide open data regarding the telecommunications infrastructure?

Brazil has made progress in creating laws, standards, policies and practices designed to open data, such as the creation of the National Open Data Infrastructure, the Access to Information Law, the Civil Framework of the Internet, Open Data Policy, Data Governance Policy, Digital Government Strategy and the implementation of the 4th National Partnership Plan with the Open Government Partnership (Brazilian Network Information Center [NIC.br] & Regional Center for Studies on the Development of the Information Society [CETIC.br], 2019). In addition, the provision of data is part of the Agency's Strategic Planning. Given this, the agency has an open data panel on infrastructure, quality, indicators, sector categories and the main telecommunication services (ANATEL, 2022a).

Is there any obligation to provide open data on backhaul pricing?

The obligation to provide information is part of a set of regulations related to access to Information and the National Open Data Policy. In addition, the agency has internal guidelines and strategies for opening data and disseminating information. Data on the portion of the population covered with an optical transport network (backhaul) are available for monitoring the Agency's 2016–2019 Multi-Year Plan Goal (Ministry of Communications, 2021c). However, there is no open data on backhaul prices.

Does regulation foresee multiple categories of telecommunications services (e.g., Internet access, broadcasting)? Are information services distinguished between themselves (content creation and content distribution)?
The regulation provides for multiple categories of telecommunications network services, as well as the use of orbit and radio frequency spectrum resources. Each type of service will be the object of a separate concession or authorisation, with a clear determination of the rights and duties of the telecom, users and the Agency. Telecommunications services are classified into services of collective interest and services of restricted interest. Services of restricted interest are subject to certain conditions so that exploration does not harm the collective interest. The legal regime for telecommunications services is classified as public and private. The public regime is the one provided by concession or permission, with attribution of universalisation and continuity obligations to its provider. Exploration is allowed only under the private regime and subject to universalisation duties.

The service modalities are defined by the Agency according to its purpose, scope of delivery, form, means of transmission, technology employed or other attributes. Information services are differentiated between: Multimedia Communication Service (SCM) and Personal Mobile Service (SMP). Within Anatel, the regulations are then organised into: SCM (Fixed Broadband), SMP (Mobile Telephony), STFC (Fixed Telephony) and SeAC (Pay TV Services) related to radio frequency and satellite, concession regulations, certification and inspection (ANATEL, n.d.-b).

Do the country's national regulations recognise community operators/ non-profit/Telecommunications operators?
The Community Broadcasting Service (RadCom), instituted by Law n° 9.612 of 1998, is characterised by frequency modulation, operates at low power and restricted coverage is regulated by concession. Thus, in Ordinance n° 1.909 and Ordinance n°1.976, new rules were established for the processing of concession requests and service provision, creating the National Concession Plan (Ministry of Science, Technology and Communications, n.d.). With the Plan, the award occurs through "selection notices," and according to the ministerial criteria, the following are included: municipalities that have no authorised entity to perform the service; and municipalities where there is an expression of interest in the provision of services.

After the publication of the Plan with the schedule of notices, the public selection is forwarded, which is analysed by the General Coordination of Community Broadcasting. During the selection, the Ministry advised the association of competing entities, if any, to jointly provide the service. The authorisation for the operating license of the station is made in the Official Gazette of the Union and forwarded to the Presidency of the Republic and the National Congress. The concession of the Community Broadcasting Service lasts for 10 years.

Is there any obligation to share infrastructure

(a) poles, cell phone towers, underground routes/tubes
(b) fibre optics sharing, telecommunication cables
(c) equipment sharing

According to the General Telecommunications Law n° 9.472 de 1997, Article 73, telecommunications service providers of collective interest will have the right to use poles, ducts, conduits and easements owned or controlled by a telecommunications service provider or other services of public interest, non discriminatory and at fair and reasonable prices and conditions.

In 2017, Anatel instituted the Regulation for Sharing the Infrastructure to Support the Provision of Telecommunications Services, in compliance with the obligations provided for in Law n° 13.116 of 2015, organised so that the service holders provide information about the infrastructure necessary to define the sharing or waiving the sharing of towers by providers. According to Anatel's Infrastructure Sharing Manual (ANATEL, 2019), the holder must make available, through the Wholesale Supply Offering System, the georeferenced technical information of infrastructures available for sharing, and include the price composition criteria and the applicable terms. Through the system, the demanding groups connect to the groups with infrastructure.

The sharing of towers, specifically, by a telecommunications service provider that uses radio transmitting stations is mandatory in situations where the distance between them is less than 500 (five hundred) meters, except when there is a technical reason.

In addition, according to the Infrastructure Sharing Regulation, it is mandatory to share excess capacity, such as: fixed physical means, such as poles or towers, surface structure and suspended structures, as well as an unobstructed line of sight between transmitter and receiver; telecommunications networks in their operational set of circuits and equipment, for the transmission and other functions essential to the operation of telecommunication services. Holders have priority in the use of infrastructure.

There is no specific obligation to share fibre optics; however, models of the FTTH type are increasingly used, and that is why it is essential to share the structure of poles with electricity distributors.

Is there any unbundling obligation? Can you be an Internet service provider and a content provider at the same time?

The provision of Internet connection services is different from the provision of telecommunications services, that is, the Internet is a Value-Added Service (VAS). As prescribed by the General Telecommunications Law and other Anatel regulations, interested parties are guaranteed the use of telecommunication service networks to provide added value services, provided that the regime is freely agreed, isonomic and non-discriminatory.[9]

[9] For more information, see Resolution n° 693 (2018) on Telecommunications Services Regulation.

Faced with complaints from consumers about the recurrence of cases in which operators charge for value-added services from telephone bills or Internet access, Anatel instituted regulatory oversight as a management tool and started promoting activities together with operators to maintain compliance with the rules. Among the actions to mitigate the problem, it was recommended that operators adopt a value-added service management system to allow better control over the contracting and collection of services. The mechanism should also allow consumers to consult collection entries.[10]

Is there any obligation to treat Internet traffic in a non-discriminatory fashion (so-called network neutrality principles)?

The General Telecommunications Law attributed to Anatel guarantees the universalisation and continuity of service provision in the public regime, allowing access to any person or institution, regardless of location and socioeconomic status. Regarding the obligation of continuity, it says about the enjoyment of the service without unjustified stoppages. Still, universalisation is a periodic goal of the agency's strategic plan, emphasising the service to the physically disabled, as well as rural, remote or precarious urban areas.

In addition, the obligation to treat Internet traffic in a non-discriminatory manner is ensured by Article 3 of the Marco Civil da Internet, Law n° 12.965 of 2014. Article 9 defines isonomy in the transmission, switching or routing of data packets, without any distinction of content, origin, destination, service or applicability. However, traffic discrimination is possible only if it is a service provision requirement or as an emergency priority. Only in those situations can the operator perform differential treatment, informing users and ensuring the transparency of conduct.

The exceptions were detailed in Decree n° 8.771 of 2016, of approval of the civil framework of the Internet, stressing the permission only for the treatment of technical issues, such as network security, congestion or for the search for alternative solutions in cases of interruption of routes official, through transparency of the measures, in addition to the indication of the management measures in the contracts signed with the user, and wide dissemination of the practices. In the case of emergencies, communication must be made by those responsible to inform of the situation of risk, calamity or disaster. The document emphasises the veto of agreements that compromise the universalisation and continuity of service provision.[11]

---

[10] For more information about regulatory oversight and value-added services, see Ministry of Communications (2022d).

[11] Cell phone and data plans, known as "zero plan" are controversial and impact net neutrality. The "zero-rating" offered by the operators is restricted to the use of certain applied, without discounting the contracted franchise. Some organisations critical of rights on the Internet, report that it is a form of positive discrimination and that it can cause imbalance in the market favouring the use of services and applications to the detriment of others. The business sector, on the other hand, argues that the practice does not violate the net neutrality.

Does the country have any specific legal or regulatory provisions regarding the Internet Access Providers' possibility to monitor the content of user communications?

Monitoring the content of users' communications is supported by the General Telecommunications Law and the General Personal Data Protection Law.

According to Article 72 of the General Telecommunications Law, the service provider will only use the information related to individual activities upon the express and specific consent of the user, justified only in the performance of their activity.

Does the country have any specific legal or regulatory provisions regarding Internet Access Providers' possibility to collect and process user personal data?

According to the General Telecommunications Law, the service provider may use information regarding the individual use of the service by the user. The provider may disclose only aggregated information to third parties to avoid user identification or violation of privacy.

The General Law on Protection of Personal Data reiterates the specific consent on the collection and use of sensitive data, informed and expressed by the data subject, as fulfilment of legal duty, expressed in the contractual obligations, to guarantee the protection of the privacy and physical integrity of the data owner or third party. Consent is dispensed when the processing of data is imperative for the fulfilment of legal duty, sharing of data aiming at the implementation of public policies with legal support, and carrying out studies by guaranteeing anonymity whenever possible. The end of the processing of personal data will occur when the processing expires, when the data subject requests the end of the processing, the purpose of the use of data is reached and verified or by judicial decision.

Therefore, the collection of data from users of telecommunications services is a measure that requires transparency, alignment with legal bases, and the monitoring of a National Data Protection Authority (provided for in Art. 55-A of the referred law) to inspect and control data processing, since the information cannot serve other purposes.

Does the country require a license to operate telecommunications networks? Is there any license exemption?

The country requires a license for the multimedia communication service, which aims to standardise telecommunications companies and Internet providers. The request is made through a process that is managed by the Anatel Station Concession and Licensing Management.

According to the regulation of the multimedia communication service,[12] the request for the issuance of a License through the Mosaic system of Anatel. Licensing is a title of charge, and allows the provision of transmission capacity, Internet connection, reception and emission of multimedia service.

[12] Resolution N° 614 of the Board of Directors of the National Telecommunications Agency (2013).

Therefore, three types of license differ in: multimedia communication service license to be taken to become an Internet provider, as it allows the provision of an Internet connection; the Fixed Switched Telephone Service is the second fixed switched telephone service license to provide the Tripple Play service, through the transmission of voice and other signals, intended for communication between certain fixed points; and the conditional access service license, when working with multimedia kits, an additional package, among other services, such as the TV offer. After the payment of fees, authorisation goes through the evaluation of the Superintendent of Concession and Installment Resources, and then it is published in the Federal Official Gazette. To issue the license, it is necessary to register the authorised and responsible stations so that the licensing is carried out. Companies with less than 5000 users in service and who make exclusive use of radiocommunication equipment with restricted or confined radiation are exempt from authorisation of the multimedia communication service, according to Resolution n° 680 of 2017.

Does the country offer a specific/simplified license for not-for-profit operators or for operators that cover specific areas (e.g., rural areas)?
The provision of the telecommunication service in rural and remote areas is supported by the General Plan of Goals for Universalization in the public regime, governed by Resolution n° 622, of August 23, 2013.

The service to the rural area, specific areas such as rural public schools, or even remote areas is included under the terms of Bidding Notice n° 004 of 2012/PVCP/SPV by Anatel, which establishes several commitments to the telecommunications service providers winners in terms of the reach of remote regions, to allow digital and social inclusion of the Brazilian population.

Operators are obliged to progressively expand telecommunications services at affordable prices, whether for voice and data connections, including a distance of up to 30 km from the limits of the municipal headquarters. Service coverage for rural public schools should be free of charge. Connections must have at least a 256-kbps download rate and 128 kbps upload rate in remote areas, and a 1 Mbps download rate and 256 kbps upload rate in rural schools.

Does the country require a license to provide satellite telecommunications services, including via non-geostationary orbit satellites?
The satellite telecommunication service is considered a limited private service of restricted interest, operated at the national and international level, which covers multiple applications, such as the transmission of scientific data, aid to meteorology, operation and space research, regulated by Resolution n° 617 of 2013.

To exploit satellite telecommunications services, it is necessary to obtain two types of authorisation from Anatel. First, the right to explore the satellite depends on authorisation through public notice and private limited service; second, the authorisation of radio frequency associated with the radiocommunication satellite service is necessary when there is communication with an earth station in the national territory.

The right to exploit the Brazilian satellite, which is made through a bidding notice for 15 years, which can be extended only once for the same period, in orbital positions that are in the process of coordination or notification on behalf of Brazil or resulting from coordination processes with the International Telecommunication Union.

The global mobile service by non-geostationary satellite is governed by Rule n° 16 of 1997 and follows the same prerogatives as the global mobile service by satellite when requesting exploration, licenses and concessions. In the case of a foreign company, it is necessary to present a Brazilian legal representative.

Has the country established an obligation to provide coverage in specific areas (e.g., rural areas that lack coverage)?

The obligation to provide coverage in specific areas is based on the General Plan of Goals for the Universalization of the Switched Fixed Telephone Service provided in the Public Regime.[13] For the plan, universalisation is understood as the right of access, regardless of location and socioeconomic condition, to essential services of public interest, upon payment of a tariff established by specific regulation. Costs for meeting targets are borne by the responsible concessionaires.

Regarding coverage in specific areas, it was defined by the type of access, they are: indigenous village, rural area outside the scope of the basic tariff, settlements of rural workers, subscribers participating in low-income programmes, remaining quilombo communities, and conservation units in sustainable use, among others.

Concerning the goals of individual and collective access, for locations with more than 300 inhabitants, or for serving commercial and educational establishments, concessionaires must implement the service within a period determined by regulation. Regarding the access targets for special classes, such as rural areas, they must offer access and guarantee technical and economic viability under Resolution n° 622 of 2013, which establishes the conditions for connection and speed.

Are there any specific cybersecurity obligations with regard to the telecommunications sector?

Decree n° 10.222 of February 2020 instituted the National Cybersecurity Strategy, which defines measures for the protection of cyberspace and national security, such as technical monitoring in the face of technological changes. In addition, Normative Instruction n° 4, 2020, established the minimum requirements for Cybersecurity that must be adopted in the establishment of 5G networks.

Anatel's Regulatory Agenda 2019–2020,[14] item 7, promotes the elaboration of analyses and studies on the regulation related to the protection and security measures of the networks and services of telecommunications operators. To support the reassessment, Public Consultation n° 13 of 2020 (ANATEL, n.d.-c) was held on the

[13] Decree n° 9.619 of 2018 revoked the General Plan of Goals for the Universalization of the Switched Fixed Telephone Service provided in the Public Regime – PGMU, approved by Decree n° 7.512, of June 30, 2011.

[14] The Regulatory Agenda was established by Ordinance No. 542 of 2019 of ANATEL's Board of Directors.

minimum requirements for cybersecurity of terminal equipment that connect to the Internet and infrastructure equipment for telecommunications networks.

In addition, since 2017, the Safer Internet Program (Portal for Good Internet Practices in Brazil [BCP], n.d.), created by the Internet Steering Committee in Brazil with the support of SindiTelebrasil (National Union of Telecommunications Companies), associations of companies and Internet access providers, and partnership with Internet Society, started to develop programmes to support the technical community of the Internet to reduce attacks on services originating in the country, such as leaking routes and falsifying addresses. It also acts to bring together teams that support network security and stability among operators.

Is there any regulation regarding cybersecurity incidents?

According to the National Cybersecurity Strategy, public administration bodies and entities are responsible for implementing strategic actions planned to format a national cybersecurity system. According to the regulation, the Institutional Security Office of the Presidency of the Republic is responsible for coordinating cybersecurity, in line with cyber defence under the responsibility of the Ministry of Defense.

It is the responsibility of the Government Cyber Treatment and Response Center—CTIR Gov, to improve the response to cyber incidents with an emphasis on emerging technologies, issuing alerts and recommendations, and the participation of critical infrastructures in cyber exercises.

The strategy is expected to improve the legal framework on cybersecurity, preventing and mitigating threats, through the management of computational incidents, detection, screening, analysis and response. For this, public and private organisations must have a treatment and response team (Computer Security Incident Response Team). Currently, Brazil has about eight centres for treatment and response to cyber incidents. The country also has two treatment and response centres under national responsibility, the Center for Studies, Response and Treatment of Security Incidents in Brazil—CERT.br, more focused on commercial networks and private institutions. With a similar assignment, but focused on government networks, there is the Center for Treatment and Response to Cyber Government Incidents—CTIR Gov35.

Normative Instruction n° 4, of March 2020, defined the basic cyber security requirements that must be adopted in the establishment of 5G mobile phone networks. The established requirements seek to increase the protection of society and national institutions, in view of the possibility of vulnerabilities and backdoors within 5G technology systems.

There is a reinforcement of the General Law on Protection of Personal Data, which provides that those who deal with private data adopt security measures against unauthorised access and accidental loss, destruction, modification or any other type of violation. The National Authority for the Protection of Personal Data has technical and decision-making autonomy to supervise and develop guidelines and norms related to the protection, collection, use, storage, and distribution of personal data of Brazilian citizens.

Anatel's Regulatory Agenda 2019–2020 provides for the regulation of aspects associated with network security and the provision of services, addressing the general aspects associated with cyber security within the scope of telecommunications networks.[15]

Does the law foresee any specific cybercrime involving the (mis)use or attack of the telecommunications infrastructure?

The normative dimension of cybercrimes in the country results in a set of important laws, such as the Marco Civil da Internet, the General Law for the Protection of Personal Data, the Cyber Crimes Law and Law n° 12.735 that creates police stations specialised in combating digital crimes. This framework has been reinforced by policies and strategies, such as the National Cybersecurity Strategy and the National Critical Infrastructure Security Policy.

However, according to the analysis of the National Security Strategy (Item 2.1), the normative dimension is insufficient and requires a national effort, given the nature of the instruments that are restricted to the Federal Public Administration, not considering the productive sector and service providers, such as telecommunications. Therefore, it is recommended to improve national cybersecurity laws.

Normative Instruction n° 4 of 2020, which defines the minimum cybersecurity requirements, includes confidentiality and liability, requiring service providers to implement malicious packet detection functions to minimise the effect of attacks and identify abnormal patterns in traffic on 5G networks. According to Article 5, the infrastructure equipment is open to auditing and processes. In the case of failures, intentional or not, that compromise personal data, the company and the subcontracting concessionaires will respond according to their responsibilities.

It is important to note that the National Policy for the Safety of Critical Infrastructures established an Integrated Data System to enable the continuity of the provision of its services, through prevention and precaution, reflecting the need to adopt security procedures in all aspects, including cyber.

Does the law foresee SIM and/or IMEI registration? What are the requirements applicable to such registration (for instance, the documents and information required for Know-Your-Customer (KYC) processes)?

According to the General Telecommunications Law, all devices that access the cellular network, that is, those that use a SIM card, must have an Anatel certification. Certification is a prerequisite for marketing telecommunications products. According to Anatel's Certification and Homologation Regulation, it is necessary to register the SIM card with the operator, providing the CPF. Telephone providers may only allow connection to devices that are certified for the mobile network, and the use of radio frequency emitting devices without certification is prohibited.

---

[15] The current regulatory agenda underwent some changes by order of the council and also, to ensure the maintenance of the actions of the previous agenda. The current Agenda now has 48 initiatives, 16 of which are new initiatives and 32 are continuations of the agenda from the previous biennium (Ministry of Communications, 2022c).

Anatel advises the user to check the International Mobile Equipment Identity before making the purchase. Since each cell phone has a specific location number, this makes it easier in case of theft or robbery. It is through this number that operators can prevent cell phone misuse. However, there is no obligation under Brazilian law. Anatel has a "Legal cell phone" programme to support consumers when purchasing irregular handsets. It is possible to check the situation of the device on the Anatel website, by inserting a sticker that is in the cell phone case, behind the battery or by typing * # 06 # on the cell phone and the call key.

The General Telecommunications Law and other regulations do not stipulate specific Know Your Customers/Client rules, as a compliance resource to analyse the risk of consumer choices. But consumers who have bought an irregular cell phone without knowing it, find support in the Consumer Protection Code, to have their rights guaranteed and to return the device through the invoice and warranty term. Especially, when buying over the Internet, the customer has 7 days from receipt of the product to make the return.

Does the country specify the prices or tariffs for provision of telecommunication services or impose any minimum or maximum limits?

The financial consideration for the provision of public services is regulated by a price ceiling model that establishes the maximum value of the tariff to be practised. There are annual readjustments, according to the combination of inflation and the fact of tariff reduction, in addition, Anatel promotes tariff reviews to maintain the balance of concession contracts. The price is given according to the service traded on the market; the monitoring and adjustments depend on the regulation that supports the contract between the user and the service provider. A calculation is made for the Telecommunications Services Index (Ministry of Communications, 2022e), which is made up of a combination of other indices in the economy and to update values associated with the provision of telecommunications services, such as public telephone tariffs, reflecting the real variations in providers' expenses, guided by Resolution n° 253 of 2009.

Another important foundation is the guarantee of equality between operators; the General Telecommunications Law imposes the obligation of interconnection between the networks (fixed and mobile) of the operators. In Act n° 9.919 of 2019,[16] the maximum values for the use of local fixed networks for the subsequent years were changed. This ensures that no telephone operator, whether fixed or mobile, refuses to make its telephone network available for call termination originating on another operator's network.

Are there any policies or regulations governing right-of-way issues, such as utilising land to dig trenches and lay fibre, for the creation of telecommunications infrastructure?

Infrastructure sharing is supported by Antenna Law n° 13.116 of 2015, which provides for the right of way and use of areas to hold fibres, such as the creation of

[16] Repealed by Decree n° 10,553 of 2020.

telecommunications infrastructure. The law establishes the general conditions for the installation and sharing of infrastructure and the mandatory permission for the passage of cables and optical fibres for the installation of telecommunications networks, as a priority treatment. However, it does not exempt the concessionaire from complying with engineering standards and requirements and with municipal, state or district laws and the courses required from installation to operation. The right of way must be authorised by regulatory bodies under whose competence the area to be occupied or crossed.

To support infrastructure sharing, Anatel approved Judgment n° 359 in 2019 of the infrastructure sharing operational manual established by the Infrastructure Sharing Regulation to Support the Provision of Telecommunications Service 2017. The manual enforces the obligations of the Law on Antennas (Berbet, 2019) by sharing the means of using the Input Supply System with information from the infrastructure. Any conflicts will be resolved by Anatel itself. The manual also lists the chances of sharing.

The government is expected to publish the decree regulating the Antenna Law to address the right of way and the sharing of critical infrastructure between energy companies, roads and railways, in addition to specifying the situation of small providers and the need for a license. The right-of-way for cables, systems and resources of telecommunications networks.

What are the regulations applicable to the setting up and operation of landing stations and international gateways to the Internet?

The licensing standards for Earth stations include gateway-type access stations. The international gateway is usually used to make calls over IP networks (VoIP) internationally. Anatel did not create rules that fit the offer of VoIP operators. VoIP is considered a multimedia communication service, as a technology and not a telephone service with the use of numbering and interconnection, so it applies the rules of the Multimedia Communication Service, Resolution n° 614 of 2013. The resolution establishes interconnection as the type of connection between compatible telecommunications networks, so that users can communicate with service users from another network or access services available on them. The operating license of the station allows and authorises telecommunications and radio frequency services, as for earth stations with access between space traffic and telecommunications networks, in an integrated manner.

Regarding the licensing of access Earth stations, Resolution n° 719 of 2020, which supports the General Licensing Regulation, provides that the process can be carried out both by the holder of the service exploitation concession and by the holder of the exploration right of the satellite operator.

Are there any regulations of the Over-the-Top (OTT) services?

Over-the-top services are those that operate at the application layer where Internet users produce, access and exchange information. Due to their functionalities of video, voice and messaging services over IP, applications compete with telecommunication services, so they must be reached by the regulatory agenda.

According to the General Telecommunications Law, Article 61, the regulatory treatment must be given between the companies with added value, that is, the one that mobilises over-the-top service, and the telecommunications operators. According to the article of the law, the value-added service is the type of activity that adds new uses to a telecommunications service, with which it should not be confused. In Brazil, the Internet is considered a value-added service and, therefore, over-the-top companies are not subject to the obligations of Anatel's telephone and regulatory companies.

There is a discussion about the definition of over-the-top within the scope of the International Telecommunication Union: first, whether the definition of over-the-top services will be in accordance with the competition with the services provided by the operators; second, whether the over-the-top concept will be redefined by the entity to impact the political agenda of member states. The question of definition and regulation seems open; thus, Anatel approved the public consultation on the numbering regulation (ANATEL, n.d.-d). According to the agency's proposal, the numbering of the personal mobile service will be used as a global mobile service; Fixed broadband will be identified according to the fixed telephone plan number as approved by the public consultation in November 2022.

What are the grounds, if any, on which the country can suspend access to the Internet or direct the blocking of access to specific websites?

The suspension of Internet access can be triggered as an interruption to improve its dimension. In the case of network maintenance, the provider must communicate the fact to consumers at least 7 days in advance, under Resolution n° 614 of 2013, to Anatel. The repair is valid for some type of system degradation that compromises the quality of the service provided.

The suspension of telecommunications and Internet services as cancellation due to default complies with rules established by Anatel, in the General Regulation of Consumer Rights of Telecommunications Services.[17] Regarding the Marco Civil da Internet (Law n° 12,965 of 2014), Article 11, there are discussions about the possibility of suspending Internet access, that is, users' telecommunication services.

According to the article, in any situation of collection, storage, treatment of registration, data, communications by providers and Internet applications in which at least one of the acts occurs in the national territory, the rights of privacy, confidentiality and protection as provided for must be respected in legislation.

The blocking of access to specific websites is accompanied by a work group signed by the partnership between Anatel and the National Cinema Agency (ANCINE) (ANATEL, 2022b) and by the National Council for Combating Piracy and crimes against intellectual property of the Ministry of Justice and Public Security. The work group recently created by the agencies aims to develop a joint regulation to administratively block sites that offer pirated audiovisual content. Thus, agencies can remove illegal sites from the Internet without the need for judicial intervention.

[17] Approved by ANATEL Resolution No. 32 Brasil, (2014).

Judicial intervention is based on Law n° 9.609 and Law n° 9.610, both of 1998, which provide for the protection of the intellectual property of computer programs, their commercialisation in the country. In addition, the National Council for Combating Piracy and Crimes against Intellectual Property of the Ministry of Justice and Public Security has been responsible for supporting the blockade guidelines.

Does the country have a specific policy or strategy promoting the development of Internet eXchange Point (IXP) and other interconnection and transmission systems?

The Brazil Internet Exchange (IX.br) is the strategy responsible for promoting a direct interconnection infrastructure between the autonomous networks that make up the Internet in the country. The Internet Steering Committee Project in Brazil was created in 2004. The project was renamed in 2015 from PTT.br to IX.br for an internationalisation process.

The initiative is coordinated by the Internet Steering Committee in Brazil (CGI.br) and by the Ponto BR Information and Coordination Center (NIC.br). It is a private service, with its independent autonomous systems, linked by Internet access and content providers, such as content distribution networks that use IPv6 and IPV4 traffic among themselves, such as academic, governmental, and financial institutions, among others. In Brazil, 33 networks are operating in different locations (IX.br, n.d.).

The interconnection between the systems is done through agreements signed between the participants within the scope of the IXP. According to the Committee, currently, São Paulo's traffic exchange points are a worldwide exponent and contain a number of interconnected networks and data traffic. Generally, the points are regional and are created to fulfil the objective of improving the costs and quality of connections in the localities, so they have data centres with simultaneous interconnection equipment for organisations. The aim is to provide the Internet faster, more cost-effectively.

Another project created by the Internet Steering Committee in Brazil (CGI.br) and the Ponto BR Information and Coordination Center (NIC.br) to support interconnection and transmission systems is OpenCDN (NIC.br & Brazilian Internet Steering Committee [CGI.br], n.d.). The project works to improve the speed, cost and quality of Internet access, shortening the distance between available content and the user. It is based on CDN (Content Delivery Networks) technology and was started in 2018, in the metropolitan region of Salvador. With the project, the CDN can install cache servers in data centres that are already connected by local Internet Exchange Points.

Have any exceptional measures been adopted to regulate the COVID-19 crisis?

Due to the COVID-19 pandemic, the government issued Law n° 13.979 of February 2020, establishing measures to deal with the public health emergency to safeguard the provision of public services and maintenance of essential activities with a view to adopting restrictive measures of the law, two decrees were issued.

Decree n° 10.282 and Decree n° 10.288, both regulated the definition of essential public services and activities, such as telecommunications and the Internet, identified by broadcasting services, postal services and telecommunications and Internet services as essential activities.

Regarding the suspension and cancellation of services due to consumer default, the rules established by the General Telecommunications Services Consumer Rights Regulation, within the scope of Anatel's duties, were maintained.

In compliance with the judicial decisions of April 2 and 7, 2020, of the judgment of the 12th Federal Civil Court of São Paulo, Anatel recommended to the fixed and mobile telephony service providers to support the provision of services during the emergency period of the COVID-19, as well as the reestablishment of the services of those consumers who have already suffered delinquency cuts. The decisions refer to Public Civil Action n° 5004662-32.2020.4.03.6100 (Instituto de Defesa do Consumidor [IDECON], 2020).

5 Access to the Spectrum

How does the country organise access to spectrum for data transmission (e.g., via auctions)?

With the General Telecommunications Law n° 9.472 of 1997, the process of privatisation of telecommunication services in the country adopted the form of auction, competition or sale of shares in public offering, as a way of organising the spectrum. Article 157 of the said law defined the radio frequency spectrum as a limited resource and as a public good, the management and use of which is Anatel's responsibility. Article 158 competes with Anatel for the Radio Frequency Allocation, Distribution and Destination Plan.

The Plan must allocate the frequency bands guided by international recommendations, serve the public interest, develop the national sector and facilitate consultation and knowledge of the spectrum with regard to decision-making by interested parties.

In 1998, Resolution n° 65 established the Bidding Regulation for the Concession, Permission and Authorization of Telecommunications Service and Authorization for the Use of Radiofrequency.

With the regulation, the telecommunications service concession is defined, and that should be made through publication in the Official Gazette and submitted to public consultation. In the next phase, all the bidders' proposals are analysed and judged according to the requirements of the invitation to bid. Then, the winning proposals and resources are enabled, and the Anatel Council awards the service award. It is worth emphasising that during the qualification of the winner, tax regularity, technical, legal, economic and financial quality are checked, including in the case of consortia. The concession is formalised by signing a contract.

The concession of permission is given in an exceptional situation by compromising the functioning of the service, which leads to intervention in the concessionaire company or by a concession. The permission is preceded by the bidding process and formalised by signing the term.

Authorisation and use of radiofrequency are administrative acts linked to the concession or permission, which assigns a fixed period of right to use radio frequency and follows the rules of the General Plan of Concessions and Regulation of Telecommunications Services of Anatel.

With the increase in applications that can be transmitted through the data transmission spectrum, Anatel keeps the Frequency Band Allocation, Destination and Distribution Plan updated, together with the band assignment table. Both thc allocation and destination of the bands are organised according to the function of the spectrum use: primary services and secondary services. Specific definitions of spectrum usage follow Resolution n° 671 of 2016.

The band frequencies and prices are stipulated by Anatel, placed in public consultation and structured in the auction call instrument. In the bidding model, Anatel splits the spectrum into parts of band frequencies and allocates services to each fraction of the spectrum. In the country, cell phone radio frequency was the first auction in 1996. In 2010, another auction was held for the mobile phone band H.[18] The fourth generation of mobile broadband (4G) that corresponds to the 700 MHz band was put up for auction in September 2014. However, the auction rules may change, the Ministry of Science, Technology, Innovations and Communications recently issued Ordinance n° 418 of 2020, with recommendations and measures for the bidding of frequency bands for the deployment of the fifth generation of mobile telephony.

Does the country offer any kind of advantage in access to the spectrum (for example, discount or compensation) for operators that use the spectrum to provide services in rural areas?

Rural service in the country has a specific regulation by Anatel. Resolution n° 622 of 2013 defined the guidelines for the provision of fixed telephone service in rural areas and remote regions, except the basic charging area. The service has a General Plan of Goals for Universalization which governs the Authorisation Terms (ANATEL, 2022d).

The provision of services in the rural area was established by the Authorisation Term linked to Bidding Notice n° 004 of 2012—Rural and urban Broadband Notice. The service providers that won the bid should assume the commitment to reach rural and remote areas, allowing the inclusion and penetration of voice and data services. Thus, providers are obliged to offer fixed telephone services and multimedia communication services with defined distance, and to serve rural public schools, providing data connection. Data transmission speeds were also established.

There are no policies or compensation devices or deeds that will offer services in rural areas. However, the General Plan of Goals for Universalization, excluded the goal of creating multifaceted service stations in the rural area, converging on the universal service obligation.

[18] For more information on past auctions, see the Senate's Journal of public hearings (Teixeira & Brasil, 2011).

Does the country offer low bureaucratic, affordable licensing for spectrum access to be used for social purposes or to provide coverage? Does this include provision of public Wi-Fi services?
The bidding rules for the right to use radio frequencies provided for in the Regulation guided by Resolution n° 671 of 2016, item 2, note that Anatel may reserve radio frequency bands or sub-bands to serve projects of social and digital inclusion, to provide use by public security, civil defence and military purposes.

Wireless technology uses the technical protocol of the Institute of Electrical and Electronic Engineers 802.11, which defines a series of transmission and coding standards for wireless communications.[19] Anatel regulates the use of radiocommunication equipment with restricted radiation, which includes the wireless network standard, which is the wireless connectivity standard for local networks. Resolution n° 680 of 2017 on the Restricted Radiation Radiocommunication Equipment Regulation, Article 62, determines that network stations supporting the provision of services of collective interest are exempted from licensing, applying to providers with up to 5000 accesses in service.

The recent Resolution n° 718 of 2020 altered the functioning of the femtocells, allowing the provider to self-configure and manage the users. The femtocells operate as fixed station radio communication, like low-power antennas and reach and cover signals, especially in indoor environments.

Does the country allow secondary use of spectrum? If so, how is it defined?
The secondary use of the spectrum is carried out according to the concession of the right to use a radio frequency. The entity that is authorised to use the frequency on a primary basis has the right to protect its communication in the event of harmful interference. Frequencies that operate on a secondary basis do not have the right to protection, so they cannot activate Anatel.

When the destination of the primary use range is followed, authorisation for secondary use is permitted. According to Resolution n° 671 of 2016, Chapter 3, the channelling and specific conditions of use of radio frequency, as secondary use, must be compatible with the activity or service to be explored, regarding the power, bandwidth and technique employed. This type of authorisation does not require public calling.

The new General Telecommunications Law n° 13,879 of 2019 changed the requirement to present a viable and compatible project in the case of authorisation of telecommunications services. Regulation facilitates the secondary spectrum market, allowing for an extension through successive authorisations for telecommunications services. For extensions of spectrum use, investment commitments will be established according to government guidelines or the payment of public value for renewal. Finally, spectrum management has also been made more flexible, as it allows the transfer of authorisation to use the banner without the bound correspondence, with the consent of Anatel.

[19] For more information on the adoption of wireless in the country, see Marques (2006).

Do the country's regulations provide for the use of unlicensed or license-free bands in specific areas, such as rural areas, or throughout the country?
According to Resolution n° 680, 2017 and n° 705, 2018 the use of radio frequency bands without a license or in specific areas, will be possible whenever the interested party complies with the regulation and authorisation, both of the use of the frequency, band or channel, in the following situations: authorisation of use nonexclusive, that is, secondary character; band association already held by the entity, in the same area and space, corresponds to another service of collective interest; primary authorisation, with verification that there is no technical limitation.

In the case of multimedia communication services, providers with up to 5000 accesses are exempted from licensing, and whose use is exclusive by confined means or restricted radiation radio equipment such as Wi-Fi.

The provision of services in rural areas follows specific Resolution n° 622 of 2013, disciplined in terms of authorisation; according to which, fixed telephone service providers must follow the general plan of goals guided by the principles of universalisation, and offer rural service plans.

6 Financial Resources

Is there any fund for universalisation (to promote the increase) of Internet access or access to Telecom services for everybody? Is there a Universal Service Fund or any other fund? If so, how are resources collected and distributed?
There are three funds to promote telecommunications services and to promote technological innovation: FUST, FINTEL and FUNTTEL.

The Telecommunications Inspection Fund (FISTEL) was created to provide resources and expenses for the Federal Government to carry out the inspection of telecommunications services. The Fund was created by Law n° 5.070 of 1966 and amended by the General Telecommunications Law in 1997, adapting the sector to the new reality, but maintaining the cost of inspection activities. Anatel took over the management of the fund when it was created.

The fund is made up of Anatel's collections: inspection and installation fees, inspection and operation fees, and provision of telecommunications services. It is possible to monitor the fund's annual collection, and the legal destinations, between Anatel, National Treasury, National Culture Fund, Telecommunications Services Universalization Fund and the National Scientific and Technological Development Fund (ANATEL, 2020a).

The Telecommunications Services Universalization Fund (FUST) aims to stimulate the expansion of services throughout the country, expanding the offer in regions with low population density, low income, and inadequate infrastructure; thus, there are no viable rates of return sufficient for investment in universalisation.

The fund for the integration of voice and data in the country was established by Law n° 9.998 of 2000, and reinforces the premise of service availability to the user, regardless of cost. Therefore, voice and data services must include the entire population, with priority for areas related to education, health, security, remote or border regions, extending access to people with special needs.

The fund consists of a contribution of 1% on the gross operating revenue on the telecommunications service provided in the public and private regimes, in addition to the funds transferred from FISTEL. The distribution of resources is applied to programmes, projects and activities carried out by fixed-line concessionaires, in areas indicated by the Superintendence of Development of the Northeast and by the Superintendence of Development of the Amazon, with 18% being applied in education, assisting the disabled.

All service providers that hold a concession, permission or authorisation to provide services, radio frequency and satellite exploration rights are required to contribute. It is possible to follow the evolution of the collection of the universalisation fund, the value of the allocations received, contributions and total charges between the years 2001 and 2020.[20]

The Fund for the Technological Development of Telecommunications (FUNTTEL) was created by Law n° 10.052 of 2000 to stimulate technological innovation among companies in the telecommunications sector, to facilitate the access of medium and small companies, and to promote professional training to increase the competitiveness of the national industry.

The fund's contribution is 0.5% of the gross revenue of protesting telecommunications services companies, excluding taxes. The funds are applied exclusively according to the interest of the telecommunications sector, directly allocated to the CPQd Foundation.

For the promotion of public broadcasting, Law n° 11.652 of 2008, Article 32, instituted the Contribution for the Promotion of Public Radio Broadcasting (CFRP), whose objective is to improve services by expanding its penetration. The funds are paid annually, in the form of instalments, and are destined for Brazil Communication Company (EBC) and Anatel is responsible for planning and monitoring the contribution. The amounts collected by the company in the exercise of its activities generate a return of 2.5% of the amount collected for Anatel (Ministry of Communications, 2022a).

Are telecommunications services taxed or subject to other specific levies? If so, how?

The sector's tax burden is on mobile telephony and broadband, and is intended to pay government taxes and the remuneration of the telecommunications sector's production chain. In accordance with Anatel, tax rates are applied to Transactions on Circulation of Goods and Services (ICMS), Social Integration Program (PIS) and Contribution to the Financing of Social Security (COFINS). These taxes may vary by state. In addition to the tax burden, income tax— corporate and social contribution on net income (CSLL) are levied. According to Anatel simulations,

[20] See Law n° 10,052 of the Executive Branch (2000).

approximately 40.3% of the value of the service is destined for the tax burden (Ministry of Communications, 2021a).

In addition, it has sector contributions through public funds to maintain the productive chair: Fund for Universalization of Telecommunications Services, Fund for Telecommunications Inspection and Fund for Technological Development of Telecommunications.

According to the World Telecommunication/ICT Indicators database, the Brazilian tax burden is the fourth largest in mobile telephony services and the largest in fixed broadband (Ministry of Communications, 2021a).

Is there any fund to provide subsidies to operators to expand coverage to underserved areas and least privileged populations?

The Telecommunications Services Universalization Fund was created to support universal service obligations for telecommunications services directly in areas where there is no efficient operation of the service. In the case of Brazil, these areas are concentrated in the north and northeast regions.

However, as the Structural Plan for Telecommunications Networks 2019–2024 (Ministry of Communications, 2022b), Anatel sent a proposal for a draft law (Grossmann, 2022) to the Directing Council of the Ministry of Science, Technology, Innovation and Communications, for the improvement of sectoral legislation to expand the use of the fund's resources. The fund currently focuses on Switched Telephone Service projects, but the sector's strategy is to make it effective for broadband policies. Therefore, more aligned with the objectives of increasing access to telecommunications services, such as the Internet.

Is any form of direct support (such as funding or tax exemptions) offered to small/micro/not-for-profit providers?

To promote the expansion of fixed broadband, Anatel, through Resolution n° 694 of 2018, instituted some incentives for the performance of small service providers. To facilitate and encourage competition between companies, the agency created the Wholesale Offers Negotiation System; in addition, it will be able to establish differentiated obligations for Small Providers (ANATEL, 2021).

The agency provided a booklet with guidelines on competitive broadband and with guidelines on how to be a telecommunications service provider (ANATEL, n.d.-a).

References

Alliance for Affordable Internet [A4AI]. (2022). *Affordability Drivers Index (ADI)*. https://a4ai.org/research/affordability-drivers-index/

Agência Nacional de Telecomunicações [ANATEL]. (2018). *Manual de Boas Práticas Regulatórias*. https://www.gov.br/casacivil/pt-br/assuntos/governanca/regulacao/boas-praticas-regulatorias/manual-de-boas-praticas-regulatorias/manualbpr-anatel.pdf/view

ANATEL. (2019). *Manual Operacional de Compartilhamento de Infraestrutura*. https://sei.anatel.gov.br/sei/modulos/pesquisa/md_pesq_documento_consulta_externa.php?eEPwqk1skrd8hSlk5Z3rN4EVg9uLJqrLYJw_9INcO5pd7dnORvfFQEeUSwhLN0vZREs-3AqCmF3tK6CIIBd_Di7fcTDBSVofLa8sECA7Jd61GwfokB7mlnOl_tUlGtS

ANATEL. (2020a). *Arrecadação*. https://www.gov.br/anatel/pt-br/regulado/arrecadacao

ANATEL. (2020b). *Plano Estrutural de Redes de Telecomunicações (PERT). Planejamento regulatório da ANATEL para a ampliação do acesso à banda larga no Brasil. PERT 2019-2024*. https://sei.anatel.gov.br/sei/modulos/pesquisa/md_pesq_documento_consulta_externa.php?eEP-wqk1skrd8hSlk5Z3rN4EVg9uLJqrLYJw_9INcO4m2N1jXIPEu1rXnv7UHJFGKd-jO_xz5ZYqyuXgvKFPZe9U7a4FRauel0Ej_GJ3pzD2sKi_sQQhtHNHQk_javEK

ANATEL. (2021). *Mercados de Atacado*. https://www.gov.br/anatel/pt-br/regulado/competicao/mercados-de-atacado

ANATEL. (2022a). *Painéis de Dados*. https://informacoes.anatel.gov.br/paineis/acessos

ANATEL. (2022b). *Anatel e Ancine reúnem-se em Brasília*. https://www.gov.br/anatel/pt-br/assuntos/noticias/anatel-e-ancine-reunem-se-em-brasilia

ANATEL. (2022c). *Relações Internacionais*. https://www.gov.br/anatel/pt-br/assuntos/atuacao-internacional/relacoes-internacionais

ANATEL. (2022d). *Plano Geral de Metas de Universalização*. https://www.gov.br/anatel/pt-br/regulado/universalizacao/plano-geral-de-metas-de-universalizacao

ANATEL. (n.d.-a). *Como ser provedor de internet*. https://www.anatel.gov.br/Portal/verificaDocumentos/documento.asp?null&filtro=1&documentoPath=sala_imprensa/17-4-2017%2D%2D17h8min27s-cartilha_como_ser_provedor_internet.pdf

ANATEL. (n.d.-b). *Legislação*. https://informacoes.anatel.gov.br/legislacao/

ANATEL. (n.d.-c). *Consulta Pública N° 13*. https://sistemas.anatel.gov.br/SACP/Contribuicoes/TextoConsulta.asp?CodProcesso=C2326&Tipo=1&Opcao=finalizadas

ANATEL. (n.d.-d). *Consulta Pública N° 41*. https://sistemas.anatel.gov.br/SACP/Contribuicoes/TextoConsulta.asp?CodProcesso=C2506&Tipo=1&Opcao=andamento%E2%80%8B%E2%80%8B

Berbet, L. (2019). *Decreto do Governo vai Regulamentar a Lei das Antena*. Tele.síntese. https://www.telesintese.com.br/decreto-do-governo-vai-regulamentar-a-lei-das-antenas/

Brasil. (2014). Resolução nº 32, de 2014. *Ministério das Comunicações*. https://antigo.mctic.gov.br/mctic/export/sites/institucional/contratos_gestao_organizacoes_sociais/arquivos/TCG/LNA/Relatorio-2014.pdf

Brazilian Internet Exchange [IX.br]. (n.d.). *Localidades atuais do IX.br*. https://ix.br/localidades/atuais

Brazilian Network Information Center [NIC.br], & Regional Center for Studies on the Development of the Information Society [CETIC.br]. (2019). *Assessing Internet Development in Brazil: Using UNESCO Internet Universality ROAM-X Indicators*. https://cetic.br/publicacao/assessing-internet-development-in-brazil-using-unesco-s-internet-universality-roam-x-indicators/

Brazilian Network Information Center [NIC.br], & Brazilian Internet Steering Committee [CGI.br]. (n.d.). *OpenCDN Shared Infrastructure [Infraestrutura Compartilhada]*. https://opencdn.nic.br/

Center for the Study, Response and Treatment of Security Incidents in Brazil. (2022). *Support Materials for Computer Security Incident Response Teams (CSIRTs) [Materiais de Apoio para Grupos de Resposta a Incidentes de Segurança em Computadores (CSIRTs)]*. Cert.br. https://www.cert.br/csirts/

Centro Regional de Estudos para o Desenvolvimento da Sociedade da Informação. (2022). Relatório Anual Cetic.br 2021. https://cetic.br/pt/publicacao/cetic-br-annual-report-2021/

Decreto n. 10.222, de 5 de fevereiro de 2020. (2020).

Decreto n. 10.405 do Poder Executivo, de 25 de junho de 2020. (2020). https://www.in.gov.br/en/web/dou/-/decreto-n-10.405-de-25-de-junho-de-2020-263473205?utm_term=ABERT+URGENTE+-++Published+decree+which+extends+deadlines+for+licensing+of+radio+and+TVstations&utm_campaign=GLOBALLIST&utm_source=e-

goi&utm_medium=email&eg_sub=126f7ff952&eg_cam=37d49d60538ed4736a3cd5d0609&eg

Decreto n. 8.771 do Poder Legislativo, de 11 de maio de 2016. (2016). https://legislacao.presidencia.gov.br/atos/?tipo=DEC&numero=8771&ano=2016&ato=070QTRq1EeZpWT2f5

Decreto n. 9.573 do Poder Executivo, de 22 de novembro de 2018. (2018). https://legislacao.presidencia.gov.br/atos/?tipo=DEC&numero=9573&ano=2018&ato=e04c3ZU9UeZpWT43c

Decreto n. 9.612 do Poder Executivo, de 17 de dezembro de 2018. (2018). http://www.planalto.gov.br/ccivil_03/_Ato2015-2018/2018/Decreto/D9612.htm

Decreto n. 9.619 do Conselho diretor da agência nacional de telecomunicações, de 20 de dezembro de 2018. (2018). https://www.anatel.gov.br/legislacao/index.php/component/content/article?id=1243

Decreto n. 9.875 do Poder Executivo, de 27 de junho de 2019. (2019). https://www.in.gov.br/en/web/dou/-/decreto-n-9.875-de-27-de-junho-de-2019-%20179414859%20#:%20~:%20text%20=%202%%20C2%%20BA%%2020O%%2020Advice%%2020National%%2020de,%20smuggling%%202C%%2020%%20C3%%20A0%20egaega%%20C3%%20A7%%20C3%%20A3o%%2020fiscal%%2020delas9602-4

Decreto n. 9.903 do Poder Executivo, de 8 de julho de 2019. (2019). http://www.planalto.gov.br/ccivil_03/_ato2019-2022/2019/decreto/D9903.htm

DECRETO REVOGADO N° 10.282 da Presidência da República. (2020). http://www.planalto.gov.br/ccivil_03/_ato2019-2022/2020/decreto/D10282.htm

Dutta, S., & Lanvin, B. (Eds.). (2022). *The Network Readiness Index 2022: Stepping into the new digital era*. Portulans Institute. https://networkreadinessindex.org/

Governo Federal. (n.d.). *Portal Brasileiro de Dados Abertos*. https://dados.gov.br/home

Grossmann, L. O. (2022, May 19). *Anatel sends projects to Minicom to use FUST resources [Anatel encaminha ao Minicom projetos para uso de recursos do FUST]*. Convergência Digital. https://www.convergenciadigital.com.br/Telecom/Anatel-encaminha-ao-Minicom-projetos-para-uso-de-recursos-do-FUST-60353.html?UserActiveTemplate=mobile

Instituto de Defesa do Consumidor [IDECON]. (2020, April). *Ação Civil Pública*. https://www.conjur.com.br/dl/juiza-federal-proibe-cortes-servicos.pdf

International Telecommunication Union [ITU]. (2017). *ICT Development Index 2017*. https://www.itu.int/net4/ITU-D/idi/2017/index.html

International Telecommunication Union [ITU]. (2019). *ICT Development Index 2019*. https://www.itu.int/en/ITU-D/Statistics/Pages/IDI2019consultation/default.aspx

Lei n. 9.998, de 17 de agosto de 2000. (2000). Brasília, DF. Recuperado de http://www.planalto.gov.br/ccivil_03/LEIS/L9998.htm

Lei n. 10.052, de 28 de novembro de 2000. (2000). Brasília, DF. Recuperado de http://www.planalto.gov.br/ccivil_03/LEIS/L10052.htm

Lei n. 11.652, de 7 de abril de 2008. (2008). Brasília, DF. Recuperado de https://presrepublica.jusbrasil.com.br/legislacao/93864/lei-11652-08

Lei n. 12.529, de 30 de novembro de 2011. (2011). Brasília, DF.

Lei n. 12.737, de 30 de novembro de 2012. (2012). Brasília, DF. Recuperado de http://www.planalto.gov.br/ccivil_03/_ato2011-2014/2012/lei/l12737.htm

Lei n. 12.965, de 23 de abril de 2014. (2014). Brasília, DF. Recuperado de https://www.jusbrasil.com.br/topicos/27363808/artigo-11-da-lei-n-12965-de-23-de-abril-de-2014

Lei n. 13.116, de 20 de abril de 2015. (2015). Brasília, DF. Recuperado de http://www.planalto.gov.br/ccivil_03/_ato2015-2018/2015/lei/L13116.htm

Lei n. 13.709, de 14 de agosto de 2018. (2018). Brasília, DF. Recuperado de http://www.planalto.gov.br/ccivil_03/_ato2015-2018/2018/lei/L13709.htm

Lei n. 13.853, de 8 de julho de 2019. (2019). Brasília, DF.

Lei n. 13.879, de 3 de outubro de 2019. (2019). Brasília, DF. Recuperado de https://www.in.gov.br/en/web/dou/-/lei-n-13.879-de-3-de-outubro-de-2019-219922078

Lei n. 13.979, de 6 de fevereiro de 2020. (2020). Brasília, DF. Recuperado de http://www.planalto.gov.br/ccivil_03/_ato2019-2022/2020/lei/L13979.htm

Lei n. 9.609, de 19 de fevereiro de 1998. (1998). Brasília, DF. Recuperado de http://www.planalto.gov.br/ccivil_03/leis/L9609.htm
Marques, F. P. (2006). The regulation of wireless internet access in Brazil [A regulação do acesso wireless à internet no Brasil]. *Revista de Economía Política de las Tecnologías de la Información y Comunicación, 8*. http://www.repositorio.ufc.br/bitstream/riufc/673/1/2006_art_%20fpjamarques_Eptic.pdf.
Ministério da Ciência, Tecnologia e Comunicações. (n.d.). Radiodifusão Comunitária. Recuperado de https://antigo.mctic.gov.br/mctic/opencms/comunicacao/SERAD/radiofusao/detalhe_tema/radiodifusao_comunitaria.html
Ministério das Comunicações. (2021a). *Carga Tributária em Telecomunicações. Recuperado de.* https://www.gov.br/anatel/pt-br/regulado/arrecadacao/carga-tributaria
Ministério das Comunicações. (2021b). *Plano Plurianual (PPA) 2020-2023*. Recuperado de https://www.gov.br/anatel/pt-br/acesso-a-informacao/acoes-e-programas/plano-plurianual-ppa
Ministério das Comunicações. (2021c). *Mapeamento de Redes de Transporte*. Recuperado de https://www.gov.br/anatel/pt-br/dados/infraestrutura/mapeamento-de-redes
Ministério das Comunicações. (2022a). *Contribuição para o Fomento da Radiodifusão Pública - CFRP e demais receitas (saldo financeiro)*. Recuperado de https://www.gov.br/anatel/pt-br/regulado/arrecadacao/cfrp
Ministério das Comunicações. (2022b). *Plano Estrutural de Redes de Telecomunicações - PERT*. Recuperado de https://www.gov.br/anatel/pt-br/dados/infraestrutura/pert
Ministério das Comunicações. (2022c). *Agenda Regulatória 2021-2022*. https://www.gov.br/anatel/pt-br/regulado/agenda-regulatoria/2021-2022
Ministério das Comunicações. (2022d). *Anatel adota nova medida cautelar contra chamadas abusivas*. https://www.gov.br/anatel/pt-br/assuntos/noticias/anatel-adota-nova-medida-cautelar-contra-chamadas-abusivas
Ministério das Comunicações. (2022e). *Valores do Índice de Serviços de Telecomunicações – IST*. https://www.gov.br/anatel/pt-br/regulado/competicao/tarifas-e-precos/valores-do-ist
Ministério do Planejamento, Desenvolvimento e Gestão. (2020). *do Monitoramento – 2019*. https://www.ebc.com.br/sites/_institucional/files/atoms/files/siop_monitoramento_espelho-monitoramento_1586979408590_1.pdf
Programa Internet + Segura (BCP). (n.d.) . https://bcp.nic.br/i+seg/sobre/
Regional Center for Studies on the Development of the Information Society [CETIC]. (2020). *Executive Summary ICT Households Survey 2020*. https://www.cgi.br/media/docs/publicacoes/2/20211124201635/executive_summary_ict_households_2020.pdf
Resolution No. 477 of the Director Council of the National Telecommunications Agency [RESOLUÇÃO N°477 do Conselho Diretor da Agência Nacional de Telecomunicações]. (2007). https://informacoes.anatel.gov.br/legislacao/resolucoes/2007/9-resolucao-477
Resolution No. 532 of the Director Council of the National Telecommunications Agency [RESOLUÇÃO N°532 do Conselho Diretor da Agência Nacional de Telecomunicações]. (2009).
Resolution No. 612 of the board of directors of the national telecommunications agency [RESOLUÇÃO N°612 do Conselho diretor da agência nacional de telecomunicações]. (2013). https://informacoes.anatel.gov.br/legislacao/resolucoes/2013/450-resolucao-612#tituloVIIIcapIII
Resolution No. 614 of the board of directors of the national telecommunications agency [RESOLUÇÃO N°614 do Conselho diretor da agência nacional de telecomunicações]. (2013). https://informacoes.anatel.gov.br/legislacao/resolucoes/2013/465-resolucao-614#:~:text=Aprova%20o%20Regulamento%20do%20Servi%C3%A7o,Direito%20de%20Explora%C3%A7%C3%A3o%20de%20Sat%C3%A9lite
Resolution No. 617 of the Director Council of the National Telecommunications Agency [RESOLUÇÃO N°617 do Conselho Diretor da Agência Nacional de Telecomunicações]. (2014).
Resolution No. 622 of the Director Council of the National Telecommunications Agency [RESOLUÇÃO N°622 do Conselho Diretor da Agência Nacional de Telecomunicações]. (2013). https://informacoes.anatel.gov.br/legislacao/resolucoes/2013/591-resolucao-622

Resolution No. 632 of the Board of Directors of the National Telecommunications Agency [RESOLUÇÃO N°632 do Conselho diretor da agência nacional de telecomunicações]. (2014). https://informacoes.anatel.gov.br/legislacao/resolucoes/2014/750-resolucao-632
Resolution No. 65 of the Director Council of the National Telecommunications Agency [RESOLUÇÃO N° 65 do Conselho Diretor da Agência Nacional de Telecomunicações]. (1998). https://www.anatel.gov.br/legislacao/resolucoes/13-1998/164-resolucao-65
Resolution No. 671 of the Board of Directors of the National Telecommunications Agency [RESOLUÇÃO N°671 do Conselho Diretor da Agência Nacional de Telecomunicações]. (2016). https://www.anatel.gov.br/legislacao/resolucoes/2016/911-resolu
Resolution No. 680 of the Board of Directors of the National Telecommunications Agency [RESOLUÇÃO N° 680 do Conselho Diretor da Agência Nacional de Telecomunicações]. (2017). https://informacoes.anatel.gov.br/legislacao/resolucoes/2017/936-resolucao-680
Resolution No. 683 of the Board of Directors of the National Telecommunications Agency. [RESOLUÇÃO N°683 do Conselho Diretor da Agência Nacional de Telecomunicações]. (2017). https://informacoes.anatel.gov.br/legislacao/resolucoes/2017/949-resolucao-683
Resolution No. 693 of the Board of directors of the national telecommunications agency [RESOLUÇÃO N°693 do Conselho diretor da agência nacional de telecomunicações]. (2018). https://informacoes.anatel.gov.br/legislacao/resolucoes/2018/1142-resolucao-693
Resolution No. 718 of the Director Council of the National Telecommunications Agency [RESOLUÇÃO N°718 do Conselho Diretor da Agência Nacional de Telecomunicações]. (2020). https://www.anatel.gov.br/legislacao/resolucoes/2020/1380-resolucao-718#art1
Secretaria de Logística e Tecnologia da Informação. (2012). *Instrução Normativa No. 4 de 12 de Abril de 2012: Institui a Infraestrutura Nacional de Dados Abertos - INDA*. Diário Oficial da União. https://www.gov.br/governodigital/pt-br/dados-abertos/InstrucaoNormativaINDA42012.pdf
Teixeira, J. C., & Brasil, T. (Eds.). (2011). The paths to expand broadband in Brazil [Os caminhos para expandir a banda larga no Brasil]. *Em discussão! Revista de audiências públicas do Senado Federal, 2*(6). https://www12.senado.leg.br/noticias/acervo-historico/em-discussao/arquivos/06/
World Trade Organisation [WTO]. (2016, March 18). *Brazil's commitments on financial services come into effect*. https://www.wto.org/english/news_e/news16_e/serv_18mar16_e.htm

Larissa Galdino de Magalhães Santos is a Yufe4Postdoc, Marie Sklodowska-Curie at the Universität Bremen. Before, she was an associate researcher at the United Nations University, Electronic Governance Unit (UNU-EGOV). Larissa also is a Researcher at the Center for Technology and Society at FGV and CyberBRICS, Law School at Fundação Getúlio Vargas. Her research is located between government technology and innovation, with a special focus on open data, smart cities, and digital transformation strategies. Co-chair of the Open Data Charter Implementation Group, she is also a Professional Fellow at Fundação Getúlio Vargas for Europe and a Ph.D. in Political Science from the State University of Campinas.

Brazil: An Analysis of the Digitalisation of Public Services

Larissa Galdino de Magalhães Santos

Abstract This chapter maps key aspects related to the digitalisation of public services in Brazil. The following elements are investigated: policy elements related to digital government strategies, declarations, programs and actions; regulatory elements related to openness, sharing and data protection laws; institutional and governance elements related to the oversight and competences of public agencies, public-private partnerships and regulatory innovations in technology; and evidence from critical sectors such as smart cities, digital ID, and digital payments.

1 National Strategies and Priorities

Is there a national strategy for digitalisation/digital transformation? Is there a specific national strategy for digitalisation of public services?

Since 2000, the Brazilian government has started a series of adaptations to the Electronic Government Program (Brazilian Government, 2019a), acting in three axes: focus on the citizen, internal management improvement, and integration with partners and suppliers.

From 2001 onwards, a set of regulations, laws, resolutions, actions, and strategies for the attributions of the Electronic Government were launched. Also, committees and working groups were created to support the Program.

In 2004 the Department of Electronic Government, Interoperability Standards in Electronic Government, and the Free Software Migration Reference Guide were created. The following year, the Electronic Government Accessibility Model was launched.

The first digital inclusion portal appeared in 2006 together with the Government Services Indicators and Metrics Methodology. In 2008, a government network for data, voice, and image transmission was implemented, with high standards of

L. Galdino de Magalhães Santos (✉)
Electronic Governance Unit (UNU-EGOV), United Nations University, Guimarães, Portugal
e-mail: larissagms@yahoo.com.br

L. Belli, L. Galdino de Magalhães Santos (eds.), *SmartBRICS*,
https://doi.org/10.1007/978-3-031-98204-0_4

performance and security, for the integration of government agencies and entities through Project Infovia (Ministry of Communications, 2022).

In the following year, the Electronic Invoice and the first purchasing services were launched. With the 2011 Access to Information Law, the government launched the Electronic Government Portal. Until 2014, the government had created initiatives to support systems of contracting and bidding.

Starting in 2015, the program was redesigned to take a citizen-centric vision towards the digital government. Subsequently, the Digital Governance Policy and the Digital Governance Strategy were created to coordinate investments to accelerate the digital transformation.

Decree No. 9319 (Decree No. 9,319 of the Presidency of the Republic, 2018) of 2018 created the National System for Digital Transformation to facilitate the governance structure and the implementation of the Brazilian Strategy for Digital Transformation with its thematic axes.

The Brazilian Strategy for Digital Transformation (E-Digital) 2016–2020 (Brazilian Government, 2018) was released in 2018 with enabling axes and digital transformation axes. The enabling axis aims at digital development of the economy, through infrastructure and access to information and communication technologies; actions in research, development and innovation; adequate regulatory environment, norms and regimes that promote trust; development of educational and professional skills, and the country's international insertion. The digital transformation axis aims at a data-based economy, proliferation of connected devices, new business models, full exercise of citizenship, and service provision.

The National Digital Governance Strategy 2016–2019 instituted in 2016 was also co-created to centralise and integrate information from the federal public administration (Brazilian Government, Ministry of Planning, Development and Management, 2018). In practice, there was a change in the alignment of policies, strongly focused on the provision of digital public services, alignment with E-Digital, and incorporation of recommendations on digital governance from the Organization for Economic Cooperation and Development (OECD).

Decree No. 9,804 of 2019 changed the governance system of E-Digital (Decree No. 9,804 of the President of the Republic, 2019). The strategy was reorganised under the scope of the Interministerial Committee for Digital Transformation, chaired by the Civil House and linked to the Presidency of the Republic, and the Ministry of Science, Technology, Innovation, and Communications was responsible for supporting the activities.

The actions and axes related to the bodies and entities of the federal public administration were instituted through the Digital Government Strategy 2020–2022 (Brazilian Government website, 2021). This strategy determined the interoperability and integration of government databases and training of public officials in their digital skills.

The Brazilian Strategy for Digital Transformation (E-Digital) for the 2022–2026 (Center for Management and Strategic Studies (CGEE), 2022) cycle was published through Ordinance No. 6,543. The new version brings a diagnosis in the previous version and new assumptions based on the discussion of CITDigital members (commission) and with the participation of actors in society (public bodies, academia, private sector) that are related to the theme of digital transformation. The Thematic Chambers (Industry, Agro, Cities, Health and Tourism) also held discussions to support the new version.

Regarding the specific strategy for the digitalisation of services, the Digital Government Strategy 2020–2022, in March 2021, the government approved the Digital Government Law that consolidated the instruments and rules for the digital transformation of the government, including the public services platform.

Is the digitalisation of any specific sector seen as a priority for the country (e.g., Central Bank Digital Currency, digital identity, online payments, deployment of Artificial Intelligence, smart cities, cybersecurity, etc.)?

Priority strategies were defined from the first Brazilian Strategy for Digital Transformation (E-DIGITAL) 2016–2020 as actions to transform government and economy, specifically, priorities for smart cities, Internet of Things, industry, agriculture and livestock, health, security and defence, education, internationalisation of companies, research, development and innovation, online platforms, the development of flexible regulatory environments and stimuli to startups.

The strategies were implemented via the National System for Digital Transformation (Decree No. 9,319 of the Presidency of the Republic, 2018) and the Interministerial Committee for Digital Transformation through plans, strategies, and thematic chambers (Brazilian Government, Ministry of Science, Technology and Innovations, n.d.-c).

In 2019, the National Internet of Things Plan (Brazilian Government, Ministry of Science, Technology and Innovations, n.d.-a) was instituted to facilitate financial investments in technologies and to promote the profiling of IoT devices, such as connected sensors, lights, and meters to collect and analyse data in Brazilian cities. The Plan created the Thematic Chamber to support the ministries in recommendations, actions, and measures to implement infrastructure that connects IoT devices for the provision of services, creating supply and demand according to the local development capacity.

The Cities 4.0 Thematic Chamber created the Brazilian Charter for Smart Cities (Brazilian Government, Ministry of Regional Development, n.d.) in 2020 as political and induction strategies through the Digital Cities Program of the Ministry of Telecommunications. The purpose of the Charter is to create a public agenda, guide and understand the impacts and potential for digital transformation in Brazilian cities. The Charter established eight strategic goals and recommendations to facilitate sustainable transformation efforts for municipalities, institutions, and people.

In 2020, the National Cyber Security Strategy (Decree No. 10,222 from the President of the Republic, 2020) was instituted (E-Ciber) based on the National Information Security Policy (Decree No. 9,637 of the President of the Republic, 2018). The strategy determined priority actions for 2020–2023, to strengthen cybersecurity actions by public and private sectors; create a centralised model of national governance; encourage a trustworthy, collaborative and participatory environment among all interested parties; raise the level of protection of critical national infrastructures and government protection; improve the legal framework and innovations in cybersecurity; expand internal and international partnerships, and raise society's level of maturity on cybersecurity.

Digital Government Strategy 2020–2022 established principles, objectives, and initiatives for digital transformation through the federal government until 2022. Some guidelines prioritise the simplification of the organisation of companies, establish quality standards for e-public services, unify the domains of government in a single portal "gov.br," integration of States (federative units of Brazil) to the Gov.br Network, implementation of digital means of payments, cataloguing of government databases, creation of a map of Brazilian companies, implementation of Artificial Intelligence resources in public services, promotion of database through blockchain, adaptation to the General Data Protection Law, and training of professionals from government teams.

The Brazilian Strategy for Artificial Intelligence (Brazilian Government, Ministry of Science, Technology and Innovations, n.d.-b) was recently created and linked to the actions of the National Strategy for Digital Transformation. The strategy aims to elaborate the ethical principles for the responsible development and use of Artificial Intelligence; promote investments in research and development; remove barriers to innovation; train professionals; and stimulate Brazilian development in an international environment. The Brazilian Strategy for Artificial Intelligence [12] was recently created and linked to the actions of the National Strategy for Digital Transformation.

Law No. 13,444 of 2017 created the National Civil Identification to facilitate citizen interaction with government and private bodies and entities. The National Civil Identification will serve as a basis for creating the digital identity. A Technical Cooperation Agreement (General Secretariat of the Republic, n.d.) signed between the Superior Electoral Court, the General Secretariat of the Presidency of the Republic, and the Ministry of Economy was established to implement the cooperation and interoperability of the database with information on users of public services offered by official Federal Government portals. A steering committee was created to support the execution of activities.

The Central Bank of Brazil established the creation guidelines (General Secretariat of the Republic, n.d.) of a Brazilian digital currency in May 2021, the "Real Digital" as "Central Bank Digital Currency." Among the guidelines, the use of smart contracts, the Internet of Things, and programmable cash for retail payments is highlighted, both for online and offline operations. The distribution of currency will be controlled by the National Financial System and the Brazilian Payment System. The legal security provided is by international standards for combating illegal operations and money laundering, in addition to banking secrecy and personal data protection rules. There is still no timetable for implementing the currency. All online payment rules are organised by the Brazilian Payment System of the Central Bank.

Recently, the Brazilian Strategy for Digital Transformation (E-Digital) for the 2022–2026 was reviewed for a new cycle as provided for in paragraph 3 of Decree

No. 9.319 of 2018 establishing the National System for Digital Transformation. The strategy brings new actions to harmonise the initiatives of the Executive Branch Federal, and reinforces actions of digital inclusion, implementation of digital infrastructures, professional training, information security, cyber security and technological development.

Is there an overall Artificial Intelligence strategy? Is there a specific national strategy for the use of Artificial Intelligence in the public sector?

The Brazilian Artificial Intelligence Strategy (Brazilian Government, Ministry of Science, Technology and Innovations, n.d.-b) was established in 2021 and has thematic and transversal axes. The scope is general, not just targeted to the public sector. The strategies aim at defining ethical principles for development and accountability, removing barriers to innovation, promoting investments in research and development, professional training for the sector, and developing an informational environment with cooperation between private, public, research and development industries.

The governance of the strategy is made up of the Ministry of Science, Technology and Innovation, the EMBRAPII network of Technologies and Digital Innovation, and Guest Institutions. The Strategy established transversal axes: legislation, ethical use and regulation; AI governance and international aspects; and vertical axes: qualification for the digital future, workforce and training, research, development, entrepreneurship and innovation, application in the productive sectors, application in public power, and public safety. In all, 73 strategic actions were defined.

Is there a specific strategy or reference to the use of social media to facilitate government activities?

In 2012, an administrative rule of the National Security Council established norms for the use of social networks in the federal public administration. The Secretariat for Social Communication created an orientation manual (Secretariat of Social Communication, 2014) for acting on social media with a standard government identity. Currently, the Special Secretariat for Social Communication, linked to the Presidency of the Republic, guides the use of social media through the Publication Manual (Special Secretariat for Social Communication, n.d.) and the Department of Content and Management of Digital Channels.

Is there a strategy or any specific policies aimed at promoting the use of open-source software/hardware by public administrations or generally?

In 2007, the Brazilian Public Software Portal was created. In 2016, Administrative Rule No. 46 (Ordinance No. 46 from the Information Technology Secretariat, 2016) established rules including the definition of government software and free software. The strategy promotes the development of software projects on the portal and defines Brazilian public software that meets the needs of modernisation of public administration and which must be made available under a free licensing model. E-PING, e-government interoperability standards architecture, sets the conditions for open standards and software solutions among government agencies.

Are there specific policies mandating interoperability requirements for the systems utilised by public administrations? Are there any strategies or recommendations to avoid vendor lock-in?

Since 2014, the federal public administration has been required to adopt standards and policies of the basic structure of electronic government, ePING (Brazilian Government portal, 2018) (Electronic Government Interoperability Standards). The architecture defines the technical specifications that regulate the use of information and communication technology in the interoperability of services and establishes the conditions for interaction with other powers.

In 2016, the Digital Governance Policy (Repealed Decree No. 8,638 of the Presidency of the Republic, 2016) was instituted to promote the execution of programs and projects related to digital governance. In 2018, the Digital Governance Strategy 2016–2019 Brazilian Government, Ministry of Planning, Development and Management, 2018) was instituted to support the implementation of the Digital Governance Policy and the Brazilian Strategy for Digital Transformation (E-Digital).

The Digital Government Strategy 2020–2022 incorporated previous strategies and policies. The Digital Government Secretariat of the Special Secretariat for De-bureaucratisation, Management, and Digital Government of the Ministry of Economy became responsible for defining the rules and interoperability of the systems.

Is there a strategy or any specific policies promoting open data (e.g., government-business data sharing, open government, and/or open data in general)?

The National Open Data Infrastructure defines the standards, technologies, procedures, and mechanisms for promoting open data. The Open Data Policy (Decree No. 8,777 of the Presidency of the Republic, 2016) guides the planning and implementation of activities. The Open Government Policy (Decree No. 10,160 of the Presidency of the Republic, 2019) addresses the Open Government Action Plans. The policies are under the management of the Office of the Comptroller General (CGU). The Digital Government Strategy 2020–2022 defined guidelines for the integration of open data portals and expansion of the quantity and quality of available databases.

Are the national strategies binding documents (i.e., adopted in the form of laws or decrees) or are they just declaratory documents?

Most strategies have a binding document framework, such as the digital government strategy and digital transformation, and the digital government law; open government program, national open data infrastructure, and national open data policy; and the access to information law. Although the country has a robust framework of strategies, policies and laws, implementation is a gap. The evaluations of multilateral entities indicate that there is no budget allocation in the documents, nor specific funds for the priority actions of the strategies (OECD, 2020).

Is there a specific policy for integration, inclusion of vulnerable groups (e.g., elderly, etc) or accessibility for people with disabilities?

The government has an Accessibility Model in Electronic Government (eMAG) (Brazilian Government, Ministry of Economy, 2022a), which consists of a set of recommendations for accessibility in government portals. The latest revision of the model is from 2014. There are other support tools (Brazilian Government, Ministry of Economy, n.d.-b), such as a translator of Libras (Official Brazilian sign language) in free software, web standards in e-government, website accessibility evaluator, and accessibility references and models (Brazilian Government, Ministry of Economy, n.d.-a). Accessibility features are aimed at people with disabilities and do not mention the inclusion of other minority or vulnerable groups.

Are the national strategies guided, or are they involved in cooperation agreements, best practices, programs, associations of organisations such as UN Agenda 2030 SDGs, OECD, World Bank?

The axes of the Brazilian Strategy for Digital Transformation were organised according to the 2030 Agenda and the Sustainable Development Goals. However, the Presidency of the Republic sanctioned the 2020–2023 Multi-Year Plan for the planning of public policies and vetoed the monitoring and evaluation mechanisms of the SDGs (Sustainable Development Goals) in the country (Chamber News Agency, 2019). E-Digital was also created to establish cooperation with the Organization for Economic Cooperation and Development Wachowicz and Canut (2018).

The Digital Government Strategy 2020–2022 incorporated criteria and recommendations of the Organization for Economic Cooperation and Development in its objectives (Objective 13). Recently, Inter-American Development Bank (IDB) (Banco Interamericano de Desenvolvimento (BID), 2021) approved a financing line of up to US$1 billion for Brazil to contribute to the digital transformation.

Are there any existing policies to zero-rate certain e-government services? Are there such policies for specific public sectors?

With the COVID-19 pandemic, the Brazilian government regulated telecommunications and the Internet as essential public services, through Decree No. 10,282 of 2020 (Repealed Decree No. 10.282 of the Presidency of the Republic, 2020), and Law No. 13,979.

However, the declaration of essentiality of telecommunications and Internet services does not impose the provision of these services, indiscriminately, even for users by default. The purpose was to safeguard the continuity of services.

Some important initiatives were adopted by both the *Agência Nacional de Telecomunicações* and the providers[1] in mid-2020. The agency and the companies signed a public commitment to maintain connections via the "*Programa Brasil Conectado*" for continuity in the provision of services. The Program is part of the

[1] For more information on the telecommunications sector and COVID-19, please check TelComp's website: https://www.telcomp.org.br/home/o-setor-de-telecomunicacoes-e-a-covid-19/

National Broadband Program (ANATEL, 2021), which seeks to increase access to broadband Internet in the country, especially in regions that lack this technology. The operators at the Agency made available to the Ministry of Health the three-digit 196, for service actions involving matters relating to COVID-19. Some companies in the telecommunications sector have temporarily released TV and streaming content services, as well as the granting of Internet bonuses for mobile phones and residential broadband.

How does the country rank on global digital adoption indices, such as the World Bank's Digital Adoption Index, the Digital Society Index, IMD World Digital Competitiveness Ranking, Global Open Data Index, etc.?
According to the World Bank's Digital Adoption Index (World Bank, 2016), the Digital Adoption Index is 68.3%, the DAI Business Subindex is 67.8%, the DAI People Subindex is 55.2%, and the DAI Government Subindex is 81.8%. According to the Digital Society Index (Dentsu Aegis Network, 2020), 76% of Brazilians consent for the use of meta-data and data use by the service provider, with 37% choosing not to receive personalised ads; 84% would stop doing business with an organisation that has lost some of its data or has used the data irresponsibly; 48% expect financial benefits from organisations using their data; 64% believe they would make payments or services using facial recognition or fingerprint technology in the future.

According to the IMD World Digital Competitiveness Ranking (IDM, 2020), Brazil occupies the 51st overall position among 63 economies. For the knowledge assessment it is 57, the classification in technologies is also 57, however the classification for future readiness is 43.

According to the Global Open Data Index (2016–2017), the country is ranked 8, with a score of 68%, among which graduates found 166 datasets available.

According to the Open Data Barometer for Latin America and the Caribbean (2020), the country's overall score is 60.20. The average score among Latin American countries is approximately 40. Considering the overall ranking from 2013 to 2020, the country is in the fourth position. The evaluation of government actions and policies is 61.21. The evaluation of the implementation of open data in public policies is 87.33. The impact assessment of the use of open data is 31.67. The assessment indicates stagnation in the open data promotion policy in the country since 2018, with a lack of resources for the maintenance of the open data portal, and a lack of social participation in the governance of the national open data policy.

According to the 2020 United Nations Electronic Government Survey (United Nations Department of Economic and Social Affairs, 2020), Brazil was ranked for the first time in the group of countries with very high EGDI, with an index of 54. The index is calculated based on the average of the telecommunications infrastructure index, index of human capital, and online service index. The online service rating index is at 0.8706, the human capital index is at 0.6558, and the technology infrastructure index is at 0.6522. Although the country obtains highly developed human capital, the state of its infrastructure may be impeding progress in the development of e-government.

Brazil is in 18th position in the E-participation ranking, and the country's index is also very high, reaching 0.9048 (United Nations, 2022). The E-Government rank is 54, and the rating is 0.7677 (United Nations, 2022).

2 Regulations

Is there any general regulation (e.g., law, decree, standards) to organise the digitalisation of public services, other than specific regulations that might apply to the key sectors identified below?

The Digital Government Law No. 14,129 of March 2021 establishes the rules and standards for the provision of public digital services (Law No. 14,129 of the Legislative Branch, 2021). The law establishes the following principles and guidelines: availability and access to services on a single platform, transparency and monitoring of the quality of services; participation, inspection and social control; accountability of public management, use of accessible language; use of technology to optimise the work of public administration; integrated action of agencies and information; simplification of procedures, universalisation and self-service; interoperability systems and promoting open data; possibility of permanence of face-to-face service; protection of personal data; standardised and qualified services; accessibility; qualification of servers and digital inclusion; technical support to other spheres of government for the adoption of digital transformation; electronic signature, government as a platform, and use of data for decision making; adequate treatment for the elderly; preference for adopting technologies in an open and free format; technological development and public sector innovation.

Is there any regulation mandating transparency audits for technologies (e.g., of platforms, algorithms, cloud services, etc.) utilised by public administrations?

The Digital Government Law determines that all bodies and entities involved in the provision of digital public services and related activities will be subject to audits. Article 49 establishes that the authorities of each body or entity of the Executive, Judiciary, and Legislative Power, including the Federal Court of Accounts, and the Federal Public Ministry, establish, implement and maintain governance practices, risk management, control, and auditing.

Among the instruments are the mechanisms of internal control, internal audit, and external audit with independent assessment and consultancy work, following internationally recognised standards. However, the Digital Government Law does not set standards for disruptive technologies or platforms.

Is there any specific regulation mandating requirements for public procurements and public tenders regarding digital public services?

Decree No. 10641 of March 2021 on the national information security policy defined the conditions for exemption from bidding in cases that could compromise national security. The Institutional Security Office of the Presidency of the Republic can determine which products should be incorporated as information security resources to maintain integrity, authenticity, and interoperability between systems.

The new Law on Public Procurement and Administrative Contracts instituted in April 2021 changed the modalities of competition, tender, auction, and competitive dialogue and added auxiliary procedures (Law No. 14.133 of the Presidency of the Republic, 2021). Therefore, it included other rules relating to the differentiated regime for hiring and trading. The law is valid for public purchases and bids for digital public services and allows the use of the Brazilian Public Key as identification and digital signature for any type of bidding process (Law No. 14,063 of the Presidency of the Republic, 2020).

Are digital public services subject to general data protection regulations? If not, is there any data protection regulation for digital public services?

Digital public services are subject to the regulations observed in the General Law for the Protection of Personal Data, Law No. 13.709 of 2018, under the protection of the Digital Government Law. The principles of the Law determine that the bodies and entities involved in public services and with the sharing of personal data must provide a safe environment by the guidelines of the General Law for the Protection of Personal Data.

Especially regarding digital government platforms, Article 25 of the Digital Government Law, Law No. 14.129 of 2021 determines that tools for transparency and control of data processing accessible to the citizen are made available. Platforms must provide information about the purpose of data processing and shared use of data, and allow citizens to make requests to data controllers. The National Data Protection Authority may issue additional rules to regulate data protection and digital public services.

According to Decree No. 9745 of 2019, the Special Secretariat for Debureaucratization, Management, and Digital Government, of the Ministry of Economy, must support actions to promote information security and protection of personal data within the scope of the Federal Public Administration, through frameworks and guides to compliance with the legal framework for the protection of personal data.

Are there any current or proposed regulations mandating the sharing of data with government agencies to enable better delivery of public services?

Decree No. 10.046 of 2019 provides for governance in data sharing, creates the Citizen Registry to unify the identification of the citizen to provide public services, and institutes the Central Data Governance Committee to support data sharing. Data-sharing governance requires government agencies to simplify the provision of public services overall. The Base Registry is the main source of information, and it integrates data from different sources to promote the offer of services.

Recently, the decree on data governance and sharing in the public sector was amended by the Federal Supreme Court in view of the risks of exposure of sensitive data and misuse (Amorim et al., 2022). The Court determined that the sharing of personal data between public administration bodies and entities must be based on legitimate, specific and explicit purposes that justify the processing of data. Purposes must be stated, and sharing must be limited to the minimum necessary. All requirements of the General Data Protection Law must be guaranteed, and security measures must be implemented, such as an electronic system with access registration that enables accountability in case of abuse. Any inappropriate use or use below the defined parameters will result in civil liability of the State and the public agents involved.

The Digital Government Law reinforces the need for integrated action between bodies and entities for the sharing of personal data, except for the protection conditions. Articles 38, 39, and 40 of the Digital Government Law determine the rules for data interoperability between public bodies, to optimise data access costs, reuse data access infrastructure, improving policy management, increase the reliability of public administration registers, facilitate the interoperability and processing of data, and create unified means of identifying citizens for the provision of public services.

3 Institutions

Is there a specific body overseeing the digitalisation of the public sector?
The Digital Government Strategy is one of the axes of E-Digital, which is monitored by the Interministerial Committee for Digital Transformation (CTDigital), chaired by the Casa Civil and linked to the Presidency of the Republic. The digital transformation plan is coordinated by the Digital Government Secretariat of the Ministry of Economy, and the digital government strategy is executed by the Special Secretariat for Modernization of the State directly related to the General Secretariat of the Presidency of the Republic. A committee monitors and evaluates activities. The governance of the strategy is defined by the National System for Digital Transformation (SinDigital) established by Decree No. 9,319 of 2018. (Decree No. 9,319 of the Presidency of the Republic, 2018).

If such a body exists, what is its status (e.g., an independent agency, a ministry, an inter-ministerial committee, an ad-hoc body, etc.)?
The Special Secretariat for State Modernization (Brazilian Government, Presidency of the Republic, 2022) is to guide all strategic modernisation of the state among all ministries and reports directly to the Presidency Secretariat General of the Republic (Repealed Decree No. 9,982 of the Presidency of the Republic, 2019).

The Digital Government strategy is monitored by the committee formed by managers of the Special Secretariat for the Modernization of the State of the General Secretariat of the Presidency of the Republic and the Secretariat of Digital Government of the Ministry of Economy (Brazilian Government, 2021). The committee is responsible for evaluating the initiatives and monitoring the execution of services.

If such a body exists, what are its prerogatives and powers?
It is incumbent upon the Special Secretariat for State Modernization to support the State Ministries in modernisation strategies, which include: coordination of the

national modernisation policy, evaluation, and supervision of actions, definition of follow-up and execution guidelines, implementation of the digital government strategy, articulation with the Brazilian Strategy of Digital Transformation, promotion of governance between ministries, State agencies, Federal District and municipalities in the agreement of actions and projects, encouraging the exchange of good practices, including with international entities (Brazilian Government, Presidency of the Republic, 2022).

Is there an evaluation system or indicators to measure the progress of development of digital government?

The Directorate of Strategy, Standardization, and Monitoring of Projects of the Special Secretariat for Modernization of the State defines and guides the project management methodology. The Institutional and Regional Modernization Secretariat coordinates and monitors the results of partnerships between Public Authorities, federative entities, and private entities.

The bipartite Digital Government Strategy Monitoring Committee, formed by the Secretariat for Modernization, the Secretary-General of the Presidency, and the Secretariat for Digital Government of the Ministry of Economy, carries out the evaluations of the initiatives, from planning to completion.

Is there a public company or any public-private partnerships working on the development of specific solutions for digitising the public sector? If the company exists, what is its function?

There is no public company or partnership responsible for developing digitalisation solutions. However, the Secretariat of Digital Government is the central organ of the Information Technology Resources Administration System of the Federal Executive Branch of the Ministry of Economy and promotes improvements in the government's IT architecture, methodologies, processes, applications, platforms, and technological bases. The Digital Government Secretariat researches new technologies to establish the values and approval of technology goods or services contracts in conjunction with the Federal Budget Secretariat (Brazilian Government, 2019b).

What are the criteria aimed at guaranteeing the independence of the "third parties" auditing digital public service providers?

The Digital Government Law provides criteria for internal auditing in the Governance, Risk Management, Control, and Audit Chapter. Article 49 defines that auditing must improve the operations of organisations through independent assessment and consultancy, by international standards, both for a risk-based approach and for the promotion of prevention, detection, and investigation of fraud practiced by agents of public or private resources in the use of federal public resources.

The Federal Court of Auditors has evaluated digital transformation and digital services since 2017. The new monitoring report was presented in March 2021 and pointed out the need to create evaluation criteria for e-services (Federal Court of Audit (TCU), 2021).

4 Key Sectors

4.1 Digital Identity

Is there a strategy to digitalise this sector or any areas of it?
There is a Cooperation Agreement between the General Secretariat of the Presidency of the Republic, the Ministry of Economy, and the Superior Electoral Court, to establish cooperation for the implementation of the national civil identification and make the digital identity available (General Secretariat of the Republic, n.d.).

Is the use of specific technologies for digital identity systems promoted or prioritised (e.g., AI, blockchain, open-source software)?
The National Civil Identification database was created by law in 2017, with technical cooperation; the bodies will support the integration of the databases to the Gov.br Platform system, which is maintained by the Ministries of Economy and the General Secretariat of the Presidency of the Republic, and the biometric data collected by the Superior Electoral Court.

The digital identity depends on the National Base conference with the government's digital services platform, where it will be made available. The Ministry of Economy is responsible for maintaining the architecture, databases, security, and confidentiality of the platform's data. The Cooperation Agreement does not specify any type of technology. The Federal Data Processing Service (Serpro) is developing a blockchain-based national identity system (LGPD Observatory, n.d.).

Is there a sectoral regulation in place (e.g., law, decree, standards) to organise the digitalisation of the sector?
The National Civil Identification is governed by Law No. 13.444 of 2017, which established the registration of citizen data under the responsibility of the Superior Electoral Court. The Technical Cooperation Agreement implements the actions of interoperability of the databases and availability of the digital identity through the government's digital services platform.

Are there any policies promoting digital sovereignty for digital identity systems (e.g., data localisation, preference or obligation to utilise domestic providers, etc.)?
There are no specific policies on the digital identity system. The digital identity will follow the standards of government platforms through the technical cooperation agreement. The agreement does not provide for any type of preference or obligation regarding data. The institution of a work plan is planned to be monitored by the executive committee.

Has the digitisation of the sector or any area of it been promoted because of the COVID-19 pandemic? If yes, then how so?
No. According to technical cooperation, the integration of databases and services is designed to match the social relevance of Decree No. 8939 of 2016, which established the Digital Citizenship Platform (Gov.br) to offer digital public services.

Is there a specific body in charge of overseeing, coordinating or promoting the digitalisation of the sector?
Supervision will be carried out by the Executive Committee, the National Civil Identification Management Committee, composed of representatives from the Federal Executive Branch, the Superior Electoral Court, the Federal Senate, the Chamber of Deputies, and the National Council of Justice.

4.2 Smart Cities and Digitised Local Administrations

Is there a smart city strategy?
The first actions on the smart city were introduced in the Brazilian Strategy for Digital Transformation and the National Internet of Things Plan, which established the creation of thematic IoT chambers, and the Chamber of Cities 4.0. Decree No. 9,612 of 2018 determined the conditions for the creation of the Digital Cities Program (Portal of the Chamber of Deputies, n.d.). The Chamber of Cities 4.0 was launched in 2019 in a joint action of the Ministry of Regional Development and the Ministry of Science, Technology, and Innovation, in addition to public and private businesses, governmental and academic institutions. Four working groups were created: Urban and Sustainable Development, Digital Solutions and Technologies for Smart and Sustainable Cities, Low-Carbon Solutions and Technologies for Smart and Sustainable Cities, and Connectivity Infrastructure for Smart and Sustainable Cities.

The City Council 4.0 started to subsidise the creation of the Brazilian Program of Sustainable Smart Cities to create a maturity model of sustainable smart cities, and indicators of economic, environmental, and sociocultural dimensions. At the same time, the Ministry of Regional Development prepared the Brazilian Charter for Smart Cities in partnership with other ministries to support the construction of a public agenda for digital transformation in Brazilian cities. The Charter established a national concept for smart cities, defined strategic objectives, and provided recommendations for Brazilian cities.

The Charter was also prepared following the Support to the National Sustainable Urban Development Agenda (Andus) Project. Andus is a technical cooperation agreement between the Brazilian and German governments to support the national urban development strategy with a focus on sustainability and climate change.

Is the use of specific smart city technologies promoted or prioritised (e.g., AI, blockchain, open-source software)?
The Brazilian Charter for Smart Cities recommends the use of Artificial Intelligence to support the analysis of large amounts of anonymised data for diagnosis and urban management. It encourages the use of open-source or free software as per the guidelines of the National System for Digital Transformation. Use of new government contracting models based on the use of free software and open source. Use of open

source and free software is based on public data-sharing platforms. Expanding the use of collaborative mapping tools is done by favouring the use of free and open-source platforms and tools.

Is there a sectoral regulation in place (e.g., law, decree, standards) to organise the digitalisation of cities and urban areas in general?

The National Internet of Things Plan is a vertical of solutions for public policies and smart cities. Smart cities are environments that tend to be highly connected, whose infrastructure is interconnected by objects to the digital network to provide services.

Article 6 on public telecommunications policies, Decree No. 9,612 of 2018, determined the implementation of infrastructure and services based on information and communication technologies for the development of digital and smart cities, which include: implementation of infrastructure and services in areas where the service does not exist; connection to public equipment and public bodies through a high-capacity network; encouraging partnerships with private entities and public authorities to promote the sustainability of the initiatives; offering free and public access points; incentives for sharing publicly accessible data; fostering local development based on digital innovation and the use of technologies.

Then, the Brazilian Charter of Smart Cities determined the guiding directives and an agenda of recommendations, such as: supporting the municipalities and other local agents, to structure the initiatives and establish directives for the data governance system, security, and privacy; ensure security standards and protocols for IoT project components; adopt innovative and inclusive governance models to support territorial intelligence; encourage financing instruments in urban development for digital transformation, research, and infrastructure implementation; and build ways to systematically understand and assess the impacts of transformation, identify challenges and correct them throughout implementation.

Are there any policies promoting digital sovereignty for smart cities (e.g., data localisation, preference or obligation to utilise domestic providers, etc.)?

There is no specific legislation on digital sovereignty in smart cities.

Has the digitisation of the sector or any area of it been promoted because of the COVID-19 pandemic? If yes, then how so?

No. Although the COVID-19 pandemic has stimulated the adoption of telework and digital public services in general, the smart cities program has existed since the first Brazilian Strategy for Digital Transformation in 2018.

Is there a specific strategy or regulation targeting the digitisation of land records or real estate records?

There are no specific regulations regarding the digitisation of land records or real estate records. On the other hand, there is a national open data policy that promotes the availability of public data and information in the country, and the access to information law to promote information transparency.

Is there a specific body in charge of overseeing, coordinating or promoting the digitalisation of the sector?
There is no specific body to oversee, coordinate and promote the digitisation of the sector. There is a joint action by the Ministry of Science, Technology, and Innovation and the Ministry of Regional and Urban Development to support actions in the City Chamber 4.0. The Brazilian Charter for Smart Cities is supported by the National Agenda for Sustainable Urban Development in collaboration with the German Cooperation Agency (GIZ). With the recreation of the Ministry of Communications, some support activities are being taken over by the body.

Is there any outstanding example of strategy or policy elaborated by a local administration?
Brazilian cities such as Florianópolis, Curitiba, Campinas, Vitória, São Caetano do Sul, Santos, Brasília, Porto Alegre, Belo Horizonte, Rio de Janeiro, and São Paulo have smart city projects (BrazilLAB, 2021). Most projects do not have a direct link with the Federal Government Program initiative. The creation of the Brazilian Charter for Smart Cities aims to support the public agenda among Brazilian cities in a joint initiative linked to the strategies of the federal government.

5 Digital Money and Payments

Is there a strategy to digitalise this sector or any areas of it, such as the Central Bank Digital Currency program?
In August 2020, Ordinance No. 108.092 created the Interdepartmental Working Group to discuss guidelines for the creation of the Brazilian digital currency (Ordinance No. 108,092 of the Ministry of Economy/Brazilian Central Bank, 2020). The discussion on Central Bank Digital Currencies aims to follow the technological evolution of the national economy, increase the efficiency of the retail payment system, promote new business models and innovations, increase the country's participation in the global and regional economic scenarios, and increase the efficiency of cross-border transactions.

The Central Bank created the PIX, a means of instant payment in which funds are transferred between accounts (Banco Central do Brasil (BCB), n.d.-b). Pix can be made from a checking account, savings account or prepaid payment account. To make Pix, the system identifies the creditor's account information by creating a key. The Pix Key previously registered can be CPF, CNPJ, e-mail, mobile number or random key (a randomly generated alphanumeric string that can be used by users who do not want to link their personal data to their transactional account information). The recipient can also generate QR Codes. The Pix can scan a QR Code and the settlement is in real time.

The Central Bank of Brazil created the Open Financial System Banking (Banco Central do Brasil (BCB), n.d.-c). The initiative's main objective is to innovate the financial system through the sharing of data and services. The user decides to share his data between financial organisations. With this, organisations can offer personalised services. Resolution n° 32 and Resolution n° 117 established the technical requirements and operational procedures for the implementation of the system. Recently, the process changed its name to "Open Finance" with the aim of disseminating the scope of the program, which includes sharing data on products, exchange services, investments, insurance and pension plans.

Is the use of specific technologies for digital money/payments promoted or prioritised (e.g., AI, blockchain, open-source software)?
The Interdepartmental Working Group Assessment highlighted guidelines for digital currency development prioritising smart contracts, the Internet of Things, and programmable money.

Is there a sectoral regulation in place (e.g., law, decree, standards) to organise the digitalisation of the sector?
The development of the Brazilian digital currency is in the consultative study phase of the Interdepartmental Working Group. The general recommendation is for adherence to all the principles and rules of privacy and security determined, particularly by Complementary Law No. 105 of 2001 (banking secrecy), and by the General Law for the Protection of Personal Data (Banco Central do Brasil (BCB), n.d.-a). Measures to prevent money laundering and compliance with court orders are planned to track illegal operations.

Are there any policies promoting digital sovereignty in digital money/payments (e.g., data localisation, preference or obligation to utilise domestic providers, etc.)?
No.

Has the digitisation of the sector or any area of it been promoted because of the COVID-19 pandemic? If yes, then how so?
No.

Is there a specific body in charge of overseeing, coordinating or promoting the digitalisation of the sector?
The Interdepartmental Working Group supports the Central Bank of Brazil in digital currency development studies. The Central Bank of Brazil is responsible for the initiative.

6 Other Relevant Examples

Is there any other sector (such as education, health, etc) where a specific strategy or policy is in place to foster and organise digitalisation?
There is no strategy or policy in place for digitising other sectors. Despite this, there is a tax reform proposal that provides for the creation of taxes for digital services. There are strategic plans to scan for specific areas of public security and defence.

Is there a strategy to digitalise this sector or any areas of it?

There is no specific strategy. E-Digital defined the development of new technologies, accompanied by scientific production to stimulate security and defence through platforms that ensure the interoperability and coordination of the national defence command and control system, prioritising radio communication tools, investment in cryptography, and safety equipment.

The National Policy on Public Security and Social defence, Law No. 13.675 of 2018 instituted the National Information System on Public Security, Prisons, Traceability of Weapons and Ammunition, Genetic Material, Digitals, and Drugs to store, process, and integrate data and information to assist in the formulation, implementation, execution, monitoring and evaluation of public security and defence policies (Law No. 13,675 of the Presidency of the Republic, 2018). The National Policy for Public Security and Social Defence recommends the development of structural projects and technological innovation, training, standardisation of structures, and equipment of interest to public security. However, there is no specific guidance on scanning.

The Strategic Plan 2020–2023 defined as strategic projects: use of analytical intelligence, not in the Big Data Analytics technology segment for integration and analysis of data and information of interest to public safety; use of applied geotechnology and remote sensing for prevention, repression and elucidation of crimes and environmental disasters; creation of the National Multibiometric Bank and the Integrated Network of Multibiometric Banks to facilitate the unification and standardisation of criminal information; implementation of methodologies and information tools to create automatic identification of crime patterns, such as routes, types of crimes, vehicle and person profiles; strengthening of the National Network of Technology Laboratories against Money Laundering through the availability of adequate technologies, database and qualification for data analysis and processing procedures; to support the Integrated Network of Genetic Profile Databases; implement an Intelligent Situational Awareness System for data search, analysis, knowledge production; creation of the Cronos Network as a secure/encrypted information channel for data extraction and analysis from mobile devices; fostering the use of videoconferencing for court hearings in the prison system; and implementation of a critical digital radio communication system between public security agencies.

Is the use of specific technologies for public security promoted or prioritised (e.g., AI, blockchain, open-source software, biometrics, facial recognition, smart surveillance, etc.)?

The orientation of the Brazilian Strategy for Digital Transformation is to prioritise radio communication tools. The actions and programs of the 2020–2023 Strategic Planning guide on promoting the use of big data and Artificial Intelligence for data analysis in the MAIS Program, applied geotechnology and remote sensing, and biometrics.

Is there a sectoral regulation in place (e.g., law, decree, standards) to organise the digitalisation of the sector?
Law No. 13.675 of 2018 created the National Public Security Fund, which determined that the federal entities that are part of the National Information System on Public, Prison, Weapons and Ammunition, Genetic Material, Digital and Drug Security (Sinesp) must update and provide data to the system upon retention of the Fund's resources. The National Policy for Public Security and Social Defence does not have a specific digitisation norm or standard.

Are there any policies promoting digital sovereignty for public security systems (e.g., data localisation, preference or obligation to utilise domestic providers, etc.)?
The orientation of the Brazilian Strategy for Digital Transformation is to ensure the development of investment in radio communication protocols, encryption, and security equipment by national companies. The National Policy on Public Security and Social defence, Law No. 13.675 of 2018 instituted the National Information System on Public Security, Prisons, Traceability of Weapons and Ammunition, Genetic Material, Digitals, and Drugs to store, process, and integrate data and information to assist in the formulation, implementation, execution, monitoring and evaluation of public security and defence policies (Law No. 13,675 of the Presidency of the Republic, 2018).

Has the digitisation of the sector or any area of it been promoted because of the COVID-19 pandemic? If so, then how so?
No.

Is there a specific body in charge of overseeing, coordinating or promoting the digitalisation of the sector?
The promotion of digitisation is the responsibility of the Ministry of Justice and Public Security.

Is there a specific personal data protection regime regulating the processing of personal data performed by entities responsible for public security?
The General Data Protection Law regulates the collection, processing, and use of information by the Public Authorities. The law allows the shared use of data by Public Power, as long as its objective is to meet specific purposes for the execution of public policies and legal attribution by public bodies and entities. According to Article 4, the law does not apply to the processing of personal data carried out exclusively for public security, national defence, state security, or activities of investigation or prosecution of criminal offences.

7 Tax Administration

Is there a strategy to digitalise this sector or any areas of it?
There is no specific strategy for taxes on digital services. There are currently proposals for the institution of a Brazilian tax that would focus specifically on digital services being processed at the congress. There are also tax claims, contributions to programs for social integration and the formation of public servants' assets, and contributions for intervention in the economic domain. Current discussions are for the creation of a unified tax, Value Added Tax, to be charged on transactions and services.

Among the proposals of Constitutional Amendment and bills, we highlight the implementation of "Cide Digital" to increase the rate of Contribution for the Financing of Social Security for digital services, and the creation of a Social Contribution on Digital Services (Araújo, R., & Anea, C., 2021). The creation of the Contribution on the Invoicing of Goods and Services has been discussed by a working group within the Ministry of Economy and which contributed to the presentation of the Tax Reform Law Project (Brazilian Government, Ministry of Economy, 2022b).

Is the use of specific technologies for tax administration promoted or prioritised (e.g., AI, blockchain, open-source software)?
No.

Is there a sectoral regulation in place (e.g., law, decree, standards) to organise the digitalisation of the sector?
The Tax Reform Bill No. 3887 of 2020 provides for the creation of a new unified tax as a social contribution on transactions with goods and services (Chamber of Deputies, 2020). According to the bill, it is a new way of taxing consumption, in line with the most modern international models of Value Added Tax, which includes taxation on digital services. Articles 5 and 6 of the bill present proposals for tax collection through digital platforms, that is, one that acts as an intermediary between suppliers and purchasers of transactions on services and goods in a non-presential manner and by electronic means. The proposal is under consideration by the plenary of the legislative power.

Are there any policies promoting digital sovereignty in tax administration (e.g., data localisation, preference or obligation to utilise domestic providers, etc.)?
No.

Has the digitisation of the sector or any area of it been promoted because of the COVID-19 pandemic? If so, then how so?
No.

Is there a specific body in charge of overseeing, coordinating or promoting the digitalisation of the sector?
Ministry of Economy.

References

Amorim, F., Carneiro, L., & Maia, F. (2022, September). *Gilmar Mendes: Government must follow LGPD when sharing personal data.* JOTA. https://www.jota.info/coberturas-especiais/protecao-de-dados/gilmar-mendes-governo-deve-seguir-lgpd-ao-compartilhar-dados-pessoais-14092022

ANATEL. (2021). *Plano Nacional de Banda Larga.* Gov.br. https://www.gov.br/anatel/pt-br/regulado/universalizacao/plano-nacional-de-banda-larga

Araújo, R., & Anea, C. (2021, January). *[Digital Services Tax: Brazil and its false tax cognates] [Imposto sobre Serviços Digitais: o Brasil e seus falsos cognatos tributários.]* JOTA. https://www.jota.info/coberturas-especiais/nova-economia/imposto-sobre-servicos-digitais-o-brasil-e-seus-falsos-cognatos-tributarios-20012021

Banco Central do Brasil (BCB). (n.d.-a). *Digital Currency of the Central Bank of Brazil. Guidelines [Moeda Digital do Banco Central do Brasil Diretrizes.]* https://www.bcb.gov.br/conteudo/home-ptbr/TextosApresentacoes/20210524_Diretrizes_CBDC_BCB_vPub.pdf

Banco Central do Brasil (BCB). (n.d.-b). *O que é Pix?.* Gov.br. https://www.bcb.gov.br/estabilidadefinanceira/pix

Banco Central do Brasil (BCB). (n.d.-c). *Open Finance.* Gov.br. https://www.bcb.gov.br/estabilidadefinanceira/openfinance

Banco Interamericano de Desenvolvimento (BID). (2021). *Brazil will accelerate digital transformation with IDB support [Brasil acelerará a transformação digital com apoio do BID].* https://www.iadb.org/pt/noticias/brasil-acelerara-transformacao-digital-com-apoio-do-bid

Brazilian Government. (2018). *Brazilian Strategy for Digital Transformation E-Digital. [Estratégia Brasileira para a Transformação Digital E-Digital.]* Gov.br. https://www.gov.br/mcti/pt-br/centrais-de-conteudo/comunicados-mcti/estrategia-digital-brasileira/estrategiadigital.pdf

Brazilian Government. (2019a, November). *Digital Government > Digital Governance Strategy > From Electronic to Digital. [Governo Digital > Estratégia de Governança Digital > Do Eletrônico ao Digital.]* Gov.br. https://www.gov.br/governodigital/pt-br/estrategia-de-governanca-digital/do-eletronico-ao-digital

Brazilian Government. (2019b, November). *Digital Government Secretariat (SGD) [Secretaria de Governo Digital (SGD).]* Gov.br. https://www.gov.br/governodigital/pt-br/sisp/secretaria-de-governo-digital-sgd

Brazilian Government. (2021, May). *Digital Government Strategy 2020-2022 has 30% of goals already completed. [Estratégia de Governo Digital 2020-2022 tem 30% das metas já concluídas].* Gov.br. https://www.gov.br/economia/pt-br/assuntos/noticias/2021/maio/estrategia-de-governo-digital-2020-2022-tem-30-das-metas-ja-concluidas

Brazilian Government Portal. (2018). *Electronic Government Interoperability Standards* - ePING *[Padrões de Interoperabilidade de Governo Eletrônico - ePING].* https://eping.governoeletronico.gov.br/#parte1

Brazilian Government, Ministry of Economy. (2022a). *Accessibility Model. [Modelo de Acessibilidade.]* Gov.br. https://www.gov.br/governodigital/pt-br/acessibilidade-digital/modelo-de-acessibilidade

Brazilian Government, Ministry of Economy. (2022b, December). *"A modern VAT would deal well with Brazil's problems in consumption taxation," says Vanessa Canado ["Um IVA moderno lidaria bem com os problemas do Brasil na tributação do consumo," afirma Vanessa Canado].* Gov.br. https://www.gov.br/economia/pt-br/assuntos/noticias/2019/12/201cum-iva-moderno-lidaria-bem-com-os-problemas-do-brasil-na-tributacao-do-consumo201d-afirma-vanessa-canado

Brazilian Government, Ministry of Economy. (n.d.-a). *Digital Accessibility. [Acessibilidade Digital.]* Gov.br. https://www.gov.br/governodigital/pt-br/acessibilidade-digital

Brazilian Government, Ministry of Economy. (n.d.-b). *Tools. [Ferramentas.]* Gov.br. https://www.gov.br/governodigital/pt-br/acessibilidade-digital/ferramentas

Brazilian Government, Ministry of Planning, Development and Management. (2018). *Digital Governance Strategy - EGD Digital Transformation: Citizenship and Government (2016-2019). [Estratégia de Governança Digital - EGD Transformação Digital: Cidadania e Governo (2016-2019).]* Gov.br. https://www.gov.br/governodigital/pt-br/estrategia-de-governanca-digital/revisaodaestrategiadegovernancadigital20162019.pdf

Brazilian Government, Ministry of Regional Development. (n.d.). *Brazilian Charter for Smart Cities.* [Ministério do Desenvolvimento Regional. (n.d.) *Carta Brasileira para Cidades Inteligentes.*] Gov.br. https://www.gov.br/mdr/pt-br/assuntos/desenvolvimento-regional/projeto-andus/carta-brasileira-para-cidades-inteligentes

Brazilian Government, Ministry of Science, Technology and Innovations. (n.d.-a). *Digital Transformation > Internet of Things.* [Ministério da Ciência, Tecnologia e Inovações (n.d.) *Transformação Digital > Internet das Coisas.*] Gov.br. https://www.gov.br/mcti/pt-br/acompanhe-o-mcti/transformacaodigital/internet-das-coisas

Brazilian Government, Ministry of Science, Technology and Innovations. (n.d.-b). *Artificial Intelligence. [Inteligência Artificial.]* Gov.br. https://www.gov.br/mcti/pt-br/acompanhe-o-mcti/transformacaodigital/inteligencia-artificial

Brazilian Government, Ministry of Science, Technology and Innovations. (n.d.-c). *Digital Transformation* [Ministério da Ciência, Tecnologia e Inovações. (n.d.) *Transformação Digital*] Gov.br. https://www.gov.br/mcti/pt-br/acompanhe-o-mcti/transformacaodigital

Brazilian Government, Presidency of the Republic. (2022, August). *Secretaria Especial de Modernização do Estado [Special Secretariat for State Modernization].* Gov.br. https://www.gov.br/secretariageral/pt-br/composicao/orgaos-especificos-singulares/seme

BrazilLAB. (2021, September). *Ranking Connected Smart Cities 2020 aponta São Paulo como a cidade mais inteligente do País [Connected Smart Cities 2020 Ranking points São Paulo as the smartest city in the country].* Ranking Connected Smart Cities. https://brazillab.org.br/noticias/ranking-connected-smart-cities-2020-aponta-sao-paulo-como-a-cidade-mais-inteligente-do-pais

Center for Management and Strategic Studies (CGEE). (2022). *Brazilian Strategy for Digital Transformation (E-Digital) Cycle 2022-2026. [Centro de Gestão e Estudos Estratégicos (CGEE). Estratégia Brasileira para a Transformação Digital* (E-Digital) Ciclo 2022-2026.] https://www.gov.br/mcti/pt-br/acompanhe-o-mcti/transformacaodigital/arquivosestrategiadigital/e--digital_ciclo_2022-2026.pdf

Chamber News Agency. (2019, December). *Bolsonaro sanctions PPA with veto to UN sustainable development goals [Bolsonaro sanciona PPA com veto a metas de desenvolvimento sustentável da ONU].* Portal of the Chamber of Deputies. https://www.camara.leg.br/noticias/629391-bolsonaro-sanciona-ppa-com-veto-a-metas-de-desenvolvimento-sustentavel-da-onu/

Chamber of Deputies. (2020). Law Project 3887/2020 [PL 3887/2020]. https://www.camara.leg.br/proposicoesWeb/fichadetramitacao?idProposicao=2258196

Decreto n. 10.160, de 9 de dezembro de 2019. (2019). Brasília, DF. Recuperado de https://www.planalto.gov.br/ccivil_03/_Ato2019-2022/2019/Decreto/D10160.htm#art13

Decreto n. 10.222, de 5 de fevereiro de 2020. (2020). Brasília, DF. Recuperado de http://www.planalto.gov.br/ccivil_03/_ato2019-2022/2020/decreto/D10222.htm

Decreto n. 8.777, de 11 de maio de 2016. (2016). Brasília, DF. Recuperado de https://www.planalto.gov.br/ccivil_03/_ato2015-2018/2016/decreto/D8777.htm

Decreto n. 9.319, de 21 de março de 2018. (2018). Brasília, DF. Recuperado de http://www.planalto.gov.br/ccivil_03/_ato2015-2018/2018/decreto/D9319.htm

Decreto n. 9.637, de 26 de dezembro de 2018. (2018). Brasília, DF. Recuperado de http://www.planalto.gov.br/ccivil_03/_Ato2015-2018/2018/Decreto/D9637.htm#art6i

Decreto n. 9.804, de 23 de maio de 2019. (2019). Brasília, DF. Recuperado de https://legislacao.presidencia.gov.br/atos/?tipo=DEC&numero=9804&ano=2019&ato=67fQTQE9keZpWT050

DECRETO REVOGADO N° 10.282 da Presidência da República. (2020). http://www.planalto.gov.br/ccivil_03/_ato2019-2022/2020/decreto/D10282.htm

DECRETO REVOGADO N° 8.638 da Presidência da República. (2016). http://www.planalto.gov.br/ccivil_03/_Ato2015-2018/2016/Decreto/D8638.htm
DECRETO REVOGADO No. 9,982 da Presidência da República. (2019). http://www.planalto.gov.br/ccivil_03/_ato2019-2022/2019/decreto/D9982.htm
Dentsu Aegis Network. (2020). *Decoding Data Dynamics Digital Society Index*. https://assets-eu-01.kc-usercontent.com/eb6a58b7-c891-0178-24ce-015bc8221f40/d2ef5fe6-3cbe-40f9-8b33-84cd18e25c18/DSI%20Report%202020_Decoding%20Data%20Dynamics.pdf
Federal Court of Audit (TCU). (2021, March). *March 3rd plenary session highlights. [Destaque da sessão plenária de 3 de março.]* Portal.tcu.Gov.br. https://portal.tcu.gov.br/imprensa/noticias/destaque-da-sessao-plenaria-de-3-de-marco.htm
IMD World Competitiveness Center. (2020). IMD World Digital Competitiveness Ranking 2020. IMD Business School. https://www.imd.org/research-knowledge/competitiveness/reports/imd-world-digital-competitivenessranking- 2020/
General Secretariat of the Republic. (n.d.). *Technical cooperation agreement signed between the general secretariat of the presidency of the republic, the ministry of economy and the superior electoral court, aiming at cooperation for the implementation of the national civil identification. [Acordo de cooperação técnica que firmam entre si a secretaria geral da presidência da república, o ministério da economia e o tribunal superior eleitoral, objetivando a cooperação para implementação da identificação civil nacional.]* https://www.tse.jus.br/++theme++justica_eleitoral/pdfjs/web/viewer.html?file=https://www.tse.jus.br/comunicacao/noticias/arquivos/act-identificacao-civil-nacional/@@download/file/TSE-ACT-ICN-.pdf
Lei n. 13.675, de 11 de junho de 2018. (2018). Brasília, DF. Recuperado de http://www.planalto.gov.br/ccivil_03/_Ato2015-2018/2018/Lei/L13675.htm
Lei n. 14.063, de 23 de setembro de 2020. (2020). Brasília, DF. Recuperado de https://www.planalto.gov.br/ccivil_03/_Ato2019-2022/2020/Lei/L14063.htm
Lei n. 14.129, de 29 de março de 2021. (2021). Brasília, DF. Recuperado de https://www.in.gov.br/en/web/dou/-/lei-n-14.129-de-29-de-marco-de-2021-311282132
Lei n. 14.133, de 1° de abril de 2021. (2021). Brasília, DF. Recuperado de http://www.planalto.gov.br/ccivil_03/_Ato2019-2022/2021/Lei/L14133.htm
Ministério da Comunicação. (2022). *Programa Norte Conectado amplia infraestrutura de comunicações para promover inclusão digital.* Gov.br. https://www.gov.br/mcom/pt-br/noticias/2022/dezembro/programa-norte-conectado-amplia-infraestrutura-de-comunicacoes-para-promover-inclusao-digital
Observatório da LGPD. (n.d.). @serpro. Recuperado de https://observatoriolgpd.com/tag/serpro-2/
OECD. (2020, October). *On the Way to the Digital Age in Brazil [A Caminho da Era Digital no Brasil]*. OECD. https://doi.org/10.1787/45a84b29-pt.
ORDINANCE No. 46 from the Information Technology Secretariat. (2016). https://www.gov.br/governodigital/pt-br/software-publico/portaria-46.pdf
Portal of the Chamber of Deputies. (n.d.). *Computerized Legislation - DECREE No. 9,612, DECEMBER 17, 2018 [Legislação Informatizada - DECRETO N° 9.612, DE 17 DE DEZEMBRO DE 2018]*. https://www2.camara.leg.br/legin/fed/decret/2018/decreto-9612-17-dezembro-2018-787469-publicacaooriginal-156998-pe.html
PORTARIA N° 108.092 do Ministério da Economia/Banco Central do Brasil. (2020). https://www.in.gov.br/en/web/dou/-/portaria-n-108.092-de-20-de-agosto-de-2020-273476769
Secretaria de Comunicação Social. (2014). *Manual de Orientação para atuação em mídias sociais: identidade padrão de comunicação digital do poder executivo federal*. https://www.gov.br/gestaodeconteudo/pt-br/arquivos/manual-de-redes-sociais-idg.pdf
Special Secretariat for Social Communication. (n.d.). https://www.gov.br/secom/pt-br
The Open Data Barometer Latin America and the Caribbean 2020. (2020). https://barometrolac.org/ilda-edicion/informe/#opendata
The World Bank. (2016). *Digital Adoption Index*. https://www.worldbank.org/en/publication/wdr2016/Digital-Adoption-Index#:~:text=The%20DAI%20is%20a%20worldwide,coverage%20and%20simplify%20theoretical%20linkages.

United Nations. (2022). *Country Selector > Brazil*. UN E-government knowledgebase. https://publicadministration.un.org/egovkb/en-us/Data/Country-Information/id/24-Brazil

United Nations Department of Economic and Social Affairs. (2020). *United Nations E-government Survey 2020 Digital Government in the Decade of Action for Sustainable Development*. https://publicadministration.un.org/egovkb/Portals/egovkb/Documents/un/2020-Survey/2020%20UN%20E-Government%20Survey%20(Full%20Report).pdf

Wachowicz, M., & Canut, L. (2018). *Analysis of the Brazilian strategy for digital transformation: comments on decree no. 9319/18 [Análise da estratégia brasileira para transformação digital: comentários ao decreto n° 9319/18]*. https://www.gedai.com.br/wp-content/uploads/2018/08/livro_An%C3%A1lise-da-estrat%C3%A9gia-brasileira-para-transforma%C3%A7%C3%A3o-digital.pdf

Larissa Galdino de Magalhães Santos is a Yufe4Postdoc, Marie Sklodowska-Curie at the Universität Bremen. Before, she was an associate researcher at the United Nations University, Electronic Governance Unit (UNU-EGOV). Larissa also is a Researcher at the Center for Technology and Society at FGV and CyberBRICS, Law School at Fundação Getúlio Vargas. Her research is located between government technology and innovation, with a special focus on open data, smart cities, and digital transformation strategies. Co-chair of the Open Data Charter Implementation Group, she is also a Professional Fellow at Fundação Getúlio Vargas for Europe and a Ph.D. in Political Science from the State University of Campinas.

Existing Trends Towards the Nationalization of Public Service Digitization in Russia

Andrey A. Schcherbovich

Abstract The article analyzes how the law on the sovereignty of the Internet affects the development of the program for the digitization of services in Russia. This data is a comparison of the digitalization of the Russian information infrastructure and public services in accordance with the methodology of the CyberBRICS project. This article discusses a roadmap for the digitization of public services through a national program, through the introduction of state restrictions on the Internet, and technological development in the context of COVID-19 and its geopolitical challenges.

1 Introduction

The crises associated with the COVID-19 pandemic, as well as the current Russian military operation in Ukraine, have given rise to two opposite trends in the development of the Internet in Russia. On the one hand, as in many other countries, the Internet industry has been further developed thanks to the COVID-19 pandemic. Zoom, Amazon, DocuSign, and Microsoft increased their market value during the time of the pandemic. According to Canalys, a market research firm, "this is again the largest quarterly expansion in dollar terms, as continuing pandemic restrictions drove intense demand for the cloud to support remote working and learning, e-commerce, content streaming, online gaming, and collaboration. At the same time, a gradual recovery in economic confidence stimulated cloud investments by organizations in all industry segments to drive digital transformation" (Top 4, 2022). However, according to The Economist, Amazon Web Services and other cloud providers are still booming, but e-commerce and web conferences are declining. Quoting, "Today the lockdown lunacy index—which includes Netflix, a streaming service; Peloton, a maker of fancy exercise bikes; Robinhood, a stock-trading app;

A. A. Schcherbovich (✉)
Faculty of Law, Department of Constitutional and Municipal Law, National Research University Higher School of Economics, Moscow, Russia

L. Belli, L. Galdino de Magalhães Santos (eds.), *SmartBRICS*,
https://doi.org/10.1007/978-3-031-98204-0_5

Shopify, an e-commerce platform; and Zoom, a videoconferencing firm—has fallen by more than 80% from its peak, far exceeding the 18% drop in the NASDAQ. Zoom and friends are trading at below pre-pandemic prices" (The Tech Winners, 2022).

Against the backdrop of declining economic indicators in all sectors of the economy, the development of the Internet industry, on the contrary, has become more significant against the background of the pandemic. The digitalization of all branches of the public sector in the Russian Federation was also actively developing. In July 2017, Russia adopted the Russia Digital Economy Program with an expected annual budget of US$1.8 billion until 2025 to address the current weaknesses preventing the country from joining global digital economy leaders. To manage the program, five basic directions for the development of the digital economy in Russia for the period until 2024 have been identified. The basic directions include normative regulation, personnel and education, the formation of research competencies and technical background, information infrastructure, and information security. According to Gritsenko and Zherebtsov (2021), p. 44, "the most recent iteration of public sector digitalization named 'Government as a platform' had been presented as a concept in April 2018 by the Russian think-tank Center for Strategic Research."

Otherwise, the trend towards the isolation of the Internet in Russia, which arose even before the war with Ukraine, with the adoption of the law on the sovereign Internet, has acquired quite significant proportions.

The development of digital public services, their real improvement in digital form, is accompanied by restrictions on the part of the state. These are two parallel trends that influence each other. The policy of restricting digital rights, which began with the adoption of the federal law "On the protection of children from information harmful to their health and development."[1] Up to this point, the Internet in Russia, unlike, say, China, was not subject to state regulation. Therefore, the inevitable improvement in the quality of the provision of digital services occurs, as it were, against the background of the inevitable introduction of appropriate restrictions generated by the idea that the Internet should be sovereign in the country. This was further facilitated by the COVID-19 pandemic, which tested restrictive practices, such as introducing digital passes for citizens and increased surveillance and control in the digital environment. Subsequently, such norms were applied in connection with the aggravation of the geopolitical situation due to the aggravation of the conflict between Russia and Ukraine in February 2022. The geopolitical aggravation also leads to sanctions that limit the supply of technologies to Russia, which affects the quality of services provided by the state in electronic form.

2 Antecedents of the Sovereign Internet Legislation

The Mir payment system appeared in Russia in 2014 after the imposition of sanctions against Russia due to the annexation of Crimea and the outbreak of war in Ukraine. The law prescribes that all payments from the state to citizens of the

[1] See Federal Law N° 436 - FZ (2010).

Russian Federation, such as salaries, pensions, and social payments, must be transferred to cards of the Mir payment system. It should be noted that the system, with a few exceptions, does not work within Russia. Cards of leading international payment systems left the Russian market during the aggravation of the conflict with Ukraine in 2022.

The localization of the personal data of Russians, introduced by amendments to the Federal Law "On Personal Data" (Law No. 242-FZ, 2014), contradicts the nature of the Internet as an international network. Even though this is technically possible, many questions arise regarding the implementation of constitutional rights and freedoms of citizens. In fact, the adoption of this law was an unprecedented measure that could affect the nature of the work of the entire Internet in Russia.

The specified law regulates the obligations of operators to ensure the recording, systematization, accumulation, storage, clarification (update, change), and extraction of personal data of citizens of the Russian Federation located in information databases located on the territory of the Russian Federation, as well as indicating information about the location of such databases.

Roskomnadzor is vested with the right, on the basis of a judicial act that has entered into force, to restrict access to information processed in violation of the legislation of the Russian Federation in the field of personal data. The law defines the procedure for restricting access to information processed in violation of the legislation of the Russian Federation in the field of personal data. For this purpose, an automated information system "Register of Violators of the Rights of Personal Data Subjects" was created.

This trend prevailed in the legislation and law enforcement practice of the Russian Federation in 2022. The Sovereign Internet Law was adopted in May 2019, and on 1 November 2019, most of its provisions came into force in Russia. The main purpose of the Sovereign Internet Law is to create an autonomous system that can support the operation of the Russian segment of the Internet in the event of disconnection from the global network.

The Sovereign Internet Law imposes several obligations on certain categories of persons [communication service providers, owners of various communication networks' infrastructure as well as information dissemination organizers (e.g., social networks, mail services)], as well as establishing a specific register of Internet exchange points. According to the Sovereign Internet Law, telecom operators are required to install state equipment at traffic exchange points for analyzing and filtering traffic (Deep Packet Inspection, DPI) within the country and communication lines crossing the Russian border (Law No. 90-FZ, 2019). It should be noted here that even though Russia is oriented toward China in the supply of DPI software and hardware, one of the consequences of the current sanctions is that the implementation of the RuNet becomes much more difficult without DPI from Western suppliers of surveillance technologies such as Sandvine, etc.

3 The Russian Strategy for Digitalization

The "Strategy for the Development of the Information Society in the Russian Federation for 2017–2030" defines the "ecosystem of the digital economy" as "a partnership of organizations ensuring the continuous interaction of their technological platforms, applied Internet services, analytical systems, information systems of public authorities of the Russian Federation, organizations and citizens."

Thus, the creation of an ecosystem of the digital economy entails the creation of a partnership of organizations between the state and the private sector. Despite this declared goal, such partnerships are not the main element of the digital economy. In any case, the leading role in the digitalization of the economy in Russia belongs to the state. For example, Rostelecom, a predominantly state-owned company, operates a nationwide *Gosuslugi* (government services) portal (Law No. 90-FZ, 2019).

In the field of digital identification, there is a Presidential Decree on the use of electronic passports (Wijermars, 2021) developed by the Ministry of Digital Development, Communications, and Mass Media of the Russian Federation. It is proposed to store an electronic passport, which can be an electronic copy of the original identity document, and other electronic identity documents on a mobile device.[2] It is also planned to develop a mobile application for this. It is expected that e-passports will be introduced in the regions no later than July 1, 2023.

As for the digitalization strategy of cities and local administrations, there are various national and federal projects on e-government and strategies. Moscow is by far the champion in bringing the smart city program to life. The Smart City of Moscow project (Merging Reality, 2022), initiated in 2018, is designed to continue the development of e-government and the digitization of services over the past decade. This strategic program, calculated up to 2030, is linked to the concept of the digital economy and sets priorities, goals, and objectives for managing and developing the digital economy in Moscow until 2030.

Online surveillance as is not permitted by Russian law and is not subject to legislation justifying the use of such technology in the event of a coronavirus crisis. Combining various elements of digital and technical infrastructure, such as the Moscow city video surveillance system, Artificial Intelligence, smartphone geodata provided by telecom operators, and a face recognition solution developed by NtechLab, this system makes it possible to track every citizen. According to the NtechLab website (NtechLab, 2022), they create solutions that help to see the full picture of events in real-time and in retrospect. In a fraction of a second, they can recognize the face of a person in a crowd of thousands, track his location by body features, or find all the frames with a car of interest from all cameras on the network. NtechLab technologies help create a safe and comfortable urban environment and increase the safety and competitiveness of enterprises in various industries. Safety in cities around the world is undergoing a process of digital rethinking, some aspects

---

[2] For example, a driver's license, car documents or a certificate of registration at the place of residence.

of which have been further accelerated by the impact of COVID-19. City leaders around the world are working with police and other first responders to realize the benefits of next-generation emergency response systems, early warning systems, real-time crime centers, digital evidence management, digital forensics and intelligence, and data-sharing platforms.

However, for the time being, surveillance will be focused on a limited list of individuals created at the federal level from lists generated by departments and operational bodies that have the right to access the system within the framework of a provision that allows surveillance and tracking of a person.

4 The COVID-19 Impact

The impact of the Internet during COVID-19 has been recognized in all countries, and Russia is no exception. Therefore, during the COVID-19 pandemic, the digitalization program did not stop but also evolved to a qualitatively new level. All areas of the public sphere, including the introduction of digital passports, public security, smart cities, local administrations, healthcare, finance, and taxation, have developed due to digitalization during the COVID-19 pandemic.

During the COVID-19 pandemic, the role of the Internet in the life of Russia responded to the two trends that were announced at the beginning of the article. On the one hand, the Internet helped maintain economic life at the proper level and saved jobs and economic activity, primarily in cities. The Internet played a significant role in maintaining the country's economy in a normal state: a lot of people used the Internet to implement labor relations, and the consumption of public services provided via the Internet increased. On the other hand, with the help of the Internet, Russia was able to implement surveillance measures for citizens and introduce the institution of QR codes and digital passes, which, in the absence of a state of emergency, the law on which was not enacted during the pandemic, was formally an illegal restriction of freedom. Nevertheless, measures to restrict the rights and freedoms of citizens in connection with the pandemic were introduced in all countries, and Russia was no exception.

We can mention the positive impact of remote work regulation. The Labor Code introduces the concept of remote work, which is the performance of a labor function defined by an employment contract outside the location of the employer, its branch, representative office, another separate structural unit (including those located in another area), outside a stationary workplace, territory or facility, directly or indirectly under the control of the employer, provided that for the performance of this labor function and for the interaction between the employer and the employee on issues related to its implementation, information and telecommunication networks, including the Internet, and public communication networks (Law No. 197-FZ, 2022).

In addition, if we keep in mind the specific impact that the Internet had during the COVID-19 pandemic, then it should be considered that the Internet was actively used by the state to control the spread of the pandemic. In most regions of the

Russian Federation, digital passes allowing people to move even within the city during the outbreak of the pandemic were introduced, which were issued online on the Moscow City public services portal.

Both surveillance and control measures, digital passes, and the Moscow automated recognition system, are based on the structure of Moscow's e-government, embodied in the Smart City of Moscow project, which has been put into practice over the past decade.

5 The Digitalization of the Russian Public Sector

Here, it is necessary to consider the problems associated with public services in digital form and the digitalization of the public sector, security, taxes, finance, healthcare, and other politically and economically important aspects of the sectors of the economy of the Russian Federation.

In the sphere of public security, the Russian SORM (System for Operative Investigative Activities) is the system designated for lawful interception interfaces of telecommunications and telephone networks that enables the targeted—but not mass—surveillance of both telephone and Internet communications in Russia. SORM was first implemented in 1995 to allow access to surveillance data for the FSB, but during Vladimir Putin's first week in office on January 5, 2000, the law was amended to allow seven other federal security agencies (apart from the FSB) to access to data gathered via SORM, including Ministry of Internal Affairs, Border patrol and customs, Police and Russia's tax police. The legality of the SORM legislation has repeatedly been questioned (Gaufman, 2021).

In the sphere of digitizing tax administrations, the concept of Development and Functioning in the Russian Federation determines the main directions for the development and functioning of the tax monitoring system in the Russian Federation. This concept is aimed at improving the quality and efficiency of tax control based on high-tech solutions, simplifying, and facilitating the interaction between tax authorities and organizations that are taxpayers, payers of fees, payers of insurance premiums, and (or) tax agents, increasing the overall transparency of the process. It should be noted that the current Prime Minister, Mikhail Mishustin, a former head of the federal tax service, is well known for having overseen the digitalization of the tax system.

In the financial sphere, federal law regulates the relations arising from the issuance, accounting, and circulation of digital financial assets, the specifics of the activities of the operator of the information system in which the issuance of digital financial assets and the operator of the exchange of digital financial assets, as well as the relations arising from the circulation of digital currency in the Russian Federation (Law No. 259-FZ, 2020).

The Russian public health sector has been under reform since 2017. Healthcare reforms include the computerization of medical institutions, the development of high-tech areas, and the unification and digitization of offline medical data. The focus is on the creation and production of domestic technologies to drive the development of the (public) health sector.

In 2017, a Federal Law of July 29, 2017, No. 242-FZ stated "On Amendments to Certain Legislative Acts of the Russian Federation" on the Application of Information Technologies in the Field of Health Protection (law on telemedicine) was adopted (Law No. 242-FZ, 2017). It is difficult to create a unified system of medical data on all citizens of Russia since there is no common data bank for all patients in both public clinics and private medical institutions.

6 The Use of Electronic Voting in the Russian Federation

The problem of using electronic voting in elections of public authorities is very important in the field of Internet governance at the national level. Electronic voting is a rather promising way of exercising the right to vote, having been used for a long time in several democratic countries. However, there is a problem of trust in electronic voting on the part of citizens of the Russian Federation, as well as on the part of candidates who, because of using electronic voting, lost elections to the State Duma of the Russian Federation. The fact is that in the elections to the State Duma of the Russian Federation in 2021, electronic voting organized using blockchain technology was selectively used in the city of Moscow and several other constituent entities of the Russian Federation.

At the same time, several problems with the use of electronic voting should be highlighted. The first problem arises from distrust of electronic voting. Electronic voting was first introduced into practice when the amendments to the Constitution of the Russian Federation were adopted; thus, voting itself raises many questions in terms of the law and procedure for its implementation. The second problem is that the electoral legislation itself is very detailed in terms of the procedure. The law regulates all electoral actions in detail, but the e-voting procedure is not spelled out in the law. The third problem is that with electronic voting, it is impossible to control the voting procedure, counting of votes, and summing up the results with an accuracy comparable to conventional electoral procedures. If a qualified observer at a regular polling station can guarantee the absence of any violations or help the commission eliminate them, then the procedures for tracking the results of voting and control over this voting by an organized community of observers, firstly, are not prescribed by law, and secondly, requires special qualification of observers in the field of information and communication technologies.

At two polling stations in the city of Moscow, where electronic voting was used, the results differed significantly from the results obtained traditionally. Interestingly, when electronic voting was not used, the candidate who competed with the opposition candidate won. When counting votes, anomalies were revealed when there was a mass vote for a pro-government candidate. Thus, in both cases, the opposition candidates were defeated.

7 The Impact of the Current Geopolitical Challenges

In accordance with the current geopolitical challenges caused by the current military conflict between Russia and Ukraine, we can see the introduction of governmental restrictions unprecedented in the entire history of the existence of the Internet in Russia. The roadmap on "The main activities of the Government of the Russian Federation for the period until 2024" that was approved within the presidential Decree on May 7, 2018, on national goals and strategic objectives of the development of the Russian Federation for the period until 2024, it is stated that the preference should be given to the utilization of domestic providers, the use of domestic data centers and locally produced equipment (Law No. 223-FZ, 2011). From January 1, 2025, government authorities and customers are prohibited from using foreign software on their significant critical information infrastructure facilities (Presidential Decree No. 166, 2022).

The isolation of the Russian segment of the Internet, followed by the implementation of the Sovereign Internet Law, affects the development of digitalization programs for public services in Russia. One of the goals of the National Digital Economy Program (2018) is "the use of predominantly domestic software by government agencies, local governments, and organizations." In the state program on Digital Economy, these measures were addressed under the rubric of information security with corresponding indicators for decreasing the share of foreign ICT equipment and software in the purchases of federal and regional government authorities and state-owned enterprises (SOEs). The new program uses different indicators for government bodies and SOEs but focuses exclusively on software, omitting ICT equipment (Government of the Russian Federation, 2018).

We can see that by itself, the idea of replacing foreign software with Russian is not a smart move. Despite the presence in Russia of a significant number of software products that are leaders in the foreign market, such as Kaspersky Lab, for example, or ABBYY, which produces software for text recognition and working in PDF, it is not necessary to talk about the availability of software that can replace foreign ones. It should be noted that interdependence between countries is also manifested here. It is better to create software in cooperation between different states. This business model is practiced by most foreign IT companies.

Another risk over the whole existence of the Internet in Russia could be the result of the sanctions that are imposed on Russia in the technological sphere. So, the United States imposed sanctions on Russia, targeting the technology sector, a sanctions evasion network, and what it called malicious "cyber actors" while paving the way to act against additional sectors in response to President Vladimir Putin's assault on Ukraine. We will continue to target Putin's war machine with sanctions from every angle until this senseless war of choice is over, Treasury Secretary Janet Yellen said in a statement (Psadelakis, 2022).

Sanctions accompanied the withdrawal of foreign technological companies from the Russian market and the impossibility of supplying new technologies to the

Russian market. These technological sanctions could throw Russia far back in technological development.

In fact, we are talking about the isolation of the Russian segment from within the Russian Federation or at least trying to do so. This directly contradicts the principles that were proclaimed in the report of the working group of the UN Secretary-General, entitled "The Age of Digital Interdependence." Authors of the report believe that our aspirations and vulnerabilities are deeply interconnected and interdependent; that no one individual, institution, corporation, or government alone can or should manage digital developments; and that we must work through our differences in order to shape our common digital future. We declare our commitment to building on our shared values and collaborating in new ways to realize a vision of humanity's future in which affordable and accessible digital technologies are used to enable economic growth and social opportunity, lessen inequality, enhance peace and security, promote environmental sustainability, preserve human agency, advance human rights and meet human needs" (United Nations, 2019).

8 Final Considerations

The Internet is developing all over the world, and the purpose of the Internet is the possibility of cross-border transmission of information. Interdependence in economic, political, and social terms is a guarantee of stable and peaceful interaction between countries, and the Internet is a key tool for ensuring such interdependence. All attempts that are being made by several states, including the Russian Federation, to close their digital space are an intrusion into the very structure of the Internet. In fact, the network that is being created in accordance with the law on the sovereign Internet will not be the Internet but will be an "Intranet" network within a particular state.

According to the German Council on Foreign Relations, calls for sovereignty in the digital domain are heard in both authoritarian countries and liberal democracies. Although such calls consist of diverse terminology and foci, they generally concern the increasing role of nation-states in Internet governance and the development of digital technologies. The term **sovereign Internet** is a Russian invention coined in the last decade during the state's endeavor to control information in the country. **Technology sovereignty**, on the other hand, is a widely used expression that describes a country's intention to develop and use homegrown technologies to avoid one-sided dependency (Epifanova & Dietrich, 2022).

Recently, the principle of ensuring the security of the Russian Federation in the creation of information systems, their operation, and the protection of the information contained in them is increasingly coming to the fore in the development of legislation in the field of information and Internet regulation, and to some extent becomes dominant in the development of new laws, in the specified area. This can be largely attributed to the complex geopolitical situation, against which officials are increasingly using the phrase "digital" or "information" sovereignty of Russia.

A number of initiatives aimed at regulating the Internet, in particular, blocking resources containing information that can be qualified as extremist or aimed at violating the current legislation on the procedure for holding rallies; provisions on the storage of data and their provision by the organizers of the dissemination of information on the Internet at the request of law enforcement agencies; initiatives of the Ministry of Digital Development, Communications and Mass Media of the Russian Federation on import substitution in the field of information technology, etc. to a large extent, they are links in the general policy of building digital (information) sovereignty of Russia Saveliev (2015).

When discussing a sovereign Internet, it should be borne in mind that despite the attempts of some countries, including Russia, to claim that it is possible to create a sovereign Internet, that is, a network that operates within one country in accordance with national Internet governance programs, does not represent value to the extent that a free Internet without fragmentation and national restrictions is of value. From a technological point of view, the Internet is a network that goes beyond the borders of any country, and Russia is no exception. Therefore, the Internet is created and maintained by the efforts of many countries, and this is normal for any high-tech system. At the same time, the digitalization of public services is possible with the use of modern technologies, including foreign ones. If we have available technologies that are produced in one country, then we should state a significant technological lag.

References

Decree of the President of the Russian Federation No. 166 of March 30, 2022. *On measures to study the technological independence and security of critical information of confidential information of the Russian Federation*. ConsultantPlus Legal Reference System.

Epifanova, A., & Dietrich, P. (2022, February 21). *Russia's quest for digital sovereignty. Ambitions, realities, and its place in the world*. German Council of Foreign Relations. Retrieved on May 12, 2022 from https://dgap.org/en/research/publications/russias-quest-digital-sovereignty

Federal Law No. 223-FZ of July 18, 2011 (as amended on April 16, 2022). *On procurement of goods, works, services by certain types of legal entities*. ConsultantPlus Legal Reference System.

Federal Law No. 242-FZ of July 21, 2014. *On Amendments to Certain Legislative Acts of the Russian Federation in Part of Clarifying the Procedure for Processing Personal Data in Information and Telecommunication Networks* (as amended on December 31, 2014). ConsultantPlus Legal Reference System.

Federal Law No. 242-FZ of July 29, 2017. *On Amendments to Certain Legislative Acts of the Russian Federation on the Application of Information Technologies in the Sphere of Health Care*. ConsultantPlus Legal Reference System.

Federal Law No. 259-FZ of July 31, 2020. *On Digital Financial Assets, Digital Currency and Amendments to Certain Legislative Acts of the Russian Federation*. ConsultantPlus Legal Reference System.

Federal Law No. 90-FZ of May 1, 2019. *On Amendments to the Federal Law 'On Communications' and the Federal Law 'On Information, Information Technologies and Information Protection'*. ConsultantPlus Legal Reference System.

Gaufman, E. (2021). Cybercrime and punishment: Security, information war, and the future of Runet. In D. Gritsenko, M. Wijemars, & M. Kopotev (Eds.), *The Palgrave handbook of digital russia studies* (pp. 115–134). Palgrave Macmillan. https://doi.org/10.1007/978-3-030-42855-6

Government of the Russian Federation. (2018). *National Program "Digital Economy of the Russian Federation"*. Retrieved on May 12, 2022 from http://government.ru/rugovclassifier/614/events/

Gritsenko, D., & Zherebtsov, M. (2021). E-Government in Russia: Plans, reality, and future outlook. In D. Gritsenko, M. Wijemars, & M. Kopotev (Eds.), *The Palgrave handbook of digital Russia studies* (pp. 33–51). Palgrave Macmillan. https://doi.org/10.1007/978-3-030-42855-6

Labor Code of the Russian Federation dated December 30, 2001, No. 197-FZ (as amended on February 25, 2022, with amendments and additions, effective from March 1, 2022). ConsultantPlus Legal Reference System.

Merging Reality and VR: How Does a Smart City Work?. (2022). The official portal of the Moscow Mayor and Moscow Government. Retrieved on May 12, 2022 from https://web.archive.org/web/20211207092950/https://www.mos.ru/en/city/projects/smartcity/

NTechLab. (n.d.). *Home*. Retrieved on October 13, 2022 from https://ntechlab.com/

Psadelakis, D. (2022, March 31). *U.S. targets Russia's technology sector in fresh sanctions*. Reuters. Retrieved on May 12, 2022 from https://www.reuters.com/world/us-imposes-additional-russia-related-sanctions-treasury-website-2022-03-31/

Saveliev, A. I. (2015). *Commentary to the Federal Law of July 27, 2006 N 149-FZ "On Information, Information Technologies and Information Protection" (item-by-article)* (p. 320). Statut.

The Ministry of Digital Development proposes to introduce electronic passports in the regions no later than July 1, 2023. (2021, March 22). D-Russia. Retrieved on May 12, 2022 from https://d-russia.ru/mincifry-predlagaet-vvesti-jelektronnye-pasporta-v-regionah-ne-pozdnee-1-ijulja-2023-goda.html

The tech winners and losers of the pandemic. (2022, September 1). *The Economist*. Retrieved on October 13, 2022 from https://www.economist.com/leaders/2022/09/01/the-tech-winners-and-losers-of-the-pandemic?itm_source=parsely-api

Top 4 Companies That Have Capitalized on the Work from Home Boom. (2021, June 10). Cascade. Retrieved on May 12, 2022 from https://www.cascade.app/blog/work-from-home-boom

United Nations. (2019). *The age of digital interdependence: Report of the UN secretary-general's high-level panel on digital cooperation*. Retrieved on May 12, 2022 from https://www.un.org/en/pdfs/DigitalCooperation-report-for%20web.pdf

Wijermars, M. (2021). The digitalization of Russian politics and political participation. In D. Gritsenko, M. Wijemars, & M. Kopotev (Eds.), *The Palgrave handbook of digital Russia studies* (pp. 15–32). Palgrave Macmillan. https://doi.org/10.1007/978-3-030-42855-6

Andrey A. Schcherbovich is an Associate Professor at the National Research University Higher School of Economics, Faculty of Law (Department of Constitutional and Municipal Law), in Moscow, Russia. His professional interests include Internet Governance, Constitutional Law, Human Rights, International Public Law and Procedure, Information Law, International Organizations, and the United Nations. Andrey graduated from the National Research University Higher School of Economics, Faculty of Law (Department of International Law) in 2008 and completed Postgraduate studies at the National Research University—Higher School of Economics (Moscow, Russia); Faculty of Law (Department of Constitutional and Municipal Law) in 2011.

Russia: An Overview of the Telecoms and Internet Access Sector

Andrey A. Schcherbovich and Anna Orlova

Abstract This chapter develops an overview of the Russian situation regarding access to Internet through the following matters: number of subscribers across different categories; affordability of services; type of technology being used; gender gap; urban-rural gap; ranking in the global ICT indices; strategy for expanding the Internet access; participation in institutions; telecommunications regulations in the country; access to the spectrum for data transmission; and financial resources.

1 Context

1.1 What Is the State of Internet Access in the Country, in Terms Of

Russia represents a significant part of the global Internet, with advanced connectivity infrastructure and high penetration of access among its population, conditioning an active online civil society. According to Statista, Russia is today (Kemp, 2020) the eighth country with the highest number of Internet users, 116.4 million (Statista, 2022), which makes it the eighth country with the highest number of Internet users among the largest countries of the world.

In 2016, Russia, along with the other 3 BRICS countries, was among the largest in the world in terms of the size of their digital economy, with eGDP[1] share of 28%

[1] eGDP (Gross Domestic Product) is an indicator proposed by the Boston Consulting Group (BCG) that calculates digital/Internet-related expenditure in private consumption, investment, government expenditure, and net export.

A. A. Schcherbovich (✉)
Faculty of Law, Department of Constitutional and Municipal Law, National Research University Higher School of Economics, Moscow, Russia

A. Orlova
São Paulo State University (UNESP), São Paulo, Brazil

L. Belli, L. Galdino de Magalhães Santos (eds.), *SmartBRICS*,
https://doi.org/10.1007/978-3-031-98204-0_6

(Cheng, 2017). Of the 10 countries with the highest eGDP share, four places were taken up by BRICS countries, putting the BRICS countries in the forefront of global digital competition.

In 2018, it was 80.9%[2] of individuals were using the Internet in Russia, according to the World Bank (2022). This number corresponds to the data of the Federal Service of State Statistics. In 2018, the share of individuals using the Internet in the population aged 15–72 stood at 81% (Abdrakhmanova et al., 2020).

Fixed Broadband

Fixed broadband is widely available and continues to expand rapidly. In the 2016 State of Broadband report by ITU (International Telecommunications Union [ITU], 2016), Russia ranked 55th among 187 nations in the fixed broadband category, with 18.77 subscriptions per 100 inhabitants. The Federal Statistics service estimated that 66.8% of households had access to broadband at 256 kbps or more.

1.1.1 Number of Subscribers Across Different Categories

Internet Penetration by Age

According to the All-Russian omnibus of GfK, by the beginning of 2019, the audience of Internet users in Russia among the population 16+ made 90 million people (+three million people from last year) and reached a point of 75.4% of the adult population of the country.

In 2018, according to the Omnibus GFK survey (Omnibus-GFK Rus, 2018) Internet penetration among young people (age 16–29 years old) is 99%, and middle-aged (age 30–54 years old) is 88% people is close to the limit values, and the growth of the Internet audience is happening mainly due to older people (55+ years old) that is 36%.

By frequency: Daily, weekly, monthly

According to NGO Public Opinion Foundation (2020) conducted between May 15 to May 17 2020 about Internet usage, 69% of Russians say that they used Internet in the last day, 4% in the last week, 1% in the last month, 1%—in the last three months, 1% in the last half a year, 2% more than a year ago, and 22% never used the Internet. The numbers of this research closely match data from the 2018 Russian Federation official Internet access rate of 80% total (published by ITU-D).

By category: Residential, business, academic

Among Internet users, the majority use mobile Internet, while 60% have Internet at home. 27% use only the mobile Internet, and 21%, only at home (Tadviser, 2022).

In 2019, 44.3% of important infrastructure facilities declared having connectivity to broadband access to the Internet, according to statistics on the national project "Digital Economy" published by Rosstat.

Schools, universities, state agencies, territorial electoral commissions, medical and obstetrical centers, and points of firefighters and police have support from the national program "Digital Economy," which, until 2021, has available 72 billion rubles to connect about 100,000 facilities.

---

[2] In percentage of population.

1.1.2 Affordability of Services

The average monthly account revenue per user (ARPU) is 359 RUB (5 USD), according to TMT consulting. In 2019, operators adjusted rates, considering an increase in the VAT, from 18% to 20%, and the regulatory requirements caused additional expenses—for example, the Yarovaya Law, which added many requirements related to vigilance and counter-terrorism (Federal Law No. 374-FZ of July 6, 2016), requiring multimillion rubles of investments.

The cost of broadband Internet has been falling continuously in Russia. In March 2016, the average monthly cost of a fixed broadband subscription was 404 rubles (~$6.3) in Russia (Public Opinion Foundation, 2020), ranging from 624 to 359 ($9.8 to $5.6). Considering the monthly average salary of just over 32,000 rubles (~$500) in January 2016, and the minimum wage of $109 set in July 2016, the cost of broadband largely meets the globally recognized affordability targets. Moreover, for residents of small villages and towns, the Russian government intends to provide subsidized subscription plans that cost only 70 US cents per month for a 10 mbit/s connection.

The cost of mobile broadband access in Russia

According to a 2019 study by analytical agency Content Review (2018), the cheapest unlimited mobile is Internet in Russia, in the rating of the cost of 1 GB, Russia took fourth place, having improved its performance compared to 2018.

Highlights:

- The average world cost of 1 gigabyte of mobile Internet was 195.5 rubles, in Russia—37.9 rubles (269.3 and 55.5 rubles in December 2018, respectively).
- The average world cost of a tariff with unlimited mobile Internet was 2791.8 (37.05 USD) rubles per month.
- Russia took first place in the ranking of countries[3] with the cheapest unlimited Internet.
- Russia entered the top five countries with the cheapest mobile Internet, moving to fourth place. The following factors affect the cost of a gigabyte: an increase in mobile traffic packages with a simultaneous decrease in their cost, introduction of unlimited tariffs, volatility of national currencies, market competition, country size, and 5G availability.

1.1.3 Type of Technology Being Used

Seventy-three million Russians aged 16+ (61% of the total adult population) use the Internet on mobile devices—tablets or smartphones. 59% use the Internet on smartphones and 14% use the Internet on tablets (Omnibus GFK Survey, 2018). And 32 million Russians (16+ years old) use the Internet only on mobile devices (smartphones or tablets)—this is 35% of all Internet users. However, the growth of the audience in itself on the Internet is not the main news. As of January 15, 2019,

[3] Corresponding tariffs are present in 26 out of 50 countries considered in the study.

within the last few years, the growth of the Internet's audience has been slow and is generally due to the users of the senior generation connecting to the network. At the same time, among youth and people of middle age, penetration of the Internet is close to its limit.

1.1.4 Gender Gap

In the period from July to September 2016, according to the Web Index Report, the monthly Internet audience included 85.6 million people, or 70% of Russians aged 12+. In line with global trends, younger age groups have been reached almost completely. For both male and female groups between 12–24, the percentage of Internet users ranges from 95% to 98%, and 92–93% for groups 25–34. The older groups have lower usage rates, declining to 18% for females 65+ and 29% for males 65 + .

1.1.5 Urban-Rural Gap

With most of its population living in cities, Russia has the highest penetration of the Internet among the CIS countries. Nevertheless, despite high penetration rates in the urban areas, there are wide discrepancies in penetration among different regions and republics of the Russian Federation. In large cities of Russia, the penetration has almost exhausted its growth potential by 2015, with several million individuals remaining unconnected in cities with less than 500,000 inhabitants and in rural areas (Yandex, 2016).

There are notable differences between small town Russia (<100,000 residents) and big town Russia (100,000+ residents), with the former having a monthly reach of 76%, and the latter only 63%. Within big towns in Russia, the largest cities, Moscow and Saint-Petersburg, stand out with higher percentages. Income group distribution also shows major differences, with 85% of self-reported income group "above average" using the Internet, as opposed to only 48% in the group "lower than average" (Digital Report, 2018).

1.2 What Is the Country's Ranking in the Global ICT Indices, such as ITU's ICT Development Index (IDI), WEF's Network Readiness Index (NRI), A4AI's Affordability Drivers Index, and GSMA's Mobile Connectivity Index (MCI)?

(a) Classification in the ITU ICT Development Index
In ITU's ICT Development Index, Russia's IDI 2017 rank is 45, with the IDI 2017 value of 7.07; (no ranks were issued in 2018 and 2019).

(b) Classification in the WEF Network Preparation Index
In 2019, Russia's NRI rank is 48 with a score of 54.98, with an upper-middle income. The group of Commonwealth of Independent States (CIS) is headed by the Russian Federation (48th). Its best performance relates to People (38th), especially the ICT usage and skills of firms and national authorities (35th in Businesses and 32nd in Governments). At the level of the subpillar, meanwhile, the country does even better when it comes to Inclusion (29th). However, the same pillar—Governance (56th)—also includes the Russian Federation's weakest dimension in the NRI: Regulation (91st). Other areas in need of improvement include Future Technologies (72nd) in the Technology (51st) pillar and Quality of Life (85th) in the Impact pillar (59th). The associated pillars, Technology and Governance, are also the two weakest dimensions of the CIS, which suggests that many countries in the region should pay more attention to promoting online safety and ICT regulation and to preparing themselves for disruptive technologies like Artificial Intelligence and Internet of Things.
(c) AI Accessibility Driver Index Classification
Russia has not been ranked in A4AI's index.
(d) Classification in the GSMA Mobile Connectivity Index
Russia's score for the GSMA's Mobile Connectivity Index for 2018 is 73.0 (the *Difference 2014–2018 score* is 6.9). The category with the highest rank was consumer readiness, earning 86.6 points (with basic skills scoring 84.0 and gender equality 88.2). The infrastructure in mobile connectivity, which included network coverage and performance among other criteria, was the weakest sector with a score of 64.6. The content and service sector has a score of 75.9.

1.3 Does the Country have a Strategy for the Expansion of Internet Access, Such as a National Broadband Plan or Similar?

Russia's strategy for Internet access expansion, along with other technological development aspects, is broadly outlined in the following set of documents and frameworks on Russia's vision for the national broadband development and digital economy:

1. National program "Russia Digital Economy Program" outlining Russia's goals for 2025
2. May 2018 Presidential Decree
3. State program of the Russian Federation "Information Society (2011–2020)"
4. The Eurasian Economic Union (EAEU) Agenda 2025

Also, until 2018, Russia had a national broadband plan that had very ambitious goals for mobile broadband coverage expansion. The aforementioned documents and agendas serve as a logical continuation of the previous national broadband plan.

There is a Decree of the President of the Russian Federation from May 7, 2018 on national goals and strategic objectives of the development of the Russian Federation for the period until 2024 (Decree of the President of the Russian Federation No. 204 of May 7, 2018). This law prescribes to the government of the Russian Federation to ensure the accelerated introduction of digital technologies in the economy and social sphere, among other national development goals of the Russian Federation for the period until 2024.

In accordance with this law, the roadmap "The main activities of the Government of the Russian Federation for the period until 2024" (2018) was approved by the government on September 27, 2018. This is the key document of the strategic planning of the government of Russia until 2024.

In section 2.1. on the "Digital Economy of the Russian Federation" of the aforementioned document, the government of the Russian Federation aims to achieve the following goals and targets of the national project "Digital Economy of the Russian Federation" in regards to the national broadband plan:

> creation of a stable and secure information and telecommunication infrastructure for high-speed transmission, processing and storage of large amounts of data, accessible to all organizations and households, including providing broadband access to the information and telecommunication network 'Internet' of households and socially significant infrastructure objects, the creation of reference data centers in federal districts, an increase in the share of the Russian Federation in the global volume of provision of data storage and processing services.

Investing in a globally competitive, secure infrastructure to support the growth of a data-driven economy remains (The World Bank, 2018) a top priority, as emphasized in the May 2018 Presidential Decree.

In July 2017, Russia adopted the Russia Digital Economy Program with an expected annual budget of US$1.8 billion until 2025 (Decree of the Government of the Russian Federation No. 1632-r of July 28, 2017) to address the current weaknesses preventing the country from joining global digital economy leaders.

To manage the program, five basic directions for the development of the digital economy in Russia for the period until 2024 have been identified. The basic directions include normative regulation, personnel and education, the formation of research competencies and technical background, information infrastructure, and information security.

The Digital Economy national program adopted by Government Order 1632-p of July 28, 2017 sets the provision of stable 5G mobile services in all major cities of Russia by 2024 as one of its major goals.

2 International Commitments

2.1 Is the Country a Member of the ITU?

Yes, Russia, the Russian Empire at the time, joined the ITU (International Telegraph Union) in 1865 (1865/12/31), and since then, the Russian Federation has been a member of the ITU, which, since 1934, is named the International Telecommunication Union.

2.2 Is the Country a Signatory to the 1988 or 2012 Version of the International Telecommunication Regulations (ITRs)?

Yes, the Union of Soviet Socialist Republics (USSR) signed the 1988 ITRs. Russia has signed the 2012 ITRs.

2.3 Does the Country have a Policy of Following ITU Recommendations and/or Technical Standards?

Article 69 on "International cooperation of the Russian Federation in the field of communications" of the Federal Law of 07.07.2003 No. 126-FZ (The Law "On Communications") defines the policy of working with ITU:

> The Communications Administration of the Russian Federation, within the limits of its authority, represents and protects the interests of the Russian Federation in the field of telecommunications and postal services, interacts with communications administrations of foreign states, intergovernmental and international non-governmental communications organizations, and also coordinates the issues of international cooperation in the field of communications carried out by the Russian Federation, by citizens of the Russian Federation and Russian organizations, ensures the fulfilment of obligations of the Russian Federation arising from international treaties of the Russian Federation in the field of communications.

"Telecommunications Administration" (administration) is the government agency or service responsible for fulfilling obligations under the Charter of the International Telecommunication Union, the Convention of the International Telecommunication Union, and the Radio Regulations. In the Russian Federation, the Ministry of Digital Development, Communications and Mass Media (until 2018, the Ministry of Telecom and Mass Communications of the Russian Federation (Minsvyaz) acts as a Telecommunications administration.

2.4 What Is the Composition of the Country's Delegations at ITU Meetings, Including Official Reunions and Study Groups (e.g., Government Only, or Multistakeholder Including Private Sector, Academia, and Civil Society Representatives)?

The composition of Russia's official delegations at ITU meetings consists of: government, private sector (namely, state (co)-owned companies), and academia (state universities).

Only one delegation representing the Administration of Communications of the Russian Federation may be sent to an international ITU event.

The composition of Russia's delegations at ITU's meetings, particularly to the Plenipotentiary Conference of ITU, world and regional conferences and assemblies, is defined by the Ministry of Information Technologies and Communications (Order of the Ministry of the Information Technologies and Communications of the Russian Federation No. 47 of December 29, 2004). The Russian Federal Communications Agency (Rossvyaz) is responsible for the formation of the delegation in cases where an international procedure for coordinating the use of radio-frequency assignments, including orbital-frequency positions for spacecraft, is carried out.

2.5 Is the Country a Member of the WTO? If So, Is the Country a Signatory to the General Agreement on Trade in Services?

The Russian Federation has been a member of the WTO since 22 August 2012. As part of its WTO accession, Russia signed the General Agreement on Trade in Services (GATS) that provides a legal framework for addressing barriers affecting trade in professional services.

2.6 Is the Country a Signatory to Any Regional Framework for Regulation of Telecommunications or a Member of Any Regional Organization for Telecommunications Regulation?

(a) The Russian Federation is a participant and a full member of the Regional Commonwealth in the Field of Communications (RCC/CIS)

RCC[4] is an international organization with the functions of the CIS interstate coordinating body in the field of electric and postal communications, and has observer status in the International Telecommunication Union (ITU) and the Universal Postal Union (UPU), and interacts with international and regional organizations, actively participating in conferences and forums.

The permanent executive body of RCC is the executive committee, whose location is Moscow, Russia. Operating parts of RCC are the commissions, councils of operators of telecommunication and a mail service, and the working groups whose activity is directed to the development and implementation of specific objectives of the commonwealth.

The RCC consists of 20 participants—12 full members and 8 observers. Participants of RCC and at the same time full members of RCC are the following countries: Azerbaijan, Armenia, Belarus, Kazakhstan, Kyrgyz Republic, Georgia, Republic of Moldova, Russian Federation, Tajikistan, Turkmenistan, Republic of Uzbekistan, Ukraine and observers Bulgaria, Lithuania, Latvia, Slovenia, Estonia, and international organization of space communication Intersputnik. In the Russian Federation, the administration of communications functions is assigned to the Ministry of Digital Development, Communications and Mass Media (2022).

(b) European Conference of Postal and Telecommunications Administrations (CEPT)

In 1994 Russian Federation became a member of CEPT[5]—the European Conference of Postal and Telecommunications Administrators.

(c) The Intersputnik International Organization of Space Communications (Intersputnik, Organization)

At present, the governments of the following twenty six countries are members of the Intersputnik International Organization of Space Communications (Intersputnik, 2022a): Republic of Azerbaijan, Islamic Republic of Afghanistan, Republic of Belarus, Republic of Bulgaria, Hungary, Socialist Republic of Vietnam, Federal Republic of Germany, Georgia, Republic of India, Republic of Yemen, Republic of Kazakhstan, Kyrgyz Republic, Democratic People's Republic of Korea, Republic of Cuba, Lao People's Democratic Republic, Mongolia, Republic of Nicaragua, Republic of Poland, Russian Federation, Romania, Syrian Arab Republic, Federal Republic of Somalia, Republic of Tajikistan, Turkmenistan, Ukraine and Czech Republic.

To date, the government of the Russian Federation has appointed the following Intersputnik Signatory: The Federal State Unitary Enterprise "Russian Satellite Communications Company" (www.rscc.ru). A Signatory is a telecommunications entity appointed by an Intersputnik Member, for which the Intersputnik Operating Agreement entered into force (Intersputnik, 2022b).

[4] Regional Commonwealth in the Field of Communications <https://en.rcc.org.ru/>. Retrieved on May 12, 2022.

[5] European Conference of Postal and Telecommunications Administrations (CEPT) <https://www.cept.org/>. Retrieved on May 12, 2022.

(d) International satellite communications organization INTELSAT (MOSS INTELSAT)
The Russian Federation is a member of the international satellite communications organization INTELSAT, the main goal of which is to continue and implement, in accordance with the intended direction, the design, development, creation, launch into orbit, operation and maintenance of the space component of the global system of commercial communications satellites, created in accordance with the provisions of the Interim Agreement and the Special agreements. The responsible ministry is the Ministry of Telecom and Mass Communications of the Russian Federation.[6]
(e) European satellite communications organization "EUTELSAT" (EOSS "EUTELSAT")
The main purpose of EUTELSAT shall be the design, development, construction, establishment, operation, and maintenance of the space segment of the European telecommunications satellite system or systems. In this context, EUTELSAT shall have as its prime objective the provision of the space segment required for international public telecommunications services in Europe.[7]
Eutelsat owns two subsidiaries in Russia, including home Internet provider Konnect. In turn, the Russian state satellite operator owns a small stake in Eutelsat itself. (Corporate documents say most of the 3.62% ownership stake corresponds to the Russian Satellite Communications Company, or RSCC) (Ling, 2022).

3 Institutions

3.1 *Does the Country have a Telecommunications Regulatory Authority? If So, Is It an Independent Body, and What Are Its Attributes?*

The telecoms sector is regulated by:

(a) the Ministry of Digital Development, Communications and Mass Media,[8] which is vested with the authority to create a general development strategy for the telecoms, information distribution, and technology industries and to issue

[6] The Agreement on the International Organization of Satellite Communications, INTELSAT, was signed at Washington on August 20, 1971.

[7] The Convention establishing the European Telecommunications Satellite Organization "EUTELSAT," including its Preamble and its Annexes, was opened for signature by governments at Paris on 15 July 1982.

[8] Until 2018 the Ministry of Telecom and Mass Communications of the Russian Federation (Minsvyaz or Mincomsvyaz).

subordinate regulations in pursuance of the main regulatory framework set by federal laws;

(b) the Federal Service for Supervision in the Sphere of Connection, Information Technologies and Mass Communications (Roskomnadzor), which is a federal agency under the Ministry and oversees compliance in these spheres.

As the main regulator in the Technology, Media, and Telecommunications (TMT) sector in Russia, the Ministry of Digital Development, Communications and Mass Media is responsible for establishing and enforcing state policy in the sphere of electronic and postal communications, for promulgating the development and introduction of new information and communication technologies, and for coordinating the work of other state agencies in this area. Legislative oversight is exercised mainly through the State Duma Committee for mass media. The Committee develops mass media-related draft laws and provides expert analysis of laws submitted by other Duma committees regarding their compliance with current media law.

Broadly, Mincomsvyaz is in charge of elaborating and implementing state policy in the TMT sector. It also, inter alia, participates in the legislative process (namely, by submitting bills to the government) and adopts secondary legislation in the area.

3.2 What Is the Allocation of Regulatory Responsibilities Between the Appropriate Government Department(s) and the Telecommunications Regulatory Authority?

The State Commission for Radio Frequencies (2022) (SCRF/GKRCh) and the Federal Radio Frequency Service, which are part of the Ministry for Digital Development, Connection and Mass Communications, are responsible for:

(a) spectrum allocation;
(b) the supervision of radio electronic equipment and radio frequency devices; and
(c) compliance control regarding the allocated spectrum and the collection of frequency-use fees, respectively.

Furthermore, three state agencies fall under the auspices of Mincomsvyaz:

- The Federal Service for Supervision of Communications, Information Technology and Mass Media (Roskomnadzor) is the main licensing authority of all types of broadcasting and telecom services in the telecommunication sector and is in charge of mass media registrations; it is in charge of the supervision of personal data protection and information distribution issues. The RKN also maintains and operates the state register of web resources blocked in Russia. It also monitors the compliance of telecom operators with the established regulatory requirements.
- The Federal Print and Mass Media Agency (Rospechat).
- The Federal Agency of Communications (Rossvyaz), which is in charge of certification in the telecom area.

3.3 If the Country Follows a Federal Structure, Is There an Allocation of Responsibilities Relating to the Telecommunications Sector Between the Central/Federal Government and the States?

Previously, the Russian regions (states) had independence in the area of information technologies since Article 73 of the Constitution of the Russian Federation secures to them the entirety of state power outside the limits of joint jurisdiction and exclusive jurisdiction of the federal center.

After the vote on changes in the Constitution of the Russian Federation took place on 1st of July 2020,[9] the Russian regions (states) formally lost independence in the area of information technologies, due to changes in Article 71[10] of the Constitution of the Russian Federation.

Particularly in Sections i) and l) of Article 71 of the Constitution of the Russian Federation, the list of exclusive jurisdictions of the Russian Federation has been supplemented with a new element—information technologies and digital data circulation.

How these changes will translate into the allocation of responsibilities between the federal center and the Russian regions is yet to be seen, as the vote was very recent.

3.4 Is There a Competition Department Within the Telecommunications Regulatory Authority?

No. The Ministry of Digital Development, Communications and Mass Media has no competition (or anti-monopoly) department.

3.5 Does the Country have a Competition Authority? If So, Is It an Independent Body, and What Are Its Attributes?

Russia's Ministry for Antimonopoly Policy and Support to Entrepreneurship (MAP Russia) was abolished on March 9, 2004, and its powers were delegated to other authorities. The functions of the federal antimonopoly body, control over the

---

[9] The changes in the Constitution of the Russian Federation came into force on the fourth of July 2020, after the President of the Russian Federation signed a Decree of the President of the Russian Federation of No. 445 of July 3, 2020 "On the official publication of the Constitution of the Russian Federation as amended."

[10] The text of the Constitution of the Russian Federation was amended by the laws of the Russian Federation on the amendment to the Constitution of the Russian Federation No. 1-FKZ dated March 14, 2020.

activity of natural monopolies, and observance of the legislation on advertising were delegated to the newly established Federal Antimonopoly Service (FAS).

Federal Antimonopoly Service (the FAS Russia) is an authorized federal executive body, which is carrying out its functions with regard to the approval of the regulatory legal acts and control over compliance with the anti-monopoly legislation, legislation in the field of natural monopolies' activity, in the field of state regulation of prices (tariffs) for the goods (services), advertising, foreign investments in the business entities of strategic importance for the Russian national defense and state security, control in the field of state defense order, purchases of goods, works and services for the state and municipal needs and procurement of goods, works and services by certain legal entities, as well as with regard to the approval of closed methods for selection of suppliers (contractors, performers).

The FAS Russia, represented by the Central Office as well as its 84 Regional Offices (which have their own functions and competences), is independent in decision-making. In the structure of public authorities, the FAS Russia reports to the government of the Russian Federation by submitting to the government an annual report on the results of its activities. FAS Russia is subordinate to the government of the Russian Federation (reports directly to the Chairman of the Government of the Russian Federation).

The FAS Russia works in conditions under which the legal framework defining its activities, together with the characteristics of its institutional position, ensures the independence of the authority from political influence.

Absence of political pressure on the FAS Russia is ensured by the fact that the authority is directly subordinated to the government of the Russian Federation, but is not a part of it. On the one hand, it determines the status of the authority that is different from the status of the federal ministry. On the other hand, as the FAS Russia controls the relevant activity of authorities, this fact ensures the FAS Russia acts independently as an anti-monopoly authority while bringing cases against authorities, primarily against federal ones.

3.6 *Does the Country have a Data Protection Authority? If So, Is It an Independent Body, and What Are Its Attributes? If Not, Which Body of the Government Takes Care of Personal Data-Related Issues?*

Yes, the national data protection authority in Russia is the Federal Service for Supervision of Communications, Information Technologies and Mass Media (Roskomnadzor). It is not independent and is under the jurisdiction of the Ministry of Digital Development, Communications and Mass Media by Decree of the President of the Russian Federation No. 1715 of December 3, 2008. A complete list of Roskomnadzor's powers can be found on the Roskomnadzor website (Roskomnadzor, 2013).

3.7 *Does the Country have a Specific Public Body Dealing with Open Data? If So, Is It an Independent Body, and What Are Its Attributions?*

The following organizations are working to coordinate and develop Open Government Data (OGD) at the federal level: the Russian Open Data Council,[11] the Ministry of Economic Development, the Ministry of Telecommunication, and the Government Analytical Center of the Russian Federation. The Open Data Council is a part of the Government Commission on Open Government; it coordinates the development of OGD through preparing government programs, proposals and recommendations, collecting and applying the best practices, promoting the idea of OGD, and creating independent feedback channels. The Ministry of Economic Development is responsible for developing the federal portal, providing operational and procedural support, and synchronizing federal and regional initiatives. The Ministry of Telecommunications is responsible for the coordination of OGD development by government bodies, including corresponding information systems, as well as the advancement of social e-services based on OGD. The Government Analytical Center of the Russian Federation monitors the OGD in the Russian Federation: the results of the analysis are published in the Open Data Bulletin (Open Data Bulletin 2015–2016) that has been issued every three months since June 2015.

In Russia, in 2013, a law[12] was adopted to ensure access to information on the activities of state bodies and local self-government bodies, according to which publication of data in the public domain has become mandatory. The basic principles for ensuring access to information on the activities of state bodies and local governments are as follows: openness and accessibility of information on the activities of state bodies; accuracy of information; freedom of searching, receiving, transmitting, and disseminating information. The law prohibits the dissemination of information containing state secrets or personal data.

In 2014, the Russian government approved the road map of IT sector development for the years 2014–2025 (ICT Road-Map 2013), and OGD development is one of the main priorities of the plan.

[11] Guidelines for the publication of open data by state bodies and local governments, as well as technical requirements for the publication of open data. Version 3.0 (Government Commission for Coordinating the Activities of the Open Government, 2014).

[12] The term "open data" was officially defined in Federal Law No. 112-FZ (2013), which formed the legal basis for the government's work with open data.

3.8 Does the Country have a Body/An Authority for Managing CyberSecurity Incidents, Such as CERTs/CSIRTs? If So, What Are Its Attributions, and What Is the Nature of Such an Entity (e.g., Governmental, Multistakeholder, Private)?

According to the European Union Agency for Network and Information Security (ENISA), there are 5 CERT teams in the Russian Federation: CERT-GIB, BI.ZONE-CERT, FinCERT, Infosecurity Incident Response Team (IN4-CERT), and RU-CERT.

RU-CERT is part of the international associations CSIRT/CERT of the centers FIRST and Trusted Introducer, and within the framework of these associations, officially acts as a contact party in the Russian Federation.

RU-CERT is the name of the Computer Security Incident Response Team RU-CERT (CSIRT /CERT team) from the Russian Federation. RU-CERT is an independent nonprofit organization; its main objective is to reduce the level of information security threats for users of the Russian segment of the Internet (.ru and .su TLDs). The organization's area of competence includes countering the use of domain names (in the ".SU" domain) to carry out phishing, unauthorized access to information systems of third parties (users, visitors), distribute malware, and manage malware (botnet control).

To achieve its objectives, RU-CERT cooperates with leading Russian IT companies, operators of operative-search activities, state authorities, and the government of the Russian Federation, foreign centers for responding to computer incidents, and other organizations operating in the field of computer and information security.

RU-CERT operates within the regulatory framework of the Russian Federation; therefore, RU-CERT is not authorized to deal with issues that are within the jurisdiction of law enforcement agencies. In these cases, one must contact the regional units of the Russian Federal Security Service (FSB) or the Ministry of Internal Affairs of the Russian Federation. RU-CERT does not have the authority to close resources, filter addresses, stop delegating domains, remove content from a particular resource, search for people involved in certain actions, etc. RU-CERT does not record or register the facts of spam messages.

3.9 Does the Country have a Coordination System Involving the Aforementioned Institutions? If So, What Is the Nature of such an Entity (e.g., Governmental, Multistakeholder, Private)?

Russia has a State System for the Detection, Prevention, and Elimination of the Consequences of Computer Attacks (GosSOPKA) that was created in accordance with the Decree of the President of the Russian Federation No. 31c of January 15, 2013.

In January 2013, President Vladimir Putin instructed the Federal Security Service (FSB) of Russia to create a system for detecting, preventing, and eliminating the consequences of computer attacks on IT resources located in Russia, as well as in diplomatic missions and consular posts of Russia abroad.

On January 1, 2018, the Federal Law No. 187-FZ of July 26, 2017 "On the Security of Critical Information Infrastructure" came into force in Russia.

The law is intended to regulate relations in the field of ensuring the security of information infrastructure facilities of the Russian Federation, the functioning of which is critically important for the state economy. According to the law, information systems and networks, as well as automated control systems operating in the following areas can be classified as critical information infrastructure objects: health; science; transport; communication; power engineering; banking and other areas of the financial market; fuel and energy complex; atomic energy; defense and rocket and space industry; mining, metallurgical and chemical industries.

Objects of critical information infrastructure, as well as telecommunication networks used to organize interaction between them, make up the concept of critical information infrastructure.

The requirements of this law affect those organizations (state bodies and institutions, legal entities, and individual entrepreneurs) that own (on the basis of ownership, lease, or another legal basis) objects of critical information infrastructure or that ensure their interaction.

The Ministry of Digital Development, Telecommunications and Communications of the Russian Federation will create special competition commissions that will determine who will and how to receive subsidies for the creation of industry centers of the State System for the Detection, Prevention and Elimination of the Consequences of Computer Attacks (GosSOPKA) and its inclusion in the system of automated exchange of information on current cyber threats. The corresponding order was published in November 2019 on the Official Portal of Legal Information of the Government of the Russian Federation (Order of the Ministry of Digital Development, Telecommunications and Mass Media of the Russian Federation No. 629 of October 30, 2019).

4 Regulations

4.1 Are the Telecommunication Regulations and Standards Openly and Publicly Accessible?

Yes, telecommunication regulations and standards (GOSTs) are publicly available. The Federal Agency for Technical Regulation and Metrology (Rosstandart) is part of the system of federal executive bodies of the Russian Federation and is administered by the Ministry of Industry and Trade of the Russian Federation.

The Federal Agency for Technical Regulation and Metrology is a federal executive body that performs the functions of rendering public services and managing state property in the field of technical regulation and metrology.

Before amendments to the legislative acts of the Russian Federation, the Federal Agency for Technical Regulation and Metrology licensed the manufacture and repair of measuring instruments, as well as the functions of state metrological control and supervision. The Federal Agency also exercises control and supervision over compliance with the mandatory requirements of national standards and technical regulations until the government of the Russian Federation decides to transfer these functions to other federal executive bodies.

It was formed in accordance with the Decree of the President of the Russian Federation No. 649 of May 20, 2004 "Issues of the structure of federal executive bodies." The Federal Agency for Technical Regulation and Metrology conducts its activities in accordance with the Regulation approved by Decree of the Government of the Russian Federation of June 17, 2004 No. 294 (2004).

Rosstandart maintains a database with existing technical regulations (Rosstandart, 2022c), a catalog of national standards (Rosstandart, 2022b), a catalog of interstate standards (Rosstandart, 2022a), and a catalog of international standards (ISO). This database is available on Rosstandard's website https://www.gost.ru/portal/gost/.

4.2 *Is There a Specific General Telecommunications Legislation?*

Yes, the Federal Law "On Communications" establishes the legal principles for activity in the sphere of communications on the territory of the Russian Federation and the territories put under the jurisdiction of the Russian Federation, and defines the authority of the state power bodies in the sphere of communications, as well as the rights and the duties of the persons who are taking part in this activity or making use of communications services.

4.3 *Are There Any Instruments Other Than Legislation and Regulations, such as License Agreements, that Govern the Provision of Telecommunication Services in the Country?*

The Law on Telecommunications establishes general principles and rules that apply to telecommunications legislation in Russia.

There are also a number of regulations adopted in furtherance of the Law on Telecommunications, e.g., by the government of the Russian Federation and the Ministry of Communications.

- Such regulations cover, inter alia, the following:
- Licensing requirements;
- Rules for the provision of specific telecommunication services;
- Rules for the operation of telecommunication networks.

In addition, other ancillary considerations affecting the provision of telecommunications services in Russia are regulated by other laws, including:

- The Federal Law "On Personal Data" No. 152-FZ dated 27 July 2006;
- The Federal Law "On Combating Money Laundering and the Financing of Terrorism" No. 115-FZ dated 07 August 2001;
- The Federal Law "On Licensing of Certain Types of Activities" No. 99-FZ dated 04 May 2011.

4.4 Is There Any Obligation to Provide Open Data Regarding the Telecommunications Infrastructure?

No, but the register of the communications infrastructure of the Russian Federation is maintained by Roskomnadzor (2012). Clause 1 of the order of the Ministry of Digital Development, Telecommunications and Mass Media of the Russian Federation of July 31, 2019 N 221 "On approval of the terms, procedure, composition and format for the provision by telecom operators, owners or other owners of technological communication networks, organizers of the dissemination of information in the information and telecommunication network" Internet, as well as other persons who have a unique identifier for the totality of communications and other technical means in the information and telecommunications network "Internet," in the electronic form of information provided for by subparagraph 4 of paragraph 8 of Article 56.2 of the Federal Law of 07.07.2003 N 126-FZ "On Communications." This law provides that telecom operators, owners or other owners of technological communication networks, the organizer of the dissemination of information in the information and telecommunications network "Internet," as well as other persons who have a unique identifier for the totality of communications and other technical means on the Internet, submit to Federal service for supervision in the field of communications, information technology and mass communications information. The law mandates to provide information about the autonomous system number they have, as well as about the network addresses belonging to the autonomous system; on interaction with telecom operators having an autonomous system number, owners or other owners of technological communication networks, other persons; about the places of connection of their means of communication to communication lines crossing the State Border of the Russian Federation; on the places of installation of their communications equipment connected to communication lines located outside the territory of the Russian Federation; about telecommunication message routes; about technical and software tools (including communication tools) functioning in order to identify the Internet network addresses corresponding to domain names; about the infrastructure of their communication network in electronic form by filling out electronic forms or posting information in XML format in a personal account on the official website of the Federal Service for Supervision of Communications, Information Technology and Mass Communications on the Internet or by organizing automatic interaction of their communication network management systems or means of communication with the information system for monitoring and managing a public communication network, created in accordance with Decree of the Government of the Russian Federation of February 13, 2019 N 136 "On the Center for Monitoring and Controlling a Public Communications Network" Ruling of the Supreme Court of the Russian Federation No. 303-ES22-6625 of May 26, 2022).

4.5 Is There Any Obligation to Provide Open Data on Backhaul Pricing?

No, but there is the register of significant objects of critical information infrastructure of the Russian Federation to identify significant objects of critical information infrastructure of the Russian Federation in the course of intersectoral activities to identify significant objects of critical confidentiality information, the implementation of critical state control in the field of security of critical information in accordance with Federal Law of July 26, 2017 No. 187-FZ "On the security of critical information infrastructure of the Russian Federation." Maintaining the Register of operations carried out to record, store, and provide information in paper and electronic form on significant objects of critical confidential information. The register is formed and maintained by the Federal Service for Technical and Export Control (Order of the FSTEC of Russia No. 227 of December 6, 2017).

4.6 Does Regulation Foresee Multiple Categories of Telecommunications Services (E.g., Internet Access, Broadcasting)? Are Information Services Distinguished Between Themselves (Content Creation and Content Distribution)?

Yes, according to the Article "29" of the Federal Law of 07.07.2003 No. 126-FZ (The Law "On Communications") and the Decree of the Government of the Russian Federation of December 30, 2020 No. 2385 (as amended on February 26, 2022) "On Licensing Activities in the Field of Provision of Communication Services and the Recognition of Certain Acts of the Government of the Russian Federation as invalid" together with the "Regulations on Licensing Activities in the Field of

Provision of Communication Services," the following 20 types of communication services and licenses corresponding to them have been established in Russia:

- Services of local telephone communication, except for services of local telephone communication using payphones and means of collective access.
- Long-distance and international telephone communication services.
- Telephone services in a dedicated communication network.
- Services of intrazonal telephone communication.
- Services of local telephone communication using payphones.
- Services of local telephone communication using means of collective access.
- Telegraphic services.
- Communication services of a personal radio call.
- Services of mobile radio communication in the public communication network.
- Services of mobile radio communication in a dedicated communication network.
- Services of mobile radiotelephone communication.
- Services of mobile satellite radio communication.
- Communication services for the provision of communication channels.
- Communication services for data transmission, except for communication services for data transmission to transmit voice information.
- Communication services for the transmission of data for transmitting voice information.
- Telematic communication services.
- Communication services for cable broadcasting purposes.
- Communication services for broadcasting.
- Communication services for wire radio broadcasting.
- Postal services.

A communication operator is a legal entity or individual entrepreneur providing telecommunication services on the basis of an appropriate license. Communication operators can be classified according to the type of service:

- Operator of universal communication services.
- Satellite telephone operator.
- Mobile operator.
- Fixed-line operator.
- Virtual mobile operator.
- Internet service provider.

An Internet service provider is a telecom operator licensed for one of the following types of services:

- Communication services for the provision of communication channels
- Communication services in the data transmission network, except for the transmission of voice information
- Communication services for the transmission of voice information in the data transmission network
- Telematic communication services

4.7 Do the Country's National Regulations Recognize Community Operators and /or Non-profit Telecommunications Operators?

No. In accordance with Article 2 of the Federal Law "On Communications," Russian legislation defines the following types of operators:

- an operator occupying a significant position in a public communications network—an operator that, together with affiliated persons, has at least 25% of the installed capacity in a geographically defined numbering zone or throughout the territory of the Russian Federation or has the ability to pass at least 25% traffic;
- communication operator—a legal entity or an individual entrepreneur providing communication services on the basis of an appropriate license;
- universal service operator—a telecom operator that provides communication services in a public communication network and which, in the manner prescribed by this federal law, is entrusted with the obligation to provide universal communication services;
- operator of obligatory publicly accessible TV channels and (or) radio channels—a communications operator that, on the basis of an agreement with a subscriber, provides communications services for the purposes of television broadcasting and (or) radio broadcasting (except for communications services for the purposes of wired radio broadcasting) and, in accordance with this federal law, is obliged to carry out broadcasting of obligatory publicly available TV channels and (or) radio channels, the list of which is determined by the legislation of the Russian Federation on mass media.

4.8 Is There Any Obligation to Share Infrastructure:

(a) poles, cell phone towers, underground routes/tubes
(b) fiber optics sharing, telecommunication cables
(c) equipment sharing

Until 2013, infrastructure sharing in Russia was limited to passive infrastructure sharing due to certain technical requirements set in the applicable regulation. Those limitations were lifted in 2013, and Russian telecoms operators have since been encouraged to share active and passive infrastructure. Amendments setting the terms of technical interconnection and the joint use of certain elements of infrastructure were introduced via a number of Ministry for Digital Development, Connection and Mass Communications orders between 2014 and 2016. The existing regulation allows for the joint ownership of frequencies and the joint certification of radio electronic equipment and high-frequency devices. However, in practice, major wireless operators are not usually eager to share infrastructure because:

(a) their existing networks cover the same geographic territories; and
(b) operators are concerned about the risks of losing subscribers to competitors.

The only area that saw and will most likely see an increase in infrastructure sharing and joint effort is the development of next-generation, long-term evolution and 5G services. Due to the high forecasted costs required to set up these networks, most of which are used by the military at present, major operators are willing to join forces.

In addition to the above, under the Rules of Non-Discriminatory Access to Infrastructure adopted by Government Decree 1284 (2014), dated November 29, 2014, natural monopolies in the telecoms industries must provide access to their infrastructure facilities by law.

4.9 Is There Any Unbundling Obligation? Can You be an Internet Service Provider and a Content Provider at the Same Time?

Under the Ministry for Digital Development, Connection and Mass Communications Order No. 54, dated May 2, 2006, operators that hold substantial positions in publicly available networks and operators of universal services and natural telecoms monopolies must keep separate accounts for:

(a) different types of activity;
(b) provided services; and
(c) different sections of the telecoms network used for the provision of such services.

4.10 Is There Any Obligation to Treat Internet Traffic in a Non-Discriminatory Fashion (So-called Network Neutrality Principles)?

Russian legislation contains no statutory requirements for net neutrality. However, the idea has been broadly discussed and is actively supported by the Federal Antimonopoly Service. In 2016, the Federal Anti-monopoly Service published a basic document on net neutrality on its website, explaining the main principles and goals therein (Federal Anti-Monopoly Service [FAS], 2016). All major mobile operators (i.e., MTS, Vimpelcom (Beeline), and MegaFon) have expressed their support for the principle of net neutrality.

Even though the Federal Anti-monopoly Service continues promoting net neutrality and seems to have the support of the market representatives, in September 2018 the Federal Service for Supervision in the Sphere of Connection, Information

Technologies and Mass Communications (Roskomnadzor) expressed a view that the development of 5G networks and their use for telemedicine and remotely controlled vehicles would require prioritizing such traffic over others. Furthermore, the association of major LTE operators (MTS, Vimpelcom (Beeline), MegaFon, and Tele2) has also expressed (Meduza, 2018) concerns about net neutrality in connection with 5G services in the official letter addressed to the Russian government in August 2018.

4.11 Does the Country have Any Specific Legal or Regulatory Provisions Regarding the Internet Access Providers' Possibility to Monitor the Content of User Communications?

Russia adopted laws aimed at establishing additional measures to counter terrorism and ensure public safety. In the media, this package of laws was called the "Yarovaya package" or the "Yarovaya law."

The expansion of the powers of law enforcement agencies lies in the fact that law enforcement agencies have the opportunity to request information from mobile operators (telephone conversation records, SMS messages, etc.) as part of the consideration of reports of crimes (Articles 2, 3, 4 of the Law No. 374-FZ).

The organizer of the dissemination of information on the Internet is obliged to store on the territory of the Russian Federation information about the facts of reception, transmission, delivery and (or) processing of voice information, written text, images, sounds, video or other electronic messages of Internet users and information about these users in within one year from the end of the implementation of such actions.

From October 1, 2018, telecom operators are required to store text, voice, video, and other user messages for 30 days. Further, the operator is obliged to increase the amount of storage by 15% per year (clause 6 of Decree of the Government of the Russian Federation of April 12, 2018 N 445 "On approval of the Rules for the storage by telecom operators of text messages of users of communication services, voice information, images, sounds, video and other messages of users communication services") (Bogodaeva, 2022).

4.12 Does the Country have Any Specific Legal or Regulatory Provisions Regarding the Internet Access Providers' Possibility to Collect and Process Users' Personal Data?

The telecom operator is obliged to terminate, under certain conditions, the service of the subscriber if, within the prescribed period, the discrepancy between the personal data of the actual users and the information stated in the subscription agreements is confirmed (Article 13 of Law No. 374-FZ). Failure to comply with this requirement entails liability in accordance with Article 13.34 of the Administrative Code of the Russian Federation.

According to the Sovereign Internet Law, telecom operators are required to install state equipment at traffic exchange points for analyzing and filtering traffic (Deep Packet Inspection; DPI) within the country and communication lines crossing the Russian border (Federal Law No. 90-FZ of May 1, 2019).

4.13 Does the Country Require a License to Operate Telecommunications Networks? Is There Any License Exemption?

As regards the telecommunication sector, further to the Federal Law No. 126-FZ (The Law "On Communications"), a license is a prerequisite for providing telecommunication services in Russia. Operators provide telecoms services in Russia under Government Decree, dated December 30, 2020 No. 2385 (as amended on February 26, 2022) "On Licensing Activities in the Field of Provision of Communication Services and the Recognition of Certain Acts of the Government of the Russian Federation as Invalid" together with the "Regulations on Licensing Activities in the Field of Provision of Communication Services," on the basis of telecoms licenses for the relevant type of service. The communication service licenses must be obtained by communication service providers wishing to conduct business in Russia. Telecoms license terms are determined and licenses are issued by Roskomnadzor; licenses can be issued for a period between three years and 25 years (Decree of the Government of the Russian Federation No. 2385 of December 30, 2020). Please refer to question No. 6 for the list of licensed activities.

Telecoms licenses are issued under the Federal Law No. 126-FZ (The Law "On Communications") in accordance with the licensing requirements under the above-mentioned Government Decree 2385. Licenses are issued on a per-territory basis, and operators that provide a variety of services must hold relevant licenses for all services and regions in which they provide services, which can sometimes number hundreds of licenses.

The listed titles are not clearly defined or exhaustively described in the Government Decree 2385 or any other regulations. In practice, this sometimes makes it difficult to reach a clear conclusion on whether a certain business activity falls under any type of licensable service (usually, a Russian telecoms consultant is engaged for such purposes).

4.14 Does the Country Offer a Specific/Simplified License for Not-for-Profit Operators or for Operators that Cover Specific Areas (E.g., Rural Areas)?

No. Russia provides for licensing according to the types of activities indicated in question 6, and not depending on the volume of services provided or their zero price.

4.15 Does the Country Require a License to Provide Satellite Telecommunications Services, Including via Non-geostationary Orbit Satellites?

Yes, the Russian Federation requires a license to provide mobile satellite services as per the Communication Law and, more specifically, Regulation of the Russian Government No. 87 dated 18 February 2005. Including via non-geostationary orbit satellites in accordance with the Order by the Ministry of Information Technologies and Communications of Russian Federation (No. 99 dated August 22, 2007) On approval of the Rules for the application of earth stations in satellite communications and broadcasting of the unified telecommunication network of the Russian Federation (as amended on June 15, 2015).

4.16 Has the Country Established an Obligation to Provide Coverage in Specific Areas (E.g., Rural Areas that Lack Coverage)?

The principle of universal access to communication services was incorporated in the Russian legislation, namely, in the Communication Law, in 2003. Encouraging universal access to communication services is one of the paramount priorities of the government's policy in the TMT area, and is mainly aimed at ensuring access to communication services in rural areas and hard-to-reach regions of Russia (which are quite numerous due to the vastness of the Russian territory).

Currently, in terms of the Communication Law, universal service includes the following types of telecommunication services:

- telephone services accessible via public payphones (coin stations) or interactive kiosks, which should be available in all residential areas all for all residents within a maximum one-hour walking distance;
- data transfer services and access to the Internet via public access points, ensuring Internet access (at 10 Mbit/s speed) in all residential areas with more than 250 inhabitants (project on "bridging the digital divide").

One of the biggest Russian telecoms operators, JSC "Rostelecom," is in charge of the project aiming at ensuring universal access to communication services, which is currently ongoing.

It is also important that all Russian communication service providers are obliged to pay contributions to the Universal Service Fund—a specific fund established to finance universal communication services.

4.17 Are There Any Specific Cybersecurity Obligations with Regard to the Telecommunications Sector?

Federal Law No. 187-FZ dated July 26, 2017 "On the Security of the Russian Federation's Critical Data Infrastructure" (2017), which introduces requirements for infrastructure security (the "CDI Law").

The law sets out the basic principles for ensuring the security of critical information infrastructure, the powers of the state bodies of Russia to ensure the security of the critical information infrastructure, as well as the rights, obligations and responsibilities of persons holding rights of ownership or other legal rights to the facilities for critical information infrastructure, communications providers and information systems providing interaction with these facilities.

The elements of the critical information infrastructure are understood to be information systems, telecommunication networks of state authorities, as well as such systems and networks for the management of technological processes that are used in state defense, healthcare, transport, communication, finance, energy, fuel, nuclear, aerospace, mining, metalworking, and chemical industries. All these industries are considered critical for the economy and should be protected against any cyber threats. The law requires such industries to implement protection measures, assign the category of protection (in accordance with the statutes), and then register with FSTEK (2022), which is now the supervisory authority in this field.

The Sovereign Internet Law was adopted (Federal Law No. 90-FZ 'On Amendments into the Communication Law and the Information Law') in May 2019, and on 1 November 2019, the majority of its provisions came into force in Russia. The main purpose of the Sovereign Internet Law is to create an autonomous system that can support the operation of the Russian segment of the Internet in the event of disconnection from the global network.

The Sovereign Internet Law imposes a number of obligations on certain categories of persons (communication service providers, owners of various communication networks' infrastructure, as well as information dissemination organizers (e.g., social networks, mail services), and establishes a specific register of Internet exchange points ("register"). The obligations imposed include:

- providing certain information to Roskomnadzor, information on the purpose of using a communication line that crosses the Russian border, and the means of communication installed on it;

- participating in drills arranged by Roskomnadzor;
- restricting interaction between networks (e.g., by allowing only the use of the Internet exchange points listed in the register) and prohibiting owners of Internet exchange points from connecting communication networks to Internet exchange points when such networks fail to comply with the requirements of the law; and,
- installing hardware and software tools that enable Roskomnadzor to monitor traffic, including access to resources blocked in Russia.

4.18 Is There Any Regulation Regarding Cybersecurity Incidents?

As a result of possible computer attacks, a special law was adopted that deals with specific measures and requirements to be implemented and adopted to ensure the safety of the critical information infrastructure (Federal Law No. 187-FZ 'On the Safety of Critical Information Infrastructure', dated 26 July 2017). Although the practical application of this new law is still not fully clear, the general idea behind it is that all critical infrastructure objects will be categorized depending on their economic, political, and social importance (that is, there will be three categories of importance). Depending on the relevant category of importance, specific rules and requirements will apply with respect to security measures to be implemented.

4.19 Does the Law Foresee Any Specific Cybercrime Involving the (Mis)use or Attack of the Telecommunications Infrastructure?

The Law No. 187-FZ dated July 26, 2017 "On the Security of the Russian Federation's Critical Data Infrastructure" foresees attacks on critical data infrastructure.

As a result of possible computer attacks, this law was adopted that deals with specific measures and requirements to be implemented and adopted to ensure the safety of the critical information infrastructure. Although the practical application of this law is still not fully clear, the general idea behind it is that all critical infrastructure objects will be categorized depending on their economic, political, and social importance (that is, there will be three categories of importance). Depending on the relevant category of importance, specific rules and requirements will apply with respect to security measures to be implemented.

4.20 Does the Law Foresee SIM and/or IMEI Registration? What Are the Requirements Applicable to Such Registration (For Instance, the Documents and Information Required for Know-Your-Customer (KYC) Processes)?

Mandatory paid registration of mobile devices by IMEI might be applied starting from first of July 2021, according to the Kommersant newspaper (Tishina, 2020), with reference to a law project that is currently under development.

The senators proposed to introduce paid registration of all mobile devices with Internet access in Russia from February 1, 2020 using the International Mobile Equipment Identity (IMEI). The corresponding bill was developed by the first deputy head of the Federation Council Committee on Constitutional Legislation, Lyudmila Bokova, with a group of parliamentarians. The bill proposes to oblige manufacturers and importers to register mobile devices by IMEI number. Individuals will be able to independently register gadgets (not only cell phones, but also tablets, laptops, and other devices) purchased abroad on the website of state services. The possibility of extending this rule to all devices is being discussed, including sensors (used, for example, in electricity and water meters), which, like a mobile phone, must have serial numbers.

Cellular operators will be obliged to block devices that are not allowed to work in networks by IMEI. According to the project, a central database of these numbers will be created. It will be synchronized with the international GSMA database.

Supposedly, several lists of devices should be created. The black list will include stolen, illegally imported phones blocked at the request of law enforcement agencies; the white list—fully functioning devices in cellular networks; the gray list and the list of exceptions—temporarily functioning phones for the period of checking the legality of import and purchase.

5 SIM Card Registration Requirements

In June 2018, Federal Law No. 245 of July 29, 2017, came into force, which prohibits the use of mobile phones without specifying passport data. All subscribers with incorrect documents risk being left without communication. These are new requirements of the communications law; the regulations came into force on June 1, 2018. The new law is intended to force market participants to properly fulfill their obligations to uniquely identify subscribers, which is already provided for by existing legislation.

In accordance with the law the telecom operator is obliged to verify the accuracy of information about the subscriber and information about the users of the communication services of the subscriber—a legal entity or an individual entrepreneur, including those provided by a person acting on behalf of the telecom operator, in accordance with this federal law and the rules for the provision of communication services.

5.1 Does the Country Specify the Prices or Tariffs for the Provision of Telecommunication Services or Impose Any Minimum or Maximum Limits?

According to Article 28 on "Regulation of tariffs for communication services" of the Federal Law No. 126-FZ dated July 07, 2003 (The Law "On communications"):

(a) Tariffs for communication services are established by the communication operator independently, unless otherwise provided by this federal law and the legislation of the Russian Federation on natural monopolies.
(b) Tariffs for public telecommunications and public postal services are subject to state regulation in accordance with the legislation of the Russian Federation on natural monopolies. The list of public telecommunications and public postal services, tariffs for which are regulated by the state, as well as the procedure for their regulation, is established by the Government of the Russian Federation. Tariffs for universal communication services are regulated in accordance with this federal law.
(c) State regulation of tariffs for communication services (except for the regulation of tariffs for universal communication services) should create conditions that provide communication operators with compensation for economically justified costs associated with the provision of communication services, and compensation for a reasonable rate of return (profitability) from the capital used in the provision of communication services, tariffs for which are set by the state.

Tariffs in the fixed-line segment are determined by the Federal Tariff Service on an annual basis, taking into consideration inflation and the operators' expenses. The price competition in the long-distance (LD) segment increased as mobile operators began implementing promotional tariffs to promote voice traffic growth after the crisis (long-distance traffic is predominantly built by corporate clients). At the same time, traditional operators had limited room for maneuver as intra-zonal and domestic LD tariffs, which are subject to regulation by the government, remained flat over the last three years. As a result, mobile operators managed to bite off a heavy share of the intraregional and long-distance market from traditional fixed-line operators, first, regional operators of Svyazinvest, which are now united under Rostelecom (Gazprombank, 2012).

5.2 Are There Any Policies or Regulations Governing Right-of-Way Issues, Such as Utilizing Land to Dig Trenches and Lay Fiber, for the Creation of Telecommunications Infrastructure?

The Land Code sets a specific category of land that can be used for communications, radio, television, and informatics services. Federal and municipal land can be leased for the construction and exploitation of communications network infrastructure. The terms for granting such rights are set in the Land Code and city planning regulations. The Land Code also contains rules on the establishment and recordation of easements on lands where telecoms infrastructure is located and way-leave rights for exploitation and repair.

There are no specific regulations or policies governing the right-of-way/servitude issues for the creation of telecommunication infrastructure. However, there are various articles of the Civil Code (1994) and Land Code of the Russian Federation (2001) that articulate steps for recovery of damages (requesting compensation for loss or damage) from temporary occupation of land plots for laying a linear communication structure with subsequent temporary (short-term) use for emergency repair cases, and laying fiber-optic telecommunication cable.

Particularly, these are Article 57 and Article 62 (paragraph 1) of the Land Code of the Russian Federation and Article 1, Article 12, and Article 15 (Clause 2) of the Civil Code of the Russian Federation.

5.3 What Are the Regulations Applicable to the Setting Up and Operation of Landing Stations and International Gateways to the Internet?

According to Article 8 on Registration of ownership and other property rights to communication objects, of the Federal Law No. 126-FZ dated July 07, 2003 "On communications":

Communication facilities that are firmly connected to the land and the movement of which is impossible without disproportionate damage to their purpose, including line-cable communications facilities, refer to real estate, the state registration of property rights, and other property rights carried out in accordance with civil law. Features of state registration of property rights and other property rights to linear-cable communication facilities are established by the government of the Russian Federation.

The setting up and operation of the international gateways to the Internet is done in accordance with the Regulation "On the procedure for joining public communication networks and the procedure for regulating the traffic pass of public communication networks" (1995). This Regulation has been developed in pursuance of a clause of the Decree of the President of the Russian Federation of 10.10.94 No. 1989 "On the Peculiarities of Public Administration of a Public Telecommunication Network" (Presented as an Appendix to the letter of the Ministry of Communications of the Russian Federation No. 54-u of March 28, 1995).

5.4 *Are There Any Regulations of the Over-The-Top (OTT) Services?*

Voice over IP (VoIP) services are not expressly regulated by Russian legislation. VoIP operators normally provide services under the terms of telecoms licenses for data transfer for voice information transmission purposes. Rules for the interconnection of telecoms networks adopted by Government Decree 161, dated March 28, 2005, allow the connection of Internet Protocol-based networks to other networks.

In terms of statutory regulations, the main trend appears to be a tightening of state control over information distribution via communications networks and the Internet, including messaging and over-the-top services and restrictions on the anonymity of communications (e.g., through identification requirements for online and electronic service users).

From 2018, the Federal Law No. 149-FZ of July 27, 2006 "On information, informational technologies and the protection of information" stipulates those users must identify themselves on messenger services like Telegram, Snapchat, and Yandex. The amendments also meant that Roskomnadzor could block messenger services—something that happened when Russia tried to block Telegram in April 2018, leading to considerable collateral damage as sections of the Russian segment of the Internet (RuNet) became unavailable to regular users.

5.5 *What Are the Grounds, If Any, on Which the Country Can Suspend Access to the Internet or Direct the Blocking of Access to Specific Websites?*

Restrictions on the content accessed by customers (network users) are mainly based on security considerations.

The Information Law contains a complex procedure for blacklisting of websites containing information the dissemination of which is prohibited under Russian law. The state regulator Federal Service for Supervision of Communications, Information Technology and Mass Media (Roskomnadzor), under 2012 amendments to the Federal Law No. 144-FZ (On information, information technologies, and protection of information) has the authority to block access to websites, but only after the warning to an Internet provider and sufficient time for the website owner to correct the wrong information. There should be a warning and three days given for the follow-up action, according to the law. However, there are precedents when Roskomnadzor has been blocking online resources abruptly, without following the standard procedure and without notice.[13]

Roskomnadzor is in charge of holding a specific unified *Register* (Roskomnadzor, 2009) of domain names, Internet website page locators, and network addresses that allow for identifying Internet websites containing information prohibited for distribution in Russia (Register).

The Information Law also imposes additional regulatory obligations on operators providing Internet access to their customers. Thus, telecommunications operators (providing Internet services to their customers) should have access to and regularly upload information from the Register, and restrict access to blacklisted websites within 24 hours starting from the moment when such a website is included in the Register. The list of grounds for the blocking of access to a web resource is constantly expanded. This measure is performed by telecoms operators that must cover all such costs.

Furthermore, the Information Law specifically prohibits the use of technologies that allow access to blocked websites (for instance, VPN services, anonymous search engines, etc.).

5.6 *Does the Country have a Specific Policy or Strategy Promoting the Development of Internet eXchange Point (IXP) and Other Interconnection and Transmission Systems?*

The principal rules of telecoms network interconnections are set out in Articles 18 to 20 of the Federal Law No. 126-FZ (The Law "On Communications"). Further, two decrees adopted by the government provide the specific technical requirements for:

(a) general network interconnections; and
(b) the interconnection of broadcasting networks, respectively.

Apart from these mandatory rules, all terms of interconnection and network-to-network access are defined and agreed on by the contracting operators. Operators of publicly available telecoms networks must provide interconnection services to other operators.

Operators considered to have a substantial position in publicly available networks (where a "substantial position" is defined as holding more than 25% of the capacity in the relevant geographic numbering area, individually or as part of a group of affiliates) must offer equal and non-discriminating terms for all connecting

[13] See the case of an independent "Fergana" news website being blocked on October 1, 2019 in Russia (Committee to Protect Journalists, 2019).

operators on the basis of standard published contracts. Operators that hold a substantial position cannot refuse interconnection, except where such connection would contradict their license terms or applicable regulations.

Network connection costs are government-regulated for operators that hold a substantial position in publicly available networks. For such operators, the Federal Agency for Communications sets the minimum and maximum costs of interconnection services per connection point.

Disputes on interconnection-related issues are resolved through standard judicial procedures in arbitrazh (i.e., commercial) courts.

The Federal Law of May 1, 2019 No. 90-FZ[14] "On Amendments to the Federal Law on Communications" and the Federal Law "On Information, Information Technologies and the Protection of Information" provide for the creation of a national Internet traffic routing system, centralized management tools, etc. One of the major changes according to this law is that telecom operators are required to install state equipment at traffic exchange points for analyzing and filtering traffic (Deep Packet Inspection—DPI) within the country and communication lines crossing the Russian border (Federal Law No. 90-FZ of May 1, 2019; Federal Law No. 31-FZ of March 18, 2019). Also, telecom operators are obliged to enter in the register and use exclusively these exchange points (the procedure is determined by the government).

5.7 *Have Any Exceptional Measures been Adopted to Regulate Internet Access in Light of the COVID-19 Crisis?*

In 2019, Russia passed the "fake news" law (Federal Law on Amendments on the Law on Information of 13.03.2019 No. 31-FZ). According to this law, distribution of deliberately unreliable socially important information in the media, as well as in information and telecommunication networks under the guise of reliable messages shall entail the imposition of an administrative fine for citizens from 30,000 to 100,000 rubles (an equivalent of US$450 and US$1500, respectively, at the time when the law was passed).

On March 31, 2020, in response to COVID-19, Russia passed amendments to legislation on "fake news," particularly regarding the spread of fake information that can threaten people's life and safety, as well as distributing deliberately false information of public significance. Violation of these amendments can imply imprisonment from three to five years (Federal Law No. 100-FZ of April 1, 2020).

---

[14]The so-called law on "Sovereign Internet" has entered into force on November 1, 2019.

6 Access to Spectrum

6.1 How Does the Country Organize Access to Spectrum for Data Transmission (E.g., Via Auctions)?

Articles 22 to 24 of the Federal Law No. 126-FZ dated July 07, 2003 (The Law "On Communications") set out general provisions on the regulation of spectrum. Under these provisions, the State Commission for Radio Frequencies (SCRF/GKRCh), under the Ministry for Digital Development, Connection and Mass Communications, is vested with the authority to regulate the use and allocation of spectrum in Russia. Spectrum frequencies are allocated in accordance with the Frequency Bandwidths Allocation Chart adopted by Government Decree 1049-34, dated December 21, 2011. In addition to setting the framework for the use of spectrum and making general decisions on the possibility of using spectrum for the provision of specific services, the SCRF issues permissions (Ministry of Digital Development, Communications and Mass Media of the Russian Federation, 2022) to use certain bandwidths and frequency channels. If a relevant radio frequency resource is limited in the territory that the operator applies for, the spectrum is allocated at auction.

The Federal State Unitary Enterprise Main Radio Frequency Centre analyses electromagnetic compatibility and issues expert evaluations of the potential allocation of spectrum to specific operators that have applied for permissions. This entity also oversees compliance with technical operation requirements for spectrum use in Russia.

Compliance with the terms of allocation of radio frequencies is supervised by the Federal Radio Frequency Service.

(a) LTE frequencies

At the beginning of the decade of 2010 (in 2012, 2013, 2014), the 4G spectrum auctions for LTE frequencies were conducted in Russia.

The largest Russian Telecom operators, such as "Rostelecom," MTS, "Megafon," and "VimpelCom" (Beeline), received LTE licenses in lower bands (e.g., 720–790 MHz, 791–862 MHz) and higher frequency bands (e.g., 2500–2690 MHz) at the 4G spectrum auction in 2012. Each winner received 2 bands in high and low bands with bandwidths of 10 MHz and 7,5 MHz, respectively. High band is usually used for LTE deployment with small cells (e.g., in big cities) while the low band is used in places where larger cell coverages are needed.

In 2014, a new form of frequency distribution through auctions was introduced in the field of frequency regulation. According to Government Decree No. 480 (2014), it was planned to hold the first auction where the LTE frequencies 2570–2595 MHz and 2595–2620 MHz (Band 38) should have been exposed. Federal Antimonopoly Service (FAS), Roskomnadzor, and the Ministry of Economic Development demanded that auctions be held on a regional basis to enable new participants to enter the market and receive more funds for regional budgets. As a result, it was decided to include both the federal lot and the regional lots (82 lots) in this action conducted in 2015.

Apart from Band 38, the shrinking number of LTE Russian operators also have licenses in the following bands: Band 20 (800 MHz), Band 3 (1800 MHz), Band 7 (2.6 GHz), Band 40 (2.3 GHz) and also Band 31 (450 MHz), a special low frequency band (initially proposed by Brazil at 3rd Generation Partnership Project (2022)), which provides maximum LTE coverage range, well-tailored for rural and remote places coverage (State Commission for Radio Frequencies [SCRF], 2017).

In Russia, commercial LTE networks have been launched in 37 regions by the end of October 2013. At the beginning of the implementation of LTE networks, LTE FDD mode was commonly adopted, in Band 7 (2600 MHz), while LTE TDD was used by MTS in Moscow in Band 38 (2600 MHz) and "Vainakhtelecom" in the Chechen Republic, Band 40 (2.3 GHz).

"Osnova Telecom" is deploying LTE TDD networks in Band 40 (2.3 GHz), which has most of the band resources (from 70 to 100 MHz, depending on the region). In accordance with licensing terms, companies should have launched networks in 40 regions by the end of January 2014. On October 3, 2013, "Osnova Telecom" prepared pre-launch networks' testing in 12 regions.

LTE networks have been deployed in all regions and federal subjects of Russia (Mforum, 2016), facilitated in part by shared investment and use of networks, such as between VimpelCom and MTS. By the end of 2015, VimpelCom reported its LTE coverage of the territory that holds 70% of the Russian population (VimpelCom, 2015).

(b) 5G frequencies

At the end of 2019, the State Commission on Radio Frequencies (SCRF/GKRCh), that is responsible for the distribution of this resource in Russia, has instructed Roskomnadzor to hold an auction for the right to obtain licenses to provide services in the 5G standard using frequencies of 25.25–25.65 GHz no later than the third quarter of 2020. The bid was supposed to be the first 5G frequency auction in Russia.

However, on March 17, 2020, the SCRF commission had a meeting (SCRF, 2020) and took a decision "On the determination of radio frequency ranges for the creation of communication networks of the 5G/IMT-2020 standard on the territory of the Russian Federation" and approved (Decision of the State Committee for Radio Frequencies No. 20-54-02, n.d.; SCRF, 2020) a new frequency distribution scheme for the development of fifth generation (5G) mobile communication networks).

Now the SCRF commission has adopted a new scheme:

1. Based on the results of research work on the topic: "Preparation of a draft plan for the conversion of the radio frequency spectrum in the interests of introducing 5G/IMT-2020 technology in the Russian Federation," determine that the radio frequency ranges 694–790 MHz, 2300–2400 MHz, 2570–2620 MHz,

4400–4990 MHz and 24.25–27.5 GHz are promising for building communication networks of the 5G/IMT-2020 standard.
2. To establish that the radio frequency spectrum available for the provision of communication services in the radio frequency range 4400–4990 MHz limits the possible number of operators of fifth-generation communication networks on the territory of the Russian Federation. The minimum required continuous section of the radio frequency spectrum for the provision of communication services in fifth-generation networks in a given territory in certain sections of the radio frequency band 4400–4990 MHz is 50 MHz.
3. To allocate a radio frequency band 24.25–24.65 GHz to an indefinite circle of persons for use by radio electronic means of the 5G/IMT-2020 standard, including for the purpose of creating technological communication networks, on the territory of the Russian Federation. Frequencies 24.25–24.65 GHz are proposed to be allocated to "an indefinite circle of persons," including "to create technological communication networks." This wording means that applicants will be able to obtain a resource without bidding by sending a corresponding application to the Russia's State Commission on Radio Frequencies (SCRF/GKRCh).
4. Allocate LLC New Digital Solutions (a joint venture between MegaFon[15] and Rostelecom to develop 5G) and FSUE NIIR[16] (OGRN 1027700120766) the radio frequency band 24.65–27.5 GHz for use by radio electronic means of fifth generation communication networks for scientific, research, experimental, experimental and design work to clarify the characteristics of radio electronic means of communication networks of the 5G/IMT-2020 standard and to determine the conditions for joint use of the radio frequency band 24.25–27.5 GHz of radio electronic equipment of communication networks of the 5G/IMT-2020 standard from radio electronic means of the State Corporation Roscosmos in the coinciding and neighboring radio frequency bands.

Earlier, representatives of the Ministry of Telecom and Mass Communications announced that they were planning to allocate a slightly narrower frequency band to a consortium of the largest Russian Telecom operators—Rostelecom, MTS, MegaFon, and VimpelCom (Beeline brand) without trading.

Operators will be able to use the frequencies they have for the construction of 5G networks without "issuing separate decisions of the State Committee for Radio Frequencies." The document indicates the bands that are currently used for the development of 2G, 3G, and 4G communications.

[15] MegaFon is the second largest mobile phone operator and the third largest telecom operator in Russia.

[16] Federal State Unitary Enterprise "Order of Labor Red Banner Russian Scientific Research Institute of Radio Named After M.I. Krivosheev" (2022).

6.2 Does the Country Offer Some Type of Advantage in the Spectrum Access (E.g., Discount or Compensation) for Operators Who Use the Spectrum to Provide Services in Rural Areas?

There is a national program "Digital Economy of the Russian Federation" (Government of the Russian Federation, 2022) that subsidizes at least 50% of the cost to mobile operators who build towers in remote areas ("In the Kuban", 2020). The Digital Economy project is planned for 5 years from 2019 to 2024 and foresees various forms of subsidies for the provision of telecommunication infrastructure and the development of the digital agenda of the Russian Federation.

6.3 Does the Country Offer Simplified (I.e., Low Bureaucratic, Affordable) Licensing for Spectrum Access to be Used for Social Purposes or to Provide Coverage to Specific Areas? Does This Include the Provision of Public Wi-Fi Services?

No, Russia does not offer simplified licensing for spectrum access for social purposes. On the contrary, as regards the provision of public Wi-Fi services, to prevent terrorist attacks (e.g., terrorists using public Wi-Fi networks to access the Internet), the following regulations were applied in 2014:

Federal Law No. 97-FZ of May 5, 2014;[17]

Decree of the Government of the Russian Federation No. 758[18] of July 31, 2014;

Decree of the Government of the Russian Federation No. 801[19] of August 12, 2014 on the identification of Wi-Fi users in public places.

According to these Regulations, the owners of free Wi-Fi points, namely: the owners of cafes, restaurants, hotels, and other places with public access to the Internet, are obliged to identify users by their phone number or passport data.

---

[17] Federal Law No. 97-FZ of May 5, 2014 (as amended on July 29, 2017) "On Amendments to the Federal Law 'On Information, Information Technologies and Information Protection' and certain legislative acts of the Russian Federation on the issues of streamlining the exchange of information using information and telecommunication networks."

[18] Decree of the Government of the Russian Federation No. 758 of July 31, 2014 "On Amendments to Certain Acts of the Government of the Russian Federation in Connection with the Adoption of the Federal Law 'On Amendments to the Federal Law On Information, Information Technologies and Information Protection' and Certain Legislative Acts of the Russian Federation on streamlining the exchange of information using information and telecommunication networks."

[19] Decree of the Government of the Russian Federation No. 801 of August 12, 2014. "On Amendments to Certain Acts of the Government of the Russian Federation."

6.4 Does the Country Allow Secondary Use of Spectrum? If So, How Is It Defined?

Regulation of the use of the radio frequency spectrum is the exclusive right of the Russian state. The use of the radio frequency spectrum is allowed only on the basis of permission (general or private). The transfer of the right to use the radio frequency spectrum (renewal of the relevant permit) is allowed only by decision of the state body. As a result, there is no radio frequency market in Russia. Lease or borrow of spectrum frequencies is prohibited.

According to Article 24 on "Allocation of radio frequency bands and assignment (assignment) of radio frequencies or radio channels" of the Federal Law No. 126-FZ dated July 07, 2003 (The Law "On Communications"), the use of the radio frequency spectrum without a permit is not allowed, unless otherwise provided by this federal law. The right to use radio frequency bands granted in accordance with this article cannot be transferred by one user of the radio frequency spectrum to another user without a decision of the state commission on radio frequencies or the body that granted this right. According to Article 35 on "Renewal of a license" of the Federal Law No. 126-FZ dated July 07, 2003 (The Law "On Communications"), a telecoms license can be transferred without additional approvals. In cases where the use of spectrum is involved, the reissue of a license to a new licensee requires a prior transfer of the spectrum use permit. Further, when applying for the reissue of a license, the applicant must inform the Federal Service for Supervision in the Sphere of Connection, Information Technologies and Mass Communications of such prior transfer. A sub-license where the original holder reserves rights or can revoke the grant of rights is impossible, as licenses are issued in the name of one holder only. According to the Decree of the Government of the Russian Federation No. 895 dated June 08, 1998 "On approval of the Regulation on payment for the use of the radio frequency spectrum in the Russian Federation," "it is not allowed to transfer to organizations regardless of the form of ownership and to individual entrepreneurs in the ownership or permanent indefinite use of the radio frequency spectrum," "the right of organization, regardless of the form property and an individual entrepreneur for the use of the radio frequency spectrum cannot be transferred to other individuals and legal entities, unless otherwise provided by the regulatory legal acts of the Russian Federation."

6.5 Do the Country's Regulations Provide for the Use of Unlicensed or License-Free Spectrum Bands in Specific Areas, Such as Rural Areas, or Throughout the Country?

The unlicensed use of spectrum is restricted to indoor use (with technologies like Wi-Fi), with few exceptions (Decision of the State Committee for Radio Frequencies under the Ministry of Information Technologies and Communications of Russia No.

07-20-03-001 of May 7, 2007). All issues related to the allocation and assignment of radio frequencies are regulated by the Federal Law of 07.07.2003 No. 126-FZ (The Law "On Communications") and a number of other legal documents. The law defines the authorization procedure for access to the radio frequency spectrum. The right to use the radio frequency spectrum is granted through the official allocation of radio frequency bands and the assignment of radio frequencies or radio frequency channels. The use of the radio frequency spectrum without an appropriate permit is not allowed.

Thus, issues related to the allocation and assignment of radio frequencies are normatively fixed and strictly regulated in the Russian Federation.

7 Financial Resources

7.1 Is There Any Fund for Universalization (To Promote the Increase) of Internet Access or Access to Telecom Services for Everybody)? Is There a Universal Service Fund or Any Other Fund? If So, How Are Resources Collected and Distributed?

The Russian Federation was considered one of the UASFs in the Asia-Pacific region that has financed fixed-broadband projects. Russia was classified as having a high level of activity according to an ITU study conducted in 2013 (ITU, 2013).

Regarding the Universal Service Fund, the Russian Federation today can be characterized as a single operator of the Universalization Fund system, where all funds go to a single company (Rostelecom). The Russian Federation has shifted from a system of a competitive tender process between 21 operators to a single-operator model (United Nations Economic and Social Commission for Asia and the Pacific, 2013).

The Universal Service Fund consists of the contributions of all Russian (Telecom) operators of 1.2% of revenue. All operators of the public communications network are obligated to make deductions (non-tax payments) quarterly (Federal Law No. 126-FZ of July 7, 2003, Article 60) to the universal service reserve to finance state support of universal telecom services development and the maintenance of the ported mobile phone number database (for the purposes provided for by the Federal Law No. 126-FZ).

In February 2014, Russian President Vladimir Putin signed amendments to the Federal Law No. 126-FZ dated July 07, 2003 (The Law "On Communications"), which appointed State telecoms company Rostelecom as Russia's single operator of universal communication services. Chapter 8 (Articles 57–61) of the Federal Law No. 126-FZ defines universal communication services, the procedure of appointment of the responsible Telecom operator (via tender or by the appointment of the state), Universal Service Reserve, and compensation for losses caused by the provision of universal communication services in the Russian Federation.

In May 2014, the Russian government announced that Rostelecom would be tasked with carrying out its broadband service program to bring Internet access to more than 13,000 towns and four million people across Russia. The Rostelecom company must commit itself to supporting the existing infrastructure of Universal Service, including payphones and access points (VRM) on the Internet. In addition to these duties, a single operator will also fight the digital divide by providing broadband at speeds of at least 10 Mbit/s to settlements of 250–500 people.

Rostelecom telecommunications operator

According to the Federal Law "On Communications," the government of the Russian Federation assigns the obligation to provide universal communications services throughout the territory of Russia to an operator occupying a significant position in the public communications network in the territories of at least 2/3 of the constituent entities of the Russian Federation. The only operator that meets these criteria is PJSC Rostelecom.

According to the announcement of the Rostelecom report 2019 on "Universal communications services and the project to eliminate the digital divide," where the priority topic is "Good Digit," respectively, the emphasis in the document is on digitalization of the country and the largest and most demanded projects implemented during 2019. However, the report is not out yet, and for the latest data, it is better to refer to the report 2018 (Rostelecom, 2018).

7.2 *Are Telecommunications Services Taxed or Subject to Other Specific Levies? If So, How?*

Taxation of Telecommunication Services

None of the Russian legal documents currently clearly defines the concept of "telecommunication services." There is a judicial interpretation of this term. Particularly, in some court decisions, it is indicated that telecommunication services can be considered as communication services (see, for example, the decision of the Moscow Arbitration Court of 12.07.2010 No. A40-36263/10-140-241). However, in fact, this is not entirely true, since the concept of "telecommunication services" is somewhat broader than the concept of "communication services."

In accordance with the Decree of the Government of the Russian Federation of September 10, 2007 N 575 "On the Approval of the Rules for the Provision of Telematic Communication Services," the information and telecommunication network is understood to mean a technological system designed to transmit information via communication lines, which is accessed using computer equipment. A similar definition is contained in paragraph 4 of Article 2 of the Federal Law No. 149-FZ of July 27, 2006. The use of the definition of "information and telecommunications" suggests that such a network is related to both communications and information.

From the above definition of information and telecommunication networks, one can derive the main features of telecommunication services as services related to the operation of information and telecommunication networks:

(a) these are services related to the functioning of information and telecommunication networks and (or);
(b) services for the reception, processing, storage, transmission, and delivery of telecommunication messages.

Russia ratified the Protocol on accession to the WTO, part of which includes the list of obligations for goods and the list of obligations for services. After ratification, these texts have become part of the international agreements of our country and now have even greater legal force than Russian regulatory legal acts. This follows from the norms of Part 4 of Article 15 of the Constitution of the Russian Federation.

This document provides a specific list of telecommunication services, which include:

- public voice telephone services: local, long-distance, and international, mobile telephony;
- data transmission services on packet-switched networks;
- data transmission services on circuit-switched networks;
- services of private leased networks;
- email services;
- voicemail services;
- online access and information search in databases;
- electronic data interchange;
- value-added services/extended faxes, including storage and search;
- encoding and converting protocols;
- online access and/or data processing (including transaction processing);
- other.

The implementation of telecommunication services is fully covered by paragraph 1 of Article 146[20] of the Tax Code of the Russian Federation, namely, 1) the sale of goods (works, services) in Russia. This transaction is recognized as a taxable item. Consequently, the contractor of these services in the general case has an obligation to calculate and pay tax. For these types of services, the general rule applies for the taxation of these services with a VAT rate of 18%. Only the sale of services in Russia is subject to VAT.

Note: this part needs re-confirmation of understanding of Russian legislation and the Russian Tax Code with a Russian lawyer/accountant.

Taxation of electronic services provided on the Internet

[20] Object of taxation. Article 146 of the Tax Code of the Russian Federation (2000).

From January 1, 2017, foreign companies will pay VAT on the sale of electronic services or content to Russians. The corresponding bill was adopted by the State Duma. The document aims to create a level playing field for Russian and foreign companies to conduct business in the Russian Federation.

Electronic services will include the provision through the Internet of rights to use computer programs, including games and databases. The list also includes the provision of advertising services on the Internet, services for placing ads, supporting electronic resources, the use of electronic books, music, videos, and others.

Article 174.2 of the Tax Code of the Russian Federation sets forth the main provisions relating to the taxation of electronic services.

On July 3, 2016, the President of the Russian Federation signed Federal Law No. 244-FZ "On Amendments to Parts One and Two of the Tax Code of the Russian Federation" (the so-called "Google Tax"). The changes, enshrined in this federal law entered into force on 01.01.2017, fixed a new procedure for calculating and levying VAT on the provision of electronic services by foreign companies to Russian consumers.

The change was due to the need to equalize foreign and Russian companies: before the amendments, foreign companies were not paying taxes for the provision of electronic services, which gave them an advantage compared to Russian companies. To circumvent the law, companies were registered in countries with the lowest tax rate (Letter of the Federal Tax Service of Russia No. SD-4-3/7937 of April 24, 2019).

Starting from January 1, 2017, foreign Internet companies that provide electronic services in Russia, and the territory of the Russian Federation is recognized as the place of sale of such services, are required to pay VAT at a rate of 18% on online transactions. As part of the so-called Google tax, companies are required to register with the Russian tax authority (clause 4.6 of Article 83 of the Tax Code) and regularly submit tax returns to the Federal Tax Service (FTS).

Under the new rule, Russian legal entities and individual entrepreneurs are not tax agents, regardless of whether the foreign organization is registered with the Russian tax authorities or not (paragraph 9 of Article 174.2 of the Tax Code of the Russian Federation, letter of the Ministry of Finance of Russia dated September 3, 2018 No. 03-07-08/62624).

The Ministry of Finance of Russia explained that this rule applies only to foreign companies (letter of the Ministry of Finance of Russia dated May 24, 2019 No. 03-07-08/37670), because registration of foreign entrepreneurs providing electronic services is not provided for by the Tax Code of the Russian Federation. The law also established that if a foreign person is not registered with the Russian tax authority, then when selling services, the place of sale of which is recognized as the territory of the Russian Federation, it is the Russian company-buyer that is to be recognized and taxed as the tax agent[21] (Article 161 of the Russian Federation Tax Code) (Utsyna, 2019).

Before the implementation of the B2B e-services rules on 1 January 2019, when nonresidents made B2B supplies of e-services into Russia, the customer was responsible for paying VAT directly to the tax authority via the withholding (tax agent) method. The change in the VAT payment rules for e-services, effective from 1 January 2019, means that Russian customers now pay Russian VAT directly to the nonresident supplier, who is in turn obliged to register in Russia and pay VAT to the tax authority via its own quarterly VAT return.

7.3 Is There Any Fund to Provide Subsidies to Operators to Expand Coverage to Underserved Areas and the Least Privileged Populations?

Until 2014, there used to be a Universal Service Fund for telecom operators. By order of the government of the Russian Federation No. 437-r of March 26, 2014, Rostelecom was appointed as the single federal operator of universal service. On May 13, 2014, a ten-year agreement was signed between the Federal Communications Agency and Rostelecom on the conditions for the provision of CMS. To implement the program to eliminate the digital divide, about 215 thousand kilometers of fiber-optic communication lines would be built.

Since 2014, as part of the reform of universal communications services (UUS) and the digital divide program, 47 subjects of the Russian Federation (RF) have signed tripartite cooperation agreements. The purpose of these agreements is to develop telecommunications infrastructure and integrated state information systems on the territories of these RF subjects. One of the main areas of cooperation is to eliminate the digital divide and ensure equal opportunities for all residents of the regions to use modern communication services, including high-speed Internet access.

To provide Internet connectivity to the isolated and hard-to-reach regions of Russia, Mincomsvyaz has been taking on various measures to provide for Internet accessibility by means of advanced information and communication technologies. Particularly to connect remote areas to the telecom networks, the Ministry of Communications has been supporting projects to build submarine fiber optic links

[21] However, by 2019, some foreign companies that are selling electronic content in Russia have encountered difficulties in paying the so-called Google tax. Russian law obliges foreign companies to pay "Google tax" directly, but Russian banks reject tax payments from foreign accounts due to the lack of full details in payment orders (although payment forms are completed according to the provided instructions).

Foreign companies pay tax from their foreign bank accounts, and the standard forms of payment orders using the SWIFT system do not provide as many digits as correspondent bank accounts, and in the budget classification codes of Russia. Companies simply do not have enough space in the payment form to indicate all the necessary details (Tax on Google, 2019).

to connect remote mainland areas along the Magadan-Sakhalin-Kamchatka route, as well as connecting telecom networks of the Kuril Islands to the Rostelecom network (the uniform telecom network of the Russian Federation). Universal broadband services will be provided in 1757 access points (105% of the plan), and 2215 healthcare facilities and schools. The total service area of access points provides free access to over 2000 additional sites of Russian Federation government bodies, government budgetary agencies, and the Common Government Services Portal of the Russian Federation through wireless networks.

There is a national program "Digital Economy of the Russian Federation" (Government of the Russian Federation, 2022) that subsidizes at least 50% of the cost to mobile operators who build towers in remote areas ("In the Kuban", 2020). The Digital Economy project is planned for 5 years from 2019 to 2024 and foresees various forms of subsidies for the provision of telecommunication infrastructure and the development of the digital agenda of the Russian Federation.

There were also regional projects, for example, the state program of the Khanty-Mansiysk Autonomous Okrug—Ugra "Information Society for 2016–2020," approved by the government of the Khanty-Mansiysk Autonomous Okrug—Ugra dated October 9, 2013 No. 424-p. Within the implementation of this program, a procedure for providing a subsidy for the reimbursement of part of the cost of building communication facilities in remote and hard-to-reach areas was developed (Department of Information Technologies and Digital Development, Khanty-Mansiysk Autonomous Okrug – Yugra, 2013).

7.4 Is Any Form of Direct Support (Such as Funding or Tax Exemptions) Offered to Small and/or Micro and/or Not-for-Profit Providers?

No. Russia does not provide direct support, funding, or tax exemptions to small and/or micro and/or not-for-profit providers.

References

The main areas of activity of the Government of the Russian Federation for the period until 2024 (approved by the Government of the Russian Federation on September 29, 2018 No. 8028p-P13).

3rd Generation Partnership Project (3GPP). (2022). https://www.3gpp.org/

Abdrakhmanova, G., Demyanova, A., Fridlyanova, S., et al. (2020) Monitoring the development of the information society in the Russian Federation. In Gokhberg, L. (Ed.) *Digital economy: Pocket data book*. National Research University Higher School of Economics. ISBN 978-5-7598-2158-8.

Agreement relating to the International Telecommunications Satellite Organization "INTELSAT," August 20, 1971., https://www.state.gov/international-telecommunications-satellite-organization-intelsat

Bogodaeva, O. E. (2022). *Review of changes introduced into the laws on the initiative of I. Yarovaya and V. Ozerov*. ConsultantPlus Legal Reference System. https://www.consultant.ru/law/podborki/zakon_yarovoj/

Cheng, W. (2017). The tale of the digital economy in China. *Presentation for the 5th IMF Statistical Forum*.

Civil Code of the Russian Federation N 51-FZ (Part one, as amended on February 25, 2022). (1994, November 30).

Committee to Protect Journalists. (2019, October 2). *Russian internet regulator blocks independent Fergana news website*. https://cpj.org/2019/10/russian-internet-regulator-blocks-independent-ferg/

Content Review. (2018, December 26). *Топ-50 стран по стоимости мобильного интернета (декабрь 2018)*. Retrieved on May 12, 2022 from http://www.content-review.com/articles/45644/

Convention establishing the European Telecommunications Satellite Organization EUTELSAT, July, 15, 1982., https://www.eutelsatigo.int/wp-content/uploads/2022/07/Convention-establishing-EUTELSAT.pdf

Decision of the State Committee for Radio Frequencies under the Ministry of Information Technologies and Communications of Russia No. 07-20-03-001 of May 7, 2007 (as amended on 11.09.2018). *"On the allocation of radio frequency bands for short-range devices"* taken at the meeting of the SCRF dated May 07, 2007 (protocol No. 07-20). Retrieved on May 12, 2022 from https://digital.gov.ru/ru/documents/4039/

Decision of the State Committee for Radio Frequencies No. 20-54-02. (n.d.). *On the determination of radio frequency ranges for the creation of communication networks of the 5G / IMT-2020 standard on the territory of the Russian Federation*.

Decree of the Government of the Russian Federation No. 1203-47 of September 18, 2019 (as amended on February 26, 2022). (2019). *On approval of the Table of allocation of radio frequency bands between radio services of the Russian Federation and invalidation of some resolutions of the Government of the Russian Federation*.

Decree of the Government of the Russian Federation No. 1284 of November 29, 2014. (2014). *On approval of Rules of non-discriminatory access to infrastructure for placement of networks of telecommunication*. http://government.ru/docs/15968/

Decree of the Government of the Russian Federation No. 161 of March 28, 2005 (as amended on January 18, 2021). (2005). *On approval of the Rules for the connection of telecommunication networks and their interaction*.

Decree of the Government of the Russian Federation No. 1632-r of July 28, 2017. (2017). *On approval of the program Digital Economy of the Russian Federation*

Decree of the Government of the Russian Federation No. 2385 of December 30, 2020 (as amended on February 26, 2022). (2020). *On Licensing Activities in the Field of Provision of Communication Services and the Recognition of Certain Acts of the Government of the Russian Federation as invalid together with the "Regulations on Licensing Activities in the Field of Provision of Communication Services,"* with rev. and add., intro. in force from March 1, 2022.

Decree of the Government of the Russian Federation No. 294 of June 17, 2004 (as amended on October 29, 2021). (2004). *On the Federal Agency for Technical Regulation and Metrology*.

Decree of the Government of the Russian Federation No. 480 of May 24, 2014 (as amended on April 17, 2021). (2014). *On tenders (auctions, competitions) for obtaining a license for the provision of communication services* (together with the "Rules for bidding (auction, competition) for obtaining a license for the provision of communication services").

Decree of the Government of the Russian Federation No. 758 of July 31, 2014. (2014). *On Amendments to Certain Acts of the Government of the Russian Federation in Connection with the Adoption of the Federal Law 'On Amendments to the Federal Law' 'On Information, Information Technologies and Information Protection' and Certain Legislative Acts of the Russian Federation on streamlining the exchange of information using information and telecommunication networks.*

Decree of the Government of the Russian Federation No. 801 of August 12, 2014. (2014). *On Amendments to Certain Acts of the Government of the Russian Federation.*

Decree of the President of the Russian Federation No. 1230 of October 16, 2001 (as amended on January 15, 2013). (2001). *Issues of the structure of federal executive bodies.*

Decree of the President of the Russian Federation No. 1715 of December 3, 2008 (as amended on May 21, 2012). (2008). *On Certain Issues of Public Administration in the Field of Communications, Information Technology and Mass Communications.*

Decree of the President of the Russian Federation No. 204 of May 7, 2018 (as amended on July 21, 2020). (2018). *On the national goals and strategic objectives of the development of the Russian Federation for the period up to 2024.*

Decree of the President of the Russian Federation No. 31c of January 15, 2013 (as amended on December 22, 2017). (2013). *On the creation of a state system for detecting, preventing and eliminating the consequences of computer attacks on information resources of the Russian Federation.*

Decree of the President of the Russian Federation No. 649 of May 20, 2004. (2004). *Issues of the structure of federal executive bodies.*

Department of Information Technologies and Digital Development, Khanty-Mansiysk Autonomous Okrug - Yugra. (2013). *Providing hard-to-reach and remote settlements with high-speed Internet access.* https://depit.admhmao.ru/deyatelnost/informatsiya-o-khode-realizatsii-investitsionnykh-proektov/329382/obespechenie-trudnodostupnykh-i-udalennykh-naselennykh-punktov-vysokoskorostnym-dostupom-v-set-inter/

Digital Report. (2018, April 18). *Russia: State of affairs report.* https://digital.report/russia-state-of-affairs-report/

European Conference of Postal and Telecommunications Administrations (CEPT) (2022) Overview. https://www.cept.org/. Accessed 12 May 2022.

Federal Antitrust Service [FAS]. (2016). *Report on the feasibility of introducing the principles of a neutrality network in telecommunication networks.* Retrieved on May 12, 2022 from http://fas.gov.ru/attachment/138176/download?1504613513

Federal Law No. 100-FZ of April 1, 2020. (2020). *On Amendments to the Criminal Code of the Russian Federation and Articles 31 and 151 of the Code of Criminal Procedure of the Russian Federation.*

Federal Law No. 112-FZ of June 7, 2013. (2013). *On Amendments to the Federal Law 'On Information, Information Technologies and Information Protection' and the Federal Law "On Ensuring Access to Information on the Activities of State Bodies and Local Self-Government Bodies".*

Federal Law No. 126-FZ of July 7, 2003 (as amended on December 30, 2021). (2003). *On Communications* (as amended and supplemented, effective from May 1, 2022).

Federal Law No. 149-FZ of July 27, 2006 (as amended on December 30, 2021). (2006). *On Information, Information Technologies and Information Protection* (as amended and supplemented, effective from January 1, 2022).

Federal Law No. 187-FZ of July 26, 2017. *On the Security of Critical Information Infrastructure.* (2017).

Federal Law No. 244 - FZ of July 3, 2016. (2016). *On Amendments to Parts One and Two of the Tax Code of the Russian Federation.*

Federal Law No. 245-FZ of July 29, 2017 (as amended on December 5, 2017). (2017). *On Amendments to the Federal Law 'On Communications'.*

Federal Law No. 31-FZ of March 18, 2019. (2019). On Amendments to Article 15.3 of the Federal Law *'On Information, Information Technologies and Information Protection'.*

Federal Law No. 374-FZ of July 6, 2016. (2016). *On Amendments to the Federal Law 'On Combating Terrorism' and Certain Legislative Acts of the Russian Federation in Part of Establishing Additional Measures to Counter Terrorism and Ensuring Public Security*

Federal Law No. 90-FZ of May 1, 2019. (2019). *On Amendments to the Federal Law 'On Communications' and the Federal Law 'On Information, Information Technologies and Information Protection'.*

Federal Law No. 97-FZ of May 5, 2014 (as amended on July 29, 2017). (2014). *On Amendments to the Federal Law 'On Information, Information Technologies and Information Protection' and certain legislative acts of the Russian Federation on the issues of streamlining the exchange of information using information and telecommunication networks.*

Federal State Unitary Enterprise "Order of Labor Red Banner Russian Scientific Research Institute of Radio Named After M.I. Krivosheev." *Home*. Retrieved on May 12, 2022 from https://niir.ru/

Gazprombank. (2012). *Rostelecom: From an outsider to a true Big 4 name*. https://docplayer.net/1820775-Rostelecom-from-an-outsider-to-a-true-big-4-name.html

Government Commission for Coordinating the Activities of the Open Government. (2014). *Minutes of the Meeting No. 4 of May 29, 2014.*

Government of the Russian Federation. (2022). *National Program "Digital Economy of the Russian Federation."* Retrieved on May 12, 2022 from http://government.ru/rugovclassifier/614/events/

In the Kuban will subsidize the installation of communication towers. (2020, January 16). Telesputnik. https://telesputnik.ru/materials/tekhnika-i-tekhnologii/news/na-kubani-prosubsidiruyut-ustanovku-vyshek-svyazi/

INTELSAT Agreement (1971) International Satellite Communications.

International Telecommunications Union. (2013). *Universal Service Funds and Digital Inclusion for All: September 2013*. https://www.itu.int/en/ITU-D/Digital-Inclusion/Pages/Digital_Inclusion_Resources/Universal_Service_Funds_Digital_Inclusion.aspx

International Telecommunications Union. (2016). *The State of Broadband 2016: Broadband Catalyzing Sustainable Development*. Retrieved on May 12, 2022 from http://www.itu.int/pub/S-POL-BROADBAND.17-2016

Intersputnik. (2022a). *About Intersputnik*. Retrieved on May 12, 2022 from https://intersputnik.int/about/organization/

Intersputnik. (2022b). *Intersputnik participants*. Retrieved on May 12, 2022 from https://intersputnik.int/about/participants/

Kemp, S. (2020, February 18). *Digital 2020: Russian Federation*. Datareportal. https://datareportal.com/reports/digital-2020-russian-federation

Land Code of the Russian Federation No. 136-FZ (as amended on May 1, 2022). (2001, October 25).

Letter of the Federal Tax Service of Russia No. SD-4-3/7937 of April 24, 2019. (2019). *On the procedure for applying VAT in the provision of services by foreign organizations in electronic form from January 1, 2019.*

Letter of the Ministry of Communications of the Russian Federation of March 28, 1995 No. 54-u. (1995). *On the procedure for connecting to public communication networks and the procedure for regulating the transmission of traffic in public communication networks.*

Ling, J. (2022, May 13). *How One Company Helps Keep Russia's TV Propaganda Machine Online*. Wired. https://www.wired.com/story/eutelsat-russia-ukraine-propaganda-denis-diderot-committee/

Meduza. (2018, August 23). *Russia's four biggest telecoms say nyet to a new initiative to codify Net Neutrality*. https://meduza.io/en/news/2018/08/23/russia-s-four-biggest-telecoms-say-nyet-to-a-new-initiative-to-codify-net-neutrality

MegaFon (n.d.) Overview of operations.

Mforum. (2016, January 11). *LTE in Russia: Preliminary results of the year*. Retrieved on May 12, 2022 from http://www.mforum.ru/news/article/116266.htm

Ministry of Digital Development, Communications and Mass Media. (2022). *Regional cooperation in communications*. Retrieved on May 12, 2022 from https://digital.gov.ru/ru/activity/directions/292

Ministry of Digital Development, Communications and Mass Media of the Russian Federation. (2022). *State Commission on Radio Frequencies*. Retrieved on May 12, 2022 from https://digital.gov.ru/ru/activity/advisories/7/

Ministry of Telecom and Mass Communications (Minsvyaz) (2018) Functions before restructuring.

Omnibus-GFK Rus. (2018). *Internet Penetration in Russia: results of 2018*. Retrieved on May 12, 2022 from https://cdn2.hubspot.net/hubfs/2405078/cms-pdfs/fileadmin/user_upload/dyna_content/ru/documents/press_releases/2019/gfk_rus_internet_audience_in_russia_2018.pdf

Order of the FSTEC of Russia of December 6, 2017 No. 227 (as amended on February 10, 2022). (2017). *"On Approval of the Procedure for Maintaining a Register of Significant Objects of the Critical Information Infrastructure of the Russian Federation"* (Registered with the Ministry of Justice of Russia on February 8, 2018 No. 49966).

Order of the Ministry of Digital Development, Telecommunications and Mass Media of the Russian Federation No. 629 of October 30, 2019. (2019). *On the Competition Commission of the Ministry of Digital Development, Telecommunications and Mass Media of the Russian Federation on the provision by the Ministry of Digital Development, Telecommunications and Mass Media of the Russian Federation of subsidies from the federal budget for the creation of an industry center of the State System for the Detection, Prevention, and Elimination of the Consequences of Computer Attacks (GosSOPKA) and its inclusion in the system of automated exchange of information about current cyber threats*. https://img.rg.ru/pril/177/93/60/56497.pdf

Order of the Ministry of Information and Communications of Russia No. 54 of May 2, 2006 (as amended on February 16, 2021). (2006). On Approval of the Procedure for Maintaining Separate Accounting of Income and Expenses by Telecom Operators for the Types of Activities Performed, Communication Services Provided and Parts of the Telecommunication Network Used to Provide These Services. (Registered in Ministry of Justice of Russia 16.05.2006 N 7838).

Order of the Ministry of Information Technologies and Communications of Russian Federation No. 99 of August 22, 2007. (2007). *On approval of the Rules for the application of earth stations in satellite communications and broadcasting of the unified telecommunication network of the Russian Federation* (as amended on June 15, 2015).

Order of the Ministry of Information Technologies and Communications of the Russian Federation No. 47 of December 29, 2004. (2004). http://docs.cntd.ru/document/901921638.

Public Opinion Foundation. (2020, May 31). *Internet and online services*. https://fom.ru/SMI-i-internet/14402

Regional Commonwealth in the Field of Communications. (2022). Overview. https://en.rcc.org.ru/. Accessed 12 May 2022.

Regulation "On the procedure for joining public communication networks and the procedure for regulating the traffic pass of public communication networks" (1995). Retrieved on May 12, 2022 from http://www.gosthelp.ru/text/Polozhenieoporyadkeprisoe.html

Roskomnadzor. (2009, August 20). *Registers*. https://eng.rkn.gov.ru/mass-communications/registers/

Roskomnadzor. (2012, November 29). *Register of the communications infrastructure of the Russian Federation*. Retrieved on May 12, 2022, from https://rkn.gov.ru/opendata/7705846236-communicationInfrastructureRF/

Roskomnadzor. (2013, January 29). *Powers of Roskomnadzor.* Retrieved on May 12, 2022 from http://eng.rkn.gov.ru/about/powers_of_roskomnadzor/

Rosstandart (Federal Agency for Technical Regulation and Metrology). (2022a). *The catalog of interstate standards*. Retrieved on May 12, 2022 from https://www.gost.ru/portal/gost/home/standarts/cataloginter

Rosstandart (Federal Agency for Technical Regulation and Metrology). (2022b). *The catalog of national standards of the Russian Federation*. Retrieved on May 12, 2022 from https://www.gost.ru/portal/gost/home/standarts/catalognational

Rosstandart (Federal Agency for Technical Regulation and Metrology). (2022c). *The list of existing technical regulations of the Russian Federation*. Retrieved on May 12, 2022 from https://www.gost.ru/portal/gost/home/standarts/technicalregulationses

Rostelecom. (2018). *Цифровая экосистема экономики будущего: Годовой отчет 2018 (Digital ecosystem of the economy of the future. Annual Report 2018)*. https://ar2018.rostelecom.ru/download/full-reports/ar_ru_annual-report_pages.pdf

Ruling of the Supreme Court of the Russian Federation No. 303-ES22-6625 of May 26, 2022 in case No. A51-5502/2021.

Russian State Commission for Radio Frequencies. (2022). *Home*. Retrieved on May 12, 2022 from http://www.grfc.ru/grfc/

Sovereign Internet Law. (2019). Implementation.

State Commission for Radio Frequencies (SCRF). (2017). *SCRF meeting of December 28, 2017 (Minutes No. 17-44)*. https://digital.gov.ru/ru/documents/5875/

State Commission for Radio Frequencies (SCRF). (2020). *SCRF meeting of March 17, 2020 (Minutes No. 20-54dsp)*. https://digital.gov.ru/ru/documents/7154/

Statista. (2022, January). *Countries with the highest number of internet users as of December 2019*. Retrieved on May 12, 2022 from https://www.statista.com/statistics/262966/number-of-internet-users-in-selected-countries/

Tadviser. (2022, September 27). *Internet access Market of Russia and CIS*. Retrieved on May 12, 2022 from https://tadviser.com/index.php/Article:Internet_access_(Russian_market)

Tax Code of the Russian Federation (Part Two) No. 117-FZ of May 8, 2000 (as amended on January 5, 2022, with amendments and additions, effective from May 16, 2022). (2000).

Tax on Google. (2019, November 19). Tadviser. https://www.tadviser.ru/index.php/%D0%A1%D1%82%D0%B0%D1%82%D1%8C%D1%8F:244-%D0%A4%D0%97_%22%D0%9D%D0%B0%D0%BB%D0%BE%D0%B3_%D0%BD%D0%B0_Google%22

The Federal Service for Technical and Export Control [FSTEC]. (2022). *Home*. https://fstec.ru/

The World Bank. (2018). *Russia Digital Economy Report, September 2018, Competing in the Digital Age: Policy Implications for the Russian Federation*. World Bank. https://openknowledge.worldbank.org/bitstream/handle/10986/30584/AUS0000158-WP-REVISED-P160805-PUBLIC-Disclosed-10-15-2018.pdf?sequence=1&isAllowed=y

The World Bank. (2022). *Individuals using the Internet (% of population) - Russian Federation*. Retrieved on May 12, 2022 from https://data.worldbank.org/indicator/IT.NET.USER.ZS?locations=RU&most_recent_value_desc=false

Tishina, Y. (2020, April 28). *Smartphones will pass the census. Registration of devices by serial number may become mandatory in 2021*. Kommersant Newspaper. https://www.kommersant.ru/doc/4333245

United Nations Economic and Social Commission for Asia and the Pacific. (2013). *The Impact of Universal Service Funds on Fixed-Broadband Deployment and Internet Adoption in Asia and the Pacific*. https://www.researchgate.net/publication/320263070_The_Impact_of_Universal_Service_Funds_on_Fixed-Broadband_Deployment_and_Internet_Adoption_in_Asia_and_the_Pacific

Utsyna, E. (2019, June 3). When purchasing electronic services from a foreign entrepreneur, a Russian organization will be considered a tax agent for VAT. *GARANT.RU*. https://www.garant.ru/news/1275462/

Vimpelcom. (2015). *Vimpelcom annual report 2015*. Beeline. Retrieved on May 12, 2022 from http://static.beeline.ru/upload/images/Annual_Report_2015_rus_final_clean.doc

Yandex. (2016). *Development of the Internet in Russian regions*. https://yandex.ru/company/researches/2016/ya_internet_regions_2016

Andrey A. Schcherbovich is an Associate Professor at the National Research University Higher School of Economics, Faculty of Law (Department of Constitutional and Municipal Law), in Moscow, Russia. His professional interests include Internet Governance, Constitutional Law, Human Rights, International Public Law and Procedure, Information Law, International Organizations, and the United Nations. Andrey graduated from the National Research University Higher School of Economics, Faculty of Law (Department of International Law) in 2008 and completed Postgraduate studies at the National Research University – Higher School of Economics (Moscow, Russia); Faculty of Law (Department of Constitutional and Municipal Law) in 2011.

Anna Orlova holds a degree in Psychology from the University of Saint Petersburg and a Master's in Psychology and Sociology. Her research has been at the intersection of academic research and volunteering in various digital activism and advocacy projects, focusing on community connectivity. Anna joined CyberBRICS as a graduate research fellow.

Russia: An Analysis of the Digitalization of Public Services

Andrey A. Schcherbovich and Anna Orlova

Abstract This chapter maps key aspects related to the digitalization of public services in Russia. The following elements are investigated: policy elements related to digital government strategies, declarations, programs and actions; regulatory elements related to openness, sharing and data protection laws; institutional and governance elements related to the oversight and competences of public agencies, public-private partnerships and regulatory innovations in technology; and evidence from critical sectors such as smart cities, digital ID, and digital payments.

1 National Strategies and Priorities

1.1 Is There a National Strategy for Digitalization/Digital Transformation? Is There a Specific National Strategy for Digitalizing Public Services?

Yes, the Russian Federation has a national strategy for the digitalization of public services, which is an ongoing activity that has been taking place for more than a decade and has been reflected in various state and federal programs, agendas, and laws.

In the early 2000s, under the Federal Target Program (hereafter FTP), "Electronic Russia (2002–2010)" e-Government was first developed as a separate reform. "The basic purposes of the Program were to create conditions for development of democracy; increasing efficiency in the functioning of the economy, State management

A. A. Schcherbovich (✉)
Faculty of Law, Department of Constitutional and Municipal Law, National Research University Higher School of Economics, Moscow, Russia

A. Orlova
São Paulo State University (UNESP), São Paulo, Brazil

L. Belli, L. Galdino de Magalhães Santos (eds.), *SmartBRICS*,
https://doi.org/10.1007/978-3-031-98204-0_7

and local management; ensuring the rights to free search, access, transmission, production and dissemination of information; and building ICT capacity."

Among the defined key and most important targets and indicators of the Federal Target Program "Electronic Russia (2002–2010)" were:

- the stages of transfer to an electronic form of the processes of providing public services by federal executive authorities;
- share of users of a single portal of state and municipal services (functions) among Internet users;
- the number of state control (supervision) bodies providing services for receiving notifications of the start of entrepreneurial activity in electronic form.

There is a Decree of the President of the Russian Federation No. 204 from May 7, 2018 on national goals and strategic objectives of the development of the Russian Federation for the period until 2024. This law prescribes to the government of the Russian Federation to ensure the accelerated introduction of digital technologies in the economy and social sphere, among other national development goals of the Russian Federation for the period until 2024.

In accordance with this law, the roadmap "The main activities of the Government of the Russian Federation for the period until 2024" was approved by the government on September 27, 2018. This is the key document of the strategic planning of the government of Russia until 2024.

In sect. 2.1. on "Digital Economy of the Russian Federation" (Government of the Russian Federation, n.d.-b) of the aforementioned document, the government of the Russian Federation aims to achieve the following goal and targets of the national project "Digital Economy of the Russian Federation" regarding the national broadband plan: "creation of a stable and secure information and telecommunication infrastructure for high-speed transmission, processing and storage of large amounts of data, accessible to all organizations and households, including providing broadband access to the information and telecommunication network 'Internet' of households and socially significant infrastructure objects, the creation of reference data centers in federal districts, an increase in the share of the Russian Federation in the global volume of provision of data storage and processing services."

Investment in a globally competitive, secure infrastructure to support the growth of a data-driven economy remains a top priority, as emphasized in the May 2018 Presidential Decree. In July 2017, Russia adopted the national "Digital Economy Program" from 2017 to 2024 with an expected annual budget of US$1.8 billion until 2025 to address the current weaknesses preventing the country from joining global digital economy leaders.

As part of the implementation of the Decrees of the President of the Russian Federation dated May 7, 2018 No. 204 "On national goals and strategic objectives of the development of the Russian Federation for the period up to 2024" and dated July 21, 2020 No. 474 "On national goals for the development of the Russian Federation for the period up to 2030 of the year," as well as aiming to solve the problem of ensuring the accelerated introduction of digital technologies in the economy and social sphere, the Government of the Russian Federation has formed a national program "Digital Economy of the Russian Federation" approved by the minutes of the meeting of the Presidium of the Council under the President of the Russian Federation for Strategic Development and National Projects from June 4, 2019 No. 7.

To manage the program, five basic directions for the development of the digital economy in Russia for the period until 2024 have been identified. The basic directions include normative regulation, personnel and education, the formation of research competencies and technical background, information infrastructure, and information security. On July 21, 2020, Russian President Vladimir Putin signed a decree on the national development goals of the country for the period up to 2030. It is aimed at increasing the population of the country, improving the standard of living of citizens, creating comfortable conditions for their residence, as well as revealing the talent of each person, according to the Kremlin's website.

One of the national goals set by President Putin for 10 years is called "Digital Transformation." The following tasks have been set within its framework:

- achieving "digital maturity" of key sectors of the economy and social sphere, including healthcare and education, as well as public administration;
- an increase in the share of mass socially significant services available in electronic form up to 95%;
- an increase in the share of households that are provided with the possibility of broadband access to the information and telecommunication network of the Internet, up to 97%;
- an increase in investments in domestic solutions in the field of information technology by four times compared to the indicator of 2019.

1.2 Is the Digitalization of Any Specific Sector Seen as a Priority for the Country (e.g., Central Bank Digital Currency, Digital Identity, Online Payments, Deployment of Artificial Intelligence, Smart Cities, Cybersecurity, Etc.)?

In July 2017, Russia adopted the Russia Digital Economy Program with an expected annual budget of US$1.8 billion until 2025 to address the current weaknesses preventing the country from joining global digital economy leaders. To manage the program, five basic directions for the development of the digital economy in Russia for the period until 2024 have been identified. The basic directions include normative regulation, personnel and education, the formation of research competencies and technical background, information infrastructure and information security.

According to Gritsenko and Zherebtsov (2021), "the most recent iteration of public sector digitalization Gosudarstvo kak platforma (government as a platform) had been presented as a concept in April 2018 by the Russian think-tank Center for Strategic Research."

1.3 Is There an Overall Artificial Intelligence Strategy? Is There a Specific National Strategy for the Use of Artificial Intelligence in the Public Sector?

The use and application of Artificial Intelligence within the digitalization of public services has been given a special focus in the past few years. However, there is no overall Artificial Intelligence strategy so far, and this is currently being debated and undergoing a phase of planning and development within the overall national strategy for digitalization/digital transformation of public services.

Artificial Intelligence (AI) driven decision-making algorithms are expected to be at the core of public service according to the concept paper "(Cyber)state for digital economy. Digital Transformation" presented in 2018 by the Center for Strategic Research think-tank, which is presumed to be a new roadmap for digital transformation of the Russian government (Gritsenko & Zherebtsov, 2021).

The Concept for the development of regulation of relations in the field of Artificial Intelligence technologies and robotics until 2024 was approved by the Order of the Government of the Russian Federation No. 2129-r of August 19, 2020 "On approval of the Concept for the development of regulation of relations in the field of artificial intelligence and robotics technologies until 2024."

The order ruled:

- to approve the Concept for the development of the regulation of relations in the field of Artificial Intelligence and robotics technologies until 2024;
- the federal executive authorities and the State Corporation for Space Activities "Roskosmos" shall be guided by the provisions of the Concept when exercising functions for the development of state policy and legal regulation in the established spheres of activity;
- the interested federal executive bodies and the State Corporation for Space Activities "Roskosmos" shall, within 3 months, submit to the Ministry of Economic Development of Russia proposals for the implementation of the Concept within the framework of the national program "Digital Economy of the Russian Federation."

The general provisions of the Concept are:

1. Objectives of the Concept
2. Goals and objectives of regulating relations in the field of Artificial Intelligence technologies and robotics
3. Principles of regulation of relations in the field of Artificial Intelligence technologies and robotics
4. Problems, general approaches, and directions of regulation of relations in the field of Artificial Intelligence technologies and robotics
5. Is there a specific strategy or reference to the use of social media to facilitate government activities?

On May 17, 2022, the State Duma adopted in the first reading a bill obliging the authorities to maintain official public pages on social networks and publish up-to-date information.

According to the initiators of the bill, this will allow citizens to freely enter direct communication with the authorities at all levels. As stated in the explanatory note, the Ministry of Digital Development will develop functionality for government agencies and organizations for automated management of accounts in social networks based on the State Services portal.

In addition, Instagram, according to media reports, began to massively block users from Russia. Page owners are notified of suspicious activity. After that, they are deprived of access to the account. Users themselves say that they did not violate any rules of the social network. The activities of the organization Meta Platforms Inc. (social networks Facebook, Instagram), recognized as extremist, are prohibited in Russia.

However, recently, some of the departments of the Moscow government started using Telegram channels to provide specific information to the citizens, specifically shortly before or right after the ban on the use of the Telegram app was lifted by the Russian court ("The State Duma", 2022).

1.4 Is There a Strategy or Any Specific Policies Aimed at Promoting the Use of Open-Source Software/Hardware by Public Administrations or Generally?

No, there is no specific policy aimed at promoting the use of open-source software/hardware by public administrations. However, on June 3, 2021, Maxim Parshin, the deputy minister of digital development, communications, and mass communications, claimed that Russia should have an open-source development strategy. Parshin stated that the strategy should not be developed by the ministry alone and should engage with the community, involving all stakeholders, noting that the state is only one of them. This process will be moderated by the Ministry of Digital Development, Communications and Mass Media of the Russian Federation Company and an official document is expected as an output. He also added that there is a need for an independent technology platform with a repository, which is clearly overdue. Parshin mentioned a possibility of cooperation with GitHub on this.

The strategy on Open Source is also expected to provide an overview of measures of support by the state. These measures are also to be outlined together with the community of stakeholders. Parshin pointed at financial and government regulation at the level of state procurement (Ministry of Digital Development, Communications and Mass Communications of the Russian Federation, 2021).

1.5 Are There Specific Policies Mandating Interoperability Requirements for the Systems Utilized by Public Administrations? Are There Any Strategies or Recommendations to Avoid Vendor Lock-in?

The "Electronic Russia (2002–2010)" Program, although demonstrating "a significant step forward in regard with digitization of the government sphere," has failed to achieve many of its objectives, such as interdepartmental electronic interaction, standardization of IT solutions, resulting in partial use of created hardware and software systems because of lacking systems interoperability.

The national standard on interoperability that was developed by the Federal State Budgetary Institution of Science Institute of Radio Engineering and Electronics named after V. A. Kotelnikov RAS (IRE named after V. A. Kotelnikov RAS) and approved and put into force by the Order of the Federal Agency for Technical Regulation and Metrology of November 13, 2012 No. 751-st in accordance with the Federal Law of December 27, 2002 No. 184-FZ "On Technical Regulation."

In the national standard of the Russian Federation on "Information technologies. Industrial automation systems and integration. Interoperability. Basic principles"[1] implemented on September 1, 2013, interoperability is defined as follows:

> Interoperability is the ability of two or more information systems or components to exchange information and use information obtained as a result of the exchange. Interoperability plays a significant role in the creation of industrial automation systems and their integration and, along with the property of portability, is the most important component of the concept of "open systems." At present, more and more attention is paid precisely to the issues of ensuring interoperability for information systems of various scales (from nanosystems to "systems of systems") and information systems (IS) in various fields of application. Interoperability is gaining more and more importance, primarily because today practically no sphere of life (public administration, healthcare, education, science, business, etc.) is complete without the use of information and communication technologies. It can be stated that ensuring interoperability is one of the main foundations for the formation and development of the information society. The main way to solve the problem of interoperability or "transparency" of a heterogeneous environment is the consistent application of the principles of open systems and the methodology of functional standardization.

This standard specifies:

- basic concepts related to the concept of "interoperability";
- approaches to achieving interoperability and existing barriers;
- a unified approach to ensuring the interoperability of a wide range of information systems;
- the main steps to achieve interoperability.

[1] GOST R 55062-2021, approved and put into effect by the Order of Rosstandart of No. 1296-st of October 25, 2021.

The aforementioned standard is intended for customers, suppliers, developers, consumers, and personnel who maintain information systems and provide software and services.

1.6 Is There a Strategy or Any Specific Policies Promoting Open Data (E.g., Government-Business Data Sharing, Open Government, and/or Open Data in General)?

On May 7, 2012, President Vladimir Putin signed Decree No. 601, the executive order to provide open government data. In 2014, the Open Government Data Portal was launched. The Open Government Data Portal has been tightly connected to another initiative—the Open Government—that was launched by President Dmitry Medvedev to ensure transparency of the legislative and executive processes in Russia (Wijermars, 2021). The Russian Open Government initiative was abolished in May 2018, and the functions of the Open Government Minister were not reassigned to another portfolio; however, this has not cancelled the obligation to publish open data.

Open Data initiative in Russia is mainly regulated by the Decree of the President of the Russian Federation (No. 601 of May 7, 2012) "On the main directions of improving the system of public administration" and the federal laws "On Information, Information Technologies and Information Protection," No. 149-FZ, which entered into force on July 27, 2006, and "On providing access to information on the activities of state and local government agencies," No. 8-FZ that entered into force on February 9, 2009, with respective amendments.

In 2015, the Open Data Council was created by the *Governmental Commission for Coordinating the Activities of an Open Government* to facilitate the implementation of the Presidential Decree No. 601. The Open Data Council served as a consultative body shaped by representatives of federal authorities, business, and universities, headed by the minister of the Open Government.

The Open Data Council, being a part of the Commission, coordinated the development of OGD through preparing government programs, proposals, and recommendations, collecting and applying the best practices, promoting the idea of OGD, and creating independent feedback channels. As the Council was established with consultative functions, all the recommendations had to be submitted to the Governmental Commission that had the power to issue final recommendations.

The Open Data Council was suspended in May 2018 when Vladimir Putin was re-elected as the President of the Russian Federation and the formation of a new government. A new council has neither been created nor a new working group appointed.

In Russia, in 2013, a law was adopted to ensure access to information on the activities of state bodies and local self-government bodies, according to which publication of data in the public domain has become mandatory. The basic principles for ensuring access to information on the activities of state bodies and local governments are as follows: openness and accessibility of information on the activities of state bodies; accuracy of information; freedom of searching, receiving, transmitting, and disseminating information. The law prohibits the dissemination of information containing state secrets or personal data.

The following organizations were working to coordinate and develop Open Government Data (OGD) at the federal level: the Russian Open Data Council, the Ministry of Economic Development, the Ministry of Telecommunication, and the Government Analytical Center of the Russian Federation. The Ministry of Economic Development was responsible for developing the federal portal, providing operational and procedural support, and synchronization of federal and regional initiatives. The Ministry of Telecommunications was responsible for the coordination of OGD development by government bodies, including corresponding information systems, as well as the advancement of social e-services based on OGD. The Government Analytical Center of the Russian Federation monitors the OGD in the Russian Federation: the results of the analysis were published in Open Data Bulletin (Open Data Bulletin, 2015–2016), which has been issued every three months since June 2015.

In 2014, the Russian Government approved the road map of IT sector development for the years 2014–2025, and Open Government Data development was one of the main priorities of the plan.

Among the most recent examples that demonstrate the continuity in open data development in Russia are the publication of open data by the Federal Tax Service of Russia, the launch of the project spending.gov.ru by the Audit Chamber of the Russian Federation, and the use of open data for interaction between the Ministry of Culture and its subordinate organizations and cultural institutions.

1.7 Are the National Strategies Binding Documents (I.e., Adopted in the Form of Laws or Decrees) or Are They Just Declaratory Documents?

The Russian national strategies are binding documents that are adopted in the form of laws and decrees.

1.8 Is There a Specific Policy for Integration, Inclusion of Vulnerable Groups (E.g., Elderly, Etc.), or Accessibility for People with Disabilities?

There are some initiatives and resolutions that have been taken in the wake of the COVID-19 pandemic to provide access to important governmental online resources and websites, as well as to grant access to participate in the court sessions using video- and web-conferencing systems.

On July 2, 2020, Russian President Vladimir Putin signed a Federal Law of July 2, 2021 No. 319-FZ "On Amendments to the Federal Law" "On Communications" providing free access to Russian socially significant websites.

On April 29, 2020, the Presidiums of the Supreme Court and the Council of Judges recommended that all Russian courts, if technically feasible, taking into account the opinions of the participants in the process, hold court sessions using not only a video-conferencing system, but also a web-conferencing system. Access to e-courts removes certain barriers to accessing justice for vulnerable groups and makes litigation more transparent and effective.

The procedure for organizing participation in a court session through the online session system is provided for by Articles 153, 153.1, and 154 of the Arbitration Procedure Code of the Russian Federation.

Only users with verified accounts in the Unified Identification and Authentication System (ESIA) can participate in the online court session. The procedure for obtaining access to online court sessions can be found on the website of the electronic service "My Arbitrator."

1.9 Are the National Strategies Guided or Are They Involved in Cooperation Agreements, Best Practices, Programs, Associations of Organizations, Such as UN Agenda 2030 SDGs, OECD, and World Bank?

Yes, Russian city, municipal, and federal governments participate in various practices and programs of the Organization for Economic Co-operation and Development (OECD), World Bank, and UN bodies.

For example, to compare its educational achievements to international standards and students' performance in other (Western) countries Russia took part in international large-scale assessments, such as of OECD's Programme for International Student Assessment (PISA), OECD's PIAAC (Programme for the International Assessment of Adult Competencies); IEA's (International Association for the Evaluation of Educational Achievement) TALIS (Teaching and Learning International Survey;) IEA's Trends in International Mathematics and Science Study (TIMMS), and IEA's Progress in International Reading Literacy Study (PIRLS). This was done after Russia received recommendations to develop centralized examinations and national surveys of education quality from the OECD and World Bank.

However, some experts note that Russia has recently lost its interest in joining the Organization for Economic Co-operation and Development (OECD), and we are yet to see how this will affect Russia's involvement and participation in international cooperation and related initiatives.

Digital Development Partnership

Specifically in relation to the national strategy on the Russian Digital Economy Program that the government had set to implement in 2017, the World Bank has cooperated with the Institute of the Information Society (IIS) and other local partners in Russia to conduct a Digital Economy Country Assessment (DECA) to identify the challenges that Russia was likely to face. This was the first global pilot of the benchmarking tool developed within the Digital Development Partnership initiative.

1.10 Are There Any Existing Policies to Zero-Rate Certain e-government Services? Are There Such Policies for Specific Public Sectors?

Yes, in the wake of the COVID-19 pandemic, on July 2, 2021 Russian President Vladimir Putin signed a Federal Law of July 2, 2021 No. 319-FZ "On Amendments to the Federal Law" (approved on 23 July 2021) "On Communications" providing free access to Russian socially significant websites.

1.11 How Does the Country Rank on Global Digital Adoption Indices, Such as the World Bank's Digital Adoption Index, the Digital Society Index, IMD World Digital Competitiveness Ranking, Global Open Data Index, Etc.?

The Digital Adoption Index is a worldwide index that measures countries' digital adoption across three dimensions of the economy: people, government, and business. The index covers 180 countries on a 0–1 scale and emphasizes the "supply-side" of digital adoption to maximize coverage and simplify theoretical linkages. The overall DAI is the simple average of three sub-indices. Each sub-index comprises technologies necessary for the respective agent to promote development in the digital era: increasing productivity and accelerating broad-based growth for business, expanding opportunities, improving welfare for people, and increasing the efficiency and accountability of service delivery for government. Russia's place for 2014 was 0.688322186, and for 2016 was 0.744089782 (The World Bank, 2016).

Russia took 23rd place in the ranking of countries for the development of the digital society (Digital Society Index, 2019). In last year's edition of the rating, it was on the tenth line. The compilers of the list explain the fall of Russia by 13 positions by the fact that in 2019, the number of countries in which the study was conducted increased from 10 to 24.

The leader of the rating was Singapore, followed by the USA and China in the second and third places. In fourth place is Denmark, the top five is closed by the United Kingdom, the leader of last year's edition of the rating. Next come the Netherlands, Norway, Finland, Estonia, and Germany. The second ten are France, Canada, Ireland, Australia, India, Spain, Poland, Mexico, Hungary, and Italy ("Russia Fell", 2019).

The IMD World Digital Competitiveness Ranking, produced by the IMD World Competitiveness Center, measures the capacity and readiness of 64 economies to adopt and explore digital technologies as a key driver for economic transformation in business, government, and wider society. Based on a mixture of hard data and survey replies from business and government executives, the digital rankings help governments and companies to understand where to focus their resources and what might be best when embarking on digital transformation. Russia's place is 42 between Poland and Cyprus (IMD World Competitiveness Center, 2022).

The Global Open Data Index (GODI) is an independent assessment of open government data publication from a civic perspective. GODI enables different open data stakeholders to track the government's progress on open data release. GODI also allows governments to get direct feedback from data users. The Index gives both parties a baseline for discussion and analysis of the open data ecosystem in their country and internationally. We encourage all interested parties to participate in an open dialogue to allow for ownership of the results and to make the Index as relevant as possible.

Russia is ranked number 38 against other places in the Index (20% Open; 43% Score) (Open Knowledge Foundation, 2016).

2 Regulations

2.1 Is There Any General Regulation (E.g., Law, Decree, Standards) to Organize the Digitalization of Public Services, Other than Specific Regulations that Might Apply to the Key Sectors Identified Below?

There is an overarching Federal Program "Information Society 2011–2020," established by Decree No. 1815-p from October 20, 2010, which sets as its key objective the digitization of all spheres of the Russian society. Also, the earlier e-Government reform (2002–2010) was harmonized with this Program.

In the Russian Federation, the entire system of providing state and municipal services is regulated by the Federal Law of July 27, 2010 No. 210-FZ "On the organization of the provision of state and municipal services." This federal law regulates relations arising in connection with the provision of state and municipal services, respectively, by federal executive bodies, bodies of state extra-budgetary funds, executive bodies of state power of the constituent entities of the Russian Federation, as well as local administrations and other bodies of local self-government exercising executive and administrative powers. This federal law establishes the features of the organization of the provision of state and municipal services in multifunctional centers, carried out on the principle of "one window," in accordance with which the provision of state or municipal services is carried out after a single application of the applicant with a corresponding request, and interaction with bodies providing state services, or by bodies providing municipal services is carried out by a multi-functional center without the participation of the applicant in accordance with regulatory legal acts and an agreement on interaction. The law contains sections devoted to the regulation of the use of information and telecommunication technologies in the provision of state and municipal services, as well as the organization of activities for the issuance and maintenance of universal electronic cards of the population. Thus, the Federal Law "On the Organization of the Provision of State and Municipal Services" introduced fundamental changes to the entire regulatory framework of relations between society and the authorities in the Russian Federation and formed a new model of a client-oriented state.

2.2 Is There Any Regulation Mandating Transparency Audits for Technologies (E.g., of Platforms, Algorithms, Cloud Services, Etc.) Utilized by Public Administrations?

Audits are part of the process of implementation of national strategy goals and expenditures of the federal budget allocated for the national strategy goals. Audits are conducted according to the Work plan of the Accounts Chamber of the Russian Federation for 2020.

The auditor of the Accounts Chamber of the Russian Federation (SP of the Russian Federation) is an official leading a certain direction of the activities of the Accounting Chamber of the Russian Federation, which covers a complex, a group, or a collection of a number of income or expenditure articles of the federal budget, united by unity of destination.

The Accounts Chamber includes 12 auditors who, in accordance with the Constitution of the Russian Federation, are appointed by the Federation Council and the State Duma on the proposal of the President of the Russian Federation. The upper and lower chambers of the Federal Assembly of the Russian Federation each appoint 6 auditors for a period of 6 years. When a vacant position of an auditor appears, it must be filled within 2 months.

The competence of the auditor of the SP of the Russian Federation includes the organization of the work chaired by him, the activities of the Accounts Chamber in accordance with the distribution of responsibilities between the auditors of the Accounts Chamber. Auditors are guided by the Federal Law "On the Accounts Chamber of the Russian Federation" and the Rules. Auditors within their competence independently solve all issues related to the areas of work that they are responsible for, as well as the results of this work. The Accounts Chamber publishes a list of audits for 2020 in the public domain.

In December 2008, a new Federal Law "On Auditing" No. 307-FZ was adopted from January 1, 2009 (separate articles—from January 1, 2010), according to which licensing of auditors was replaced by compulsory membership in the audit of self-regulating organization of auditors (SROs).

2.3 Is There Any Specific Regulation Mandating Requirements for Public Procurements and Public Tenders Regarding Digital Public Services?

In 2005, a new procurement law was introduced on the federal level, the Federal Law 94-FZ of July 21, 2005 No. 94-FZ "On placing orders for the supply of goods, performance of work, provision of services for state and municipal needs." This law mandated the creation of transparent and available information access.

The given federal law is applied in the cases of procurement of goods, works and services for state and municipal needs and the needs of budget-funded organizations, except when such services are provided by international financial organizations formed under the international treaties to which the Russian Federation is a signatory, as well as international financial organizations, with which the Russian Federation has concluded international treaties.

2.4 Are Digital Public Services Subject to General Data Protection Regulations? If Not, Is There Any Data Protection Regulation for Digital Public Services?

Yes, digital public services are subject to data protection regulations.

2.5 Are There Any Current or Proposed Regulations Mandating the Sharing of Data with Government Agencies to Enable Better Delivery of Public Services?

On February 9, 2009, Federal Law No. 8-FZ "On the access to information on the activity of the state and local authorities" was issued. According to the law, all citizens of the Russian Federation, as well as legal entities and public associations, have the right to receive reliable information about the activities of any government body.

In accordance with the state strategy for the development of information technologies and building an information society (2002–2010), the Internet was defined as one of the key channels of access to information. According to the law, each state body, including regional divisions, should have an official website on the Internet, where information for all categories of citizens, legal entities, and other users is posted in the public domain.

The published information must include static data on the activities of the state body, including statistical data and indicators characterizing the state and the dynamics of development of economic, social, and other spheres of life, the regulation of which is attributed to the powers of this body.

Also, an Order of the Government of Russia No. 478 from June 15, 2009, "On the unified system of information and reference support of citizens and organizations on questions concerning their cooperation with the state and local authorities by means of the Internet," and the Presidential Decree No. 721 from September 9, 2009 have brought changes into the FTP "Electronic Russia 2002–2010" to enable a unified technical infrastructure for the Russian e-Government.

On February 9, 2009, the Federal Law No. 8-FZ "On the access to information on the activity of the state and local authorities" has been issued, together with an Order of the Government of Russia No. 478 from June 15, 2009, "On the unified system of information and reference support of citizens and organizations on questions concerning their cooperation with the state and local authorities by means of the Internet," and the Presidential Decree No. 721 from September 9, 2009, has brought changes into the FTP "Electronic Russia 2002–2010" to enable a unified technical infrastructure for the Russian e-Government.

3 Institutions

3.1 Is There a Specific Body Overseeing the Digitalization of the Public Sector?

The Ministry of Digital Development, Communications and Mass Media of the Russian Federation and the Ministry of Economic Development of the Russian Federation.

In accordance with the Decree of the President of the Russian Federation of May 7, 2018 No. 204 "On national goals and strategic objectives of the development of the Russian Federation for the period up to 2024," the national program "Digital economy of the Russian Federation" has been formed.

One of the objectives of the program is to create a system of legal regulation of the digital economy based on a flexible approach in each area. The federal project "Normative regulation of the digital environment," which is supervised by the Ministry of Economic Development of the Russian Federation, is dedicated to the implementation of this task.

The federal project provides for the development and adoption of a number of regulatory legal acts aimed at removing the priority barriers that hinder the development of the digital economy. It is also planned to settle the cross-cutting issues for various branches of legislation related to the identification of subjects of legal relations in the digital environment, electronic document management, and data circulation, including personal data.

The Digital Economy Development Department coordinates the work of the participants in the federal project. In addition, the Department is responsible for the development of a number of documents, including bills on the long-term storage of electronic documents, on the national data management system, on regulatory sandboxes, the concept of regulation of Artificial Intelligence and robotics, and other regulations.

Currently, within the framework of a federal project, the conditions for the collection, storage and processing of data using new technologies have been formed, the peculiarities of processing personal data permitted by the subject of personal data for distribution have been established, which will increase the control of the subject of personal data over the processing of his personal data permitted by him for distribution (Federal Law of December 30, 2020 No. 519-FZ)

3.2 If Such a Body Exists, What Is Its Status (E.g., an Independent Agency, a Ministry, an Inter-ministerial Committee, an Ad-hoc Body, Etc.)?

The system for managing the development and implementation of programs, as well as monitoring their implementation, includes:

(a) the Presidium of the Government Commission on Digital Development, the Use of Information Technologies to Improve the Quality of Life and the Conditions for Doing Business (hereinafter referred to as the Presidium of the Commission);
(b) Ministry of Digital Development, Telecommunications and Mass Media of the Russian Federation;
(c) Ministry of Finance of the Russian Federation;
(d) Ministry of Health of the Russian Federation;
(e) Ministry of Labor and Social Protection of the Russian Federation;
(f) Competence center for program coordination—a state institution under its jurisdiction determined by the Ministry of Digital Development, Telecommunications and Mass Media of the Russian Federation;
(g) government agencies responsible for digital transformation (Decree of the Government of the Russian Federation No. 1646 of October 10, 2020).

3.3 If Such a Body Exists, What Are Its Prerogatives and Powers?

Presidium of the Commission:

(a) determine the composition of the federal executive bodies, which should be guided in their activities by this Regulation;
(b) considers and approves:

model job regulations of the deputy head of the state body responsible for digital transformation;

model regulation on an independent structural unit of the state body responsible for digital transformation;

standard form of the program;

model regulation on the management of digital transformation projects;

unified technical policy for the implementation of programs;

methodological documents necessary to ensure the functioning of the system for managing the development and implementation of programs, as well as monitoring their implementation, including:

guidelines for the preparation of programs by state bodies in accordance with the standard form of the program;

guidelines for the formation and submission, in accordance with this Regulation, by state bodies of information on informatization activities;

rules for checking information about informatization activities;

the procedure for generating the program event code;

a program change request form, as well as methodological recommendations for the preparation of program change requests by government agencies.

The standard form of the program, as well as methodological recommendations for the preparation of programs by state bodies in accordance with the standard form of the program, are approved by the Presidium of the Commission based on the results of their consideration at the same time;

(c) considers draft programs and disagreements on draft programs after their approval by state bodies with the Ministry of Digital Development, Communications and Mass Media of the Russian Federation, and makes a decision on the approval of draft programs;
(d) considers a summary report on the results of the implementation of the programs approved by state bodies in accordance with this Regulation and decides on the level of achievement by state bodies of the goals of digital transformation, including assessing the efficiency and effectiveness of the activities of the relevant deputy head of the state body responsible for digital transformation;
(e) based on the results of monitoring the implementation of programs, approves, if necessary, changes in the goals of digital transformation, provided for in paragraph 16 of these Regulations;
(f) makes decisions aimed at ensuring the functioning of the system for managing the processes of developing and implementing programs, as well as monitoring their implementation.

Ministry of Digital Development, Telecommunications and Mass Media of the Russian Federation:

(a) prepares draft documents specified in subparagraph "b" of paragraph 7 of these Regulations, and submits them for consideration and approval to the Presidium of the Commission;
(b) considers, with the participation of the center of competence for the coordination of programs, draft programs and makes a decision on their approval;
(c) requests, if necessary, from state bodies additional documents and materials on issues within the competence of the Presidium of the Commission and the

Ministry of Digital Development, Communications and Mass Media of the Russian Federation;

(d) through the federal state information system for the coordination of informatization, the functioning of which is carried out in accordance with the Decree of the Government of the Russian Federation of November 14, 2015 No. 1235 "On the federal state information system for the coordination of informatization," verification of information on informatization activities submitted by state bodies;

(e) monitors the implementation of programs with the participation of the competence center for program coordination, including following the results of its implementation:

submits a quarterly report on the implementation of digital transformation projects in case of deviations from the planned progress in the implementation of digital transformation projects;

prepares a consolidated report on the results of the implementation of programs, and annually submits the said summary report for consideration to the Commission's presidium;

(f) at the request of the Presidium of the Commission and (or) state bodies, organizes, with the participation of the competence center for program coordination, an expert assessment of the results of the implementation of individual program activities;

(g) for the purpose of information support for the implementation of the processes of development, coordination, review, approval and implementation of programs, including monitoring their implementation, forms functional requirements, ensures the operation and development of the federal state information system for the coordination of informatization, develops and approves, if necessary, regulatory legal acts, organizational—administrative and methodological documents regulating the functioning of this system;

(h) submit proposals to the Presidium of the Commission on changing the goals of digital transformation.

The Ministry of Finance of the Russian Federation, the Ministry of Health of the Russian Federation (in the part relating to the Federal Compulsory Medical Insurance Fund) and the Ministry of Labor and Social Protection of the Russian Federation (in the part relating to the Pension Fund of the Russian Federation and the Social Insurance Fund of the Russian Federation) review programs in in accordance with this Regulation.

The Competence Center for Program Coordination performs:

(a) organizational and technical, expert-analytical, methodological and informational support of the functions and powers of the Ministry of Digital Development, Communications and Mass Media of the Russian Federation, provided for by this Regulation, including ensuring the collection of proposals from state bodies on draft documents specified in subparagraph "b" paragraph 7 of these Regulations, as well as on their basis, the formation and submission of generalized proposals in the form of drafts of these documents to the Ministry of Digital Development, Communications and Mass Media of the Russian Federation;

(b) consideration of draft programs and submission to the Ministry of Digital Development, Telecommunications and Mass Media of the Russian Federation of draft relevant decisions based on the results of the coordination of draft programs;

(c) ensuring the implementation of monitoring of the implementation of programs and the preparation of a draft summary report on the results of the implementation of programs, as well as the preparation of draft reports on the results of monitoring;

(d) preparation of proposals for the development of a federal state information system for the coordination of informatization to ensure, through this system, the effective implementation of the processes of developing and implementing programs, monitoring their implementation, as well as ensuring the implementation of the powers of the Ministry of Digital Development, Communications and Mass Media of the Russian Federation for the development and operation of the federal state information system of informatization coordination;

(e) carrying out activities for information and methodological support of state bodies in terms of the development and implementation of programs by them, including through the organization of thematic conferences, meetings, seminars, and webinars.

State bodies:

(a) in accordance with the documents specified in subparagraph "b" of paragraph 7 of these Regulations, develop and adopt legal acts approving:

job regulations of the deputy head of the state body responsible for digital transformation;

regulation on an independent structural unit of the state body responsible for digital transformation;

regulation on the management of digital transformation projects;

(b) adopt legal acts that establish the procedure for organizing the development, approval, and implementation of programs, which, among other things, determine the deputy heads of the state body responsible for achieving the values of digital transformation performance indicators provided for by the program;

(c) carry out, in accordance with these Regulations, the development, coordination, approval and implementation of consolidated programs, including the preparation of reports to monitor the results of their implementation;

(d) carry out the development of draft programs and ensure the implementation of a unified technical policy approved by the Presidium of the Commission;

(e) send draft programs for approval to the Ministry of Digital Development, Communications and Mass Media of the Russian Federation, and consideration and approval by the Presidium of the Commission;

(f) send draft programs to the Ministry of Finance of the Russian Federation as part of information on the rationale for the distribution of planned budget appropriations according to the corresponding code of types of expenses for the classification of expenses of the budgets of the Russian Federation for the purchase of goods, works, services in the field of information and communication technologies and approve the draft programs approved by the Presidium of the Commission;

(g) submit to the Ministry of Digital Development, Telecommunications and Mass Media of the Russian Federation for verification information on informatization activities;

(h) ensure the implementation of informatization activities, including digital transformation projects, in accordance with the legislation of the Russian Federation on information, information technologies, and information protection;

(i) when planning and implementing informatization activities, ensure:

accounting for all information systems created, developed, and operated by state bodies (including information technologies, technical means, and information and telecommunication networks necessary for their operation) and components of the information and telecommunications infrastructure at all stages of the life cycle of information systems and information and telecommunications infrastructure;

inclusion of programs for electronic computers developed by state bodies as a result of the creation and development of information systems, together with design, technical, accompanying, and methodological documentation for such programs, in the national fund of algorithms and programs;

reuse of information and communication technologies created at the expense of the federal budget and the budgets of state extra-budgetary funds;

compatibility of information and communication technologies and interconnectedness of state information resources used in various state bodies;

reducing technological dependence, including through the use of Russian information and communication technologies, as well as free software in the creation, development, and operation of information systems and information and telecommunications infrastructure;

(j) use the federal state information system for the coordination of informatization to carry out the processes of developing, coordinating, reviewing, approving, and implementing programs (including project management of the implementation of program activities), monitoring and controlling their implementation, generating and presenting information about informatization activities;

(k) create a technical customer service and carry out the implementation of program activities, including the management of digital transformation projects provided for by the programs (Decree of the Government of the Russian Federation No. 1646 of October 10, 2020).

3.4 Is There an Evaluation System or Indicators to Measure the Progress of the Development of Digital Government?

When developing a draft program, the state bodies involved in its development ensure that the program is developed taking into account the goals and objectives of the state programs of the Russian Federation, national projects and other strategic planning documents implemented in the relevant areas, as well as taking into account the values of the target indicators established in these documents, and the timing of the implementation of activities in accordance with the methodological recommendations for the preparation of programs by state bodies in accordance with the standard form of the program.

3.5 Is There a Public Company or Any Public-Private Partnerships Working on the Development of Specific Solutions for Digitizing the Public Sector? If the Company Exists, What Is Its Function?

The "Strategy for the Development of the Information Society in the Russian Federation for 2017–2030" defines the "ecosystem of the digital economy" as "a partnership of organizations ensuring the continuous interaction of their technological platforms, applied Internet services, analytical systems, information systems of public authorities of the Russian Federation, organizations and citizens." Thus, the creation of the ecosystem of the digital economy entails the creation of "a partnership of organizations." However, a partnership is not the main element of the digital economy. Regardless of whether enterprise owners of digital technologies, Internet portals, and servers form or do not form a partnership, the economy does not cease to be digital (Wijermars, 2021). For example, Rostelekom operates the "State Services" nationwide portal.

3.6 What Are the Criteria aimed at Guaranteeing the Independence of the "Third Parties" Auditing Digital Public Service Providers?

No, when providers are taking part in the State programs of digitalization, the audit is performed by the Accounts Chamber of the Russian Federation—the auditing structure under the supervision of the Parliament of the Russian Federation. The audit of state programs of the Russian Federation (federal targeted programs) is used to assess the quality of their formation and implementation in terms of:

- compliance of the course and results of their implementation with the specified requirements.
- validity and compliance with the schedules for the implementation of individual stages of work and information about resource support.
- correlation of results with expended federal resources (Federal Law No. 41-FZ of April 5, 2013).

4 Key Sectors

4.1 *Digital Identity*

4.1.1 Is There a Strategy to Digitalize This Sector or Any Areas of It?

According to the announcement made on 7 June 2021 by the head of the department of the Ministry of Digital Development, Communications and Mass Media of the Russian Federation, Maksut Shadayev (Government of the Russian Federation, n.d.-a), the technical project on the electronic passport has been completed (Draft Decree of the President of the Russian Federation as of March 19, 2021) by the Ministry and further coordinated with the Ministry of Internal Affairs and the Federal Security Service of Russia to come up with the technical solution. The project proposes to replace the paper passport with a smart card and a mobile application. The tests will start in December 2021; first, only residents of Moscow will be able to obtain an electronic passport of a citizen of Russia. Further, this project will spread to the entire territory of Russia. The electronic passports are expected to be introduced in the regions no later than July 1, 2023 (The Ministry of Digital Development, 2021), according to the Ministry.

The Presidential Decree on the use of electronic passports was developed by the Ministry of Digital Development, Communications and Mass Media of the Russian Federation; it proposes to store the electronic passport, which actually might be an electronic copy of the original identification documents,[2] and other electronic identification documents on the mobile device. It is also planned to develop a mobile application for this purpose.

Previously, the Ministry published a preliminary (not final) draft decision tied to authentication in the Multifunctional Center[3] (MFC) and biometric data. After verification, the user must be able to get access to a Mobile application that would verify identity in instances like booking tickets, registering as an individual entrepreneur, or, for example, during police checks on the road.

It is worth noting that the government approved the first concept of switching to an electronic passport eight years ago, and the dates for the start of the experiment were postponed several times. The official strategy for the digital identity was launched in 2013.

---

[2] For example, a driver's license, car documents or a certificate of registration at the place of residence.

[3] Multifunctional center for the provision of state and municipal services.

4.1.2 Is the Use of Specific Technologies for Digital Identity Systems Promoted or Prioritized (E.g., AI, Blockchain, Open-Source Software)?

The identity card contains restricted information (personal data). In this regard, the information support of the identity card and the entire application infrastructure must guarantee the integrity, availability, and confidentiality of the information being processed.

The integrity of the data placed on the electronic carrier of the identity card is ensured using cryptographic methods of information protection, as well as authentication and authorization mechanisms. Confidentiality of data when accessing them directly or through electronic applications is provided by authentication and authorization mechanisms. The availability of data is determined by the reliability indicators of the software and hardware of the identity card, which are established at the stage of integrated design.

When using a cryptographic electronic application, the standards adopted in the Russian Federation in accordance with GOST 34.10-2012 and GOST 34.11-2012 are implemented. A cryptographic electronic application undergoes a conformity assessment in conjunction with an identity card as an operating environment in the manner prescribed by the legislation of the Russian Federation (Decree of the Government of the Russian Federation No. 1699-r of September 19, 2013).

4.1.3 Are There Any Policies Promoting Digital Sovereignty for Digital Identity Systems (E.g., Data Localization, Preference or Obligation to Utilize Domestic Providers, Etc.)?

As part of solving the priority task of import substitution, as well as in accordance with the plan for guaranteed purchases of Russian civilian microelectronic products in terms of providing computing devices and hardware and software systems in 2016, the Russian Ministry of Communications carried out work to transfer the central node of the "Mir" system—an interdepartmental redundant processing center data (MRTSOD), which provides information interaction of departmental segments of the Mir system with each other, as well as with external information systems, for the use of free software (FOS) and equipment of domestic companies. More than 100 servers built on domestic processors of the Elbrus architecture, Rubicon-K firewalls manufactured by the Russian company NPO Echelon, as well as solutions based on open-source software, are used as part of the import-substituting solutions of the interdepartmental redundant processing center data (Ministry of Digital Development, Communications and Mass Media of the Russian Federation, 2018).

4.1.4 Is There a Sectoral Regulation in Place (E.g., Law, Decree, Standards) to Organize the Digitalization of the Sector?

The Government of the Russian Federation approved the Concept for the introduction in the Russian Federation of an identity card of a citizen of the Russian Federation, issued in the form of a plastic card with an electronic information carrier, as the main document proving the identity of a citizen of the Russian Federation on the territory of the Russian Federation (hereinafter referred to as the electronic passport), and a plan for its implementation (Decree of the Government of the Russian Federation dated September 19, 2013 No. 1699-R).

As follows from this Concept, the issuance of electronic passports was planned from January 1, 2016, and the end of the issuance of a passport of a citizen of the Russian Federation on paper—from January 01, 2025 (with a possible revision of the indicated deadlines) (sections I, VI of the Concept).

Subsequently, it was decided to postpone the measures for the introduction of electronic passports on the territory of the Russian Federation (clause 23b of the Decree of the Government of the Russian Federation of April 16, 2016 No. 315) (ABC of Law, 2022).

4.1.5 Has the Digitization of the Sector or Any Area of It Been Promoted Because of the COVID-19 Pandemic? If Yes, then How So?

Since the beginning of the pandemic, the Russian government has made several attempts to introduce the QR-code system; however, until today, it has not been able to put it into work, and on Friday, 16 July 2021, the Mayor of Moscow has announced a cancellation of the decree on the use of QR-codes in the restaurants and cafes of Moscow. It was expected that only citizens who possess QR-codes proving completed vaccination from COVID-19 would be able to visit and dine at restaurants and cafes of Moscow.

The Moscow government received the Runet Prize for the system of digital solutions aimed at countering the coronavirus pandemic in the Technologies vs Coronavirus category.

4.1.6 Is There a Specific Body in Charge of Overseeing, Coordinating, or Promoting the Digitalization of the Sector?

The Ministry of Digital Development, Communications and Mass Media of the Russian Federation is in charge of overseeing, coordinating, or promoting the digitalization of the sector.

4.2 *Smart Cities and Digitized Local Administrations*

4.2.1 Is There a Smart City Strategy?

Although various national and federal projects on electronic government and strategies, Moscow by far has been the champion in putting the smart city agenda into action. Moscow Smart City project (Moscow City Hall, n.d.), initiated in 2018, is to continue e-government developments and digitization of services of the last decade. This strategic program, planned until 2030, is aligned with the digital economy framework and sets priorities, goals, and objectives for the governance and development of the digital economy in Moscow up to 2030. Moscow aims to digitize all city processes and "establish a new administration in Moscow as the smart city platform. In 2019, Moscow becomes the main city to implement the national AI beta-programmes."

Moscow, the capital city, is an example of an "ideal smart city," with its strategic program "Smart City 2030" that was started in 2018 with a discussion on the Internet between businesses and citizens. The main idea is to digitalize all city processes and establish a new administration in Moscow as the smart city platform. In 2019, Moscow becomes the main city to implement the national AI beta-programs.

Moscow's electronic government framework is embodied in a Moscow Smart City project that has been put into practice over the last decade.

4.2.2 Is the Use of Specific Smart City Technologies Promoted or Prioritized (E.g., AI, Blockchain, Open-Source Software)?

Decree of the Government of the Russian Federation of August 19, 2020 No. 2129-r assumes the use of Artificial Intelligence and robotics systems to implement the concept of "smart city."

To this end, it is necessary to identify and remove regulatory barriers, including those that prevent:

automation of housing and communal services and utilities (accounting for meter readings and the implementation of a "flexible" supply of resources depending on variable indicators, automatic detection of noise levels, pollution and its analysis, equipment operation control, etc.);

introduction of "smart" urban transport (in terms of the development of "unmanned" transport and the development of the infrastructure accompanying it—systems for photo and video recording of offenses, systems for the automatic administration of urban parking spaces, systems for automatic control of traffic flows depending on the congestion of the roadway, automatic control systems for the state of the roadway and road transport infrastructure, public transport routing systems based on big data analysis, etc.);

creation of digital platforms and services to involve citizens in the management of urban processes (introduction of voting on specific issues, analysis of textual appeals using Artificial Intelligence systems to identify a general attitude to the problem or the problems themselves, analysis of public opinion expressed);

introduction of intelligent public security systems (video surveillance systems with biometric identification functions, etc.);
general planning and planning for the development of territories based on Artificial Intelligence and big data processed by it.

At the same time, special attention should be paid to revising the approach to the mandatory participation of a person in decision-making in the designated areas (from the need for a person to participate in a specific action to operational and strategic goal setting and control by a person) (Decree of the Government of the Russian Federation No. 2129-r of August 19, 2020).

4.2.3 Is There a Sectoral Regulation in Place (E.g., Law, Decree, Standards) to Organize the Digitalization of Cities and Urban Areas in General?

The implementation period for the activities provided for by this Smart City standard, except the introduction of a digital platform for involving citizens in solving urban development issues, is determined in the passport of the regional project and the state program of the constituent entity of the Russian Federation based on the analysis of the key problems of the urban economy, the solution of which is possible through the implementation the specified activities.

The activities specified in this Smart City standard are provided for the implementation, in compliance with the requirements established by the legislation of the Russian Federation, for the protection of information and information systems in cities with a population of over 100,000 people and cities that are the administrative centers of the constituent entities of the Russian Federation and may be also implemented in settlements with a population of less than 100,000 people.

The activities provided for by this Smart City standard are carried out taking into account the existing infrastructure, including that built as part of the Safe City APK, and the implemented functionality of the state information system for housing and communal services, and the information resources developed based on their results are built, as a rule, on the basis of state information systems for ensuring urban planning activities, and if such construction is impossible, they are synchronized with state information systems for ensuring urban planning activities and, if necessary, other state information systems (Ministry of Construction of Russia, 2019).

4.2.4 Are There Any Policies Promoting Digital Sovereignty for Smart Cities (E.g., Data Localization, Preference or Obligation to Utilize Domestic Providers, Etc.)?

Regarding the smart cities agenda, there is an obligation to utilize domestic providers.

4.2.5 Has the Digitization of the Sector or Any Area of It Been Promoted Because of the COVID-19 Pandemic? If Yes, then How So?

The Russian law defines an emergency as a situation in a certain territory developed from a spread of a disease that poses a danger to others, among other causes, that could result in or results in human casualties, damage to human health or the environment, significant material losses and disruption of human activity (Federal Constitutional Law on Emergencies of May 30, 2001 No. 3-FKZ). During the period when all working activities were stopped by the presidential decree, the high readiness regime was initially active till the end of April 2020 with prolongation till the end of May 2020, financial losses along with the severe limitations to people's living conditions—in addition to the risk of infection—all together became a massive problem for Russian population.

Under Article 18 of the aforementioned Law on Emergencies, which lists the rights and obligations of citizens in case of emergency, Russian citizens are entitled to medical care and compensation for damages. Given that there was a spread of the COVID-19 disease, danger posed to others, human casualties, damage to people's health, significant material losses, and limitations of the living conditions of people, the current situation in Russia can be clearly defined as an emergency. However, the state of emergency, which would oblige Russian authorities to reimburse financial losses to the millions of Russian citizens, was not declared.

The reluctance of the Russian state to declare a state of emergency and therefore enforce a quarantine in Russia can also be explained by the unwillingness of the state to further delay the public vote for the proposed changes in the constitution of the Russian Federation.

In whichever light we perceive these issues, there are already clear indications that Russian citizens disagree with the governmental stance and demand the declaration of a state of emergency and provision of financial aid to the people.

4.2.6 Is There a Specific Strategy or Regulation Targeting the Digitization of Land Records or Real Estate Records?

As part of the digitalization program, the law assumes the transfer of documents contained in register files (including cadastral files opened before January 1, 2017, cases of title documents), the storage of which is (was carried out) in the form of documents on paper, into the form of electronic images of such documents, as well as the development, implementation and information support of electronic services necessary for the provision of services in the field of state cadastral registration, state registration of rights and provision of information contained in the Unified State Register of Real Estate (including the personal account of the copyright holder of the property), as well as the provision of such services through these electronic services (Federal Law No. 218-FZ of July 13, 2015).

4.2.7 Is There a Specific Body in Charge of Overseeing, Coordinating, or Promoting the Digitalization of the Sector?

The Ministry of Digital Development, Communication and Mass Media, the Ministry of Construction, and the governments of the federal subjects and local administrations.

4.2.8 Is There Any Outstanding Example of Strategy or Policy Elaborated by a Local Administration?

According to experts, IoT solutions will massively penetrate "smart cities" with populations of more than one million people by 2025, while the economic effect will increase up to 375 billion rubles. Technologies optimize the interaction between the main city stakeholders—business, residents, and the city authorities—and make the Quadruple and quintuple innovation helix frameworks include the media and natural environment, making urban space more transparent and convenient. Moscow, the capital city, is an example of an "ideal smart city," with its strategic program "Smart City 2030" that was started in 2018 with a discussion on the Internet between businesses and citizens. The main idea is to digitalize all city processes and establish a new administration in Moscow as the smart city platform. In 2019, Moscow becomes the main city to implement the national AI beta-programs. A common secure digital space (the smart city platform) is planned in St. Petersburg as well, followed by other cities. A "safe city" system includes tools for monitoring basic real and artificial threats, and is already in use (e.g., in Nizhny Tagil, telemetry systems are used in schools; in Kursk and Vologda, intelligent security systems detect threats to public safety, etc.). These are joint projects of private IT companies, authorities, industry associations, and universities as the basic members of data systems.

4.3 *Digital Money and Payments*

4.3.1 Is There a Strategy to Digitalize This Sector or Any Areas of It, Such as the Central Bank Digital Currency Program?

Yes, there is a strategy by the Central Bank to introduce a project on digital ruble; this project should include technological and legal parts. According to Russia's central bank governor, Elvira Nabiullina, "digital currencies will be the future of financial systems" (Ng, 2021). According to Nabiullina, there is a need for cheap and fast payment systems, and the proposed Central Bank digital currencies are to fill that gap. Moscow aims to have a digital ruble prototype ready by the end of 2021, to start pilots and trials already in 2022. The project entails the development of a sovereign digital currency, which is different from cryptocurrencies, such as Bitcoin.

The Russian Central Bank digital currency is to be issued and controlled by the authorities, and the value of one digital ruble will equal one cash ruble, according to the Consultation paper (Bank of Russia, 2020) on "A Digital Rouble" issued by the Bank of Russia.[4]

4.3.2 Is the Use of Specific Technologies for Digital Money/Payments Promoted or Prioritized (E.g., AI, Blockchain, Open-Source Software)?

As the digital money/payments are still being discussed, the consultation paper "Digital Rouble" (Bank of Russia, 2020) on the development of the central bank digital currency (CBDC), prepared by the Bank of Russia in 2020, discusses several possible models of CBDCs and technologies for their implementation. When exploring mechanisms for the technical implementation of a CBDC in Sect. 4.2. Design of a CBDC using distributed ledger technology (DLT) is discussed. The accounting entity in distributed ledgers is a token. According to the Glossary section of the consultation paper, a token is a unit of accounting in the blockchain network used to represent a digital balance in a particular asset or to account for interchangeable digital assets. Tokens are usually used to create derivatives based on distributed ledgers.

4.3.3 Is There a Sectoral Regulation in Place (E.g., Law, Decree, Standards) to Organize the Digitalization of the Sector?

Yes, the federal law regulates the relations arising from the issuance, accounting and circulation of digital financial assets, the specifics of the activities of the operator of the information system in which the issuance of digital financial assets and the operator of the exchange of digital financial assets, as well as the relations arising from the circulation of digital currency in the Russian Federation (Federal Law No. 259-FZ of July 31, 2020).

4.3.4 Are There Any Policies Promoting Digital Sovereignty in the Sphere (E.g., Data Localization, Preference or Obligation to Utilize Domestic Providers, Etc.)?

One of the goals of the National Digital Economy program (2018) is "the use of predominantly domestic software by government agencies, local governments, and organizations." In the state program on Digital Economy (2017), "these measures

---

[4] The digitalization of the economy and the development of financial technologies generate public demand for new, advanced payment methods (Bank of Russia, 2020).

were addressed under the rubric of information security with corresponding indicators for decreasing the share of foreign ICT equipment and software in the purchases of federal and regional government authorities and state-owned enterprises (SOEs). The new program uses different indicators for government bodies and SOEs but focuses exclusively on software, omitting ICT equipment."

4.3.5 Has the Digitization of the Sector or Any Area of It Been Promoted Because of the COVID-19 Pandemic? If Yes, Then How So?

The Troika digital pass card (vs. cash) payment system in the Moscow subway was promoted (and specifically the use of a personalized digital card[5] passes was enforced) since the beginning of the COVID-19 pandemic. Moscow city's smart ticket system includes several ways to pay for transit rides. The Troika card is one of the most used ways of payment in the Moscow transportation system (up to 90% of all travel). This system has recently won some global awards (Transport Ticketing Global, 2020).

4.3.6 Is There a Specific Body in Charge of Overseeing, Coordinating, or Promoting the Digitalization of the Sector?

Ministry of Economic Development, Central Bank of Russia.

4.4 *Other Relevant Examples*

4.4.1 Is There Any Other Sector (Such as Education, Health, Etc.) Where a Specific Strategy or Policy Is in Place to Foster and Organize Digitalization?

The Russian public health sector has been under reform since 2017. Healthcare reform includes computerization of medical institutions, development of high-tech areas, and unification and digitization of offline medical data. The focus is on the creation and production of domestic technologies to drive the development of the (public) health sector.

In 2017, a Federal Law of July 29, 2017 No. 242-FZ on "On Amendments to Certain Legislative Acts of the Russian Federation on the Application of Information Technologies in the Field of Health Protection" (Law on Telemedicine) was adopted. At the time, there was a challenge to the homogeneous collection and storage of

[5] Troika payment option is currently available in the form of a card, a key ring, a ring, or a bracelet, which was personalized in November 2020; now it can be attached to the user's account in the My Moscow app. In case the card is lost, the remaining balance will be transferred to a new card.

medical data by the state, whereas some 80 scientific research institutes had their own information arrays, for example. There is a lack of a functioning electronic system for the exchange of information among public and private medical institutions.

While medical information is monopolized by the state, it is heterogeneous: for example, about 38 million personal electronic medical data sets are filed in accordance with different classifications, and about 80 scientific research institutes have their own independent information arrays, etc. There has been no functioning electronic system that would allow the exchange of medical information between various public and private medical institutions. However, the development of the Unified State Information System in Public Health (EGIS) should solve these problems. The Russian healthcare reform requires the development of a legislative framework for advances like telemedicine technologies. In 2017, a federal law on telemedicine was adopted. According to the industrial experts, mobile mHealth technologies will be in demand in Russia no earlier than in 2020, after laws and standards for the exchange of medical data are adopted, EGIS is completed, and protocols and methods for e-consultations are created. This would be possible only with state support.

The Supervisory Board of the Digital Economy organization, which met on June 27, 2019 in Moscow, approved the decision to create sectoral working groups for the digital industry, digital education and digital health, and selected their business co-chairs.

4.5 *Public Security*

4.5.1 Is There a Strategy to Digitalize This Sector or Any Areas of It?

In accordance with the roadmap of the Russian Government "The main activities of the Government of the Russian Federation for the period until 2024" in relation to the economic development and innovation-driven economy, "Ensuring stability and operational safety Russian digital infrastructure requires the organization and construction of a system of data processing and storage centers on the territory of the country, taking into account the possibilities of forming the export potential of these services, contributing to the development and increase of competitiveness digital economy of Russia."

The development of digitalization of the economy and social sphere requires strengthening the security measures of the information environment. The current level of use by the population of information security means, provision of routing of network traffic of the Russian segment of the information and telecommunication network "Internet," the use of domestic developments and technologies in software is insufficient and requires additional measures to ensure protection of the rights and interests of individuals, businesses, and the state in cyberspace.

According to the roadmap, by 2024, the government of the Russian Federation is to ensure the solution of the following tasks in the economic sphere:

ensuring information security based on domestic developments in the transfer, processing, and storage of data, which guarantees the protection of the interests of the individual, business, and the state.

Increasing security in the information environment for citizens, businesses, and government bodies will be achieved through:

- provision of routing of network traffic of the information and telecommunication network "Internet" on the territory of the Russian Federation;
- stimulating the development and further use of domestic software in the activities of state authorities, state corporations, and companies with state participation;
- updating the regulatory requirements for the stability and security of communication networks and equipment of public authorities and organizations, adopting a set of standards in the field of information security;
- formation of specialized resources aimed at prevention and counteraction to cyber threats in the information environment, including ensuring the integrity, stability and security of the functioning of the Russian segment of the information and telecommunication network "Internet," operational interaction with law enforcement agencies on the facts of committing illegal actions in the digital environment, creating a system for filtering Internet traffic when using information resources by children, providing citizens with access to information about cases of using them personal data, etc.

4.5.2 Is the Use of Specific Technologies for Public Security Promoted or Prioritized (E.g., AI, Blockchain, Open-Source Software, Biometrics, Facial Recognition, Smart Surveillance, Etc.)?

According to the Federal Law "On Operative Investigative Activities," the list of types of special technical means intended for secretly obtaining information while carrying out Operative Investigative Activities is established by the government of the Russian Federation (Federal Law No. 144-FZ of August 12, 1995). These could include special technical means for secretly receiving and recording acoustic information, for covert visual observation and documentation, for eavesdropping on telephone conversations, for covert interception and registration of information from technical communication channels, for covert control of postal messages and items, for covert research of objects and documents, for secret penetration and examination of premises, vehicles and other objects, for covert control over the movement of vehicles and other objects, for secretly obtaining (changing, destroying) information from the technical means of its storage, processing and transmission, and for covert identification of a person (Decree of the Government of the Russian Federation No. 770 of July 1, 1996).

4.5.3 Is There a Sectoral Regulation in Place (E.g., Law, Decree, Standards) to Organize the Digitalization of the Sector?

The system of technical means for ensuring operational-search activities (SORM) is created based on the Federal Law "On Operative Investigative Activities" and the Federal Law "On Communications" and is designed to provide technical support for the implementation of these activities on networks (services) of documentary telecommunications (SDES), used to provide data transmission and telematic services, including the Internet (State Communications Committee of Russia, 1999).

The Russian state does not have the capabilities to carry out mass surveillance. Russian SORM (System for Operative Investigative Activities) is the system designated for lawful interception interfaces of telecommunications and telephone networks that enables the targeted—but not mass—surveillance of both telephone and Internet communications in Russia. SORM was first implemented in 1995 to allow access to surveillance data for the FSB, but during Vladimir Putin's first week in office on January 5, 2000, the law was amended to allow seven other federal security agencies (apart from the FSB) to access to data gathered via SORM, including Ministry of Internal Affairs, Border patrol and customs, Police and Russia's tax police. The legality of the SORM legislation has always been questioned, and in December 2015 the European Court of Human Rights ruled unanimously that those Russian legal provisions "do not provide for adequate and effective guarantees against arbitrariness and the risk of abuse which is inherent in any system of secret surveillance," especially given that this risk "is particularly high in a system where the secret services and the police have direct access, by technical means, to all mobile telephone communications," thus violating Art. 8 of the European Convention on Human Rights that stipulates a right to respect for one's "private and family life, his home and his correspondence" (Gaufman, 2021).

4.5.4 Are There Any Policies Promoting Digital Sovereignty for Public Security Systems (E.g., Data Localization, Preference or Obligation to Utilize Domestic Providers, Etc.)?

From March 31, 2022, customers (except for organizations with municipal participation) making purchases in accordance with the Federal Law of July 18, 2011 No. 223-FZ "On the Procurement of Goods, Works, Services by Certain Types of Legal Entities," cannot purchase foreign software, including as part of software and hardware systems, for its use at significant objects of the critical information infrastructure of the Russian Federation belonging to them (hereinafter referred to as critical information infrastructure), as well as the purchase of services necessary for the use of this software at such facilities, without agreeing on the possibility of making purchases with the federal executive body authorized by the Government of the Russian Federation.

In the roadmap on "The main activities of the Government of the Russian Federation for the period until 2024" that was approved within the presidential Decree from May 7, 2018 on national goals and strategic objectives of the development of the Russian Federation for the period until 2024, it is stated that the preference should be given to the utilization of domestic providers, the use of domestic data centers and locally produced equipment. According to the Roadmap:

- provision of routing of network traffic of the information and telecommunication network "Internet" on the territory of the Russian Federation;
- stimulating the development and further use of domestic software in the activities of state authorities, state corporations, and companies with state participation;
- updating the regulatory requirements for the stability and security of communication networks and equipment of public authorities and organizations, adopting a set of standards in the field of information security.

4.5.5 Has the Digitization of the Sector or Any Area of It Been Promoted Because of the COVID-19 Pandemic? If So, then How?

Online surveillance is not authorized by Russian law and does not fall under the legislation that justifies the use of such technology in the case of a coronavirus crisis. Combining various elements of digital and technical infrastructure, such as Moscow's city CCTV system, Artificial Intelligence, smartphone geodata provided by telecom operators, and a face recognition solution developed by NtechLab, this system offers the capability to track every citizen. However, so far, the tracking will be focused on a limited list of people, created at the federal level (from the lists formed by agencies/operating bodies with the right to access the system), within the provision that allows surveillance and tracking of a person.

Both the surveillance and control measures—digital pass and Moscow's automated recognition system—are based on Moscow's electronic government framework embodied in a Moscow Smart City project that has been put into practice over the last decade (Orlova & Shcherbovich, 2020).

4.5.6 Is There a Specific Body in Charge of Overseeing, Coordinating, or Promoting the Digitalization of the Sector?

Ministry of Digital Development Communication and Mass Media, Federal Security Service, Office of the Prosecutor General of the Russian Federation.

4.5.7 Is There a Specific Personal Data Protection Regime Regulating the Processing of Personal Data Performed by Entities Responsible for Public Security?

Yes, the Federal Law of July 27, 2006 No. 152-FZ "On Personal Data" regulates relations related to the processing of personal data carried out by federal state authorities, state authorities of the constituent entities of the Russian Federation, other state bodies, local self-government bodies, municipal bodies that are not part of the system of local self-government bodies, legal entities, individuals using automation tools or without using such tools, if the processing of personal data without using such tools corresponds to the nature of the actions (operations) performed with personal data using automation tools.

The State Duma will consider amendments regarding the processing and transfer of personal data of Russians. The explanatory note to the bill states that it is aimed at combating the identification of military personnel and law enforcement officers.

Amendments to the law "On Personal Data" change the procedure for cross-border transfer of personal data. The ability to transmit information in this way will now depend on the territory of which foreign state the recipient is located. "A cross-border transfer of personal data can be considered any process in which data is transferred from Russia to a foreign recipient, including from server to server."

If adopted, the amendment will primarily hit Russian companies that use cloud products of IT companies from the United States: "They will use servers located on the territory of the Russian Federation more, as well as products of IT companies from Russia and countries that provide adequate protection of personal data" (Samokhina, 2022).

4.6 *Tax Administration*

4.6.1 Is There a Strategy to Digitalize This Sector or Any Areas of It?

The Concept of Development and Functioning in the Russian Federation determines the main directions for the development and functioning of the tax monitoring system in the Russian Federation. This Concept is aimed at improving the quality and efficiency of tax control based on high-tech solutions, simplifying and facilitating the interaction between tax authorities and organizations that are taxpayers, payers of fees, payers of insurance premiums and (or) tax agents, increasing the transparency of the payers.

4.6.2 Is the Use of Specific Technologies for Tax Administration Promoted or Prioritized (E.g., AI, Blockchain, Open-Source Software)?

(a) a combination of a decentralized and centralized approach to processing payer data, including taking into account the standards for processing big data arrays, the development of which is provided for under the national program "Digital Economy of the Russian Federation."

The centralization of the processing of payers' data should be carried out at the level of information flows that affect the completeness, reliability, and immutability of the processed data.

Decentralized processing of payers' data, including information on transactions (transactions), primary documents confirming transactions, and other facts of economic life stored in the information systems of the payers, should be carried out in the information systems of the payers;

(b) expanded information interaction based on the organization of access of tax authorities to information systems of payers in real time.

When organizing extended information interaction, restrictions should be taken into account, including those established by the Tax Code of the Russian Federation, namely, the Law of the Russian Federation "On State Secrets," the Federal Law "On Commercial Secrets," the Federal Law "On Information, Information Technologies and Information Protection," and the Federal Law "On Personal Data."

(c) tax declarations, calculations, reports, registers of documents and other documents (information) must be generated in the information systems of payers and must be submitted to the tax authorities via telecommunication channels through an electronic document management operator using cryptographic information protection (Decree of the Government of the Russian Federation No. 381-r of February 21, 2020).

4.6.3 Is There a Sectoral Regulation in Place (E.g., Law, Decree, Standards) to Organize the Digitalization of the Sector?

Digitalization of tax administration and integration of all sources of information into a single information space in the Main Directions of the Budgetary, Tax and Customs Tariff Policy for 2020 and for the planning period of 2021 and 2022 is defined as a measure aimed at eliminating unfair competitive advantages of the shadow sector and income growth budgets of the budget system (Ministry of Finance of Russia, n.d.).

4.6.4 Are There Any Policies Promoting Digital Sovereignty in Tax Administration (E.g., Data Localization, Preference or Obligation to Utilize Domestic Providers, Etc.)?

From January 1, 2025, government authorities and customers are prohibited from using foreign software on their significant critical information infrastructure facilities (Decree of the President of the Russian Federation No. 166 of March 30, 2022).

4.6.5 Has the Digitization of the Sector or Any Area of It Been Promoted Because of the COVID-19 Pandemic? If So, then How?

Situational centers for operational interaction with business, monitoring the state of the economy and budget revenues have been created. Over the entire period of the pandemic, they processed more than 20,000 applications, which helped the government develop the necessary solutions to support taxpayers. Debt centers that specifically target taxpayers help regulate the provision of installment and arrears payments. Since April 2019, such organizations have been operating in nine regions: Vologda, Volgograd, Kaliningrad, Murmansk, Saratov, Ulyanovsk regions, Bashkortostan, the Udmurt Republic, and Primorsky Krai. According to the head of the Federal Tax Service, Daniil Yegorov, such centers will appear after October 1, 2020 in nine more constituent entities of the Russian Federation. The number of complaints related to tax disputes handled by the agency fell by 17.2% during the pandemic. At the same time, a system was launched to collect information daily on any applications related to the provision of state support measures. This information was used to solve problems for changing certain parameters and rules for conducting online support activities. In the future, this experience will be used in solving the problem of the pre-trial block—the development of feedback on the source of the dispute. During a meeting with the President of the Russian Federation, the head of the Federal Tax Service, Daniil Egorov, also spoke about the development of a unified state register of civil status records (EGRP). More than 77 million records of all types registered in 2006–2018 were withdrawn from regional systems. This figure is 99.94% of the planned number of conversions set by the Russian Ministry of Justice (Salkina & Semenova, 2020).

4.6.6 Is There a Specific Body in Charge of Overseeing, Coordinating, or Promoting the Digitalization of the Sector?

Ministry of Finance of Russia, Federal Tax Service.

References

ABC of Law. (2022). *Is it possible to get an electronic passport of a citizen of the Russian Federation?*.

Bank of Russia. (2020). *A Digital Ruble: Consultation paper*. http://cbr.ru/StaticHtml/File/113008/Consultation_Paper_201013_eng.pdf

Decree of the Government of the Russian Federation No. 1646 of October 10, 2020 (as amended on February 17, 2022). (2020) “On measures to ensure the effectiveness of measures for the use of information and communication technologies in the activities of federal executive authorities and management bodies of state extra-budgetary funds [together with the ‘Regulation on departmental digital transformation programs’].”

Decree of the Government of the Russian Federation No. 1699-r of September 19, 2013 (as amended on May 22, 2018). On approval of the Concept for the introduction in the Russian Federation of an identity card of a citizen of the Russian Federation, issued in the form of a plastic card with an electronic storage medium, and an action plan for the implementation of the Concept (together with the “Concept for the introduction in the Russian Federation of an identity card of a citizen of the Russian Federation, issued in the form of a plastic card with an electronic storage medium, as the main document proving the identity of a citizen of the Russian Federation on the territory of the Russian Federation”) (2013).

Decree of the Government of the Russian Federation No. 2129-r of August 19, 2020. On approval of the Concept for the development of regulation of relations in the field of artificial intelligence technologies and robotics until 2024. (2020).
Decree of the Government of the Russian Federation No. 381-r of February 21, 2020. On approval of the Concept for the development and functioning of the tax monitoring system in the Russian Federation. (2020).
Decree of the Government of the Russian Federation No. 770 of July 1, 1996 (as amended on July 15, 2002). On Approval of the Regulation on Licensing the Activities of Individuals and Legal Entities Not Authorized to Carry Out Operative-Search Activities Related to the Development, Production, Sale, Acquisition for the Purpose of Sale, import into the Russian Federation and export outside of it of special technical means intended (designed, adapted, programmed) for secretly obtaining information, and the List of types of special technical means intended (designed, adapted, programmed) for secretly obtaining information in the process of implementing Operative Investigative Activities. (1996).
Decree of the President of the Russian Federation No. 166 of March 30, 2022. On measures to study the technological independence and security of critical information of confidential information of the Russian Federation. (2022).
Decree of the President of the Russian Federation No. 204 of May 7, 2018 (as amended on July 21, 2020). "On the national goals and strategic objectives of the development of the Russian Federation for the period up to 2024". (2018).
Decree of the President of the Russian Federation No. 601 of May 7, 2012. On the main directions for improving the system of public administration. (2012).
Draft Decree of the President of the Russian Federation as of March 19, 2021 (project ID 14.04.03-21.00114294). On the passport of a citizen of the Russian Federation containing an electronic information carrier (prepared by the Russian Ministry of Digital Development). (2021).
Federal Law No. 144-FZ of August 12, 1995 (as amended on April 1, 2022). On Operative Investigative Activities. (1995).
Federal Law No. 184-FZ of December 27, 2002 (as amended on July 2, 2021). On Technical Regulation (as amended and supplemented, effective from December 23, 2021). (2002).
Federal Law No. 218-FZ of July 13, 2015 (as amended on May 1, 2022). On State Registration of Real Estate. (2015).
Federal Law No. 223-FZ of July 18, 2011 (as amended on April 16, 2022). On Procurement of Goods, Works, Services by Certain Types of Legal Entities. (2011).
Federal Law No. 242-FZ of July 29, 2017. On Amendments to Certain Legislative Acts of the Russian Federation on the Application of Information Technologies in the Sphere of Health Care. (2017).
Federal Law No. 259-FZ of July 31, 2020. On Digital Financial Assets, Digital Currency and Amendments to Certain Legislative Acts of the Russian Federation. (2020).
Federal Law No. 41-FZ of April 5, 2013 (as amended on April 30, 2021). On the Accounts Chamber of the Russian Federation. (2013).
Gaufman, E. (2021). Cybercrime and punishment: Security, information war, and the future of runet. In D. Gritsenko, M. Wijermars, & M. Kopotev (Eds.), *The Palgrave handbook of digital Russia studies* (pp. 115–134). https://doi.org/10.1007/978-3-030-42855-6
Government of the Russian Federation. (n.d.-a). Maksut Shadayev, Minister of Digital Development, Communications and Mass Media of the Russian Federation. Retrieved on May 12, 2022 from http://government.ru/en/gov/persons/627/events/
Government of the Russian Federation. (n.d.-b). *National Program "Digital Economy of the Russian Federation*." Retrieved on May 12, 2022 from http://government.ru/rugovclassifier/614/events/
Gritsenko, D., & Zherebtsov, M. (2021). E-Government in Russia: Plans, reality, and future outlook. In D. Gritsenko, M. Wijermars, & M. Kopotev (Eds.), *The Palgrave handbook of digital Russia studies* (pp. 33–51). https://doi.org/10.1007/978-3-030-42855-6
IMD World Competitiveness Center. (2022). *The IMD World Digital Competitiveness Ranking*. Retrieved on May 12, 2022 from https://www.imd.org/centers/world-competitiveness-center/rankings/world-digital-competitiveness/

Ministry of Construction of Russia. (2019). *Smart City Standard "Basic and additional requirements for smart cities."*

Ministry of Digital Development, Communications and Mass Communications of the Russian Federation. (2021, August 2). *Maxim Parshin: "Open Source will be one of the themes of the International Collegiate Programming Contest (ICPC) Championship finals."* https://digital.gov.ru/ru/events/41202/

Ministry of Digital Development, Communications and Mass Media of the Russian Federation. (2018, September 6). *Digital passports*. Retrieved on May 12, 2022 from https://digital.gov.ru/ru/activity/directions/52/

Ministry of Finance of Russia. (n.d.). *The main directions of the budget, tax and customs tariff policy for 2020 and for the planning period of 2021 and 2022.*

Moscow City Hall. (n.d.). *Merging Reality and VR: How Does a Smart City Work?*. Retrieved on May 12, 2022 from https://www.mos.ru/en/city/projects/smartcity/

National Standard of the Russian Federation GOST R 55062-2021. Information technologies, Interoperability, Basic provisions (approved and put into effect by the Order of Rosstandart No. 1296-st of October 25, 2021).

Ng, A. (2021, June 1). Digital currencies are the future for Russia's financial system, central bank governor says. CNBC. Retrieved on May 12, 2022 from https://www.cnbc.com/2021/06/02/digital-currencies-are-the-future-for-russia-central-bank-chief-says.html

Open Knowledge Foundation. (2016). *Global Open Data Index – Russia*. Retrieved on May 12, 2022 from https://index.okfn.org/place/ru.html

Orlova, A. & Shcherbovich, A. (2020). Russia during COVID-19: Information warfare, digital passes and digital protest. In Belli, L., Pahwa, N., & Manzar, O. (Eds.). *The value of internet openness in times of crisis: Official outcome of the UN IGF Coalitions on Net Neutrality and on Community Connectivity* (pp. 81–88). https://bibliotecadigital.fgv.br/dspace/handle/10438/29865

Russiafell13placesintheDigitalSocietyIndex.(2019,April18).TSSOnline.RetrievedonMay12,2022 from https://www.tssonline.ru/news/rossiya-upala-na-13-mest-v-ratinge-digital-society-index

Salkina, A., & Semenova, A. (2020). The impact of COVID-19 on the tax system of Russia. *International Journal of Humanities and Natural Sciences, 12-2*(51).

Samokhina, S. (2022, April 7). From food to real estate one step. How, after the scandal with Yandex, the State Duma rules the law on personal data. *BBC News*. https://www.bbc.com/russian/features-61015440?ocid=wsrussian.social.in-app-messaging.telegram..russiantelegram_.edit

State Communications Committee of Russia. (1999). *General technical requirements for the system of technical means to ensure the functions of operational-search activities on the networks (services) of documentary telecommunications* (approved by Order No. 47 of March 27, 1999).

The Ministry of Digital Development proposes to introduce electronic passports in the regions no later than July 1, 2023. (2021, March 22). D-Russia. Retrieved on May 12, 2022 from https://d-russia.ru/mincifry-predlagaet-vvesti-jelektronnye-pasporta-v-regionah-ne-pozdnee-1-ijulja-2023-goda.html

The State Duma adopted in the first reading a law obliging state bodies to maintain public pages in social networks. (2022, May 18). 27 Region. Retrieved on May 12, 2022 from https://27r.ru/news/russia/95667-gosduma-prinyala-v-i-chtenii-zakon-obyazyvayushchij-gosorgany-vesti-pabliki-v-sotssetyakh

The World Bank. (2016). *Digital Adoption Index*. Retrieved on May 12, 2022 from https://www.worldbank.org/en/publication/wdr2016/Digital-Adoption-Index

Transport Ticketing Global. (2020). *Best Smart Ticketing Programme 2020*. https://www.transport-ticketing.com/2020-awards-winners

Wijermars, M. (2021). The digitalization of Russian politics and political participation. In Gritsenko, D., Wijermars, M., & Kopotev, M. (Eds.). *The Palgrave handbook of digital Russia studies* (pp. 15–32). doi:https://doi.org/10.1007/978-3-030-42855-6.

Andrey A. Schcherbovich is an Associate Professor at the National Research University Higher School of Economics, Faculty of Law (Department of Constitutional and Municipal Law), in Moscow, Russia. His professional interests include Internet Governance, Constitutional Law, Human Rights, International Public Law and Procedure, Information Law, International Organizations, and the United Nations. Andrey graduated from the National Research University Higher School of Economics, Faculty of Law (Department of International Law) in 2008 and completed Postgraduate studies at the National Research University—Higher School of Economics (Moscow, Russia); Faculty of Law (Department of Constitutional and Municipal Law) in 2011.

Anna Orlova holds a degree in Psychology from the University of Saint Petersburg and a Master's in Psychology and Sociology. Her research has been at the intersection of academic research and volunteering in various digital activism and advocacy projects, focusing on community connectivity. Anna joined CyberBRICS as a graduate research fellow.

Understanding State-Level Variations in India's Digital Transformation

Smriti Parsheera

Abstract India's digital transformation is often described in terms of the country's vast Internet penetration, growing mobile connectivity, and widespread uptake of digital payments and other online services. Undoubtedly, India has made tremendous progress on all these fronts over the last few years. But digitalisation narratives founded upon aggregate national statistics bear the risk of assuming a homogeneity of digital access and experience in the country. This article highlights some of the state-level differences in digital access, skills, and infrastructure across India—as a basis for dispelling assumptions about the homogeneity and universality of India's digital transformation. The article draws attention to the varying levels of digital readiness within India, and to the need to account for these variations in the design and implementation of the country's digital initiatives.

1 Introduction

The Constitution of India describes the country, in Article 1, as "a Union of States" (Republic of India, 1950). The country is divided into 28 states and eight union territories, with the responsibility to administer different functional areas in these territories divided between the central and state governments. At the central level, India's digital transformation strategy is built on the foundational blocks of strengthening access, the adoption of e-governance initiatives, and the empowerment of citizens. These key objectives are articulated in the government's Digital India programme, which has been in operation since 2015 (Government of India, n.d.-a). Digital India brings together a number of different schemes and initiatives that include projects with a pan-Indian application, as well as those developed or implemented at the level of state governments.

The success of the Digital India programme is often reported in terms of statistics about the country's growing Internet access, mobile penetration, adoption of

S. Parsheera (✉)
School of Public Policy, Indian Institute of Technology Delhi, New Delhi, India

L. Belli, L. Galdino de Magalhães Santos (eds.), *SmartBRICS*,
https://doi.org/10.1007/978-3-031-98204-0_8

digital services, and booming start-up culture (Kaka et al., 2019; Prasad, 2022). India has indeed seen tremendous developments on all these fronts. Yet a study of the country's digital trajectory is incomplete without the inclusion of a more localised understanding of how the digital story is playing out in the country's different states (Singh et al., 2013).

Accordingly, this article focuses on the differences in digital adoption and implementation across India's states, and how those differences may contribute to differentiated outcomes for citizens. Based on a review of the available data and literature, this article notes that, in addition to administrative variations, digitisation outcomes are also influenced by factors like the country's rural-urban divide, varying levels of digital literacy and skills, and other socio-economic considerations. All of these play a role in determining how a diverse spectrum of user groups across the country experience, in varying ways, India's digital transformation.

2 A "Mobile First" Approach to Digital Transformation

Being the second most populous country in the world, it is unsurprising that many of India's digital achievements are highlighted in terms of the size of its user base. According to official estimates, India currently has more than 1.15 billion mobile connections and almost 830 million Internet subscribers (TRAI, 2022). These developments have spurred a "mobile first" strategy that can be seen in the design of services offered by the government, as well as in private offerings. For instance, the government's UMANG (Unified Mobile Application for New-age Governance) app emphasises a "mobile first" approach while seeking to bring together all e-governance initiatives on its platform (MeitY, n.d.). The Jan Dhan-Aadhaar-Mobile (JAM) scheme offers another important example. JAM focuses on leveraging India's mobile phone strength (Press Trust of India, 2022) and enrolments in its digital identity programme, Aadhaar (UIDAI, 2022), to push for the adoption of banking services in the country (PM India, n.d.), on the assumption that most individuals already have a mobile phone and digital identity, thus paving the way for the adoption of other digitally enabled services.

The central government's Direct Benefit Transfer (DBT) scheme is an example of such a service. Under the DBT scheme, disbursements of various welfare benefits are made directly to the bank accounts of individuals, with Aadhaar being the "preferred" mode of authentication (Government of India, n.d.-b). In August 2021, the government also introduced a new digital payment solution called e-RUPI, which is a pre-paid digital voucher that can be received by a beneficiary on their phone as an SMS or QR code. It is meant to be used only for certain designated purposes, such as an e-RUPI transfer by the Health Ministry to avail health services at designated hospitals that have agreed to redeem the e-RUPI vouchers. The government's long-term plan is to connect e-RUPI with several other disbursements under the DBT scheme (Ministry of Finance, 2021), meaning that the mobile phone will play an even more central role in an individual's ability to access their welfare entitlements.

The assumption about near-ubiquitous mobile adoption in the country is also visible in the widespread use of one-time passwords (OTPs), received via SMS, for accessing various products and services. In some cases, this electronic means of verification coexists with offline alternatives. For instance, the Income Tax Department currently allows individuals to verify their tax filings through various electronic means, including an Aadhaar-based OTP, as well as by using traditional postal services. But an offline option is not always provided. When the government launched its CoWin portal to manage the administration of COVID-19 vaccinations, all users needed to complete an OTP check to log onto the system. Access to vaccination bookings was, therefore, predicated on a user having either their own mobile phone or the ability to seek assistance from others who had a phone and were willing to help. The rush for limited vaccination slots in the early days of the vaccination rollout made it clear that the digital-only strategy inevitably favoured mobile-savvy citizens over others (Santuka, 2021).

The assumption about ubiquitous access has, therefore, been challenged in the light of available evidence on the inequities that exist in India's digital ecosystem. The country's digital divide has most notably been demonstrated with respect to both gender (Barboni et al., 2018) and the rural-urban divide (Pandey, 2020; Singh et al., 2013). The latest Mobile Gender Gap Report by GSMA found a 14% gap between Indian men and women for mobile ownership and a 41% gap for mobile Internet usage (GSMA, 2022). With respect to the rural-urban divide, 2021 data released by the Telecom Regulatory Authority of India (TRAI) showed rural and urban Internet densities (subscriptions per 100 people in the population) standing, respectively, at 37% and 104% (TRAI, 2022). This gap is significant in itself, given that the majority of India's population (approximately 65%) resides in its rural areas (World Bank, n.d.). The differences become all the starker when the data is disaggregated at the level of different states.

3 Understanding State-Level Variations

For the purposes of telecommunications licensing, India is divided into 22 service areas. This demarcation broadly corresponds to the boundaries of India's states, subject to some variations. For instance, states such as Madhya Pradesh, Andhra Pradesh, and Bihar, which have each been bifurcated into two separate states, continue to exist as one service area. Further, a service area may consist of multiple smaller states, as seen in the case of the North Eastern service area, which includes six states from that region (Arunachal Pradesh, Manipur, Meghalaya, Mizoram, Nagaland, and Tripura).

The data points to significant variations in the state of access across different parts of the country. According to TRAI's reports, Internet access density—the number of Internet subscribers per 100 people—ranges widely, from the highest figure of 186% in Delhi to the lowest figure of 36% in the Bihar service area (TRAI, 2022). Further, except for one service area (Kerala, which has a rural Internet density of 149 per 100 people and an urban Internet density of 64 per 100 people), the figures for rural Internet density are lower than for urban density in all service areas.

Intra-service area variations can also be seen in cases where two or more states are part of the same service area. The service area of Bihar, which, as noted above, has the poorest Internet density in the country, consists of two states—Bihar and Jharkhand—that have widely different Internet densities, of 43% and 10% respectively. Similarly, Chhattisgarh, which forms part of the Madhya Pradesh service area, performs significantly worse than its counterpart state, Madhya Pradesh, in the same service area. Chhattisgarh has the country's lowest Internet density, at 7%, while Internet density in Madhya Pradesh stands at 63% (TRAI, 2022). Finally, data released by the government in 2021, about villages that remain outside the grid of mobile connectivity, found that there were 25,000 unconnected villages, and the majority of these villages were concentrated in the states of Odisha, Madhya Pradesh, and Maharashtra (Srivastava, 2021).

Another general trend that emerges is that the regions that fare worst in terms of inclusiveness in Internet access also perform relatively poorly on other human development indicators (Bhardwaj, 2021; Parsheera, 2019b). A more granular subdivision, down to the levels of districts, blocks, and villages—which are smaller units of administration within a state—can be expected to reflect a similar trend. TRAI's data on Internet subscriptions does not go down to the level of these units, but other sources offer relevant indications. Intra-state variations have, for instance, been observed in the rollout of the government's BharatNet project, which seeks to provide broadband connectivity to most of India's villages. In the state of Himachal Pradesh, all the Gram Panchayats (village-level units) selected for coverage in the first phase of the project were situated "in the relatively better-off districts of Hamirpur, Mandi and Solan" (Parsheera, 2019a)—thus excluding large portions of the state's tribal groups, which are concentrated in the districts of Lahaul-Spiti, Kinnaur, and Chamba.

In addition, the network experience of users in less developed regions has been found to be poorer, compared to service areas with a higher revenue-earning potential. India's North Eastern Region, which has historically been among the country's most neglected and underdeveloped areas (Gokhale, 2022; Barua, 2011), offers an example. According to an analysis by Open Signal, the average data download and upload speeds in the North Eastern Region were, respectively, 23.4% and 43.3% lower than the national average (Khatri, 2022). The neighbouring state of Assam, which also lies in India's North Eastern Region (although it is a separate telecommunications service area), displayed similar results. This may partially be explained by the unwillingness on the part of telecommunication providers to invest in infrastructure in remote and inaccessible areas with comparatively low revenue potential. In addition to commercial considerations, state-level policies (as discussed in the next section) also influence the quality of digital access available to their residents.

It has also been found that the ability of different user groups to benefit from e-governance solutions is highly dependent on their level of digital skills. In this context, researchers have found that only 38% of households in India are digitally literate—61% in urban areas and 25% in rural areas (Mothkoor & Mumtaz, 2021). (A household is regarded as digitally literate if at least one person can operate a computer and use the Internet.) In certain regions—such as Uttar Pradesh, Madhya Pradesh, Chhattisgarh, Bihar, and parts of Jammu and Kashmir—the rural digital literacy rates are less than 20%. In contrast, states such as Goa and Kerala have achieved more than 70% digital literacy in both rural and urban areas. The researchers attribute this to specific digital literacy initiatives undertaken by those states, such as a computer literacy programme in Kerala and a memorandum of understanding to promote digital literacy entered into by the state of Goa with Google (Mothkoor & Mumtaz, 2021).

4 Right-of-Way Policies

Ensuring "broadband for all" is contingent upon the establishment of the necessary infrastructure in the form of optical fibre, copper cables, telecommunication towers, and other apparatus required for the operation of networks. The establishment of such infrastructure requires permissions for the use of public land and public rights-of-way. In terms of India's constitutional dispensation, the legislative responsibilities are divided between the central government and the states, with some sectors driven by the former and others by the latter. The power to make laws relating to posts, telegraphs, and communications is vested in the central government (Entry 31, List 1, Seventh Schedule, Constitution of India, 1950). But responsibility for land use policy, law, and regulation, which have an important bearing on the setting up of telecommunications infrastructure, falls under the domain of state governments (Entry 18, List 2, Seventh Schedule, Constitution of India, 1950). This allows the states to determine the policies, costs, and timelines for land-related permissions for laying down telecommunications infrastructure.

The inconsistent implementation of right-of-way policies in India has been found to delay the expansion of India's telecommunications infrastructure (GSMA, 2020; Marwah, 2019). This has been a problem not only for private operators but also for the roll-out of the government's own BharatNet project, which, as noted above, aims to achieve universal broadband access (TRAI, 2016). In addition to permissions from state governments (and local authorities within them), right-of-way permissions are sometimes also required from central government bodies like the National Highway Authority of India and the Indian Railways (TRAI, 2016). As a result, the requirement of authorisations from multiple authorities often results in extensive delays and exorbitant fees.

In some cases, government functionaries have observed a direct correlation between low broadband penetration and non-alignment of right-of-way rules by the state governments (Aulakh, 2021). Right-of-way challenges also contribute to the low rate of fiberisation of telecommunications towers in the country, i.e., the low proportion of towers that are connected to a fibre-based backhaul. At present, only about 30% of India's towers (and fewer than 7% of households) are connected to fibre (Surya, 2021). The rates of fiberisation are lowest in mountainous states such as Himachal Pradesh, and in remote parts of the North Eastern Region (The Economic Times, 2022).

In a bid to streamline these processes, the central government issued the Indian Telegraph Right of Way Rules in 2016, providing for the expedited processing of applications for setting up underground and above-ground infrastructure (Government of India, 2016). The rules provide for mechanisms such as a single window clearance system (option of a single electronic application process for facilitating approvals by all authorities within a state), fixed timelines for processing, and a cap on the fees for administrative expenses. However, the implementation of the rules remains under the domain of the state governments, and the practices that have evolved have not been consistent or sufficiently effective (Dua, 2020; Standing Committee on Communications and Information Technology, 2021). Through the Draft Indian Telecommunication Bill, 2022, the central government proposed legislative changes to streamline the right-of-way permissions involving both public and private properties (Department of Telecommunications, 2022). This was brought into effect through the Telecommunications Act, 2023.

In another attempt to address the right-of-way backlogs, the government recently launched the GatiShakti Sanchar Portal, which is described as a "collaborative institutional mechanism between all stakeholders" to act as a single interface for right-of-way approvals (Department of Telecommunications, n.d.). If successful, this initiative can play an important role in the delivery of the BharatNet project and in the forthcoming roll-out of 5G services, which require fiberisation levels far beyond the country's current levels.

5 Conclusion

India is characterised by great diversity in the living conditions of its population—a diversity that is also reflected in variations in digital access, digital skills, and digital outcomes. The importance of addressing these differences risks being obscured in digitisation initiatives founded upon aggregate national statistics that paint a picture of robust mobile penetration and Internet access. This article has sought to highlight some of the state-level differences present in respect of digital access, skills, and infrastructure across India—as a basis to dispel assumptions about the homogeneity and growing universality of the country's digital transformation.

However, the article's objective is not to make a case against the pursuit of digital transformation on these grounds. Rather, the aim is to highlight the realities of India's federal structure and the varying levels of digital readiness that need to be accounted for in the design and implementation of the country's growing number of digital initiatives.

References

Aulakh, G. (2021, December 16). DoT Secy asks field units to expedite RoW permissions for fast broadband rollout. *The Live Mint*. https://www.livemint.com/industry/telecom/dot-secy-asks-field-units-to-expedite-row-permissions-for-fast-broadband-rollout-11639651989591.html.

Barboni, G., Field, E., Pande, R., Rigol, N., Schaner S., & Troyer Moore, C. (2018). A tough call: Understanding barriers to and impacts of women's mobile phone adoption in India. Harvard Kennedy School. https://epod.cid.harvard.edu/sites/default/files/2018-10/A_Tough_Call.pdf.

Barua, S. (2011, December 13). Why northeast is lagging behind the rest of India? *The Shillong Times*. https://theshillongtimes.com/2011/12/13/why northeast-is-lagging-behind-the-rest-of-india.

Bhardwaj, A. (2021). HDI: How states fare in human development. Center for Economic Data and Analysis (CEDA), Ashoka University. https://ceda.ashoka.edu.in/hdi-How-states-fare-in-human-development.

Department of Telecommunications. (n.d.). About us. https://sugamsanchar.gov.in/about-us.

Department of Telecommunications. (2022) Indian Telecommunication Bill, 2022. https://dot.gov.in/relatedlinks/indian-telecommunication-bill-2022.

Dua, T. R. (2020). Right of way (RoW) for digital communications infrastructure. Presentation on behalf of Tower and Infrastructure Providers Association. BRI Workshop with East and Northeast Region States. https://icrier.org/pdf/2-March-2020/TAIPA.pdf.

Gokhale, N. A. (2022, February 3). The neglected states of the nation. Outlook. https://www.outlookindia.com/website/story/the-neglected-states-of-the-nation/220206.

Government of India. (2016). The Indian Telegraph Right of Way Rules, 2016. https://dot.gov.in/sites/default/files/Consolidated%20Indian%20Telegraph%20Right%20of%20Wa-1_1.pdf?download=1.

Government of India. (n.d.-a). Digital India. https://www.digitalindia.gov.in.

Government of India. (n.d.-b). Direct Benefit Transfer (DBT): About us. https://dbtbharat.gov.in/page/frontcontentview/?id=MTc.

GSMA. (2020). Rights of way (RoW) in India: A submission from the GSMA relating to India mobile sector. https://dipa.co.in/reports/GSMA%20Paper%20on%20RoW%20Sep%272020.pdf.

GSMA. (2022). The mobile gender gap report 2022. https://www.gsma.com/r/wp-content/uploads/2022/06/The-Mobile-Gender-Gap-Report-2022.pdf.

Kaka, N., Madgavkar, A., Kshirsagar, A., Gupta R., Manyika J., Bahl K., & Gupta, S. (2019). Digital India: Technology to transform a connected nation. McKinsey Global Institute. https://www.mckinsey.com/capabilities/mckinsey-digital/our-insights/digital-India-technology-to-transform-a-connected-nation.

Khatri, H. (2022, July 21). Analyzing the mobile network experience in India's telecom circles. Opensignal. https://www.opensignal.com/2022/07/21/analyzing-the-mobile-network-experience-in-indias-telecom-circles.

Marwah, A. M. (2019, July). RoW Roadblocks: Exploring solutions to expedite fibre roll-out. Tele.net. https://tele.net.in/row-roadblocks.

Ministry of Electronics and Information Technology (MeitY). (n.d.). UMANG: About this app.https://play.google.com/store/apps/details?id=in.gov.umang.negd.g2c&hl=en_IN&gl=US.

Ministry of Finance. 2021, August 6). Know all about e-RUPI, the new digital payment instrument. Press Information Bureau Mumbai. https://pib.gov.in/PressReleasePage.aspx?PRID=1743056.

Mothkoor, V., & Mumtaz, F. (2021, March 23). The digital dream: Upskilling India for the future. Ideas for India. https://www.ideasforindia.in/topics/governance/the-digital-Dream-upskilling-india-for-the-future.html.

Pandey, K. (2020, July 30). COVID-19 lockdown highlights India's great digital divide. Down to Earth https://www.downtoearth.org.in/news/governance/covid-19-lockdown-highlights-india-s-great-digital-divide-72514.

Parsheera, S. (2019a, July 5). Go to Lahaul-Spiti for "internet ka vanvaas." Digital India & telecom companies skipped it. The Print. https://theprint.in/opinion/go-to-lahaul-spiti-for-internet-ka-vanvaas-digital-india-telecom-companies-skipped-it/258707
Parsheera, S. (2019b, October 17). India's on a digital sprint that is leaving millions behind. BBC World. https://www.bbc.com/news/world-asia-india-49085846.
PM India. (n.d.). Leveraging the power of JAM: Jan Dhan, Aadhar and Mobile. https://www.pmindia.gov.in/en/government_tr_rec/leveraging-the-power-of-jam-jan-dhan-aadhar-and-mobile.
Prasad, R. S. (2022, June 2). The Digital India transformation. The Indian Express. https://indianexpress.com/article/opinion/columns/digital-india-eight-years-on-narendra-modi-5g-aadhaar-7948202.
Press Trust of India. (2022, February 22). India to have 1 billion smartphone users by 2026: Deloitte. The Hindu. https://www.thehindu.com/business/india-to-have-1-billion-smartphone-users-by-2026-deloitte/article65075151.ece.
Republic of India. (1950). Constitution of India. https://legislative.gov.in/sites/default/files/COI.pdf.
Santuka, Y. (2021, June 26). The story of CoWIN: How a vaccination strategy for digital India failed to bridge the digital divide. The Bastion. https://thebastion.co.in/covid-19/the-story-of-cowin-how-a-vaccination-strategy-for-digital-india-failed-to-bridge-the-digital-divide.
Singh, N., Zhou, Y., Williams, K., Kendall, J., & Kaushik, P. D. (2013). Bridging the digital divide in rural India: Lessons from a survey in four states. *Review of Market Integration, 5*(1), 1–42. https://doi.org/10.1177/0974929213496499
Standing Committee on Communications and Information Technology. (2021). India's preparedness for 5G. Twenty-first Report. Seventeenth Lok Sabha. https://eparlib.nic.in/bitstream/123456789/799780/1/17_Information_Technology_21.pdf.
Srivastava, R. (2021, March 18). Over 25000 villages in India still lack internet connectivity, Lok Sabha told. India Today. https://www.indiatoday.in/technology/news/story/over-25000-villages-in-india-still-lack-internet-connectivity-lok-sabha-told-1780758-2021-03-18.
Surya, S. (2021, March 1). Standing committee report: India's preparedness for 5G summary. PRS Legislative Service. https://prsindia.org/policy/report-summaries/india-s-Preparedness-for-5g.
Telecom Regulatory Authority of India (TRAI). (2016, February). Recommendations on implementation strategy for BharatNet. https://www.trai.gov.in/sites/default/files/Recommendations%20on%20BharatNet%2001.02.2016%20FINAL.pdf
TRAI (2022, May 4). The Indian telecom services performance indicators: October–December, 2021. https://www.trai.gov.in/sites/default/files/QPIR_05052022.pdf.
The Economic Times. (2022, April 29). India's low fiberisation may lead to wastage of spectrum resource in 5G rollout. ET Government. https://government.economictimes.indiatimes.com/news/technology/indias-low-fiberisation-may-lead-to-wastage-of-spectrum-resource-in-5g-rollout-coai/91170918.
Unique Identification Authority of India (UIDAI). (2022). A unique identity for the people. https://uidai.gov.in/images/Aadhaar_Brochure_July_22.pdf.
World Bank. (n.d.). Rural population (% of total population)—India. https://data.worldbank.org/indicator/SP.RUR.TOTL.ZS.

Smriti Parsheera is a lawyer and independent researcher working on issues at the intersection of technology and society. Her areas of interest include privacy and data governance, internet governance, digital public infrastructure and protection of human rights in the digital sphere. This research was conducted between 2020-23 while she was a Fellow with the CyberBRICS Project at Fundação Getulio Vargas Law School, Brazil. Prior to that she has worked with organizations such as the National Institute of Public Finance & Policy, New Delhi, the Competition Commission of India and the United Nations Development Programme. Smriti graduated from the National Law School of India University, Bangalore, and obtained her LLM from the University of Pennsylvania along with a Certificate in Law and Business from the Wharton School. She is currently pursuing a PhD in public policy from the Indian Institute of Technology Delhi.

India: An Overview of the Telecoms and Internet Access Sector

Smriti Parsheera

Abstract This chapter develops an overview of the Indian situation regarding access to Internet through the following matters: number of subscribers across different categories; affordability of services; type of technology being used; gender gap; urban-rural gap; ranking in the global ICT indices; strategy for expanding the Internet access; participation in institutions; telecommunications regulations in the country; access to the spectrum for data transmission; and financial resources.

1 Context

What is the state of internet access in the country, in terms of:

(a) Number of subscribers across different categories

India has the second-largest Internet user base in the world. As per data released by the Telecom Regulatory Authority of India (TRAI), there were 718.74 million Internet subscribers at the end of 2019 (Telecom Regulatory Authority of India [TRAI], 2019b), and that figure had gone up to 836.86 million by June 2022 (TRAI, 2022). These Internet subscription figures indicate the total number of subscriptions and not the actual number of unique and active Internet users in the country. A study by the Internet and Mobile Association of India (IAMAI) and Nielsen (2019) placed this figure of active users in the range of about 504 million (IAMAI & Nielsen, 2019). Digital in India, 2019. This is about 70% of the total subscriptions reported by TRAI around that period. It is also important to note that even though there has been a significant increase in Internet subscription and usage figures in the last few years, India still sees a vast digital divide. This divide became even more evident due to the inescapable push towards digital services during the COVID-19 crisis.

In a population of 1.35 billion, an active use base of 504 million implies that only about 37% of the population is actively using the Internet. This may be due to a

S. Parsheera (✉)
School of Public Policy, Indian Institute of Technology Delhi, New Delhi, India

L. Belli, L. Galdino de Magalhães Santos (eds.), *SmartBRICS*,
https://doi.org/10.1007/978-3-031-98204-0_9

number of supply and demand-side factors. The supply side factors include affordability and availability of Internet access services and devices that can be used to connect to the Internet. On the other hand, the demand side variables include various economic, socio-cultural and demographic factors, such as income, gender, education, language, and age (Parsheera, 2019a).

The IAMAI-Nielsen study found that the highest proportion of Internet users is in the age group of 20–29 years, followed by the next age bracket of 30–39 years. Notably, Internet use among the population over 50 years of age was much lower than all the other groups, which is indicative of old age being one of the barriers to Internet access (Table 1).

The level of access also varies across different regions of the country. For the administration of telecommunications services, the country has been divided into 22 telecom service areas. While the capital region of Delhi has a very high Internet density of 198% (number of subscriptions for every hundred people in the population), there are other areas like Bihar, Jharkhand, Uttar Pradesh, Jammu & Kashmir, and Assam where the Internet density is much lower, being in the range of 35 to 45% (TRAI 2022). Further details of the rural-urban variations in the subscriber density are discussed subsequently.

Moreover, variations in Internet access are also shaped by the socioeconomic class of users. The IAMAI-Nielsen study used the New Consumer Classification System, which classifies households based on the level of education and ownership of various consumer durables, to assess the role of socio-economic factors in Internet access. They found that 57% of the Internet users belonged to categories A and B of the classification, which signified that they were the wealthier households with higher education levels. This proportion was even higher in the urban areas, where 71% of the users fell into these two segments. However, they also found that many of the new users who were coming online, particularly from small towns and rural areas, belonged to the C, D and E classifications, which indicates a broad base of the user profile.

Finally, the data shows that even among those who have Internet access, there are differences in the nature and extent of use. While 77% of urban users reported that they used the Internet every day, this was only 61% in the case of rural consumers.

Table 1 Age-wise number of active Internet users

Age group	Number of users (millions)	%
5–11 years	71	14.08
12–15 years	60.62	12.02
16–19 years	73.61	14.60
20–29 years	147.22	29.21
30–39 years	86.6	17.18
40–49 years	38.97	7.73
50+ years	25.98	5.15
Total	504	100

Source: IAMAI-Nielsen, Digital in India Report 2019 - Round 2

In fact, 13% of rural users noted that they used the Internet less than once a week. In terms of activities for which the Internet was being used, the highest number of users reported chatting and social networking, followed by entertainment, online news and email.

(b) Affordability of services

India is known to have the lowest cost of wireless Internet access in the world. As per a comparative assessment of mobile data plans from across the globe, the average price of one gigabyte (GB) of mobile data in India was US$0.09, while the global average rate was about US$5 (Cable.co.uk, 2020). Table 2 shows the comparative mobile data prices in India and other BRICS countries.

Affordability of Internet access is, however, shaped not only by the cost of the service but also by the affordability of the device that is to be used for accessing the Internet. The GSMA's Mobile gender gap report found that the highest percentage of the survey respondents from India reported handset cost to be one of the important barriers to mobile ownership and mobile Internet use (GSMA, 2022).

As per a 2019 study, the compounded annual growth rate (CAGR) of mobile phone sales volume in India between 2007 to 2018 was 6.66%. During the same period, the average selling price of phones decreased only by a CAGR of 0.11%. The study also notes that despite the gradual increase in adoption of smartphones, the Indian market remains dominated by feature phones, which constitute over 50% of the sales volume (Kathuria et al., 2019).

One of the notable developments in this segment has been the launch of Reliance Jio's smart feature phones in 2017, which support 4G services on Jio's wireless network. Reports indicate that over 100 million units of the JioPhone had been sold by 2020 (Prabhjot, 2020). Since then, Jio has launched an affordable smartphone in collaboration with Google, and the two companies have announced their plans to launch a new 5G device. However, the proliferation of such offers by dominant Internet service providers could also lead to competition concerns in the medium to long term, in addition to privacy concerns arising from the possibility of data sharing between Jio and Google.

(c) Type of technology being used

Table 2 Cost of mobile data in BRICS countries

Country	Average price/GB (Local currency)	Average price/ GB (US$)
Brazil	BRL 5.64	1.01
Russia	RUB 38.33	0.52
India	INR 6.66	0.09
China	CNY 4.30	0.61
South Africa	ZAR 101.91	7.19

Source: cable.co.uk (2020)

As in many other parts of the developing world, the Internet access market in India is propelled mainly by wireless services. About 97% of the Internet subscribers in India are connected to the Internet through wireless services (TRAI, 2022). Until around the middle of 2016, most wireless users were using low-speed narrowband Internet services. However, this has come to change in light of the large-scale adoption of 4G services in the last few years. At present, 95% of the access market consists of users of broadband services. It may be noted here that Indian regulations currently define broadband to mean download speeds of over 512 Kbps, which happens to be a lower benchmark compared to many other countries.

Figure 1 depicts how the technology-wise Internet user base in India evolved during the period from 2014 to 2018, with many users moving directly from 2G to 4G services (TRAI, 2019c). Besides the number of subscribers, the technology-wise data usage trends also point to the importance of the 4G services, which now constitute 95% of the wireless Internet consumption in the country (TRAI, 2022). This goes to show that, along with the steady decline in the number of narrowband users, their share in the country's total data consumption has also been decreasing.

In the case of wireline Internet access services, the total number of subscribers has increased from about 20 million in 2015 to 28.7 million by the middle of 2022. While the overall trend in this sector is not comparable to the scale of growth in the wireless Internet segment, one of the notable developments that can be seen from the chart below is the significant rise in the number of fibre connections (Table 3).

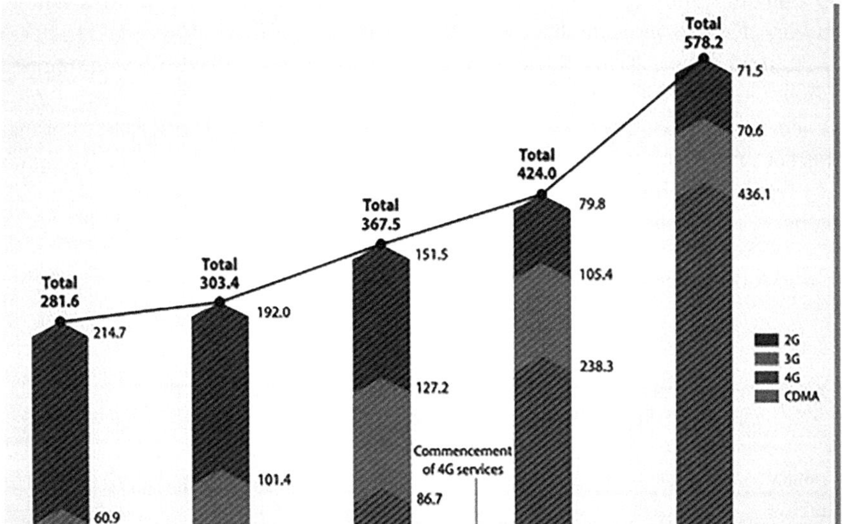

Fig. 1 Technology-wise trend in the number of wireless subscribers. Source: TRAI Wireless Data Service Report (2019)

Table 3 Technology trends in wired Internet access

Technology	Subscribers in millions (December 2015)	Subscribers in millions (June 2022)
Direct subscriber line	13.17	2.79
Ethernet/ LAN	2.18	3.58
Dial-up	3.23	0.00
Fibre	0.20	21.21
Cable modem	1.13	0.94
Leased line	0.06	0.20
Total	19.97	28.73

Source: TRAI's Performance Indicator Reports for the period ending in June 2022 and December 2015

Table 4 Mobile Internet use and ownership in India

Type	Male population (%)	Female population (%)	Gender gap (%)
Mobile owners	83	71	14
Internet users	51	30	41

Source: GSMA Mobile Gender Gap Report (2022)

(d) Gender gap

As per GSMA's Mobile Gender Gap Report (2022), the South Asian region has a mobile gender gap of 41% (GSMA, 2022). This implies that women in the region are 41% less likely to use mobile Internet compared to men. In the context of India, the report notes that although the penetration of mobile Internet use among women has been increasing, and saw a significant spike during the first 2 years of the COVID-19 pandemic, men's mobile Internet use has increased at a greater pace. The study found that while 51% of men used mobile Internet services, this figure was just 30% for women, indicating a mobile gender gap of 41% (Table 4).

Further, as shown in Table 4, there was also a gender gap of 14% in terms of mobile ownership (down from 20% in 2020). The phone ownership status of men and women also varies by type of device, with 49% of males but only 26% of females owning a smartphone. The type of device has a bearing on whether and the extent to which one can engage with the Internet.

Researchers have noted that this mobile gender gap is driven by a mix of economic factors and normative barriers arising from social norms, customs, and perceived gender roles (Barboni et al., 2018). While the Internet gender gap in India remains stark, it is encouraging to note that this gap has been narrowing over time—it has narrowed from 68% in 2017 to the current figure of 41%.

(e) Urban-rural gap

Approximately 65% of India's population lives in rural areas. However, at present, only about 40% of the total number of Internet subscribers in India come from rural areas. Further, the Internet density figures show that there are only 37.8 rural

Internet subscribers per hundred people in rural areas, as compared to 103.2 in the case of urban subscribers (TRAI, 2022). This shows that much of the adoption of Internet services has been concentrated in the urban areas. A comparison with the rural subscription figures a few years back, however, shows that there is a trend of increased adoption in rural areas, although the pace of growth in the urban segment has undeniably been much higher. For instance, at the end of 2015, India had only 112.16 million rural subscribers as opposed to the figure of 339.3 million five years later.

There are also significant inter-regional differences in the rural and urban Internet density figures. For instance, the north-eastern state of Assam has an urban density of 115% but a rural density of just 33%. A similarly wide gap is also seen in other states, including Bihar, Chhattisgarh and Rajasthan. On the other hand, there are smaller states and regions like Goa, Sikkim and Delhi that reflect a high rural as well as urban Internet density (TRAI, 2022).

What is the country's ranking in the global ICT indices, such as ITU's ICT Development Index (IDI), WEF's Network Readiness Index (NRI), A4AI's Affordability Drivers Index, and GSMA's Mobile Connectivity Index (MCI)? (Table 5).

Does the country have a strategy for the expansion of Internet access, such as a national broadband plan or similar?

The Digital India mission is a flagship programme of the Indian government. It includes a number of initiatives which have been brought under nine key pillars that include the creation of broadband highways, securing mobile connectivity for all and the creation of public Internet access (Digital India, n.d.). One of the components of the broadband highways mission is the BharatNet Project for the creation of a national optical fibre network. The project aims to provide broadband connectivity to 250,000 village Panchayats, or village-level local governance institutions. A government undertaking called Bharat Broadband Network Limited has been created to manage the rollout of the BharatNet Project. Once this infrastructure has been created, all service providers will be allowed non-discriminatory access to it to launch services in rural areas.

The implementation of the project has been much slower than anticipated. The project is now in its second phase, and as of November 2022, only 188,243 of the 250,000 village Panchayats had been declared to be service-ready (Bharat Broadband Network Limited, 2022). The reasons given by the government for the delay in the project include delays in commencement due to field surveys and pilot testing of the technology, right-of-way issues and delays being caused at the state government level in the latest phase of the project (Government of India, 2020).

The National Digital Communications Policy (NDCP) announced by the Department of Communications (DoT) in 2018 also recognises the provisioning of broadband access for all as one of its strategic objectives (Department of Telecommunications, 2018a). It articulates that the following mission is to be achieved by the year 2022—*To promote Broadband for All as a tool for*

Table 5 Ranking in global ICT indexes

Index	Rank	Observations
ITU's ICT Development Index (2017)	134 of 176	The index consists of three subcomponents. India's scores were as follows: Access sub-index—3.60 Use sub-index—1.62 Skills sub-index—4.73 The ITU has not published a revised version of the index since then, although work in this direction is reportedly in progress
Network Readiness Index (2021)	61 of 131	India received a score of 51.19 on the index. The index consists of four pillars, across which India received the following scores: Technology—48.8 Impact—55 People—50.9 Governance—50.9 This index was previously released by the World Economic Forum. However, since 2019, this has been led by the Portulans Institute (PI)
A4AI's Affordability Drivers Index (2021)	10 out of 72	India received a score of 72.32 out of 100 on this index. Its scores on the communications infrastructure and access sub-indexes were as follows: Communications infrastructure—60.8 (rank 12) Access sub-index—75.5 (rank 13) Affordability index—72.3 (rank 10)
GSMA's Mobile Connectivity Index (2022)	94 of 170	India received a score of 61.3 on the index, which consists of the following sub-components: Infrastructure—59 Affordability—69 Consumer readiness—47 Content and services—74

socio-economic development, while ensuring service quality and environmental sustainability.

Some of the specific goals that have been laid down in the policy include universal broadband connectivity for all citizens at 50 Mbps, 1 Gbps connectivity to all Gram Panchayats, enabling 100 Mbps broadband on demand to all key development institutions, including all educational institutions, and deployment of public Wi-Fi Hotspots to reach 10 million people by 2022. In terms of institutional mechanisms, the NDCP speaks of the creation of a National Broadband Mission that will implement the rural connectivity and public Wi-Fi initiatives, as well as a Fibre First Initiative to focus on fibre to the home development in Tier I, II and III towns and rural clusters.

2 International Commitments

Is the country a member of the ITU?

India has been a member of ITU since January 1, 1869, and has been a regular member of the ITU Council since 1952. It was last re-elected to the Council in 2018 for a 4-year term from 2019 to 2022 (Press Information Bureau, 2018a). At present, there are 20 ITU members from India, which include government organisations, service providers, academic institutions and other entities. The Department of Telecommunications (DoT) is the nodal agency for coordinating with the ITU from India.

In September 2018, ITU announced the establishment of an ITU South Asia Area Office and Technology Innovation Centre in New Delhi. Besides India, this office will serve eight other countries in the region, namely, Afghanistan, Bangladesh, Bhutan, Iran, Maldives, Nepal, Pakistan, and Sri Lanka (Press Information Bureau, 2018b).

Is the country a signatory to the 1988 or 2012 version of the ITRs?

India is a signatory to the International Telecommunication Regulations (ITR) of 1988. It, however, did not sign the 2012 version of the ITRs adopted at the World Conference on International Telecommunications in Dubai (Masnick, 2012).

Does the country have a policy of following ITU recommendations and/or technical standards?

The Unified License agreement, through which the government of India authorises a telecom operator to carry out telecommunications services in the country, contains certain references to the ITU's standards. It requires that the licensee can only use such equipment or products that meet the standards specified by the DoT's Telecom Engineering Centre (TEC). Where no such mandatory standards have been laid down by TEC, the licensee can only use equipment and products that meet the relevant standards set by recognised international standardisation bodies, including the ITU (Department of Telecommunications, 2016b).

The TEC's standardisation guide sets out the process for ratifying/ adopting national standards in India based on the standards developed by the Telecommunications Standards Development Society, India (TSDSI) or international standards transposed by them. The TSDSI is an autonomous, multi-stakeholder body that is recognised by the DoT as India's National Telecom Standards Development Organisation (Department of Telecommunications, 2018c). It carries out standards development for telecom and information communication technology (ICT) products and services in India (Telecommunications Standards Development Society, India [TSDSI] 2022b). The examples of international standards listed in the guide include those published by bodies such as the Organisation for International Standardisation (ISO), International Electro-technical Commission (IEC) and the ITU.

As per a presentation made by the Executive Director of TSDSI in 2016, some examples of ITU standards-based products in India include the telephony signalling protocols, Signaling System No. 7, the integrated services digital network (ISDN), Gigabit-capable passive optical networks (GPON) and Intelligent Networks (Chauhan, 2016).

What is the composition of the country's delegations at ITU meetings, including official reunions and study groups (e.g. government only, or multistakeholder including private sector, academia and civil society representatives)?

As the technical wing of DoT, the TEC represents it in international bodies like the ITU (Telecom Engineering Centre, 2017). In addition, it is also possible for individuals from other organisations like the TSDSI, industry and academia to be a part of the delegation (Biswas, 2017). For instance, the TSDSI provides an online form through which one can solicit information for participating in ITU-T's study groups 13, 5, 17 and 20 (TSDSI, 2022a).

Further, the DoT has also constituted National Working Groups on ITU's study groups to contribute to the ITU's activities, keeping in view the interests of India's telecommunications sector (Telecom Engineering Centre, 2017). The role of these working groups is to build consensus and harmonise the interests of various stakeholders and proactively make contributions to ITU's relevant study group meetings (Telecom Engineering Centre, 2022).

Is the country a member of the WTO? If so, is the country a signatory to the General Agreement on Trade in Services?

India has been a member of the WTO since 1 January 1995. It has also been a signatory to the General Agreement on Trade in Services since it entered into force in 1995. India has listed specific requirements relating to the telecommunications sector in its Schedule of Specific Commitments. The requirements relating to this sector have been indicated in the original Schedule of Specific Commitments dated 15 April 1994 and were later updated on 11 April 1997 (GATS/SC/42, 1994; GATS/SC/42/Suppl. 3, 1997).

Is the country a signatory to any regional framework for regulation of telecommunications or a member of any regional organisation for telecommunications regulation?

The DoT is a member of the Asia-Pacific Telecommunity (APT), which was founded jointly by the United Nations Economic and Social Commission for Asia and the Pacific (UNESCAP) and the ITU. The APT has a strength of 38 Members, 4 Associate Members and 137 Affiliate Members (Asia-Pacific Telecommunity, 2022). Its activities include assisting members in the preparation of global conferences and promoting regional harmonisation of programmes and activities in the region. In 1997, the APT and ITU Regional Office for Asia and the Pacific came together to create the South Asian Telecommunication Regulators' Council, involving 9 South Asian countries (Mahmood, 2017). In the case of India, the SATRC Membership is held by the Telecommunication Regulatory Authority of India (TRAI).

3 Institutions

Does the country have a Telecommunications Regulatory Authority? If so, is it an independent body, and what are its attributes?
TRAI, which was constituted under the TRAI Act (1997), is the statutory body responsible for the regulation of telecommunication services in India. This refers to any service that involves the transmission of signs, signals, writing, etc. by wire, radio, visual or other electromagnetic means (TRAI Act, 1997, Section 2(k)). TRAI has been vested with recommendatory and regulatory functions. Its regulatory functions include monitoring compliance with the terms of telecom licenses, interconnection between service providers, monitoring quality of services and ensuring compliance with universal service obligations (TRAI Act, 1997, Section 11(a)). It has also been given the power to notify the rates at which telecommunication services can be provided. However, at present, the Authority follows a tariff forbearance policy in most segments of the market. This means the prices are left to be decided by market forces. Besides these regulatory functions, TRAI also has a statutory responsibility to make recommendations to the government on various aspects like licensing terms, introduction of new players in the market, facilitating competition, technological improvements, and efficient spectrum management (TRAI Act, 1997, Section 11(a)).

Following an amendment to the TRAI Act in 2000 and a subsequent notification issued by the government, broadcasting services were also included within TRAI's regulatory ambit. The same amendment also created an appellate tribunal called the Telecom Disputes Settlement and Appellate Tribunal (TDSAT). The TDSAT has the authority to adjudicate disputes between the government, as the licensor of telecom services, and service providers, as well as among service providers themselves.

The Indian government recently put out a new draft Indian Telecommunication Bill (2022) for public comments that proposes certain amendments to the powers of the TRAI. Specifically, the draft bill seeks to remove the requirement under the current TRAI Act requiring the government to seek the recommendations of the TRAI before issuing a new telecommunications license (Draft Indian Telecommunication Bill, 2022, Section 46).

While TRAI is organised as an autonomous statutory body, it cannot be regarded as being completely independent of the government in terms of its constitution and funding structure. TRAI consists of a Chairperson, up to two full-time members and up to two part-time members, all of whom are appointed by the Central Government (TRAI Act, 1997, Section 3). Further, the funds required for TRAI's functioning also come from the Central Government, from out of the Consolidated Fund of India (TRAI Act, 1997, Section 21). This refers to an account that consists of all revenues and receipts earned by the government. Any expenditure made by the government from this fund requires authorisation from the Parliament (Office of the Chief Controller of Accounts, n.d.). As per Section 25 of the TRAI Act, the government has the power to issue directions to TRAI on matters of policy. A similar provision is seen in the legislation applicable to most statutory regulators in India.

The head office of TRAI is located in New Delhi, in addition to which it has five regional offices in the cities of Hyderabad, Kolkata, Bengaluru, Bhopal and Jaipur. The administrative functioning of TRAI at the head office level is divided into various divisions like financial and economic analysis, consumer affairs and quality of service, networks, spectrum and licensing, technological development, and legal.

What is the allocation of regulatory responsibilities between the appropriate government department(s) and the Telecommunications Regulatory Authority?

Telecommunications services in India are regulated jointly by the DoT in the Ministry of Communications and TRAI. In addition, TRAI also regulates the broadcasting sector, which is included in the definition of telecommunications service, jointly with the Ministry of Information and Broadcasting (MIB).

TRAI's key functions were discussed in the previous response. The DoT is responsible for the granting and administration of telecom licenses, spectrum management policies, and overall enforcement of laws applicable to this sector. As per the government's allocation of business rules, some of its specific responsibilities include all policy, licensing and coordination matters relating to telecommunications; promotion of standardisation, research and development, and investments; and international cooperation in related matters (Government of India, 1961). The Wireless Planning and Coordination Wing (WPC) in the DoT is responsible for the management of spectrum and licensing activities.

The Digital Communications Commission (previously referred to as the Telecom Commission), which was created through a government order in 1989, is also an important non-statutory body in this sphere (Resolution of the Cabinet Secretariat No. 15/1/2/87 of April 11, 1989). It is responsible for formulating and implementing policies for the DoT, which are then approved by the government. The Commission is headed by the Secretary of DoT and has a set of full-time members along with several part-time members. These part-time members belong to other government departments like the Ministry of Finance and the Ministry of Electronics & Information Technology (Department of Telecommunications, 2022).

If the country follows a federal structure, is there an allocation of responsibilities relating to the telecommunications sector between the central/federal government and the states?

The Constitution of India sets out the allocation of legislative responsibilities between the Union Government and the States. As per this, the power to make laws relating to "posts and telegraphs; telephones, wireless, broadcasting and other like forms of communication" has been vested in the Central Government (The Constitution of India, 2022, Entry 31, List 1 (Union List), Seventh Schedule). However, some aspects of telecom regulation might relate to other subjects that fall in the State List or in the Concurrent List, which means that both the Union and the State Government can regulate such matters. The subject of land, which is an important area in terms of right-of-way policies for telecom infrastructure, is one such example of a subject that falls under the domain of State Governments (The Constitution of India, 2022, Entry 18, List 2 (State List), Seventh Schedule).

Is there a competition department within the Telecommunications Regulatory Authority?

TRAI does not have a separate competition division, but issues relevant to competition in the telecom sector could be taken up by different divisions. For instance, in February 2018, TRAI issued an amendment to its telecommunication tariff order to include provisions on significant market power and predatory pricing (TRAI, 2018d). It provided that any service provider that holds more than 30% market share would be barred from offering services at a price which is below the average variable cost, with a view to reducing competition in the relevant market. This order was struck down by the TDSAT for lack of transparency and based on the observation that specifying a threshold of 30% amounts to the abdication of TRAI's regulatory powers (IANS, 2019).

Through the draft Telecommunication Bill (2022), the government has proposed to give TRAI an explicit competition mandate. This refers to the proposed power to direct licensees to "abstain from predatory pricing that is harmful to the overall health of the telecommunication sector, competition, long term development and fair market mechanism" (Draft Indian Telecommunication Bill, 2022, Section 46(k)).

Does the country have a Competition Authority? If so, is it an independent body and what are its attributions?

The Competition Commission of India (CCI), which is a statutory body constituted under The Competition Act (2002), is the country's competition regulatory authority. It is responsible for investigating cases relating to anti-competitive agreements, abuse of dominance and regulating combinations that might have an appreciable adverse effect on competition. The Commission consists of a Chairperson and between two to six other members appointed by the Central Government (The Competition Act, 2002, Section 8). These selections are to be made based on the recommendations of a selection committee headed by the Chief Justice of India (The Competition Act, 2002, Section 9). CCI's work is supported by a separate investigative wing called the Office of the Director General.

In addition to its regulatory functions, CCI also has an advocacy mandate, which includes providing advice to the government in response to a request seeking inputs on the competition implications of policy actions and creating awareness regarding competition issues (The Competition Act, 2002, Section 49). In exercise of its functions under this provision, CCI has issued guidelines for the competition assessment of economic legislation and policies. As a part of this exercise, CCI is reported to have commissioned a market study on the telecom sector, which will cover issues like the adoption of new technologies, concentration levels and vertical integration ("Competition Commission Initiates", 2020).

Does the country have a Data Protection Authority? If so, is it an independent body and what are its attributes? If not, which body of the government takes care of personal data-related issues?

At present, India does not have a data protection authority. A proposal to create such a body was first brought to the table under the draft Personal Data Protection (PDP) Bill (2019) that was introduced in the Parliament in December 2019 (PDP Bill,

2019). The proposed Data Protection Authority of India under the 2019 PDP Bill was to consist of a Chairperson and not more than six full-time members, to be appointed by the Central Government (PDP Bill, 2019, Section 42). The proposed functions of this agency included laying down regulations, protecting the interests of individuals in respect of their personal data and preventing its misuse, ensuring compliance with the provisions of the law, and promoting data protection awareness (PDP Bill, 2019, Section 49). However, in August 2022, the government decided to withdraw the PDP Bill (2019) and replaced it with the draft Digital Personal Data Protection Bill (2022) (DPD Bill).

The DPD Bill replaced the idea of a Data Protection Authority with that of a Data Protection Board of India. This Board woud be entrusted with a much narrower scope of functions, mainly focused on enforcing compliance with the law and addressing situations of data breach (draft DPD Bill, 2022, Section 20). The bill was also much weaker in terms of clarity about the composition and procedures of the Data Protection Board. It enabled the government will make rules relating to the strength and composition of the Board, the process of selection, terms and conditions of appointment and service, removal of its Chairperson and other Members in the future (draft DPD Bill, 2022, Section 19). The DPD Bill was enacted as the Digital Personal Data Protection Act in August 2023.

Pending the implementation of this new legislation, limited protections for personal data are available under Section 43A of the Information Technology Act, 2000 (IT Act). This section provides for the payment of compensation to individuals for any wrongful loss suffered due to a body corporate's failure to maintain reasonable security practices while dealing with sensitive personal data. Further details regarding the implementation of this requirement have been laid down by the government under the Information Technology Rules (Reasonable Security Practices and Procedures and Sensitive Personal Data or Information) (2011).

In addition, various sector-specific regulators also regulate issues relating to data protection in their respective sectors. In the telecom sector, certain data protection-related provisions are contained in telecom licenses as well as in legislations such as the IT Act and The Telegraph Act, 1885. This includes protection of the privacy of communications and restrictions on any unauthorised interception of messages (The Telegraph Act, 1885, Section 25; TRAI, 2017a).

Does the country have a specific public body dealing with open data? If so, is it an independent body and what are its attributions?

The Right to Information Act [RTI Act] (2005) creates the statutory framework for bringing about transparency and accountability in the functioning of public authorities. It mandates all public authorities to publish details about the organisation, directory of officials, budget allocations, rules, regulations and manuals, etc., on a *sub-moto* basis (RTI Act, 2005, Section 4). In addition, citizens have the right to request any specific information from the designated public information officials required to be appointed by each public agency (RTI Act, 2005, Section 6). There are, however, some limitations on the extent of information that can be sought. This includes any personal information the disclosure of which has no relationship to any public activity or which would cause an unwarranted invasion of an individual's privacy (RTI Act, 2005, Section 8(1)(j)). The DPD Act, 2023 changed the scope of this provision to exclude all personal information, while removing the language that balances the privacy rights of an individual against the larger public interest in disclosure of a certain piece of information.

Furthermore, the RTI Act provides for the creation of a Central Information Commission and State Information Commissions that are responsible for inquiring into any non-compliance with the law by various public authorities. This may include situations where a public information officer has not been appointed, a request for information has been denied or inaccurate information has been provided (RTI Act, 2005, Section 18). To ensure the independence of these bodies, the appointment of the Chief Information Commissioner and other information commissioners is to be done directly by the President based on the recommendations of a committee consisting of the Prime Minister, the Leader of Opposition and a Union Cabinet Minister (RTI Act, 2005, Section 12). However, in a controversial move, the Parliament made certain amendments to the RTI Act in 2019, which allow the government to vary the terms of appointment and salaries of the commissioners (Sinha, 2019).

The National Data Sharing and Accessibility Policy (NDSAP) adopted by the Department of Science and Technology in 2010 is another important development in the open data context. The document creates a framework for ensuring the public availability of data that has been created through the use of public resources provided by the government of India either directly or through various departments, agencies and autonomous bodies (Department of Science and Technology, 2012). The adoption of this policy was accompanied by the creation of the portal https://data.gov.in/ that serves as the open government data platform. A few state governments have also created similar portals at the state level.

In May 2022, the Indian government put out a Draft National Data Governance Framework Policy to create a mechanism for the pooling and sharing of non-personal data and anonymised data from government and private sources (voluntarily in the case of private entities) (Ministry of Electronics and Information Technology, 2022). The policy seeks to create a body known as the India Data Management Office (IDMO) to be set up under the Digital India Corporation, a corporate entity under the Ministry of Electronics and Information Technology (MeitY). The IDMO will develop metadata rules, sharing standards and guidelines for the implementation of the data sharing policy.

Does the country have a body/an authority for managing cybersecurity incidents such as CERTs/CSIRTs? If so, what are its attributes and what is the nature of such an entity (e.g. governmental, multistakeholder, private)?

The Indian Computer Emergency Response Team (CERT-In) is India's national cyber incident response agency. Its functions include the collection and analysis of information on cyber incidents, emergency measures for handling such cases and developing information security-related procedures and practices (The Information Technology Act [IT Act], 2000). To discharge these functions, CERT-In has the power to call for any relevant information and give directions to service providers, intermediaries, data centres, and others. CERT-In consists of a Director General and such other officers as may be prescribed by the government, and it functions under the administrative control of the Ministry of Electronics and Information Technology (Information Technology [The Indian Computer Emergency Response Team and Manner of Performing Functions and Duties] Rules (2013)). As per the rules notified by this Ministry, CERT-In is supposed to interact with and coordinate among a range of stakeholders, including intermediaries, industry players, academia, law enforcement agencies, international CERTs and the DoT. The rules also provide for the creation of an Advisory Council to guide CERT-In on policy matters. This Council consists of ten members and two special invitees. Most of the members are representatives of government agencies, such as the Ministry of Home Affairs, Defence, Law and Justice and DoT. However, there is also provision for the inclusion of one industry representative, to be selected on a rotational basis among different Indian industry associations.

Does the country have a coordination system involving the aforementioned institutions? If so, what is the nature of such an entity (e.g. governmental, multistakeholder, private)?
India does not have a designated coordination body or system for coordination among different statutory agencies. The absence of such a mechanism has led to instances of regulatory uncertainty in the past. This was notably seen in a dispute relating to the jurisdiction of CCI and TRAI in a case relating to the alleged denial of interconnection by incumbent operators to a new player. The Supreme Court decided in this case that only once TRAI, as the specialised sector regulator, has looked into the technical aspects of the issue, should the CCI step in to examine whether there was any violation of competition law (Competition Commission of India vs. Bharti Airtel, 2019; Sanghi, 2018). While doing so, the Court noted the need to maintain 'comity' between the sectoral regulator and the market regulator, CCI.

Certain limited elements of coordination are reflected in the laws governing various agencies. For instance, the Competition Act enables the CCI and other statutory regulators to make references to one another, although the provision is hardly ever used in practice (Parsheera, 2018a). The previous draft of the data protection bill also provided for coordination between the proposed DPA and other regulatory authorities (PDP Bill, 2019, Section 56). The proposed mechanics for such coordination consisted of mandatory consultation on issues of concurrent jurisdiction and the option to enter into a memorandum of understanding. However, these proposals have been done away with in the enacted version of the DPD Act.

4 Regulations

Are the telecommunication regulations and standards openly and publicly accessible?
According to the TRAI Act, TRAI is meant to exercise transparency in all its functioning. In pursuance of this, the regulations made by TRAI, recommendations made by it to the government, and the consultation papers and responses to the consultation are publicly accessible on its website. In addition to this, the legislation and rules administered by the DoT (Department of Telecommunications, n.d.-a) and the telecommunication standards developed and adopted by the TSDSI (Telecommunications Standards Development Society, India, 2022c) are also available on their respective websites.

Is there a specific general telecommunications legislation?
Until 2023, the Telegraph Act and the TRAI Act were the primary telecommunications legislations in India. In addition to this, the telecommunications sector was also governed by the Wireless Telegraphy Act (1933), as well as provisions of the IT Act.

Under the Telegraph Act, a telegraph refered to any apparatus used for transmission or reception of signs, signals, writing, images and sounds or intelligence of any nature through various means (The Telegraph Act, 1885, Section 1AA). The Act provided that the government had the exclusive privilege of operating telegraphs in India, but it could grant a license to any other person to carry out such services (The Telegraph Act, 1885, Section 4). This provision formed the basis for the license agreements entered into between TSPs and the government. The other key provisions of the Act included the framework for interception of messages, provisions relating to universal service obligations and the government's powers to make rules for the conduct of telegraphs. The TRAI Act, as discussed previously, provides for the creation of TRAI and its powers and functions.

Next, the Wireless Telegraphy Act created a licensing requirement for the possession of any apparatus or material used in wireless communication (The Wireless Telegraphy, 1933, Section 3). Finally, the IT Act contains several provisions that apply specifically to intermediaries, which include TSPs. Notably, Section 79 of the IT Act exempts intermediaries from liability for third-party content, where they are not involved in the creation or modification of such content.

In 2023, India adopted a new Telecommunications Act, 2023 to amend and consolidate the laws governing telecommunication services. It repealed and replaced the provisions of the Indian Telegraph Act, 1885, the Indian Wireless Telegraphy Act, 1933 and the Telegraph Wires (Unlawful Possession) Act (1950).

Are there any instruments other than legislation and regulations, such as license agreements, that govern the provision of telecommunication services in the country?
The telecom license agreement entered into between TSPs and the government is an important document that lays down the terms and conditions on which such

authorisation has been granted. The license agreement grants the service provider the non-exclusive right to offer specified categories of services. Historically, the step-by-step liberalisation of the telecom sector meant that there were several different categories of license agreements, depending on the type of services being provided by an entity and the point at which it received the authorisation (Parsheera, 2018b). These included the Cellular Mobile Telephone Service license, the Unified Access Service License, and stand-alone ISP licenses.

Following the adoption of the National Telecom Policy (2012), the government introduced the Unified License, which is meant to account for the convergence of different types of services. For licensing and spectrum allocation purposes, the territory of India has been divided into 23 telecom service areas (Department of Telecommunications, n.d.-b). The Unified License has created a streamlined framework through which an applicant can apply for multiple services and service areas (Department of Telecommunications, 2016a). This license agreement sets out requirements relating to the ownership structure of the licensee, conditions on use of spectrum, the license term and covered area, as well as various other financial, technical, and operating conditions (Department of Telecommunications, n.d.-c). Any violation of the license terms could attract a financial penalty that may range from one to ten million Rupees per service area.

Is there any obligation to provide open data regarding the telecommunications infrastructure?

TSPs are not under an obligation to provide open data regarding their telecommunications infrastructure. However, Airtel, which is one of the largest service providers in India, has voluntarily adopted what it calls an "open network" policy. Its website contains an interactive map through which one can find the details of its current towers and tower upgrade status in different parts of the country (Airtel, 2016). In addition to this, DoT has partnered with the industry to create a portal called Tarang Sanchar (2023). Its main objective is to provide information to the public regarding electromagnetic fields (EMF) signals, but it also allows users to view the telecom tower details in their area and their EMF safety status. The information on the website appears to be incomplete in terms of coverage and is accessible only after the user completes a verification process, providing their email address and phone number.

Is there any obligation to provide open data on backhaul pricing?

There is no specific obligation relating to the provision of open data on backhaul pricing. Neither is this data being voluntarily provided by service providers.

Does regulation foresee multiple categories of telecommunications services (e.g. Internet access, broadcasting)? Are information services distinguished between themselves (content creation and content distribution)?

In 2013, the DoT adopted the universal license regime, which recognises the following categories of services: (i) access service, (ii) Internet service, (iii) national long-distance service, (iv) international long distance service, (v) global mobile personal communication by satellite, (vi) public mobile radio trunk service, (vii) very small aperture terminal closed user group service, (viii) INSAAT MSS-reporting service, and (ix) resale of international private leased circuit service. A provider can apply for a license to carry out one or more of these services or apply for a universal licence, which covers access, Internet, national long-distance and international private leased circuit services (Department of Telecommunications, 2016a). In 2016, the government also issued license guidelines for virtual network operators (VNOs), which refer to operators who rely on the network of other infrastructure providers for providing telecom services to end users/customers. There is also a separate registration framework for telecom infrastructure providers who provide dark fibre, right of way, and duct space on lease to licensed telecom operators.

The licensing of broadcasting services falls under the domain of the MIB. The MIB issues licenses/ permissions for the following categories of services: (i) direct-to-home (DTH) services, (ii) multi system operators (MSO), (iii) head-end in the sky (HITS) services, (iv) setting up of teleports by TV channels, (v) uplinking/ downlinking of TV channels from India, (vi) down linking of TV channels uplinked from abroad, and (vii) community radio stations (Ministry of Information and Broadcasting, n.d.). All these players perform different functions in the broadcasting system. DTH platforms distribute multi-channel TV programmes directly to the subscribers, MSOs downlink the signals from broadcasters and provide a bundled feed to the local cable operators, and HITS operators uplink TV broadcasts to a satellite, which is then downlinked by local cable operators and distributed to individual subscribers (National Institute of Public Finance and Policy, 2017).

The licensing requirements do not extend to the creation of content, although content creators do have to adhere to other applicable laws, such as criminal laws, the IT Act, copyright laws, etc. Further, television content is also regulated by the Cable Television Networks (Regulation) Act 1995. This law provides for the registration of cable TV operators and requires that all such operators should act in accordance with the advertisement and programme code formulated under the law. These codes prohibit the carriage of programmes or advertisements that offend morality, are obscene or defamatory, contempt of court, affect the integrity of the nation, denigrate women or children, etc. (Dua & Dhwaj, 2016). In addition to this, there are a number of self-regulatory initiatives by industry bodies such as the News Broadcasters Association, News Broadcasters Federation, Broadcasting Content Complaints Council, and Consumer Complaint Council (Agarwal, 2020). A group of leading online content providers also came together in 2020 to adopt a self-regulatory code for online media platforms ("Netflix, Amazon Prime", 2020).

Do the country's national regulations recognise community operators/ non-profit/telecommunications operators?

While India's licensing regime does not have a separate licensing process for community or non-profit telecom operators, in 2016, the government introduced a new category called virtual network operators (VNOs). These operators, which have to be set up as a company, are permitted to offer Internet services using another ISP's network. Accordingly, a small business has the option to either obtain a Unified License to act as an ISP or apply for a VNO Unified License. However, it has been noted that there is some lack of clarity regarding whether VNOs are permitted to enter into agreements with more than one network operator. In a recommendation made to the DoT, TRAI suggested that the licence agreement should be clarified to state that there is no restriction on collaborating with multiple operators for the provision of Internet access services (TRAI, 2017b).

More generally, researchers have pointed to how the complexity of spectrum management processes, limited availability of unlicensed spectrum, and licensing requirements act as barriers in the development of community networks (Srivastava, 2017). In 2018, the DoT issued the NDCP, which refers to the need for reforms in the country's licensing and regulatory regime to promote innovation, investments and ease of doing business. One of the components of this plan relates to the promotion of public Wi-Fi access through the creation of Public Data Office Aggregators and Public Data Offices (Department of Telecommunications, 2018a). This follows from a recommendation made by TRAI on this subject.

In the case of the radio broadcasting sector, there is a specialised framework to govern community radio stations, which are seen as a mechanism for the distribution of locally relevant content. As per the MIB's guidelines, educational institutions and non-profit organisations like civil society and voluntary organisations are among the entities that are permitted to operate such stations. To facilitate the growth of such stations, the government has a scheme for providing financial assistance to community radio stations, and a Community Radio Facilitation Centre has also been set up to advise applicants through various stages of the licensing process (National Institute of Public Finance and Policy, 2017). There are over 250 such radio stations operating in India.

Is there any obligation to share infrastructure:
(a) poles, cell phone towers, underground routes/tubes
(b) fibre optics sharing, telecommunication cables
(c) equipment sharing

India has adopted a voluntary framework for the sharing of infrastructure among service providers. TSPs are permitted to share active as well as passive infrastructure among themselves based on mutual agreements. Further, the Infrastructure Provider Category-I (IPC-I) framework allows registered infrastructure providers to provide passive infrastructure, namely dark fibre, duct space, towers on lease, and right of way to multiple TSPs, on mutually agreed terms. The IPC-I providers are not permitted to possess or share any active infrastructure, as the possession of wireless telegraphy equipment requires a license under the Wireless Telegraphy Act. However, an IPC-I provider can install active infrastructure (limited to antenna, feeder cable, Node B, Radio Access Network (RAN) and transmission media) on behalf of TSPs, the ownership of which must vest in the TSP (TRAI, 2020b).

In a consultation paper issued in 2020, TRAI raised the issue of whether IPC-I providers should also be allowed to offer common sharable active infrastructure and which elements of active infrastructure this should include (TRAI, 2020b). Enhancing the scope of infrastructure providers to enable the deployment of common sharable infrastructure—both passive as well as active—was also among the strategies articulated by the government in the NDCP (2018). In 2021, the government decided to amend the telecommunications license to adopt further liberalisation in the active sharing of infrastructure between telecommunication providers to also include infrastructure relating to the core network. In addition, Very Small Aperture Terminal (VSAT) were permitted to provide backhaul connectivity for cellular mobile services ("DoT Amends Norms", 2021).

Is there any unbundling obligation? Can you be an Internet service provider and a content provider at the same time?

At present, India does not impose an unbundling obligation on service providers, although it does create an enabling framework that allows for a certain level of segregation between different layers. Segregation between the infrastructure and network layers is made possible by the IPC-I category registration for stand-alone infrastructure providers. Similarly, the VNO license allows for the segregation of the network and service layers. In the NDCP (2018), the DoT has referred to the unbundling of different layers (infrastructure, network, services and applications) through differential licensing as one of its strategies. In line with this, the DoT referred to TRAI, and TRAI conducted a consultation on whether the licensing regime should allow for the separation of the network and service layers (TRAI, 2020c).

In August 2021, TRAI submitted its recommendation to the government on enabling unbundling of different layers through differential licensing (TRAI, 2021). It recommended creating a separate authorisation for Access Network Providers—operators in the network layer that would provide network services on a wholesale basis to service delivery operators for retailing purposes.

Is there any obligation to treat Internet traffic in a non-discriminatory fashion (so-called network neutrality principles)?

India has adopted one of the most robust net neutrality frameworks in the world. In February 2016, TRAI notified the Prohibition of Discriminatory Tariffs for Data Services Regulations (TRAI, 2016). The Regulation prohibits TSPs from offering differential pricing for data services based on the type of content being accessed by the user, hence barring any form of zero-rating practices. This was followed by a consultation on the other key aspects of net neutrality, including practices like blocking, throttling and prioritisation of content. This resulted in a decision by the DoT to amend the telecom licenses in July 2018, to adopt comprehensive net neutrality obligations (Department of Telecommunications, 2018d). As per this amendment, TSPs are prohibited from engaging in any discriminatory treatment of content, including based on the sender or receiver, the protocols being used or the user equipment. Further, TRAI has made recommendations to DoT on the creation of a multi-stakeholder body to advise the government on the enforcement of net neutrality requirements and on traffic management practices. However, the government is yet to take action on this.

Does the country have any specific legal or regulatory provisions regarding the Internet Access Providers' possibility to monitor the content of user communications?

The interception of telecommunication messages and Internet traffic is governed by the provisions of the Telegraph Act and the IT Act, respectively (The Telegraph Act, 1885, Section 5(2); IT Act, 2000, Section 69). Particularly, Section 5 of the Telegraph Act and Section 69 of the IT Act and the rules made under them empower the government to order service providers to carry out the interception of messages and information on certain specified grounds. This can be done with the approval of the home secretary, and in some cases, the joint secretary, both at the central and state government levels. These provisions have been criticised for their failure to meet the standards laid down by the Supreme Court while upholding the right to privacy, and petitions in this regard are currently pending before the Supreme Court (Bailey et al., 2018).

Further, the telecom licenses contain references to a Central Monitoring System (CMS), which is a centralised system to monitor communications on mobile phones, landlines and the Internet in the country. As per the license agreement, each service provider is required to put in place dedicated infrastructure to connect its systems with the regional monitoring centres of the CMS.[1] This is meant to facilitate frictionless access to data by law enforcement agencies, which is supposed to be done while acting in accordance with the legal provisions referred to above.

Does the country have any specific legal or regulatory provisions regarding the Internet Access Providers' possibility to collect and processing user personal data?

Section 43A of the IT Act, requires all body corporates to maintain reasonable security practices while dealing with sensitive personal data of individuals. This provision is applicable to all body corporates, which also includes TSPs and ISPs. As per the rules made under this section, the processing of data can only take place with the informed consent of the individual; the use of the data is subject to collection and purpose limitations and adherence to specified security practices (Government of India, 2011). Further, the Unified License (and other categories of licenses) also contain provisions relating to the confidentiality and privacy of user information. These include the requirement to protect the privacy of communications, ensure that unauthorised interception does not take place, and maintain security conditions to protect privacy.[2]

Does the country require a license to operate telecommunications networks? Is there any license exemption?

Any operation of telecommunication networks can be done only after obtaining a license from the government. Please see response to questions 2, 3 and 6 of this section for details of the licensing framework.

---

[1] Condition 8.2, Part II of the Unified License Agreement (Department of Telecommunications, 2013).

[2] Conditions 37 & 39, Part I, Unified License (Department of Telecommunications, n.d.-d).

Does the country offer a specific/simplified license for not-for-profit operators or for operators that cover specific areas (e.g. rural areas)?

A telecom operator can choose to provide its services at the national level, at the level of telecom circle/metro area (India is divided into 22 such circles) or at the level of the secondary switching area, which refers to a subdivision of a telecom circle. An ISP that only wants to serve a smaller local area, which could be up to four secondary switching areas, can apply for a Category "C" ISP license. The financial requirements for applying for this type of license, in terms of the entry fees, bank guarantees and application processing fees, are significantly lower compared to other categories of licenses. This is also the case with VNO licenses. However, there is no special category of licenses that applies specifically to rural areas.

Does the country require a license to provide satellite telecommunications services including via non-geostationary orbit satellites?

India's Department of Space is the administrative ministry responsible for the overall regulation of space activities. The provision of satellite communications services requires authorisation from the Department of Space, along with separate licenses to be issued by the DoT and MIB for telecommunication and broadcasting services, respectively. The activities for which an authorisation is required from the Department of Space include the establishment of communications systems over India, using Indian or non-Indian orbital resources, establishment and utilisation of non-geostationary orbit satellite communication systems, and establishment of ground segments for space asset operations (Department of Space, 2020).

Has the country established an obligation to provide coverage in specific areas (e.g. rural areas that lack coverage)?

The rollout obligations imposed on telecom licensees and the mandatory requirement of contribution towards the Universal Service Obligation Fund (USOF) are two of the ways in which the regulatory framework seeks to secure the coverage of rural and remote areas. The allocation of spectrum bands to TSPs is accompanied by specified minimum roll-out obligations, which determine the schedule of deployment required to be followed by the TSP across different areas. These requirements tend to vary across different technologies and bands (Jain & Dara, 2017). For instance, the allotment of the 2100 MHz spectrum in 2010 was based on the condition that the provider had to roll out to 50% of the district headquarters, of which 15% should be in rural areas. Subsequently, in the allotment of 700 MHz spectrum in 2016, the conditions stated that the operators would have to cover all towns and villages having a specified population within 5 years and all villages with a specified population by 7 years (Jain & Dara, 2017).[3] Details of the USOF are discussed in response to question 1 of the Financial Resources section.

[3] The 700 MHz spectrum, however, did not see any takers in this auction.

Are there any specific cybersecurity obligations with regard to the telecommunications sector?

The license conditions specify various security-related requirements to be followed by TSPs.[4] These requirements include the need to have an organisational policy on security and security management, conduct regular security audits, deployment of only certified equipment, and creation of facilities for monitoring any intrusions, attacks and fraud on technical facilities. If an operator fails to adopt such measures, leading to a security breach, it would be liable to pay a penalty of up to Rs. 500 million. In addition to this, the TSP is also bound by the general cybersecurity or negligence-related provisions under other laws such as the Telegraph Act, the IT Act and criminal laws. For instance, Section 69B of the IT Act provides that every intermediary, which includes TSPs, has to provide technical assistance to an authorised government agency for monitoring and collecting traffic data or information to enhance cyber security or deal with any computer contaminant in the country.

Is there any regulation regarding cybersecurity incidents?

The responsibility of cyber incident response in the country vests with CERT-In. As per the provisions of the IT Act and rules formulated under it, CERT-In is supposed to act as the trusted referral agency responding to cyber security incidents and adopting measures to reduce their risk, including through audits, awareness and training initiatives (Information Technology [The Indian Computer Emergency Response Team and Manner of Performing Functions and Duties] Rules (2013)). In 2018, there were reports of the creation of a sector-specific CERT for the telecommunications sector (Kala, 2018). However, as of now, no formal steps are known to have been taken in this regard.

CERT-In is supposed to exchange relevant information relating to attacks, vulnerabilities and solutions affecting critical sectors with the National Critical Information Infrastructure Protection Centre (NCIIPC). The NCIIPC is a statutory body created under the IT Act for undertaking measures for the protection of critical sectors, the disruption of which would result in a debilitating impact on the national security, governance, economy and social well-being of the nation (IT Act, 2000, Section 70). The telecom sector has been designated as a critical information infrastructure by the NCIIPC. The prescribed rules for designated protected systems include requirements for the constitution of an Information Security Steering Committee to approve the system's information security policies and carry out a vulnerability/ threat/ risk analysis of its cybersecurity architecture (Ministry of Electronics and Information Technology, 2018).

Does the law foresee any specific cybercrime involving the (mis)use or attack of the telecommunications infrastructure?

As noted above, the telecommunications sector has been designated as a critical information infrastructure. As per Section 70(3) of the IT Act, any person who secures access or attempts to secure access to a protected system in contravention of

[4] Condition 39, Part I, Unified License (Department of Telecommunications, n.d.-d).

the provisions of the law may be punished with imprisonment of up to 10 years and would also be liable for a fine. This is in addition to the general provisions relating to designation of cybercrimes under the IT Act, which cover any unauthorised access to a computer, computer system or network, concealing or tampering with computer source documents, and indulging in cyber terrorism. The Telegraph Act also makes it an offence to trespass into or obstruct the signal room or office of a telegraph operator, and to intentionally damage or tamper with messages or equipment. Being a much older legislation, the text of the law, however, does not refer specifically to cybercrimes.

Does the law foresee SIM and/or IMEI registration? What are the requirements applicable to such registration (for instance, the documents and information required for Know-Your-Customer (KYC) processes?
Under Section 4 of the Telegraph Act, every license holder is required to identify any person to whom it provides its services using any of the following means—(a) online or offline authentication using Aadhaar, (b) passport or (c) any other officially valid document or modes of identification as may be notified by the government.[5] It should be the voluntary choice of the person who is sought to be identified to pick any of these options. While this provision was introduced in the law only in 2019, TSPs were already required to conduct a know your customer (KYC) verification for all subscribers under the terms of the license agreements and rules made by the DoT.

The DoT has also specified a customer application form (CAF) containing all the information that must be provided by the customer. In case of an electronic KYC process, the DoT has specified a list of over 33 parameters that the licensee needs to include in the subscriber database (Circular of the Department of Telecommunications No. 800-26/2016-AS.II, 2019). This includes data such as the mobile number allotted, CAF number, name, gender, address, nationality, details of local reference (for outstation customers) and SIM activation date. An additional set of requirements has been specified for the issuance of bulk connections to entities (rather than individuals) using the digital KYC route (Circular of the Department of Telecommunications No. 800-26/2016-AS.II, 2020). This includes documentary proof of the entity's name and address, authorisation from the authorised signatory, and the list of end users. In addition, the physical coordinates of the office also need to be recorded and physically verified before activating the bulk SIM cards.

Does the country specify the prices or tariffs for the provision of telecommunication services or impose any minimum or maximum limits?
The TRAI Act empowers TRAI to notify the rates at which telecommunications services are to be provided (TRAI Act, 1997, Section 11(2)). In pursuance of this, TRAI has notified an instrument called the Telecommunication Tariff Order, which has been amended from time to time, to set out the conditions governing telecom tariffs. While in the initial years TRAI followed the practice of specifying tariffs for

[5] This provision was added to the law by the Aadhaar and Other Laws (Amendment) Act (2019).

different types of services, it has now transitioned to a forbearance regime for almost all categories of services. Currently, TRAI specifies tariffs for the following types of services—national roaming, fixed rural telephony, USSD and leased lines (TRAI, 2018a).

Are there any policies or regulations governing right-of-way issues, such as utilising land to dig trenches and lay fibre, for the creation of telecommunications infrastructure?

Since land is a state subject under the Indian Constitution, the power to make laws and regulations governing the use of land vests with the state governments. Accordingly, each state government has been following its own practices for issuing RoW permissions, which also tend to vary at the local and municipal levels within a state. This is reported to be the cause of delays and exorbitant costs in the rollout of telecom infrastructure (TRAI, 2019a).

In a bid to address these issues, in 2016, DoT adopted the Indian Telegraph Right of Way Rules, which aim to create a streamlined process for issuance of RoW permissions. The rules, which include requirements relating to the online application process, limits on application fees, and time-bound decision-making, cover the setting up of both underground and overground infrastructure. Initially, the rules applied only to TSPs, but this was revised in 2018 to also cover infrastructure providers like tower companies ("DoT Includes Tower Cos", 2018). As per a Parliamentary Standing Committee Report, as of August 2018, only seven states had adopted policies to bring their RoW regime in line with these rules (Standing Committee on Information Technology, 2018). A subsequent report stated that this figure had risen to 16 states, but a smaller number of them had agreed to the uniform RoW pricing suggested under the DoT's rules (Kurup, 2020).

The new Telecommunication Act contains a chapter dedicated to right-of-way permissions. It includes provisions relating to non-discriminatory and non-exclusive grant of right of way, process for permissions involving public and private property, the government's power to establish common ducts and cable corridors, and dispute resolution mechanisms. In addition to this, the government has announced an initiative called the GatiShakti Sanchar Portal (2022) to serve as a collaborative institutional mechanism for right-of-way approvals.

What are the regulations applicable to the setting up and operation of landing stations and international gateways to the Internet?

DoT has issued guidelines for the setting up of submarine cable landing stations for international gateways to the Internet (Department of Telecommunications, 2007). While seeking permission, the ISP must provide details of all the ISPs that would be connected to the landing station, and any additions to that can only be made with the prior written permission of the authority. Only internet traffic is allowed to be carried through the landing station, and it should not be used for any unlawful activities or against the public interest. Further, the landing station must adhere to various other requirements specified by the government, such as ensuring that there is no bulk encryption of traffic by any ISP, monitoring and security requirements, and filtering of traffic based on keywords and addresses defined by security agencies (Department of Telecommunications, 2007).

TRAI has mandated that access to the cable landing station has to be made available in a fair, non-discriminatory and transparent manner (TRAI, 2007). The cable landing station also has to submit the terms and conditions of access facilitation and co-location facilities to TRAI for its approval. The landing station then has to publish the approved reference interconnect offer, based on which an access seeker can approach the landing station for its services. Subsequently, through an amendment to this regulation in 2012 and a new regulation on facilitation and co-location charges, TRAI notified that it would be setting the facilitation, operation and maintenance and co-location charges that may be charged by cable landing stations. Following a judicial challenge to these regulations, in 2018, TRAI released a new schedule of applicable charges under these regulations (TRAI, 2018b).

Are there any regulations for the Over-The-Top (OTT) services?

In 2020, TRAI concluded a four-year-long consultation process on the regulation of OTT communication services (TRAI, 2020a). In March 2016, DoT had asked TRAI for its recommendations on issues relating to net neutrality and whether there is a need for a regulatory framework for OTT services. TRAI concluded that it was not an opportune moment to recommend any sort of comprehensive regulatory framework for OTT services and that market forces should be allowed to take their course. It also referred to the sufficiency of the extant laws and regulations in this regard. Some of the provisions that are applicable to OTT entities, among other covered entities, include requirements relating to data protection and supporting lawful information requests under the IT Act, as well as copyright and criminal laws.

However, the government has decided to take a different route in terms of bringing OTT players under the fold of regulation. The definition of telecommunication service under the draft bill includes OTT communication services (draft Telecommunication Bill, 2022, Section 2(21)), which implies that all the provisions applicable to telecommunications services might also apply to this category of service providers. Further clarity in this regard is awaited from the government, which has made statements to indicate that only OTT players that provide services comparable to telecommunication services might be covered under a "light-touch" regulatory framework ("Regulation of OTT", 2022).

In addition, OTT providers that qualify as online intermediaries are also governed by the IT Act and the Information Technology (Intermediary Guidelines and Digital Media Ethics Code) Rules (Ministry of Electronics and Information Technology, 2021). The rules contain requirements relating to content moderation, provision of information to users, and grievance redress. Further, entities that qualify as significant intermediaries are bound by additional requirements relating to the appointment of designated officers and the identification of the first originator of content by social media platforms.

What are the grounds, if any, on which the country can suspend access to the Internet or direct the blocking of access to specific websites?

Section 69A of the IT Act authorises the government to issue orders for the blocking of content on the following grounds—sovereignty, integrity and defence of India, security of the State, friendly relations with foreign States, public order or for preventing incitement to the commission of any cognisable offence relating to the above. An intermediary that fails to comply with these directions can be punished with imprisonment of up to 7 years in addition to a fine. Further, the telecom licence agreement also contains a requirement to prevent the carriage of objectionable, obscene, or infringing content once specific instances of such infringement are reported to it by the government.[6]

The detailed process of implementation of blocking requirements is laid down in the Information Technology Rules (Procedure and Safeguard for Blocking for Access of Information by Public) (2009). A blocking order may be issued at the request of a government organisation, in which case it needs to be considered by an inter-ministerial review committee, or based on directions issued by a court. The rules also require that the blocking order has to be kept confidential, which leads to a lack of transparency in the process.

In addition to the blocking of specific websites and content, government agencies in India can also suspend or shut down Internet access in particular areas. The large number of such shutdowns draw their legal basis from Section 144 of the Code of Criminal Procedure (1973). This provision contains broad powers allowing the authorised officer to "direct any person to abstain from a certain act or to take certain order" to prevent injury, danger to human life, health or safety, disturbance of public tranquillity or a riot. In 2017, DoT issued the Temporary Suspension of Telecom Services (Public Emergency or Public Safety) Rules (Department of Telecommunications, 2017), which lay down the process through which an Internet suspension order can be issued and reviewed. In a challenge against the long Internet shutdown imposed in Kashmir, the Supreme Court has emphasised the need for transparency of shutdown orders. The Court noted that such orders must adopt the proportionality-based approach principle and a review of the order must be carried out every 7 days (Anuradha Bhasin vs. Union of India, 2019; Gulam Nabi Azad vs. Union of India, 2020).

Does the country have a specific policy or strategy promoting the development of Internet eXchange Point (IXP) and other interconnection and transmission systems?

In 2003, the Department of Information Technology established the National Internet Exchange of India (NIXI) as a not-for-profit organisation to encourage peering among ISPs in India for the purpose of routing the domestic traffic within the country (National Internet Exchange of India, 2022). As a body set up by the government, NIXI has been allowed to operate without any license requirements and falls outside the purview of DoT and TRAI regulations on quality of service,

[6] Condition 38.1, Part I, Unified License (Department of Telecommunications, n.d.-d).

tariff, and interconnection port charges (TRAI, 2011). Besides NIXI, there are a few other IXPs that are operating in India. However, it is reported that as of now, only a fraction of the country's overall Internet traffic flows through these IXPs (Deep, 2020).

In 2011, TRAI had recommended to DoT that IXPs should be brought within the licensing regime to ensure their proper functioning, including mandatory interconnection of ISPs at IXPs (TRAI, 2011). But to date, there remains uncertainty regarding the legal framework applicable to IXPs. While some IXPs are operating under an ISP license, there are others that claim that no such license is required since NIXI is also operating without a license (Deep, 2020).

Have any exceptional measures been adopted to regulate the COVID-19 crisis?

The following are some of the COVID-19-related developments and measures relevant to the telecom sector:

1. Telecommunication, Internet, broadcasting and cable services were exempted from the lockdown restrictions imposed by the government to deal with COVID-19 to allow the continuous functioning of these essential services (Pathak et al., 2020). In addition, some of the states took specific measures to enable the smooth functioning of mobile networks. For instance, the Maharashtra State Electricity Regulatory Commission reduced commercial electricity tariffs by 10 to 15% (Pathak et al., 2020). In Kerala, the government took an initiative to monitor the regular supply of diesel to telecom towers that relied exclusively on diesel generator sets (Bhandari, 2020).
2. DoT suspended the testing of the mandatory telecom rollout obligations of TSPs in light of the delays reported by the operators in the acquisition of approvals, import of network equipment and physical deployment of the infrastructure ("India's Private Telcos" 2020).
3. In the initial weeks of the lockdown TSPs undertook measures like extending the validity of prepaid numbers and providing free talktime and messaging benefits. These measures were targeted towards the low ARPU users whom the TSPs believed were in more need of such relief, although TRAI had indicated a preference to make the relief packages available to all prepaid users (Sengupta, 2020).
4. The Cellular Operators Association of India wrote to DoT and various OTT video providers seeking their cooperation in mitigating network congestion that may arise due to the increase in video streaming. The OTT players responded by declaring that they would take temporary steps to ease the pressure on mobile networks (Parsheera, 2018b).
5. The industry body referred to above (see #4) also proposed that the government should enable free access to certain critical websites, such as those relating to health services and providing COVID-19-related information (Parsheera, 2018b). This was proposed to be done using the available exemptions for public emergencies under the regulations on discriminatory tariffs for data services. However, this request is not known to have been actioned upon by TRAI or DoT.

5 Access to the Spectrum

How does the country organise access to spectrum for data transmission (e.g. via auctions)?

Frequency allocations in India are determined based on the table of frequency allocations set out under the National Frequency Allocation Plan announced by the DoT (2018b). Each frequency band is allocated to one or more radio communication services, which include cellular mobile service, Wi-Fi, sound and television broadcasting, radio navigation for aircraft and ships, defence and security communications, disaster relief, satellite communications, etc. (Department of Telecommunications, 2018b). The further assignment of various spectrum bands to different users is determined by the WPC in the DoT, which is India's national radio regulatory authority.

A large part of the spectrum remains reserved for government agencies such as defence purposes, police agencies, railways and the Department of Space. As per a 2015 estimate, nearly 60% of the total available spectrum available for access networks had been assigned for government purposes, and 40% was available for commercial telecom services (TRAI 2015). This has led to calls for the periodic reassessment of the actual spectrum usage by government agencies, which can enable better harmonisation and re-farming of the spectrum (Parsheera, 2019a).

India has experimented with a number of different spectrum allotment practices for commercial cellular and mobile services before it settled on the current practice of allotment through auctions. In the initial years after the opening up of the market to private players, spectrum was allocated through auctions. There was a policy change in 2001, and until the year 2010, India moved to the practice of administrative allotment of spectrum by the DoT on a first-come-first-serve basis. However, following an incident of corruption and mismanagement of 2G spectrum, the policy regime has fully shifted toward spectrum auction as the preferred mode of allotment for cellular mobile services. The reserve price for such auctions is fixed by the DoT, based on recommendations made by TRAI. At present, spectrum prices in India are noted to be among the highest in the world ("Price of 5G" 2019).

The preference for allotment through auctions finds support from the observations made by the Supreme Court while cancelling the improperly issued 2G telecom licenses. As per the court, the alienation of natural resources like spectrum should be supported by the method of auction, which allows all eligible persons to participate in the process (Centre for Public Interest Litigation and Others vs. Union of India, 2012). However, the Court subsequently clarified that it did not intend to impose auctions as the preferred method, as this was a policy decision, but the government is bound to ensure that the adopted means are not arbitrary in nature ("Natural Resources Allocation", 2012).

Does the country offer any kind of advantage in access to the spectrum (for example, discount or compensation) for operators that use the spectrum to provide services in rural areas?

There is no special policy or concession for operators relating to the use of spectrum in rural areas. However, researchers and businesses have been making a case for allowing the secondary use of unutilised TV white spaces for providing better connectivity in rural areas. In 2015 and 2016, the DoT granted experimental licenses to various entities, including four academic institutions and Microsoft, to carry out pilot studies involving the use of TV white spaces. However, the DoT subsequently announced that it would not allocate the 470–582 MHz spectrum band for the commercial deployment of TV white spaces technology (Bhandari, 2018). Similarly, researchers have also been making a case for the opening up of unutilised V-band (57 GHz–64 GHz) and E-band (71–76 GHz and 81–86 GHz) spectrum, which has applications in both dense urban clusters and rural areas (Rai et al., 2018).

Does the country offer low bureaucratic, affordable licensing for spectrum access to be used for social purposes or to provide coverage? Does this include provision of public Wi-Fi services?

Recognising the social and welfare benefits of allowing unlicensed usage of spectrum to support services like Wi-Fi applications, DoT has designated certain unlicensed bands that are free to be used by anyone. In 2005, the DoT declared that use of wireless services in the frequency band 2.4–2.4835 GHz would be permitted without a license, subject to adherence with specified power and antenna height limits. Subsequently, the use of frequencies in the 5.150–5.350 GHz and 5.725–5.875 GHz range was permitted for indoor uses (Srivastava, 2017). In 2018, the government announced that spectrum in the 5.1–5.3 GHz and 5.7–5.8 GHz bands was unlicensed both for indoor and outdoor uses ("Government Frees Spectrum" 2018).

India currently lags behind other countries in terms of the proliferation of public Wi-Fi networks. The recommendations made by TRAI in this regard include the introduction of a new class of entities called Public Data Office Aggregators that would be allowed to provide public Wi-Fi services without the need for a specific license (TRAI 2018c). Promoting the adoption of open public Wi-Fi access is one of the key objectives set out by the DoT in the NDCP. The proposed strategies in this regard include the use of public-private partnerships to roll out one million public Wi-Fi Hotspots in urban areas and two million in rural areas.

Does the country allow secondary use of spectrum? If so, how is It defined?

The National Frequency Allocation Plan provides that each frequency allocation to a service is categorised as a primary or a secondary allocation. Accordingly, secondary use is allowed for the purposes that have been permitted under certain frequency bands. However, this is permitted in only a limited set of cases, and the DoT itself has noted in the NDCP that there is a need for promoting more efficient co-use/secondary use of spectrum. In addition, the sharing and trading of spectrum between licensed service providers is also allowed. Spectrum sharing is permitted among service providers who have authorisation to operate in a particular service area and are utilising spectrum in the same band (Department of Telecommunications, 2015).

Do the country's regulations provide for the use of unlicensed or license-free bands in specific areas, such as rural areas, or throughout the country?
See response to question 3 above for details of unlicensed bands. These are available throughout the country.

6 Financial Resources

Is there any fund for universalization (to promote the increase) of the Internet access or access to Telecom services for everybody? Is there a Universal Service Fund or any other fund? If so, how are resources collected and distributed?
The USOF was created under the Indian Telegraph (Amendment) Act (2003) to provide access to basic telegraph services to people in rural and remote areas at affordable and reasonable prices. Subsequently, in 2006, the scope of universal service obligations was amended to include all telegraph services, hence allowing the fund to be utilised for the provision of Internet access and broadband services. As per the Indian Telegraph Rules, the management of the USOF, which includes entering into agreements with service providers for the utilisation of the fund, lies with a fund administrator created under the rules (Indian Telegraph (Amendment) Rules, 2004).

The selection of the universal service provider for any particular project is to be done based on a bidding process, which is open to all eligible operators (Indian Telegraph Rules, 1951, Rule 526). However, the DoT may exercise its discretion not to follow this process in certain circumstances. For instance, this was done in the context of awarding the state-run operator, Bharat Sanchar Nigam Limited, the right to build telecom connectivity along a popular pilgrimage route. This decision was based on factors such as the remoteness of the area, commercial non-viability and national security considerations (Ministry of Communications and Information Technologies, 2015).

The BharatNet Project, formerly referred to as the National Optical Fibre Network, has been one of the largest applications of USOF. The project aims to provide connectivity to 250 thousand Gram Panchayats, a unit of governance at the village level, in the country. The project was launched in 2011, and over a decade later, only about 188 thousand of the Gram Panchayats had been connected (Bharat Broadband Network Limited, 2022). This is reflective of the project's slow rollout. While the first phase of the project focused only on optical fibre connectivity, the ongoing second phase is also looking at satellite connectivity. Further, unlike the first phase, which had a public sector-led model, in the second phase, different states have been given the option to choose their preferred model, including a state government-led model, a private sector-led model and public-private partnerships.

Are telecommunications services taxed or subject to other specific levies? If so how?
Licensed service providers are required to pay an annual license fee at the rate of 8% of their Adjusted Gross Revenue (AGR). Of this, 5% goes towards the USOF while 3% goes to the DoT. In addition, wireless service providers must also pay annual spectrum usage charges. The quantum of spectrum charges is determined based on the bandwidth allotted to the cellular operator and is charged as a percentage of their AGR. This results in providers paying between 3 to 5% of their AGR as a spectrum usage charge to the DoT ("TRAI Issues", 2020). The telecommunications sector is also subject to Goods and Services Tax at the rate of 18%.

Telecom operators have raised a demand for the rationalisation of these levies and taxes, citing the financial burden being cast on the industry and the large unutilised corpus in the USOF (Aryan, 2020). This issue became particularly significant in light of a Supreme Court decision that accepted the government's position that AGR is to be calculated based on all revenues earned by service providers and is not limited to direct revenues relating to their telecom operations only. This had created a significant backlog of revenue payments due to be paid by the operators.

Is there any fund to provide subsidies to operators to expand coverage to underserved areas and least privileged populations?
The USOF is meant to be used for expanding coverage in rural and remote areas. See response to question 1 above for more details.

Is any form of direct support (such as funding or tax exemptions) offered to small/micro/not-for-profit providers?
In the initial years of the sector, telecommunication services were entitled to a tax deduction while computing the total income for taxation purposes. The deduction applied to any provider that commenced its business between April 1995 to March 2005 and allowed them a deduction of 100% of the profits and gains for the first 5 years and 30% for the next 5 years (Income Tax Act, 1961 [Section 80IA]). However, it was noted that at least in the first few years, most of the major companies were not able to claim this benefit. This was either because they were operating under losses or they were being assessed under special provisions of the Act, which did not allow for the deductions under this provision (Comptroller and Auditor General of India, 2008).

References

Agarwal, A. (2020, September 22). Regulate digital news media before cracking down on TV news: Govt to Supreme Court. *Medianama*. https://www.medianama.com/2020/09/223-mib-supreme-court-regulation-of-digital-news-media/.

Airtel. (2016). *Open network*. https://www.airtel.in/opennetwork.

Anuradha Bhasin vs. Union of India. (2019). WP(C) 1031/2019.

Aryan, A. (2020, September 21). DoT unlikely to agree on lower licence fee recommended by TRAI, alter AGR definition. Indian Express. https://indianexpress.com/article/business/dot-unlikely-to-agree-on-lower-licence-fee-recommended-by-trai-alter-agr-definition-6604146/.

Asia-Pacific Telecommunity. (2022, October 19). Introduction. https://www.apt.int/APT-Introduction.

Bailey, R., Bhandari, V., Parsheera, S., & Rahman, F. (2018, August 1). Use of personal data by intelligence and law enforcement agencies. Macro/Finance Group NIPFP. https://macrofinance.nipfp.org.in/PDF/BBPR2018-Use-of-personal-data.pdf.

Barboni, G., Field, E., Pande, R., Rigol, N., Schaner, S., & Moore, C. T. (2018). *A tough call: Understanding barriers to and impacts of women's mobile phone adoption in India.* Harvard Kennedy School.

Bhandari, V. (2018, June 9). White space Spectrum in India: An untapped opportunity for rural connectivity. *Invest India.* https://www.investindia.gov.in/team-india-blogs/white-space-spectrum-india-untapped-opportunity-rural-connectivity.

Bhandari, V. (2020, September 22). Improving internet connectivity during the COVID-19 pandemic. The Leap Blog. https://blog.theleapjournal.org/2020/09/improving-internet-connectivity-during.html.

Bharat Broadband Network Limited. (2022). BharatNet Status as on November 28, 2022. http://www.bbnl.nic.in/BharatNet.pdf.

Biswas, R. (2017, June 22). COAI receives WP-5D of the ITU approval for connecting rural cities in India with high-speed mobile broadband. *Telecom Talk.* https://telecomtalk.info/coai-wp-5d-itu-approval-for-connecting-rural-cities-in-india-with-high-speed-mobile-broadband/165081/.

Cable.co.uk. (2020). *Worldwide mobile data pricing.* https://www.cable.co.uk/mobiles/worldwide-data-pricing/.

Centre for Public Interest Litigation and Others vs. Union of India. (2012). 3 SCC 1.

Chauhan, B. S. (2016). Role of standardisation in a developing economy. Regional Standardization Forum for Bridging the Standardization Gap. https://www.itu.int/en/ITU-T/Workshops-and-Seminars/bsg/201609/Documents/BSG%20AO%20India_TSDSI%20BSC%2020160916_Final.pdf.

Circular of the Department of Telecommunications No. 800-26/2016-AS.II. (2019, August 19). https://dot.gov.in/sites/default/files/D-KYC%20%20CAF%20and%20Databse%20format.pdf?download=1.

Circular of the Department of Telecommunications No. 800-26/2016-AS.II. (2020, September 18). https://dot.gov.in/sites/default/files/18-09-2020.pdf?download=1.

Competition Commission Initiates Studies on Telecom Sector, M&A in Digital Market. (2020, June 8). Live Mint. https://www.livemint.com/industry/telecom/competition-commission-initiates-studies-on-telecom-sector-m-a-in-digital-market-11591620332608.html.

Competition Commission of India vs. Bharti Airtel. (2019). 2 SCC 521.

Comptroller and Auditor General of India. (2008). *Report No. PA 7 of 2008.* https://cag.gov.in/uploads/old_reports/union/union_performance/2007_2008/Direct_Taxes/Report_no_7/chap_3.pdf.

Deep, A. (2020, August 26). Key takeaways: What it's like running an internet exchange in India. *Medianama.* https://www.medianama.com/2020/08/223-internet-exchange-india/.

Department of Science and Technology. (2012). National Data Sharing and Accessibility Policy. *The Gazette of India*, No. 11, p. 93. https://data.gov.in/sites/default/files/NDSAP.pdf.

Department of Space. (2020, October 2). Draft Space Based Communication Policy of India. https://www.isro.gov.in/sites/default/files/draft_spacecom_policy_2020.pdf.

Department of Telecommunications. (n.d.-a). *Act & rules.* https://dot.gov.in/act-rules.

Department of Telecommunications. (n.d.-b). *Details service areas.* https://dot.gov.in/sites/default/files/list%20of%20unifiedaccess%20licensees_0.pdf?download=1.

Department of Telecommunications. (n.d.-c). *Unified license agreement.* https://dot.gov.in/sites/default/files/Unified%20Licence_0.pdf.

Department of Telecommunications. (n.d.-d). *Unified license, Part I*. https://dot.gov.in/sites/default/files/UnifiedLicence_0.pdf.
Department of Telecommunications. (2007). Guidelines and general information for setting up of submarine cable landing stations for international gateways for internet. https://dot.gov.in/dataservices/guidelines-and-general-information-setting-submarine-cable-landing-stations.
Department of Telecommunications. (2013, October 11). Amendment for the Unified License agreement regarding Central Monitoring System. http://dot.gov.in/sites/default/files/DOC231013.pdf?download=1.
Department of Telecommunications. (2015). Guidelines for sharing of access spectrum by access service providers. https://dot.gov.in/sites/default/files/Guidelines%20for%20Access%20Spectrum%20Sharing.pdf.
Department of Telecommunications. (2016a). Guidelines for grant of unified license. https://dot.gov.in/sites/default/files/First%20Link%202016_03_28%20ULG%20AS-I.pdf.
Department of Telecommunications. (2016b). License agreement for unified license. https://dot.gov.in/sites/default/files/2016_03_30%20UL-AS-I.pdf?download=1s.
Department of Telecommunications. (2017, August 8). Notification. The Gazette of India, No. 679, p. 3. https://dot.gov.in/sites/default/files/Suspension%20Rules.pdf.
Department of Telecommunications. (2018a). National Digital Communications Policy 2018. https://dot.gov.in/sites/default/files/EnglishPolicy-NDCP.pdf.
Department of Telecommunications. (2018b). National Frequency Allocation Plan - 2018. https://dot.gov.in/sites/default/files/NFAP%202018.pdf?download=1.
Department of Telecommunications. (2018c). Telecommunications standards development society, India (TSDSI). https://dot.gov.in/telecommunications-standards-development-society-india-tsdsi.
Department of Telecommunications. (2018d). Regulatory framework on net neutrality. https://tinyurl.com/y6chtqjr.
Department of Telecommunications. (2022). Profile. https://dot.gov.in/profile.
Digital India. (n. d.). How Digital India will be realized: Pillars of Digital India. https://digitalindia.gov.in/content/programme-pillars.
DoT Amends Norms to Allow Active Infrastructure Sharing Among Telcos. (2021, September 24). ET Telecom. https://telecom.economictimes.indiatimes.com/news/active-sharing-of-infrastructure-to-facilitate-faster-rollout-of-services-coai/86475918.
DoT Includes Tower Cos in Right of Way Rules, Industry Welcomes Move. (2018, May 23). Economic Times https://economictimes.indiatimes.com/industry/telecom/telecom-policy/dot-includes-tower-cos-in-right-of-way-rules-industry-welcomes-move/articleshow/64293364.cms?from=mdr.
Draft Indian Telecommunication Bill. (2022). https://dot.gov.in/sites/default/files/Draft%20Indian%20Telecommunication%20Bill%2C%202022.pdf.
Dua, A., & Dhwaj, G. (2016, March 14). India: Framework for content on television. *Mondaq*. https://www.mondaq.com/india/broadcasting-film-tv-radio/473716/framework-for-content-on-television.
GatiShakti Sanchar Portal. (2022). *Home*. https://sugamsanchar.gov.in/.
General Agreement on Trade in Services - India: Schedule of Specific Commitments [GATS/SC/42]. (1994, April 15). Department of Commerce. https://commerce.gov.in/wp-content/uploads/2020/11/India-%E2%80%93-Schedule-of-Specific-Commitments.pdf.
General Agreement on Trade in Services - India: Schedule of Specific Commitments Supplement 3 [GATS/SC/42/Suppl.3]. (1997, April 14). Department of Commerce. https://commerce.gov.in/wp-content/uploads/2020/11/India-%E2%80%93-Schedule-of-Specific-Commitments-%E2%80%93-Supplement-3.pdf.
Government Frees Spectrum for Wifi, 5G Services in 5 Ghz Band from Licence. (2018, October 22). The Economic Times https://economictimes.indiatimes.com/industry/telecom/telecom-news/government-frees-spectrum-for-wifi-5g-services-in-5-ghz-band-from-licence/articleshow/66322128.cms?from=mdr.

Government of India. (1961). Government of India (allocation of business) rules, 1961. https://cabsec.gov.in/writereaddata/allocationbusinessrule/completeaobrules/english/1_Upload_1187.pdf.

Government of India. (2011). Information Technology (Reasonable Security Practices and Procedures and Sensitive Personal Data or Information) Rules, 2011.

Government of India. (2020). *Lok Sabha Question No. 53 to be answered on 5th February, 2020.* http://164.100.24.220/loksabhaquestions/annex/173/AS53.pdf.

GSMA. (2022). The mobile gender gap report 2022. gsma.com/r/gender-gap/.

Gulam Nabi Azad vs. Union of India. (2020, January 10). WP(C) 1164/2019.

IANS. (2019, January 2). TRAI moves SC against TDSAT ruling on predatory pricing. CNBC. https://www.cnbctv18.com/telecom/trai-moves-sc-against-tdsat-ruling-on-predatory-pricing-1849511.htm.

India's Private Telcos Can't Meet Minimum Rollout Obligations. (2020, May 19). Disruptive Asia. https://disruptive.asia/india-private-telcos-cant-meet-minimum-rollout-obligations/.

Indian Telegraph (Amendment) Rules. (2004). https://dot.gov.in/sites/default/files/26th%20March%202004_1.pdf?download=1.

Indian Telegraph Rules. (1951).

Information Technology (The Indian Computer Emergency Response Team and Manner of Performing Functions and Duties) Rules. (2013). https://www.meity.gov.in/writereaddata/files/G_S_R%2020%20%28E%292_0.pdf.

IAMAI & Nielsen. (2019). *Digital in India, 2019 - Round 2.* https://cms.iamai.in/Content/ResearchPapers/2286f4d7-424f-4bde-be88-6415fe5021d5.pdf.

Jain, R., & Dara, R. (2017, June). Framework for evolving spectrum management regimes: Lessons from India. *Telecommunications Policy, 41*(5–6) https://www.sciencedirect.com/science/article/pii/S030859611730126X

Kala, R. R. (2018, March 30). Cyber security*: Telecom sector set to have own emergency response team.* Financial Express. https://www.financialexpress.com/industry/technology/cyber-security-telecom-sector-set-to-have-own-emergency-response-team/1115627/.

Kathuria, R., Kedia, M., & Bagchi, K. (2019). Competition issues in India's Mobile handset industry. Indian Council for Research on International Economic Relations. https://icrier.org/pdf/Competition-Issues-in-India-Mobile-Handset-Industry.pdf.

Kurup, R. (2020, July 22). Seven states, two UTs agree to uniform pricing on right of way. The Hindu Business Line. https://www.thehindubusinessline.com/info-tech/seven-states-two-uts-agree-to-uniform-pricing-on-right-of-way/article32156346.ece.

Mahmood, S. (2017). The Context of South Asian Telecommunication Regulators' Council. https://www.itu.int/en/ITU-D/Conferences/GSR/Documents/GSR2017/SATRC%20Presentation%20for%20GSR-17.pdf.

Masnick, M. (2012, December 14). Who Signed The ITU WCIT Treaty... And Who Didn't. Tech Dirt. https://www.techdirt.com/articles/20121214/14133321389/who-signed-itu-wcit-treaty-who-didnt.shtml.

Ministry of Communications and Information Technologies. (2015). Indian Telegraph (Amendment) Rules, 2015. Notification of the Department of Telecommunications of August 25, 2015. https://dot.gov.in/sites/default/files/2016_09_29%20AMD-I%20Restructuring.PDF?download=1.

Ministry of Electronics and Information Technology. (2018). Information Technology (Information Security Practices and Procedures for Protected System) Rules, 2018. https://nciipc.gov.in/documents/Rules_procedures_new201.

Ministry of Electronics and Information Technology. (2021). Information Technology (Intermediary Guidelines and Digital Media Ethics Code) Rules, 2021. https://www.meity.gov.in/writereaddata/files/Intermediary_Guidelines_and_Digital_Media_Ethics_Code_Rules-2021.pdf.

Ministry of Electronics and Information Technology. (2022). National Data Governance Framework Policy Draft. https://www.meity.gov.in/writereaddata/files/National-Data-Governance-Framework-Policy.pdf.

Ministry of Information and Broadcasting. (n.d.). *Citizen's Charter 2018–19*. https://mib.gov.in/sites/default/files/CITIZEN%27S%20CHARTER%20%282018-19%29.pdf
National Internet Exchange of India [NIXI]. (2022). *Home*. https://nixi.in.
National Institute of Public Finance and Policy. (2017). Telecom Regulatory Authority of India: A Twenty Year Odyssey 1997-2017. TRAI. https://trai.gov.in/sites/default/files/A_TwentyYear_Odyssey_1997_2017.pdf.
Natural Resources Allocation, In re, Special Reference No. 1 of 2012. (2012). 10 SCC 1.
Netflix, Amazon Prime Video and 13 Other Online Platforms Sign Up for Self-Regulation Code. (2020, September 4). Scroll. https://scroll.in/latest/972260/netflix-amazon-prime-video-and-13-other-online-platforms-sign-up-for-self-regulation-code.
Office of Chief Controller of Accounts. (n.d.). *Government Accounts*. https://ccaind.nic.in/govt_accounts.asp.
Parsheera, S. (2018a). Challenges of competition and regulation in the Telecom Sector. *Economic & Political Weekly, 53*(38) .
Parsheera, S. (2018b). Net neutrality in India: Sighting the finish line. *EPW, 53*(25) .
Parsheera, S. (2019a, January 11). Policy issues in the telecom sector. Pune International Centre. https://puneinternationalcentre.org/wp-content/uploads/2019/04/Telecom_Smriti-Parsheera-1.pdf.
Pathak, A., Sagar, F. A., Rathore, V., & Deshpande, A. (2020, May 8). COVID-19: Its impact on the telecommunications sector in India. Cyril Amarchand Mangaldas. https://corporate.cyrilamarchandblogs.com/2020/05/covid-19-its-impact-on-the-telecommunications-sector-in-india/#_ftn15.
Prabhjot, G. (2020, July 20). JioPhone is Google and Ambani's second go at launching a smartphone—this time with help from Qualcomm. Business Insider. https://www.businessinsider.in/tech/mobile/news/jio-google-qualcomm-deal-for-new-4g-smartphone-jiophone/articleshow/76992941.cms.
Press Information Bureau. (2018a, November 6). "*India elected as a Member of the International Telecommunications Union (ITU) Council for another 4-year term (2019–2022)": Manoj Sinha*. https://pib.gov.in/PressReleseDetail.aspx?PRID=1552012.
Press Information Bureau. (2018b, September 18). ITU South Asia Area Office and Technology Innovation Centre to be established in New Delhi: Manoj Sinha. https://pib.gov.in/Pressreleaseshare.aspx?PRID=1546527.
Price of 5G Spectrum in India 30–40% Higher Than Global Rates: COAI. (2019, June 4). The Hindu Businessline. https://www.thehindubusinessline.com/info-tech/price-of-5g-spectrum-in-india-30-40-higher-than-global-rates-cellular-operators-body/article27460659.ece.
Rai, S., Muttreja, D., Banerjee, S., & Mishra, M. (2018). *The economics of releasing the V-band and E-band Spectrum in India*. National Institute of Public Finance and Policy. NIPFP Working Paper No. 226. https://macrofinance.nipfp.org.in/PDF/DMSS2018-Spectrum.pdf.
Regulation of OTT Apps to be Clarified in Revised Telecom Bill: Report. (2022, December 9). Business Standard. https://www.business-standard.com/article/current-affairs/regulation-of-ott-apps-to-be-clarified-in-revised-telecom-bill-report-122120900355_1.html.
Resolution of the Cabinet Secretariat No. 15/1/2/87 of April 11. 1989. https://dot.gov.in/sites/default/files/2016_05_26%20Res%20Policy-I.pdf?download=1%3Cbr%20/%3E.
Sanghi, A. (2018, December 21). CCI vs TRAI: Apex Court Does The Balancing Act. Live Law. https://www.livelaw.in/cci-vs-trai-apex-court-does-the-balancing-act/.
Sengupta, D. (2020, April 9). Covid 19: Telcos push back on Trai diktat for more offers. *Economic Times*. https://economictimes.indiatimes.com/industry/telecom/telecom-news/covid-19-telcos-push-back-on-trai-diktat-for-more-offers/articleshow/75067189.cms?from=mdr.
Sinha, R. (2019, July 29). Explainer: The right to information (amendment) Bill, 2019. PRS Legislative Research. https://www.prsindia.org/theprsblog/explainer-right-information-amendment-bill-2019.
Srivastava, R. (2017). Community networks: Regulatory issues and gaps—experiences from India. Internet Society. https://www.internetsociety.org/resources/doc/2017/community-networks-regulatory-issues-gaps-experiences-india/.

Standing Committee on Information Technology. (2018). Progress on implementation of BharatNet, Fiftieth Report. http://164.100.47.193/lsscommittee/Information%20Technology/16_Information_Technology_50.pdf.
Tarang Sanchar. (2023). Home. https://tarangsanchar.gov.in/.
Telecom Engineering Centre. (2017). Standardization guide: Adoption of TSDSI/International Telecom Standards. https://tec.gov.in/pdf/M2M/Standardisation%20guide.pdf.
Telecom Engineering Centre. (2022). National Working Group-2: Operational aspects of service provision and telecommunication management. https://www.tec.gov.in/nwg-2.
The Competition Act. (2002). https://www.cci.gov.in/legal-framwork/act.
The Constitution of India. (2022). https://legislative.gov.in/sites/default/files/COI_English.pdf.
The Digital Personal Data Protection Bill. (2022). https://www.meity.gov.in/writereaddata/files/The%20Digital%20Personal%20Data%20Potection%20Bill%2C%202022_0.pdf.
The Income Tax Act. (1961).
The Information Technology Act [IT Act]. (2000).
The Personal Data Protection Bill [PDP Bill]. (2019). http://164.100.47.4/BillsTexts/LSBillTexts/Asintroduced/373_2019_LS_Eng.pdf.
The Right to Information Act [RTI Act]. (2005).
The Telecom Regulatory Authority of India Act [TRAI Act]. (1997). https://www.trai.gov.in/sites/default/files/The_TRAI_Act_1997.pdf.
The Telegraph Act. (1885).
The Wireless Telegraphy Act. (1933).
Telecom Regulatory Authority of India [TRAI]. (2007). *International telecommunication access to essential facilities at cable landing stations regulations*. https://www.trai.gov.in/sites/default/files/Regulation_07june07.pdf.
Telecom Regulatory Authority of India [TRAI]. (2011). Recommendations on telecommunications infrastructure policy. https://trai.gov.in/sites/default/files/Rec_Infrastructurel_1.pdf.
Telecom Regulatory Authority of India [TRAI]. (2015). Recommendations on delivering broadband quickly: What do we need to do? https://trai.gov.in/sites/default/files/Broadband%3D17.04.2015.pdf.
Telecom Regulatory Authority of India [TRAI]. (2016). Prohibition of discriminatory tariffs for data services regulations. https://trai.gov.in/sites/default/files/Regulation_Data_Service.pdf.
Telecom Regulatory Authority of India [TRAI]. (2017a). Consultation paper on privacy, Security and Ownership of the Data in the Telecom Sector. https://trai.gov.in/sites/default/files/Consultation_Paper%20_on_Privacy_Security_ownership_of_data_09082017.pdf.
Telecom Regulatory Authority of India [TRAI]. (2017b). Recommendations Proliferation of Broadband Through Mahanagar Door Sanchar Bhawan, Jawahar Lal Recommendations on Proliferation of Broadband Through Public Wi-Fi Networks. https://trai.gov.in/sites/default/files/WiFi_Recommendation_09032017.pdf.
Telecom Regulatory Authority of India [TRAI]. (2018a). Explanatory Memorandum to the Telecommunication Tariff (Sixty Third Amendment) Order, 2018. https://www.trai.gov.in/sites/default/files/TTO_Amendment_Eng_16022018.pdf.
Telecom Regulatory Authority of India [TRAI]. (2018b). International Telecommunication Cable Landing Stations Access Facilitation Charges and Co-location Charges (Amendment) Regulations, 2018. https://www.trai.gov.in/sites/default/files/RegulationAFCCLC28112018_0.pdf.
Telecom Regulatory Authority of India [TRAI]. (2018c). Report on TRAI public open Wi-fi pilot. https://trai.gov.in/sites/default/files/WiFiPilotReport05042018.pdf.
Telecom Regulatory Authority of India [TRAI]. (2018d). Telecommunication Tariff (Sixty Third Amendment) Order, 2018. https://www.trai.gov.in/sites/default/files/TTO_Amendment_Eng_16022018.pdf.
Telecom Regulatory Authority of India [TRAI]. (2019a). Recommendations on an approach to rural telephony—suggested measures for an accelerated growth. https://www.trai.gov.in/sites/default/files/09Mar_Recommendation_19Mar09.pdf.

Telecom Regulatory Authority of India [TRAI]. (2019b). The Indian Telecom Services Performance Indicators October—December, 2019. https://www.trai.gov.in/sites/default/files/PIR_30062020.pdf.
Telecom Regulatory Authority of India [TRAI]. (2019c). Wireless Data Services in India. https://www.trai.gov.in/sites/default/files/Wireless_Data_Service_Report_21082019_0.pdf.
Telecom Regulatory Authority of India [TRAI]. (2020a). Recommendations on Regulatory Framework for Over-The-Top (OTT) Communication Services. https://trai.gov.in/sites/default/files/Recommendation_14092020_0.pdf.
Telecom Regulatory Authority of India [TRAI]. (2020b). Recommendations on enhancement of scope of infrastructure providers category-I (IP-I) registration. https://trai.gov.in/sites/default/files/Recommendations_13032020.pdf.
Telecom Regulatory Authority of India [TRAI]. (2020c). Consultation paper on enabling unbundling of different layers through differential licensing. https://trai.gov.in/sites/default/files/Consultation_Paper_20082020.pdf.
Telecom Regulatory Authority of India [TRAI]. (2021). Recommendations on enabling unbundling of different layers through differential licensing. https://www.trai.gov.in/sites/default/files/Recommendation_19082021_0.pdf.
Telecom Regulatory Authority of India [TRAI]. (2022). The Indian telecom services performance indicators April—June, 2022. https://www.trai.gov.in/sites/default/files/QPIR_23112022.pdf.
TRAI Issues Spectrum Usage Charges Sop. (2020, August 18). The Telegraph. https://www.telegraphindia.com/business/trai-issues-spectrum-usage-charges-sop/cid/1789412.
Telecommunications Standards Development Society, India. (2022a). *ITU-T SG13/15/17/20 Registration Form*. https://tsdsi.in/itu-t-sg13-15-17-20/.
Telecommunications Standards Development Society, India. (2022b). *Overview of TSDSI*. https://tsdsi.in/about/.
Telecommunications Standards Development Society, India. (2022c). *Published Standards*. https://tsdsi.in/published-standards

Smriti Parsheera is a lawyer and independent researcher working on issues at the intersection of technology and society. Her areas of interest include privacy and data governance, internet governance, digital public infrastructure and protection of human rights in the digital sphere. This research was conducted between 2020-23 while she was a Fellow with the CyberBRICS Project at Fundação Getulio Vargas Law School, Brazil. Prior to that she has worked with organizations such as the National Institute of Public Finance & Policy, New Delhi, the Competition Commission of India and the United Nations Development Programme. Smriti graduated from the National Law School of India University, Bangalore, and obtained her LLM from the University of Pennsylvania along with a Certificate in Law and Business from the Wharton School. She is currently pursuing a PhD in public policy from the Indian Institute of Technology Delhi.

India: An Analysis of the Digitalisation of Public Services

Smriti Parsheera

Abstract This chapter maps key aspects related to the digitalisation of public services in India. The following elements are investigated: policy elements related to digital government strategies, declarations, programs and actions; regulatory elements related to openness, sharing and data protection laws; institutional and governance elements related to the oversight and competences of public agencies, public-private partnerships and regulatory innovations in technology; and evidence from critical sectors such as smart cities, digital ID, and digital payments.

1 National Strategies and Priorities

Is there a national strategy for digitalisation/digital transformation? Is there a specific national strategy for digitalisation of public services?

India has adopted several initiatives geared towards increased digitisation and digital transformation over the last two decades. The National Policy on Information Technology, adopted in 2012, focused on strategies for the deployment of information and communication technologies (ICT) in all sectors of the economy and strengthening India's position as an IT hub (Ministry of Electronics and Information Technology [MeitY], 2012). Since 2014, the Government of India has been running a flagship programme called Digital India that operates with a "vision to transform India into a digitally empowered society and knowledge economy" (MeitY, 2022f). The programme brought together several existing and new initiatives operated by different Ministries and Departments of the government under a common umbrella. Digital India consists of nine pillars, which include the creation of broadband highways, universal access to mobile connectivity, e-governance reforms and building capacity in electronics manufacturing.

Before this, the National e-Governance Plan (NeGP), which was launched in 2006, was a similar umbrella initiative to bring together over 30 government

S. Parsheera (✉)
School of Public Policy, Indian Institute of Technology Delhi, New Delhi, India

L. Belli, L. Galdino de Magalhães Santos (eds.), *SmartBRICS*,
https://doi.org/10.1007/978-3-031-98204-0_10

projects in areas like education, health, public distribution system, to make the services more accessible to the common person (MeitY, 2021). In 2015, the NeGP was refashioned into a programme called e-Kranti, which translates to electronic revolution, targeted at "Transforming e-Governance for Transforming Governance." The key principles of e-Kranti include a focus on government process reengineering, without which a project may not be sanctioned, adoption of cloud services by default, a 'mobile first' approach to enable service delivery through phones, and adherence to prescribed cyber security measures (National e-Governance Division, n.d.-c). This is accompanied by the e-governance pillar of Digital India, which also focuses on the need for government business process re-engineering through the use of IT to improve transactions, simplification of forms, online tracking, and integration of services and platforms. The government has also launched an electronic database called the Electronic Transaction Aggregation & Analysis Layer (e-Taal) that offers a real-time aggregated view of the volume of e-services being delivered at different levels of the government (MeitY, 2022d; National Informatics Centre, 2018).

In 2020, the Ministry of Electronics and Information Technology (MeitY) released a consultation white paper on formulating a strategy for National Open Digital Ecosystems (NODEs) (MeitY, 2020b). The document describes NODEs as a new paradigm of GovTech 3.0, which follows the earlier generations of e-governance, labelled as GovTech 1.0 and 2.0. GovTech 1.0 is related to a phase of automation in which the service delivery remained largely offline, but some parts of the user experience were shifted online. The next phase of GovTech 2.0 focused on end-to-end digitisation of public service delivery. Building on these developments, the proposed NODEs model intends to follow an ecosystems approach involving the use of open APIs and interoperable platforms to connect different parts of the government system and allow private players to build new services on top of those systems (MeitY, 2020b). However, the NODEs proposal is still at the stage of being a discussion document and has not yet been translated into a definitive strategy or policy document.

Is the digitalisation of any specific sector seen as a priority for the country (e.g. Central Bank Digital Currency, digital identity, online payments, deployment of artificial intelligence, smart cities, cybersecurity, etc.)?

Digitisation initiatives are taking place across multiple sectors and are being implemented by different ministries and departments at the central and state levels. For instance, the e-Kranti programme referred to above consists of 44 Mission Mode Projects (MMPs) that are grouped into central, state and integrated projects. Each MMP is focused on strengthening e-governance in one particular area, such as banking, income tax, land records modernisation, e-courts, and e-procurement (MeitY, 2022c). The key thrust areas identified for the e-Kranti under the Digital India programme include education, health, geographic information system (GIS)-based decision-making, technology for financial inclusion, and technology for justice (National e-Governance Division, n.d.-b).

Is there an overall Artificial Intelligence strategy? Is there a specific national strategy for the use of Artificial Intelligence in the public sector?

The government think tank, NITI Aayog, released an approach document on Principles of Responsible AI in February 2021 (NITI Aayog, 2021b), followed by an approach document on Operationalizing Principles for Responsible AI in August (NITI Aayog, 2021c). Both these developments follow the process initiated in June 2018 through a discussion paper on India's National Strategy for Artificial Intelligence (NITI Aayog, 2018). In 2018, the MeitY also constituted four expert committees to propose actions in the areas of Platform and Data for AI, Leveraging AI for National Missions in Key Sectors, Mapping Technological Capabilities and Skilling, and Cyber Security, Safety, Legal & Ethical issues (MeitY, 2018). Since then, each of the four committees has submitted its recommendations, which have been put out by MeitY in the public domain (MeitY, 2022e).

The 2018 discussion paper by NITI Aayog identified the development of #AIforAll as its main goal and identified the following five sectors where AI could play a particularly important role in solving societal needs: healthcare, agriculture, education, smart cities and infrastructure and smart mobility and transportation. The paper also focused on the need to build AI research capabilities through the setting up of a Centre of Research Excellence focused on core AI research and International Centers of Transformational AI for the development and deployment of new applications. Following this, the AI principles document highlights various systems and societal considerations relating to AI, and based on that, identifies seven broad principles for responsible management of AI. This includes principles on safety and reliability, equality, inclusivity and non-discrimination, privacy and security, transparency, accountability and protection of positive human values. The most recent document that came out in August 2021 then builds on this to identify various mechanisms for operationalising the seven principles, divided among three stakeholders—governments, the private sector and research institutions.

Some of the known initiatives relating to AI in the public sector include the setting up of the Centre for Artificial Intelligence & Robotics under the Defence Research and Development Organisation (2022) and the creation of the Responsible AI for Youth program that seeks to democratise access to AI tools and demystify AI concepts for young students enrolled in government schools (National e-Governance Division, 2022). A more comprehensive mapping of Automated Decision-Making Systems that are in effect in India, as well as the challenges posed by them, is available as part of the AI Observatory created by researcher Divij Joshi (AI Observatory, n.d.).

Is there a specific strategy or reference to the use of social media to facilitate government activities?

The Government of India released a set of guidelines for the use of social media by government organisations in 2012 (Department of Electronics and Information Technology, 2012). The document highlights enhanced reach, individual engagement, real-time response and managing perceptions as some of the benefits of the use of social media by public agencies. It then goes on to identify seven core values, of identity, authority, relevance, professionalism, openness, compliance and privacy, that need to be kept in mind while using social media for official purposes. The document also contains guidance on the creation and organisation of official accounts, governance of content, data and information security, and engagement analysis.

Is there a strategy or any specific policies aimed at promoting the use of open-source software/hardware by public administrations or generally?
The "Policy on Adoption of Open Source Software for Government of India" was released in 2014 (Department of Electronics & Information Technology, 2014a). The open-source policy makes it mandatory for government agencies to "endeavour" to adopt open-source software, where the code is available for study and modification and the software is free of royalty, in all e-governance systems. However, an exception, with justification, can be made where open-source software meeting essential functional requirements may not be available or is not able to meet the urgent/strategic needs. Before this, the National Policy on Information Technology (2012) had also emphasised the importance of adopting open standards and technologies.

Are there specific policies mandating interoperability requirements for the systems utilised by public administrations? Are there any strategies or recommendations to avoid vendor lock-in?
India adopted a "Policy on Open Application Programming Interfaces (APIs) for Government of India" in 2015. As per the policy document, its objective is to create "an interoperable ecosystem of data, applications and processes which will make the right information available to the right user at the right time" (Department of Electronics & Information Technology, 2014b). The policy advocates the use of open APIs to promote interoperability among all e-governance applications, providing easier access to data and promoting participation of all stakeholders. It applies to all central government organisations, and it is also open for adoption by state governments.

In terms of practical application, the IndiaStack framework has led to the development and use of APIs in several areas such as biometric authentication and digital payments (IndiaStack, n.d.). Further, the NODEs discussion paper referred to earlier also proposes the creation of interoperable digital delivery platforms. As per the explanation provided by MeitY, the term "open" in this context refers to principles of openness in terms of transparency, accessibility, interoperability, open APIs and standards and open-source code, where appropriate (MeitY, 2020b). Further, a Working Group on Digital Service Standards had also recommended that open API-based ecosystems must be explored as a method of first choice while designing a portfolio of services in any sector (MeitY, n.d.).

Is there a strategy or any specific policies promoting open data (e.g. government-business data sharing, open government, and/or open data in general)?

The National Data Sharing and Accessibility Policy (NDSAP) adopted by the Department of Science and Technology creates a framework for ensuring the public availability of public data (Ministry of Science and Technology, 2012). It covers data that has been created using public resources provided by the Government of India either directly or through various departments, agencies and autonomous bodies (MeitY, 2012). The adoption of this policy was accompanied by the creation of the portal https://data.gov.in/ that serves as the open government data platform. In addition, a few state governments have also created similar portals at the state level.

Further, the Right to Information Act, 2005 (RTI Act) creates a statutory framework for bringing about transparency and accountability in the functioning of public authorities. It mandates all public authorities to publish details about the organisation, directory of officials, budget allocations, rules, regulations and manuals, etc., on a sub-moto basis (The Right to Information Act [RTI Act], 2005, Section 4). In addition, citizens have the right to request any specific information from the designated public information officials required to be appointed by each public agency (RTI Act, 2005, Section 6).

The government had also constituted an expert committee to make recommendations on the governance of non-personal data (MeitY, 2020a). This includes public non-personal data, namely data generated and held by government agencies during their operations, such as anonymised health data of patients, land records, vehicle registration details, etc. As per the recommendations, government and private organisations that collect and manage data will qualify as a data business and will be bound by certain requirements, like sharing details of the metadata collected by them and making data sets that are designated as High-value Datasets available to requesting entities.

In May 2022, the Indian government put out a Draft National Data Governance Framework Policy to create a mechanism for the pooling and sharing of non-personal data and anonymised data from government and private sources (voluntarily in the case of private entities) (MeitY, 2022g). The policy seeks to create a body known as the India Data Management Office (IDMO) to be set up under the Digital India Corporation, a corporate entity under the Ministry of Electronics and Information Technology (MeitY). The IDMO will develop metadata rules, sharing standards, and guidelines for the implementation of the data sharing policy.

Are the national strategies binding documents (i.e. adopted in the form of laws or decrees) or are they just declaratory documents?

Strategies and policy documents like the National Data Sharing and Accessibility Policy, the Policy on Open Application Programming Interfaces and the Policy on Adoption of Open Source Software are issued by the government without any statutory basis. Such policies are not enforceable before a court of law.

Is there a specific policy for integration, inclusion of vulnerable groups (e.g. elderly, etc) or accessibility for people with disabilities?

The Rights of Persons with Disabilities Act (2016) requires the central and state governments to ensure that audio, print and electronic media content should be made available in an accessible format and provision of electronic media should be supported by services like audio description, sign language interpretation and close captioning (The Rights of Persons with Disabilities Act, 2016, Section 42). The Department of Empowerment of Persons with Disabilities has also launched a universal accessibility programme called Accessible India that includes ICT ecosystem accessibility as one of its components (Department of Empowerment of Persons with Disabilities, 2022). Although these protections exist in the law and in government policies, the results are not always reflected in actual practice. For instance, a study conducted in 2016 found that out of the 7800 websites that were tested, 1985 websites failed to open, and most of the remaining 5815 websites had some sort of accessibility barriers (Narasimhan et al., 2016).

Are the national strategies guided or are they involved in cooperation agreements, best practices, programs, associations of organizations such as UN Agenda 2030 SDGs, OECD, World Bank?

The Digital India programme does not make any specific reference to international cooperation and best practices, either in its aims or in the key pillars. However, linkages between Digital India and the fulfilment of the SDGs have been drawn in other policy documents. For instance, a recent report on India's performance on the SDGs by the NITI Aayog refers to the implementation of the National Digital Health Mission, which involves the creation of a digital health ID and systems for electronic health records management, as a step toward achievement of the SDG 3 on health reforms (NITI Aayog & United Nations, 2021). Further, Target 9c of the SDGs relates to universal ICT access. The NITI Aayog document links this to the goal of universal access to mobile connectivity, which is one of the pillars of Digital India. Some commentators have also linked India's digitally-enabled policy initiatives to an improvement in the country's performance in the World Bank's Ease of Doing Business Index (Gupta & Auerswald, 2019).

India is not an OECD member but is recognised as one of its key partners. A 2018 publication by the OECD recognises India's participation in various OECD committees, including those relating to the digital economy (Organization for Economic Cooperation and Development [OECD], 2018). As a founding member of the Global Partnership on Artificial Intelligence (GPAI) and a G20 member, Indian has also endorsed the OECD recommendations on AI that have been adopted by both these forums (Parsheera, 2021). Further, India also has a history of adopting the standards and guidance issued by the International Telecommunication Union (ITU) in its telecommunication policy. This is reflected in the terms of the Unified License agreement and the standardisation guide set out by the Telecom Engineering Centre (Department of Telecommunications, n.d., Chap. 1, Clause 2.2(ii)). The National Digital Communications Policy released in 2018 also contained several references to the adoption of international best practices (Department of Telecommunications, 2018).

Are there any existing policies to zero rate certain e-government services? Are there such policies for specific public sectors?

In February 2016, TRAI notified the Prohibition of Discriminatory Tariffs for Data Services Regulations (Telecom Regulatory Authority of India [TRAI], 2016). The Regulation prohibits TSPs from offering differential pricing for data services based on the type of content being accessed by the user, hence barring any form of zero-rating practices. In the early days of the COVID-19 crisis, the Cellular Operators Association of India wrote to the Department of Telecommunications (DoT) suggesting that the government should enable free access to certain critical websites, such as those relating to health services and providing COVID-19-related information (Parsheera, 2020). This was proposed to be done using the available exemptions for public emergencies under the regulations on discriminatory tariffs for data services. However, this request is not known to have been actioned upon by the telecom regulator, TRAI, or the DoT.

How does the country rank on global digital adoption indices, such as the World Bank's Digital Adoption Index, the Digital Society Index, IMD World Digital Competitiveness Ranking, Global Open Data Index etc.?

India was among the 43 countries classified under Group A (GovTech leaders) in the World Bank's GovTech Maturity Index published in 2021 (Dener et al., 2021). Among the various sub-components of the index, it fared the best on the GovTech Enablers Index (0.86/1), which includes digital skills, enabling and safeguarding institutions, laws and regulations, strategy, cybersecurity, digital signature, and innovation in the public sector. It fared relatively poorly on the Core Government Systems Index (0.77/1), which measures success in aspects like government cloud, interoperability platforms, enterprise architecture, open-source solutions, and disruptive technologies.

It fared more modestly in the World Bank's Digital Adoption Index. In 2016, India had an overall score of 0.51/1 on the index. Of the three sub-indices, it fared the poorest on the sub-index relating to expanding opportunities and improving welfare for people (0.22/1), followed by productivity and growth for businesses (0.5/1) and performed the best on increasing efficiency and accountability of service delivery for government (0.8/1) (The World Bank, 2022).

India ranked 46th out of the 64 economies covered in the IMD World Digital Competitiveness Ranking. In terms of the different components, it was placed at rank 41 in knowledge, rank 44 in technology, and rank 50 in future readiness (International Institute for Management Development, 2022).

India received a score of 47% in the Global Open Data Index, placing it at rank 32 out of 94 analysed countries. It received a 100% score on two parameters—data about government budgets and air quality (Open Knowledge Foundation, 2016).

Finally, the United Nations E-Government Survey of 2020 gave India a score of 0.59 on the E-Government Index, placing it at rank 100 out of the 193 countries covered in the survey. It scored 0.85 on the online service index, 0.35 on the telecommunications infrastructure index and 0.58 on the human capital index (United Nations Department of Economic and Social Affairs, 2020). The report reflects on the high level of online services delivery in India despite there being only moderate infrastructure development.

2 Regulations

Is there any general regulation (e.g. law, decree, standards) to organise the digitalisation of public services, other than specific regulations that might apply to the key sectors identified below?
The Information Technology Act, 2000 (IT Act) is the main law governing digital transactions in India. Chapter 2 of the IT Act deals with the subject of "electronic governance," containing provisions relating to legal recognition of electronic records and signatures and use of electronic records by government agencies. It provides that any legal requirement relating to the provision of written information or the retention of records can be met in an electronic form (The Information Technology Act, 2000, Sections 4, 7). It also enables the filing of forms, the issue of licences and certifications, and receipt or payment involving government agencies to be made in an electronic format (IT Act, 2000, Section 6). But the law also clarifies that these are only enabling provisions and do not confer a right upon individuals to demand the use of electronic documents or payments by government agencies (IT Act, 2000, Section 9). The Indian government is currently in the process of preparing a draft Digital India Bill that proposes to replace the IT Act with a new law that will reportedly focus on ensuring "openness of internet, safety, trust, and accountability as basic principles" (ENS Economic Bureau, 2022).

Specifically in the context of electronic service delivery, an Electronic Delivery of Services Bill (2011) was introduced in the Parliament in 2011 (PRS Legislative Research, n.d.). The bill contained provisions that would require public authorities to deliver all public services electronically and create a mechanism for redress for non-delivery or deficiency in electronic services. However, this bill has lapsed and was not converted into a law.

Is there any regulation mandating transparency audits for technologies (e.g. of platforms, algorithms, cloud services, etc.) utilised by public administrations?
The Comptroller and Auditor General (CAG) of India is a constitutional authority under the Indian Constitution. The CAG's office is responsible for carrying out financial and performance audits of various government departments and agencies in line with the constitutional mandate and provisions of The Comptroller Auditor-General's (Duties, Powers and Conditions of Service) Act (1971). The CAG's powers to conduct systems audits include the audit of IT systems. A specialised IT audit wing has been set up for this purpose. The process and guidelines for the same are recorded in a Manual of Information Technology Audit released by the CAG (Office

of the Comptroller & Auditor General of India, n.d.). The Manual emphasises the importance of general as well as application controls. General controls relate to controls over data centre operations, acquisition and maintenance of software, and access security, while application controls relate more specifically to individual transactions. The CAG's website contains details of all IT audits that have been conducted by the office at the central and state levels, in addition to a function classification based on the operational domain of the relevant project. This includes categories such as e-governance initiatives, electricity boards and companies, land records computerisation, and computerisation of treasuries (International Centre for Information Systems and Audit [iCISA], 2022).

Is there any specific regulation mandating requirements for public procurements and public tenders regarding digital public services?
Public procurement is governed mainly by the General Financial Rules (2017) and the Manual for Procurement of Goods (2017) set out by the Ministry of Finance. The rules are treated as executive instructions that need to be observed by all government departments and organisations. The definition of "goods" covered by the rules includes "intangible products like software, technology transfer, licenses, patents or other intellectual properties purchased or otherwise acquired for the use of Government."[1] The rules lay down certain monetary thresholds allowing purchases below those limits to be made directly by the ministry, without inviting bids or through a limited tender enquiry (Mara & Deshpande, 2020). In addition to these rules, certain state governments have enacted state-specific procurement legislation. Further, in 2013, the IT Ministry notified a policy for granting preferential market access in government procurement for domestically manufactured electronic products (Department of Expenditure, 2017b). Similarly, the Ministry has also issued an order granting a preference to Indian businesses and startups in the public procurement of cybersecurity products under the Make in India policy (MeitY, 2019c).

Are digital public services subject to general data protection regulations? If not, is there any data protection regulation for digital public services?
Any privacy implications arising from personal data processing by the state would be subject to the tests laid down by the Supreme Court while declaring privacy to be a fundamental right. But, in terms of the statutory framework, the current data protection framework under Section 43A of the IT Act applies only to body corporates and hence does not cover the provision of digital services by government agencies. This is sought to be remedied through the enactment of a comprehensive data protection law, which will cover all government and private entities that process personal data. The Personal Data Protection Bill (2019) that was introduced in the Parliament in December 2019 was referred to a Joint Parliamentary Committee that submitted its recommendations in December 2021 (Lok Sabha Secretariat, 2020). But in August 2022, the Indian government decided to withdraw the 2019 bill and later replaced it with a new draft in 2022 that went on to be passed as the Digital

[1] Rule 143 of the General Financial Rules (Department of Expenditure, 2017a).

Personal Data Protection Act, 2023 (DPDP Act). The provisions of the DPDP Act remain problematic due to the broad exemptions for government agencies, particularly under Section 17(2), which allows for the exemption of any instrumentality of the state from the applicability of all provisions of the law (The Digital Personal Data Protection Act, 2023).

In addition, there are certain sector or product-specific data protection guidelines that are already in place. For instance, the digital identity project Aadhaar is governed by privacy protections available under the Aadhaar (Targeted Delivery of Financial and other Subsidies, Benefits and Services) Act (2016). The launch of the Ayushman Bharat Digital Mission has also been accompanied by a Health Data Management Policy that is meant to set out the basic standards of data protection in the digital health ecosystem (Ayushman Bharat Digital Mission, n.d.). However, unlike the Aadhaar Act, this is not a statutory framework and therefore serves only as a guidance document that is not enforceable by citizens against state agencies or private actors.

Are there any current or proposed regulations mandating the sharing of data with government agencies to enable better delivery of public services?
The PDP Bill (2019) contained a provision (Section 91) that would have enabled the government to direct any data fiduciary or data processor to provide any personal data anonymised or other non-personal data (all data other than personal data) to the government. This power was to be exercised to enable better targeting of the delivery of services or the formulation of evidence-based policies by the government. In line with the existence of this power under the draft bill, the Joint Parliamentary committee had recommended that the PDP Bill and the proposed Data Protection Authority under it should be restructured to become an overarching law on data governance, not limited to personal data. The final DPDP Act has, however, done away with this suggestion and limits its focus only to digital personal data.

There is a separate proposal for bringing about a more comprehensive legal and regulatory framework for the governance of non-personal data in the country. The IT Ministry constituted the Kris Gopalakrishnan committee of experts for this purpose, which submitted its recommendations in July 2020, followed by a revised draft in December 2020. Among other things, the recommendations suggest making it mandatory to share data that is necessary for the creation of 'high value datasets' for public good purposes (MeitY, 2020a).[2] The recommendations under these two processes will ultimately have to be reconciled to develop a consistent approach to data governance. In addition to this, the draft National Data Governance Framework, which is primarily meant for data standardisation, pooling and sharing involving public agencies, will also allow for voluntary data contribution by private entities (MeitY, 2022g).

---

[2] A detailed comparison of the two versions of the recommendations is available at Ikigai Law (2021).

3 Institutions

Is there a specific body overseeing the digitalisation of the public sector?
As noted earlier, the Digital India programme provides the umbrella structure for the promotion of digital initiatives, including in the e-governance space. The Programme Management Structure for Digital India includes a Monitoring Committee headed by the Prime Minister, an Advisory Group headed by the Minister of Communications and IT and an Apex Committee headed by the Cabinet Secretary (Digital India, 2022). In addition to this, MeitY has set up a non-profit entity called the Digital India Corporation that is meant to provide strategic support to various government departments through capacity building for e-governance projects and encouraging Public-Private Partnerships (Digital India Corporation, 2022). In terms of ministerial responsibilities, MeitY is responsible for all policy matters relating to information technology, electronics and the Internet. Further, each ministry or department that adopts a digitisation project will have its own governance structure in place for the implementation of the project, but MeitY may offer assistance to other departments in the promotion of e-governance initiatives (MeitY, 2019a).

If such a body exists, what is Its status (e.g. an independent agency, a ministry, an inter-ministerial committee, an ad-hoc body, etc.)?
The Digital India Corporation (formerly called Media Lab Asia) is a not-for-profit company set up by MeitY. The company was incorporated on September 20, 2001, as a Company Limited by Guarantee, not having share capital (Digital India Corporation, 2018). Its name was changed from "Media Lab Asia" to "Digital India Corporation" in September 2017. The company is fully under the control of the government, with its current board of directors consisting of Ministers and senior officials from MeitY.

If such a body exists, what are its prerogatives and powers?
The objective of the Digital India Corporation is to "bring the benefits of most advanced Information and Communication Technologies (ICT) to the common man." The objectives also include promotion of the Digital India programme of the government and promoting the use of technology for eHealth/Telemedicine, e-agriculture, e-payments, etc. (Digital India Corporation, 2018). The company consists of three main divisions—the Technology Development & Deployment Division, the National e-Governance Division and the MyGov Division that operates the MyGov participatory governance platform (Digital India Corporation, 2022). The government has also proposed that a new office called the India Data Management Office will be set up under the Digital India Corporation to implement the National Data Governance Framework (MeitY, 2022g).

Is there an evaluation system or indicators to measure the progress of development of digital government?
India adopted a National e-Governance Service Delivery Assessment (NeSDA) framework in 2018 (Department of Administrative Reforms and Public Grievances,

2019). The framework, developed by the Department of Administrative Reforms & Public Grievances in collaboration with industry body NASSCOM, is used to measure the effectiveness of e-governance mechanisms. It assesses the service portals offered at the state and central levels on parameters such as accessibility, content availability, ease of use, information security & privacy and end-service delivery. The first edition of the NeSDA was carried out in 2019 (Department of Administrative Reforms and Public Grievances, 2019). It focused on the provision of G2C and G2B services in six sectors—finance, labour & employment, education, local government, social welfare (including agriculture & health) and environment. The 2021 edition of the NeSDA will also cover certain other sectors like public procurement, home affairs and tourism (Department of Administrative Reforms and Public Grievances, 2022). The new assessment parameters proposed for NeSDA 2021 include open government data, e-participation, alignment to SDGs, and cyber resilience (Department of Administrative Reforms and Public Grievances, 2021).

Separately, an audit of government websites was also conducted by the Standardisation Testing and Quality Certification (STQC) Directorate in 2016. The STQC is a government undertaking that conducts testing, audit and certifications for IT & e-governance services. Its audit of 957 government websites based on the Guidelines of Indian Government Websites found that only 31 of the websites complied with the guidelines at that point (Varshney, 2016).

In 2017, a Working Group on Digital Service Standards recommended the need to put in place a set of standards for defining, designing, developing, delivering and measuring the value created by digital services (MeitY, n. d.). The document includes specific recommendations on measurement and assessment criteria for digital services, such as volume of digital transactions, turnaround times, distribution across geographies and coverage of remote areas. It also contains guidelines for the measurement of quality and outputs against basic characteristics of good governance like participation, rule of law, transparency, efficiency, and accountability.

Is there a public company or any public-private partnerships working on the development of specific solutions for digitizing the public sector? If the company exists, what is its function?

The National e-Governance Division of the DIC supports the IT Ministry in the management and implementation of e-governance projects. The division's responsibilities include providing technical assistance to e-governance projects, either directly or in collaboration with professional consultants. It is also responsible for undertaking technical appraisals of such projects, developing tender documents and private-public partnership models, carrying out impact assessments, e-readiness measurements and training and development initiatives (National e-Governance Division, n.d.-a, n.d.-b, n.d.-c). Further, the National Informatics Centre (NIC), which also falls under the IT Ministry, acts as a technology partner to the Government of India. Its responsibilities include the design of IT systems for the government and the provision of ICT infrastructure. Its products and services include ICT solutions like e-courts, e-hospitals, and e-transport, operation of a pan-India communication network called NICNET for the government, multiple National Data Centres and cloud services (National Informatics Centre, 2022). In addition to these government undertakings, there are also private initiatives like the eGov Foundation that develop technological solutions for the implementation of e-governance projects (eGov Foundation, n.d.).

What are the criteria aimed at guaranteeing the independence of the "third parties" auditing digital public service providers?
The Indian Computer Emergency Response Team (CERT-In) has a process for the empanelment of IT security auditing organisations for conducting audits and vulnerability assessment of various IT systems (CERT-In, n.d.). CERT-In, however, does not play a role in the contracting process between the empanelled organisation and the auditee. Moreover, there is little information in the public domain about third-party auditing of digital public services. The Working Group on Digital Service Standards referred to earlier also suggested the need for a security audit of digital services, but did not make any specific recommendations about the independence of such auditors. They, however, suggested the creation of frameworks for audit and certification of organisations and the establishment of a process for empanelment of professional companies to undertake audits of digital services (MeitY, n. d.). They also proposed that the government should notify the formats and templates for the audit.

4 Key Sectors

4.1 Digital Identity

Is there a strategy to digitalise this sector or any areas of it?
India has a biometric digital identity system called Aadhaar that has been in operation since 2010. It currently has over 1.3 billion people enrolled in it. Aadhaar is in the nature of a foundational ID, which means that its main objective is to establish and enable verifiability of a person's identity as opposed to serving a specific function like a driving license, passport or tax ID. The Aadhaar ID consists of a 12-digit number that is issued to individuals upon collection of their demographic and biometric information (fingerprint, iris scan and facial photo) that is used to carry out a de-duplication exercise to try and ensure that a unique identity is issued to each individual.

In a strategy overview released in April 2010, the Unique Identification Authority of India (UIDAI) referred to exclusions and inconvenience caused due to non-availability of valid identification proofs and loss to the exchequer because of difficulties in identification of legitimate beneficiaries as the main justifications for having a digital ID system (Unique Identification Authority of India [UIDAI] Planning Commission, 2010). The UIDAI offers an Aadhaar-based authentication service that can be used by government and private entities to authenticate the identity of individuals against the data held in UIDAI's Central Identities Data Repository

(CIDR). The authentication can be carried out using the person's biometrics, demographic information, a One Time Pin (OTP) or through a combination of these modes (Unique Identification Authority of India [UIDAI], 2022). Aadhaar can be used for online electronic know your customer (e-KYC) checks or offline e-KYC using a digitally signed XML file that can be downloaded from the UIDAI's website.

The Aadhaar project has raised many serious concerns, including on account of deficiencies in its legal process, privacy concerns, denial of benefits due to mandatory linkage of Aadhaar with social benefits, and the lack of participative decision-making. These concerns became the basis for a constitutional challenge to the validity of Aadhaar, which was upheld by the Supreme Court in the 2018 Puttaswamy case while imposing certain restrictions and legal changes.[3] The court allowed Aadhaar to be made mandatory for the delivery of benefits and welfare schemes financed by the government, but imposed restrictions on its use by private entities. Subsequent legislative changes by the government and the UODA, however, allow voluntary use of Aadhaar by entities like banks, mutual funds, and telecom companies.

Is the use of specific technologies for digital identity systems promoted or prioritised (e.g. AI, blockchain, open source software)?

Aadhaar uses open APIs to allow authorised entities to connect with its systems for authentication and e-KYC purposes. The UIDAI describes the Aadhaar architecture as being "open and scalable" in nature. It also notes that to avoid dependence on specific hardware, storage, operating system and database vendors or technologies, Aadhaar has been built using open source or open technologies (UIDAI, 2022).

Separately, there is also a private initiative known as the Modular Open Source Identity Platform (MOSIP) that is hosted at the International Institute of Information Technology, Bangalore and funded by organisations like the Bill & Melinda Gates Foundation, Sir Ratan Tata Trust and Omidyar Network (MOSIP, n.d.). Described as a "global public good," MOSIP seeks to support other countries in the design of digital, foundational identity systems based on principles such as modularity, Privacy by Design, open APIs to enable interoperability, vendor neutrality and cost-effectiveness. While MOSIP is not directly linked to Aadhaar, there are clear linkages between the design features and architects of the two projects (Mehta, 2020).

Is there a sectoral regulation in place (e.g. law, decree, standards) to organise the digitalisation of the sector?

The Aadhaar project is governed by The Aadhaar (Targeted Delivery of Financial and Other Subsidies, Benefits and Services) Act (2016). Although Aadhaar's enrolment and authentication systems have been in operation since 2010, the enabling statutory framework for it came into effect only in 2016. Before this, the setting up and operation of the UIDAI was done on the basis of an executive order. A prior attempt at framing a law on this subject was made through the National Identification Authority of India Bill (2010), which was introduced in the Rajya Sabha in 2010.

---

[3] Justice Puttaswamy (Retd.) and Anr. v Union of India and Ors (2018).

However, the bill met with several objections from a Parliamentary Standing Committee and remained pending with the government for several years. Subsequently, the Aadhaar Act was brought into effect in 2016 as a money bill. This route, which is reserved for particular types of bills, allows the lower house of the Parliament, called the Lok Sabha, to adopt the bill without approval from the Rajya Sabha.

The Aadhaar Act contains provisions relating to enrolments and use of Aadhaar, functions and composition of the UIDAI, protection of data and circumstances in which it may be shared, and offenses and penalties for unauthorised access and use. The Act was amended in 2019 to bring some of the provisions in line with the Supreme Court's directions in the Puttaswamy case (The Aadhaar and other laws (Amendment) Act, 2019). In addition to the Aadhaar Act, the operation of the Aadhaar system is also governed by various rules framed by the government and regulations formulated by the UIDAI itself. This includes rules relating to terms and conditions of the UIDAI chairperson and members, filing of returns and annual reports, and preparation of statements of account.

In 2020, the government issued a new set of rules allowing Aadhaar authentication to be used voluntarily for ensuring good governance, prevention of dissipation of social welfare benefits, and enablement of innovation and the spread of knowledge (MeitY, 2020c). A proposal for such uses can be initiated by a department of a central or state government, but the "requesting entity" that is subsequently authorised could include private entities. This has been called out for amounting to a violation of the Supreme Court's directions (Internet Freedom Foundation, 2021).

Are there any policies promoting digital sovereignty for digital identity systems (e.g. data localisation, preference or obligation to utilise domestic providers etc.)?

As per the submissions made by the UIDAI before the Supreme Court, Aadhaar data is stored, kept and processed only on the UIDAI servers within its data centres ("Aadhaar data kept", 2017). The UIDAI currently has two data centres—in Bengaluru and Manesar—located within India. Furthermore, entities seeking to use the Aadhaar authentication facility as requesting entities are required to comply with the requirements and eligibility conditions specified by the UIDAI. In this regard, the eligibility conditions for authorisation as an Authentication User Agency specify that the entity should have its backend infrastructure, such as servers, databases, etc., that are required specifically for the purpose of Aadhaar authentication, located within the territory of India (UIDAI, 2016, Schedule A). Despite these conditions, in 2019, reports surfaced about the use of Aadhaar data of residents in the States of Telangana and Andhra Pradesh by an entity called IT Grids for use by a political party. The complaint filed by the UIDAI against IT Grids notes that the entity had hosted the data using the US-based Amazon Web Services, which is in contravention of the Aadhaar framework (Prasad, 2019).

Has the digitisation of the sector or any area of It been promoted because of the Covid19 pandemic? If yes, then how so?
Aadhaar has been used as one of the modes for verification of identity in the administration of COVID-19 vaccines in India. While it is not the sole permitted proof of identity as per the vaccination policy, there have been reports of vaccination centres mandatorily insisting on Aadhaar. This became the subject of a public interest litigation filed before the Supreme Court (India News, 2021). The petition was ultimately dismissed by the Supreme Court based on submissions made by the government that submitting Aadhaar details was not a precondition for getting a vaccine through the government's CoWin portal for vaccination delivery (India News, 2022). The court directed the government to ensure that authorities should not insist on the production of the Aadhaar card as the only proof of identification.

Separately, it was reported that in many cases, people who registered for the vaccination using Aadhaar were automatically issued a digital health identity, without specific information or consent (Ghosh, 2021). Further, the pandemic has also been used as an opportunity for pilot testing of the facial recognition feature of Aadhaar, which creates serious human rights concerns ("Digital Rights Bodies", 2021).

Is there a specific body in charge of overseeing, coordinating or promoting the digitalisation of the sector?
The UIDAI is the body in charge of overseeing and implementing the Aadhaar project. Before acquiring a statutory basis under the Aadhaar Act (2016), the UIDAI was set up as an attached office under the erstwhile Planning Commission of India. Chapter 4 of the Aadhaar Act, which came into effect in 2016, deals with the composition and functions of the UIDAI. It provides that the Authority will consist of a Chairperson, two part-time Members, and a chief executive officer (CEO). The CEO, who is a public official, is responsible for the day-to-day administration of the authority and implementation of its work programmes. Further, Section 23 of the Aadhaar Act lays down the various powers and functions of the UIDAI, which include specifying the types of demographic and biometric information required for enrolment, generating and assigning Aadhaar numbers, performing Aadhaar authentication, maintaining the CIDR, and specifying various processes for data management, security protocols and other technology safeguards relating to Aadhaar.

4.2 *Smart Cities and Digitised Local Administrations*

Is there a smart city strategy?
The Ministry of Housing and Urban Affairs launched an initiative called the Smart Cities Mission in 2015. As per its mission statement and guidelines, "the objective is to promote cities that provide core infrastructure and give a decent quality of life to its citizens, a clean and sustainable environment and application of 'Smart' Solutions" (Ministry of Urban Development, 2015). The document also elaborates on the meaning of the terms core infrastructure and smart solutions. The former

consists of 10 areas, including water and electricity supply, sanitation, mobility and public transport, housing, and e-governance and citizen participation. Further, it provides a non-exhaustive list of the types of interventions that may be regarded as smart solutions in each of these areas. For instance, smart solutions for water management include smart meters, leakage identification and water quality monitoring.

Under the mission, 100 cities in India have been selected through a competitive process for development as smart cities. The geographical distribution is not evenly distributed across states. The following large states contain the greatest number of selected cities—Tamil Nadu, Uttar Pradesh, Maharashtra, Karnataka, Madhya Pradesh and Gujarat (Aijaz, 2021). Each selected city has to develop a proposal setting out the specific solutions that it proposes to implement. The projects adopted may be in any field of area-based development—city improvement (retrofitting), city renewal (redevelopment) and city extension (greenfield development). In addition, there should also be a plan for pan-city development, which implies the application of smart solutions to city-wide infrastructure so that the project is useful for all the city's residents. The financing responsibilities for the projects are to be shared by the central government and state/urban local governments.

The original duration of the mission was from 2015 to 20, which now stands further extended. A recent assessment of the implementation status conducted by the Observer Research Foundation found that of the total amount for which tenders have been issued under the mission, only about 23 percent of funds have been released (Aijaz, 2021). Further, only a portion of the released funds have actually been utilised. This points to the need for significant improvement in the implementation of the project, which is expected to be achieved during its extended duration.

In addition to the mission dedicated specifically to the development of smart cities, several other projects and schemes have also been introduced to improve urban governance. For instance, the National Smart Grid Mission launched in 2015 to promote the use of smart meters and other data-management solutions in the delivery of utilities (MeitY, 2019b). Another initiative known as the Atal Mission for Rejuvenation and Urban Transformation is focusing on universal coverage of water supply and sewerage connections to all households in selected cities. The reform agendas under this project include the use of energy-efficient LED street lights in cities and conducting an energy audit of water pumps (Atal Mission for Rejuvenation and Urban Transformation, 2022).

Is the use of specific smart city technologies promoted or prioritised (e.g. AI, blockchain, open source software)?

The mission statement and guidelines of the Smart Cities Mission state that smart responses involve "the use of technology, information and data to make infrastructure and services better" (Ministry of Urban Development, 2015). The government has identified the introduction of shareable APIs and digital tools for improved urban e-governance in local bodies as a focus area (MeitY, 2019b). There is a proposal for the creation of a National Urban Innovation Stack that will be a common national platform to guide cities in the adoption of technological infrastructures (National Institute of Urban Affairs, n.d.). Its suggested components include core infrastructure in the form of registries and data infrastructure, core services like payments, authentication and GIS systems, a data exchange using open standards and APIs, and a functional solutions layer.

Further, the National Strategy for Artificial Intelligence discussion paper issued by the NITI Aayog in 2018 had identified smart cities and mobility as one of the focus areas (NITI Aayog, 2018). In addition to this, the Smart Cities Mission itself issued a concept note on the use of AI in 2020. The discussion note documented the existing and proposed uses of AI by some Indian cities/states and suggested that a more detailed roadmap for this purpose should be laid down under the guidance of a working committee for assessing the AI solutions for urban India (Smart Cities Mission, 2020). It further noted that such a strategy should cover issues relating to data architectures, system design, infrastructure and procurement routes and regulatory checks for accelerating AI. The document, however, remained silent on the privacy and civil liberty concerns that also tend to arise from the integration of AI initiatives in smart city projects.

Is there a sectoral regulation in place (e.g. law, decree, standards) to organise the digitalisation of cities, and urban areas in general?
There is no specific law for the digitisation of cities, but the ability to undertake such initiatives flows from the general allocation of powers between the centre, states and local bodies. The Constitution of India recognises the important role of rural and urban local bodies in the field of governance. Accordingly, each state government is required to constitute municipalities, which are institutions of local self-governance, in urban areas (Constitution of India, 1950, Art. 243Q). The establishment, governance and powers of these bodies are detailed in state-wise laws. The relevant laws at the state level consist of the State Town and Country Planning Acts, Municipal Corporation Acts, Municipalities Acts, and Urban Areas Development Acts (NITI Aayog, 2021a). Subject to state-specific exceptions, in most cases, the powers conferred upon urban local bodies include areas like public health, solid waste management, provision of urban amenities and facilities, registration of births and deaths, water supply, roads, etc. (Chaubey, 2003). Accordingly, the power to initiate digitisation initiatives in these areas would also vest in the relevant local bodies. In addition to the state laws governing urban local bodies, there are several other laws that play a role in urban planning, development and management, covering areas such as registration, real estate, and environment (NITI Aayog, 2021a).

Are there any policies promoting digital sovereignty for smart cities (e.g. data localisation, preference or obligation to utilise domestic providers etc.)?
The Indian government's Meghraj initiative to promote the use of cloud services by government agencies requires that all data provided to the cloud service provider be stored within India. This will also apply to data belonging to different government agencies in the context of smart city projects. Further, it has been found that several smart cities are opting for "hyper localisation" silos to store data within their cities or states. Conditions in this regard are provided in the tender documents issued by the cities for the procurement of data services (Mehrotra, 2018). In addition, the Public Procurement (Preference to Make in India) Order applies to procurements

done by departments and agencies of the central government (MeitY, 2022b). However, the functionaries of the Smart Cities Mission have observed that since the Central Ministry of Urban Affairs is not the nodal authority for procurement activities of smart cities and suggested that separate Make in India preference clauses will have to be incorporated in the tender documents (Kapoor et al., 2020).

Has the digitisation of the sector or any area of It been promoted Because of the Covid19 pandemic? If yes, then how so?

As per the Smart Cities Mission, they have been actively involved in providing support for rapid response in COVID-19 management. This includes the use of the Integrated Command and Control Centers set up in various Smart Cities for real-time monitoring and management of the pandemic, exchange of best practices, use of location and contact details for food distribution, shelter homes and kitchens, which was made accessible via Google maps (Smart Cities Mission, 2021a). Similar developments are also documented in a report published by the World Economic Forum that compares the COVID responses adopted by three smart cities in India (Bengaluru, Surat and Pimpri Chinchwad) with select global cities (Tel Aviv, Lisbon and New York City) (World Economic Forum, Ministry of Housing and Urban Affairs & Deloitte, 2020). While commending the development of COVID-19 War Rooms in Indian cities, utilising the existing technology and systems, the report also highlights important gaps in terms of the need for capacity building and workforce-related constraints, complex procurement processes, and data security and protection concerns.

Is there a specific strategy or regulation targeting the digitisation of land records or real estate records?

There has been a long-running programme, which is currently called the Digital India Land Records Modernisation Programme, focused on the modernisation of the land records system in India (Department of Land Resources, 2018). The activities being undertaken under this programme include computerisation of records, digitisation of cadastral maps, land surveys, modernisation of record rooms, computerisation of registration systems, and connectivity between land records offices. The government has announced two other recent initiatives in this field. First, the field testing of a National Generic Document Registration System to make the property document registration system more efficient, reduce delays and enable integration with systems like e-sign, e-KYC, payment gateways, and data standardisation. Second, pilot testing of the Unique Land Parcel Identification Number System, which will be an alphanumeric unique ID for each land parcel (Press Information Bureau, 2021a).

Is there a specific body in charge of overseeing, coordinating or promoting the digitalisation of the sector?

The Smart Cities Mission is a centrally sponsored scheme operationalised by the Ministry of Urban Development in the Central Government. But the actual planning, implementation, management, and evaluation activities of the mission are to be done at the city level by a Special Purpose Vehicle (SPV) created in each smart city. The SPV is to be headed by a full-time CEO and has nominees of the central government, state government and urban local body on its board. The SPV has to be a corporate entity with 50:50 equity shareholding by the state and the urban local body (Smart Cities Mission, 2021b). In addition to this, there are monitoring structures set up at the national, state and city level, namely the Apex Committee at the national level, the state-level High Powered Steering Committee, and the Smart City Advisory Forum at the city level (Smart Cities Mission, 2021b).

Is there any outstanding example of strategy or policy elaborated by a local administration?
The India Smart Cities Awards 2020, given by the government in June 2021, can be viewed as an indicator of the performance of various smart cities (Press Information Bureau, 2021b). The cities of Indore and Surat were jointly declared to be the overall top performers in this survey, while Vadodara, Thane and Bhubaneswar earned the top three slots under the smart city governance initiatives category. The initiatives that earned them this recognition were a Geospatial enabled civic services platform created in Vadodara (Vadodara Smart City, n.d.), the Digi-Thane (Thane Smart City Limited, 2020) program that enables city residents to receive personalised services through a mobile app and portal, and a similar initiative undertaken by the city of Bhubaneswar (Bhubaneswar Smart City Limited, n.d.).

4.3 *Digital Money and Payments*

Is there a strategy to digitalise this sector or any areas of it, such as a Central Bank Digital Currency program?
Promotion of digital payments is one of the key focus areas of the digital transformation process in India. It forms part of the Digital India goal of achieving "Faceless, Paperless, Cashless" transactions. The Cashless India initiative lists 10 methods of digital payments that include the Aadhaar-enabled Payment System (AEPS), which allows banking transactions using Aadhaar authentication and the Unified Payments Interface (UPI), a system that allows immediate money transfers through a mobile device using APIs and a virtual payment ID. The UPI initiative constitutes the cashless layer of India Stack. In addition, other forms of digital payments, such as debit and credit cards, Unstructured Supplementary Service Data (USSD) for feature phones, Internet and mobile banking, mobile wallets and micro-ATMs are also included in the list. The government has created a dashboard called Digidhan for monitoring and analysis of all these different types of digital payment transactions (MeitY, 2022a). The Reserve Bank of India (RBI)—Digital Payments Index is another tool that has been developed to track the growth in the digital payments sector (Reserve Bank of India, 2021a). While these tools point to a significant uptake in digital transactions over the last few years, cash remains the most popular option for payments in India (Reserve Bank of India, 2020).

India's banking and payments regulator, RBI, has periodically released its vision documents for the payments sector since 2002. In its latest edition of the Payment and Settlement Systems Vision 2019–2021, the RBI identified four goals to meet the vision to "empower every Indian with access to a bouquet of e-payment options that is safe, secure, convenient, quick and affordable" (Reserve Bank of India, 2019a). The identified goals were: i) enhancement of competition in the payment systems landscape; ii) achieving optimal cost for the customers; iii) multiple payment system options to cater to the requirement of convenience; and iv) addressing security vulnerabilities to retain customer confidence. In June 2022, the RBI issued its next vision document called the Payments Vision 2025 with the core theme of "E-Payments for Everyone, Everywhere, Everytime" (Department of Payment and Settlement Systems, 2022). The document identifies five goal posts: integrity, inclusion, innovation, institutionalisation, and internationalisation, to achieve its objectives of furthering deeper access to e-payments.

In addition to the RBI's vision documents, a number of government committees have looked into the policy issues and development of digital payments. Notable among these are the Watal Committee on Digital Payments (2016), constituted by the Ministry of Finance, and the Nilekani Committee on Deepening of Digital Payment set up by the Reserve Bank of India (RBI) (2019b). The Watal Committee offered short- to medium-term recommendations on legislative changes, regulatory changes by the RBI and policy and executive steps to be taken by the Ministry of Finance and other ministries. This included the need for structural reforms to make the regulation of payments independent from the function of central banking and to foster greater interoperability between banks and non-banks. In 2019, another committee constituted by the Ministry of Finance provided detailed recommendations on expanding the reach of fintech services in the country, its role in financial inclusion, general policy and technology-related actions, and organisational and administrative measures (Department of Economic Affairs, 2019).

India has also seen some discussions on the introduction of a central bank digital currency (CBDC). In November 2017, a High-Level Inter-Ministerial Committee constituted by the Ministry of Finance recommended the introduction of CBDC as a digital form of fiat money in India (Sankar, 2021). Subsequently, the Report on Currency and Finance published by India's central bank, the RBI, in Feb 2021, had referred to the advantages and risks of CBDC. The report observed that "it is imperative for the Reserve Bank to monitor global developments, explore the possibility of the need for introduction of CBDC and remain in readiness to operationalise CBDC, as and when necessary" (Reserve Bank of India, 2021b). After this, the RBI is known to have written to the government in October 2021 seeking legal changes to enhance the scope of the definition of 'bank note' to include currency in digital form.

As per the information presented by the Minister of State for Finance before the Parliament, the RBI has been examining CBDC use cases and is working on a phased strategy for its implementation (ENS Economic Bureau, 2021). These deliberations resulted in the release of a Concept Note on Central Bank Digital Currency by the RBI in October 2022 (Reserve Bank of India, 2022). The stated purpose of the note is to create awareness about CBDCs and lay out the features of India's proposed digital Rupee (e₹). The note states that the digital Rupee will imbibe all the possible features of physical currency, and its design choices will vary based on the type of use (wholesale or retail), models of issuance, degree of anonymity required, and the form of the instrument (token-based or account-based).

Is the use of specific technologies for digital money/payments promoted or prioritised (e.g. AI, blockchain, open source software)?
Standard APIs for UPI transactions, biometric authentication, QR codes, and near-field communication (NFC) are among the various technologies being used in the Indian payments sector. The focus on standardisation is most evident in the case of the UPI architecture, which has been built upon a set of standard APIs to facilitate interoperable payment transactions. In another example, the RBI in 2020 issued directions requiring that all payment system operators that use proprietary QR codes would have to shift to interoperable QR codes by March 31, 2022. This is designed to enable interoperability among payment apps and services (Vasudevan, 2020). Further, the 2019 Report of the Steering Committee on Fintech Related Issues that was discussed earlier had identified the following technologies as forming the underpinnings of fintech—encryption, blockchain and distributed ledgers, digital currencies and tokens, smartphones, Artificial Intelligence, open APIs, IoT and big data (Department of Economic Affairs, 2019).

Is there a sectoral regulation in place (e.g. law, decree, standards) to organise the digitalisation of the sector?
Payment systems in India are regulated by the Payment and Settlement Systems Act, 2007 (PSS Act) and the regulations framed under it in 2008. The Act requires that any payment system operating in India needs to be authorised by the RBI. It sets out the procedures in this regard and authorises the RBI to determine standards for payment systems and carry out other supervisory activities. While the PSS Act and rules deal with several procedural aspects, many of the substantive legal prescriptions for payment systems and operators have been issued through directives, circulars and notifications by the RBI. This is often criticised on the ground that obligations of such a nature should flow from the primary legislative framework rather than being left to the discretion of the regulator (Ahmed & Babele, 2021). Further, the Watal Committee referred to earlier also made a case for legislative amendments to the PSS Act to make the regulation of payments independent from the function of central banking and explicitly include provisions relating to competition and innovation, open access and interoperability, consumer protection, data protection and security and regulatory governance in the PSS Act (Committee on Digital Payments, 2016).

Are there any policies promoting digital sovereignty in digital money/payments (e.g. data localisation, preference or obligation to utilise domestic providers etc.)?
In April 2018, the RBI issued a data localisation directive that required all payment system providers to ensure that the entire data relating to payment systems is stored

only in India. This includes data such as transaction details, information collected and processed as part of the message and payment instructions (Dave, 2018). The release of these instructions without any consultations, unclear articulation of the problem and no analysis of costs and benefits became the subject of much criticism (Bailey & Parsheera, 2021). Subsequently, the RBI issued some clarifications in this regard, including to specify that in the case of cross border transactions, which consist of a foreign and domestic component, a copy of the domestic component would be allowed to be stored abroad (Reserve Bank of India, n.d.-a). In exercise of its powers under this directive, the RBI has imposed restrictions on the on-boarding new domestic customers by Mastercard due to its failure in complying with the norms (Dayal, 2021a).

In addition, the issue of preferential treatment by the government has come up in the context of the government's promotion of the indigenously developed card payment system called RuPay. Card networks like Visa and MasterCard have raised concerns about the promotion of RuPay as being a type of protectionist policy that creates an uneven playing field for them (Iyer, 2021).

Has the digitisation of the sector or any area of It been promoted because of the Covid19 pandemic? If yes, then how so?

The general slowdown in economic activity during the COVID crisis, particularly during lockdown periods, led to a slowing down of digital transactions, especially in the case of large value transactions (Reserve Bank of India, 2021c). However, it also triggered greater use of certain forms of digital instruments, such as UPI transactions, contactless cards, and number of Points of Sale (PoS) terminals (Aggarwal, 2020). The RBI's annual report for 2021–21 records some of the actions taken by the regulator to enhance or simplify digital payments during this period (Reserve Bank of India, 2021c). This includes organising consumer awareness campaigns on digital payments, introduction of 24x7 real time gross settlement, increase in the permitted transaction limit for contactless transactions through NFC enabled cards (Reserve Bank of India, 2019a).

Further, the test phase of RBI's regulatory sandbox on the theme of retail payments was also carried out during this period. Through a press release issued in September 2021, the RBI announced that all the six products that were evaluated during the first cohort of the sandbox were found to be viable within the boundary conditions defined during testing and allowed the products to be considered for adoption by regulated entities. The products tested in this phase included an offline digital cash product solution to help in digitisation of payments in rural areas, an NFC-based prepaid card, and a feature phone-based payment solution for transfers using Interactive Voice Response (IVR) (Dayal, 2021b). However, it is pertinent to note that although the testing was conducted during the pandemic period, the RBI's regulatory sandbox was announced before that and does not constitute a COVID-specific response.

Is there a specific body in charge of overseeing, coordinating or promoting the digitalisation of the sector?

India's central bank, the RBI, is the regulator for the payments sector. The RBI is a statutory regulator constituted under the Reserve Bank of India Act (1934). The Board for Regulation and Supervision of Payment and Settlement Systems, a sub-committee of RBI's Central Board, is the highest policymaking body on payment systems. It is empowered to issue authorisations, prescribe policies, and conduct supervision of all the payment and settlement systems. The Department of Payment and Settlement Systems inside the RBI serves as the Secretariat to this Board (Reserve Bank of India, n.d.-b).

In addition, an entity known as the National Payments Corporation of India (NPCI), which is described as an initiative of RBI and the Indian Banks' Association (IBA), acts as an umbrella entity for operating various retail payment systems in India (National Payments Corporation of India, 2022). The NPCI has been set up as a not-for-profit company, and its shareholding is held predominantly by banks, although in the last few months a portion of its shares has also been issued to non-bank payment service providers. The NPCI owns and operates initiatives like UPI and RuPay, which have been described in the preceding responses. In addition to being an operator of these systems, NPCI also acts as a quasi-regulator of the digital payments sector—it sets the standards and terms for inclusion into the payments systems operated by it and monitors compliance with the set standards (CUTS International, n.d.). This dual role of being an operator as well as quasi-regulator, concentration of power in the hands of the NPCI, and the lack of public accountability pose a cause for concern (Parsheera, 2022).

4.4 Other Relevant Examples

Is there any other sector (such as education, health, etc) where a specific strategy or policy is in place to foster and organise digitalisation?

India is witnessing a push for digital transformation in many other sectors, examples of two of which—health and agriculture—are described below. In addition to these, digitalisation measures have also been adopted in several other areas like justice delivery, education and taxation.

In September 2021, the Ministry of Agriculture & Farmers Welfare announced the Digital Agriculture Mission 2021–2025, which is supposed to lead to the adoption of new technologies like Artificial Intelligence, blockchain, remote sensing and GIS in the agricultural sector. The information released by the Ministry on this subject also refers to the signing of pilot projects with five private entities and the move for the creation of a federated Farmers Database. This database is meant to be linked to the land records of farmers using a unique Farmer ID created for this purpose and is proposed to be used for providing benefits to farmers in the future (Press Information Bureau, 2021c). These announcements follow the release of a consultation paper by the Department of Agriculture, Cooperation & Farmer Welfare on the

InDEA Digital Ecosystem of Agriculture in July 2021 (Department of Agriculture, Cooperation & Farmer Welfare, 2021).

A similar initiative to issue digital health IDs is also underway under the Ayushman Bharat Digital Mission, which was announced by the Prime Minister in August 2020. The mission aims to create a national digital health ecosystem that will enable the interoperability of health information across stakeholders based on the consent of the individual (Ministry of Health & Family Welfare, 2020). The following are regarded to be the building blocks of this mission—HealthID, DigiDoctor, Health Facility Registry, Personal Health Records, e-Pharmacy & Telemedicine. In terms of administrative structure, a non-statutory body called the National Health Authority has been made responsible for the design and implementation of the mission.

There are some common concerns emanating from both initiatives. They include the lack of adequate representation in the formulation of each initiative, over-reliance on technical solutions, ability of misuse of personal data in the hands of the state and private actors, and risks of excursion and harms arising from the lack of effective choice and control in the hands of individuals.

References

Aadhaar data kept, processed only on own secure servers: UIDAI. (2017, August 30). Economic Times https://economictimes.indiatimes.com/news/politics-and-nation/aadhaar-data-kept-processed-only-on-own-secure-servers-uidai/articleshow/60295134.cms?from=mdr.

Aggarwal, S. (2020, May 12). #TechFightsCovid: Top 5 digital payment methods - a boon amid crisis. Community by Nasscom Insights. https://community.nasscom.in/communities/digital-transformation/fintech/techfightscovid-top-5-digital-payment-methods-a-boon-amid-crisis.html

Ahmed, S. & Babele, A. (2021, October 4). *Modernising the law for payment services in India: Preparing for the future of retail payments*. Vidhi Centre for Legal Policy https://vidhilegalpolicy.in/research/modernising-the-law-for-payment-services-in-india-preparing-for-the-future-of-retail-payments/.

AI Observatory. (n.d.). Home. https://ai-observatory.in/.

Aijaz, R. (2021). India's smart cities Mission, 2015–2021: A stocktaking. *ORF Special Report, 155*. Observer Research Foundation https://www.orfonline.org/research/indias-smart-cities-mission-2015-2021-a-stocktaking/.

Atal Mission for Rejuvenation and Urban Transformation. (2022, December 29). About Reforms. http://amrut.gov.in/content/innerpage/about-reforms.php.

Ayushman Bharat Digital Mission. (n.d.). *National Digital Health Mission: Health Data Management Policy*. https://abdm.gov.in/publications/policies_regulations/health_data_management_policy.

Bailey, R., & Parsheera, S. (2021). Data localization in India: Paradigms and processes. *CSI Transactions on ICT, 9*(3), 137–150. https://doi.org/10.1007/s40012-021-00337-4

Bhubaneswar Smart City Limited. (n.d.). Home. https://www.bhubaneswar.me/.

Chaubey, P. K. (2003, December 29). *Urban local bodies in India: Quest for making them self-reliant* [Paper]. National Seminar on Municipal Finances, New Delhi. https://fincomindia.nic.in/writereaddata/html_en_files/oldcommission_html/predocs/speech/chaubey_ulb.pdf.

Committee on Digital Payments. (2016). Medium term recommendations to strengthen digital payments ecosystem report. https://dea.gov.in/sites/default/files/watal_report271216.pdf.
CUTS International. (n.d.). Competition and regulatory concerns in payment systems ecosystem in India: Brief note based on initial literature review. https://cuts-ccier.org/pdf/Preliminary_literature_review_on_payments_systems.pdf.
Dave, N. S. (2018, April 6). Notification: Storage of Payment System Data. Reserve Bank of India. https://www.rbi.org.in/scripts/NotificationUser.aspx?Id=11244.
Dayal, Y. (2021a, July 14). Reserve Bank of India takes supervisory action on Mastercard Asia / Pacific Pte. *Ltd. Reserve Bank of India*. https://www.rbi.org.in/Scripts/BS_PressReleaseDisplay.aspx?prid=51895
Dayal, Y. (2021b, September 13). Regulatory sandbox (RS): First cohort on 'Retail Payments'—Exit. *Reserve Bank of India*. https://www.rbi.org.in/Scripts/BS_PressReleaseDisplay.aspx?prid=52217.
Defence Research and Development Organisation. (2022). Centre for Artificial Intelligence & Robotics (CAIR). https://www.drdo.gov.in/labs-and-establishments/centre-artificial-intelligence-robotics-cair.
Dener, C., Nii-Aponsah, H., Ghunney, L. E. & Johns, K. D. 2021. GovTech maturity index: The state of public sector digital transformation. World Bank. https://openknowledge.worldbank.org/handle/10986/36233.
Department of Administrative Reforms and Public Grievances. (2019). National e-Governance Service Delivery Assessment 2019: E-Governance Landscape—India's Transformative Journey. https://dmeo.gov.in/sites/default/files/2020-08/NeSDA_2019_Final_Report.pdf.
Department of Administrative Reforms and Public Grievances. (2021). National eGovernance Service Delivery Assessment 2021: Reaching citizens through seamless service delivery. https://nesda.gov.in/publicsite/NeSDA2021_Report.pdf.
Department of Administrative Reforms and Public Grievances. (2022). About NeSDA. https://nesda.gov.in/publicsite/about_nesda.php.
Department of Agriculture, Cooperation & Farmer Welfare. (2021). *Consultation paper on IDEA (India Digital Ecosystem of Agriculture)*. https://agricoop.nic.in/sites/default/files/IDEA%20Concept%20Paper_mod01062021_1.pdf.
Department of Economic Affairs. (2019). Report of the Steering Committee on Fintech Related Issues. https://dea.gov.in/sites/default/files/Report%20of%20the%20Steering%20Committee%20on%20Fintech_1.pdf.
Department of Electronics and Information Technology. (2012). Framework & guidelines for use of social media for government organisations. https://www.meity.gov.in/writereaddata/files/Approved%20Social%20Media%20Framework%20and%20Guidelines%20_2_.pdf.
Department of Electronics and Information Technology. (2014a). Policy on adoption of open source software for government of India. https://www.meity.gov.in/writereaddata/files/policy_on_adoption_of_oss.pdf.
Department of Electronics and Information Technology. (2014b). *Policy on Open Application Programming Interfaces (APIs) for Government of India*. www.meity.gov.in/writereaddata/files/Open_APIs_19May2015.pdf.
Department of Empowerment of Persons with Disabilities. (2022, April 25). Accessible India Campaign. https://disabilityaffairs.gov.in/content/page/accessible-india-campaign.php.
Department of Expenditure. (2017a). General financial rules 2017. https://finance.py.gov.in/sites/default/files/gfr2017.pdf.
Department of Expenditure. (2017b). Manual for procurement of goods. https://doe.gov.in/sites/default/files/Manual%20for%20Procurement%20of%20Goods%202017_0_0.pdf.
Department of Land Resources. (2018). The digital India land records modernization programme (DILRMP): Guidelines, technical manuals and MIS (2018-19). https://dolr.gov.in/sites/default/files/Final%20%20Guideline%20of%20DILRMP%2002-01-2019.pdf.

Department of Payment and Settlement Systems. (2022). Payments Vision 2025. https://rbidocs.rbi.org.in/rdocs/PublicationReport/Pdfs/PAYMENTSVISION2025844D11300C884DC4ACB8E56B7348F4D4.PDF.

Department of Telecommunications. (2018). National Digital Communications Policy 2018. https://dot.gov.in/sites/default/files/EnglishPolicy-NDCP.pdf.

Department of Telecommunications. (n.d.). *Unified license agreement*. https://dot.gov.in/sites/default/files/2016_03_30%20UL-AS-I.pdf?download=1s.

Digital India Corporation. (2018). Digital India corporation annual report (2017-2018). https://dic.gov.in/images/stories/annual/AR_2017-18_Eng.pdf.

Digital India Corporation. (2022, December 27). Organisation Profile. https://dic.gov.in/index.php/about/organisations/profile.

Digital India. (2022). Management structure. https://www.digitalindia.gov.in/content/management-structure.

Digital Rights Bodies Warn Against Use of Facial Recognition Technology in Vaccination Drive. (2021, April 14). The Wire. https://thewire.in/rights/covid-19-vaccination-facial-recognition-technology-aadhaar-vaccine.

eGov Foundation. (n.d.). *About us*. https://egov.org.in/about-us/

ENS Economic Bureau. (2021, November 30). RBI for widening scope of 'bank note' to include digital currency. The Indian Express. https://indianexpress.com/article/business/banking-and-finance/rbi-for-widening-scope-of-bank-note-to-include-digital-currency-7648080/.

ENS Economic Bureau. (2022, December 9). Draft Digital India Bill by Dec-end: Chandrasekhar. *The Indian Express*. https://indianexpress.com/article/business/economy/draft-digital-india-bill-by-dec-end-chandrasekhar-8314416/.

Ghosh, A. (2021, October 1). Used Aadhaar for Covid vaccine? Modi govt created your digital health ID without asking you. The Print. https://theprint.in/health/used-aadhaar-for-covid-vaccine-modi-govt-created-your-digital-health-id-without-asking-you/742958/.

Gupta, A., & Auerswald, P. E. (2019, May 6). The ups and downs of India's digital transformation. Harvard Business Review. https://hbr.org/2019/05/the-ups-and-downs-of-indias-digital-transformation.

Ikigai Law. (2021, January 5). Summary of the revised report of the committee of experts on Non-Personal Data. https://www.ikigailaw.com/summary-of-the-revised-report-of-the-committee-of-experts-of-non-personal-data/#acceptLicense.

India News. (2021, October 2). Supreme Court notice to govt on Aadhaar for Covid-19 vaccination. *The Hindustan Times*. https://www.hindustantimes.com/india-news/sc-seeks-centre-s-response-on-aadhaar-requirement-for-covid-19-vaccination-101633112977197.html.

India News. (2022, February 7). Aadhaar Not Mandatory For Covid Vaccination, Centre Tells Supreme Court. NDTV. https://www.ndtv.com/india-news/aadhaar-not-mandatory-for-covid-vaccination-centre-tells-supreme-court-2753764.

Indian Computer Emergency Response Team [CERT-In]. (n.d.). *Home - Empanelment of Information Security Auditing Organisations by CERT-In*. https://cert-in.org.in/certEmpanelment.jsp.

IndiaStack. (n.d.). *Home*. https://www.indiastack.org/about/

International Centre for Information Systems and Audit [iCISA]. (2022, December 30). *It Audit Reports*. Retrieved on December 30, 2022 from https://cag.gov.in/icisa/en/icisa-it-audit-reports?rept=st.

International Institute for Management Development. (2022). Digital competitiveness: India. https://worldcompetitiveness.imd.org/countryprofile/IN/digital.

Internet Freedom Foundation. (2021, April 27). Bad Rules for Good Governance. https://internetfreedom.in/bad-rules-for-good-governance/.

Iyer, P. (2021, December 1). *Why has RuPay rattled visa and MasterCard?*. Money Control. https://www.moneycontrol.com/news/business/why-has-rupay-rattled-visa-and-mastercard-7777841.htm.

Justice Puttaswamy (Retd.) and Anr. v Union of India and Ors. (2018), AIR 2018 SC (SUPP) 1841.

Kapoor, R., Mittal, G., Singh, G., Dhanda, P., & Singh, R. (2020, June 30). Discussion points tech clinic webinar series: Understanding preference for Make in India procurement norms for Smart cities ICT projects. https://smartnet.niua.org/sites/default/files/post_event_insights_tc-7_30th_june.pdf.

Lok Sabha Secretariat. (2020). Report of the Joint Committee on the Personal Data Protection Bill, 2019. http://164.100.47.193/lsscommittee/Joint%20Committee%20on%20the%20Personal%20Data%20Protection%20Bill,%202019/17_Joint_Committee_on_the_Personal_Data_Protection_Bill_2019_1.pdf.

Mara, P., & Deshpande, D. (2020, May 8). India: Public Procurement 2019. Mondaq. https://www.mondaq.com/india/government-contracts-procurement-ppp/930884/public-procurement-2019

Mehrotra, K. (2018, December 24). In Local vs Cloud: Most Smart Cities take to data hyper-localisation. *The Indian Express*. https://indianexpress.com/article/india/in-local-vs-cloud-most-smart-cities-take-to-data-hyper-localisation-5506579/.

Mehta, R. (2020, January 20). Engaging MOSIP at IndiaOS. Medium. https://rushabh-mehta.medium.com/engaging-mosip-at-indiaos-891e740b1a60.

Ministry of Electronics and Information Technology [MeitY]. (2012). *National Policy on Information Technology*. https://www.meity.gov.in/writereaddata/files/National_20IT_20Policyt%20_20.pdf.

Ministry of Electronics and Information Technology. (2018). Office Memorandum: Constitution of four committees for promoting Artificial Intelligence (AI) initiatives and developing a policy framework. https://www.meity.gov.in/writereaddata/files/constitution_of_four_committees_on_artificial_intelligence.pdf.

Ministry of Electronics and Information Technology. (2019a, December 12). MeitY Business Rules. https://www.meity.gov.in/meity-business-rules.

Ministry of Electronics and Information Technology. (2019b). India's trillion dollar digital opportunity. https://www.meity.gov.in/writereaddata/files/india_trillion-dollar_digital_opportunity.pdf.

Ministry of Electronics and Information Technology. (2019c). Public procurement (preference to make in India) order 2019 for cyber security products. https://www.meity.gov.in/writereaddata/files/public_procurement-preference_to_make_in_india-order_2019_for_cyber_security_products.pdf.

Ministry of Electronics and Information Technology. (2020a). Report by the Committee of Experts on non-personal data governance framework. https://static.mygov.in/rest/s3fs-public/mygov_160922880751553221.pdf.

Ministry of Electronics and Information Technology. (2020b). Strategy for National Open Digital Ecosystems (NODE)—Consultation White Paper. https://static.mygov.in/rest/s3fs-public/mygov_158219311451553221.pdf.

Ministry of Electronics and Information Technology. (2020c). The Aadhaar authentication for good governance (social welfare, Innovation, Knowledge) Rules. https://uidai.gov.in/images/Aadhaar_Authentication_for_Good_Governance_Rules_2020.pdf.

Ministry of Electronics and Information Technology. (2021, June 7). National e-Governance Plan. https://www.meity.gov.in/divisions/national-e-governance-plan.

Ministry of Electronics and Information Technology. (2022a, April 10). *DigiDhan Dashboard*. Retrieved on December 30, 2022 from http://digipay.gov.in/dashboard/default.aspx#

Ministry of Electronics and Information Technology. (2022b, December 27). *Notification of electronic products under the public procurement (preference to make in India)* Order 2017. https://www.meity.gov.in/esdm/ppo.

Ministry of Electronics and Information Technology. (2022c, December 5). Mission Mode Projects. https://www.meity.gov.in/content/mission-mode-projects.

Ministry of Electronics and Information Technology. (2022d, November 25). eTall. https://www.meity.gov.in/etaal.

Ministry of Electronics and Information Technology. (2022e, November 29). Artificial Intelligence Committees Reports. https://www.meity.gov.in/artificial-intelligence-committees-reports.

Ministry of Electronics and Information Technology. (2022f). Digital India: Power to empower. Digital India Portal. https://www.digitalindia.gov.in/.
Ministry of Electronics and Information Technology. (2022g). National Data Governance Framework Policy: Draft. https://www.meity.gov.in/writereaddata/files/National-Data-Governance-Framework-Policy.pdf.
Ministry of Electronics and Information Technology. (n.d.). *Digital Service Standard*. https://egov-standards.gov.in/sites/default/files/2021-07/Digital%20Service%20Standard%20Version%20 1.0.pdf.
Ministry of Health & Family Welfare. (2020, August 15). *Hon'ble Prime Minister announces National Digital Health Mission on India's 74th Independence Day: Press Release*. https://abdm.gov.in:8081/uploads/a2c54ea050abefd682937e87e8a18b58_a660b5727d.pdf.
Ministry of Science and Technology. (2012). National Data Sharing and Accessibility Policy. https://data.gov.in/sites/default/files/NDSAP.pdf
Ministry of Urban Development. (2015). Smart cities: Mission Statement & Guidelines. https://smartnet.niua.org/sites/default/files/resources/smartcityguidelines.pdf.
MOSIP. (n.d.). *Home*. https://www.mosip.io/index.php.
Narasimhan, N., Sharma, M., & Kaushal, D. (2016). Accessibility of government websites in India. The Centre for Internet & Society. https://g3ict.org/publication/accessibility-of-government-websites-in-india
National e-Governance Division. (2022). Responsible AI for youth 2022: About. https://responsibleaiforyouth.negd.in/about.
National e-Governance Division. (n.d.-a). *About National e-Governance Division*. https://negd.gov.in/node/67.
National e-Governance Division. (n.d.-b). *Implementation strategy of e-Kranti*. https://negd.gov.in/sites/default/files/ImplementationStrategy.pdf.
National e-Governance Division. (n.d.-c). *e-Kranti*. Retrieved on December 30, 2022 from https://negd.gov.in/e-kranti
National Institute of Urban Affairs. (n.d.). *National urban innovation stack: Strategy & approach*. https://smartnet.niua.org/sites/default/files/resources/national_urban_innovation_stack_web_version.pdf
National Informatics Centre. (2018). eTaal Portal. https://etaal.gov.in/etaal2/Aboutus.aspx.
National Informatics Centre. (2022, December 27). Home. https://www.nic.in/.
National Payments Corporation of India. (2022). About us. https://www.npci.org.in/who-we-are/about-us.
NITI Aayog & United Nations. (2021). SDG India index & dashboard 2020-21: Partnerships in the decade of action. https://sdgindiaindex.niti.gov.in/assets/Files/SDG3.0_Final_04.03.2021_Web_Spreads.pdf.
NITI Aayog. (2018). National Strategy for Artificial Intelligence #AIforAll. https://www.niti.gov.in/sites/default/files/2019-01/NationalStrategy-for-AI-Discussion-Paper.pdf.
NITI Aayog. (2021a). Reforms in urban planning capacity in India: Final report. https://www.niti.gov.in/sites/default/files/2021-09/UrbanPlanningCapacity-in-India-16092021.pdf.
NITI Aayog. (2021b). Responsible AI #AIforAll: Approach document for India—Part 1: Principles for responsible AI. https://www.niti.gov.in/sites/default/files/2021-02/Responsible-AI-22022021.pdf.
NITI Aayog. (2021c). Responsible AI #AIforAll: Approach document for India—Part 2: Operationalizing principles for responsible AI. https://www.niti.gov.in/sites/default/files/2021-08/Part2-Responsible-AI-12082021.pdf.
Office of the Comptroller & Auditor General of India. (n.d.). *Manual of information technology audit*. https://cag.gov.in/uploads/media/ITAM-Vol-I-20210331113105.pdf.
Open Knowledge Foundation. (2016). *Global open data index—India*. Retrieved on December 28, 2022 from https://index.okfn.org/place/in/.
Organization for Economic Cooperation and Development [OECD]. (2018). *Active with India*. https://www.oecd.org/india/Active_with_India.pdf.

Parsheera, S. (2020, May 18). Net neutrality in India: Ensuring openness amidst the crisis. Medianama. https://www.medianama.com/2020/05/223-net-neutrality-india-openness/.
Parsheera, S. (2021). Codes and coalitions: Path to global governance of artificial intelligence? In T. Ray & R. J. Rajagopalan (Eds.), *Digital debates: CyFy Journal*. https://www.orfonline.org/wp-content/uploads/2021/10/Digital-Debates__CyFy2021.pdf
Parsheera, S. (2022). India's policy responses to big tech: And an eye on the rise of 'lt ig ech'. *Indian Journal of Law and Technology, 15*(1), 1–34. https://www.ijlt.in/journal/india%E2%80%99s-policy-responses-to-big-tech%3A-and-an-eye-on-the-rise-of-%E2%80%98alt-big-tech%E2%80%99.
Prasad, B. (2019, April 12). Communiqué to the Station House Officer of Madhapur Police Station. https://ia903001.us.archive.org/20/items/UIDAI_Communique/278-19.pdf.
Press Information Bureau. (2021a, February 9). *Digital India Land Records Modernization Programme has been extended up to 2020–21 at a total cost of Rs. 950 crores*. https://pib.gov.in/PressReleasePage.aspx?PRID=1696503.
Press Information Bureau. (2021b, June 25). *6 years of urban transformation*. https://www.pib.gov.in/PressReleasePage.aspx?PRID=1730341
Press Information Bureau. (2021c, September 14). *Ministry of Agriculture and Farmers welfare signs 5 MOUs with private companies for taking forward Digital Agriculture*. https://pib.gov.in/PressReleasePage.aspx?PRID=1754848
PRS Legislative Research. (n.d.). *The electronic delivery of services bill, 2011*. https://prsindia.org/billtrack/the-electronic-delivery-of-services-bill-2011.
Reserve Bank of India. (2019a). Payment and settlement systems in India: Vision—2019-2021. https://www.rbi.org.in/Scripts/PublicationVisionDocuments.aspx?Id=921.
Reserve Bank of India. (2019b). Report of the High Level Committee on Deepening of Digital Payments. https://rbi.org.in/Scripts/PublicationReportDetails.aspx?UrlPage=&ID=922.
Reserve Bank of India. (2020). Assessment of the progress of digitisation from cash to electronic. https://www.rbi.org.in/Scripts/PublicationsView.aspx?id=19417.
Reserve Bank of India. (2021a, July 28). Reserve Bank of India announces Digital Payments Index (RBI-DPI) for March 2021. https://www.rbi.org.in/Scripts/BS_PressReleaseDisplay.aspx?prid=51962.
Reserve Bank of India. (2021b). Report on currency and finance 2021: Reviewing the monetary policy framework. https://rbidocs.rbi.org.in/rdocs/Publications/PDFs/RCF26022021FUL14763733401448089D2B70141732D717.PDF.
Reserve Bank of India. (2021c). Reserve Bank of India Annual Report (2020-2021). https://rbidocs.rbi.org.in/rdocs/AnnualReport/PDFs/0RBIAR202021_F49F9833694E84C16AAD01BE48F53F6A2.PDF.
Reserve Bank of India. (2022). Concept note on Central Bank Digital Currency. https://rbi.org.in/Scripts/PublicationReportDetails.aspx?UrlPage=&ID=1218.
Reserve Bank of India. (n.d.-a). *Frequently asked questions: Storage of payment system data*. Retrieved on December 29, 2022 from https://m.rbi.org.in/scripts/FAQView.aspx?Id=130.
Reserve Bank of India. (n.d.-b). *Payment and settlement systems: Overview of payment systems in India*. https://www.rbi.org.in/scripts/PaymentSystems_UM.aspx.
Sankar, T. R. (2021, July 22). *Central Bank digital currency—is this the future of money* [keynote address]. Vidhi Centre for Legal Policy Webinar, New Delhi. https://www.rbi.org.in/Scripts/BS_SpeechesView.aspx?Id=1111.
Smart Cities Mission. (2020). Artificial Intelligence: An opportunity for smart cities. https://static.mygov.in/rest/s3fs-public/mygov_159411657151553221.pdf.
Smart Cities Mission. (2021a). Indian urban pandemic preparedness and response (Covid-19). https://smartcities.gov.in/COVID-19_Response_in_Smart_Cities.
Smart Cities Mission. (2021b). *SPVs*. https://smartcities.gov.in/implementation.
Telecom Regulatory Authority of India [TRAI]. (2016). *Prohibition of discriminatory tariffs for data services regulations*. https://trai.gov.in/sites/default/files/Regulation_Data_Service.pdf.
Thane Smart City Limited. (2020, January 31). Digit-Thane. https://thanesmartcity.in/digi-thane/.

The Aadhaar (targeted delivery of financial and other subsidies, benefits and services) Act. (2016). https://uidai.gov.in/images/targeted_delivery_of_financial_and_other_subsidies_benefits_and_services_13072016.pdf.
The Aadhaar and other laws (Amendment) Act. (2019). https://uidai.gov.in/images/news/Amendment_Act_2019.pdf.
The Constitution of India, as of May 2022. (1950). https://legislative.gov.in/sites/default/files/COI_English.pdf.
The Digital Personal Data Protection Act (2023). https://www.meity.gov.in/static/uploads/2024/06/2bf1f0e9f04e6fb4f8fef35e82c42aa5.pdf.
The Information Technology Act [IT Act]. (2000). https://www.indiacode.nic.in/handle/123456789/1999.
The Right to Information Act [RTI Act]. (2005).
The Rights of Persons with Disabilities Act. (2016).
The World Bank. (2022). Digital adoption index. https://www.worldbank.org/en/publication/wdr2016/Digital-Adoption-Index.
Unique Identification Authority of India (UIDAI) Planning Commission. (2010). *UIDAI strategy overview: Creating a unique identity number for every resident in India*. https://prsindia.org/files/bills_acts/bills_parliament/2010/UIDAI_STRATEGY_OVERVIEW.pdf.
Unique Identification Authority of India. (2016). Aadhaar (authentication) regulations, 2016. https://uidai.gov.in/images/regulation_1_to_5_15092016.pdf.
Unique Identification Authority of India. (2022). Authentication ecosystem. https://uidai.gov.in/en/ecosystem/authentication-ecosystem.html.
United Nations Department of Economic and Social Affairs. (2020). E-government survey 2020: Digital government in the decade of action for sustainable development - with addendum on COVID-19 response. https://publicadministration.un.org/egovkb/Portals/egovkb/Documents/un/2020-Survey/2020%20UN%20E-Government%20Survey%20(Full%20Report).pdf.
Vadodara Smart City. (n.d.). *Vadodara City GIS: A geospatial enabled civic services platform*. http://vadodarasmartcity.in/vscdl/assets/report/Vadodara%20City%20GIS.pdf.
Varshney, R. (2016, May 31). *Digital India: Over 920 out of 957 government websites fail quality audit*. Express Computer https://www.expresscomputer.in/news/digital-india-over-920-out-of-957-government-websites-fail-quality-audit/17706/.
Vasudevan, P. (2020, October 20). Notification: Digital payment transactions—streamlining QR code infrastructure. Reserve Bank of India. https://www.rbi.org.in/Scripts/NotificationUser.aspx?Id=11987&Mode=0.
World Economic Forum, Ministry of Housing and Urban Affairs & Deloitte. (2020). *Technology and data governance in cities: Indian cities at the forefront of the fight against COVID-19*. https://www.weforum.org/reports/technology-and-data-governance-in-cities-indian-cities-at-the-forefront-of-the-fight-against-covid-19.

Smriti Parsheera is a lawyer and independent researcher working on issues at the intersection of technology and society. Her areas of interest include privacy and data governance, internet governance, digital public infrastructure and protection of human rights in the digital sphere. This research was conducted between 2020-23 while she was a Fellow with the CyberBRICS Project at Fundação Getulio Vargas Law School, Brazil. Prior to that she has worked with organizations such as the National Institute of Public Finance & Policy, New Delhi, the Competition Commission of India and the United Nations Development Programme. Smriti graduated from the National Law School of India University, Bangalore, and obtained her LLM from the University of Pennsylvania along with a Certificate in Law and Business from the Wharton School. She is currently pursuing a PhD in public policy from the Indian Institute of Technology Delhi.

The Chinese-Style Modernisation Imperative: Data-Empowered State Capitalism as Social Governmentality

Wayne Wei Wang

Abstract The article interrogates what has prompted China to establish its digital state as a sort of orientalism distinct from the Western route of postcolonial datafication by questioning how Chinese modernisation perceptions have led to digital transformation. As the article methodically traces the genealogy of law and policy reforms as a catalyst for social change, it demonstrates how China adopts its "whole-of-nation" system, or more precisely, (party-)state capitalism, and prototypes its modern strategy to digitise native public services, particularly through the digital identity infrastructure, as an institutional concentration that exemplifies the positive and exclusionary nature of social big data in streamlining administrative procedures. Two driving variables behind China's digital transformation are identified: quasi-neoliberal market processes and technology's social change spillover effects. Since its inception, the contemporary Chinese state has created a cybernetic justification for social governmentality as a method of redressing the information imbalance in the process of ruling the state polity. Thus, data provides a top-down correctivist paradigm of social relationships with a delicate granularity that is susceptible to digital non-scarcity when technology, integrated into data-empowered state capitalism, is beyond the sociotechnical imagination.

1 Introduction

A crucial component of socialism with Chinese characteristics is the term modernisation (Xian Dai Hua, 现代化), which used to be ideologically embedded in the earliest-phase national strategy that the Four Modernisations (四个现代化) were and would continue to be an integral element of the Chinese economic and political

W. W. Wang (✉)
University of Hong Kong, Pokfulam Road, Hong Kong SAR

CyberBRICS Project, FGV Rio Law School, Fundação Getúlio Vargas, Rio de Janeiro, Brazil
e-mail: drirwang@connect.hku.hk

L. Belli, L. Galdino de Magalhães Santos (eds.), *SmartBRICS*,
https://doi.org/10.1007/978-3-031-98204-0_11

agenda on poverty reduction and growth of the economy.[1] Among the Four Modernisations was the Scientific and Technological (S&T) Modernisation playing a centric role. As Deng Xiaoping noted, the mastery of S&T was imperative for socialist modernisation (Schneider, 1981), which somehow signalled the embryonic form of Chinese cybernetics in the national innovation system and the institutional intention of Marxism to include technology under political authority (Cong & Thumfart, 2022, p. 4). The Fifth Modernisation—Modernising the State Governance System and Capacity was later coined in 2013 in the Decision on Major Issues Concerning Comprehensively Deepening Reforms (Central Committee of the Chinese Communist Party, 2013) as an enabler to adjusting the State-Government-Market relationship to improve social governance. Over the years since then, technology has gradually and synchronously evolved from being an innovative element as a driving force for economic growth to being a governance tool that rules society, thus transforming the bureaucratic structure of China's public administration.

By asking how the Chinese modernisation perceptions have led to digital transformation, the article explores what has motivated China to develop its digital state as a form of orientalism that differs from the "western path"[2] of postcolonial datafication. As the article methodologically traces the genealogy of law and policy reforms as a catalyst for social change, it shows how China adopts its "whole-of-nation" system ("举国体制"), or more precisely, (party-)state capitalism (Y. Huang, 2008; Milhaupt & Zheng, 2014; Hsueh, 2016; Pearson et al., 2021) and prototypes its modern revisionist strategy to digitise native public services, particularly through the digital identity infrastructure, as an institutional concentration that illustrates the positive and exclusionary nature of social big data in streamlining the grassroots bureaucracy and assembling the digital state infrastructure as social governmentality.

2 Driving Forces of Digitalising Public Services

China's overall score on the World Bank's Digital Adoption Index was 0.59/1.00 as of 2016, with a comparatively high DAI Government Sub-index of 0.69/1.00. In 2020, the United Nations released the E-Gov Survey, which revealed that China's online services index, which measures E-Gov maturity, climbed dramatically to the "very high" level, ranking ninth in the world. The 2021 World Bank GovTech Maturity Index placed China in Group B with a significant focus on GovTech. The

[1] Before establishing the long-term "Reform and Opening-up" tactic, Deng Xiaoping furthered the Four Modernisations first proposed by Zhou Enlai in 1954 as an economic means of strengthening China's agriculture, industry, defence, and science and technology sectors.

[2] The latest report of the CCP's 20th Congress in 2022, for instance, which said "Promoting the Great Revival of the Chinese Nation with Chinese-Style Modernisation," specifically highlighted narratives about moving away from a monolithic development model and towards diversification to conceptualise state capacity building.

2021 IMD World Digital Competitiveness Ranking placed China fifteenth out of sixty-four economies. Following is a documentation of how China has completed its substantial and phased digital transformation at a pace that is described by some as a Schumpeterian industrial policy model of technological leapfrogging and catching-up (Lee, 2022).

2.1 *Stage One: State Informatisation Towards Office Automation (The 1990s)*

The Chinese government first employed state informatisation—namely, state-directed IT-facilitated modernisation (Zou, 1997, p. 6)—to establish a top-down telecommunications network across all levels of government to manage economic databases and improve administrative efficiency. For example, the 1993 "Three Goldens Projects" (三金工程) consisted of the Golden Bridge Project (金桥工程), the Golden Customs Project (金关工程), and the Golden Card Project (金卡工程), creating the infrastructural groundwork for the telecommunications, international commerce, and financial systems (Zhao, 1995).

Although the then IT systems empowered a government-centric, bureaucratic, confidential state with office automation only in the internal administration and without information technologies organisationally embedded in the substantial governmentality, the state informatisation established the model of "state-directed co-developed standardised interconnection" (Zou, 1997, p. 6) to underpin the all-level administration's better statistics-informed macro-control capabilities.

2.2 *Stage Two: E-Governments as Data Silos (2000–2014)*

As an e-gov incubator, China began the "Government Internet Access Project" (政府上网工程) in 1999 to liberate public Internet resources, create an enriched online Chinese content ecosphere, and generate added value by stimulating the software ecosystem (i.e. ISP/ICP) for public information processing (Wen & Yachang, 1999). The Chinese E-Gov Guidance and Framework were released in 2002 and 2006, respectively, to accelerate institutional changes and improve the service quality and efficiency of central and local governments (Office of the Central Committee of the Chinese Communist Party, 2002; National Informatization Leading Group, 2006), resulting in the expansion of informatisation architecture from "Three Golden Projects" to "Two Nets, One Website, Four Databases, and Twelve Golden Projects (两网，一站，四库，十二金工程)."[3]

[3] "Two Nets, One Website, Four Treasures, and Twelve Gold Projects" means Two Nets (Government Intranet and Government Extranet), One Website (gov.cn), Four Databases

As part of Stage Two, e-governments were analogously built within an Internet-enabled information marketplace where power is exercised. On the one hand, the Open Government Information Regulation (政府信息公开条例), introduced in 2007,[4] marked a turning point in the bureaucratic system in favour of mandatory disclosure of public information previously classified as confidential. On the other hand, the increase in civic participation in (new) social media—such as the creation of the first Sina Weibo Gov Account in 2009 (Yu, 2016)—set forth the political legitimacy demands for monitoring social sentiments and improving the public's access to information.

Accordingly, the conventional information asymmetry of power in Chinese hierarchical systems was somewhat reduced; however, the hierarchy's organisational structure resulted in e-governments forming data silos because both vertical and horizontal administrative departments built and maintained data pools independently without standardising inter-unit data sharing protocols (Zheng, 2007, p. 119).

2.3 *Stage Three: Digital China's User-Friendliness (2014–cont.)*

As part of China's 14th five-year plan, which outlines the country's long-term goals through 2035, Section Five emphasises the importance of accelerating digital growth and creating a digital China (Xinhua News Agency, 2021). Before that, The 19th CCP Central Committee's Fourth Plenary Session urged the establishment of a state-wide digital government (Xinhua News Agency, 2019). The motorisation of public services was the driving force behind the change, which was preceded by a series of policy documents promoting the development of a national integrated

(Population, Legal Entity, Spatial Geography and Natural Resources, Macro-economy) and Twelve Golden Projects on Financial System, Social Welfare, Agriculture, etc. (China E-Government Network, 2018).

[4] The Open Government Information Regulation was introduced in 2007 (State Council, 2007) and amended in 2019 (State Council, 2019b), with the core principle of "disclosure as the norm, non-disclosure as the exception" explicated.

online government service platform,[5] "all-in-one" portal[6] and a cross-provincial digital public service platform.[7]

The deployment of e-governments also continued in conjunction with the 12th and 13th five-year plans by adjusting and switching national databases on demography, legal entities, natural resources, spatial geography, macroeconomics, cultural content, and social credits (H. Huang, 2020b, p. 12). However, some databases were scrapped during construction or merged with a more centralised system (H. Huang, 2020a, pp. 50–51). Due to the lack of audits and evaluations of government websites, the Chinese government's efforts to expand e-services and bridge the digital divide between rural and urban areas were also unsuccessful (H. Huang, 2020a, pp. 51–52). In response, administrative campaigns to achieve web transparency (Office of the State Council, 2013) and the actions on building a "New Media Matrix" and palmtop services (Office of the State Council, 2018a) formed the omni-directional channels, including gov.cn, WeChat public accounts, Weibo public accounts and WeChat mini apps and administrative mobile apps (New Media Matrix for Government Affairs, n.d.).

Government as Apps is, in a sense, a consequence of Chinese state capitalism, or to be more precise, of public-private partnership. China adopted the 2015 "Internet Plus" initiative using the Internet as an empowering infrastructure to enhance mass productivity and galvanise state innovation and entrepreneurship (State Council, 2015b). As part of the initiative, the national "Internet + Public Services" plan, intended to revolutionise the public sector, was prototyped after the procedural design model of user-friendly e-commerce platforms (Office of the State Council, 2018b). At the same time, the central government also introduced the national plan on "Internet + Regulations,"[8] enabled in part by Alibaba's cloud service (Aliyun) to implement social risk warning, regulatory effectiveness assessment and credit modelling.[9] It marked a significant shift in the way the Chinese government reshaped

[5] See the 2018 Guiding Opinions of the State Council on Speeding up the Construction of the National Integrated Online Government Service Platform (国务院关于加快推进全国一体化在线政务服务平台建设的指导意见) (State Council, 2018), the 2019 Provisions of the State Council on Online Government Service (国务院关于在线政务服务的若干规定) (State Council, 2019a), and the 2021 Guide to the Construction of the Mobile End of the National Integrated Government Service Platform (全国一体化政务服务平台移动端建设指南) (Office of the State Council, 2021).

[6] See the 2018 Implementation Plan on Deepening "Internet + Government/Public Service" and Promoting the Reform of "one Web Portal, one Door and one Time" of Government Affairs Service (进一步深化"互联网 + 政务服务"推进政务服务"一网、一门、一次"改革实施方案) (Office of the State Council, 2018b).

[7] See the 2020 Guidance of the General Office of the State Council on Accelerating the "Cross-provincial" Government Services (国务院办公厅关于加快推进政务服务"跨省通办"的指导意见) (Office of the State Council, 2020a).

[8] The "Internet + Regulations" System literally refers to the National Integrated Online Regulatory Platform. See the Platform Portal at http://www.jianguan.gov.cn/

[9] See the overview of the solution demo for the Aliyun-powered "Internet + Regulations" model (Aliyun, n.d.).

bureaucratic governance by utilising emerging technological tools (e.g. big data analytics) and market-based mechanisms (e.g. norm entrepreneurship).

Therefore, digital administration in China also takes advantage of user-friendliness, which is a crucial characteristic of private platforms' business models. On the one hand, it has been a longstanding tradition of the Chinese government to promote barrier-free access to information at the national level. Back in 2008, the modified Disabled Persons Protection Law introduced Articles 52 and 54 to codify the government's commitment to creating conditions for barrier-free information exchange for disabled people. In 2020, policy documents advocated bridging the digital divide and promoting socially inclusive development by popularising mobile apps for ageing people.[10] Accessibility to the disabled and marginalised was widened in the 14th five-year sub-plans on State Informatisation and Public Services in 2022.

On the other hand, due to a lack of technological readiness, local governments tended to collaborate with domestic Internet companies to build Government as a Platform (GaaP). For example, Alibaba offered the governmental affairs intermediary as a customisable and low-code encapsulated component for the Zhejiang government platform (Zhong, 2020). That being said, the intermediary intends to enable governments to build e-commerce-like storefronts without depending on technological implementation. Sharing a platform-as-a-service infrastructure with functional modules and APIs enables the integration of interoperable identification data and crowdsourced databases into new apps using low-code custom programming.

3 A Centralised Approach to Digitalising Identity Infrastructure

A power-concentrated body, the National Informatisation Leading Group, was created in 1996 to oversee China's transition to digital technology (Office of the State Council, 1996). The Ministry of Industry and Information Technology (MIIT) integrated its general office in 2008 (Wang, 2014). It was decided in 2014 to reclassify MIIT's Informatization Promotion Department as the Cyberspace Administration of China (CAC), signalling that the CAC (especially its Information Development Bureau) would be responsible for the coordination of China's e-government initiatives, in concert with other agencies playing a variety of roles in digitising public services (H. Huang, 2020a, p. 50). The 2018 Plan for Deepening the Reform of

[10] In 2020, the Ministry of Industry and Information Technology and the China Disabled Persons' Federation (2020) jointly announced the Guiding Opinions on Promoting Information Accessibility (关于推进信息无障碍的指导意见) with the goal of "bridging the digital divide and promoting social inclusive development," followed by the Implementation Plan for Effectively Solving the Difficulties of the Elderly in Using Intelligent Technology (关于切实解决老年人运用智能技术困难的实施方案) (Office of the State Council, 2020b) and Special Action Programme on Ageing-friendly and Barrier-free Adaptation of Internet Apps (互联网应用适老化及无障碍改造专项行动方案) (Ministry of Industry and Information Technology, 2020).

Party and State Institutions shows that the Central Cyberspace Affairs Commission oversees the country's cybersecurity and informatisation (Central Committee of the Chinese Communist Party, 2018). As such, the CCAC is an inter-ministerial committee that serves as a deliberative and policy-making body.

A broad variety of government organisations, each with a particular role to play in the process, are also included in the digitisation of public/government services. The National Development and Reform Commission, more precisely the State Information Centre, makes plans that primarily reflect sharing information resources at the national level (H. Huang, 2020a, p. 51). At the same time, the General Office of the State Council is responsible for overseeing the disclosure of government information (i.e. the Operational Centre for gov.cn) (Office of the State Council, 2008). The Ministry of Industry and Information Technology continues to collaboratively coordinate the development of telecommunications, the Internet, and private communication networks following the 2018 Plan for Deepening the Reform of Party and State Institutions (Central Committee of the Chinese Communist Party, 2018).

3.1 Principle: Centralised Data Interoperability or Interconnectivity

As the examples above demonstrate, the central government made steps to streamline government data stewardship; yet, because traditional Chinese administration paid little attention to cross-departmental collaboration, information and/or data ramparts continue to exist. Administrations did not simply perceive power divisions as the rationale for a physical separation of data but instead as an inherently different model of data structures.

In the meantime, China's digital transformation is currently undergoing a transition in which it moves from governing society with data to regulating data for society. As discussed previously, data was traditionally viewed as a catalyst for emerging technologies such as big data analytics, Artificial Intelligence, and blockchain technology in the context of the national innovation system. In 2015, the State Council issued the Action Plan for Promoting the Development of Big Data (State Council, 2015a), which clearly states that data is a "fundamental strategic state resource." In March 2020, the CPC Central Committee and the State Council released Opinions on Strengthening the Institutional Mechanism for Market-Based Allocation of Elements (Central Committee of the Chinese Communist Party & State Council, 2020), which define data as a key market element. In a sense, the Chinese bureaucracy sees data both as bottom-up information feedback and as a complement to its top-down state-dominated capitalism and, as never before, as a productivity material that can be subject to state-drawn ownership rules and thus constructed as a data market.

This perception, mentioned earlier, has, to some extent, led legislators to develop and improve data-related rules, which deal in particular with the issue of data silos. In 2021, the Data Security Law (DSL) went into effect, establishing incentives for the open data movement. It is expressly stated in Article 42 of the DSL that the state has a role to play in formulating the use of government data. Following the DSL, as noted earlier, the "open data movement" has been confirmed by a series of 14th five-year sub-plans, such as the National Informatization Plan (NIP) (National Development and Reform Commission, 2021b), Public Service Plan (PSP) (National Development and Reform Commission, 2021a), and Digital Economy Plan (DEP) (State Council, 2021), which have demonstrated the significance of open data in unlocking the digital dividend between the public and private sectors.

Unlike the private sector, where the interoperability of large private platforms has been, to some extent, enforced by the competition authority (Chi, 2021), the public sector places more emphasis on a centralised model of interoperability or, more precisely, interconnectivity. In the latest policy document on constructing a national integrated big data system for government affairs (Office of the State Council, 2022), the central government mentions that as of October 2022, 31 provinces have established specialised government data authorities, generally referred to as big data bureaus. The big data system is based on a "1 + 32 + N" framework structure, including the national government affairs big data platform, the 32 provincial government affairs data platforms, and many of the State Council's department-specific big data platforms.

3.2 *Infrastructure: Digital Identities vs Transformative Fusion of Social Big Data*

Such institutional concentration relies on constructing a basic digital identity database, including personal and legal-person information, etc., by China's earlier national informatisation process and shows its intention to unleash the economic potential of the vast amount of data exploited upon the correlational metadata from the pan-population.

In modern China, digital identity, in a narrow sense, generally refers to two primary identifiers or credentials maintained by the Ministry of Public Security. The Third Research Institute of the Ministry of Public Security created the eID system based on Art. 2 of the Electronic Signature Law, emphasising the promising trade-off between safeguarding personal information and adapting to the openness and circulation of data in cyberspace (The Third Research Institute of the Ministry of Public Security, 2018, pp. 7–8). Following the "Internet Plus" initiative, the First Research Institute of the Ministry of Public Security piloted Version 1.0 of the Cyber Trusted Identity (CTID) system in 2016.[11] With the original aspiration of

[11] See the brief history of the CTID Platform at Anicert (n.d.-b).

privacy-enhanced technology in the core, the CTID platform desensitises and de-identifies the personal identifiers in the legal identity files, generates an irreversible data file devoid of plaintext information, and maps the documents to the legal identity files one by one.[12] The CTID uses SIM Card Digital Identity, blockchain, two-dimensional code, cryptography, and facial recognition to enable online identification without requiring the user to disclose personal information (Bao & Wu, 2020, p. 117; Gao et al., 2021, p. 91).

During the COVID-19 epidemic, China's Health Code system, with a three-colour dynamic interface, which was developed based on the underlying CTID technology in 2020, further strengthened the process of using digital identity for social governance. As opposed to the underlying digital identity or trusted credential, the former is a secondary development based on the latter (CTID, 2021). Since it is connected to the National Integrated Big Data Platform and relies on widely used payment apps like Alipay and WeChat Pay (Liang, 2020, p. 1), it has a federal character in use. Health codes go beyond identification, and their combination of personal information, health status, residence, travel history, exposure history, and other supporting data plays a socio-technical role in epidemic risk ranking and migration control in epidemic prevention (Cong, 2021, p. 4).

According to the latest policy document (Office of the State Council, 2022), likewise, China's extensive collection of big data is focused on two main categories—basic databases and thematic databases. For example, the basic databases are expected to contain population, legal persons, natural resources, economy, electronic certificates, etc., while the thematic databases are planned to cover medical and health care, government services, social security, ecological and environmental protection, credit system, emergency management, supervision of state-owned assets, etc. The process of centralised data collection and cleansing is known as fusion and aggregation (归集, *Gui Ji*), while governmental data integration attempts to facilitate transformative data fusion by distinguishing at the policy level between narrowly defined government data (data generated and collected in the course of government operations itself), industrial data (sectoral data collected by official units), public data (data collected and generated by public utilities), and social data (data collected and generated by third-party Internet platforms).

4 Conclusion and Further Discussions

There is, however, a lack of normative sense in the data catalogues mentioned above, as the tension between the use of social big data for governance and the commercialisation of social big data has also been territorially reflected in how data sovereignty is perceived in China. For example, the determination of critical information infrastructure in China has had a gradual evolution from the cybersecurity

[12] See the definition of the CTID Platform at Anicert (n.d.-a).

law to a complex system of rules involving Personal Information Protection Law, Data Security Law, and regulations on the security protection of critical information infrastructure, which show that the national security involved in data is regarded as more relevant than the comparative advantage of market-based data. Meanwhile, data grades and classifications, established in the Data Security Law, created the data catalogues by classifying data as core data, important data, and general data,[13] which are in less normative and pragmatic alignment with the national big data classification system.

As a result of social big data, Chinese state capitalism has been invigorated, whereby data replaces real-time information feedback loops developed through grassroots civic participation. This paper identifies two driving forces behind the Chinese digital transformation: quasi-neoliberal market mechanisms and technology's spillover effects on social change. The modern Chinese state has developed a distinct cybernetic rationale for social governmentality since its formation as a means of redressing the imbalance of information quid pro quo in the process of ruling the state polity. Technology has also been perceived, sometimes as a probative catalyst for ideology, sometimes as a geopolitical symbol of sovereign independence, sometimes as an economic element of innovation, and even more frequently as a normative or soft-law instrument of government. However, in the case of the public sector's digital transformation, data is frequently more than just data; it represents a top-down correctivist paradigm of social relations. The state's constitutional foundations and, as a result, citizens' rights may be somewhat vulnerable as a result of the digital non-scarcity that develops when the state gathers enough data, for example, through the decentralised/federalist abuse of digital technology (Horwitz, 2022). This dichotomy between positive and exclusionary use of social big data, or culturally and economically reimagined monitoring, thus deserves further normative and empirical investigation so that it can be dismantled, understood and remedied at a micro level, at a behavioural level, and at a cognitive level beyond socio-technical imagination.

References

Aliyun. (n.d.). 互联网+监管解决方案 [*Internet + regulatory solutions*]. https://cn.aliyun.com/solution/govcloud/intetregulation?from_alibabacloud=

Anicert. (n.d.-a). *CTID Network Certificate*. http://www.anicert.cn/identity.html

Anicert. (n.d.-b). *CTID Platform*. http://www.anicert.cn/platform.html?md=2

Bao, M., & Wu, Y. (2020). 如何证明你是你?——数字身份识别在金融中的应用 [How to prove that you are you? - Application of digital identification in finance]. 金融市场研究 *[Financial Market Research], 5*, 113–120.

Central Committee of the Chinese Communist Party. (2013). 关于全面深化改革若干重大问题的决定 [*Decision on several major issues of comprehensively deepening reform*]. http://www.gov.cn/jrzg/2013-11/15/content_2528179.htm

[13] See Article 21 of the Chinese Data Security Law.

Central Committee of the Chinese Communist Party. (2018). 深化党和国家机构改革方案 [*Plan for deepening the reform of party and state institutions*]. http://www.gov.cn/zhengce/2018-03/21/content_5276191.htm#1

Central Committee of the Chinese Communist Party & State Council. (2020). 关于构建更加完善的要素市场化配置体制机制的意见 [*Opinions on strengthening the institutional mechanism for market-based allocation of factors*]. http://www.gov.cn/zhengce/2020-04/09/content_5500622.htm

Chi, S. (2021). Alibaba: Punishment and collaboration. *Verfassungsblog*. https://verfassungsblog.de/alibaba/

China E-Government Network. (2018, May 21). *National two nets, one website, four treasures, and twelve gold projects*. http://www.c-gov.org.cn/article-166340.html

Cong, W. (2021). From pandemic control to data-driven governance: The case of China's health code. *Frontiers in Political Science, 3*. https://doi.org/10.3389/fpos.2021.627959

Cong, W., & Thumfart, J. (2022). A Chinese precursor to the digital sovereignty debate: Digital anti-colonialism and authoritarianism from the post–cold war era to the Tunis agenda. *Global Studies Quarterly, 2*(4), ksac059. https://doi.org/10.1093/isagsq/ksac059

CTID. (2021). 公安部一所参与制定的个人健康信息码国家标准发布 [*A national standard for personal health information codes, developed with the participation of the Ministry of Public Security, was released*]. Weixin Official Accounts Platform. https://tinyurl.com/y9jqkmwm

Gao, L., Li, J., Guo, W., Kang, L., Li, N., & Wang, Y. (2021). 创新社会治理 赋能数字经济——可信数字身份创新成果巡礼 [Innovative social governance empowering the digital economy—Trusted digital identity innovation achievement tour]. 警察技术 *[Police Technology], 3*, 90–93.

Horwitz, J. (2022). Chinese officials punished for changing health codes of bank depositors. *Reuters*. https://www.reuters.com/article/china-banks-henan-idINL4N2YA03D

Hsueh, R. (2016). State capitalism, Chinese-style: Strategic value of sectors, sectoral characteristics, and globalization. *Governance, 29*(1), 85–102. https://doi.org/10.1111/gove.12139

Huang, H. (2020a). 中国"数字政府"的政策演变——兼论"数字政府"与"电子政务"的关系 [The policy evolution of "digital government" in China: The relationship between "digital government" and "E-government"]. 行政论坛 *[Administrative Tribune], 27*(03), 47–55.

Huang, H. (2020b). 数字政府:政策、特征与概念 [Digital government: Policies, characteristics and concepts]. 治理研究 *[Governance Studies], 36*(03), 6–15+2.

Huang, Y. (2008). *Capitalism with Chinese characteristics: Entrepreneurship and the state* (1st ed.). Cambridge University Press.

Lee, K. (2022). *China's technological leapfrogging and economic catch-up: A Schumpeterian perspective*. Oxford University Press.

Liang, F. (2020). COVID-19 and health code: How digital platforms tackle the pandemic in China. *Social Media + Society, 6*(3) 2056305120947657. https://doi.org/10.1177/2056305120947657

Milhaupt, C. J., & Zheng, W. (2014). Beyond ownership: State capitalism and the Chinese firm. *Georgetown Law Journal, 103*, 665.

Ministry of Industry and Information Technology. (2020). *[互联网应用适老化及无障碍改造专项行动方案] Special action programme on ageing-friendly and barrier-free adaptation of internet apps*. http://www.gov.cn/zhengce/zhengceku/2020-12/26/content_5573472.htm

Ministry of Industry and Information Technology & China Disabled Persons' Federation. (2020). 关于推进信息无障碍的指导意见 [*Guiding opinions on promoting information accessibility*]. http://www.gov.cn/gongbao/content/2020/content_5570087.htm

National Development and Reform Commission. (2021a). "十四五"公共服务规划 [*The 14th five-year public service plan*]. https://www.ndrc.gov.cn/xxgk/zcfb/ghwb/202201/P020220110357049883156.pdf

National Development and Reform Commission. (2021b). "十四五"推进国家政务信息化规划 [The *14th five-year national informatization plan*]. http://www.gov.cn/zhengce/zhengceku/2022-01/06/5666746/files/cbff2937df654b44a04c6ef9d43549e9.pdf

National Informatization Leading Group. (2006). 国家电子政务总体框架 [*The overall framework of national e-government*]. https://www.mct.gov.cn/whzx/zxgz/whbwlaqhxxhgz/xxhjs_whaq/201111/t20111129_800690.htm

New Media Matrix for Government Affairs. (n.d.). *Home*. https://app.www.gov.cn/govdata/zwxmtjz.html

Office of the Central Committee of the Chinese Communist Party. (2002). 国家信息化领导小组关于我国电子政务建设指导意见 [*Guidance from the National Informatization Leading Group on the construction of e-government in China*]. https://www.neac.gov.cn/seac/zcfg/200406/1075051.shtml

Office of the State Council. (1996). *Notice concerning establishing the state council leading group for informatization work*. https://digichina.stanford.edu/work/state-council-general-office-notice-concerning-establishing-the-state-council-leading-group-for-informatization-work/

Office of the State Council. (2008). 国务院办公厅主要职责内设机构和人员编制规定的通知 [*State Council Office circular on the regulations on the establishment and staffing of the main functions*]. http://www.gov.cn/zhengce/content/2008-07/17/content_7616.htm

Office of the State Council. (2013). 关于进一步加强政府信息公开回应社会关切提升政府公信力的意见 [*Opinions on strengthening government information disclosure and enhancing the credibility of the government*]. http://www.gov.cn/zhengce/content/2013-10/18/content_1219.htm

Office of the State Council. (2018a). 关于推进政务新媒体健康有序发展的意见 [*Opinions on promoting the healthy and orderly development of new media for government affairs*]. http://www.gov.cn/zhengce/content/2018-12/27/content_5352666.htm

Office of the State Council. (2018b). 进一步深化"互联网+政务服务"推进政务服务"一网、一门、一次"改革实施方案 [*Implementation plan on deepening "Internet + Government/Public Service" and promoting the reform of "one web portal, one door and one time" of Government Affairs Service*]. http://www.gov.cn/zhengce/content/2018-06/22/content_5300516.htm

Office of the State Council. (2020a). 国务院办公厅关于加快推进政务服务"跨省通办"的指导意见 [*Guidance of the General Office of the State Council on accelerating the "cross-provincial" government services*]. http://www.gov.cn/zhengce/zhengceku/2020-09/29/content_5548125.htm

Office of the State Council. (2020b). 关于切实解决老年人运用智能技术困难的实施方案[*Implementation plan for effectively solving the difficulties of the elderly in using intelligent technology*]. http://www.gov.cn/zhengce/content/2020-11/24/content_5563804.htm

Office of the State Council. (2021). 国务院办公厅关于印发全国一体化政务服务平台移动端建设指南的通知 [*Guide to the construction of the mobile end of the national integrated government service platform*]. http://www.gov.cn/zhengce/zhengceku/2021-11/12/content_5650485.htm

Office of the State Council. (2022). 全国一体化政务大数据体系建设指南 [*Guidelines for the construction of a national integrated big data system for government services*]. http://www.gov.cn/zhengce/content/2022-10/28/content_5722322.htm

Pearson, M., Rithmire, M., & Tsai, K. S. (2021). Party-state capitalism in China. *Current History, 120*(827), 207–213. https://doi.org/10.1525/curh.2021.120.827.207

Schneider, L. A. (1981). Science, technology and China's four modernizations. *Technology in Society, 3*(3), 291–303. https://doi.org/10.1016/0160-791x(81)90001-4

State Council. (2007). 中华人民共和国政府信息公开条例 [*Open government information regulation*]. http://www.gov.cn/zwgk/2007-04/24/content_592937.htm.

State Council. (2015a). 关于印发促进大数据发展行动纲要的通知 [*Action plan for promoting the development of big data*]. http://www.gov.cn/zhengce/content/2015-09/05/content_10137.htm

State Council. (2015b). 关于积极推进"互联网+"行动的指导意见 [*Guiding opinions on actively promoting internet plus actions*]. http://www.gov.cn/zhengce/content/2015-07/04/content_10002.htm

State Council. (2018). *Guiding opinions of the State Council on speeding up the construction of the national integrated online government service platform [国务院关于加快推进全国一体化在线政务服务平台建设的指导意见]*. http://www.gov.cn/zhengce/zhengceku/2018-07/31/content_5310797.htm

State Council. (2019a). 国务院关于在线政务服务的若干规定 [*Provisions of the State Council on online government service*]. http://www.gov.cn/gongbao/content/2019/content_5389312.htm

State Council. (2019b). 中华人民共和国政府信息公开条例 [*Regulations of the People's Republic of China on open government information*]. http://www.gov.cn/zhengce/content/2019-04/15/content_5382991.htm

State Council. (2021). "十四五"数字经济发展规划 [*The 14th five-year digital economy plan*]. http://www.gov.cn/zhengce/content/2022-01/12/content_5667817.htm

The Third Research Institute of the Ministry of Public Security. (2018). *EID数字身份体系白皮书 [eID 数字身份体系白皮书]*. https://tinyurl.com/2zjkknzg

Wang, Y. (2014). 我国信息化领导小组的发展和演变 [The development and evolution of the informatization leading group]. *CNII*. https://web.archive.org/web/20180208182757/http://www.cnii.com.cn/informatization/2014-03/10/content_1319483.htm

Wen, C., & Yachang, H. (1999). 网络社会第一站——从启动"政府上网工程"谈起 [The first stop of the internet society—Starting with the launch of the "government internet access project"]. 中国计算机用户 *[China Computer Users], 05*, 37–39.

Xinhua News Agency. (2019). 中共中央关于坚持和完善中国特色社会主义制度 推进国家治理体系和治理能力现代化若干重大问题的决定 [*Decision of the Central Committee of the Chinese Communist Party on several major issues concerning the adherence to and perfection of the socialist system with Chinese characteristics and the advancement of the modernization of the state governance system and the ability to govern*]. http://www.gov.cn/zhengce/2019-11/05/content_5449023.htm

Xinhua News Agency. (2021). 中华人民共和国国民经济和社会发展第十四个五年规划和 *2035* 年远景目标纲要. *[Outline of the 14th Five-Year Plan for National Economic and Social Development of the People's Republic of China and the 2035 Long-Range Objectives]*. https://www.gov.cn/xinwen/2021-03/13/content_5592681.htm

Yu, Y. (2016). 政务微博待补三大短板 [Three shortcomings of government microblogs to be filled]. *People.Cn* [人民网]. http://politics.people.com.cn/n1/2016/0128/c1001-28090656.html

Zhao, Z. (1995). 信息安全与"三金工程" [Information security and "three Golden projects"]. 科技导报 *[Science & Technology Review], 13*(9504), 29–32. http://www.kjdb.org/CN/abstract/abstract5566.shtml

Zheng, L. (2007). Enacting and implementing open government information regulations in China: Motivations and barriers. *Proceedings of the 1st International Conference on Theory and Practice of Electronic Governance* (pp. 117–120). https://doi.org/10.1145/1328057.1328083.

Zhong, J. (2020). 数字政务"云钉一体"的实践 [The integration of clouding and dingding for government affairs]. *China Daily*. https://caijing.chinadaily.com.cn/a/202009/17/WS5f631fc6a3101e7ce9725000.html

Zou, J. (1997). 加快推进国家信息化 [Accelerating state informatization]. 信息系统工程 *[CC News], 11*, 6–7.

Wayne Wei Wang is a PhD candidate in Law and Technology at the University of Hong Kong and a CyberBRICS Fellow at the FGV Center for Technology and Society (Brazil). With an interdisciplinary background in Engineering and Law, his research focuses on Intellectual Property, Data Protection, AI Governance, and Science & Technology Studies, with an emphasis on Law, Innovation, Sustainability, and Technology (LIST) in the Global South. Wayne holds an LLM from WIPO-QUT (Australia) and is an Associate Fellow of the UK Higher Education Academy.

China: An Overview of the Telecoms and Internet Access Sector

Ikeng Lin

Abstract This chapter develops an overview of the Chinese situation regarding access to Internet through the following matters: number of subscribers across different categories; affordability of services; type of technology being used; gender gap; urban-rural gap; ranking in the global ICT indices; strategy for expanding the Internet access; participation in institutions; telecommunications regulations in the country; access to the spectrum for data transmission; and financial resources.

1 Context

What is the state of Internet access in the country, in terms of:

a. Number of subscribers across different categories

Until March 2020, Internet users in China had amounted to 904 million with an Internet access rate of 64.5%; 75.08 million new users added since June 2019, contributing to a 4.9% rise in the Internet access rate.[1] Comparably, as per the 47th China Statistical Report on Internet Development (also applying to some latest data in the following), the number of Internet users in China reached 989 million by December 2020, an increase of 85.4 million compared to March 2020, and the penetration rate reached 70.4%, an increase of 5.9 percentage points compared to March 2020 (Cyberspace Administration of China [CAC], 2021b).

Likewise, by March 2020, cellular network users had amounted to 847 million, 29.84 million more than in 2019. However, cell phone Internet users in China

[1] The COVID-19 pandemic did result in a 50% surge in Internet traffic in China, and over 60% rise in Wuhan, according to the Information and Communication Development Department of the Ministry of Industry and Information Technology. However, it does not seem to contribute to the expansion of Internet access, which has been maintaining a 2 to 4% growth each year.

I. Lin (✉)
NTPU Program on International Trade Negotiation, Taipei, Taiwan

L. Belli, L. Galdino de Magalhães Santos (eds.), *SmartBRICS*,
https://doi.org/10.1007/978-3-031-98204-0_12

reached 986 million in December 2020, up 88.85 million from March 2020. Cell phones accounted for 99.7% of Internet users.

1. As of December 2020, the size of China's non-Internet users was 416 million, a decrease of 80.73 million from March 2020. Regionally, China's non-Internet users were still mainly in rural areas, and the proportion of non-Internet users in rural areas was 62.7%, which was 23.3 percentage points higher than the proportion of the national rural population. Comparably, the number of non-Internet users in China was 496 million until March 2020, 40.2% of those were from urban areas and 59.8% were from rural areas; 51.6% of non-Internet users do not use Internet due to the lack of knowledge of computers and the Internet, 19.5% lack input methods (Pin-Yin), 13.4% of them do not have access to devices such as computers, 14.0% is due to age (too young or too old), 8.8% feel the usage is unnecessary or uninterested, 7.3% report they do not have the time for it. The previous report on the same issue in 2019 stated that 44.6 of non-Internet users do not use Internet due to the lack of knowledge on computers and Internet, 36.8% lacks input methods (Pin-Yin), 15.3% of them do not have devices such as computers, 14.2% is due to age (too young or too old), 10.6% feel the usage is unnecessary or uninterested, 9.4% report they do not have the time for it, and 5.4% do not have access to Internet locally. In comparison to the data published in 2019, most categories in the 2020 report do not seem to change much, except that in 2019, there was a category of "not having access to the Internet locally," which seemingly was added to the category of lack of knowledge of computers and the Internet in 2020.

b. Affordability of services

China is actively promoting Internet access with Policies on Facilitating Faster and More Affordable Internet Connection. The Premier of the State Council of the People's Republic of China, Li Keqiang, stated on May 28th, 2020 that the average annual income in China is 30,000 RMB (approximately 4200 USD), and 600 million people live on an annual income of 12,000 RMB (approximately 1686 USD).

c. Type of technology being used

Until December 2018, users of fibre to the home (FTTH/O) in China amounted to 368 million households, taking up 90.4% of broadband Internet connection users.

Until March 2020, 99.3% of network users in China accessed the Internet via cell phones, having a 0.7% growth in comparison to December 2018; 42.7% of network users accessed the Internet via desktop computers, dropping 48% in December 2018; 35% of network users accessed the Internet via laptop computers, a 0.8% decrease compared to December 2018; 29% of Internet users accessed the Internet via tablet computers, a slight regression of 0.8% compared to December 2018; 32% of network users accessed the Internet via TV, a 1% increase to that of December 2018.

d. Gender gap

As of December 2020, the ratio of male to female Internet users in China was 51.0:49.0, which was basically consistent with the ratio of male to female in the overall population. Until March 2020, 51.9% of the users are men while 48.1% are women, also until June 202, 52.7% of the users are men while 47.3% are women, quite similar to the 52.4% versus 47.6% ratio in December 2018.

e. Urban-rural gap

As of December 2020, the number of rural Internet users in China was 309 million, accounting for 31.3% of all Internet users, up 54.71 million from March 2020; the number of urban Internet users was 680 million, accounting for 68.7% of all Internet users, up 30.69 million from March 2020. The number of urban Internet users was 680 million, accounting for 68.7% of the total number of Internet users, an increase of 30.69 million compared with March 2020. Until March 2020, rural areas contributed 28.2% (255 million) of Internet users, while 71.8% (649 million) were from urban areas, in comparison to June 2019 when rural areas contributed 26.3% (225 million) of Internet users, while 73.7% (630 million) were from urban areas.

What is the country's ranking in the global ICT indices, such as ITU's ICT Development Index (IDI), WEF's Network Readiness Index (NRI), A4AI's Affordability Drivers Index, and GSMA's Mobile Connectivity Index (MCI)?
In 2017, China's IDI ranked 80th worldwide with the value of 5.60 (global average being 5,11), and is one of the fastest-growing countries. (International Telecommunication Union [ITU], 2017) China ranked 59 in the WEF's Network Readiness Index (NRI) with a value of 4.2 (Portulans Institute, 2022) while ranking 35 out of 61 countries in A4AI's Affordability Drivers Index with a value of 52.25 out of 100 (Alliance for Affordable Internet [A4AI], 2021). China scored 74.3 in the GSMA's Mobile Connectivity Index, scoring 73.9, 67.3, 76.3, 80.2 in infrastructure, affordability, consumer readiness and content and services, respectively (GSMA, n.d.).

Does the country have a strategy for the expansion of Internet access, such as a national broadband plan or similar?
In May 2020, the Cyberspace Administration of China, the National Development and Reform Commission, State Council Leading Group Office of Poverty Alleviation and Development, Ministry of Industry and Information Technology of the People's Republic of China jointly issued the 2020 working plan of poverty alleviation through Internet services (Cyberspace Administration of China [CAC], 2020). The working plan aims to improve Internet and broadcasting infrastructure in rural and poor areas; through projects like Extending Radio and TV Broadcasting Coverage to Every Village Project (National Development and Reform Commission, Ministry of Finance & General Administration of Radio, Film and Television, n.d. (村村通), the literal translation is connection between villages, the project is not limited to radio and TV broadcasting coverage) as well as nationwide trials of providing universal telecommunication service, rural areas and poor areas in China started to

enjoy the convenience of Internet and information society. Until October 2019, the fibre optic network and 4G network have over 98% coverage in administrative villages, while poor villages have 99% broadband coverage. In 2013, China issued the "Broadband China" strategy and Implementation Plan, the plan has five main goals: to promote regional broadband development, to accelerate the optimisation and upgrade of broadband networks, to improve the application of broadband networks, to promote the development of broadband industry chain, and improve the capacity of maintaining broadband network security. Take promoting regional broadband networks development as an example, the goal was divided into three different sectors, eastern, central and western, and rural farm areas. For the eastern part of China, the goal is to actively utilise optical fibre and the new generation of mobile telecom technology, as well as TV broadcasting technology, to improve the performance of broadband networks, ultimately catching up with developed countries. Central and western areas focus on broadband network infrastructures, improving the capacity of backbone networks and inter-network interconnection capabilities, and broadening the coverage of broadband networks. As for rural farm areas, the goal is to take broadband into the coverage of universal telecommunication services, and further enforce the Extending Radio and TV Broadcasting Coverage to Every Village Project mentioned above; different technologies such as fibre optic, copper wire, coaxial cable, 3G/LTE, microwave, satellite transmissions have been adopted to speed up the expansion of broadband networks in administrative areas and natural villages (The Central People's Government of the People's Republic of China, 2013b).

2 International Commitments

Is the country a member of the ITU?
China has been a member of ITU since 1920, and first sent a delegation to attend the Plenipotentiary Conference of ITU in Madrid, where China signed the International Telecommunication Convention.[2]

Is the country a signatory to the 1988 or 2012 version of the ITRs?
China is a signatory to the 2012 version of the ITR.

Does the country have a policy of following ITU recommendations and/or technical standards?
Yes, most of China's telecommunications related legislation and regulations is in accordance with ITU standards, for example the Measures for the Management of Filing, Coordination, Registration and Maintenance of Satellite Networks Article 1 states: To strengthen and standardise the declaration, coordination, registration and maintenance of satellite networks, these Measures are formulated in accordance

[2] The full list of member states of the ITU can be accessed at the ITU website (ITU, 2022b).

with the "Regulations of the People's Republic of China on Radio Management" and the regulations of the International Telecommunication Union (hereinafter referred to as ITU) (Ministry of Industry and Information Technology, 2017b). The Technical Requirements for the Average Loudness and True-Peak Audio Level of Digital Television Programmes of China also follows ITU Recommendation BS.1864–0 (03/2010) (The State Administration of Press, Publication, Radio and Television, 2014).

What is the composition of the country's delegations at ITU meetings, including official reunions and study groups (e.g. government only, or multi-stakeholder including private sector, academia and civil society representatives)?

The delegation of China at ITU meetings is composed of Bureau of Radio Regulation of the Ministry of Industry and Information Technology (the State Radio Office), the State Radio Monitoring Center, the State Radio Spectrum Management Center, the China Academy of Information and Communications Technology, National Radio and Television Administration, Bureau of Telecommunications Regulation of Macau, Office of the Communications Authority of Hong Kong, related telecom corporations, satellite operators and manufacturers (Industrial Culture Development Center of the Ministry of Industry and Information Technology, 2019).

Is the country a member of the WTO? If so, is the country a signatory to the General Agreement on Trade in Services?

China is a member of the WTO but is not a contracting party of GATT 1994 (World Trade Organization [WTO], 2022). China joined the WTO on 11 December 2001 after years of preparation and debates over the jurisdiction of GATT.[3] The WTO's General Agreement on Trade in Services (GATS) sets binding rules on barriers to trade in services related to market access and national treatment, but does not regulate members' domestic regulatory practices in trade in services. On December 2, 2021, 67 WTO members, including China, the European Union and the United States, held a meeting at the level of heads of delegations of each participating party to the WTO on the joint declaration initiative on domestic regulation of trade in services, and jointly issued the Declaration on the Completion of Negotiations on Domestic Regulation of Trade in Services. The rules related to domestic regulation of trade in services aim to optimise the process of approval of licenses related to trade in services, enhance the transparency and convenience of government regulation, reduce business operating costs, and improve the global business environment for trade in services (China Council for the Promotion of International Trade, 2022).

Is the country a signatory to any regional framework for the regulation of telecommunications or a member of any regional organisation for telecommunications regulation?

Since joining the APEC in 1991, the Ministry of Industry and Information Technology of the People's Republic of China (hereinafter the People's Republic of

[3] To see the members and observers' list of the WTO, see WTO (2023).

China) has been actively participating in the APEC Telecommunications and Information working group (Department of International Cooperation, 2022). China is also signatory country of the APEC-TEL Mutual Recognition Arrangement (MRA), which, is a multilateral arrangement between economies in the APEC region, as well as The MRA for Equivalence of Technical Requirements, which was endorsed by the APEC Telecommunications Ministers (Asia-Pacific Economic Cooperation, 2021) China is also a member state of the International Mobile Satellite Organization (2022), International Telecommunications Satellite Organization (Ministry of Foreign Affairs, 2023), International Maritime Satellite Organization (with Beijing Maritime Communication & Navigation Co.—MCN representing China), and the Internet Corporation for Assigned Names and Numbers (The Central People's Government of the People's Republic of China, 2013a).

3 Institutions

Does the country have a Telecommunications Regulatory Authority? If so, is it an independent body, and what are its attributes?

The Ministry of Industry and Information Technology is the primary telecommunication regulatory authority in China.[4] Subordinate to the Ministry are, among others, the Info-communication Management Bureau, in charge of supervising telecommunications and Internet services, which also controls the entry to telecommunications and Internet services market (Ministry of Industry and Information Technology, 2015b); the Communications Development which coordinates the development of public and special-use communication networks and the Internet, drafts network-technology development policies, and drafts rules and oversees telecom service fees (Ministry of Industry and Information Technology, 2008b); Cybersecurity Bureau of which is responsible for organising the security plans, policy and standards, of telecommunication and Internet, it also is in charge of the establishment and usage management of telecommunications, Internet and information security technology platform, and to monitor, notice and respond to emergencies in telecommunications and Internet (Ministry of Industry and Information Technology, 2008a); Radio Regulatory Bureau (State Radio Office) which divides, distributes, and assigns radio frequencies, oversees radio station operations, coordinates and manages civilian satellite positioning, coordinates with the military on radio management issues, and manages issues related to foreign radio. The Ministry is not an independent body; rather, it is subordinate to the State Council.

[4] Regulation on Telecommunications of the People's Republic of China Article 3 paragraph 1: The competent department of information industry of the State Council is responsible for the nationwide supervision and administration of telecommunications in accordance with this Regulation (State Council of the People's Republic of China, 2016).

What is the allocation of regulatory responsibilities between the appropriate government department(s) and the Telecommunications Regulatory Authority?

See the answer to the previous question.

If the country follows a federal structure, is there an allocation of responsibilities relating to the telecommunications sector between the central/federal government and the states?

China does not follow a federal structure; the two special administrative regions of Hong Kong and Macau, however, are autonomous to some degree (Basic Law of the Macao Special Administrative Region of the People's Republic of China 1993). Article 17 of the Basic Law of the Hong Kong Special Administrative Region of the People's Republic of China reads: The Hong Kong Special Administrative Region shall be vested with legislative power. Laws enacted by the legislature of the Hong Kong Special Administrative Region must be reported to the Standing Committee of the National People's Congress for the record. The reporting for record shall not affect the entry into force of such laws (Basic Law of the Hong Kong Special Administrative Region of the People's Republic of China, 2021). Thus, giving power to the Legislative Council of the Hong Kong Special Administrative Region to legislate regulations such as the Communications Authority Ordinance, which regulates issues regarding telecommunications in Hong Kong, as well as the establishment of the Communications Authority (Communications Authority, 2012). The Communications Authority is independent of the Ministry of Industry and Information Technology (Communications Authority, 2021). Macau on the other hand, has the Basic Telecommunications Law, which was decreed by The Legislative Assembly, in terms of the subsection 1) of the 71st Article of the Basic Law of the Special Administrative Region of Macao to define the bases of the telecommunications policy of the Special Administrative Region of Macao, as well as the general framework which regulates the establishment, management and exploration of telecommunications networks and the telecommunications services rendered.[5] The telecommunications authority in Macau is the Bureau of Telecommunications Regulation, which was established in accordance with the Administrative Regulation No. 5/2006 (repealed and replaced by Administrative Regulation No. 29/2016). The Bureau is in charge of providing postal public services and regulating, monitoring, promoting, and coordinating all activities related to the telecommunications industry.

Is there a competition department within the Telecommunications Regulatory Authority?

As per the portal of MIIT, its Information and Communication Administration Bureau reportedly announced some campaign-like enforcement against online unfair competition (Xinhuanet News, 2021). At the same time, MIIT's Department

[5] To learn more, see the Basic Telecommunications Law (2001).

of Industrial Policy and Regulations used to make policies on enterprise mergers (Ministry of Industry and Information Technology, n.d.).

Does the country have a Competition Authority? If so, is it an independent body, and what are its attributes?

Before the institutional reform in 2018, the competence of anti-monopoly work was divided among three departments, with the Anti-monopoly Bureau of the Ministry of Commerce, the Price Supervision, Inspection and Anti-monopoly Bureau of the National Development and Reform Commission, and the Anti-monopoly and Anti-unfair Competition Enforcement Bureau of the State Administration for Industry and Commerce exercising anti-monopoly functions.

Among those, the major competition authority in China was the Anti-Monopoly Bureau, which was subordinate to the Ministry of Commerce of the People's Republic of China. In 2021, The State Antimonopoly Bureau was established as a national bureau under the State Council and became subordinate to the State Administration for Market Regulation. The new Bureau reportedly includes the Competition Policy Coordination Division, Anti-monopoly Enforcement Division I, and Anti-monopoly Enforcement Division II.

- The Division of Competition Policy Coordination coordinates competition policy implementation and antimonopoly investigation on a comprehensive basis (State Administration for Market Regulation, 2021c);
- The First Division of Anti-monopoly Enforcement is responsible for anti-monopoly enforcement of monopoly agreements, abuse of dominant market position and abuse of intellectual property rights to exclude and restrict competition (State Administration for Market Regulation, 2021a);
- The Second Division of Anti-monopoly Enforcement is responsible for the anti-monopoly review of operator concentration in accordance with the law. It also investigates and handles cases of operator concentrations that violate the law, as well as cases that do not meet the declaration standards but may be able to exclude or restrict competition (State Administration for Market Regulation, 2021b).

Does the country have a Data Protection Authority? If so, is it an independent body, and what are its attributes? If not, which body of the government takes care of personal data-related issues?

Before the Personal Information Protection Law was introduced, China did not have a data protection authority, the allocation of data protection responsibility was scattered between sectors such as Cyberspace Administration, Industry and Ministry of Information Technology, Public Security Organs, State Post Bureau, the People's Bank of China, etc., thus with the widely distributed power and responsibility and troubles of coordination between sectors, it used to be difficult to form a top down data protection system. However, the PIPL came into effect in 2021, with its Article 60 saying that the Cyberspace Administration of China plays a coordinating role in protecting personal information and some other ministry-level departments exercise data protection authority in their specific sectors. For example, the Network Security

Bureau of the Ministry of Industry and Information Technology sometimes takes care of personal data-related issues.

Does the country have a specific public body dealing with open data? If so, is it an independent body, and what are its attributes?

China does not have a specific body dealing with open data. The Cyberspace Administration of China (Office of the Central Cyberspace Affairs Commission), National Development and Reform Commission, and Ministry of Industry and Information Technology joint issued the "Work Plan for the Pilot Program of Opening of Public Information Resources (unofficial translation),"(公共信息资源开放试点工作方案) which determined Beijing, Shanghai, Zhejiang province, Fujian province, and Guizhou province as regions under the pilot program to carry out the pilot program of opening of public information resources (CAC, n.d.). In the "Action Outline for Promoting the Development of Big Data" (State Council of the People's Republic of China, 2015), the State Council stated that one of the main tasks is to accelerate the opening and sharing of government data, promoting the integration of resources, and enhancing the governance capacity, and establishing a national unified open platform for government data by the end of 2018 to make public data resources available to the public in a reasonable and moderate.

Does the country have a body/an authority for managing cybersecurity incidents, such as CERTs/CSIRTs? If so, what are its attributes and what is the nature of such an entity (e.g. governmental, multi-stakeholder, private)?

The National Computer Network Emergency Response Technical Team/Coordination Center of China (CNCERT/CC) (2013) manages cyber security incidents. In 2017, the Ministry of Industry and Information Technology (2017d) issued the Public Internet Network Security Incident Emergency Response Plan (unofficial translation)(公共互联网网络安全突发事件应急预案), the Plan stated that under the coordination of the Cyberspace Administration of China, the Office of the Central Leading Group for Cyberspace Affairs will lead the work of responding to public Internet network security incidents, and is responsible for commanding and coordinating in occurrence of major cybersecurity incidents. The National Computer Network Emergency Response Technical Team/Coordination Center of China is a non-governmental, non-profit cybersecurity technical centre.

Does the country have a coordination system involving the aforementioned institutions? If so, what is the nature of such an entity (e.g. governmental, multi-stakeholder, private)?

The leading group for national informatization is the coordination body of the institutions, with Xi Jinping as the leader of the group (General Office of the State Council, 1999). The group consists of General Secretary of the Communist Party of China Central Committee, Premier of the State Council, Director General of National Radio and Television Administration, Chairman of the Office of the Central Cyberspace Affairs Commission, Secretary of the Leading Party Members' Group of the Ministry of Science & Technology and Ministers of Ministry of Foreign Affairs, Ministry of Industry and Information Technology, Ministry of Finance and so on. The goal of the group is to act as the leader between major cybersecurity and informatisation problems between different fields and to strategise the development of national cybersecurity and informatisation (Office of the Central Cyberspace Affairs Commission, n.d.).

4 Regulations

Are the telecommunication regulations and standards openly and publicly accessible?
The telecommunication regulations and standards are openly and publicly accessible. According to Article 4 of the Regulation on Telecommunications of the People's Republic of China (State Council of the People's Republic of China, 2016): The supervision and administration of telecommunications shall be carried out according to the principles of separation of the Government and enterprises, anti-monopoly, development promotion, openness, fairness and impartiality.

Is there a specific general telecommunications legislation?
The general telecommunication legislation is the Regulation on Telecommunications of the People's Republic of China, issued in 2000 and revised in 2016. The regulation is formulated to regulate the order of the telecommunications market, to protect the lawful rights and interests of telecommunications users and service providers and to ensure the safety of telecommunications networks and information to promote the healthy development of telecommunications (State Council of the People's Republic of China, 2016).

Are there any instruments other than legislation and regulations, such as license agreements, that govern the provision of telecommunication services in the country?
Yes, for example, the Internet Society of China (n.d.) once called for wide signatories of the Telecommunications and Internet Industry Network Data Security Self-Regulation Convention.

Is there any obligation to provide open data regarding the telecommunications infrastructure?
Yes, Urgent notice regarding co-location and sharing of the telecommunication infrastructure (unofficial translation) (关于推进电信基础设施共建共享的紧急通知) stated that State/City Communication Administration should establish a telecommunication infrastructure database accessible to basic telecommunication businesses (Ministry of Industry and Information Technology, 2008c).

Is there any obligation to provide open data on backhaul pricing?
Article 25 of the Telecommunication Regulation of the People's Republic of China (2016) states: The service providers shall, at the request of the competent department of information industry of the State Council and other telecommunications administrative authorities, provide complete and correct information and data on the

cost of service they provide. Article 25 of the 2016 Telecommunication Regulation derived from Article 26 of the 2000 Telecommunication Regulation of the People's Republic of China; in the 2016 version the sentence "The standard for fixed and guideline prices shall be formulated by holding hearings in which service providers, end-users and other sectors can exchange their opinion" was deleted, seemingly skipping the process of taking in opinions of service providers and users (State Council of the People's Republic of China, 2016).

Does regulation foresee multiple categories of telecommunications services (e.g. Internet access, broadcasting)? Are information services distinguished between themselves (content creation and content distribution)?

China has yet to have a set of comprehensive telecommunication laws; current telecommunication regulations reside in administrative laws and rules. The Telecommunication Regulation of the People's Republic of China regulates the telecommunication market order, maintains service users and service providers' legal interests, guarantees network and information safety, promotes the growth of the telecommunication industry and so on (State Council of the People's Republic of China, 2016). The Ministry of Industry and Information Technology issued several administrative rules in accordance with the Telecommunication Regulation of the People's Republic of China, including Measures for the Administration of Telecommunications Business Licensing, Measures for the Network Access Management of Telecommunication Equipment, Provisions on Protecting the Personal Information of Telecommunications and Internet Users, Provisions on the Registration of True Identity Information of Telephone Subscribers, Interim Measures for the Quality Supervision and Management of the Telecommunications Service; but as the telecommunication industry grows, the emergence of new technologies results in new challenges in cybersecurity, personal data protection, consumers' protection, thus, law at the upper level of the legal hierarchy is needed, and was thus discussed in the Standing Committee of the 13th National People's Congress (Office of Central Cyberspace Affairs Commission/Cyberspace Administration of China [CAC], 2015).

There are two ways to distinguish information services, on the one hand, in a narrower sense, information services are divided into content services, entertainment, business and locating information, and so on. Users of information services can be users of fixed communication, users of mobile communication, Internet users, or users of other data transmitting network; in this modality of distinguishing, information services are classified as one of the value-added business of telecommunications services; from the point of view of responsibilities of Ministry of Information Industry (superseded by Ministry of Industry and Information Technology), information services should not only include traditional telecommunications services, Internet, and software services, rather, they should also include radio and TV (Ministry of Industry and Information Technology, 2015a). On the other hand, a broader sense of distinguishing information services is to divide them into categories such as production of electronic information equipment, distribution and renting of electronic information equipment, electronic information transmitting services, computer services, and other information related services according to the Interim Provisions on the Classification of Information Related Industries (unofficial translation) (统计上划分信息相关产业暂行规定); electronic information transmitting services, computer services, and other information related services are opposed to the general information services according to the Interim Provisions; from the perspective of business, information services include telecommunications related services, Internet information services, radio and TV transmitting services, satellite transmitting services, computer and software related services, news publishing related services, libraries and archives related services.

Do the country's national regulations recognise community operators/ non-profit/Telecommunications operators?

Article 8 of the Regulation on Internet Information Service of the People's Republic of China states: A non-profitable Internet information service provider shall file for record its activities at telecommunications administrative authorities of the provinces, autonomous regions and cities under the direct control of the Central Government or the Ministry of Information Technology (MII), and the following documents shall be submitted:

1. basic information of the service provider and its person-in-charge;
2. the website address and services provided;
3. having obtained the approval of the competent industry authorities in case its service falls within the scope as provided in Article 5 (State Council of the People's Republic of China, 2011).

Upon submitting all the above documents, it shall be recorded and given a file number.

Is there any obligation to share infrastructure?

(a) poles, cell phone towers, underground routes/tubes,
(b) fibre optics sharing, telecommunication cables,
(c) equipment sharing?

Urgent notice regarding co-location and sharing of the telecommunication infrastructure (unofficial translation) (关于推进电信基础设施共建共享的紧急通知) regulates obligations of sharing infrastructure:

1. Existing poles and towers have to be shared, those that are not capable of sharing should adopt measures such as technical upgrades. Owners of existing poles and towers should respond within 10 days and provide reasons if they are not able to share. It is forbidden to construct new towers and poles if the location already has existing towers and poles, construction needs to be approved by the provincial coordinating body if there are special needs to construct new poles and towers.
2. New poles and towers need to be co-built.
3. Other infrastructures should be co-built and shared. Transmission line, including tubes, poles, fibre-optic cable, and base station, should be co-built; existing base

station infrastructure and transmission line should be shared with other telecommunication companies (Ministry of Industry and Information Technology, 2008c).

Is there any unbundling obligation? Can you be an Internet service provider and a content provider at the same time?
There is no unbundling obligation, according to Article 6 of Measures for the Administration of Telecommunications Business Licensing (Ministry of Industry and Information Technology, 2017a), an applicant for operating the value-added telecommunications business shall satisfy the following requirements:

1. It is a legally formed company.
2. It has the funds and professionals suitable for its business activities.
3. It has the credibility or capability of providing customers with long-term services.
4. Its registered capital is one million yuan or more if it is to operate the business within a province, autonomous region or municipality directly under the Central Government; and its registered capital is ten million yuan or more if it is to operate the business nationwide or across provinces, autonomous regions and/or municipalities directly under the Central Government.
5. It has the necessary sites, facilities and technical schemes.
6. The company and its major investors and major business managers are not included in the list of enterprises with dishonest telecommunications business operations.
7. Other requirements as prescribed by the state.

An example of an Internet service provider acting as a content provider is China Mobile. While being one of the three largest Internet service providers in China, China Mobile also launches a platform called Mobile Market, which provides users with software, music, games, videos, and comics through a multipurpose application market [AM1].

Is there any obligation to treat Internet traffic in a non-discriminatory fashion (so-called network neutrality principles)?
No, there is no obligation to treat Internet traffic in a non-discriminatory fashion in China, given the existence of the Great Fire Wall (Frisch, 2017).

Does the country have any specific legal or regulatory provisions regarding the Internet Access Providers' possibility to monitor the content of user communications?
Yes, there are regulations prohibiting monitoring, Article 8 of the China Internet Sector Self-Discipline Convention: Consciously safeguard the lawful rights and interests of consumers. Preserve users' information and secrets; do not use information provided by users to engage in any activity that has no relationship with the commitments made to users, and do not use technological or other superiority to infringe the lawful interests of consumers or users. (The Central People's Government of the People's Republic of China, 2010) However, regulations for

monitoring the content of user communications can be seen in administrative rules. Paragraph 7 of the Decision of the Standing Committee of the National People's Congress on Preserving Computer Network Security mentioned: Any unit that engages in the computer network business shall carry out activities in accordance with law and, when it discovers illegal or criminal acts or harmful information on the computer network, shall take measures to suspend transmission of harmful information and report the matter to the relevant authority without delay (Standing Committee of the National People's Congress, 2000). Article 5 of the Administrative Measures for the Security Protection of Computer Information Networks Linked to the Internet started: No unit or individual shall use the international networking to produce, duplicate, search and disseminate the following information: (1) information that instigates the resistance and disruption of the implementation of the Constitution, laws and administrative regulations; (2) information that instigates the subversion of the state political power and overthrow of the socialist system; (3) information that instigates the splitting up of the country and sabotage of national unity; (4) information that instigates hatred and discrimination among nationalities and sabotages solidarity among nationalities; (5) information that fabricates or distorts facts, spreads rumours and disrupts social order; (6) information that propagates feudalistic superstitious, obscenity, pornographic, gambling, violence, murder and terror and instigates crimes; (7) information that openly insults others or fabricates facts to slander others; (8) information that damages the reputation of state organs; and (9) other information that violates the Constitution, laws and administrative regulations (State Council of the People's Republic of China, 1997a).

Does the country have any specific legal or regulatory provisions regarding the Internet Access Providers' possibility to collect and process users' personal data?

General regulations of data protection: In 2012, Standing Committee of the National People's Congress issued the Decision of the Standing Committee of the National People's Congress on Strengthening Information Protection on Networks (The Central People's Government of the People's Republic of China & Xinhua News Agency, 2012), laying down rules of personal data collection and usage; in 2013 the Law of the People's Republic of China on the Protection of Consumer Rights and Interests was amended to add regulations regarding consumers' data protection; sector 17 of the 2015 Amendment of criminal law of the people's Republic of China (nine) adds provisions on the illegal sale or provision of a citizen's personal information and provides the punishment for committing or facilitating such crimes (Order No. 30 by the President of the People's Republic of China, 2015); the 2016 Cybersecurity Law not only further regulates the collection and usage of personal data, but also clarified obligations and responsibilities of network operators regarding personal data security; during the Fifth Session of the Twelfth National People's Congress in 2017, personal data has been listed as one of the civil rights under the protection of the General Principles of the Civil Law of the People's Republic of China. The Chinese Civil Code and the PIPL were enacted in 2020 and 2021, respectively, to establish the core framework of personal data protection.

Data protection on telecommunication: Provisions on Protecting the Personal Information of Telecommunications and Internet Users is the regulation that oversees data protection in telecommunications. The provision was issued in 2013 by the Ministry of Industry and Information Technology due to the rapid development of telecommunications and the Internet, also issues like leaks of personal data spurred the legislation of personal data protection (Ministry of Industry and Information Technology, 2013a). The provision can further perfect telecommunications and Internet personal data protection by regulating the collection and usage of users' personal data when Internet information service providers fail to do so. The issuing of the provision is also implementing the Decision of the Standing Committee of the National People's Congress on Strengthening Information Protection on Networks (The Central People's Government of the People's Republic of China & Xinhua News Agency, 2012), further making clear the rules of personal data usage and collection of telecommunication operators and Internet information service providers.

Does the country require a license to operate telecommunications networks? Is there any license exemption?
Yes, operating telecommunications networks in China requires a license according to the Measures for the Administration of Telecommunications Business Licensing (Ministry of Industry and Information Technology, 2017a) issued in 2017 by the Ministry of Industry and Information Technology, the license, according to the Telecommunication Regulation of the People's Republic of China 2016, shall use the method of tender when granting.[6] There is no exemption from the licensing.

Does the country offer a specific/simplified license for not-for-profit operators or for operators that cover specific areas (e.g. rural areas)?
No.

Does the country require a license to provide satellite telecommunications services, including via non-geostationary orbit satellites?
Yes, Article 5, paragraph 2 of the Administrative Provisions on the Establishment of Satellite Communication Networks as Well as the Setup and Use of Earth Stations states: the domestic space station to be used has been approved by the MIIT and for which a wireless station license has been obtained. While Article 3 states that "The state applies the licensing system to the establishment of satellite communication networks. The establishment of satellite communication networks shall be subject to the approval of the Ministry of Industry and Information Technology of the People's Republic of China (hereinafter referred to as 'MIIT'). No entity or individual may establish any satellite communication network without approval" (Order No. 7 by the Ministry of Industry and Information Technology of the People's Republic of China, 2009). Also, the Service Guide to the approval of the Establishment of Satellite Communication Networks as Well as the Setup and Use

[6] Article 12 of the Telecommunication Regulation of the People's Republic of China (State Council of the People's Republic of China, 2016).

of Earth Stations (unofficial translation) Paragraph 16 mentions that the approval of establishment of a satellite communication network will be a permit or approval document for the use of radio frequencies (Ministry of Industry and Information Technology, 2012).

Has the country established an obligation to provide coverage in specific areas (e.g. rural areas that lack coverage)?
There is no obligation in doing so, but it is encouraged for telecommunication operators to provide better rates for users in rural areas or underprivileged users according to the Notice of the Ministry of Industry and Information Technology on Further Regulating Activities to Market Telecommunications Tariff Schemes (unofficial translation) (工业和信息化部关于进一步规范电信资费营销行为的通知) (Ministry of Industry and Information Technology, 2018).

Are there any specific cybersecurity obligations with regard to the telecommunications sector?
The 2017 Cybersecurity Law Article 21 states: The state shall implement the rules for graded protection of cybersecurity. Network operators shall, according to the requirements of the rules for graded protection of cybersecurity, fulfil the following security protection obligations, to ensure that the network is free from interference, damage or unauthorised access, and prevent network data from being divulged, stolen or falsified.

1. Developing internal security management rules and operating procedures, determining the persons in charge of cybersecurity, and carrying out the responsibility for cybersecurity protection.
2. Taking technical measures to prevent computer viruses, network attacks, network intrusions and other acts endangering cybersecurity.
3. Taking technical measures to monitor and record the status of network operation and cybersecurity incidents, and preserving relevant weblogs for not less than six months as required.
4. Taking measures such as data categorisation, and back-up and encryption of important data.
5. Performing other obligations as prescribed by laws and administrative regulations.

In light of Article 21, the Ministry of Public Security issued the Notice of the Cyberspace Administration of China on Regulations on the Classified Protection of Cybersecurity (Consultation Paper) (unofficial translation) (CAC, 2021a) to further implement the protection of cybersecurity.

The 2021 Cybersecurity Review Measures aims to enhance the secure and controllable level of critical information infrastructure and safeguard national security; the regulation regulates the purchase of network products and services by critical information infrastructure, which affects or may affect national security.

The previous version of the 2020 Cybersecurity Review Measures was revised in 2021, most notably the addition of the provision "Article 7: Online platform operators holding the personal information of more than 1 million users and newly listing on foreign markets must report for cybersecurity review with the Cybersecurity Review Office" (CAC et al., 2022).

Is there any regulation regarding cybersecurity incidents?
National Contingency Plans for Cyber Security Incidents oversees cybersecurity incidents. The regulation aims to establish a healthy national cybersecurity contingency system, to strengthen the ability to cope with cybersecurity incidents, to prevent and decrease losses of cybersecurity incidents, and to protect public interests, national security, public safety, and social order. Each province's (including districts and cities) sectors should notify related units and report the possible cybersecurity incidents when deemed necessary while monitoring and analysing information; the early warning includes types of incidents, level of the warning, starting time, possible affected scope, responses to be taken and so on (CAC, 2017b).

Does the law foresee any specific cybercrime involving the (mis)use or attack of the telecommunications infrastructure?
Yes, the Critical Information Infrastructure Security Protection Regulations (unofficial translation) (关键信息基础设施安全保护条例) foresee cybercrime involving the (mis)use or attack of the telecommunications infrastructure (CAC, 2017a).

Does the law foresee SIM and/or IMEI registration? What are the requirements applicable to such registration (for instance, the documents and information required for Know-Your-Customer (KYC) processes)?
The Provisions on the Registration of True Identity Information of Telephone Subscribers Article 3 states: The term "registration of true identity information of telephone subscribers" as mentioned in these Provisions refers to the activity in which a telecommunications service operator truthfully registers the true identity information provided by a subscriber when it handles network access procedures for the subscriber's fixed or mobile telephone service (including wireless network cards, same below), concludes an agreement or confirms the provision of service with this subscriber. Thus, the true identity of an individual when registering for the service is mandatory (Ministry of Industry and Information Technology, 2013b). To register, according to Article 7, an individual may provide any of the following valid identity documents:

1. A resident identity card, a temporary resident identity card, or a booklet of permanent residence;
2. An identity card for servicemen of the Chinese People's Liberation Army or an identity card for policemen of the Chinese People's Armed Police Force;
3. A Mainland travel permit for Hong Kong and Macau residents, a Mainland travel permit for Taiwan residents, or any other valid travel documents;
4. The passport of a foreign citizen; or.
5. Any other valid identity documents as prescribed in laws, administrative regulations, and provisions of the state. The range of the provisions includes fixed or mobile telephone service, and wireless network card (Ministry of Industry and Information Technology, 2013b).

The Ministry of Industry and Information Technology also issued the Notice on Related Works of Further Perfecting the Management of Real-name Registration of Phone Users (unofficial translation) (关于进一步做好电话用户实名登记管理有关工作的通知), requiring telecommunication companies to implement face recognition starting 2019/12/1, only after the face recognition process can the individual access the network; the Notice also forbids the reselling of SIM cards (Ministry of Industry and Information Technology, 2019).

Does the country specify the prices or tariffs for the provision of telecommunication services or impose any minimum or maximum limits?

China does not regulate the prices of telecommunication services. Since the 2016 version of the Regulation on Telecommunications of the People's Republic of China, service fees will be determined by the market (Article 23: Telecommunication services shall be subject to market-regulated pricing. Telecommunication operators shall fully consider the production and operation costs, the supply and demand situation in the telecommunication market, and other factors to reasonably determine the charging rates for telecommunication services. The Article replaced Article 24 of the 2000 version) (State Council of the People's Republic of China, 2016) rather than being set by fixed, guideline or market prices stated in the 2000 version of the Regulation on Telecommunications of the People's Republic of China (Article 24: Charges for telecommunications services are set by fixed, guideline or market prices. Charges for basic telecommunications services can be set by fixed or guideline prices set by the government or by market prices. Charges for value-added telecommunications services can be set by market prices or guideline prices set by the government. Charges for telecommunications services involving full market competition can be set by market prices. The Catalogue of Charges for telecommunications services set by fixed, guideline or market prices shall be formulated by MII after consulting the State Planning Commission (State Council of the People's Republic of China, 2000). However, Chinese government still encourages the lowering of prices for telecommunication services with policies such as Notice of the Ministry of Industry and Information Technology on Further Regulating Activities to Market Telecommunications Tariff Schemes (Ministry of Industry and Information Technology, 2018), the Notice encourages telecommunication service providers to provide different plans regarding their usage, and encourages service providers to act in accordance with the requirements of the Policies on Facilitating Faster and More Affordable Internet Connection.

Are there any policies or regulations governing right-of-way issues, such as utilising land to dig trenches and lay fibre, for the creation of telecommunications infrastructure?

There are policies governing the right-of-way for the creation of telecommunication infrastructure in China. The Notice on Strengthening the Planning of Urban Basic Telecommunication Infrastructure (unofficial translation) (关于加强城市通信基础设施规划的通知) acts as the source of the planning of telecommunication infrastructure building. The notice was jointly issued by the Ministry of Housing and Urban-Rural Development and the Ministry of Industry and Information Technology in 2015. It aims to push forward the development of urban telecommunication infrastructure, to support the healthy advancement of the information telecommunication industry, and to promote the development of industrialisation, informatisation, and urbanisation. The notice acknowledges that integrating planning of telecommunication fibre optic cable, tower, cables, data centres, and base centres into the Urban and Rural Planning Law is essential for the promotion of constructing national information infrastructure and the implementation of the "Broadband China" strategy. When developing road traffic, underground cable, and green space, government sectors should incorporate the construction of telecommunication cables, base stations, and towers into the plan and the coordination in accordance with the Guiding Opinions of the General Office of the State Council on Promoting the Urban Underground Utility Tunnel Construction (Office of the State Council, 2015). When planning Urban Underground Common Trench, it is needed to consider leaving space for cables and wires for telecommunications infrastructures; when planning public infrastructures such as railways, bus stations, scenic areas and transportation hubs, it is needed to simultaneously plan and construct various kind of telecommunications infrastructures; when planning municipal infrastructures such as roads and its protective green lands and street lights, government sectors need to comply with related national regulations and save space for base stations and towers while considering the needs for the conducting of power to perfect the connection between the planning of telecommunications infrastructures and power sources (Ministry of Industry and Information Technology, 2015c).

What are the regulations applicable to the setting up and operation of landing stations and international gateways to the Internet?
Ministry of Industry and Information Technology on Provisions on Strengthening the Protection of International Communication Network Structure (unofficial translation) (关于加强国际通信网络架构保护的若干规定) Article 4 regulates measures that basic telecommunication operators have to adopt for the protection of international transmission networks such as international communication accesses (including cable land points and earth stations of satellites), submarine cables, and cables (Ministry of Industry and Information Technology, 2010).

Are there any regulations for the Over-The-Top (OTT) services?
Yes, there are five main technical requirements: General technical requirements for OTT TV, Technical requirements for OTT TV integration platform, Technical requirements and interface specification for program integrating system of OTT TV integration platform, Technical requirements and interface specification for accounting management system of OTT TV integration platform, and Technical requirements for OTT TV content service platform (Department of Science and Technology, 2020).

1. What are the grounds, if any, on which the country can suspend access to the Internet or direct the blocking of access to specific websites?

The Interim Regulation of the People's Republic of China on the Management of International networking of Computer Information (State Council of the People's

Republic of China, 1997b) in 1996 gives power to the government to block websites, Article 6 reads: To carry out international networking of computer information, the output and input channels provided by the Ministry of Posts and Telecommunications in its public telecommunication network shall be used. No units or individuals shall establish or use other channels for international networking on their own accord. In 2017, the Notice of the Ministry of Industry and Information Technology on Cleaning Up and Regulating the Internet Access Service Market (Ministry of Industry and Information Technology, 2017c) was issued, the Notice states that business operations such as Conducting business without license, conducting business beyond territorial scope, conducting business beyond business scope, and subleasing or transferring business license, include enterprises providing the IDC (Internet data centre), ISP (Internet service provider) and CDN (content distribution network) services. The Interim Regulation of the People's Republic of China on the Management of International Networking of Computer Information and the Notice of the Ministry of Industry and Information Technology on Cleaning Up and Regulating the Internet Access Service Market include the provisions that impose the Internet blockade commonly known as the Great Fire Wall of China.

Does the country have a specific policy or strategy promoting the development of Internet eXchange Point (IXP) and other interconnection and transmission systems?

Since 2000, China has been actively setting up Internet exchange points in Beijing, Shanghai,[7] and Guangzhou ("Is the new", 2019); and after 2015, as the need for interconnections between networks increases, Internet-corporations-directed Internet exchange points emerged, for example, several Internet corporations established content acceleration platforms to open up communications between private network providers. In 2019, China established the National New Internet Exchange Point in Hangzhou, to realise "one point to access them all" (一点接入、全网联通) and therefore improving the capability of the Internet and lower the price of Internet access and data transmission cost (Ministry of Industry and Information Technology, 2020). As of 2020 and 2021, three additional New Internet Exchange Points were created in Zhongwei (Ningxia), Qianhai (Shenzhen), and Shanghai respectively (Ningxia Hui Autonomous Region Communications Administration, 2020; Ministry of Industry and Information Technology, 2021a; China News Network, 2021).

Have any exceptional measures been adopted to regulate Internet access in light of the COVID-19 crisis?

Since the outbreak of COVID-19, China has actively blocked combinations of words throughout the Internet, for example on the livestream platform YY, multiple words such as "武漢不明肺炎" (unknown Wuhan pneumonia) 、"武漢海鮮市場" (Wuhan seafood market) 、"沙士變異" (SARS mutation) 、"爆發SARS疫情" (SARS outbreak) 、"武漢衛生委員會" (Wuhan Municipal Health Commission)

[7] The research on the innovation and supervision of Internet exchange center.

、"P4病毒實驗室" (Wuhan P4 Laboratory) have been blacklisted; Weibo, since January, have blocked words and phrases such as 中國政府防疫措施 (China's work against the pandemic)、港澳台防疫工作 (Hong Kong, Macau, and Taiwan's works against the pandemic)、李文亮 (Li Wenliang); other phrases such as "human to human transmission," and "Xi Jinping goes to Wuhan" have all been blocked (BBC News, 2020). Local governments have been actively censoring the Internet, too. Until June 23rd, 2020, the Guangdong Administration for Market Regulation had blocked 17,226 pieces of information related to wild animal trade (South+Client, 2020).

5 Access to the Spectrum

How does the country organise access to spectrum for data transmission (e.g. via auctions)?

In 2002, China tried allocating spectrum via bidding; however, in the past 15 years, the spectrum has been allocated via authorisation through administrative examination and approval (State Radio Regulation of China, 2018). The newly revised Telecommunication Regulations establish a system of coexistence of administrative distribution and auction. For radio frequency licenses related to national security and public interest, the administrative distribution method will continue to be used for key protection. The newly revised Telecommunication Regulations stipulate that the allocation of radio frequency resources can be carried out in both administrative and market methods. In the past, frequency allocation in China relied more on administrative examination and approval. The revision of the Telecommunication Regulations establishes bidding and auction as a system, clarifying that commercial frequencies such as terrestrial public mobile communications can be allocated through bidding and auction (Ali Cloud Developer Community, 2017).

Does the country offer some type of advantage in the spectrum access (e.g. discount or compensation) for operators who use the spectrum to provide services in rural areas?

Two major projects provide services in rural areas: the Extending Radio and TV Broadcasting Coverage to Every Village Project and the Pilot Program of the Universal Telecommunications Service. These two projects enable the vast Chinese rural population to connect to the rest of the information society via the Internet and telecommunications.

It is proclaimed by the Chinese government that "where there are people, there is 4G signal." The confidence came from the concept of universal service, meaning that anyone can have access to the Internet anywhere with affordable prices, with the main goal being to uphold the public interest of society. The telecommunications infrastructure in rural areas can be an example; they cost more to build but also charge less. "These builds are money-losing from the perspective of economic efficiency," said Shu Hua Ying, a member of the China Institute of Communications.

He also notes, “In countries such as the US and Canada, the telecommunications industry is highly privatized, therefore economic value will more often than not be the main consideration. However, in China, all the telecommunications companies are state owned, and public welfare is a social responsibility incumbent upon the state” (Office of Central Cyberspace Affairs Commission/ Cyberspace Administration of China [CAC], 2019).

Does the country offer low bureaucratic, affordable licensing for spectrum access to be used for social purposes or to provide coverage? Does this include the provision of public Wi-Fi services?
Regarding the spectrum allocation of the Extending Radio and TV Broadcasting Coverage to Every Village Project, contracting businesses of the Program can have priority when distributing telecom frequencies. For the price standards for rural communications, telecommunications businesses can flexibly formulate various forms of preferential policies, the new price standards should be reported to the Ministry of Information Industry (now Ministry of Industry and Information Technology) or the provincial communications administrations for approval or filing; taking into account the affordability for the villagers, it is required that the price of rural communication shall not be higher than the current price.

The provincial communications administrations are responsible for the coordination, monitoring, inspection, guidance and promotion of local village communication projects, and conduct target assessment of local village communication projects, while businesses implement village communication projects independently. The Ministry of Information Industry (now Ministry of Industry and Information Technology) and provincial communications administrations only conduct target assessment and acceptance; they also do not participate in the operation process of businesses (National Development and Reform Commission, Ministry of Finance & General Administration of Radio, Film and Television, n.d.).

Provincial communications administrations are responsible for public Wi-Fi services. Pinggu District near Beijing, for example, has been promoting district-wide informatisation that provides Wi-Fi to every household with over 130 Wi-Fi hotspots established (Beijing Daily, 2016).

Does the country allow secondary use of spectrum? If so, how is it defined?
China is still working towards marketised management regarding access to spectrum, which includes secondary use and trading of spectrum (State Radio Regulation of China, 2018).

Do the country’s regulations provide for the use of unlicensed or license-free bands in specific areas, such as rural areas, or throughout the country?
No, China does not provide regulations for the use of unlicensed or license-free bands in specific areas; there is no mention of such exceptions in regulations such as the Regulation on Telecommunications of the People’s Republic of China or the Regulation on Internet Information Service of the People’s Republic of China.

6 Financial Resources

Is there any fund for universalisation (to promote the increase) of Internet access or access to Telecom services for everybody? Is there a Universal Service Fund or any other fund? If so, how are resources collected and distributed?

Yes, there are funds for the universalisation of Internet access and telecommunication services, the Pilot Measures for the Management of Telecommunications Universal Service Subsidy Funds provide funds for the universalisation of Internet access and telecommunication services, which includes the construction and maintenance fees for fibre optic and broadband network in rural areas, through arrangements of Ministry of Finance of the people's Republic of China (Ministry of Finance, 2019). In 2019, the Ministry of Finance issued over 3.2 billion RMB, which then provided funds for over 20 thousand 4G base stations (Xinhua News Agency, 2019), according to the Notice on the Subsidy Funds of the Universalization of Telecommunication Service (Ministry of Finance, 2019). Also, telecommunications operators have provided over 40 billion RMB for the universalisation of telecommunication services since 2015 in response to the government's funds (China News Network, 2017). The funds will be distributed in accordance with the Measures of the Administration for Special Transfer Payments from the Central Government to Local Governments and regulations of the National Treasury Centralized Payment System (e.g. the Measures for the Administration of Payment Services for Intermediary Receipt of State Treasury Funds (People's Bank of China, 2019).

Are telecommunications services taxed or subject to other specific levies? If so, how?

According to notice number 106 of the Ministry of Finance in 2013, telecommunication industry will no longer be paying business tax, rather, they should be paying value-added tax; the notice includes companies that provide speech, pictures, messages transmission through various communications networks such as cable/wireless electromagnet system or electro-optical system; the notice also includes basic telecommunication services and value-added services. The tax rate for basic telecommunication services is 11% while the tax rate for value-added services is 6% (Ministry of Finance and State Administration of Taxation, 2014).

Is there any fund to provide subsidies to operators to expand coverage to underserved areas and the least privileged populations?

To support the construction of network coverage in China, the Ministry of Finance issued subsidies in accordance with the context of the Notice of the Ministry of Finance and the Ministry of Industry and Information Technology on Further Carrying Forward the Pilot Program of the Universal Telecommunications Service (unofficial translation) (关于深入推进电信普遍服务试点工作的通知) (Ministry of Finance, 2018). for example, operators establishing pilot programs of the universal telecommunications service in rural administrative village will be subsidised with 30% of both constructing cost and cost for six years of operation; for operators establishing pilot programs of the universal telecommunications service in border areas will be subsidised with 30% of both constructing cost and cost for ten years of operation. (Ministry of Finance, 2018).

Is any form of direct support (such as funding or tax exemptions) offered to small, micro, or not-for-profit providers?
There are only five telecommunications operators in China, none of which are small or micro providers. There is no direct support for non-profit operators either.

References

ADMINISTRATIVE REGULATION No. 5. (2006). *By organization and operation of the telecommunications authority*. https://bo.io.gov.mo/bo/i/2006/15/regadm05_cn.asp#5

ADMINISTRATIVE REGULATION No. 29. (2016). *By organization and operation of the telecommunications regulatory authority*. https://bo.io.gov.mo/bo/i/2016/51/regadm29_cn.asp

Ali Cloud Developer Community. (2017). *MIIT systematically introduces an auction mechanism: 5G spectrum allocation may be tested*. https://developer.aliyun.com/article/167095

Alliance for Affordable Internet (A4AI). (2021). *The affordability report 2021*. Web Foundation. https://a4ai.org/report/2021-affordability-report/.

Asia-Pacific economic cooperation. (2021). *Telecommunications and information*. https://www.apec.org/Groups/SOM-Steering-Committee-on-Economic-and-Technical-Cooperation/Working-Groups/Telecommunications-and-Information

Basic Law of the Hong Kong Special Administrative Region of the People's Republic of China. (2021). https://www.basiclaw.gov.hk/tc/basiclaw/index.html

Basic Law of the Macao Special Administrative Region of People's Republic of China. (1993). https://bo.io.gov.mo/bo/i/1999/leibasica/index_cn.asp

Basic Telecommunications Law, n° 14 of the Legislative Assembly (2001). https://bo.io.gov.mo/bo/i/2001/34/lei14_en.asp

BBC News (2020, March). *Coronavirus: Hundreds of keywords blocked on Chinese social media*. https://www.bbc.com/zhongwen/trad/chinese-news-51765305

Beijing Daily. (2016). *Pinggu 2017 Wi-Fi access for every village*. https://beijing.qianlong.com/2016/1229/1259145.shtml

Communications Authority Ordinance. (2012). *Hong Kong e-Legislation*. https://www.elegislation.gov.hk/hk/cap616!en-zh-Hant-HK

Communications Authority. (2021, February). *Roles and functions*. https://www.coms-auth.hk/tc/about_us/role_functions/index.html

China Council for the Promotion of International Trade. (2022, February). *Overview and main contents of negotiations on domestic regulation of trade in services*. https://www.ccpit.org/a/20220211/20220211n9ee.html

China News Network. (2017). *Ministry of industry and information technology: 90% of poverty-stricken villages will be connected to broadband ahead of schedule*. http://www.gov.cn/xinwen/2017-10/14/content_5231656.htm

China News Network. (2021, December 21). The National (Shanghai) New Internet Exchange Center was put into operation. *China News*. https://www.sh.chinanews.com.cn/jinrong/2021-12-21/94549.shtml

Civil Code of the People's Republic of China. (2020). http://www.npc.gov.cn/englishnpc/c23934/202012/f627aa3a4651475db936899d69419d1e/files/47c16489e186437eab3244495cb47d66.pdf

Cyberspace Administration of China [CAC]. (2017a). *The critical information infrastructure security protection regulations*. http://www.cac.gov.cn/2017-07/11/c_1121294220.htm
Cyberspace Administration of China [CAC]. (2017b). *The national contingency plans for cyber security incidents*. http://www.cac.gov.cn/2017-06/27/c_1121220113.htm
Cyberspace Administration of China [CAC]. (2019). *The 44th China statistical report on internet development*. http://www.cac.gov.cn/2019-08/30/c_1124938750.htm
Cyberspace Administration of China [CAC]. (2020). *The 45th China statistical report on internet development*. http://www.cac.gov.cn/2020-04/27/c_1589535470378587.htm
Cyberspace Administration of China [CAC]. (2021a). *Notice of the Cyberspace Administration of China on regulations on the classified protection of cybersecurity (Consultation paper)*. http://www.cac.gov.cn/2021-11/14/c_1638501991577898.htm
Cyberspace Administration of China [CAC]. (2021b). *The 47th China statistical report on internet development*. https://tinyurl.com/2zpkxxnw
Cyberspace Administration of China (CAC). (n.d.) *Public information resources open pilot work program*. http://www.cac.gov.cn/wxb_pdf/20180105006.pdf
Cyberspace Administration of China, National Development and Reform Commission of the People's Republic of China, Ministry of Industry and Information Technology of the People's Republic of China, Ministry of Public Security of the People's Republic of China, Ministry of State Security of the People's Republic of China, Ministry of Finance of the People's Republic of China, Ministry of Commerce of the People's Republic of China, People's Bank of China, State Administration for Market Regulation, State Administration of Radio and Television, China Securities Regulatory Commission, State Secrets Service & State Cryptography Administration. (2022). *Cybersecurity review measures*. http://www.cac.gov.cn/2022-01/04/c_1642894602182845.htm
Cybersecurity Law of the People's Republic of China. (2015). http://www.cac.gov.cn/2016-11/07/c_1119867116.htm
Department of International Cooperation. (2022, May 13). *Introduction to the Asia-Pacific Economic Cooperation (APEC) and its mechanisms in the field of industry and information*. Ministry of Industry and Information Technology. https://www.miit.gov.cn/jgsj/gjs/hzjzlw/art/2022/art_6565bc05b16643c0b1ae969cc4685b2a.html
Department of Science and Technology. (2020). *Notice of the Science and Technology Department of the State Administration of Radio and Television on publicizing the drafts for approval of five radio and television industry standards including "overall technical requirements for Internet TV."* http://www.nrta.gov.cn/art/2020/5/7/art_113_51003.html
Frisch, N. (2017, December). A future without net neutrality? Welcome to China. *The New York Times China*. https://cn.nytimes.com/opinion/20171215/net-neutrality-china-internet/
GSMA. (n.d.). *GSMA mobile connectivity index*. https://www.mobileconnectivityindex.com/
General Office of the State Council. (1999). *On the establishment of the national informatization: Notification of the leading group of work*. http://www.gov.cn/gongbao/content/2000/content_60619.htm
Hui, D. (2020). Legislative choice of administrative regulation for personal information protection in China. *Jiaotong University Law, 2*, 140–152. https://lawreview.sjtu.edu.cn/ch/reader/view_abstract.aspx?file_no=20200208
Industrial Culture Development Center of the Ministry of Industry and Information Technology. (2019). *Zhang Feng led the Chinese delegation to attend the opening of the 2019 World Radiocommunication Conference*. https://www.miit-icdc.org/info/1009/9489.htm
International Telecommunication Union (ITU). (2017). *ICT development index 2017 rank*. https://www.itu.int/net4/ITU-D/idi/2017/index.html
International Telecommunication Union (ITU). (2022a, November). *General Secretariat of ITU*. https://www.itu.int/online/mm/scripts/gensel8
International Telecommunication Union (ITU). (2022b, November). *List of Member States*. https://www.itu.int/en/about/Pages/default.aspx

International Mobile Satellite Organization (IMSO). (2022). *Member States*. https://imso.org/member-states/

Internet Society of China. (n.d.) *Convention on self-regulation of network data security in the telecommunications and internet industries*. https://www.isc.org.cn/resource/editor/attached/file/20201013/20201013103800_81527.pdf

Is the new Internet exchange a blessing or a curse? [新型互联网交换中心到底是福是祸?]. (2019, September 20). *LinktoCN Law Firm*. http://www.linktocn.com/newsinfo/1665816.html

Law of the People's Republic of China on the Protection of Consumer Rights and Interests. (2013). http://en.pkulaw.cn/Display.aspx?lib=law&Cgid=6384&EncodingName=big5

Ministry of Industry and Information Technology. (2008a). *Cybersecurity administration*. https://www.miit.gov.cn/jgsj/waj/jgzz/art/2020/art_4646354791574be7b6971ba29254e910.html

Ministry of Industry and Information Technology. (2008b). *Information and communication development division*. https://www.miit.gov.cn/jgsj/txs/jgzz/art/2020/art_1d802067efbe47debdc646f242f7152c.html

Ministry of Industry and Information Technology. (2008c). *Urgent notice regarding co-location and sharing of the telecommunication infrastructure*. https://www.miit.gov.cn/jgsj/txs/wlfz/art/2020/art_7408230123e5455a902194f539b890c9.html

Ministry of Industry and Information Technology. (2010). *Provisions on strengthening the protection of international communication network structure*. http://www.gov.cn/zwgk/2010-10/25/content_1729534.htm

Ministry of Industry and Information Technology. (2012). *Service guide to the approval of the establishment of satellite communication networks as well as the setup and use of Earth stations*. http://www.gov.cn/bumenfuwu/2012-11/12/content_2598520.htm

Ministry of Industry and Information Technology. (2013a). *Provisions on protecting the personal information of telecommunications and internet users*. http://web.archive.org/web/20180220211816/http://www.miit.gov.cn/n1146285/n1146352/n3054355/n3057724/n3057729/c4700145/content.html

Ministry of Industry and Information Technology. (2013b). *Provisions on the registration of true identity information of telephone subscribers*. http://www.gov.cn/zhengce/2022-08/23/content_5722716.htm

Ministry of Industry and Information Technology. (2015a). *Classification catalogue of telecommunications services (Version 2015)*. https://www.miit.gov.cn/jgsj/xgj/gzdt/art/2020/art_e6824c9e756c43f7be263a3fe78c36f0.html

Ministry of Industry and Information Technology. (2015b). *Institutional responsibilities of the information and communications authority*. https://www.miit.gov.cn/jgsj/xgj/jgzz/art/2020/art_a6900ae503854dc789cdd939e406c3d5.html

Ministry of Industry and Information Technology. (2015c). *Notice on strengthening the planning of urban basic telecommunication infrastructure*. http://www.gov.cn/xinwen/2015-09/25/content_2939011.htm

Ministry of Industry and Information Technology. (2017a). *Measures for the administration of telecommunications business licensing (2017 revision)*. http://www.lawinfochina.com/display.aspx?id=29652&lib=law&EncodingName=big5

Ministry of Industry and Information Technology. (2017b). *Notice on the measures for the management of filing, coordination, registration and maintenance of satellite networks*. http://www.gov.cn/xinwen/2017-01/23/content_5162652.htm#1

Ministry of Industry and Information Technology. (2017c). *Notice of the Ministry of Industry and Information Technology on cleaning up and regulating the internet access service market*. https://www.miit.gov.cn/jgsj/xgj/gzdt/art/2020/art_6dd0e345bc3947b2a7c88509c4951cd0.html

Ministry of Industry and Information Technology. (2017d). *Notice of the Ministry of Industry and Information Technology on the issuance of the public internet network security incident emergency response plan*. http://web.archive.org/web/20180429134331/http://www.miit.gov.cn/n1146295/n1652858/n1652930/n3757016/c5925919/content.html

Ministry of Industry and Information Technology. (2018). *Notice of the Ministry of Industry and Information Technology on further regulating activities to market telecommunications tariff schemes*. http://www.gov.cn/xinwen/2018-08/24/content_5316168.htm
Ministry of Industry and Information Technology. (2019). *Notice on related works of further perfecting the management of real-name registration of phone users*. http://www.miit.gov.cn/n1146285/n1146352/n3054355/n3057724/n3057728/c7448683/content.html
Ministry of Industry and Information Technology. (2020). *The national (Hangzhou) new Internet exchange center was completed and opened*. https://www.miit.gov.cn/jgsj/xgj/gzdt/art/2020/art_cd9440c91f964435ba41e74626b4b29d.html
Ministry of Industry and Information Technology. (2021a). *Liu Liehong attended the unveiling ceremony of the National (Shenzhen Qianhai) New Internet Exchange Center*. https://www.miit.gov.cn/xwdt/gxdt/ldhd/art/2021/art_730a8eeaa85841899925fd669bda0b0b.html
Ministry of Industry and Information Technology. (2021b). *Specific responsibilities of the Radio Authority (National Radio Office)*. https://www.miit.gov.cn/jgsj/wgj/jgzz/art/2020/art_1dcfd8e75a4c4f40ab80d65b6d18dfeb.html
Ministry of Industry and Information Technology. (n.d.). *Mergers And Reorganizations*. https://www.miit.gov.cn/jgsj/zfs/jbzz/index.html
Ministry of Finance and State Administration of Taxation. (2014). Pilot program of the universal telecommunications service (unofficial translation). [关于深入推进电信普遍服务试点工作的通知] http://www.chinatax.gov.cn/n810341/n810765/n812141/n812262/c1078947/content.html
Ministry of Finance. (2018). *Notice on further promoting the pilot program of telecom universal service*. http://www.gov.cn/xinwen/2018-06/02/content_5295665.htm
Ministry of Finance. (2019). *Pilot measures for the management of telecommunications universal service subsidy funds*. http://www.gov.cn/xinwen/2019-01/15/content_5357943.htm
Ministry of Foreign Affairs. (2023). *China's relations with the International Telecommunication Union*. https://www.mfa.gov.cn/web/wjb_673085/zzjg_673183/gjs_673893/gjzz_673897/gjdx_674095/gx_674099/
National Bureau of Statistics. (2004). *Interim provisions on the classification of information related businesses*. http://www.stats.gov.cn/tjsj/tjbz/200402/t20040210_8659.html
National Computer Network Emergency Response Technical Team/Coordination Center of China (CNCERT/CC). (2013). *About us page*. https://www.cert.org.cn/publish/english/index.html
National Development and Reform Commission, Ministry of Finance & General Administration of Radio, Film and Television. (n.d.) "*'Eleventh five-year plan' national radio and television village access project construction plan*." https://www.ndrc.gov.cn/fggz/fzzlgh/gjjzxgh/200804/P020191104623751015283.pdf
Ningxia Hui Autonomous Region Communications Administration. (2020). *The National (Zhongwei) New Internet Exchange Center was officially inaugurated*. Ministry of Industry and Information Technology. https://www.miit.gov.cn/xwdt/gxdt/dfgz/art/2020/art_a23d0bd2ec614b54936a5bb6a1ac2d1a.html
Office of the Central Cyberspace Affairs Commission. (n.d.) *Office leader*. http://www.cac.gov.cn/bgs/A0902index_1.htm
Office of the Central Cyberspace Affairs Commission. (2015) *Accelerate the legal system construction of my country's network security and informatization*. http://www.cac.gov.cn/2015-06/04/c_1115516273.htm
Office of Central Cyberspace Affairs Commission/Cyberspace Administration of China (CAC). (2019) *Why do remote mountain villages in China have access to the Internet?* http://www.cac.gov.cn/2019-11/13/c_1575177563378061.htm
Office of the State Council. (2015). *Guiding opinions of the General Office of the State Council on promoting the construction of urban underground comprehensive pipe gallery*. http://www.gov.cn/zhengce/content/2015-08/10/content_10063.htm
Order No. 30 by the President of the People's Republic of China. (2015). http://www.gov.cn/zhengce/2015-08/30/content_2922323.htm

Order No. 66 of the President of the People's Republic of China. (2015). http://www.npc.gov.cn/zgrdw/npc/xinwen/2017-03/15/content_2018721.htm
Order No. 7 by the Ministry of Industry and Information Technology of the People's Republic of China. (2009). http://www.gov.cn/flfg/2009-03/10/content_1255644.htm
People's Bank of China. (2019). *Relevant person in charge of the People's Bank of China answered questions from reporters on the "Administrative Measures for Treasury Fund Collection and Payment Services (Trial).*" http://www.gov.cn/zhengce/2019-12/13/content_5460946.htm
Personal Information Protection Law of the People's Republic of China. (2021). http://en.npc.gov.cn.cdurl.cn/2021-12/29/c_694559.htm
Portulans Institute. (2022) *Network readiness index 2022.* https://networkreadinessindex.org/country/south-africa/
Standing Committee of the National People's Congress. (2000). *Decision of the Standing Committee of the National People's Congress on preserving computer network security.* http://lawinfochina.com/display.aspx?id=14400&lib=law
State Administration for Market Regulation. (2021a). *Antitrust Enforcement Division I.* https://www.samr.gov.cn/jg/sjzz/202111/t20211118_336964.html
State Administration for Market Regulation. (2021b). *Antitrust Enforcement Division II.* https://www.samr.gov.cn/jg/sjzz/202111/t20211118_336965.html
State Administration for Market Regulation. (2021c). *Competition Policy Coordination Division.* https://www.samr.gov.cn/jg/sjzz/202111/t20211118_336963.html
State Council of the People's Republic of China. (1997a). *Administrative measures for the security protection of computer information networks linked to the internet.* http://www.gov.cn/gongbao/content/2011/content_1860856.htm
State Council of the People's Republic of China. (1997b).
State Council of the People's Republic of China. (2000). *Regulation on telecommunications of the People's Republic of China.* Law Info China. http://www.lawinfochina.com/display.aspx?lib=law&id=1667
State Council of the People's Republic of China. (2011). *Regulation on Internet Information Service of the People's Republic of China (2000–2011 Annotation Version).* PKU Law. https://www.pkulaw.com/en_history/compare/Annotation_Version-475.html
State Council of the People's Republic of China. (2015). *Notice of the State Council on printing and distributing the action plan for promoting the development of big data no. 50.* http://www.gov.cn/zhengce/content/2015-09/05/content_10137.htm
State Council of the People's Republic of China. (2016). *Telecommunication regulation of the People's Republic of China (2016 revision).* Law Info China. http://www.lawinfochina.com/display.aspx?id=22402&lib=law&EncodingName=big5
State Radio Regulation of China. (2018). *Implementing dynamic spectrum management to improve resource utilization efficiency.* http://www.srrc.org.cn/article20512.aspx
Statistical Report on the Development of the Internet in China. (2019). China Internet Network Information Center (CNNIC). http://www.cac.gov.cn/wxb_pdf/0228043.pdf
South+Client. (2020). *Cut off the network transaction chain! Guangzhou blocked and deleted more than 17,000 pieces of wild animal trading information.* http://www.gd.gov.cn/gdywdt/zwzt/fkyq/gdzxd/content/post_3021930.html
The Central People's Government of the People's Republic of China. (2010). *"China internet industry self-discipline convention" signed.* http://www.gov.cn/lssdjt/content_1565171.htm
The Central People's Government of the People's Republic of China & Xinhua News Agency. (2012). *Decision of the National People's Congress on Strengthening the network information protection.* http://www.gov.cn/jrzg/2012-12/28/content_2301231.htm
The Central People's Government of the People's Republic of China. (2013a, April). *Shang Bing delivered a speech at the opening ceremony of the 46th ICANN meeting in Beijing.* http://www.gov.cn/gzdt/2013-04/08/content_2372832.htm

The Central People's Government of the People's Republic of China. (2013b, August). *Circular of the State Council on printing and distributing the "broadband china" strategy and implementation plan.* http://www.gov.cn/zwgk/2013-08/17/content_2468348.htm
The Central People's Government of the People's Republic of China. (2018) *Order of the Ministry of Transport of the People's Republic of China.* http://www.gov.cn/gongbao/content/2019/content_5366478.htm
The National People's Congress of the People's Republic of China. (n.d.) *The Political Bureau of the Central Committee of the Communist Party of China held a meeting on democratic life Xi Jinping, General Secretary of the Central Committee of the Communist Party of China, presided over the meeting and delivered an important speech.* Congress of China magazine. http://www.npc.gov.cn/
The National People's Congress of the People's Republic of China. (2016, January). *Xi Jinping holds discussions with non-party personages and welcomes the New Year together.*
The State Administration of Press, Publication, Radio and Television. (2014). *Technical requirements for the average loudness and true-peak audio level of digital television programmes* (数字电视节目平均响度和真峰值音频电平技术要求) http://www.nrta.gov.cn/module/download/downfile.jsp?classid=0&filename=1603081615168884904.pdf
"2020 key points of online poverty alleviation work issued and implemented" (2020, March). Cyberspace Administration of China (CAC) http://www.cac.gov.cn/2020-03/18/c_1586073208099659.htm
Xinhua News Agency. (2019). *In 2019, my country will support the construction of about 20,000 4G base stations.* http://www.gov.cn/xinwen/2019-04/16/content_5383497.htm
Xinhuanet News. (2021). *The Ministry of Industry and Information Technology will carry out special rectification actions for unfair competition in the industry, focusing on malicious shielding, forced bundling and other acts.* http://www.xinhuanet.com/legal/2021-04/30/c_1127394348.htm
World Trade Organization (2023). *Members and observers.* https://www.wto.org/english/thewto_e/whatis_e/tif_e/org6_e.htm
World Trade Organization. (2022). *The 128 countries that had signed GATT by 1994.* https://www.wto.org/english/thewto_e/gattmem_e.htm

Ikeng Lin is a graduate student in Public International Law at the University of Amsterdam and National Taipei University. He graduated in law from National Chengchi University and undertook an international student exchange to FGV during that time. His interests are in the Law of the Sea and Cyber Warfare in International Humanitarian Law, and he will be focusing on cyberattacks at sea for his master's thesis. He worked as an assistant researcher for the NTPU Program on International Trade Negotiation, and a BBNJ Research Project of a Study on the Development of the BBNJ Marine Genetic Resources Regulations from the Perspective of the Interplay between the UNCLOS and CBD. He also interned at the Ministry of Foreign Affairs, Republic of China (Taiwan), and the Taiwan Shilin District Court.

China: An Analysis of the Digitalisation of Public Services

Wayne Wei Wang

Abstract This chapter maps key aspects related to the digitalisation of public services in China. The following elements are investigated: policy elements related to digital government strategies, declarations, programs and actions; regulatory elements related to openness, sharing and data protection laws; institutional and governance elements related to the oversight and competences of public agencies, public-private partnerships and regulatory innovations in technology; and evidence from critical sectors such as smart cities, digital ID, and digital payments.

1 National Strategies and Priorities

1. Is there a national strategy for digitalisation/digital transformation? Is there a specific national strategy for the digitalisation of public services?

With the establishment of the government's information infrastructure and the emergence of e-government, the digital government in China gets off to a state-led start. It has been in operation since the early 1990s. China's E-Government Construction has been defined in part by the Guiding Opinions of the National Informatization Leading Group on E-Government [国家信息化领导小组关于我国电子政务建设指导意见] (2002) and the Overall Framework of National E-Government [国家电子政务总体框架] (Ministry of Industry and Information Technology, 2006), which aims to simultaneously digitise public administration and build information infrastructure, culminating in the 2006 official launch of the portal (gov.cn) of the Central People's Government of China.

In 2012 and 2017, under the guidance of the "12th Five-Year Plan" ["十二五"规划] (Xinhua News Agency, 2011) and the "13th Five-Year Plan," ["十三五"规划]

W. W. Wang (✉)
University of Hong Kong, Pokfulam Road, Hong Kong SAR

CyberBRICS Project, FGV Rio Law School, Fundação Getúlio Vargas, Rio de Janeiro, Brazil
e-mail: drirwang@connect.hku.hk

L. Belli, L. Galdino de Magalhães Santos (eds.), *SmartBRICS*,
https://doi.org/10.1007/978-3-031-98204-0_13

(Xinhua News Agency, 2016a), the National Development and Reform Commission released their "National Government Information Project Building Plans," laying out major components of national e-government development. Particularly in the context of the 13th Five-Year Plan ["十三五"规划] (Xinhua News Agency, 2016a), it was proposed to lay the foundation for a comprehensive government affairs information system that satisfies the requirements of modernising the national system and building governance capacity, as well as to develop a top-level structure of large platform sharing, big-data-driven social governance, and process co-governance.

Following the State Council's Guidance on Actively Promoting "Internet Plus" [国务院关于积极推进"互联网+"行动的指导意见] (State Council of the People's Republic of China, 2015d), the national initiative on "Internet + Public Services" [进一步深化"互联网+政务服务," 推进政务服务"一网、一门、一次"改革实施方案] (General Office of the State Council of the People's Republic of China, 2018a) was modelled after the procedural design model of user-friendly e-commerce platforms while the central government also introduced the "Internet + Regulation" (国务院办公厅关于运用大数据加强对市场主体服务和监管的若干意见) initiative, as per Premier Minister Li Keqiang (2015) to "provide good services, effectively supervise and create a level playing field."

The fourth plenary session of the 19th Central Committee of the CPC, in its decision on "Upholding and improving the system of socialism with Chinese characteristics and modernizing the system and capacity of state governance," [中共中央关于坚持和完善中国特色社会主义制度，推进国家治理体系和治理能力现代化若干重大问题的决定] (2019b) put forward "Establishing and improving systems and rules for administration by means of the Internet, big data, artificial intelligence, and other technological means... advancing the construction of a digital government." China's 14th Five-Year Plan ["十四五"规划] (Xinhua News Agency, 2021a), which lays the groundwork for the country's long-term goals until 2035, underlined the importance of "accelerating digital growth" and "creating a digital China" in Section 5 in 2021, heralding the launch of the Digital China Initiative.

China's Central Cyberspace Affairs Commission, or the Cyberspace Administration of China, presented a key policy document on National Informatization in late 2021 as part of China's 14th Five-Year Plan, defining and enhancing its state-led incentives for digital transformation. The 14th Five-Year National Informatization Plan (NIP) ["十四五"国家信息化规划] (Cyberspace Administration of China [CAC], 2021b) includes ten primary targets across eight categories, seventeen significant initiatives, and ten priority actions. Data, infrastructure, innovation, societal governance, digital public services, and the digital marketplace are among the topics that are addressed in this NIP, with such overall aims as enhancing people's digital skills and competencies, digitalising urbanisation and societal governance, achieving sustainable and green climate goals, furthering digital inclusion in financial services, as well as improving digital healthcare for the elderly (China Cyberspace Network, 2021).

2. Is the digitalisation of any specific sector seen as a priority for the country (e.g. Central Bank Digital Currency, digital identity, online payments, deployment of Artificial Intelligence, smart cities, cybersecurity, etc.)?

Along with the aforementioned "Digital China Initiative," China has been constructing a comprehensive plan for digital transformation, beginning with a government-led "smart plus" campaign that will use Artificial Intelligence and big data to revolutionise a broad range of sectors.

Concerning the incentive for digital economic growth, China proposed a more effective use of massive data and a more precise classification of application scenarios of technologies to facilitate the deep integration of digital technology into the real economy, enable the transformation and upgrading of traditional industries, and stimulate the emergence of new business models.[1] In its 14th Five-Year Plan ["十四五"规划] (Xinhua News Agency, 2021a), the Chinese government stressed the facilitation of key technologies such as cloud computing, Internet of Things, industrial Internet, blockchain, Artificial Intelligence, and augmented reality, along with the promotion of new consortia, such as the open-source community of digital technology, as well as efforts to improve the open-source intellectual property system and encourage enterprises to open up software source code, hardware design, and app services.

In addition to setting the foundation for China's digital society, as mentioned beforehand, the Chinese government has also encouraged the public sector to pursue "Internet + Public Services." [进一步深化"互联网+政务服务,"推进政务服务"一网、一门、一次"改革实施方案] (General Office of the State Council of the People's Republic of China, 2018a). Public services are evolving into product-like operating models, with major attention given to e-education, e-health, and smart courts. Chinese digital urbanisation, including the Smart City initiative, has been performed hierarchically and categorically at the central and local levels to increase administrative efficiency, for instance, through the Internet of Things and municipal data brains that involve most sectors.[2]

According to the 14th Five-Year National Informatization Plan ["十四五"国家信息化规划] (CAC, 2021b), 5G ecosystems will be created, the Internet of Things will be implemented, a network spanning air, space, and ocean will be established, and a national integrated big data centre system will have been put in place to increase computing capacity for open data sharing.

3. Is there an overall Artificial Intelligence strategy? Is there a specific national strategy for the use of Artificial Intelligence in the public sector?

For the first time, Artificial Intelligence was named as a crucial aim in the State Council's July 2015 "Guiding Opinions on Actively Promoting Internet Plus Actions." [国务院关于积极推进"互联网+"行动的指导意见] (State Council of the People's Republic of China, 2015d). Until July 2017, the State Council released

[1] See Chapter 15 of the 14th Five-Year Plan (Xinhua News Agency, 2021a).

[2] See Chapter 16 of the 14th Five-Year Plan (Xinhua News Agency, 2021a).

the "Plan for the Development of Next-Generation Artificial Intelligence" [新一代人工智能发展规划] (State Council of the People's Republic of China, 2017) as China's national strategy for AI, through which China has fostered a fast-developing AI core industry worth 1 trillion yuan, promoted national research and development, and established the framework for AI-related legislation and regulation.

Since 2020, the Party Central Committee, the State Council, and other agencies have produced over ten policies on Artificial Intelligence, and AI has been featured in four consecutive years' central government annual reports. These policy documents, for example, the Three-Year Action Plan for Promoting the Development of the Next-Generation Artificial Intelligence Industry (2018–2020) [促进新一代人工智能产业发展三年行动计划(2018–2020年)] (Ministry of Industry and Information Technology, 2017), with the Colleges and Universities Artificial Intelligence Innovation Action Plan [高等学校人工智能创新行动计划] (Ministry of Education, 2018), established the aims of integrating AI into the actual economy, supporting AI-related research and development, and enhancing AI education across the nation.

Moreover, the State Council released the Notice on the Action Plan for Promoting the Development of Big Data [促进大数据发展行动纲要] (2015b) in 2015 with the goal of developing a new model of social governance that is characterised by accurate monitoring and multi-party coordination. The communiqué of the 19th CPC Central Committee's fourth plenary session [第十九届中央委员会第四次全体会议公报] (2019a) in 2019 emphasised AI as a foundation of constructing a "Digital China."

4. Is there a specific strategy or reference to the use of social media to facilitate government activities?

The Chinese authorities have facilitated the "civilization of cyberspace" as one of its overarching principles for Internet regulation for a long period of time. For instance, the most recent enunciation was included in the Opinions on Strengthening the Construction of Cyberspace Civilization [关于加强网络文明建设的意见] (Xinhua News Agency, 2021b, September 14), which aimed to aid in the promotion of critical public policies, the cultivation of Internet culture, the enforcement of good virtue, and online behaviour, as well as ecological governance in cyberspace (i.e. platform regulation).

Meanwhile, China's Gov New Media system evolved alongside the government transparency action. On October 1, 2013, the General Office of the State Council announced the Opinions on Further Strengthening Government Information Disclosure in Response to Social Concerns and Enhancing the Government's Credibility [关于进一步加强政府信息公开，回应社会关切，提升政府公信力的意见] (2013b), naming the first batch of "new media for government affairs": Gov Weibos and Gov WeChat public accounts.

In December 2018, the General Office of the State Council issued the Opinions on Promoting the Healthy and Orderly Development of New Media for Government Affairs [关于推进政务新媒体健康有序发展的意见] (2018b), which for the first time made a comprehensive, standardised and systematic conceptual expression and functional positioning of "new media for government affairs." Additionally, the Opinions identified three functions of AI with a key role to play—improving disclosure of government information, encouraging real-time interaction with inquirers, and upgrading palmtop services.

On April 18, 2019, the General Office of the State Council once again formulated and issued the "Government Websites and New Government Media Inspection Indicators" and "Annual Assessment Indicators for the Supervision of Government Websites and New Government Media" [政府网站与政务新媒体检查指标 & 政府网站与政务新媒体监管工作年度考核指标] (2019a), accelerating scientific management and standardised guidance at the central policy level by arithmetically measuring the activeness, timeliness, and friendliness of new media operators.

According to the 47th Statistical Report on China's Internet Development [第47次中国互联网络发展状况统计报告] (China Internet Network Information Center, 2021) in 2021, there were 140,837 Weibo accounts verified by the Sina platform for government organisations as of December 2020. As of December 2020, all 31 Chinese provinces have established government-run Weibo accounts. As of December 2020, 82,958 government affairs accounts have been established on Toutiao by governments at all levels. As of December 2020, 26,098 government Douyin (the Chinese version of TikTok) accounts have been established at all levels.

5. Is there a strategy or any specific policies aimed at promoting the use of open-source software/hardware by public administrations or generally?

As mentioned above, China has stepped up its efforts to incubate an open-source culture to establish AI as a New Infrastructure,[3] which involves 5G networks, data centres, Artificial Intelligence, the industrial Internet of Things, ultra-high voltage (UHV) power transmission, high-speed rail and electric vehicle charging infrastructure (Li, 2020). Additionally, the open-source ecosystem has been considered as a support mechanism for the national innovation system's pursuit of technical independence. China has not reached a zero breakthrough in developing the first indigenous open-source foundation until 2020 (Long & Wang, 2021). China's open-source development history is very young in comparison to the rest of the globe. Open-source businesses are only beginning to take off.

In this light, the 14th Five-Year Plan ["十四五"规划] (Xinhua News Agency, 2021a) for Economic and Social Development made a strong commitment to fostering the growth of open-source digital technologies. It was primarily intended to encourage "deep learning frameworks and open source algorithmic platforms" to stimulate national innovation and research in Artificial Intelligence. Additionally, fostering an open-source community culture, developing open-source-related legislation, such as intellectual property rules, and encouraging enterprises to

[3] In 2018, the Central Economic Work Conference was held in Beijing, which redefined infrastructure, defining 5G, Artificial Intelligence, industrial Internet, and Internet of Things as "new Infrastructure" (Xinhua Net, 2019).

open-source software/hardware design and application services were identified as critical initiatives for enhancing innovation in some digital technologies.

The Chinese central government advocated in the 2021 National Standardization Development Outline [国家标准化发展纲要] (Xinhua News Agency, 2021d) to develop machine-readable standards and open-source standards to accelerate digital transformation in standardisation. In late 2021, the Ministry of Industry and Information Technology issued the 14th Five-Year Software and Information Technology Services Development Plan ["十四五"软件和信息技术服务业发展规划] (2021) that advocates a blueprint for a flourishing indigenous open-source ecosystem.

6. Are there specific policies mandating interoperability requirements for the systems utilised by public administrations? Are there any strategies or recommendations to avoid vendor lock-in?

The Guidance on E-government Construction [国家信息化领导小组关于我国电子政务建设指导意见] (National Informatization Leading Group, 2005) signalled the early stages of the "Two Nets, One Website, Four Databases, and Twelve Gold Projects"[4] (两网，一站，四库，十二金工程) initiative.

When the Government Information Disclosure Regulations (GIDR) was implemented in 2007, the goal was to increase administrative transparency. Most public services were still delivered offline, though.

The initiative of "Internet + Government/Public Services" was piloted in the State Council Guidance on Accelerating the Promotion of "Internet + Government/Public Services" [国务院关于加快推进"互联网+政务服务"工作的指导意见] (2016b) following the initiative of "Internet Plus," which promoted the digital transformation of public services by leveraging cross-regional, cross-level, and cross-departmental data sharing and relying on data flow to carry out the process of government service reengineering. The General Office of the State Council issued the Guide to the Construction of the Technical system of "Internet + Government/Public Service" ["互联网+政务服务"技术体系建设指南] (2016b), whose Chapter 6 highlighted the mechanism for central-local data aggregation and sharing systems, cross-unit data docking systems, as well as the massive "basic resource" data pools.

The 19th Party Central Committee's Fourth Plenary Session urged the establishment of a state-wide digital government. The initiative of mobilising public services moulded the change, which was preceded by a series of policy documents encouraging a national integrated online government service platform (General Office of the State Council of the People's Republic of China, 2021; State Council of the People's Republic of China, 2018, 2019) and "all-in-one" portal (General Office of

[4] "Two Nets, One Website, Four Treasures, and Twelve Gold Projects" means Two Nets (Government Intranet and Government Extranet), One Website (gov.cn), Four Databases (Population, Legal Entity, Spatial Geography and Natural Resources, Macro-economy) and Twelve Gold Projects on Financial System, Social Welfare, Agriculture, etc. (China E-Government Network, 2018).

the State Council of the People's Republic of China, 2018a), as well as "cross-provincial" digital public services (General Office of the State Council of the People's Republic of China, 2020b).

7. Is there a strategy or any specific policies promoting open data (e.g. government-business data sharing, open government, and/or open data in general)?

In the State Council General Office's Essentials of Government Information Disclosure Work [2015年政府信息公开工作要点] (2015a) and the Opinions on Comprehensively Promoting Open Government Work [关于全面推进政务公开工作的意见] (2016c), the opening of government data was regarded as an enabler to expanding the scope of government information disclosure. And in the following documents such as "Notice on the Action Plan for Promoting the Development of Big Data" [促进大数据发展行动纲要] (State Council of the People's Republic of China, 2015b), "the 13th Five-Year Plan" (Xinhua News Agency, 2016a) and "Outline of National Informatization Development Strategy" [国家信息化发展战略纲要] (Xinhua News Agency, 2016b), open data has become one of the key initiatives to implement the national big data strategy and build Digital China.

However, the three documents outlined the practical implementation standards for open data sharing, including the Interim Measures for the Management of Government Information Resource Sharing [政务信息资源共享管理暂行办法] (State Council of the People's Republic of China, 2015a), the Implementation Plan for the Integration and Sharing of Government Information Systems [政务信息系统整合共享实施方案] (General Office of the State Council of the People's Republic of China, 2017b), and the Guidelines for the Preparation of Government Information Resource Catalogues (Trial) [政务信息资源目录编制指南(试行)] (National Development and Reform Commission & Cyberspace Administration of China, 2017). Paralleling this, the "National e-Government Standards System Construction Guide" [国家电子政务标准体系建设指南] (General Office of the State Administration for Market Regulation, 2020) was released in June 2020, and its subsystem of government data sharing and openness standards explicitly addresses data security and other standards for government data stewardship.

In March 2020, the CPC Central Committee and the State Council issued Opinions on Strengthening the Institutional Mechanism for Market-based Allocation of Factors [关于构建更加完善的要素市场化配置体制机制的意见] (Xinhua News Agency, 2020), which explicitly defined data as a market key factor.

The Data Security Law (DSL) (数据安全法), which was enacted and took effect in 2021, is the first national law to provide incentives for the open data movement. Article 42 of the DSL provides specifically the state's role in formulating the utilisation of government data (National People's Congress of the People's Republic of China [NPC], 2021).

Following the DSL, as noted earlier, the "open data movement" was confirmed by a series of 14th Five-Year sub-plans including the National Informatization Plan (NIP) ["十四五"国家信息化规划] (National Development and Reform Commission, 2021), the Public Service Plan (PSP) ["十四五"公共服务规划] (National Development and Reform Commission, 2022), and the Digital Economy

Plan (DEP) [“十四五”数字经济发展规划] (State Council of the People’s Republic of China, 2021b), which indicated the role of open data in unleashing the digital dividend between the public and private sectors.

8. Are the national strategies binding documents (i.e. adopted in the form of laws or decrees) or are they just declaratory documents?

Digital China or Chinese national strategies of digital transformation were largely set out in the laws (法律) made by the National People’s Congress and semi-binding administrative regulations (行政法规), ministerial regulations (部门规章), regional regulations (地方性法规), local government regulations (地方政府规章) and others (其他规范性文件) (Legislation Law of the People’s Republic of China, 2015), along with policy declarations (政策).

For instance, China’s National People’s Congress introduced the Data Security Law, a law (法律) that places greater regulatory emphasis on the security aspects of open data but puts forward more declarative narratives in regards to data sharing and aggregation. The Government Information Disclosure Regulations (GIDR) and the Plan for Development of Next-Generation Artificial Intelligence were made by the State Council as Administrative Regulations (行政法规). The departments/ministries of the State Council issued ministerial regulations (部门规章) like the Colleges and Universities Artificial Intelligence Innovation Action Plan. The series of 5-year plans/sub-plans, on the other hand, are policy papers that are not legally enforceable but serve as navigational guides for legislators at all central and local levels. The narratives about data use in the main policy documents echo the narratives in regional regulations such as those in Shanghai Municipal Data Regulations (上海市数据条例) and those in Shenzhen Special Economic Zone Data Regulations (深圳经济特区数据条例).

9. Is there a specific policy for integration, inclusion of vulnerable groups (e.g. elderly, etc.) or accessibility for people with disabilities?

In 2008, the modified Protection of Disabled Persons Law (残疾人保障法) took effect, including Articles 52 and 54 to codify the government’s commitment to assembling circumstances for barrier-free information exchange for disabled people.[5] In 2012, the State Council further adopted an Administrative Regulation on the Construction of a Barrier-Free Environment [无障碍环境建设条例] (State Council of the People’s Republic of China, 2012), which included a Chapter 3 outlining the situations that would need and ensure barrier-free information exchange.

In 2020, the Ministry of Industry and Information Technology and the China Disabled Persons’ Federation jointly announced the Guiding Opinions on Promoting Information Accessibility [关于推进信息无障碍的指导意见] (2020) with the goal of “bridging the digital divide and promoting social inclusive development,” followed by the Implementation Plan for Effectively Solving the Difficulties of the Elderly in Using Intelligent Technology [关于切实解决老年人运用智能技术困

[5] Those government’s obligations remained in effect in the latest amendment of 2018 (NPC, 2018).

难的实施方案] (General Office of the State Council of the People's Republic of China, 2020c) and Special Action Programme on Ageing-friendly and Barrier-free Adaptation of Internet Apps [互联网应用适老化及无障碍改造专项行动方案] (Ministry of Industry and Information Technology, 2020).

In compliance with the Special Action Programme on Ageing-friendly and Barrier-free Adaptation of Internet Apps [互联网应用适老化及无障碍改造专项行动方案] (Ministry of Industry and Information Technology, 2020), as noted earlier, in 2021, the General Office of the Ministry of Industry and Information Technology produced an Implementation Plan outlining the standard specifications for retrofit and the evaluation requirements for websites and mobile applications, respectively (General Office of the Ministry of Industry and Information Technology, 2021).

The 14th Five-Year National Informatization Plan (NIP) ["十四五"国家信息化规划] (National Development and Reform Commission, 2021) proposed to construct more Information Accessibility (信息无障碍) facilities to enhance digital literacy and ensure people's digital empowerment. One of its Digital Public Service Optimization and Upgrading Projects, as highlighted in Column 16, promoted "omnidirectional" ends, including smart terminals, websites, and apps, while also deploying information accessibility tags across the country and facilitating an online service platform for the disabled. The 14th Five-Year Protection and Development Plan for the Disabled ["十四五"残疾人保障和发展规划] (State Council of the People's Republic of China, 2021c) placed a similar emphasis on information accessibility.

The 14th Five-Year Public Service Plan (National Development and Reform Commission, 2022), released in 2022, outlines a clear strategy for accelerating the construction of information accessibility, effectively resolving the difficulties faced by the elderly and other special groups when utilising intelligent technology, and assisting the elderly, disabled, and others in sharing digital life. While emphasising the critical role of the National Integrated Government/Public Service Platform, the Plan proposes to encourage the use of modern information technology to facilitate service delivery while maintaining necessary on-site service windows for the elderly, disabled, and other special populations.

10. Are the national strategies guided or are they involved in cooperation agreements, best practices, programs, associations of organisations such as UN Agenda 2030 SDGs, OECD, World Bank?

Despite the absence of a narrative in those national policies that explicitly relate incentives to international cooperation agreements, the Chinese governmental reports have demonstrated support for international organisations' actions. Among the publications that make it abundantly obvious that they want to harness digital innovation to meet international obligations are those that establish the Chinese narrative on cyberspace and the Chinese SDGs agenda for 2030.

In 2015, Chinese President Xi Jinping stressed in his keynote speech on "Building a Community with a Shared Future in Cyberspace" (共同构建网络空间命运共同

体) at the opening ceremony of the second World Internet Conference that constructed the appeals for "infrastructure connectivity," "digital economy for common prosperity" and "equity/justice in cyberspace" ("Chinese President Xi…," 2015).

Since 2016, the Ministry of Foreign Affairs has been hosting a specific website for the collection of documents on the 2030 Agenda for Sustainable Development. The list starts by introducing China's 2016 position paper and 2016 national plan on the Implementation of the 2030 Agenda for Sustainable Development (Ministry of Foreign Affairs, 2016a, 2016b). Three biannual Progress Reports (Center for International Knowledge on Development, 2021; Ministry of Foreign Affairs, 2017, 2019) and one VNR report on the agenda (Ministry of Foreign Affairs, 2021), together with an annual series of case studies on Big Earth Data in Support of the Sustainable Development Goals (Chinese Academy of Sciences, 2019, 2020, 2021) were also included to reflect on and analyse China's commitment, demonstrating how China has been bridging the digital gap, eradicating extreme poverty, boosting digital education, growing the digital economy, and constructing digital infrastructure for connection, among other things.

Following such reports, the 14th Five-Year Plan ["十四五"规划] (Xinhua News Agency, 2021a) and its sub-plans were developed. For instance, the 14th Five-Year National Informatization Plan (NIP) ["十四五"国家信息化规划] (Cyberspace Administration of China, 2021b) emphasised the need to enhance the capacity for sustainable development in poverty-stricken areas through the creation of digital villages and the improvement of farmers' digital literacy.

11. Are there any existing policies to zero-rate certain e-government services? Are there such policies for specific public sectors?

Yes, since three ministerial authorities released the Notice on Standardizing the Management of E-government Platform Fees (Central People's Government, 2011), China has exercised full zero-rate e-gov services. As per the Notice, it was highlighted that:

- People's governments at all levels, as well as their departments and units, are prohibited from using the e-government platform for commercial purposes. Enterprises, individuals, and the general public should be able to use e-government platforms for free.
- Administrative organs at all levels, public institutions acting as government functions, social organisations, and other organisations that need to introduce third-party electronic authentication services in the process of providing public services through the e-government platform shall not participate in the operation of such services or charge fees in any form. Enterprises or individuals shall not be required to purchase these services by means of coercion or disguised coercion.
- Those organs must strictly follow the "Government Information Disclosure Regulations" (政府信息公开条例) and "Notice on Relevant Issues such as Charging for Providing Government Public Information" [财政部、国家发展改革委关于提供政府公开信息收取费用等有关问题的通知] (Ministry of

Finance & National Development and Reform Commission, 2008). They are thus prohibited from charging running service costs disguised as technical maintenance, service, or electronic media cost fees.[6]

After China launched the National Integrated Government Service Platform [全国一体化政务服务平台] (2022) and the "All-in-one" Portal project ["一网通办"], people no longer have to pay additional money for e-government services. The adjustment was made in compliance with the Circular on Strengthening the Management and Collection of Government Non-Tax Revenue in the Cross-Provincial Universal Handling of Government Affairs Services [关于加强政务服务"跨省通办"涉及政府非税收入收缴管理事项的通知] (Ministry of Finance et al., 2021). Specifically, the provisions in the Circular state that relevant departments at all levels are prohibited:

- From charging additional fees other than postage and other costs associated with collecting non-tax revenues
- From imposing conditions or charges for cross-province administrative services
- From substituting paid services for free services, from substituting voluntary services for mandatory services and
- From substituting fee-paying approval for administrative approval

12. How does the country rank on global digital adoption indices, such as the World Bank's Digital Adoption Index, the Digital Society Index, IMD World Digital Competitiveness Ranking, Global Open Data Index, etc.?

As per the World Bank's Digital Adoption Index (2016), China had an overall score of 0.59/1.00. Of the three subscores, China had a modest fluctuation, including DAI Business Sub-index (0.55/1.00), DAI People Sub-index (0.52/1.00), and the relatively higher DAI Government Sub-index (0.69/1.00). In the Hong Kong Special Administrative Region (SAR) and Macau Special Administrative Region (SAR), the Business and People indices both achieved reasonably high ratings (Table 1).

According to the United Nations E-Government Survey 2020, the international ranking of China's e-government development index (EGDI) rose from 65th in

Table 1 DAI Index

	DAI Business Sub-index	DAI People Sub-index
Hong Kong SAR, China	0.85/1.00	0.91/1.00
Macau SAR, China	0.78/1.00	0.87/1.00

[6] When the notice was published in 2011, the 2007 Government Information Disclosure Regulations remained in effect, stating in Article 27 that administrative organs providing government information on request shall not charge any additional fees, except for the cost of retrieval, reproduction, postage, and other costs. However, it was changed in 2019 to include an information processing charge under Article 42 if the applicant's demands for government information obviously exceed a reasonable range.

2018 to 45th in 2020 (United Nations Department of Economic and Social Affairs, 2020). The online services index, which is the primary metric used to assess a country's degree of e-government development, has risen dramatically from 34th to 9th in the world, with China's online service reaching the worldwide "very high" level.

China was one of 59 countries classified under Group B (High: Significant focus on GovTech) in the World Bank's GovTech Maturity Index published in 2021, with its Special Administrative Regions—Hong Kong SAR in Group A (Very high: GovTech leaders) and Macau SAR in Group C (Medium: Some focus on GovTech) (Dener et al., 2021).

According to the 2021 IMD World Digital Competitiveness Ranking, China ranked 15th overall out of 64 economies, with its knowledge, technology, and future preparedness components ranking sixth, twentieth, and seventeenth, respectively (International Institute for Management Development, 2021a). Simultaneously, Hong Kong SAR China ranked second overall, with knowledge, technology, and future-readiness components placing fifth, first, and tenth, respectively (International Institute for Management Development, 2021b).

2 Regulations

1. Is there any general regulation (e.g. law, decree, standards) to organise the digitalisation of public services, other than specific regulations that might apply to the key sectors identified below?

Although there is no such blanket legislation coordinating the digital transformation of public services, as previously said, certain domains are regulated by Chinese authorities through particular provisions in legislation (national laws and administrative regulations included), decrees (for example, notices or circulars), and standards.

The first regulatory package focuses on administrative procedures, including enacting and amending:

- The Administrative Licensing Law (行政许可法)[7] and
- Government Information Disclosure Regulations (政府信息公开条例)

The second emphasises the importance of information/data security and encryption. China framed its e-gov within critical infrastructure subject to national security obligations, by introducing, for example:

- The 2017 Cybersecurity Law (网络安全法)

[7] "Administrative organs should establish and improve the system, the implementation of e-government, administrative licensing matters announced on the website of the administrative organs to facilitate applicants to take data messages and other means of administrative licensing applications; should share information on administrative licensing with other administrative organs to improve efficiency" (Administrative Licensing Law, 2003, Art. 33).

- The 2020 Cryptography Law (密码法)
- The 2021 Regulations on the Security Protection of Critical Information Infrastructure (CII Rules) (关键信息基础设施安全保护条例) and
- The 2021 Data Security Law (数据安全法)

The third dimension concerns the practical implementation of E-Government, "Internet + Government/Public Services," and the National Integrated Government Service Platform. Table 2 details the legislative and policy-making history by indicating the enactment year, the title, and the efficacy hierarchy of some key regulatory documents.

2. Is there any regulation mandating transparency audits for technologies (e.g. of platforms, algorithms, cloud services, etc.) utilised by public administrations?

In 2016, the General Office of the State Council introduced the Guide to the Construction of the Technical System of "Internet + Government/Public Service" ["互联网+政务服务"技术体系建设指南], which set out the mechanism of Electronic Monitoring and Management (电子监察管理).

In 2020, the Guidelines for the Development of the National New Generation Artificial Intelligence Standard System [国家新一代人工智能标准体系建设指南] (Standardization Administration of the People's Republic of China et al., 2020) were also released, emphasising the importance of standardising intelligent applications in government affairs to ensure "open, transparent, and shared government information" in the Smart Gov services.

Additionally, there is a trend toward requesting technological transparency audits as part of the cybersecurity review. For example, Article 10 of the Cybersecurity Review Measures [网络安全审查办法] (CAC et al., 2021) requires the authority to conduct a review of "the security, openness, transparency, diversity of sources of products and services, the reliability of supply channels, and the risk of supply disruptions due to political, diplomatic, trade, and other factors" for national security purposes. As mentioned previously, a few sets of recommended standards for e-government platforms have been developed to navigate public technologists, setting non-mandatory transparency-related criteria. For instance, Part 5 of the Standardized Guidelines for E-Government [电子政务标准化指南 第5部分:支撑技术] (Standardization Administration of the People's Republic of China, 2014) states that application/service integration must comply with the following technical requirements:

- Enabling interoperability between applications
- Providing application portability in a distributed environment
- Providing application access **transparency** in a distributed environment; and
- Adhering to open-source standards

Meanwhile, national legislation regulating the use of algorithms has grown in recent years. For example, the Guidance on Strengthening the Comprehensive Governance of Internet Information Service Algorithms [关于加强互联网信息服务算法综合治理的指导意见] (State Information Office of the People's Republic

Table 2 Key regulatory documents overview

Enactment year	Document title
Governance through big data	
2015	Notice on the Action Plan for Promoting the Development of Big Data [促进大数据发展行动纲要] (State Council of the People's Republic of China, 2015b)
2015	Opinions of the General Office of the State Council on Using Big Data to Strengthen the Service and Supervision of Market Subjects [国务院办公厅关于运用大数据加强对市场主体服务和监管的若干意见] (General Office of the State Council of the People's Republic of China, 2015b)
"Internet plus"/"internet + gov/public services"	
2015	The State Council's Guidance on Actively Promoting "Internet Plus" [国务院关于积极推进"互联网+"行动的指导意见] (State Council of the People's Republic of China, 2015d)
2016	The State Council's Guiding Opinions on Accelerating the Work of "Internet + Government Services" (国务院关于加快推进"互联网+政务服务"工作的指导意见] (State Council of the People's Republic of China, 2016c)
2016	Guide to the Construction of the Technical System of "Internet + Government/Public Service" ["互联网+政务服务"技术体系建设指南] (General Office of the State Council of the People's Republic of China, 2016b)
2018	Implementation Plan on Deepening "Internet + Government/Public Service" and Promoting the Reform of "one Website Portal, one Door and one Time" of Government Affairs Service [进一步深化"互联网+政务服务"推进政务服务"一网、一门、一次"改革实施方案] (General Office of the State Council of the People's Republic of China, 2018a)
E-gov/national integrated government service platform	
2018	Guiding Opinions of the State Council on Speeding up the Construction of the National Integrated Online Government Service Platform [国务院关于加快推进全国一体化在线政务服务平台建设的指导意见] (State Council of the People's Republic of China, 2018)
2019	Provisions of the State Council on Online Government Service [国务院关于在线政务服务的若干规定] (State Council of the People's Republic of China, 2019)
2020	National e-Government Standards System Construction Guide (国家电子政务标准体系建设指南] (General Office of the State Administration for Market Regulation, 2020)
2021	Guide to the Construction of the Mobile End of the National Integrated Government Service Platform [全国一体化政务服务平台移动端建设指南] (General Office of the State Council of the People's Republic of China, 2021)
Selected standards	
GB/T National Recommended Standards on the Management, Design, and Standardization of (Cloud-Computing-based) E-Government[a]	

[a]For example, see those GB/T standards like the General/Management/Service/Security/Technical Specification of Electronic Government Common Platform Based on Cloud Computing (基于云计算的电子政务公共平台总体/管理/服务/安全/技术规范)

of China, 2021) was published to promote the openness and transparency of algorithms, with a focus on the commercial sector. A similar approach was echoed in the 2022 Internet Information Service Algorithmic Recommendation Management Provisions (互联网信息服务算法推荐管理规定] (CAC, 2021a).

3. Is there any specific regulation mandating requirements for public procurements and public tenders regarding digital public services?

The rules for public procurement for the government information system have remained mostly unchanged since the Interim Measures for the Administration of Government Procurement in the Government Information System [政务信息系统政府采购管理暂行办法] (Ministry of Finance, 2018) were implemented in 2018.

- The Interim Measures, especially in Articles 5 and 6, called for the engagement of experts or a third party, as well as data interoperability with the National Data Sharing Platform and open data with characteristics, such as machine readability and reusability by society.
- Article 7 further establishes the notion that government information systems should be constructed in cloud computing mode if they do not hold state secrets and offer services to the general public.
- Particularly, Article 9 outlined the conditions for public tenders, stating that if the government information system is obtained via bidding, the comprehensive scoring technique must be used; if not, competitive negotiation or single-source procurement must be used.

Following that, the 2020 Measures for the Construction and Management of National Government Informatization Projects [国家政务信息化项目建设管理办法] (General Office of the State Council of the People's Republic of China, 2020d) were published to clarify the organising and overseeing bodies in charge of planning, budgeting, and procurements, as well as measuring the progress of information sharing, funding, cryptography, and cybersecurity, among other things.

Most importantly, by combining the use of the Cybersecurity Law (2017, Art. 35), Cryptography Law (2019, Art. 27), and Regulations on the Security Protection of Critical Information Infrastructure (CII Rules) (Creemers et al., 2021, Art. 19), China has created a security-based review of public procurements for a critical information infrastructure that covers most e-government projects.

4. Are digital public services subject to general data protection regulations? If not, is there any data protection regulation for digital public services?

In 2021, the Data Security Law (DSL) and Personal Information Protection Law (PIPL), which supplement the data protection provisions in the Chinese Civil Code (CCC) and Cybersecurity Law (CSL), were enacted at the national level (i.e. by the National People's Congress). In terms of regulating data processing (especially personal information processing) by public sectors, the CSL, DSL, and PIPL have major implications for digital public services. The relevant articles of the three laws are laid out in Table 3.

Table 3 Selected articles on personal information in digital public services in the CSL, DSL, and PIPL

Article no.	The legal text
Cybersecurity Law[a]	
Art. 28	Network operators shall provide technical support and assistance to public security organs and national security organs that are safeguarding **national security** and investigating **criminal activities** in accordance with the law
Art. 30	Information obtained by cybersecurity and informatization departments and relevant departments performing cybersecurity protection duties can only be used as **necessary** for the protection of cybersecurity, and **must not be used in other ways**
Art. 37	**Critical information infrastructure** operators that gather or produce **personal information** or **important data** during operations within the mainland territory of the People's Republic of China, shall store it **within mainland China**. Where due to business requirements it is truly necessary to provide it outside the mainland, they shall follow the measures jointly formulated by the State cybersecurity and informatization departments and the relevant departments of the State Council to conduct a **security assessment**
Data Security Law[b]	
Art. 7	The State is to protect the data-related rights and interests of individuals and organizations; encourage lawful, reasonable, and effective data use; ensure the lawful and orderly free flow of data; and promote the development of the **digital economy** with data as a key factor
Art. 14	The State is to implement a **big data** strategy, advancing **data infrastructure** construction, and encouraging and supporting the innovative application of data in all industries and all fields Provincial-level and higher people's governments shall include **digital economy** development in their respective level's people's economic and social development plans, and formulate **digital economy development plans** as needed
Art. 15	The State is to support the development and use of data to increase the intelligentization level of **public services**. When providing intelligentized public services, the needs of **elderly people** and **people with disabilities** shall be fully considered, to avoid creating obstacles in the daily lives of elderly people and people with disabilities
Art. 21	The State is to establish a **categorized and graded protection system** for data, implementing categorized and graded protection according to the **data's degree of importance** in economic and social development, as well as the degree of danger to **national security, public interests, or the lawful rights and interests of individuals**[c] **or organizations** brought about if it is altered, destroyed, leaked, or illegally obtained or used
Art. 31	The provisions of the **Cybersecurity Law** of the PRC apply to the outbound security management of **important data** collected or produced by **critical information infrastructure** operators operating within the mainland territory of the PRC
Art. 35	Where public security authorities and national security authorities obtain data as necessary to safeguard **national security** or investigate **crimes** in accordance with law, they shall undergo strict approval procedures according to relevant State provisions and proceed in accordance with law, and relevant organizations and individuals shall cooperate

(continued)

Table 3 (continued)

Article no.	The legal text
Art. 36	The competent authorities of the PRC are to handle **foreign justice or law enforcement institution requests** for the provision of data, according to **relevant laws and treaties or agreements** concluded or participated in by the PRC, or in accordance with the principle of **equality and reciprocity**. Domestic organizations and individuals must not provide data stored **within** the mainland territory of the PRC to the justice or law enforcement institutions of foreign countries without the **approval** of the competent authorities of the PRC
Chapter 5	Security and Openness of **Government Data**
Art. 38	**State authorities** that need to collect or use data to perform their **legally-prescribed** duties shall do so within the scope of their legally-prescribed duties and in accordance with the conditions and procedures provided by law and administrative regulations; they shall preserve the **confidentiality**, in accordance with law, of data such as personal private [data], **personal information**, commercial secrets, and confidential commercial information; and they must not divulge or illegally provide it to others
Art. 40	**State authorities** entrusting **others** to construct or maintain e-government systems, or to store or process government data, shall undergo strict **approval** procedures, and shall supervise entrusted parties' performance of data security protection obligations. Entrusted parties shall perform data security protection obligations according to the provisions of laws, administrative regulations, and contractual agreements, and must not retain, use, divulge, or provide others with government data without **authorization**
Personal Information Protection Law[d]	
Art. 33	This Law applies to **State organs**' activities of handling **personal information**; where this Section contains specific provisions, the provisions of this Section apply
Art. 34	**State organs** handling **personal information** to fulfil their statutory duties and responsibilities shall conduct them according to the powers and procedures provided in laws or administrative regulations; they may not exceed the **scope or extent necessary** to fulfil their statutory duties and responsibilities
Art. 35	**State organs** handling **personal information** for the purpose of fulfilling statutory duties and responsibilities shall fulfil **notification** duties, **except where circumstances as provided in Article 18, Paragraph I,**[e] of this Law exist, or where the **notification will impede** State organs' fulfilment of their statutory duties and responsibilities
Art. 36	**Personal information** handled by **State organs** shall be stored **within** the mainland territory of the People's Republic of China. If it is truly necessary to provide it abroad, a **security assessment** shall be undertaken. Relevant authorities may be requested to support and assist with a security assessment
Art. 37	The provisions of this Law regarding **personal information** handling by **State organs** apply to the handling of personal information in order to fulfill statutory duties by **organizations authorized by laws and regulations to manage public affairs functions**

[a]The English translation of CSL was adopted from the version made by Stanford DigiChina Project (Creemers et al., 2018)

[b]The English translation of DSL was adopted from the version made by Stanford DigiChina Project (2021)

[c]As per Art. 21, personal information can thus constitute important data in some cases

(continued)

Table 3 (continued)

[d]The English translation of PIPL was adopted from the version made by Stanford DigiChina Project (Creemers & Webster, 2021)

[e]The Article 18, Para I: "Personal information handlers handling personal information are permitted not to notify individuals about the items provided in Paragraph 1 of the previous Article under circumstances where laws or administrative regulations provide that confidentiality shall be preserved or notification is not necessary"

5. Are there any current or proposed regulations mandating the sharing of data with government agencies to enable better delivery of public services?

As mentioned in the preceding section, statutory restrictions on "sharing" data for the purposes of "safeguarding national security or investigating crimes" exist in Art. 28 of the CSL and Art. 35 of the DSL to allow greater protection of national security and public safety. Similarly, according to applicable rules, Art. 52 compels critical information infrastructure operators to disclose cybersecurity monitoring and early warning information.

Different government agencies are requesting data sharing from the private sector as part of the "Internet + Regulation" Initiative. These mandatory requests are made in sectors including tax, customs, financial services, e-commerce platforms, and energy and carbon reduction, among others. For example, Article 28 of the Electronic Commerce Law (电子商务法) stipulates that the platform is obliged to submit tax-related information to the tax authorities. Article 22 of the Measures for the Supervision and Administration of Online Trading [网络交易监督管理办法] (State Administration for Market Regulation, 2021) states that "an online trading business shall, according to…, provide such data and information as price, sales volume and sales amount of commodities or services in a specific period of time, specific category and specific region."

3 Institutions

1. Is there a specific body overseeing the digitalisation of the public sector?

Yes, the National Informatization Leading Group (国家信息化领导小组) was established in 1996 as the early supervising body. Later, in 2008, after the national ministry system reform was launched, the Ministry of Industry and Information Technology (MIIT) absorbed its general office.[8] However, in 2014, the MIIT's Informatization Promotion Department, which oversaw e-government operations, was reclassified as the Cyberspace Administration of China (CAC) (中央网络安全和信息化委员会办公室), signalling that CAC (especially its Information Development Bureau) would take the lead in coordinating China's e-government

[8] See the terminology of the Informatization Office of the State Council at Baidu Baike (2021).

development, with other agencies playing a variety of roles in digitising public services (Huang, 2020, pp. 47–50).

2. If such a body exists, what is its status (e.g. an independent agency, a ministry, an inter-ministerial committee, an ad-hoc body, etc.)?

The Cyberspace Administration of China is also the Office of the Central Cyberspace Affairs Commission (CCAC) (中央网络安全和信息化委员会), as stated in the 2018 Plan for Deepening the Reform of Party and State Institutions [深化党和国家机构改革方案] (Central Committee of the Communist Party of China, 2018). The 2018 Plan also shows that the Central Cyberspace Affairs Commission takes the lead in overseeing the country's cybersecurity and informatisation. On this point, CCAC is an inter-ministerial committee that serves as one of the central policy-making and deliberative coordinating bodies.

3. If such a body exists, what are its prerogatives and powers?

To be specific, CCAC, like its predecessor, the Central Cyberspace Affairs Leading Group (中央网络安全和信息化领导小组), is reportedly responsible for assuming a central and unified leadership role to solve the governance problem of "Nine Dragons Rule the Waters" (九龙治水), coordinating major cybersecurity and informatisation issues across multiple fields, formulating and implementing national cybersecurity and information technology development strategies, macro-planning, and major policies, and continuously enhancing security capabilities (Xinhuanet, 2014).

As the CCAC's Office, the CAC's predecessor, State Internet Information Office (国家互联网信息办公室) had long been responsible for content moderation, which took over from the Bureau of Internet News Regulation (互联网新闻监管局) in 2011 (Miao & Lei, 2016, p. 337). In terms of digitising public services, the CAC's Information Development Bureau is responsible for the nation's E-Government construction (Huang, 2020, p. 50). Additionally, the CAC is the primary enforcement agency for the Cybersecurity Law (performing national security reviews of critical information infrastructures, for example), as well as the Data Security Law and Personal Information Protection Law (as the coordinating agency).

The digitalisation of public/government services also includes a wide range of government entities, each with a specific role to play in the process. The sharing of information resources at the national level is mainly reflected in the Plans made by the National Development and Reform Commission (i.e. State Information Center), while the oversight of government information disclosure falls to the General Office of the State Council (i.e. the Operational Center for gov.cn) (Huang, 2020, p. 52). As per the 2018 Plan for Deepening the Reform of Party and State Institutions (Central Committee of the Communist Party of China, 2018), the Ministry of Industry and Information Technology continues to play an active role in coordinating the construction of telecommunications, Internet, and private communication networks.

4. Is there an evaluation system or indicators to measure the progress of the development of digital government?

Yes, there have been quite a few official and trial evaluation systems/indicators available for measuring digital government development.

The first sort of evaluation program is the strategy-tracing approach. Since 2017, the Cyberspace Administration of China has produced an annual report on the advancement of Digital China (China Cyberspace, 2020, 2021; CNBC, 2019; Xinhua, 2018). As the 2020 Digital China Development Report (China Cyberspace, 2021) demonstrates, all critical initiatives toward building a Digital China (such as digital governments) were included, along with numerical state-wide statistics, regulatory campaigns, best practices, and future blueprints, while also introducing the Evaluation System of the Effectiveness of Informatization Development in Different Regions—namely Informatization Development Index and Provincial Ranking of Informatization Development Levels.

The second is a way of evaluation or internal supervision, as exemplified in Table 4.

5. Is there a public company or any public-private partnerships working on the development of specific solutions for digitising the public sector? If the company exists, what is its function?

As previously stated, official entities such as the State Information Center and the Operational Center for Gov Web are responsible for central-level digitisation. However, four primary strategies for digitising the public sector have been created in the local context in line with provincial goals.

According to the 2020 Annual Report on China's Rule-of-Law Government (2020中国法治政府发展报告) published by the Research Institute of Rule-of-Law Government at the China University of Political Science and Law, local governments were piloting the establishment of a dedicated agency for big data administration as the coordinating unit for data interconnectivity and lifecycle monitoring of

Table 4 Evaluation systems

Year	Title
2016	Guide to the Construction of the Technical System of "Internet + Government/Public Service" ["互联网+政务服务"技术体系建设指南] (General Office of the State Council of the People's Republic of China, 2016b)
2017	Circular on the Inspection of the National Internet Government Service Platform—National Internet Government Service Platform Inspection Indicators [全国互联网政务服务平台检查指标] (General Office of the State Council of the People's Republic of China, 2017a)
2018	(GB/T 37273-2018) General principles for the evaluation of public service effect [公共服务效果测评通则]
2019	Opinions of the General Office of the State Council on Establishing a "Good and Bad Review" System for Government Services to Improve the Level of Government Services [国务院办公厅关于建立政务服务"好差评"制度提高政务服务水平的意见] (General Office of the State Council of the People's Republic of China, 2019b)

digital government development (CUPL Research Institute of Rule-of-Law Government, 2020, pp. 229–231). Simultaneously, to seek the support of technology, funding, and human resources, local governments experimented with at least two types of public-private partnerships, including "Social Service Procurement by Governments" (conventional public procurement) and "Procurement from Professional Building and Operating Centers." The former is subject to the Government Procurement Law, whilst the latter varies according to the nature of the private party (i.e. whether it is state-owned or not) and the government and corporate parties' investment share (CUPL Research Institute of Rule-of-Law Government, 2020, pp. 231–233).

6. What are the criteria aimed at guaranteeing the independence of the "third parties" auditing digital public service providers?

As per the Guide to the Construction of the Technical System of "Internet + Government/Public Service" ["互联网+政务服务"技术体系建设指南] (General Office of the State Council of the People's Republic of China, 2016b), its section on "third-party assessment" demonstrates that the supply side and demand side evaluation indices are used to evaluate digital public service providers.

The supply-side evaluation index is primarily used to assess the coverage of online government affairs services offered by the government and departments, the accuracy of published information, and the application level of the integrated platform. The assessment data is gathered primarily by real-time data monitoring, department filling, background system inspection, and scaping.[9]

The demand side evaluation index primarily measures natural and legal entities' satisfaction with government departments at all levels for providing online government services, as well as government departments' ease in providing government services. The goal of this review is to determine public satisfaction with online government services. This indicator should include the whole population of public service receivers, namely the perception and assessment of natural and legal persons on the service quality, friendliness, level of service, and capability of online government services. The assessment data are gathered primarily by data collection, questionnaire surveys, online service evaluations, and telephone (SMS) follow-up visits (General Office of the State Council of the People's Republic of China, 2016b).

[9] See Section 8—"Supervision and Assessment of Online Government Services" of the Guide to the Construction of the Technical System of "Internet + Government/Public Service" (General Office of the State Council of the People's Republic of China, 2016b).

4 Key Sectors

4.1 Digital Identity

1. Is there a strategy to digitalise this sector or any areas of it?

Yes, the Chinese Ministry of Public Security has developed two systems of digital identity.

The Third Research Institute of the Ministry of Public Security created the eID [公民网络电子身份标识] (2021) system on the basis of Art. 2 of the Electronic Signature Law,[10] emphasising the promising balance between safeguarding personal information and adapting to the openness and circulation of data in the network society (Third Research Institute of the Ministry of Public Security, 2018).

Following the "Internet Plus" initiative, the First Research Institute of the Ministry of Public Security piloted Version 1.0 of the CTID [居民身份网络可信凭证] (Anicert, 2022) system in 2016. The CTID platform desensitises and de-identifies the identity information included in the legal identity document, and generates an irreversible data file that is devoid of plaintext information and maps with the legal identity document one by one. It enables online identification without requiring the user to disclose personal information.

2. Is the use of specific technologies for digital identity systems promoted or prioritised (e.g. AI, blockchain, open-source software)?

Yes, as the developmental history of the CTID system shows, it has been promoting its sub-system of SIM Card Digital Identity as well as a project named "Personal ID + Blockchain" (Anicert, 2021). The CTID system's core technology is based on Two-Dimensional Code and cryptography (Gao et al., 2021, pp. 90–91). Facial recognition has also been integrated into the process of establishing an authentic CTID for entities, according to the public list of CTID industrial standards.[11]

3. Is there a sectoral regulation in place (e.g. law, decree, standards) to organise the digitalisation of the sector?

Yes.

Article 2 of the Electronic Signature Law, which was first enacted in 2004, laid the groundwork for the development of digital identity systems by recognising the legally binding significance of electronic signatures in contract agreements.

Users of Internet services are required to register with Internet service providers using their real names in accordance with Article 24 of the Cybersecurity Law, to which it is stated that "the State is committed to the implementation of a strategy of

[10] "The 'Electronic Signature' as mentioned in the present Law shall refer to the data included and attached in the data message in electronic form, for the use of identifying the identity of the signatory and showing that the signatory has recognized the contents therein" (Electronic Signature Law, 2015, Art. 2).

[11] The CTID industrial standards can be found by search at https://std.samr.gov.cn/hb/hbQuery.

trusted identities in cyberspace, provides support for research and development of secure and convenient technologies for electronic identity authentication, and promotes mutual recognition between different electronic identity authentication schemes."

It is also noted in Article 62 of the Personal Information Protection Law that the Cyberspace Administration of China should facilitate the research, development, and application of techniques to provide electronic identity authentication that is safe, convenient, and protect personal information, and establish public services for network identity authentication.

Additionally, in conjunction with the eID system, the National Information Security Standardization Technical Committee enacted a set of nationally recommended eID standards in 2019, titled Information security technology—Security technique requirements for citizen cyber electronic identity (National Public Service Platform for Standards Information, 2018). Similarly, in 2020, the CTID system was augmented with a set of sector-specific standards on Cyber Authentication Service for Resident Identity (National Public Service Platform for Standards Information, 2021).

4. Are there any policies promoting digital sovereignty for digital identity systems (e.g. data localisation, preference or obligation to utilise domestic providers, etc.)?

Yes. Given that the Ministry of Public Security stores digital identity-related data, it is reasonable to assume that those data are collected by Critical Information Infrastructure Operators (CIIOs) in accordance with Article 37 of the Cybersecurity Law, which requires CIIOs to store personal information and critical data locally or subject them to a security assessment. Let alone, digital identity is likely to fall under the definition of personal information, requiring data localisation or a security assessment by the CAC under Article 40 of the Personal Information Protection Law.

In general, Article 10 of the Government Procurement Law requires the obligation to utilise domestic providers. However, foreign-invested firms have an equal opportunity to engage in the government procurement market under Article 16 of the Foreign Investment Law. Article 15 of the Foreign Investment Regulations says further that firms receiving foreign investment should not be disadvantaged as a result of unjust conditions such as ownership structure, organisational structure, investor nationality, or product brand.

5. Has the digitisation of the sector or any area of it been promoted because of the COVID-19 pandemic? If yes, then how so?

With the outbreak of a worldwide pandemic and the rapid growth of mobile payment, China has accelerated its digital transformation, for example, by upgrading digital identity-centric systems (e.g. CTID and eID) and developing health QR codes. A few cities started developing and experimenting with health codes based on QR code technology in early February 2020 (Cong, 2021). Its colour varies from red to yellow to green based on an algorithmic computation of the individual's data, which includes traffic data, SIM card data, financial transaction data, and user-submitted data (MPayPass, 2020). In 2020, The Standards on Health Codes were grounded mainly on the CTID system and would be connected to the National Integrated Government Service Platform (Guo, 2021).

6. Is there a specific body in charge of overseeing, coordinating or promoting the digitalisation of the sector?

Yes, as previously stated, the Ministry of Public Security is the primary accountable agency for digital identity. However, the Cyberspace Administration of China may also be responsible for completing security assessments on the condition that DigiID data must be sent outside of China. Simultaneously, the CAC oversees the security of sensitive personal information (including biometrics) in accordance with Chapter II Section II of the PIPL.

4.2 *Smart Cities and Digitised Local Administrations*

1. Is there a smart city strategy?

Yes.

In 2012, China's urban digital transformation was formally launched with the issuance of the first policy document, Interim Measures for the Administration of National Smart City Pilots [国家智慧城市试点暂行管理办法] (General Office of the Ministry of Housing and Urban-Rural Development, 2012b). "Internet Plus" and "Internet + Public/Government Services" have been linked to the development of Digital Government, as has the Big Data Plan, among other efforts, as the smart city program proceeds forward.

The Smart City initiative's infancy began with digital urbanisation. In 2014, the state issued the National New Urbanization Plan (2014–2020)—国家新型城镇化规划 (2014–2020年) (Xinhua News Agency, 2014) and suggested the development of new communities that are environmentally friendly, intelligent, and humanistic. The same year, a coalition of ministerial agencies led by the National Development and Reform Commission issued the Notice of Guidance for Healthy Development, which acknowledged issues such as cybersecurity concerns. In 2016, the State Council released the Circular on Further Promoting Some Opinions on New Urbanization [国务院关于深入推进新型城镇化建设的若干意见] (State Council of the People's Republic of China, 2016a) to establish the "Broadband China" Initiative and encourage sustainable and environmentally compatible new cities. The process of digital urbanisation has been further expanded into policies on facilitating smart rural regions (General Office of the State Council of the People's Republic of China, 2016a; General Office of the Central Committee of the Communist Party of China & General Office of the State Council of the People's Republic of China, 2019) and grassroots social governance (Central Committee of the Communist Party of China & State Council of the People's Republic of China,

2017, 2021a), which have been enriched via infrastructure development and the use of new technology.

Since 2021, the Smart City Initiative has been expanded to include areas such as smart mobility (Central Committee of the Communist Party of China & State Council of the People's Republic of China, 2021b; State Council of the People's Republic of China, 2021a), sustainable energy vehicles (General Office of the State Council of the People's Republic of China, 2020a), green urbanisation (General Office of the Central Committee of the Communist Party of China & General Office of the State Council of the People's Republic of China, 2021), and the digital economy (State Council of the People's Republic of China, 2021b).

2. Is the use of specific smart city technologies promoted or prioritised (e.g. AI, blockchain, open-source software)?

Yes, some latest policy documents embedding smart city technologies are listed in Table 5.

3. Is there a sectoral regulation in place (e.g. law, decree, standards) to organise the digitalisation of cities, and urban areas in general?

The digitalisation of cities in China has been promoted by decrees (particularly the Ministerial Regulations, 部门规章) and secured by a set of national standards. The list can be found in the following list.

The Ministerial Regulations
The Circular of the General Office of the Ministry of Housing and Urban-Rural Development on Carrying out the Nationwide Pilot Work of Smart Cities [住房和城乡建设部办公厅关于开展国家智慧城市试点工作的通知] (2012a). It includes two attached documents:

- Interim Measures for the Administration of the National Pilot Project of Smart Cities (国家智慧城市试点暂行管理办法)
- National Pilot Index System for Smart Cities (Districts/Towns) (Trial)—国家智慧城市(区、镇)试点指标体系(试行)

The Circular of the National Development and Reform Commission, the Ministry of Industry and Information Technology, the Ministry of Science and Technology and Other Eight Departments on the Issuance of Guidance on Promoting the Healthy Development of Smart Cities [国家发展和改革委员会、工业和信息化部、科学技术部等八部门关于印发促进智慧城市健康发展的指导意见的通知] (National Development and Reform Commission, 2014a).

The Circular of the General Office of the National Development and Reform Commission, the Secretary Bureau of the Cyberspace Administration of China, and the Office of the Standardization Administration of China on Organizing the Evaluation of New-type Smart Cities to Promote the Healthy and Rapid Development of New-type Smart Cities in a Pragmatic Manner [关于组织开展新型智慧城市评价工作务实推动新型智慧城市健康快速发展的通知] (National Development

Table 5 Policy documents on smart city technologies

Year	Document title	Smart city technology
2022	The 14th Five-Year Plan on the Development of Modern Comprehensive Transportation System [“十四五”现代综合交通运输体系发展规划] (State Council of the People’s Republic of China, 2021a)	5G, Internet of Things, Big Data, Cloud Computing, Artificial Intelligence
2021	The 14th Five-Year Plan on the Development of the Digital Economy [“十四五”数字经济发展规划] (State Council of the People’s Republic of China, 2021b)	Big Data, Edge Computing, Digital Twins Tech
2021	Opinions on Promoting the Green Development of Urban and Rural Construction [关于推动城乡建设绿色发展的意见] (General Office of the Central Committee of the Communist Party of China & General Office of the State Council of the People’s Republic of China, 2021)	Urban Information Model
2021	The Outline of National Comprehensive Three-Dimensional Transportation Network Planning [国家综合立体交通网规划纲要] (Central Committee of the Communist Party of China & State Council of the People’s Republic of China, 2021b)	Transportation Logistics, Intelligent Networked Vehicle
2020	Development Plan of New Energy Automotive Industry (2021–2035)—新能源汽车产业发展规划(2021–2035年) (General Office of the State Council of the People’s Republic of China, 2020a)	New Energy Vehicle
2017	Plan for the Development of Next-Generation Artificial Intelligence [新一代人工智能发展规划] (State Council of the People’s Republic of China, 2017)	Artificial Intelligence, Intelligent Building, Big Data, Smart
2015	The Notice on the Action Plan for Promoting the Development of Big Data [促进大数据发展行动纲要] (State Council of the People’s Republic of China, 2015b)	Big Data, Internet of Things, Cloud Computing
2015	Opinions on Promoting the Innovative Development of Cloud Computing and Cultivating New Business Models of the Information Industry [关于促进云计算创新发展培育信息产业新业态的意见] (State Council of the People’s Republic of China, 2015c)	Cloud Computing, Big Data
2013	Medium- and Long-term Development Plan for the National Satellite Navigation Industry [国家卫星导航产业中长期发展规划] (China National Space Administration, 2013)	Satellite Navigation (Particularly Vehicle Navigation)
2013	Guiding Opinions on Promoting the Orderly and Healthy Development of the Internet of Things [关于推进物联网有序健康发展的指导意见] (General Office of the State Council of the People’s Republic of China, 2013a)	Internet of Things

and Reform Commission, 2016). It includes four attached documents on how to assess the construction of smart cities.

The Notice of the National Bureau of Surveying, Mapping and Geographic Information on Accelerating the Pilot Work of Promoting the Construction of Spatio-Temporal Big Data and Cloud Platform in Smart Cities [国家测绘地理信息局关于加快推进智慧城市时空大数据与云平台建设试点工作的通知] (2017).

National Standards

For example, the overall design
GB/T 34678-2017 Smart city—Technical reference model—智慧城市 技术参考模型

GB/T 37043-2018 Smart city—Terminology—智慧城市 术语
GB/T 36332-2018 Smart city—Domain knowledge model—Core conceptual model—智慧城市 领域知识模型 核心概念模型
GB/T 36333-2018 Smart city—Top-level design guide—智慧城市 顶层设计指南

The list can go on with some industry-specific standards, like Internet of Things (IoT).[12]

4. Are there any policies promoting digital sovereignty for smart cities (e.g. data localisation, preference or obligation to utilise domestic providers, etc.)?

Yes. According to the Cybersecurity Law, Article 37 requires a restricted data localisation for both personal information and important data pertaining to the smart city operators if they are designated Critical Information Infrastructure Operators (CIIO). Data localisation requirements stated in Article 40 of the Personal Information Protection Law apply to smart city operators, even though they are not CIIOs, if they process personal data exceeding the amount of the threshold set by the Cyberspace Administration of China (CAC).

At the same time, because smart city-related data may come within the category of important data, the smart city program is likely to succumb to the Data Security Law and any subsequent rules to be set by the CAC.

Certain industry-specific regulations apply to smart city data as well. The regulations include:

- Interim Measures for the Administration of Online Ride-Hailing Service
- Provisions on Safety Management of Automobile Data (Trial)
- Map Management Regulations

As indicated in Sect. 4.1, if the smart city builder is a government-characteristic entity, the Government Procurement Law will likely apply, requiring domestic suppliers to be favoured. The most recent version of the Science and Technology Progress Law maintains the standard established by the Government Procurement Law, and adds that, for the first time in the market, government procurement should take the lead in purchasing domestic products, rather than being limited by commercial performance (Article 91).

5. Has the digitisation of the sector or any area of it been promoted because of the COVID-19 pandemic? If yes, then how so?

[12] See GB/T 36620-2018 Internet of Things (IoT) based technical application guide for smart city—面向智慧城市的物联网技术应用指南.

The COVID-19 epidemic sparked the digitisation of smart city sectors such as online education, telemedicine, and home offices, as well as the development of a complete contact tracing system (epidemiological mapping, health codes, and digital travel records).

COVID-19 has facilitated the establishment of smart cities in the digital epidemic prevention industry, according to the New Smart City Industry Mapping Research Report (China Academy of Information and Communications Technology, 2021). The infrastructure layer includes platforms for public health emergency management, apps and minor processes for epidemic prevention, telemedicine platforms, and voice-based information systems. The Intelligent terminal layer's hardware components include intelligent medical equipment, a smart thermometer, unmanned vehicles, unmanned aerial aircraft, and nucleic acid detection equipment. At the software level, applications such as integrated solutions, vaccinations, electronic health vouchers, epidemiological big data, and other digital epidemic prevention services are covered (i.e. application services).

6. Is there a specific strategy or regulation targeting the digitisation of land records or real estate records?

Yes. The Property Law (物权法), which first took effect on October 1, 2007, proposes that the state establish a uniform real estate registration system. In November 2013, the former Ministry of Land and Resources was clearly defined by the executive meeting of the State Council as responsible for guiding and supervising the national unified registration of real estate, such as land, housing, grassland, forest land, and sea area (Xinhua Net, 2014). In September 2014, the 26th Ministerial Conference of the former Ministry of Land and Resources considered and adopted in principle the general framework for the construction of the "Land and Resources Cloud," which is the abbreviation of the Unified Registration Information System for Land and Resources and Real Estate (China Economic Weekly, 2018). Simultaneously, the Interim Real Estate Registration Regulations (不动产登记暂行条例) were adopted in 2014 and revised in 2019, mandating that the real estate register utilise electronic means where possible. 2018 saw the launch of the National Real Estate Registration Information Management Platform, which is part of the "Law and Resources Cloud" (Xian News, 2018).

7. Is there a specific body in charge of overseeing, coordinating or promoting the digitalisation of the sector?

Yes. Since 2014, the Smart City Initiative has been led by an inter-ministerial committee, namely the Smart City Interministerial Coordination Working Group (State Information Center & Smarter City Development and Research Center, 2014). For instance, as per the 2014 Notice of Guidance for Healthy Development [关于促进智慧城市健康发展的指导意见] (National Development and Reform Commission, 2014b), the Smart City initiative has been stimulated by an assembly of ministries to foster sector-specific policies, including the National Development and Reform Commission, the Ministry of Industry and Information Technology, the Ministry of Science and Technology, the Ministry of Public Security, the Ministry of Finance, the Ministry of Land and Resources,[13] the Ministry of Transport and the Ministry of Housing and Urban-Rural Development.

To illustrate, the usage of geographical data is a suitable example. The National Bureau of Surveying and Mapping Geographic Information, which was later absorbed by the Ministry of Natural Resources (MNR), piloted the spatiotemporal big data platform in 2017, and the MNR published the Technical Outline for the Construction of a Smart City Spatiotemporal Big Data Platform.

8. Is there any outstanding example of strategy or policy elaborated by a local administration?

Yes. Since China unveiled the plan for Smart Cities and Digital China, which includes big data, open data, digital government, and smart cities, a number of local governments have pioneered legislation and policymaking, with some enacting smart city-specific regional regulations (for example, Haikou, Yingtan, Datong, Jining, and Yinchuan).

The Ministry of Housing and Urban-Rural Development, in collaboration with the Ministry of Industry and Information Technology, has chosen two sets of pilot cities to coordinate the development of smart city infrastructure and intelligent networked vehicles. Beijing, Shanghai, Guangzhou, Wuhan, Changsha, and Wuxi are included in the first (Ministry of Housing and Urban-Rural Development & Ministry of Industry and Information Technology, 2021a); Chongqing, Shenzhen, Xiamen, Nanjing, Jinan, Chengdu, Hefei, Cangzhou, Wuhu, and Zibo are included in the second (Ministry of Housing and Urban-Rural Development & Ministry of Industry and Information Technology, 2021b).

Shenzhen is a standout example of a Smart City that has been at the cutting edge of innovation, serving as the socialist demonstration zone with Chinese features specified by the Chinese central government (Central Committee of the Communist Party of China & State Council of the People's Republic of China, 2019). Shenzhen has been fulfilling its role as one of China's most innovative cities with the implementation and/or amendment of the following legislative measures:

- Regulations of Shenzhen Special Economic Zone on the Construction of Barrier-free Cities (2021)
- Shenzhen Special Economic Zone Data Regulations (2021)
- Shenzhen Special Economic Zone Quality Regulations (amended in 2019)

---

[13] In 2018, the Ministry of Land and Resources was abolished, and the National Bureau of Surveying and Mapping Geographic Information was absorbed by the Ministry of Natural Resources.

4.3 Digital Money and Payments

1. Is there a strategy to digitalise this sector or any areas of it, such as the Central Bank Digital Currency program?

Yes. The initiative for Digital Currency/Electronic Payments (DC/EP) began in 2014 (Working Group on E-CNY Research and Development of the People's Bank of China, 2021, p. 1). DC/EP will be utilised as a cash supplement, with a two-tier operation mechanism that leverages digital technological advancement to provide anonymity and controllability (Chai & Ren, 2022). And it has been tested in a number of places, including Shenzhen (Zhou, 2020a), Suzhou (Zhou, 2020b), and others. Along with the establishment of 261 million digital wallets, the e-yuan was utilised in transactions worth 87.6 billion yuan (US $13.8 billion) (Tang, 2022). It was accepted by over 8 million retailers as of the end of December 2021 (Tang, 2022). In early 2021, the People's Bank of China's Digital Currency Institute joined the m-CBDC Bridge initiative (People's Bank of China Digital Currency Institute, 2021).

By the end of June 2021, the number of digital Yuan pilot scenarios had allegedly surpassed 1.32 million, encompassing living expenditures, catering services, transportation, shopping and consumption, and government services, among other sectors. Over 20.87 million personal wallets and 3.51 million corporate wallets were opened, resulting in over 70.75 million transactions and a total value of approximately 34.5 billion yuan (Li & Lu, 2022).

2. Is the use of specific technologies for digital money/payments promoted or prioritised (e.g. AI, blockchain, open-source software)?

Yes. According to Yifei Fan, the People's Bank of China's then-deputy governor, the E-CNY uses a controlled anonymous system, with the People's Bank of China holding all information. Big data and Artificial Intelligence enable the analysis of transaction data and capital movements, the prevention and prosecution of unlawful and criminal actions such as money laundering, terrorist funding, and tax evasion, and the effective maintenance of financial stability (Fan, 2020).

According to the Briefing Meeting on publishing *the Progress of E-CNY Research Development in China* (People's Bank of China, 2021), E-CNY is organised in a centralised manner. The central bank is the conduit for all transactions between institutions. E-CNY expressions utilise an encrypted string. E-CNY may use alliance chain technology to establish a centralised dispersed account. To fully use E-CNY's "payment as settlement," its system combines blockchain and programmable smart contracts to enable automatic reconciliation and error management. By using the irreversibility of hash algorithms, blockchain accounts create data separation between various operational agencies, balancing privacy and financial data security.

3. Is there a sectoral regulation in place (e.g. law, decree, standards) to organise the digitalisation of the sector?

In August 2020, the State Council approved the Ministry of Commerce's "Overall Scheme for Comprehensively Deepening the Innovation and Development of Service Trade" [全面深化服务贸易创新发展试点总体方案] (Ministry of Commerce, 2020) to initiate the central bank digital currency pilot work in the Beijing-Tianjin-Hebei region, the Yangtze River Delta region, the Guangdong-Hong Kong-Macao Greater Bay Area, and the central and western regions, subject to certain conditions.

In October 2020, the modified People's Bank of China Law (Draft for Comments) was produced, which says in Article 19 that Renminbi (CNY) can exist in both physical and digital form, establishing a legal foundation for the issuing of digital currency.

4. Are there any policies promoting digital sovereignty in digital money/payments (e.g. data localisation, preference or obligation to utilise domestic providers, etc.)?

As banking services are likely to fall within the definition of Critical Information Infrastructure in Article 2 of the Regulations on Critical Information Infrastructure Security Protections, the E-CNY data are likely to succumb to stringent data localisation requirements or, alternatively, a security assessment by CAC.

Furthermore, personal financial information is controlled specifically under the People's Bank of China's Circular on the Protection of Personal Financial Information by Banking Financial Institutions. It states that personal financial information gathered in China should be stored, processed, and analysed in China. Unless otherwise specified by applicable laws and regulations and the People's Bank of China, banking and financial institutions are prohibited from transferring domestic personal financial information abroad.

5. Has the digitisation of the sector or any area of it been promoted because of the COVID-19 pandemic? If yes, then how so?

The 2003 SARS epidemic accelerated China's path to launch e-commerce and digital payments (Huddleston Jr., 2020). The emergence of large-scale cloud computing and the COVID-19 pandemic has placed a heightened emphasis on digital currencies and payment services. In certain instances, such as the transfer of real estate and housing interests, recent amendments to the Electronic Signature Law permit the use of electronic signatures. Customers are gaining an enhanced understanding of property information through augmented reality/virtual reality technologies and live online sales during the COVID-19 pandemic in 2020 (Yiou, 2021). Particularly, electronic signatures and cloud contracts make it possible to take traditionally offline activities, such as real estate transactions, into the digital realm. CBIRC's Notice on Further Improving Financial Services for Epidemic Prevention and Control [中国银保监会办公厅关于进一步做好疫情防控金融服务的通知] (General Office of the China Banking and Insurance Regulatory Commission, 2020), for example, suggests optimising and enriching "non-contact service" channels, and offering secure and convenient "at-home" financial services. It would appear that banks and other financial institutions are employing blockchain technology, big data technology, cloud computing, and other emerging technologies to enhance their online risk assessment and control capabilities. A further advantage of cloud computing is that firms provide more data for the construction of an ideal credit system and, as a result, reduce monetary transaction costs on both sides.

The scenarios outlined above were also echoed in the Progress of E-CNY Research Development in China report, which emphasises that E-CNY is a prompt response to the COVID-19 and the call for "new retail payment infrastructures that are safe, inclusive, and adaptive to the digital era" (Working Group on E-CNY Research and Development of the People's Bank of China, 2021, p. 1).

6. Is there a specific body in charge of overseeing, coordinating or promoting the digitalisation of the sector?

Yes. As previously stated, the People's Bank of China (China's central bank) is the primary regulatory body overseeing the digitalisation of e-Yuan. Until now, the Central Bank's coordinating unit has been its Digital Currency Research Institute.

For example, a central-local collaboration facilitated the digitisation of E-Yuan. In June 2018, the Central Bank's Digital Currency Institute registered and formed Shenzhen Financial Technology Co., Ltd. as a fully owned subsidiary. Nanjing Financial Science and Technology Research and Innovation Center was established in September 2018 with the five-party cooperation between the Central Bank, local governments, banks, and universities. Yangtze River Delta Financial Science and Technology Co., Ltd. was created in March 2019 in collaboration with relevant Suzhou entities (Zhou, 2020c).

4.4 Other Relevant Examples

1. Is there any other sector (such as education, health, etc.) where a specific strategy or policy is in place to foster and organise digitalisation?

China is planning to further digitalise quite a few industrial sectors as per the 14th Five-Year National Informatization Plan.

It also included a project to integrate the "Internet + Education" Cloud Network to make educational resources easier to share, reduce the gap between rural and urban schools, and enhance educational equality. In addition, 5G technology has been reworked to improve instructional AR/VR content development.

Digital health was also mentioned in the Plan. Specifically, social governance experiments of medical Artificial Intelligence were presented as a means of applying AI to healthcare. Telehealth was recommended to enhance medical inclusion by implementing national healthcare big data financing, creating a source directory, and strengthening the grading evaluation system for smart hospitals and online medical services. Improvements in infectious disease surveillance and public health crises, as well as in the adequacy of evaluation and monitoring, are all part of the strategy, which is aimed at enhancing the ability to detect threats in real time and to issue early warnings.

In addition, the Central Committee's 2021 "Rule-of-Law (RoL) China Construction Plan (2020–2025)" [法治中国建设规划2020–2025年] (Xinhua News Agency, 2021c) specifically emphasised the full use of big data, cloud computing, Artificial Intelligence, and other technical methods while establishing an RoL Digital Transformation Project for "smart legal public services."

References

Administrative Licensing Law of the People's Republic of China. (2003). Asian Legal Information Institute. http://www.asianlii.org/cn/legis/cen/laws/allotproc500/#:~:text=The%20Administrative%20License%20Law%20of%20the%20People%27s%20Republic,Jingtao%2C%20President%20of%20the%20People%27s%20Republic%20of%20China.

Anicert. (2021). *CTID平台 平台介绍 [CTID platform—Introduction to the platform]*. Retrieved December 27, 2022, from http://web.archive.org/web/20210413001502/http://www.anicert.cn/platform.html?md=2.

Anicert. (2022). *居民身份网络可信凭证是什么? [What is a resident network trusted credential?]*. http://web.archive.org/web/20220924051840/http://www.anicert.cn/identity.html.

Center for International Knowledge on Development. (2021). *China's progress report on implementation of the 2030 agenda for sustainable development*. https://www.fmprc.gov.cn/mfa_eng/topics_665678/2030kcxfzyc/202109/P020211019152754484797.pdf.

Central Committee of the Communist Party of China. (2018). *Plan for deepening the reform of party and state institutions*. http://www.gov.cn/zhengce/2018-03/21/content_5276191.htm#1.

Central Committee of the Communist Party of China. (2019a). *Communiqué of the fourth plenary session of the 19th Central Committee of the Communist Party of China*. Xinhua Net. http://www.xinhuanet.com/politics/2019-10/31/c_1125178024.htm.

Central Committee of the Communist Party of China. (2019b). *Decision of the CPC Central Committee on upholding and improving the system of socialism with Chinese characteristics and modernizing the system and capacity of state governance*. http://www.gov.cn/zhengce/2019-11/05/content_5449023.htm.

Central Committee of the Communist Party of China & State Council of the People's Republic of China. (2017). *Opinions on strengthening and improving community governance in urban and rural areas*. http://www.gov.cn/xinwen/2017-06/12/content_5201910.htm.

Central Committee of the Communist Party of China & State Council of the People's Republic of China. (2019). *Opinions on supporting the construction of Shenzhen demonstration zone with Chinese characteristics*. http://www.gov.cn/zhengce/2019-08/18/content_5422183.htm.

Central Committee of the Communist Party of China & State Council of the People's Republic of China. (2021a). *Opinions on strengthening the modernization of the grass-roots governance system and capacity*. http://www.gov.cn/zhengce/2021-07/11/content_5624201.htm.

Central Committee of the Communist Party of China & State Council of the People's Republic of China. (2021b). *Outline of national comprehensive three-dimensional transportation network planning*. http://www.gov.cn/zhengce/2021-02/24/content_5588654.htm.

Central People's Government. (2011). *Notice on standardizing the management of E-government platform fees*. The National People's Congress of the People's Republic of China. http://www.npc.gov.cn/zgrdw/npc/zt/qt/rdxxhjs/2015-07/28/content_1942055.htm.

Chai, Z., & Ren, X. (2022, January 6). *数字人民币APP来了 有哪些亮点? [What are the highlights of the digital RMB app?]*. Xinhua Net. Retrieved February 14, 2022, from http://www.xinhuanet.com/money/20220106/96b3308054c7463b927f89f3031a5cfa/c.html.

China Academy of Information and Communications Technology. (2021). 新型智慧城市产业图谱研究报告 *[New smart city industry mapping research report]*. Retrieved February 13, 2022, from http://www.caict.ac.cn/kxyj/qwfb/ztbg/202112/t20211229_394777.htm.

China Cyberspace. (2020, October 9). *Digital China construction and development progress report (2019)*. Cyberspace Administration of China. http://www.cac.gov.cn/2020-09/10/c_1601296274273490.htm.

China Cyberspace. (2021, February 7). *Cyberspace Administration of China releases Digital China Development Report (2020)*. Cyberspace Administration of China. http://www.cac.gov.cn/2021-06/28/c_1626464503226700.htm.

China Cyberspace Network. (2021). *Relevant responsible comrades of the Cyberspace Administration of the Central Committee answered reporters' questions on the "14th Five-Year Plan" for National Informatization*. Cyberspace Administration of China. http://www.cac.gov.cn/2021-12/27/c_1642205312620820.htm.

China Economic Weekly. (2018, August 28). 不动产登记全国联网，下一步:开征房地产? [Real estate registration clouded nationwide, next step: levy real estate tax?]. *People.cn*. Retrieved February 11, 2022, from http://finance.people.com.cn/n1/2018/0828/c1004-30254674.html.

China E-Government Network. (2018). *Two nets, one website, four databases, and twelve gold projects*. http://www.e-gov.org.cn/article-166340.html.

China Internet Network Information Center. (2021). *The 47th China statistical report on internet development*. http://www.cac.gov.cn/2021-02/03/c_1613923423079314.htm.

China National Space Administration. (2013). *Medium- and long-term development plan for the national satellite navigation industry*. http://www.cnsa.gov.cn/n6758823/n6758839/c6796174/content.html

Chinese Academy of Sciences. (2019). *Big earth data in support of the sustainable development goals*. https://www.fmprc.gov.cn/mfa_eng/topics_665678/2030kcxfzyc/201909/P020210525474856809656.pdf.

Chinese Academy of Sciences. (2020). *Big earth data in support of the sustainable development goals*. https://www.fmprc.gov.cn/mfa_eng/topics_665678/2030kcxfzyc/202009/P020210525474890736702.pdf.

Chinese Academy of Sciences. (2021). *Big earth data in support of the sustainable development goals*. https://www.fmprc.gov.cn/mfa_eng/topics_665678/2030kcxfzyc/202109/P020211019152777729038.pdf.

Chinese President Xi delivers keynote speech at world internet conference. (2015). *World internet conference—Wuzhen Summit*. https://www.wuzhenwic.org/communitywithasharedfutureincyberspace_5.html

CNBC. (2019, June 5). *"Digital China construction and development report (2018)": The scale of online payment users in China has reached 600 million*. Cyberspace Administration of China. http://www.cac.gov.cn/2019-05/06/c_1124457115.htm.

Cong, W. (2021). From pandemic control to data-driven governance: The case of China's health code. *Frontiers in Political Science, 3*. https://www.frontiersin.org/articles/10.3389/fpos.2021.627959/full.

Creemers, R., Sacks, S., & Webster, G. (2021, August 18). *Translation: Critical information infrastructure security protection regulations (effective Sept. 1, 2021)*. https://digichina.stanford.edu/work/translation-critical-information-infrastructure-security-protection-regulations-effective-sept-1-2021/.

Creemers, R., & Webster, G. (2021, August 20). *Translation: Personal information protection law of the People's Republic of China—Effective Nov. 1, 2021*. DigiChina. https://digichina.stanford.edu/work/translation-personal-information-protection-law-of-the-peoples-republic-of-china-effective-nov-1-2021/.

Creemers, R., Webster, G., & Triolo, P. (2018, June 29). *Translation: Cybersecurity law of the People's Republic of China (effective June 1, 2017)*. DigiChina. https://digichina.stanford.edu/work/translation-cybersecurity-law-of-the-peoples-republic-of-china-effective-june-1-2017/.

Cryptography law of the People's Republic of China. (2019). National People's Congress. http://www.npc.gov.cn/englishnpc/c23934/202009/dfb74a30d80b4a2bb5c19678b89a4a14.shtml.

CUPL Research Institute of Rule-of-Law Government. (2020). *Annual report on China's rule-of-law government*.

Cyberspace Administration of China. (2021a). *Internet information service algorithmic recommendation management provisions*. http://www.cac.gov.cn/2022-01/04/c_1642894606364259.htm.

Cyberspace Administration of China. (2021b). *The 14th Five-Year National Informatization Plan (NIP)*. http://www.cac.gov.cn/2021-12/27/c_1642205314518676.htm.

Cyberspace Administration of China, National Development and Reform Commission, Ministry of Industry and Information Technology, Ministry of Public Security, Ministry of State Security, Ministry of Finance, Ministry of Commerce, People's Bank of China, State Administration for Market Regulation, State Administration of Radio and Television, China Securities Regulatory Commission, State Administration of State Secrets & State Cryptography Administration. (2021). *Cybersecurity review measures*. http://www.gov.cn/zhengce/zhengceku/2022-01/04/content_5666430.htm.

Data Security Law of the People's Republic of China. (2021). http://www.npc.gov.cn/npc/c30834/202106/7c9af12f51334a73b56d7938f99a788a.shtml.

Dener, C., Nii-Aponsah, H., Ghunney, L. E., & Johns, K. D. (2021). *GovTech Maturity Index: The state of public sector digital transformation*. World Bank. https://openknowledge.worldbank.org/handle/10986/36233.

DigiChina. (2021, June 29). *Translation: Data Security Law of the People's Republic of China (Effective Sept. 1, 2021)*. https://digichina.stanford.edu/work/translation-data-security-law-of-the-peoples-republic-of-china/.

eID Secure Authentication. (2021). *Index*. http://web.archive.org/web/20211201022421/https://eid.cn/index.html.

Fan, Y. (2020, September 15). 关于数字人民币M0定位的政策含义分析 [An analysis of the policy implications of the M0 orientation of E-CNY]. *Financial News*. Retrieved February 14, 2022, from http://web.archive.org/web/20220308171510/https://www.financialnews.com.cn/pl/zj/202009/t20200915_200890.html.

Gao, L., Li, J., Guo, W., Kang, L., Li, N., & Wang, Y. (2021). 创新社会治理 赋能数字经济——可信数字身份创新成果巡礼 [Innovating social governance and enabling digital economy: Innovation achievements of trusted digital identity]. *Police Technology, 90*.

General Office of the Central Committee of the Communist Party of China & General Office of the State Council of the People's Republic of China. (2019). *Strategic outline of digital rural development*. http://www.gov.cn/zhengce/2019-05/16/content_5392269.htm.

General Office of the Central Committee of the Communist Party of China & General Office of the State Council of the People's Republic of China. (2021). *Opinions on promoting green development in urban and rural areas*. http://www.gov.cn/zhengce/2021-10/21/content_5644083.htm.

General Office of the China Banking and Insurance Regulatory Commission. (2020). *Notice on further improving financial services for epidemic prevention and control*. http://www.gov.cn/zhengce/zhengceku/2020-02/16/content_5479561.htm.

General Office of the Ministry of Housing and Urban-Rural Development. (2012a). *Circular on carrying out the nationwide pilot work of smart cities*. http://www.gov.cn/zwgk/2012-12/05/content_2282674.htm.

General Office of the Ministry of Housing and Urban-Rural Development. (2012b). *Interim measures for the administration of national smart city pilots*. https://baike.baidu.hk/item/%E5%9C%8B%E5%AE%B6%E6%99%BA%E6%85%A7%E5%9F%8E%E5%B8%82%E8%A9%A6%E9%BB%9E%E6%9A%AB%E8%A1%8C%E7%AE%A1%E7%90%86%E8%BE%A6%E6%B3%95/303729.

General Office of the Ministry of Industry and Information Technology. (2021). *Circular on further improving the implementation of the special actions for the aging-friendly and barrier-free transformation of internet applications*. http://www.gov.cn/zhengce/zhengceku/2021-04/13/content_5599225.htm.

General Office of the State Administration for Market Regulation. (2020). *National e-government standards system construction guide*. https://gkml.samr.gov.cn/nsjg/bzjss/202006/W020200619303475665607.pdf.

General Office of the State Council of the People's Republic of China. (2013a). *Guiding opinions on promoting the orderly and healthy development of the internet of things*. http://www.gov.cn/zwgk/2013-02/17/content_2333141.htm.

General Office of the State Council of the People's Republic of China. (2013b). *Opinions on further strengthening government information disclosure in response to social concerns and enhancing the government's credibility*. http://www.gov.cn/zhengce/content/2013-10/18/content_1219.htm.

General Office of the State Council of the People's Republic of China. (2015a). *Essentials of government information disclosure work*. http://www.gov.cn/zhengce/content/2015-04/21/content_9644.htm.

General Office of the State Council of the People's Republic of China. (2015b). *Opinions of the General Office of the State Council on Using Big Data to Strengthen the Service and Supervision of Market Subjects*. http://www.gov.cn/zhengce/content/2015-07/01/content_9994.htm.

General Office of the State Council of the People's Republic of China. (2016a). *Circular on accelerating the upgrading of radio and television villages to household access*. http://www.gov.cn/zhengce/content/2016-04/21/content_5066526.htm.

General Office of the State Council of the People's Republic of China. (2016b). *Guide to the construction of the technical system of "internet + government/public service*." http://www.gov.cn/zhengce/zhengceku/2017-01/12/content_5159174.htm.

General Office of the State Council of the People's Republic of China. (2016c). *Opinions on comprehensively promoting open government work*. http://www.gov.cn/zhengce/content/2016-11/15/content_5132852.htm.

General Office of the State Council of the People's Republic of China. (2017a). *Circular on the inspection of the national internet government service platform—National internet government service platform inspection indicators*. http://www.gov.cn/zhengce/zhengceku/2017-11/03/content_5236744.htm.

General Office of the State Council of the People's Republic of China. (2017b). *Implementation plan for the integration and sharing of government information systems*. http://www.gov.cn/zhengce/content/2017-05/18/content_5194971.htm.

General Office of the State Council of the People's Republic of China. (2018a). *Implementation plan on deepening "internet + government/public service" and promoting the reform of "one website portal, one door and one time" of Government Affairs Service*. http://www.gov.cn/zhengce/zhengceku/2018-06/22/content_5300516.htm.

General Office of the State Council of the People's Republic of China. (2018b). *Opinions on Promoting the Healthy and Orderly Development of New Media for Government Affairs*. http://www.gov.cn/zhengce/content/2018-12/27/content_5352666.htm.

General Office of the State Council of the People's Republic of China. (2019a). *"Government websites and new government media inspection indicators" and "annual assessment indicators for the supervision of government websites and new government media."* http://www.gov.cn/zhengce/content/2019-04/18/content_5384134.htm.

General Office of the State Council of the People's Republic of China. (2019b). *Opinions of the General Office of the State Council on Establishing a "Good and Bad Review" System for government services to improve the level of government services*. http://www.gov.cn/gongbao/content/2020/content_5467511.htm.

General Office of the State Council of the People's Republic of China. (2020a). *Development plan of new energy automotive industry (2021-2035)*. http://www.gov.cn/zhengce/content/2020-11/02/content_5556716.htm.

General Office of the State Council of the People's Republic of China. (2020b). *Guidance on accelerating the "cross-provincial" government services*. http://www.gov.cn/zhengce/zhengceku/2020-09/29/content_5548125.htm.

General Office of the State Council of the People's Republic of China. (2020c). *Implementation plan for effectively solving the difficulties of the elderly in using intelligent technology*. http://www.gov.cn/zhengce/content/2020-11/24/content_5563804.htm.

General Office of the State Council of the People's Republic of China. (2020d). *Measures for the construction and management of national government informatization projects*. http://www.gov.cn/zhengce/content/2020-01/21/content_5471256.htm.

General Office of the State Council of the People's Republic of China. (2021). *Guide to the construction of the mobile end of the national integrated government service platform*. http://www.gov.cn/zhengce/zhengceku/2021-11/12/content_5650485.htm.

Guo, W. (2021, May 24). 公安部一所参与制定的个人健康信息码国家标准发布 (Publication of national standards for personal health information codes). 安信*CTID*. Retrieved February 9, 2022, from https://tinyurl.com/y9jqkmwm.

Huang, H. (2020). 中国"数字政府"的政策演变—兼论"数字政府"与"电子政务"的关系 [The policy evolution of China's "digital government"—Also on the relationship between "digital government" and "E-government"]. 行政论坛 [*Administrative Tribune*], 27.

Huddleston Jr., T. (2020, March 26). The SARS epidemic threatened Alibaba's survival in 2003—Here's how it made it through to become a $470 billion company. *CNBC*. Retrieved January 26, 2022, from https://www.cnbc.com/2020/03/26/chinas-2002-2003-sars-outbreak-helped-alibaba-become-e-commerce-giant.html.

Informatization Office of the State Council. (2021, December 11). *Baidu Baike*. https://web.archive.org/web/20221215183821/https://baike.baidu.com/item/%E5%9B%BD%E5%8A%A1%E9%99%A2%E4%BF%A1%E6%81%AF%E5%8C%96%E5%B7%A5%E4%BD%9C%E5%8A%9E%E5%85%AC%E5%AE%A4/3463404.

International Institute for Management Development. (2021a). *Digital competitiveness ranking: China*. https://worldcompetitiveness.imd.org/countryprofile/CN/digital.

International Institute for Management Development. (2021b). *Digital competitiveness ranking: Hong Kong*. https://worldcompetitiveness.imd.org/countryprofile/HK/digital.

Legislation Law of the People's Republic of China. (2015). Law Info China. http://web.archive.org/web/20220604101541/http://lawinfochina.com/display.aspx?id=19023&lib=law.

Li, K. (2015). *Li Keqiang: Give birth to new momentum to achieve development and upgrading*. http://www.gov.cn/guowuyuan/2015-10/16/content_2947730.htm.

Li, Y. (2020). '新基建，是什么？(What Is New Infrastructure)' (Xinhua Net, 2020) http://www.xinhuanet.com/2020-04/26/c_1125908061.htm accessed 27 January 2022.

Li, N., & Lu, Q. (2022, April 1). 数字人民币(试点版)APP来了，已上架各大应用商店 [E-CNY App is being piloted, and it has appeared in major app stores]. *People.cn*. Retrieved February 14, 2022, from http://finance.people.com.cn/n1/2022/0104/c1004-32323727.html.

Long, Y., & Wang, X. (2021, June 25). 构建"开源"创新体系，助力我国关键数字技术"弯道超车" [Building "open source" innovation system to help China's key digital technologies "bend and overtake"]. *ST Daily*. Retrieved January 30, 2022, from http://www.stdaily.com/index/h1t14/2021-06/25/content_1163056.shtml.

Miao, W., & Lei, W. (2016). Policy review: The Cyberspace Administration of China. *Global Media and Communication, 12*.

Ministry of Commerce. (2020). *Overall scheme for comprehensively deepening the innovation and development of service trade*. http://www.gov.cn/zhengce/zhengceku/2020-08/14/5534759/files/206b8f5f563c4ed5a066d6dd7a833e95.pdf.

Ministry of Education. (2018). *Colleges and universities artificial intelligence innovation action plan*. http://www.moe.gov.cn/srcsite/A16/s7062/201804/t20180410_332722.html.

Ministry of Finance. (2018). *Interim measures for the administration of government procurement in the government information system*. http://www.gov.cn/xinwen/2018-01/03/content_5252794.htm.

Ministry of Finance, Ministry of Human Resources and Social Security & Ministry of Natural Resources. (2021). *Circular on strengthening the management and collection of government*

non-tax revenue in the cross-provincial universal handling of Government Affairs Services. http://www.gov.cn/zhengce/zhengceku/2021-03/09/content_5591836.htm
Ministry of Finance & National Development and Reform Commission. (2008). *Notice on relevant issues such as charging for providing government public information*. https://www.mee.gov.cn/ywgz/fgbz/gz/200806/t20080623_124444.shtml.
Ministry of Foreign Affairs of the People's Republic of China. (2016a). *China's National Plan on Implementation of the 2030 Agenda for Sustainable Development*. https://www.fmprc.gov.cn/mfa_eng/topics_665678/2030kcxfzyc/201704/P020210525474822784501.pdf.
Ministry of Foreign Affairs of the People's Republic of China. (2016b). *China's position paper on the Implementation of the 2030 Agenda for Sustainable Development*. https://www.fmprc.gov.cn/mfa_eng/topics_665678/2030kcxfzyc/201811/t20181129_701773.html.
Ministry of Foreign Affairs of the People's Republic of China. (2017). *China's progress report on Implementation of the 2030 Agenda for Sustainable Development*. https://www.fmprc.gov.cn/mfa_eng/topics_665678/2030kcxfzyc/201708/P020210525474841044350.pdf.
Ministry of Foreign Affairs of the People's Republic of China. (2019). *China's progress report on Implementation of the 2030 Agenda for Sustainable Development*. https://www.fmprc.gov.cn/mfa_eng/topics_665678/2030kcxfzyc/201909/P020210525474868189879.pdf.
Ministry of Foreign Affairs of the People's Republic of China. (2021). *China's VNR report on Implementation of the 2030 Agenda for Sustainable Development*. https://www.fmprc.gov.cn/mfa_eng/topics_665678/2030kcxfzyc/202107/P020210912747378573318.pdf.
Ministry of Foreign Affairs of the People's Republic of China. (n.d.). *The 2030 Agenda for Sustainable Development*. https://www.fmprc.gov.cn/mfa_eng/topics_665678/2030kcxfzyc/.
Ministry of Housing and Urban-Rural Development & Ministry of Industry and Information Technology. (2021a). *Notice on determining the first batch of pilot cities for the coordinated development of smart city infrastructure and intelligent network vehicles*. http://www.gov.cn/zhengce/zhengceku/2021-05/07/content_5605031.htm.
Ministry of Housing and Urban-Rural Development & Ministry of Industry and Information Technology. (2021b). *Notice on determining the second batch of pilot cities for the coordinated development of smart city infrastructure and intelligent network vehicles*. https://wap.miit.gov.cn/xwdt/gxdt/sjdt/art/2021/art_2aeec69fc4594eea8c6e6f0aa073a8ed.html.
Ministry of Industry and Information Technology. (2006). *Overall framework of national E-government*. https://www.mct.gov.cn/gtb/index.jsp?url=https://www.mct.gov.cn/whzx/zxgz/whbwlaqhxxhgz/xxhjs_whaq/201111/t20111129_800690.htm.
Ministry of Industry and Information Technology. (2017). *Three-year action plan for promoting the development of the next-generation artificial intelligence industry (2018-2020)*. http://www.cac.gov.cn/2017-12/15/c_1122114520.htm.
Ministry of Industry and Information Technology. (2020). *Special action programme on ageing-friendly and barrier-free adaptation of internet apps*. http://www.gov.cn/zhengce/zhengceku/2020-12/26/content_5573472.htm.
Ministry of Industry and Information Technology. (2021). *14th Five-Year Software and Information Technology Services Development Plan*. http://www.gov.cn/zhengce/zhengceku/2021-12/01/content_5655205.htm.
Ministry of Industry and Information Technology & China Disabled Persons' Federation. (2020). *Guiding opinions on promoting information accessibility*. http://www.gov.cn/gongbao/content/2020/content_5570087.htm.
MPayPass. (2020, April 24). 健康码未来将走向何方? [Where will the health code go in the future?]. *The Paper*. Retrieved February 10, 2022, from https://www.thepaper.cn/newsDetail_forward_7117399.
National Bureau of Surveying, Mapping and Geographic Information. (2017). *Notice on accelerating the pilot work of promoting the construction of spatio-temporal big data and cloud platform in smart cities*. http://fgcx.bjcourt.gov.cn:4601/law?fn=chl541s581.txt&dbt=chl.
National Development and Reform Commission. (2014a). *Circular of the National Development and Reform Commission, the Ministry of Industry and Information Technology, the Ministry of*

Science and Technology and other eight departments on the issuance of guidance on promoting the healthy development of smart cities. Cyberspace Administration of China. http://www.cac.gov.cn/2014-08/27/c_1112850680.htm.

National Development and Reform Commission. (2014b). *Notice of guidance for healthy development*. Cyberspace Administration of China. http://www.cac.gov.cn/2014-08/27/c_1112850680.htm.

National Development and Reform Commission. (2016). *Circular of the General Office of the National Development and Reform Commission, the Secretary Bureau of the Cyberspace Administration of China, and the Office of the Standardization Administration of China on organizing the evaluation of new-type smart cities to promote the healthy and rapid development of new-type smart cities in a pragmatic manner*. https://www.ndrc.gov.cn/xxgk/zcfb/tz/201611/t20161128_962791.html?code=&state=123.

National Development and Reform Commission. (2021). *14th Five-Year National Informatization Plan (NIP)*. http://www.gov.cn/zhengce/zhengceku/2022-01/06/5666746/files/cbff2937df654b44a04c6ef9d43549e9.pdf.

National Development and Reform Commission. (2022). *14th Five-Year Public Service Plan (PSP)*. https://www.ndrc.gov.cn/xxgk/zcfb/ghwb/202201/P020220110357049883156.pdf.

National Development and Reform Commission & Cyberspace Administration of China. (2017). *Guidelines for the preparation of government information resource catalogues (trial)*. https://www.gov.cn/xinwen/2017-07/13/5210203/files/2415d43d2bcb4dfe9c3f1e1b5c0626c1.pdf.

National Informatization Leading Group. (2002). *Guiding opinions concerning our country's E-government construction*. China Copyright and Media. https://chinacopyrightandmedia.wordpress.com/2002/08/05/national-informatization-leading-group-guiding-opinions-concerning-our-countrys-e-government-construction/.

National Informatization Leading Group. (2005). *Guidance on e-government construction*. China Information Technology Security Evaluation Center. http://www.itsec.gov.cn/fgbz/xgfg/200507/t20050711_15267.html.

National Integrated Government Service Platform. (2022). *Home*. http://gjzwfw.www.gov.cn/.

National People's Congress of the People's Republic of China. (2018). *Law of the People's Republic of China on the protection of persons with disabilities*. http://www.npc.gov.cn/zgrdw/npc/xinwen/2018-11/05/content_2065632.htm.

National People's Congress of the People's Republic of China. (2021). *Data Security Law—Official English translation*. http://www.npc.gov.cn/englishnpc/c23934/202112/1abd8829788946ecab270e469b13c39c.shtml.

National Public Service Platform for Standards Information. (2018). *Information security technology—Security technique requirements for citizen cyber electronic identity*. https://tinyurl.com/y9zcr785.

National Public Service Platform for Standards Information. (2021). *Cyber authentication service for resident identity*. https://tinyurl.com/yb7evxda.

People's Bank of China. (2021). 中国数字人民币的研发进展白皮书媒体吹风会文字实录 [The progress of research development of E-CNY in China: A transcript of the white paper media briefing]. http://www.pbc.gov.cn/rmyh/3963412/3963426/4294165/index.html.

People's Bank of China Digital Currency Institute. (2021, February 25). 中国人民银行数字货币研究所加入多边央行数字货币桥研究项目 [The People's Bank of China Digital Currency Research Institute joined the Multilateral Central Bank Digital Currency Bridge Research Project]. *Shanghai Local Financial Supervision Administration*. Retrieved February 14, 2022, from http://jrj.sh.gov.cn/ZXYW178/20210225/e94237dbb06a47adb54f6f5f54ebed0f.html.

Standardization Administration of the People's Republic of China. (2014). *Standardized guidelines for E-government—Part 5: Underlying technology*. http://openstd.samr.gov.cn/bzgk/gb/newGbInfo?hcno=420004A7A5ED6ECA9C5196D17B4691AA.

Standardization Administration of the People's Republic of China, Cyberspace Administration of China, National Development and Reform Commission, Ministry of Science and Technology & Ministry of Industry and Information Technology. (2020). *Guidelines for the development of the national new generation artificial intelligence standard system*. http://www.gov.cn/zhengce/zhengceku/2020-08/09/content_5533454.htm.

State Administration for Market Regulation. (2021). *Measures for the supervision and administration of online trading*. https://gkml.samr.gov.cn/nsjg/fgs/202103/t20210315_326936.html.

State Council of the People's Republic of China. (2012). *Administrative regulation on the construction of a barrier-free environment*. http://www.gov.cn/zwgk/2012-07/10/content_2179864.htm.

State Council of the People's Republic of China. (2015a). *Interim measures for the management of government information resource sharing*. http://www.gov.cn/zhengce/content/2016-09/19/content_5109486.htm.

State Council of the People's Republic of China. (2015b). *Notice on the action plan for promoting the development of big data*. http://www.gov.cn/zhengce/content/2015-09/05/content_10137.htm.

State Council of the People's Republic of China. (2015c). *Opinions on promoting the innovative development of cloud computing and cultivating new business models of the information industry*. http://www.gov.cn/zhengce/content/2015-01/30/content_9440.htm.

State Council of the People's Republic of China. (2015d). *State council's guidance on actively promoting "internet plus*." http://www.gov.cn/zhengce/content/2015-07/04/content_10002.htm.

State Council of the People's Republic of China. (2016a). *Circular on further promoting some opinions on new urbanization*. http://www.gov.cn/zhengce/content/2016-02/06/content_5039947.htm039947.htm.

State Council of the People's Republic of China. (2016b). *Guidance on accelerating the promotion of "internet + government/public services*." http://www.gov.cn/zhengce/zhengceku/2016-09/29/content_5113369.htm.

State Council of the People's Republic of China. (2016c). *The State Council's guiding opinions on accelerating the work of "internet + government services*." http://www.gov.cn/zhengce/content/2016-09/29/content_5113369.htm.

State Council of the People's Republic of China. (2017). *Plan for the development of next-generation artificial intelligence*. http://www.gov.cn/zhengce/content/2017-07/20/content_5211996.htm.

State Council of the People's Republic of China. (2018). *Guiding opinions of the State Council on speeding up the construction of the national integrated online government service platform*. http://www.gov.cn/zhengce/zhengceku/2018-07/31/content_5310797.htm.

State Council of the People's Republic of China. (2019). *Provisions of the State Council on online government service*. http://www.gov.cn/gongbao/content/2019/content_5389312.htm.

State Council of the People's Republic of China. (2021a). *14th Five-Year Plan on the Development of Modern Comprehensive Transportation System*. http://www.gov.cn/zhengce/content/2022-01/18/content_5669049.htm.

State Council of the People's Republic of China. (2021b). *14th Five-Year Plan on the Development of the Digital Economy*. http://www.gov.cn/zhengce/content/2022-01/12/content_5667817.htm.

State Council of the People's Republic of China. (2021c). *14th Five-Year Protection and Development Plan for the Disabled*. http://www.gov.cn/gongbao/content/2021/content_5629604.htm.

State Information Center Smarter City Development and Research Center. (2014). 促进智慧城市健康发展部际协调工作组第一次会议在国家信息中心举行 [*The first meeting of the Interministerial Coordination Working Group on promoting the healthy development of smart cities was held at the National Information Center*]. http://scdrc.sic.gov.cn/News/339/4080.htm.

State Information Office of the People's Republic of China. (2021). *Guidance on strengthening the comprehensive governance of internet information service algorithms*. http://www.moe.gov.cn/jyb_xxgk/moe_1777/moe_1779/202109/t20210929_568182.html.

Tang, F. (2022, January 21). As US wades into digital currency arena, China's E-Yuan already has a big head start. *South China Morning Post*. Retrieved February 14, 2022, from https://www.scmp.com/economy/china-economy/article/3164283/us-wades-digital-currency-arena-chinas-e-yuan-already-has-big.

The World Bank. (2016). *Digital Adoption Index*. https://www.worldbank.org/en/publication/wdr2016/Digital-Adoption-Index.

Third Research Institute of the Ministry of Public Security. (2018). *White paper on the eID digital identity system*. http://web.archive.org/web/20181212193421/https://eid.cn/digid/introduce.html.

United Nations Department of Economic and Social Affairs. (2020). *E-government survey 2020: Digital government in the decade of action for sustainable development with addendum on COVID-19 response*. https://publicadministration.un.org/egovkb/Portals/egovkb/Documents/un/2020-Survey/2020%20UN%20E-Government%20Survey%20(Full%20Report).pdf.

Working Group at Peking University & Huang, H. (2020). 平台驱动的数字政府:能力、转型与现代化 [Platform-driven digital government: Capacity, transformation and modernization]. 电子政务 *[E-Government], 2*.

Working Group on E-CNY Research and Development of the People's Bank of China. (2021). *Progress of research & development of E-CNY in China*. http://www.pbc.gov.cn/en/3688110/3688172/4157443/4293696/2021071614584691871.pdf.

Xian News. (2018, June 18). 全国不动产登记信息管理平台已实现全国联网 [The national real estate registration information management platform has been connected to the national network]. *CNR*. Retrieved February 11, 2022, from http://www.cnr.cn/sxpd/shgl/20180618/t20180618_524273650.shtml.

Xinhua. (2018, April 23). *The Digital China Development Report (2017) was released*. Cyberspace Administration of China. http://www.cac.gov.cn/2018-04/23/c_1122728917.htm.

Xinhua Net. (2014). 不动产统一登记制度启动在即 *[The unified real estate registration system is about to start]*. Retrieved February 11, 2022, from http://www.xinhuanet.com/house/sh/zt/140411_bdc/140411_bdc.html.

Xinhua Net. (2019, December 21). *Central economic work conference held in Beijing: Xi Jinping and Li Keqiang made important speeches*. http://www.xinhuanet.com/politics/leaders/2018-12/21/c_1123887379.htm.

Xinhua News Agency. (2011). *Outline of the 12th Five-Year Plan for National Economic and Social Development*. http://www.gov.cn/2011lh/content_1825838.htm.

Xinhua News Agency. (2014, March 16). *National new urbanization plan (2014-2020)*. Central Government Portal. http://www.gov.cn/zhengce/2014-03/16/content_2640075.htm.

Xinhua News Agency. (2016a). *Outline of the 13th Five-Year Plan for National Economic and Social Development of the People's Republic of China*. http://www.gov.cn/xinwen/2016-03/17/content_5054992.htm.

Xinhua News Agency. (2016b, July 27). *The General Office of the CPC Central Committee and the General Office of the State Council issued the outline of the National Informatization Development Strategy*. State Council of the People's Republic of China. http://www.gov.cn/zhengce/2016-07/27/content_5095336.htm.

Xinhua News Agency. (2020, September 4). *CPC Central Committee and State Council opinions on strengthening the institutional mechanism for market-based allocation of factors*. http://www.gov.cn/zhengce/2020-04/09/content_5500622.htm.

Xinhua News Agency. (2021a). *Outline of the 14th Five-Year Plan for National Economic and Social Development of the People's Republic of China and the long-range goals for 2035*. http://www.gov.cn/xinwen/2021-03/13/content_5592681.htm.

Xinhua News Agency. (2021b, September 14). *The General Office of the CPC Central Committee and the General Office of the State Council issued the "opinions on strengthening the construction of cyberspace civilization."* State Council of the People's Republic of China. http://www.gov.cn/xinwen/2021-09/14/content_5637195.htm.

Xinhua News Agency. (2021c, October 1). *The Central Committee of the Communist Party of China issued the Rule-of-Law (RoL) China Construction Plan (2020-2025)*. State Council of the People's Republic of China. http://www.gov.cn/zhengce/2021-01/10/content_5578659.htm.

Xinhua News Agency. (2021d, October 10). *The CPC Central Committee and the State Council issued the National Standardization Development Outline*. http://www.gov.cn/zhengce/2021-10/10/content_5641727.htm.

Xinhuanet. (2014, February 27). 中央网络安全和信息化领导小组成立:从网络大国迈向强国 [Establishment of the Central Cyberspace Affairs Leading Group: From a cyber gigantic country to a cyber powerful country]. *People.com*. Retrieved February 7, 2022, from http://cpc.people.com.cn/n/2014/0227/c64094-24486382.html.

Yiou. (2021). *2021 China VR/AR industry research report and China innovation 50 companies list*. https://pdf.dfcfw.com/pdf/H3_AP202107121503391467_1.pdf?1626129540000.pdf.

Zhou, C. (2020a, October 20). China digital currency: Shenzhen consumers spend 8.8 million yuan in largest trial of digital yuan. *South China Morning Post*. Retrieved February 14, 2022, from https://www.scmp.com/economy/china-economy/article/3106265/china-digital-currency-shenzhen-consumers-spend-88-million?module=inline&pgtype=article.

Zhou, C. (2020b, December 5). China digital currency: Suzhou to hand out 20 million yuan of virtual red packets as part of trial. *South China Morning Post*. Retrieved February 14, 2022, from https://www.scmp.com/economy/china-economy/article/3112724/chinese-city-hand-out-virtual-red-packets-part-digital-yuan?module=inline&pgtype=article.

Zhou, Z. (2020c, September 29). 落子上海，央行数研所将成立第四家金融科技公司 [In Shanghai, a fourth fintech company will be set up by the Central Bank's Research Institute]. *LeiPhone*. Retrieved February 14, 2022, from https://www.leiphone.com/category/fintech/7o0pVU6M6sfiYii8.html.

Wayne Wei Wang is a PhD candidate in Law and Technology at the University of Hong Kong and a CyberBRICS Fellow at the FGV Center for Technology and Society (Brazil). With an interdisciplinary background in Engineering and Law, his research focuses on Intellectual Property, Data Protection, AI Governance, and Science & Technology Studies, with an emphasis on Law, Innovation, Sustainability, and Technology (LIST) in the Global South. Wayne holds an LLM from WIPO-QUT (Australia) and is an Associate Fellow of the UK Higher Education Academy.

Digital Transformation Reality Check: Addressing the Internet Usage Gap in South Africa

Senka Hadzic

Abstract The paper explores Internet access in South Africa, highlighting its reliance on affordable prepaid mobile data and the affordability divide caused by income inequalities. It examines infrastructure and policy developments, addressing barriers to digital transformation as the country aims to lead in the Fourth Industrial Revolution.

1 Introduction

Internet access in South Africa is predominantly mobile, and one of the reasons is the availability of prepaid (top-up on demand) data packages that can be purchased incrementally at relatively low cost, instead of committing to a monthly subscription. Affordability remains the major obstacle to higher Internet penetration rates in the country. According to the UN Broadband Commission, affordability of data prices is defined as the price of 1 GB of data having to be less than 2% of disposable income. In South Africa, due to the large inequalities and disparities in disposable income, it is the affordability divide between the low-income and high-income South Africans that is creating barriers to connecting the unconnected. At the same time, the country is looking to become a leader in implementing the Fourth Industrial Revolution. This paper presents an overview of the current state of Internet access in South Africa, underlying infrastructure and policy developments, to understand the bottlenecks for proceeding with the digital transformation agenda—which does not come without its own controversies.

S. Hadzic (✉)
Research ICT Africa, Cape Town, South Africa

CyberBRICS, Law School, Fundação Getúlio Vargas, Rio de Janeiro, Brazil

L. Belli, L. Galdino de Magalhães Santos (eds.), *SmartBRICS*,
https://doi.org/10.1007/978-3-031-98204-0_14

2 South Africa's Digital Transformation

In 2017, the (former) Department of Telecommunications and Postal Services (DTPS)—now Department of Communications and Digital Technologies (DCDT)—developed the National e-Government Strategy and Roadmap (DTPS, 2017a) aimed at modernising and transforming future public service delivery. The strategy was developed in terms of the Electronic and Communications Transaction Act and the National Integrated ICT Policy White Paper (2016). In this document, e-Government refers broadly to the use of information and communication technologies to link citizens and the public sector and facilitate collaborative and efficient governance. It was published together with an enabling coordinated and integrated National e-Strategy (DTPS, 2017b), which cuts across government departments and sectors, and guides the national e-government strategy. The purpose of the National e-Government Strategy and Roadmap is to guide the digital transformation of public service in South Africa into an inclusive digital society.

In April 2019, the Presidential Commission on the Fourth Industrial Revolution (PC4IR) was appointed to develop a 4IR strategy for South Africa. The PC4IR report (PC4IR, 2020) can be seen as a broader digital transformation strategy as it addresses issues beyond government services. The Commission, chaired by the President, is tasked with identifying relevant policies, strategies and action plans to help South Africa become a major player in 4IR. The Commission comprises thirty members from a variety of stakeholder groups (including government, business, labour, civil society, academia) and needs to act accordingly to guarantee alignment with the National Development Plan. The Department of Communications and Digital Technologies is the lead department within the government tasked with driving 4IR readiness for the country.

Multiple entities are involved in the country's innovation-related policies and programmes: Department of Science and Innovation (DSI) (formerly the Department for Science and Technology (DST)), the Department for Trade, Industry and Competition (DTIC), the Department of Planning, Monitoring and Evaluation, and the Technology Innovation Agency (TIA). In addition, a number of other ministries are involved in broader elements of related policy development and implementation. These government entities cooperate with various actors, such as research councils, universities, and industry associations, in developing national policies and programmes.

PC4IR was appointed in April 2019, and 4IR became clearly the priority for the country's newly elected government in May 2019: since then, every new digital policy, independent of the sector, has been shaped around the 4IR context. As all efforts were suddenly concentrated on developing a 4IR policy, some ongoing developments were somewhat abandoned, including the critical allocation of high-demand spectrum, which at that moment was crucial for broadband expansion and affordable access. The excessive attention given to the topic has been widely criticised—mostly for its technological lens leading to digital paradox and amplified inequalities, the fact that digital policies are being developed in siloes, instead of an integrated approach across sectors (Gillwald, 2019b), and for eventually being a distraction from unfinished policy processes and institutional failures (Gillwald, 2019a). Further critique includes focus on 4IR and technologies which do not acknowledge the inequalities in schools, differences in educational performance, and lack of facilities and basic resources in South African schools (Carrim, 2022). While the science, technology and innovation landscape may be characterised by strong institutions, the lack of interaction among the key actors poses a challenge in South Africa's path to a leadership position in 4IR (Jegede, 2021; Jegede & Ncube, 2021).

The Centre for the Fourth Industrial Revolution (C4IR) is an initiative of the South African government, acting through the Department of Science and Innovation. It is hosted by the Council for Scientific and Industrial Research (CSIR) and is part of a global network of centres for 4IR (C4IR Network), via a collaboration agreement with the World Economic Forum (WEF). The C4IR Network facilitates the sharing of global insights and best practices in technology governance among members. The centre was founded in 2021 and serves as a multistakeholder hub, enabling collaboration between businesses, government and academia.

3 Challenges to the 4IR Agenda

It is necessary to highlight the obstacles to implementing the 4IR agenda in a sustainable manner. The major challenge is undoubtedly the current state of Internet access in the country, but there are also other policy-regulatory, infrastructural and financial challenges.

3.1 The Context of Internet Access and Usage

According to the global information and communication technology (ICT) indices[1] South Africa, in most cases, ranks in the middle globally; however, in the African context, it often ranks significantly higher than other African states. Some of these indices reveal that South Africa has a relatively strong ICT governance framework and generally favourable policies, even though these remain largely unimplemented. At the same time, the country performs poorly on demand-side indices such as Internet uptake, skills and digital awareness.

For example, the World Economic Forum's Network Readiness Index (NRI) focuses on international competitiveness. In the 2021 evaluation, South Africa was

[1] Global ICT indices include International Telecommunication Union (ITU) ICT Development Index (IDI), World Economic Forum (WEF) Network Readiness Index (NRI), Alliance for Affordable Internet (A4AI) Affordability Drivers Index, GSMA's Mobile Connectivity Index (MCI).

ranked 70th out of 130 countries, with an overall score of 48.88 (Portulans Institute, 2022). The score on 'governance'—which includes regulation—was relatively high—61.25; however, due to the low uptake (the score on 'people' and 'impact' was 46.42 and 42.25, respectively), the overall rank dropped significantly. The 'technology' score was 45.59.

GSMA's Mobile Connectivity Index (2022) looks at mobile Internet uptake. South Africa scored 64.5 in the 2021 evaluation of the index, scoring 65, 53.9, 74.0, 67.0 in infrastructure, affordability, consumer readiness and content and services, respectively (GSMA, 2021).

The infrastructure index calculation is based on network coverage (90.8), network performance (60.4), other enabling infrastructure (67.4) and spectrum (30.7). Obviously, the fact that South Africa has failed to release high-demand spectrum contributes to the low overall infrastructure index. Favourable taxation (85.4) does not compensate for extremely high levels of income inequality (0.0) and high mobile tariffs; hence, the affordability index is the weakest of all four components. The affordability index is additionally composed of handset price (47.9) and mobile tariffs (74.7). The consumer readiness index is calculated based on mobile ownership (75.5), basic skills (61.9) and gender equality (85.4). Content and services index calculation is based on local relevance (64.6), availability (63.6) and online security (78.5).

According to Research ICT Africa's After Access survey data from 2017 (Gillwald et al., 2021), 53% of South Africans have access to the Internet. A more recent figure, the ITU estimate from 2020, suggests that 70% of South Africans are online (World Bank, 2020).

Demand-side data (such as those gathered by the After Access survey) is essential for getting an accurate picture of broadband availability, adoption, and usage. They complement supply-side data and together form the basis for good policy-making. The fact that data collection generally is a labour-intensive and costly process leads to the situation where demand-side data tends to be most incomplete in underserved places—and those would benefit most from new interventions. It is equally critical to have up-to-date information about the demand side, especially having in mind the fast-changing technological development and uptake of digital tools, services and platforms. After extensive data collection in 2017 in seven African countries, Research ICT Africa is performing another African After Access Survey in 2022.

3.2 *Institutional and Regulatory Aspects: Spectrum*

One of the crucial access policy issues that kept being deferred is the auction of high-demand spectrum, which is directly contributing to the affordability of mobile broadband. The developments around spectrum regulation reflect institutional instability in the sector. Since 2010, the Independent Communications Authority of South Africa (ICASA) has attempted to convene a spectrum auction three times during a decade—each time the auction was withdrawn. There are multiple causes of these serial auction failures, but one of them is clearly the lack of coherent vision from the Ministry, which has seen a high turnover of different ministers—thirteen ministers in 13 years—which has led to disputes between ICASA (the regulator) and the Ministry. Along with the repeated change in leadership, which caused disruption and discontinuity, ongoing clashes between ICASA's mandate and government (Ministerial) preferences on how and to whom spectrum should be allocated, together with constant legal battles between ICASA and the mobile operators, have been impeding progress in South Africa's telecommunications industry for over a decade.

One of the disruptions in spectrum allocation was due to COVID-19. After the South African government proclaimed a state of disaster at the end of March 2020, ICASA made additional radio spectrum available to ensure that the network could keep up with additional demand during the lockdown. The pace at which the temporary spectrum assignment was completed was eliciting hopes for a prompt realisation of the long-overdue permanent auction. Another act that demonstrated progressive thinking was offering TV white space (TVWS) portions of the spectrum—for the first time since the final TVWS regulations (Independent Communications Authority of South Africa [ICASA], 2018) were published in May 2018, three operators were granted access to secondary spectrum. Nevertheless, with the constant prolongation of the state of disaster and national lockdown, ICASA (2021b) kept extending the duration of the temporary spectrum assignment, and pushing back the auction deadline until early 2021, only to be met by two of the four national operators announcing a court case to stop the auction (Howell & Potgieter 2021). Eventually, the auction process resumed in early 2022 and was successfully completed with the Telkom lawsuit settled.

In September 2022, the DCDT published a new draft spectrum policy for public comment (DCDT, 2022). The Next Generation Radio Frequency Spectrum Policy for Economic Development (Spectrum Policy) supports the deployment and licensing of alternative infrastructure networks, and aims to adopt spectrum management approaches that promote participation of local small and medium enterprises (SMEs) and the emergence of new entrants into the ICT sector. Although still only a draft, it is a very progressive and inclusive spectrum policy, aiming to address gaps and limitations, including the failure to lower the cost of communications.

In such a dynamic sector as telecom regulation, both administrative decisions and the commercial interests for challenging them (as it has been done by operators) can be overtaken by sometimes unpredictable events. The integrity of regulatory functions is a matter of public interest. To fulfil the rationale of independent regulation, this is determined through public consultation. Indeed, it is the regulator's mandate to defend its decision against vested interests, public or private, if it believes it is safeguarding the public interest or fulfilling public policy objectives by which it is bound.

3.3 Infrastructure

Despite regulatory delays and deferred policy processes, the South African telecommunications sector has performed relatively well when it comes to infrastructure rollout, both regarding network extension and technology upgrades. The two major mobile operators, Vodacom and MTN provide mobile broadband coverage to over 95% of the South African population.

However, it is more than 5% of the population that remains unconnected, but approximately six times more. This is nothing unusual: the latest research by GSMA shows that on a global scale, mobile coverage has reached 95%. At the same time, 3.2 billion people, or 40% of the global population, who live in areas covered by mobile broadband, still face challenges in actually getting online ("Mobile Internet's…", 2022).

The challenges to connecting South Africa's remaining 30% of the population are, for the most part, demand-side challenges, a major barrier being the affordability of both prepaid data packages as well as smart devices. Further barriers include the lack of digital literacy skills and the lack of relevant content and services (Gillwald et al., 2021).

The fact that there is 95% coverage and yet a significant part of the population remains unconnected suggests evident flaws with the current approach, which fails to bring affordable connectivity to South Africans. Literature suggests that the almost universal mobile coverage is the result of market forces, and not necessarily a policy outcome (Lewis, 2017). The costs to roll out infrastructure to provide coverage to the remaining 5% of the population are disproportional. Existing operators are not eager to expand infrastructure into remote areas with low population density, where they do not see a business case and return on investment. Current regulations do not accommodate complementary access solutions such as community networks, which are bottom-up connectivity solutions deployed and owned by the communities themselves (Rey-Moreno & Pather, 2020).

Good quality infrastructure is, without doubt, the backbone for digital transformation. However, if this infrastructure does not provide affordable access to everyone, the perks of digitalisation may end up benefiting only the few.

3.4 Funding Universal Access and Service

South Africa's Universal Service and Access Fund (USAF) is managed by the Universal Service and Access Agency of South Africa (USAASA) and is financed by contributions from all holders of electronic communications network service (ECNS) and electronic communications service (ECS) licenses. The fund was established under the Electronic Communications Act (ECA, 2005) to fund projects and programmes that aim to achieve universal service and access to ICTs by all South African citizens. These are substantial funds and are solely meant to subsidise the provision of universal access to telecommunications services for people in underserviced areas, schools and further education and training institutions. As such, it is primarily focused on infrastructure initiatives—an additional focus includes subsidising the establishment and operation of centres where access to electronic communications networks can be obtained.

The Department of Communications and Digital Technologies tasked USAASA with a significant portion of the implementation of its Broadcasting Digital Migration (BDM) project. South Africa's migration from analogue to digital terrestrial television has encountered numerous delays and difficulties, resulting in the country missing the International Telecommunication Union's 2015 deadline to complete the full switch. The delays in the spectrum auction discussed in the previous section are also linked to the delayed analogue switch-off implementation. USAASA's task is to assist poor TV-owning households by subsidising the cost to acquire Set-Top Boxes and antennas for receiving digital terrestrial television at their homes. Installation services are provided through the USAF; however, the roll-out has been extremely inefficient and spending is non-transparent. This instance is one of the several cases where USAASA has faced repeated allegations of corruption and mismanagement.

On the other side, ICASA also failed to establish a coherent framework for the calculation of annual licence fees and USAF contributions, which led to the creation of loopholes that allow licensees to delay their payments. Overall, the regulator is facing a challenge to enforce compliance (Lewis, 2020).

The 4IR strategy itself highlights the current inefficient use of existing funds. The PC4IR report proposed that the effectiveness of this fund be reviewed and linked to a more integrated approach to digital infrastructure development, which includes skills development.

4 Conclusion

South Africa has developed some of the most progressive policies in promoting both broadband and digital transformation; however, significant challenges have been experienced in their implementation. Shifting departmental structures, frequent ministerial turnover and delayed auctioning of high-demand spectrum and mismanagement of universal service funds are some of the institutional challenges.

The PC4IR report acknowledges the role the telecommunication sector plays in 4IR initiatives, however mostly through the 5G lens. But whether 5G will support South Africa's *inclusive* transition into the 4IR is debatable. ICASA's report on readiness for 5G focuses largely on industrial applications (ICASA, 2021a). In that sense, it is not entirely clear what the specific 5G use cases are in the South African context that will benefit the end user. The new draft spectrum policy gives hope that the sector is moving in the right direction it remains to be seen what the consultation process brings and how the eventual implementation moves ahead.

Digital communication infrastructure is increasingly becoming an integral part of other sectors such as finance, health, education, and others—and this is not only the case in South Africa but globally. Broadband policies need to incorporate issues from these sectors, and the other way around (Broadband Commission for Sustainable Development, 2021).

References

Broadband Commission for Sustainable Development. (2021, September). *The state of broadband: People-centred approaches for universal broadband*. ITU. Retrieved March 14, 2023, from https://www.itu.int/dms_pub/itu-s/opb/pol/S-POL-BROADBAND.23-2021-PDF-E.pdf.

Carrim, N. (2022, February 10). 4IR in South Africa and some of its educational implications. *Journal of Education, 86*, 3–20. http://www.scielo.org.za/scielo.php?script=sci_arttext&pid=S2520-98682022000100002.

Department of Communications and Digital Technologies [DCDT]. (2022). *Next generation radio frequency spectrum draft policy*. Government Gazette No. 46873 (pp. 4–29). https://www.gov.za/documents/communications-and-digital-technologies-next-generation-radio-frequency-spectrum-policy.

Department of Telecommunications and Postal Services [DTPS]. (2017a). *National e-government strategy and roadmap*. Government Gazette No. 40772 (pp. 490–584). https://www.dtps.gov.za/images/phocagallery/Popular_Topic_Pictures/40772_7-4_NationalGovernment(1).pdf.

Department of Telecommunications and Postal Services [DTPS]. (2017b). *National e-strategy: Technology working for the people to build an information and knowledge society*. Government Gazette No. 40772 (pp. 586–614). https://www.dtps.gov.za/images/phocagallery/Popular_Topic_Pictures/40772_7-4_NationalGovernment(1).pdf.

Gillwald, A. (2019a, October 4). *SA must be wary of big promises made about 4IR*. TechCentral. Retrieved March 13, 2023, from https://techcentral.co.za/sa-must-be-wary-of-big-promises-made-about-4ir/180191/.

Gillwald, A. (2019b, July 8). *4IR in SA is too important to remain in the domain of the elite*. Research ICT Africa. Retrieved March 13, 2023, from https://researchictafrica.net/2019/07/08/4ir-in-sa-is-too-important-to-remain-the-domain-of-the-elite/.

Gillwald, A., Mothobi, O., & Rademan, B. (2021, September 11). *After access: The state of ICT in South Africa*. Research ICT Africa. Retrieved March 13, 2023, from https://researchictafrica.net/publication/state-of-ict-in-south-africa/.

GSMA. (2021). *GSMA Mobile Connectivity Index: South Africa*. Retrieved March 14, 2023, from https://www.mobileconnectivityindex.com/#year=2021&zoneIsocode=ZAF.

GSMA. (2022). *GSMA Mobile Connectivity Index 2022*. Retrieved March 14, 2023, from https://www.mobileconnectivityindex.com/.

Howell, B., & Potgieter, P. (2021, January 1). Spectrum shortage and merger by any other name in South Africa. In *23rd biennial conference of the International Telecommunications Society (ITS)*. https://openaccess.wgtn.ac.nz/articles/conference_contribution/Spectrum_shortage_and_merger_by_any_other_name_in_South_Africa/19567210.

Independent Communications Authority of South Africa [ICASA]. (2018). *Regulations on the use of television white spaces 2018*. Government Gazette No. 41512 (pp. 1913–1930). https://www.icasa.org.za/legislation-and-regulations/regulations-on-the-use-of-television-white-spaces-2018.

Independent Communications Authority of South Africa [ICASA]. (2021a). *The state of 5G in South Africa: From readiness to recommendations*. https://www.icasa.org.za/uploads/files/ICASA-2021-5G-Annual-Report.pdf.

Independent Communications Authority of South Africa [ICASA]. (2021b, August 30). *Three months grace period to allow licensees to wind down their use of temporary radio frequency spectrum*. Retrieved March 13, 2023, from https://www.icasa.org.za/news/2021/three-months-grace-period-to-allow-licensees-to-wind-down-their-use-of-temporary-radio-frequency-spectrum.

Jegede, O. (2021, September). Backdrop of research and innovation in South Africa: Implications for Fourth Industrial Revolution. In F. Matos, M. F. Ferreiro, A. Rosa, & I. Salavisa (Eds.), *Proceedings of the 16th European conference on innovation and entrepreneurship ECIE 2021* (pp. 452–459). Academic Conferences International Limited. https://www.researchgate.net/publication/354330883_Backdrop_of_Research_and_Innovation_in_South_Africa_Implications_for_Fourth_Industrial_Revolution.

Jegede, O., & Ncube, C. (2021). Science, Technology, innovation management for industrial development in South Africa: Implications for the Fourth Industrial Revolution. *International Journal of Innovation, Creativity and Change, 15*(9), 673–695. https://www.ijicc.net/images/Vol_15/Iss_9/15965_Jegede_2021_E_R.pdf

Lewis, C. (2017). *Universal access and service in South Africa: Policy success, policy failure and policy impact*. SSRN. https://ssrn.com/abstract=2980803.

Lewis, C. (2020). *Regulating telecommunications in South Africa: Universal access and service*. Palgrave Macmillan. https://link.springer.com/book/10.1007/978-3-030-43527-1

Mobile internet's 'usage gap' is almost eight times the size of the 'coverage gap', GSMA research reveals. (2022, October 19). *GSMA*. Retrieved March 13, 2023, from https://www.gsma.com/newsroom/press-release/mobile-internets-usage-gap-is-almost-eight-times-the-size-of-the-coverage-gap-gsma-research-reveals/.

Portulans Institute. (2022). *Network Readiness Index: South Africa*. Retrieved March 14, 2023, from https://networkreadinessindex.org/countries/south-africa/.

Presidential Commission on the Fourth Industrial Revolution [PC4IR]. (2020). *Summary report & recommendations*. Retrieved March 14, 2023, from https://www.gov.za/sites/default/files/gcis_document/202010/43834gen591.pdf.

Rey-Moreno, C., & Pather, S. (2020). Advancing rural connectivity in South Africa through policy and regulation: A case for community networks. In *2020 IST-Africa conference (IST-Africa)* (pp. 1–10).

World Bank. (2020). *Individuals using the internet (% of population)—South Africa*. Retrieved March 14, 2023, from https://data.worldbank.org/indicator/IT.NET.USER.ZS?locations=ZA.

Senka Hadzic is a Senior Associate at Research ICT Africa, where she primarily researches alternative spectrum policies to enable small-scale operators and community networks. She was a post-doctoral fellow at the ICT for Development Centre at the University of Cape Town from 2016 to 2018. Her expertise is in low-cost connectivity solutions in the Global South, and she has consulted for a variety of organizations, including the International Telecommunication Union and Engineering for Change. Dr. Hadzic completed her PhD in Electronics and Telecommunications Engineering at the University of Aveiro (Portugal) in early 2014, and since then, she has been working at the intersection of technology, design, and policy. She is a CyberBRICS Fellow.

South Africa: An Overview of the Telecoms and Internet Access Sector

Senka Hadzic

Abstract This chapter develops an overview of the South African situation regarding access to Internet through the following matters: number of subscribers across different categories; affordability of services; type of technology being used; gender gap; urban-rural gap; ranking in the global ICT indices; strategy for expanding the Internet access; participation in institutions; telecommunications regulations in the country; access to the spectrum for data transmission; and financial resources.

1 Context

What is the state of Internet access in the country, in terms of

This section is based on data from Research ICT Africa's report 'State of ICTs in South Africa' (Gillwald et al., 2018) and the policy brief 'After Access 2022: Internet usage trends in South Africa' (Research ICT Africa, 2022).

Number of subscribers across different categories

The share of South Africans using the Internet increased from 49% in 2018 to 76% in 2022. Education and income are the major determinants of mobile and Internet connectivity and use. The main barriers to Internet access are a lack of awareness and knowledge of how to use it. For those who are already online, the main barrier to using the Internet more is overwhelmingly the high cost of data.

The real gap is a poverty gap. The socially and economically marginalised are unable to harness the Internet to enhance their social and economic well-being. Despite mobile broadband, the digital divide between the poor and the rich is significant in South Africa.

According to ITU data from 2017, 2.84% of the population uses fixed broadband, while there are 58.62% active mobile broadband subscriptions.

S. Hadzic (✉)
Research ICT Africa, Cape Town, South Africa

CyberBRICS, Law School, Fundação Getúlio Vargas, Rio de Janeiro, Brazil

L. Belli, L. Galdino de Magalhães Santos (eds.), *SmartBRICS*,
https://doi.org/10.1007/978-3-031-98204-0_15

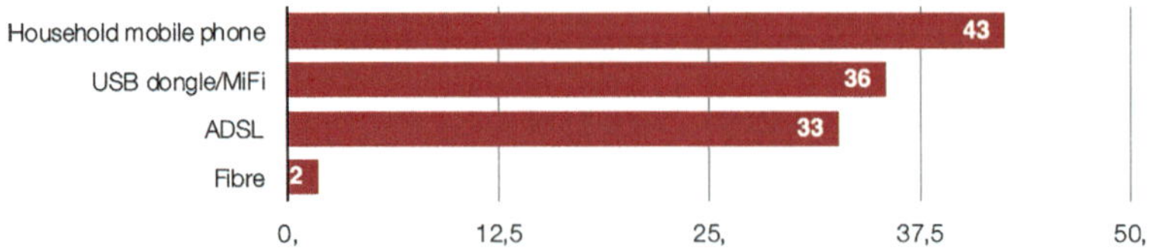

Fig. 1 'State of ICTs in South Africa'. Source: Research ICT Africa (2022)

Affordability of services

According to the UN Broadband Commission, affordability of data prices is defined as the price of 1 GB of data having to be less than 2% of disposable income (Alliance for Affordable Internet, 2018). In South Africa, due to the large inequalities and disparities in disposable income, some studies have shown that in 2016, in rural low-income areas, certain populations spent as much as 22% of their disposable income only to be able to make a few short phone calls and send some SMSes (Rey-Moreno et al., 2016).

The affordability divide between the low-income and high-income South Africans is creating barriers to connecting the low-income earners. RIA's African mobile pricing or RAMP project tracks the cheapest baskets of 1 GB of prepaid data in several African countries. In the last quarter of 2012, the cheapest pack of 1 GB data in South Africa was around 4.65 USD (Research ICT Africa, n.d.).

Type of technology being used

During the After Access Survey (household and individual user survey, analysing the demand side) in 2017, 62% of households reported one or more members having access to or using the Internet. However, most of this access (57%) takes place 'using mobile devices', with just over 10% of households reporting Internet access 'at home'.

Mobile devices, such as USB dongles, portable hotspots and mobile phones, are the primary tools that are used by those households that do access the Internet, while fibre is only used by 2% of the population.

One of the reasons why mobile wireless technology is dominant is the availability of data services that can be purchased incrementally at low cost, such as top-up on demand—instead of committing to a prescribed monthly fee (Fig. 1).

Gender gap

While the GDP per capita figure masks extreme inequalities in South Africa, the country performs well in relation to gender equity. The gender gap in Internet use in South Africa was 12% in 2017. Since then, until 2022, it has become almost negligible.

In contrast to other African countries, where all ICT indicators favour males, in South Africa, females (85%) are more likely to own a mobile phone than men (83%). However, males are more likely to own a smartphone than females. This suggests that men are more likely to be able to afford more expensive phones and that most women are unable to buy smartphones due to income disparities. This, in turn, would imply that females are less likely to access the Internet.

Urban-rural gap

While the gender gap seems to be fading, disparities in access still exist between urban and rural populations. However, over the period between 2018 and 2022, the rural gap decreased from 22% to 10%.

What is the country's ranking in the global ICT indices, such as ITU's ICT Development Index (IDI), WEF's Network Readiness Index (NRI), A4AI's Affordability Drivers Index, and GSMA's Mobile Connectivity Index (MCI)?

The ICT Development Index (IDI) is a composite indicator launched by ITU in 2009 to assess and benchmark the developments in information and communication technology (ICT) across countries and over time. In the last edition from 2017, South Africa ranked 92nd globally (Research ICT Africa, n.d.), out of 176 assessed countries (data from 2017), with the IDI value 4.96.

Since then, ITU launched a process for revision of the indicators included in the IDI, and a new version of the IDI (ITU, 2020) will be published soon.

WEF's Network Readiness Index (NRI) focuses on international competitiveness.

In the 2021 evaluation, South Africa was ranked 70th out of 130 countries (Portulans Institute, 2022), with an overall score of 48.88. Again, the score on 'governance' (which includes regulation) was relatively high—61.25; however, due to the low uptake (the score on 'people' and 'impact' was 46.42 and 42.25, respectively), the overall rank dropped significantly. The 'technology' score was 45.59.

A4AIs Affordability Drivers Index (*The Affordability Report* 2021) looks more at affordability, and out of 72 countries that were evaluated in 2021, South Africa was 27th. SA scored 68.51 on the access sub-index, 49.50 on the infrastructure sub-index, and 62.58 on the affordability driver index (where it climbed up one rank since the last evaluation).

GSMA's Mobile Connectivity Index (GSMA, 2021) looks at mobile Internet uptake.

South Africa scored 64.5 in the 2021 evaluation of the index, scoring 65, 53.9, 74.0, 67.0 in infrastructure, affordability, consumer readiness and content and services, respectively.

The infrastructure index calculation is based on network coverage (90.8), network performance (60.4), other enabling infrastructure (67.4) and spectrum (30.7). Obviously, the fact that South Africa has failed to release high-demand spectrum contributes to the low overall infrastructure index. Favourable taxation (85.4) does not compensate for extremely high levels of income inequality (0.0) and high mobile tariffs; hence, the affordability index is the weakest of all four components. The affordability index is additionally composed of handset price (47.9) and mobile tariffs (74.7). The consumer readiness index is calculated based on mobile ownership (75.5), basic skills (61.9) and gender equality (85.4). Content and services index calculation is based on local relevance (64.6), availability (63.6) and online security (78.5).

Essentially, in terms of these indices, South Africa generally ranks somewhere in the middle globally, but in the African context often significantly ahead of other African states.

Does the country have a strategy for the expansion of Internet access, such as a national broadband plan or similar?
Broadband expansion has been prioritised in the National Development Plan. The government adopted a national broadband policy in a document entitled 'SA Connect: Creating Opportunities, Ensuring Inclusion' (Electronic Communications Act 2005).

The four central strategies adopted in the policy are:

1. Digital readiness
2. Digital development
3. Building the digital future
4. Realising digital opportunity

The strategy is designed to provide universal accessibility across the country at a cost and quality that meets the needs of citizens, business and the public sector, as well as access to the creation and consumption of a wide range of converged applications and services required for effective economic and social participation.

The SA Connect document contains several targets expressed as 'broadband access in Mbps user experience'. The targets also differentiate between targets for the population as a whole and targets for schools, health facilities and government facilities.

Essentially, the targets are as follows:

However, the strategy failed to meet 2016 targets as well as 2020 targets (Table 1).

Besides SA Connect, the other main policy initiative was the protracted National Integrated ICT Policy White Paper, which was finalised in 2016 and accepted by Cabinet and Parliament. It focuses on improving access to infrastructure, competition (particularly in the services market), and inclusion of all citizens in the digital economy. The white paper covers everything from revised institutional arrangements for the sector to universal access and service and cybersecurity (National Integrated ICT Policy White Paper 2016).

2 International Commitments

Is the country a member of the ITU?
Yes. South Africa became a member of the ITU in 1881. In 1965, following the Montreux Plenipotentiary Conference, South Africa was excluded from participating in meetings of the Organisation but continued to remain a member of the organisation. A follow-up decision taken at the 1989 Plenipotentiary Conference in Nice resolved that South Africa would continue to be excluded from all conferences, meetings and activities of the ITU until apartheid policies were eliminated. This

Table 1 SA Connect targets for 'broadband access in Mbps user experience'

Target	Penetration measure	Baseline (2013)	By 2016	By 2020	By 2030
Broadband access in Mbps user experience	% of population	33.7% Internet access	50% at 5 Mbps	90% at 5 Mbps 50% at 100 Mbps	100% at 10 Mbps 80% at 100 Mbps
Schools	% of schools	25% connected	50% at 10 Mbps	100% at 10 Mbps 80% at 100 Mbps	100% at 1 Gbps
Health facilities	% of health facilities	13% connected	50% at 10 Mbps	100% at 10 Mbps 80% at 100 Mbps	100% at 1 Gbps
Government facilities	% of government offices		50% at 5 Mbps	100% at 10 Mbps	100% at 100 Mbps

resolution was set aside by the Executive Council on 9 May 1994 and formally adopted during the 1994 Plenipotentiary Conference.

South Africa submitted instruments of accession to the Constitution, Convention and Optional Protocol of the ITU on 30 June 1994, thus permitting its full participation in the ITU with effect from the 1994 Plenipotentiary Conference held in Japan. At that conference and at the subsequent conferences in Minneapolis, in 1998, and Marrakech, in 2002, South Africa was nominated and elected to membership of the Council (PATU/ATU, 2004b).

In 2018, South Africa was elected (South African Government, 2018) into the International Telecommunications Union (ITU) Executive Council and Radio Regulations Board (RRB).

Before the establishment of the Department for Communications and Digital Technologies (DCDT) in 2019, the Department of Communications (DoC) was responsible for setting electronic communications policy, overseeing radio frequency spectrum and representing South Africa in international fora such as the International Telecommunications Union (ITU).

Is the country a signatory to the 1988 or 2012 version of the International Telecommunication Regulations (ITRs)?

Yes. South Africa signed (ITU, 2004a) the 2012 version of the International Telecommunications Regulations.

Does the country have a policy of following ITU recommendations and/or technical standards?

South Africa supports various ITU initiatives (Cwele, 2018):

- Since 2015, South Africa has been serving as an active member of the UN Broadband Council for Sustainable Development under the leadership of the ITU and UNESCO Secretaries General.

- South Africa has been actively participating in various ITU committees and regional meetings.
- In 2018, the ITU Telecoms World Conference was hosted in Durban, South Africa.
- As a legacy of this conference and with the support of ITU and other international organisations, the African Digital Transformation Centre was launched in the capital city of Pretoria. This Centre's objective is to incubate enterprise talent, harness innovation and prepare the African continent to take full advantage of the Fourth Industrial Revolution. It will assist African Small, Medium and Micro Enterprises (SMMEs) with conformance testing, standardisation and protection of their intellectual property. It will contribute to the development and utilisation of African-produced ICT solutions designed to meet local needs.

The Independent Communications Authority of South Africa's mandate (ICASA, n.d.) is to regulate the telecommunications, broadcast and postal services in the public interest and ensure affordable services of a high quality for all South Africans.

In regulating the industry, ICASA aligns its actions, policies and regulations with frameworks set by international and regional bodies to which it is affiliated, including the ITU.

Although overall high-level spectrum policy and international country interaction with the ITU are clearly under the Ministry's domain, regulatory practice in many jurisdictions with independent sector regulators (or spectrum agencies) leaves spectrum management and band planning within the ambit of such a specialised agency, along with regulation, assignment, licensing, charging, monitoring and enforcement in relation to spectrum.

What is the composition of the country's delegations at ITU meetings, including official reunions and study groups (e.g. government only, or multistakeholder including private sector, academia and civil society representatives)?

The composition of South Africa's official delegations at ITU meetings (2022a, b) consists of: government, private sector (both state (co)-owned companies and fully private) and academia (state universities).

The administrative body is the Department of Communications and Digital Technologies, with the support of the Independent Communications Authority of South Africa (ICASA) and the Ministry of Communications and Digital Technologies.

The private sector is represented by three major operators (Telkom, Vodacom and MTN), Sentech (signal distributor for the South African broadcasting sector), and engineering companies GEW Technologies and Orbicom.

The academic sector is represented by the Council for Scientific and Industrial Research (CSIR).

Is the country a member of the WTO? If so, is the country a signatory to the General Agreement on Trade in Services?

Yes. South Africa was a member of the GATT and participated in the Uruguay Round of negotiations. The country ratified the Marrakesh Agreement in December

1994 and thus became a founding member of the WTO when the Organisation was established.

Is the country a signatory to any regional framework for the regulation of telecommunications or a member of any regional organisation for telecommunications regulation?
South Africa is represented in international fora such as the International Telecommunications Union (ITU), the African Telecom Union (ATU), and the Communication Regulators' Association of Southern Africa (CRASA).

Pan-Africa Telecommunications Union (PATU)/(ATU) was established as a specialised agency of the Organisation of African Unity (OAU) on 7 December 1977 to harmonise and co-ordinate the development of telecommunications networks and services in Africa.

At the fourth Extraordinary Session of the Conference of Plenipotentiaries of PATU on 7 December 1999, in Cape Town, the African Telecommunications Union (ATU, 2022) was established as the successor to PATU. South Africa signed the Constitution and Convention of the ATU at that time (PATU/ATU, 2004b).

ICASA, the South African regulator, represents South Africa at CRASA (CRASA, n.d), the Communication Regulators' Association of Southern Africa. CRASA has thirteen active members, namely regulators from the following SADC (Southern African Development Community, n.d.) countries: Angola, Botswana, Democratic Republic of Congo, Lesotho, Malawi, Mauritius, Mozambique, Namibia, South Africa, Swaziland, Tanzania, Zambia, and Zimbabwe. Based in Gaborone, Botswana, CRASA's focus is to harmonise the Information Communications and Technologies (ICT) regulatory environment in the SADC region to improve the ICT business environment and investment climate in SADC countries (Southern African Development Community [SADC], n.d.).

The country is also a member of the International Telecommunications Satellite Organization (ITSO) and the International Mobile Satellite Organization (IMSO).

3 Institutions

Does the country have a Telecommunications Regulatory Authority? If so, is it an independent body, and what are its attributions?
The Independent Communication Authority of South Africa (ICASA) is a product of statute, the Independent Communication Authority of South Africa Amendment Act of 2000, amended in 2005. The ICASA Act, Act 13 of 2000, establishes the Independent Communications Authority of South Africa (ICASA). ICASA exercises the regulatory powers and functions provided for in the Electronic Communications Act (ECA) (Act 36 of 2005), the Broadcasting Act (Act 4 of 1999), and the Postal Services Act (Act 124 of 1998).

ICASA was established in July 2000, as a merger of the telecommunications regulator, the South African Telecommunications Regulatory Authority (SATRA) and the Independent Broadcasting Authority (IBA).

The ICASA Amendment Act 2005 also provided for the incorporation of the Postal Regulator into ICASA. The Amendment Act of 2005 also increased ICASA's council complement from seven to nine councillors.

ICASA's mandate is to:

- grant licences to electronic communications operators and service providers;
- monitor licensee compliance with licence terms and conditions;
- develop regulations;
- plan and manage the radio frequency spectrum;
- protect consumers.

What is the allocation of regulatory responsibilities between the appropriate government department(s) and the Telecommunications Regulatory Authority?

Roles for the sector are divided between the government (the Ministry), which is responsible for policy formulation, and the national regulatory agency ICASA.

In 2014, the Department of Communications split into two departments: the Department of Communications (DoC), which was responsible for broadcasting services and new media, and the Department of Telecommunications and Postal Services (DTPS), which dealt with the ICT sector, Internet access policies, and infrastructure. In this rearrangement of the institutions, responsibility for the regulator was assigned to the DoC, and the DTPS was left with no direct line to the regulator, which is essentially the implementer of its policy. During that time, ICASA was reporting to the Minister of Communications, but the Minister of the DTPS was responsible for the key sectors over which ICASA is expected to preside (telecommunications, post and the Internet). A lot of time was spent trying to unravel the legislation. Eventually, in 2019, the two departments merged again to operate as one central ministry leading the country's ICT agenda, under the name of the Department of Communications and Digital Technologies.

ICASA is a Chapter 9 institution (an institution that supports democracy) in terms of the South African Constitution and is a portfolio organisation of the Department of Communications (DoC).

Besides ICASA, other entities that report to this ministry are:

- ZADNA, domain name authority—the statutory regulator and manager of the .za country code top-level domain.
- FPB - Film and Production Board.
- USAAFA, Universal Service and Access Agency of South Africa (USAASA) and the Universal Service and Access Fund (USAF).
- Broadband Infraco, a wholesale provider of backhaul connectivity.
- National Electronic Media Institute of South Africa (NEMISA).
- Sentech, the signal distributor for the South African broadcasting sector.
- South African Broadcasting Corporation SOC Limited (SABC).

- South African Post Office (SAPO).
- State Information Technology Agency (SITA).
- Telkom.

The ICT Policy White Paper (or specifically the resulting ICT Sector Commission and Tribunal Bill) proposes to merge ICASA, zaDNA and FPB into one single regulator. The new economic regulator will be answerable to the department, while retaining independent regulation of broadcasting and content. The new regulator would essentially resemble ICASA, and it would additionally assume many of the functions of other bodies.

If the country follows a federal structure, is there an allocation of responsibilities relating to the telecommunications sector between the central/ federal government and the states?

The provincial governments of the nine provinces of South Africa have their own executive and legislative branches, but not separate judicial systems. In terms of the telecommunications sector, there is no separation of responsibilities between the national government and the provinces.

Is there a competition department within the Telecommunications Regulatory Authority?

One of ICASA's strategic objectives is to promote competition by implementing measures to facilitate effective, competitive markets in the sector. This ex-ante regulation is designed to protect consumers by safeguarding fair competition and by preventing anti-competitive behaviour. Ex post regulation, which deals with failures after they occur, is within the scope of the Competition Commission and Tribunal.

However, ICASA's failure to impose ex ante regulation and act effectively on competition issues has resulted in the Competition Commission (The Competition Commission South Africa, n.d.) being identified as the agency best suited to deal with such issues.

Does the country have a Competition Authority? If so, is it an independent body, and what are its attributions?

The Competition Commission is one of three independent statutory bodies established in terms of the Competition Act, No. 89 of 1998, to regulate competition between firms in the market. The other bodies are the Competition Tribunal and the Competition Appeal Court (CAC). The Competition Commission is the investigating and prosecuting agency in the competition regime, while the Competition Tribunal is the court. The CAC hears appeals against decisions of the Tribunal. Although each of the bodies functions independently of each other and the State, the Commission and Tribunal are administratively accountable to the Economic Development Department (EDD), while the CAC is part of the judiciary.

Does the country have a Data Protection Authority? If so, is it an independent body, and what are its attributions? If not, which body of the government takes care of personal data-related issues?
The Information Regulator is an independent body established in terms of Section 39 of the Protection of Personal Information Act 4 of 2013 (POPIA). It is accountable to the National Assembly and has jurisdiction throughout the Republic of South Africa.

The Regulator is responsible for the promotion and protection of the right to privacy as it relates to the protection of personal information and the right of access to information. The Information Regulator is, among other authorities, empowered to monitor and enforce compliance by public and private bodies with the provisions of the Promotion of Access to Information Act (PAIA) and the POPIA.

In June 2020, South African President Cyril Ramaphosa announced that the bulk of the Protection of Personal Information Act would come into force on 1 July 2020, seven years after the Act was passed.

Does the country have a specific public body dealing with open data? If so, is it an independent body, and what are its attributions?
The national data and information governance framework provides the legal basis for accessing government information in the public interest. Section 32(1) of the Constitution provides for the right to access information, stating that "everyone has the right to access any information that is held by the state; and any information that is held by another person and that is required for the exercise or protection of any rights."

The Promotion of Access to Information Act (PAIA) was enacted by Parliament in 2000 to give effect to this constitutionally-recognised right. The act recognises that the system of government in South Africa before 1994 resulted in a secretive and unresponsive culture in the public and private bodies, which would often lead to an abuse of power and human rights violations. PAIA seeks to change that state of affairs by establishing clear rules regarding the right to access information. The Information Regulator has the mandate to provide guidelines that would be accessible to everyone. PAIA also mandates all bodies to publish a manual which sets out the categories of documents that they may disclose or refuse to disclose.

To foster a culture of transparency and accountability in *both* the public and private sectors, PAIA does not cater only for the accessibility of publicly held information but also makes provisions for accessing information that is held by private bodies in South Africa. Part 2 of the Act is aimed at access to records of public bodies, while part 3 is dedicated to the access to records of private bodies. Many provisions in parts 2 and 3 are substantially similar.

The Information Regulator has been given oversight of both this law and the data protection law (POPIA).

PAIA does not state anything explicitly on open government data except for saying departments must state which records they 'voluntarily and proactively' disclose. The Department of Public Service and Administration (DPSA) has the Open Government Partnership (OGP) mandate. OGP is a multilateral initiative that aims to secure concrete commitments from national and subnational governments to promote open government, empower citizens, fight corruption, and harness new technologies to strengthen governance.

Does the country have a body/an authority for managing cybersecurity incidents, such as CERTs/CSIRTs? If so, what are its attributions, and what is the nature of such an entity (e.g. governmental, multistakeholder, private)?
The National Cybersecurity Policy Framework (NCPF) is the overarching cybersecurity strategy in South Africa. The Cybersecurity Hub (CSIRT, 2016) was established by the Department of Telecommunications and Postal Services in 2015. It is South Africa's National Computer Security Incident Response Team (CSIRT), and is working with stakeholders from government, the private sector, civil society and the public with a view to identifying and countering cybersecurity threats.

Does the country have a coordination system involving the aforementioned institutions? If so, what is the nature of such an entity (e.g. governmental, multistakeholder, private)?
No.

4 Regulations

Are the telecommunication regulations and standards openly and publicly accessible?
The telecommunication regulations and standards are openly and publicly accessible. ICASA publishes all the acts, final and underway regulations, inquiries, notices and radio frequency spectrum plans on their website.

Is there a specific general telecommunications legislation?
These laws set out the general legal framework for telecommunications in South Africa:

- Independent Communications Authority of South Africa Act, 12 of 2000 (ICASA Act).
- Telecommunications Act 103 of 1996.
- Electronic Communications and Transactions Act 25 of 2002 (ECT Act).
- Electronic Communications Act of 2005.

They contain a detailed institutional framework, including the creation of the telecommunications regulatory authority (ICASA). They include licensing, competition policy, quality service, interconnection, scarce resources management, universal service, tariffs regulation, penalties and sanctions and dispute resolution. They also cover electronic communications and transactions.

Are there any instruments other than legislation and regulations, such as license agreements, that govern the provision of telecommunication services in the country?

ICASA is responsible for regulating the telecommunications sector, and these regulations cover electronic communications, licensing, consumer protection, radio frequency spectrum, broadcasting and postal services.

Other considerations affecting the provision of telecommunications services in South Africa are regulated by other laws, including the POPI Act, RICA, Consumer Protection Act.

Is there any obligation to provide open data regarding the telecommunications infrastructure?

There is no obligation. Most mobile operators publish their coverage data, but not the data on tower locations, etc.

Is there any obligation to provide open data on backhaul pricing?

No.

Does regulation foresee multiple categories of telecommunications services (e.g. Internet access, broadcasting)? Are information services distinguished between themselves (content creation and content distribution)?

The Electronic Communications Act differentiates between broadcasting services, electronic communication network services and electronic communications services.

ICASA is the official regulator of the South African broadcasting, telecommunications and postal services sectors. In terms of telecommunications, ICASA's main responsibilities relate to licensing, consumer protection and telecommunication numbering. In terms of regulations for the broadcasting industry, ICASA issues licences to service providers, plans and manages the radio frequency spectrum, and protects consumers against poor-quality services.

The Electronic Communications Act defines 'electronic communications' as 'the emission, transmission or reception of information, including without limitation, voice, sound, data, text, video, animation, visual images, moving images and pictures, signals or a combination thereof by means of magnetism, radio or other electromagnetic waves, optical, electromagnetic systems or any agency of a like nature, whether with or without the aid of tangible conduct, but does not include content service'.

The ECT Act regulates the liability of information system service providers such as ISPs, and (clearly) distinguishes between the different roles played by content providers, content platforms and Internet Access Providers.

Based on these definitions, the ECTA states that an "information system service provider" is an intermediary and that an intermediary is neither a content provider nor a content consumer.

Section 70 of the ECT Act notes that, for the purposes of Chapter 11, a *"service provider" means any person providing information system services.*

'information system services' includes the provision of connections, the operation of facilities for information systems, the provision of access to information systems, the transmission or routing of data messages between or among points specified by a user and the processing and storage of data, at the individual request of the recipient of the service.

"information system" means a system for generating, sending, receiving, storing, displaying or otherwise processing data messages and includes the Internet.

Do the country's national regulations recognise community operators and/or non-profit Telecommunications operators?

In May 2018, South Africa became the first country on the continent to support community networks as a viable communication system provider. The minister of communications highlighted in a speech that the community ownership model advances components of the ICT Development Index and development goals.

Non-profit operators are recognised and mentioned in the Electronic Communications Act as eligible for license exemption.

Is there any obligation to share infrastructure

a. poles, cell phone towers, underground routes/tubes,
b. fibre optics sharing, telecommunication cables,
c. equipment sharing?

Chapter 8 of the ECA, read with the Electronic Communications Facilities Regulations 2010, obliges an ECNS licensee to lease a facility to another licensee/licence-exempt person on request, subject to that request being commercially and technically feasible. 'Electronic communications facilities' defined in the act include:

a. masts (poles),
b. wires and cables (including fibre),
c. equipment which can be used for, or in connection with, electronic communications.

Is there any unbundling obligation? Can you be an Internet service provider and a content provider at the same time?

Generally, there is no unbundling obligation, and an ISP can also act as a content provider. However, in the case of dominant operators, there are certain unbundling obligations. In the fixed line sector, Telkom was required to unbundle.

MTN, another incumbent, had started offering content service and even zero-rated it. This move was challenged on anti-competition grounds.

One can say that there are constraints on major players who are also holders of Electronic Communications Network Service (ECNS) licences; however, an ISP operator is only licensed by registration for an Electronic Communications Service (ECS) licence, so formally they are not so regulated, and there are no compulsory unbundling requirements.

Is there any obligation to treat Internet traffic in a non-discriminatory fashion (so-called network neutrality principles)?
There was an attempt to introduce net neutrality rules in the ICT Policy White Paper and the amendments to legislation that were meant to result.

The White Paper calls for net neutrality on all South African operators and service providers to "ensure that all lawful and legal Internet traffic is treated equally, without discrimination, restriction or interference." The white paper, which is a precursor to legislation, said that ICASA will be required to hold an inquiry, in consultation with the competition authorities, into the extent to which regulatory intervention is required to uphold the principles of an open Internet. Among other things, the policy directs ICASA to consider if it will be necessary to introduce rules or guidelines on zero-rating, barring, throttling or paid prioritisation of traffic and, if so, what exclusions to this would be in the public interest (such as zero-rating of access to defined public interest content and services).

The objectives of the white paper-based framework include promoting the Internet as a platform for freedom of expression, access to information, innovation and economic growth as well as protecting the rights of users to freely access legal content, applications and services on the Internet and barring intermediaries from unreasonably interfering with or in any way disadvantaging users' access to the Internet.

However, probably due to the ECA amendment act being caught up with spectrum issues, there was no reference to the subject of net neutrality in the amendment bill.

Does the country have any specific legal or regulatory provisions regarding the Internet Access Providers' possibility to monitor the content of user communications?
According to the ECTA, there is no general obligation to monitor.

When providing electronic communication services, there is no general obligation on a service provider to monitor the data that it transmits or stores, or actively seek facts or circumstances indicating an unlawful activity.

The Minister may, subject to section 14 of the Constitution, prescribe procedures for service providers to:

(a) inform the competent public authorities of alleged illegal activities undertaken, or information provided by the recipients of their service.
(b) to communicate to the competent authorities, at their request, information for enabling the identification of recipients of their service.

The Regulation of Interception of Communications and Provision of Communication-Related Information Act (Regulation of Interception of Communications and Provision of Communication-Related Information Act 70 of 2002), RICA Act regulates the interception and monitoring of direct and indirect communications. RICA contains exceptions relating to where interception and monitoring take place with the consent of the parties involved, or where it is carried out by law enforcement personnel. In September 2019, the High Court declared a number of sections of South Africa's interception law unconstitutional.

While a service provider is under no obligation to monitor the data which it transmits or stores or to seek out facts or circumstances which indicate an unlawful activity, once it becomes aware of such facts or circumstances, it is obligated to respond thereto with reasonable expediency.

Does the country have any specific legal or regulatory provisions regarding the Internet Access Providers' possibility to collect and process users' personal data?

South Africa's data protection law, the Protection of Personal Information Act (POPI Act), is an all-inclusive piece of legislation that safeguards the integrity and sensitivity of private information. Entities operating in sectors that require them to handle personal particulars—including telecommunications and, accordingly, ISPs—are required to carefully manage the data capture and storage process. Companies also have to get permission to keep data, and disclose the reason that they need it.

POPI establishes eight conditions, which need to be met for the processing of personal data to be lawful. These conditions include: accountability, processing limitation, purpose specification, further processing limitation, information quality, openness, security safeguards, and data subject participation.

Does the country require a license to operate telecommunications networks? Is there any license exemption?

ICASA's mandate is to grant licences to operators and service providers. This includes registration, transfer and granting of service licences and licence exemption. Generally, a licence or licence exemption is required whenever communications are carried from one point to another. Licenses exist to make sure that scarce resources like numbers or frequencies are efficiently allocated, but also to protect consumers when dealing with service providers.

In South Africa, there are two categories of licenses regarding electronic communications:

- Electronic Communications Service (ECS) licences to provide services to customers (such as the provision of voice and data services) either over its own or over another licensee's network. Example: an ISP that uses someone else's infrastructure.
- Electronic Communications Network Service (ECNS) licences which allow the holder to establish, roll out and operate a physical network, based on any technology, like radio equipment for wireless networks, copper or fibre cable. ECNS licensees are also able to enter into commercial arrangements with other ECNS licensees, so that they can benefit from and use each other's network infrastructure.

At the same time, both ECS and ECNS can be either Individual or Class. Individual ones are national in scope, and Class licenses are regional, e.g. District Municipality.

Besides the general annual license fee, the USAF Regulations require licensees to pay an annual contribution of 0.2% of annual turnover (Independent Communications Authority of South Africa [ICASA], 2018).

Does the country offer a specific/simplified license for not-for-profit operators or for operators that cover specific areas (e.g. rural areas)?
There are certain conditions under which one can get a license exemption.

One can be exempted from holding an ECS license if:

- A person or company that provides services does that on a non-profit basis.
- In case of a reseller who provides services on behalf of another licensee.
- In case of an ancillary service which includes elements of electronic communications service, but these elements do not constitute its major purpose, for example tracking, alarm and similar services. → they all use electronic communications in a way but that is not their primary purpose.

One can be exempted from an ECNS license if:

- It is a Small Electronic Communications Network (SECN), or a network that lies within a limited area, and is used by a specific user group (must use frequencies which are licence exempt).
- A Private Electronic Communications Network (PECN) is a network used primarily for providing electronic communications for the owner's own use. Where a PECN resells, leases or otherwise makes available any spare capacity on its network to a third party, such resale, lease or other provisioning of spare capacity is subject to additional regulations.

Does the country require a license to provide satellite telecommunications services, including via non-geostationary orbit satellites?
According to the Electronic Communications Act, satellite systems are considered electronic communication networks; hence, the standard license rules apply.

Has the country established an obligation to provide coverage in specific areas (e.g. rural areas that lack coverage)?
Yes. According to the Electronic Communications Act, the money in the Universal Service and Access Fund must be utilised exclusively for the payment of subsidies to any electronic communications network service licensee to finance the construction or extension of electronic communications networks in underserviced areas, where these geographical areas are defined by ICASA.

Are there any specific cybersecurity obligations with regard to the telecommunications sector?
The Cybercrimes Bill will place obligations on electronic communication service providers (which includes any entity or person who is declared by the Ministry of State to own or control a critical information infrastructure) which become aware that its electronic communication network is being used to commit an offence to immediately report the matter in the prescribed manner to the South African Police

Services and preserve all information/evidence that will be relevant to the investigation of the offence.

Is there any regulation regarding cybersecurity incidents?
According to the POPI Act, the responsible party is required to take appropriate technical and organisational measures to prevent unlawful access to personal information in its possession or control. This includes the obligations to take measures to monitor, detect, prevent or mitigate incidents.

Does the law foresee any specific cybercrime involving the (mis)use or attack of the telecommunications infrastructure?
There is no legislation in force that specifically relates to cybersecurity requirements applicable to national critical infrastructure at present. The latest version of the Cybercrimes Bill that was passed by the National Assembly has removed references to national critical information infrastructures (which were referenced in the previous versions of the bill).

If a provider becomes aware that their telecommunications infrastructure has been used to commit an offence, the provider has the obligation to report the matter in the prescribed manner to the South African Police Services and preserve all information/evidence that will be relevant to the investigation of the offence.

Does the law foresee SIM and/or IMEI registration? What are the requirements applicable to such registration (for instance, the documents and information required for Know-Your-Customer (KYC) processes)?
Under the 2002 Regulation of Interception of Communications and Provision of Communication-Related Information Act (Regulation of Interception of Communications and Provision of Communication-related Information Act 70 of 2002) (RICA), providers of electronic communications services are required to obtain certain information from subscribers in the sign-up process, known as the Know-Your-Customer process. A South African citizen must provide his or her name, address and identity number. For non-citizens, a name, address and passport number are required.

Does the country specify the prices or tariffs for the provision of telecommunication services or impose any minimum or maximum limits?
Under Chapter 10 of the Electronic Communications Act (Competition matters), ICASA is empowered to address retail price controls as pro-competitive licence conditions upon licensees having significant market power. A licensee has significant market power with regard to the relevant market or market segment where the Authority finds that the particular individual licensee or class licensee:

(a) is dominant;
(b) has control of essential facilities; or.
(c) has a vertical relationship that the Authority determines could harm competition in the market or market segments applicable to the particular category of licence.

Are there any policies or regulations governing right-of-way issues, such as utilising land to dig trenches and lay fibre, for the creation of telecommunications infrastructure?
Under Chapter 4 of the Electronic Communications Act, ECNS licensees have broad rights to enter upon land for the purpose of constructing, maintaining, altering or removing electronic communications facilities, subject to environmental and other applicable regulations.

The Minister must, in consultation with the Minister of Provincial and Local Government, the Minister of Land Affairs, the Minister of Environmental Affairs, the Authority and other relevant institutions, develop guidelines for the rapid deployment and provisioning of electronic communications facilities. These guidelines must provide procedures and processes for:

(a) obtaining any necessary permit, authorisation, approval or other governmental authority, including the criteria necessary to qualify for such permit, authorisation, approval or other governmental authority; and
(b) resolving disputes that may arise between an electronic communications network service licensee and any landowner, to satisfy the public interest in the rapid rollout of electronic communications networks and electronic communications facilities.

In 2020, the minister of communications and digital technologies published a draft policy for the rapid deployment of electronic communications facilities, and it is an attempt on the part of the government to bring greater balance to the interaction between licensees on the one hand and landowners on the other hand.

If licensees want to roll out facilities using public (municipal) land, they have to apply for what is referred to as a wayleave—the permission from the local authority to dig up the pavement to lay the fibre or to erect a base station on that land.

In case of private land, compensation is payable to a landowner where a licensee comes onto the land and uses it for a purpose that disrupts the rights of the landowner. The policy talks about reasonable compensation, where the landowner is not able to exploit the licensee, and the licensee is not able to exploit the landowner. Ultimately, it throws the detail of the question of compensation down to the regulator, ICASA, which will, over the next year, have to develop a set of regulations that clarify how that compensation will be calculated.

What are the regulations applicable to the setting up and operation of landing stations and international gateways to the Internet?
According to the ECA, Chapter 8, ICASA must prescribe a list of essential facilities, including international electronic communications facilities such as submarine cables and satellite earth stations. It also states that:

An electronic communications network service licensee may not enter into any agreement or other arrangement with any person for access to, or use of, any international electronic communications facilities, including submarine cables and satellites, that—

(a) contains an exclusivity provision;

(b) contains provisions that create undue barriers to access to and use of such international communication facilities; or.
(c) otherwise restricts any party to such agreement or other arrangement from—

(i) leasing;
(ii) selling; or
(iii) otherwise entering into an agreement with any licensee under this Act or person providing services pursuant to a licence exemption for access to, and use of such international electronic communications facilities.

Are there any regulations for the Over-The-Top (OTT) services?
South Africa's dominant operators have been seeking regulatory intervention on the grounds of creating an equal playing field and have argued that OTTs have no licence or tax obligations. A parliamentary discussion (PMG, 2016) was held in January 2016 to address the question of the appropriate governance of Over-the-Top (OTT) services. Several stakeholders agreed that part of the problem is not having a globally accepted standard definition of OTT services.

What are the grounds, if any, on which the country can suspend access to the Internet or direct the blocking of access to specific websites?
There are no grounds upon which Internet access can be suspended, unless there is a state of emergency that could suspend the constitution. Interestingly, regulations in terms of the current state of disaster due to the global pandemic cannot suspend the constitution.

Does the country have a specific policy or strategy promoting the development of Internet eXchange Point (IXP) and other interconnection and transmission systems?
The National Integrated ICT Policy White Paper (Department of Telecommunications and Postal Services 2016a, 2016b) includes the following as objectives for policy intervention for Internet exchange points (IXPs):

- To keep continental traffic continental, regional traffic regional and local traffic local;
- To ensure efficient Internet traffic management across the continent, the SADC region and within South Africa;
- To increase the speed of inter-country exchange of data;
- To reduce the costs associated with exchanging data between countries in Africa, the SADC region and within South Africa;
- To facilitate peering between ISPs in South Africa; and.
- To encourage South African ISPs to peer in the SADC region.

The Internet Service Providers Association (ISPA) launched South Africa's first Internet exchange point in Johannesburg in 1996. INX-ZA (2022), a division of ISPA, operates community-run Internet exchange points in Johannesburg, Cape Town, and Durban.

The African Peering and Interconnection Forum (AFPIF, n.d.) addresses the key interconnection, peering, and traffic exchange opportunities and challenges on the continent and gathers infrastructure providers, Internet service providers, IXPs, international financial institutions, policymakers, and regulators.

Chapter 7 of the Electronic Communications Act is dedicated to interconnection. ICASA issued the Interconnection Regulations (ICASA, n.d.-a, n.d.-b) in 2010, which gave effect to that chapter. The purpose of these regulations is to:

1. To facilitate the conclusion of interconnection agreements by stipulating: (i) agreement principles, (ii) timeframes and processes to be followed by parties and (iii) the procedures for the submission, review and filing of agreements.
2. To provide for and require the provision of interconnection services to enable licensees to interconnect with each other.
3. To encourage interoperability.

The setting of pricing principles governing interconnection is essential in facilitating the entrance of competition into the market.

Have any exceptional measures been adopted to regulate Internet access in light of the COVID-19 crisis?

ICASA requested all network service providers to heed the call to enable the country to mitigate the spread of COVID-19 by facilitating easy and affordable (and/or free) access to data. In this regard, they engaged the sector on possible ways of radio frequency spectrum relief for the duration of the declared state of disaster to ease congestion, ensure good quality of broadband services, and enable licensees to lower the cost of access to consumers (particularly in relation to education, emergency and other social services).

After the SA government proclaimed a state of disaster at the end of March, ICASA made additional radio spectrum available to ensure that the network could keep up with additional demand during the lockdown. ICASA also called on all service providers who meet the minimum certification requirements for TV white spaces to make use of the TVWS database for the purposes of providing affordable and/or free access to data to rural consumers during this period.

ICASA also considered the relaxation of the tariff notification filing requirements to enable the speedy roll-out of specifically tailored data packages to respond to the pandemic.

5 Access to Spectrum

How does the country organise access to spectrum for data transmission (e.g. via auctions)?

The Department of Communications and Digital Technologies is responsible for interaction with the ITU and represents South Africa at the World Radio Communication Conferences convened by the ITU every four years. The Minister of Communications has the ultimate authority over the band plan, which sets out the uses to which the various frequency bands can be put by the users thereof. South

Africa falls within ITU Region 1 and the band plan will largely accord with that agreed to under the ITU's auspices.

The Minister also controls the use of frequency for security services and other Government uses. ICASA is responsible for the administration, management and licensing of all radio spectrum that has not been allocated for government or security uses. Spectrum is awarded subject to the allocation set out in the national radio frequency plan. The national radio frequency plan must be updated and amended when necessary to keep the plan current.

Initially, ICASA followed a first-come-first-served basis, but started working on regulations setting out the mechanisms to be employed in assigning frequency in bands where demand exceeds supply. Since 2010, the South African regulator has attempted to convene a spectrum auction three times, and each time the auction has been withdrawn. There are multiple causes of these serial auction failures. One is the lack of a coherent vision from the Ministry of Communications, which has seen 13 different ministers in 13 years, that, in turn, has led to disputes between the regulator and the ministry. During all this time, basically over a decade, operators were deploying 4G services in bands that were not originally meant for it, which ended up ultimately costing them more, and these costs were passed on to the consumers. Another reason is delays in digital migration and freeing up the high-demand spectrum, namely the 700 and 800 MHz digital dividend bands.

After another delay due to the COVID-19 pandemic, the auction process was finally completed in 2022 (ICASA, 2022).

Spectrum is awarded on a technology-neutral basis, subject to the allocation set out in the national radio frequency plan.

Does the country offer some type of advantage in the spectrum access (e.g. discount or compensation) for operators who use the spectrum to provide services in rural areas?

No. However, the country does impose some coverage obligations, principally for those bidding for spectrum in the 700 MHz or 800 MHz bands (which are in the process of being auctioned).

ICASA employs Administrative Incentive Pricing (AIP) to try and promote the efficient use of spectrum.

Does the country offer simplified (i.e. low bureaucratic, affordable) licencing for spectrum access to be used for social purposes or to provide coverage to specific areas? Does this include the provision of public Wi-Fi services?

No. However, in September 2022, the DCTD published a new draft spectrum policy ("Communications and Digital Technologies" 2022) for public comment. The Next Generation Radio Frequency Spectrum Policy for Economic Development (Spectrum Policy) supports the deployment and licensing of alternative infrastructure networks, and aims to adopt spectrum management approaches that promote participation of local small and medium enterprises (SMEs) and the emergence of new entrants into the ICT sector. Although still only a draft, it is a very progressive and inclusive spectrum policy, aiming to address gaps and limitations, including the failure to lower the cost of communications.

Does the country allow secondary use of spectrum? If so, how is it defined?
Secondary use of spectrum is only allowed in the TV white space frequencies (470–694 MHz). The regulation requires a Geo-location Spectrum Database (GLSD) to control the availability of channels to White Space Devices (WSDs) requiring access to spectrum. The regulations also define permitted maximum power levels of the devices and the maximum allowed antenna height.

The ITA issued in October 2020 states that 'In cases that the spectrum is not fully utilised by the licensee within 5 years of issuance of the Radio Frequency Spectrum Licences, the Authority will initiate the process for the Licensee to share unused spectrum in all areas with ECNS licensees who may, inter alia, combine licensed spectrum in any innovative combinations in order to address local and rural connectivity in some municipalities including by entrepreneurial SMMEs.'

Do the country's regulations provide for the use of unlicensed or license-free spectrum bands in specific areas, such as rural areas, or throughout the country?
ICASA has issued regulations setting out bands which may be used without a frequency licence, subject to certain technical restrictions.

The most important of these bands for telecommunications purposes are the 2.4 GHz and 5.8 GHz ISM bands, which are used extensively for the provision of Wi-Fi services in rural areas.

6 Financial Resources

Is there any fund for universalisation (to promote the increase) of Internet access or access to Telecom services for everybody? Is there a Universal Service Fund or any other fund? If so, how are resources collected and distributed?
The Universal Service and Access Agency of South Africa (USAASA, 2022) is a state-owned entity of government established through the Electronic Communications Act.

In terms of the ECA, the Agency must:

- strive to promote the goal of universal access and universal service;
- encourage, facilitate and offer guidance in respect of any scheme to provide universal access, universal services or telecommunication services in terms of the Reconstruction and Development Plan (RDP);
- foster the adoption and use of new methods of attaining universal access and universal service;
- make recommendations to enable the Minister to determine what constitutes universal access, universal service and underserviced areas;
- conduct research into and keep abreast of developments in the Republic and elsewhere on information communication technology, electronic communications services and electronic communications facilities;

- continually survey and evaluate the extent to which universal access and service have been achieved;
- make recommendations to the Minister in relation to policy on any matter relating to universal access and universal service;
- advise the Authority (ICASA) on any matter relating to universal access and universal service;
- continually evaluate the effectiveness of this Act and things done in terms thereof towards the achievement of the goal of universal access and universal service;
- manage the Universal Service and Access Fund (USAF) in accordance with the provisions of the Act;
- submit annual reports on its operations, budget and expenses to the Minister;
- utilise the USAF exclusively for the payment of certain subsidies; and,
- provide incentives to network licensees to construct, operate and maintain networks in areas declared underserviced by ICASA.

In 2010, the determinations (Gov Gazette: 32939, 2012) of universal access and universal service targets for Electronic Communications Services (ECS), Electronic Communications Networks Services (ECNS) were issued. The determinations for Universal Access targets for data ECS are as follows:

- at least one public broadband Internet access point for every 10,000 people in a geographically defined community; and
- access to a data ECS at a public access point within a range of 2 km from any person residing in such a community.

The following criteria apply: "the service (defined as including access to broadband and being able to use the Internet for at least 20 hours per month, of which no fewer than 10 hours are within peak times or being able to consume at least 500 MB per month) is available to 90% of households on demand and is affordable to 60% of households, that is, the cost does not exceed 5% of the households total expenditure."

The Universal Service and Access Fund (USAF) is managed by USAASA and is financed by contributions from all telecommunications licensees except community broadcasting service licensees. The USAF's sole mandate is to make payments for subsidies towards the provision of ICT equipment and services, and construct and extend electronic communication and broadcasting networks for needy persons in underserviced areas.

The ECA requires all licensees to contribute to the USAF in accordance with regulations issued by ICASA, which remains the body responsible for prescribing the basis and manner of contributions, albeit by law they may not exceed 1% of a licensee's annual turnover.

The Digital Development Fund Bill proposes to dissolve the Universal Service and Access Agency of South Africa, which manages the Universal Service Access Fund, and replace it with a new digital development fund. The widened scope of the Digital Development Fund Bill enables it to act as a medium for private funds to flow to underserved areas.

Are telecommunications services taxed or subject to other specific levies? If so, how?

In October 2018, the National Treasury issued regulations prescribing electronic services for the purpose of the definition of electronic services in section 1(1) of the Value-Added Tax Act (1991). It is proposed that telecommunications services should be excluded from the definition of "electronic services" in the regulations. The proposed 2020 update defines "telecommunications services" as:

'the transmission, emission or reception, and the transfer or assignment of the right to use capacity for the transmission, emission or reception, of signals, writing, images, sounds or information of any kind by wire, cable, radio, optical or other electromagnetic system, or by a similar technical system, and includes access to global information networks but does not include the content of the telecommunication'.

Currently, the VAT Act and Regulations do not provide for "intermediaries" and "platforms" to be the principal supplier of the electronic services. To broaden the scope, further amendments are proposed in the VAT Act and Regulations to specifically deal with "intermediaries" and "platforms."

Is there any fund to provide subsidies to operators to expand coverage to underserved areas and the least privileged populations?

The Universal Service and Access Fund (USAF) is designed to fund projects and programmes that strive to achieve universal service and access to ICTs by all South African citizens. In accordance with the ECA, this fund is utilised exclusively for the payment of subsidies for:

- Assistance of needy persons towards the cost of the provision to or the use by them of broadcasting and electronic communications services,
- Financing the construction or extension of electronic communications networks in under-serviced areas,
- The procurement of broadcasting and electronic communications network services and access to electronic communications networks for schools and further education and training institutions,
- The establishment and operation of broadcasting services and the establishment and operation of, including training of and the payment of allowances to personnel of centres where access to electronic communications networks can be obtained.

Every holder of a license granted or deemed to have been granted in terms of the ECA is mandated to make prescribed contributions to the USAF.

Is any form of direct support (such as funding or tax exemptions) offered to small and/or micro and/or not-for-profit providers?

If a person or company provides services on a non-profit basis, they can be exempted from holding an Electronic Communications Service (ECS) license. An Electronic Communications Network Service (ECNS) license exemption is possible for a Private Electronic Communications Network (PECN).

If exempted from holding a license, one is exempt from paying registration, renewal and annual fees. Annual fees are based on revenue, and for the lowest group with the annual turnover of USD 0 to USD 3,000,000, the annual fee is 0.15% of revenue. One is also allowed co-location of equipment in an incumbent's towers, which is something they allow to license holders only.

If registered as a cooperative (which is often the case for community networks), there might be additional benefits for the provider: all the profit (if any) does not go to the shareholders, but is invested back into the community to achieve the co-operative's goals, then there is no obligation to pay 0.2% of annual turnover as a contribution to the Universal Service and Access Funds.

ECS licence exemption from all these fees and compliance requirements is possible for different reasons, among them "a person or company who provides ECS on a non-profit basis," as well as ECNS exemptions for a Private Electronic Communications Network (PECN).

References

African Peering & Interconnection Forum (AFPIF). (n.d.). https://www.afpif.org/

Alliance for Affordable Internet. (2018, January). *UN Broadband Commission Adopts A4AI "1 for 2" Affordability Target*. A4AI. https://a4ai.org/news/un-broadband-commission-adopts-a4ai-1-for-2-affordability-target/

Alliance for Affordable Internet (A4AI). (2021) *The Affordability Report 2021*. Web Foundation. https://a4ai.org/report/2021-affordability-report/

Communications and Digital Technologies: Next generation radio frequency spectrum policy for economic development: Written submissions invited. (2022, October). South African Government. https://www.gov.za/documents/communications-and-digital-technologies-next-generation-radio-frequency-spectrum-policy

Communications Regulators' Association of Southern Africa (CRASA). (n.d.). https://www.crasa.org/

Cwele, S. (2018). *South Africa Speech at the ITU PP-18*. https://www.itu.int/web/pp-18/en/speech/174

Department of International Relations & Cooperation of the Republic of South Africa. (2004a, February). *International Telecommunication Union (ITU) History and Present Status*. http://www.dirco.gov.za/foreign/Multilateral/inter/itu.htm

Department of International Relations & Cooperation of the Republic of South Africa. (2004b, February). *Pan-Africa Telecommunications Union (PATU)/African Telecommunications Union (ATU) History and Present Status*. http://www.dirco.gov.za/foreign/Multilateral/africa/patu.htm

Department of Telecommunications & Postal Services of South Africa. (2016a, October). *National Integrated ICT Policy White Paper*. https://www.gov.za/sites/default/files/gcis_document/201610/40325gon1212.pdf

Department of Telecommunications & Postal Services of South Africa. (2016b). *Official website of the South African National CSIRT*. https://www.cybersecurityhub.gov.za/

Electronic Communications Act, 2005 (ACT NO. 36 OF 2005). (2013, December). *South Africa Connect: Creating opportunities, ensuring inclusion South Africa's Broadband Policy*. Government Notice from the Department of Communications. https://www.gov.za/documents/electronic-communications-act-south-africa-connect-creating-opportunity-ensuring-inclusion

Gillwald, A., Mothobi, O., & Rademan, B. (2018, July). *The State of ICT in South Africa*. ResearchICTafrica.net. https://researchictafrica.net/after-access-south-africa-state-of-ict-2017-south-africa-report_04/
GSMA. (2021). *GSMA mobile connectivity index*. Mobileconnectivityindex.com. https://www.mobileconnectivityindex.com/
Independent Communication Authority of South Africa (ICASA). (2022, March). *ICASA concludes successful spectrum auction and collects more than R14.4 Billion Proceeds*. https://www.icasa.org.za/news/2022/icasa-concludes-successful-spectrum-auction-and-collects-more-than-r14-4-billion-proceeds
Independent Communication Authority of South Africa (ICASA). (n.d.-a). *Our Mandate*. https://www.icasa.org.za/pages/our-mandate
Independent Communication Authority of South Africa (ICASA). (n.d.-b). *Interconnection Regulations 2010*. https://www.icasa.org.za/legislation-and-regulations/interconnection-regulations
Independent Communications Authority of South Africa (ICASA). (2018, October). Regulations in respect of prescribed annual contributions of licensees to the universal service and access fund. *Government Gazette, Volume 520* (No. 31499) https://www.ellipsis.co.za/wp-content/uploads/2011/02/USAF-regulations.pdf
Independent Communications Authority of South Africa (ICASA) Act, 2000 As amended by: Broadcasting Amendment Act, No. 64 of 2002. (No. 13 of 2000). (n.d.). https://www.icasa.org.za/uploads/files/Independent-Communications-Authority-of-South-Africa-Act-2000.pdf
International Telecommunication Union (ITU). (2020, September). *ICT Development Index 2020: A proposal*. https://www.itu.int/en/ITU-D/Statistics/Documents/events/egti2020/IDI2020_BackgroundDocument_E.pdf
International Telecommunications Union (ITU). (2022a). *General Secretariat*. ITU Committed to connecting the world. https://www.itu.int/en/general-secretariat/Pages/default.aspx
International Telecommunications Union (ITU). (2022b). *South Africa*. ITU Committed to connecting the world. https://www.itu.int/online/mm/scripts/gensel9?_ctryid=1000100478&_ctryname=South%20Africa
INX-ZA. (2022, March). https://wiki.inx.net.za/
Parliament Monitoring Group (PMG). (2016, January). *Over-the-Top (OTT) policy and regulatory options*. https://pmg.org.za/committee-meeting/21942/
Portulans Institute. (2022). *South Africa Performance Overview*. Network Readiness Index. https://networkreadinessindex.org/country/south-africa/
Regulation of Interception of Communications and Provision of Communication-related Information Act 70 of 2002. (2022). *South African Government*. https://www.gov.za/documents/regulation-interception-communications-and-provision-communication-related-information%2D%2D13
Regulations Prescribing Electronic Services for the Purpose of the Definition of "Electronic Services" in Section 1 of the value-added Tax Act, 1991. No. R. (2018). https://www.treasury.gov.za/legislation/regulations/Electronic%20services/
Research ICT Africa. (2022, November). *After Access 2022: Internet usage trends in South Africa*. https://researchictafrica.net/wp/wp-content/uploads/2022/12/SA-After-Acess-2022_Policy-Brief-High-level-findings-3Dec2022.pdf
Research ICT Africa. (n.d.). *Research ICT Africa Mobile Pricing (RAMP)*. https://researchictafrica.net/research-ict-africa-ramp-index-2/
Rey-Moreno, C., Blignaut, R., Tucker, W., & May, J. (2016). An in-depth study of the ICT ecosystem in a South African rural community: Unveiling expenditure and communication patterns. *Information Technology for Development, 22*(Supplement 1), 101–120. https://doi.org/10.1080/02681102.2016.1155145
South African Government. (2018, November). *South Africa elected into International Telecommunications Union Executive Council and Radio Regulations Board*. https://www.

gov.za/speeches/south-africa-elected-international-telecommunications-union-itu-executive-council-and-radio
The Competition Commission South Africa. (n.d.). https://www.compcom.co.za/
Universal Service and Access Agency of South Africa (USAASA). (2022). *Homepage*. http://www.usaasa.org.za/

Senka Hadzic is a Senior Associate at Research ICT Africa, where she primarily researches alternative spectrum policies to enable small-scale operators and community networks. She was a postdoctoral fellow at the ICT for Development Centre at the University of Cape Town from 2016–2018. Her expertise is in low-cost connectivity solutions in the Global South, and she has consulted for a variety of organizations, including the International Telecommunication Union and Engineering for Change. Dr. Hadzic completed her PhD in Electronics and Telecommunications Engineering at the University of Aveiro (Portugal) in early 2014, and since then, she has been working at the intersection of technology, design, and policy. She is a CyberBRICS Fellow.

South Africa: An Analysis of the Digitalisation of Public Services

Senka Hadzic

Abstract This chapter maps key aspects related to the digitalisation of public services in South Africa. The following elements are investigated: policy elements related to digital government strategies, declarations, programmes and actions; regulatory elements related to openness, sharing and data protection laws; institutional and governance elements related to the oversight and competences of public agencies, public-private partnerships and regulatory innovations in technology; and evidence from critical sectors such as smart cities, digital ID, and digital payments.

1 National Strategies and Priorities

Is there a national strategy for digitalisation/digital transformation? Is there a specific national strategy for digitalisation of public services?

In 2017, the (former) Department of Telecommunications and Postal Services—DTPS (now Department of Communications and Digital Technologies) developed a national e-government strategy (2017a) aimed at modernising and transforming future public service delivery. The strategy was developed in terms of the Electronic and Communications Transaction Act (2002) and the National Integrated ICT Policy white paper (2016). In this document, e-government refers broadly to the use of information and communication technologies to link citizens and the public sector and facilitate collaborative and efficient governance. It was published together with an enabling coordinated and integrated e-strategy (Department of Telecommunications and Postal Services [DTPS], 2017b) which cuts across government departments and sectors, and guides the national e-government strategy.

The purpose of the National e-Government Strategy and Roadmap is to guide the digital transformation of public service in South Africa into an inclusive digital

S. Hadzic (✉)
Research ICT Africa, Cape Town, South Africa

CyberBRICS, Law School, Fundação Getúlio Vargas, Rio de Janeiro, Brazil

L. Belli, L. Galdino de Magalhães Santos (eds.), *SmartBRICS*,
https://doi.org/10.1007/978-3-031-98204-0_16

society. The Department is supporting SITA—State Information Technology Agency—as the implementing agency, creating an enabling ICT environment for government departments to provide electronic services (e-services) to the citizens of South Africa. SITA is responsible for the acquisition, installation, implementation, and maintenance of information technologies in the public sector.

E-government includes the following programmes:

Government to Government (G2G): interaction between different levels of government and collaboration with government agencies;
Government to Citizen (G2C): interaction between the government and its citizens;
Government to Employee (C2G): relationship between the government and its employees;
Government to Business (G2B): supporting business activities.

The national e-government strategy is the result of an evolution dating back to 1995, when the White Paper on the transformation of public services was released. In 2001, the Department of Public Service and Administration (DPSA) produced an e-government policy document entitled 'Electronic Government: The Digital Future—A Public Service IT Policy Framework' (Department of Public Service and Administration [DPSA], 2022). In 2012, SITA developed an e-government framework and started offering e-services. In 2014, the South African government transferred administration of the legislation that enables the State IT Agency (SITA) from the Department of Public Service and Administration (DPSA) to the Department of Telecommunications and Postal Services (DTPS). In 2015, two South African provinces—Gauteng and Western Cape—developed their provincial e-government strategies. In 2016, the National ICT Integrated Policy White Paper was approved: it had an emphasis on digital transformation of public service and the need to develop a National e-Government Strategy and Roadmap.

Six guiding principles for developing and implementing e-government initiatives and services are interoperability, ICT security, economy of scale, elimination of duplication, inclusion of indigenous languages in ICT applications, and digital inclusion.

In terms of digital transformation in general, in April 2019, the Presidential Commission on the Fourth Industrial Revolution (DTPS, 2019) (PC4IR) was appointed to develop a 4IR strategy for South Africa.

Is the digitalisation of any specific sector seen as a priority for the country (e.g. Central Bank Digital Currency, digital identity, online payments, deployment of Artificial Intelligence, smart cities, cybersecurity, etc.)?
The Presidential Commission on the Fourth Industrial Revolution (PC4IR) was appointed in April 2019 to develop a 4IR strategy. 4IR became clearly the priority for the country, and since then, every new digital policy, independent of the sector, has been shaped around the 4IR context. Unfortunately, some ongoing developments were somewhat abandoned, as all efforts were suddenly concentrated on developing a 4IR policy.

Smart cities and the financial services sector are explicitly mentioned in the report.

Some of the technologies driving this revolution are Artificial Intelligence (AI), blockchain, cloud computing, Internet of Things, 3D printing and autonomous vehicles. A major common thread through many of the different technological pillars of the 4IR is data. The Draft Cloud and Data Policy (Electronic Communications Act 2005) was published in April 2021 and provides recommendations on data governance in the 4IR context.

Is there an overall Artificial Intelligence strategy? Is there a specific national strategy for the use of Artificial Intelligence in the public sector?
The Presidential Commission on 4IR recommended the establishment of a National AI Institute, which would be the facility for training, research and development, and advance the use of AI in tackling challenges that South Africa faces.

Data is central to the application of AI and is the key asset. The use of AI requires that data must comply with the FAIR principles: be findable, accessible, interoperable and reusable.

The Draft Cloud and Data Policy (Electronic Communications Act 2005) from 2021 states it would empower the AI Strategy, which will be pursued in the AI Institute.

In November 2022, the launch of the Artificial Intelligence Institute of South Africa and AI hubs was announced (South African Government, 2022).

The launch of the AI Institute is the realisation of one of the recommendations of the Presidential Commission on the Fourth Industrial Revolution (PC4IR) and aims to place South Africa as a leading country in the world in digital technologies.

Is there a specific strategy or reference to the use of social media to facilitate government activities?
Identifying channels of customers' preference is a critical success factor for effective e-government. The national e-government strategy lists the following channels:

- Internet, where all government services shall be made available online through the e-government central portal, 24/7365 days are year.
- Mobile, where services are available via Mobi site, mobile apps and Unstructured Supplementary Service Data (USSD).
- Phone/call centre.
- Digital TV.
- Common service centres.

While social media are not listed as an official channel, the strategy document encourages social media tools for citizen participation, their use as a tool for raising awareness about e-government services, and for providing feedback on the National e-Government Central Portal (South Africa E-Service Portal, n.d.).

In the context of local governments, the Department of Cooperative Governance and Traditional Affairs (CoGTA) has been promoting (Cooperative Governance Traditional Affairs, 2018) the use of GovChat (2021) by municipalities to use social media as a way to address weaknesses in current participation mechanisms and to encourage 'active citizenship'. The GovChat community engagement platform integrates popular communication tools like WhatsApp, and in rural communities where connection may be slower, it is available via the Unstructured Supplementary Service Data (USSD) channel. GovChat is also exploring the use of AI to enhance government efficiency and responsiveness (Plantinga et al., 2019).

Is there a strategy or any specific policies aimed at promoting the use of open-source software/hardware by public administrations or generally?

In 2002 and 2003, the South African Cabinet adopted policies from the Government IT Officer's Council (GITOC) regarding Free and Open Source Software (FOSS). After additional research and consultation, a revised policy was issued in 2007. The policy on free and open- source software use for South African Government (DPSA, 2006) recommends implementation of FOSS unless proprietary software is significantly superior, migration of current proprietary software in SA government to FOSS whenever comparable software exists, development of all new software using FOSS principles, implementation of Open Content Licensing, and promotion of FOSS in South Africa. Apart from lowering administration costs, this strategy was also aiming to enhance local IT skills and eventually convert South Africa from a predominant consumer of technology to a supplier/producer.

However, despite the efforts to increase the use of FOSS in government, migration had various degrees of success across departments (Itweb Business Technology Media Company, 2019).

The Draft Cloud and Data Policy (Electronic Communications Act 2005) from 2021 suggests that the overall policy framework on data and cloud must be biased towards open standards and open systems, including open-source frameworks, rather than closed and exclusive systems.

Are there specific policies mandating interoperability requirements for the systems utilised by public administrations? Are there any strategies or recommendations to avoid vendor lock-in?

Section 7(6) of the SITA Act amendment from 2002 requires the Agency to set standards for the interoperability of information systems and standards for a comprehensive information systems security environment for departments.

The national e-government policy lists six guiding principles for e-government services, one of which is interoperability. All government ICT systems, including networks, platforms, applications and data, must be part of an interoperable system where information sharing, communication across platforms and collaborative applications run seamlessly.

Government tender procedures and procurement practices must seek to enforce the policy of interoperability of systems. The applicable Minimum Interoperability Standards (MIOS) policy ensures that all ICT goods or services must be compatible with existing and planned government systems.

Competition ensures that government service delivery is not exclusively dependent on any single ICT provider and thereby avoids vendor lock-in. Interoperability should be achieved without compromising essential ICT security concerns.

Implementing these policies is of utmost importance because the approach to digital transformation adopted by different branches of government is not synchronised. Most existing systems were not designed to share information across branches and government departments.

The Draft Cloud and Data Policy (Electronic Communications Act 2005) from 2021 supports the development of an interoperability framework between government and businesses.

Is there a strategy or any specific policies promoting open data (e.g. government-business data sharing, open government, and/or open data in general)?

The national data and information governance framework provides the legal basis for accessing government information in the public interest. Section 32(1) of the Constitution provides for the right to access information, stating that "everyone has the right to access any information that is held by the state; and any information that is held by another person and that is required for the exercise or protection of any rights."

The Promotion of Access to Information Act (PAIA) was enacted by Parliament in 2000 to give effect to this constitutionally-recognised right. The act recognises that the system of government in South Africa before 1994 resulted in a secretive and unresponsive culture in the public and private bodies, which would often lead to an abuse of power and human rights violations. PAIA seeks to change that state of affairs by establishing clear rules regarding the right to access information. The Information Regulator has the mandate to provide guidelines that would be accessible to everyone. PAIA also mandates all bodies to publish a manual which sets out the categories of documents that they may disclose or refuse to disclose.

To foster a culture of transparency and accountability in both the public and private sectors, PAIA does not cater only for the accessibility of publicly held information but also makes provisions for accessing information that is held by private bodies in South Africa.

PAIA does not state anything explicitly on open government data except for saying departments must state which records they 'voluntarily and proactively' disclose. The Department of Public Service and Administration (DPSA) has the Open Government Partnership (OGP) mandate. OGP is a multilateral initiative that aims to secure concrete commitments from national and subnational governments to promote open government, empower citizens, fight corruption, and harness new technologies to strengthen governance.

Currently, government departments, public agencies and universities are paying other state agencies for data—these often also have appropriate research functions related to their mandate. Some may have obligations to report data to international bodies, particularly the UN and the ITU, but not much of it ends up in the public domain.

The White Paper on Science, Technology and Innovation (2019) emphasises the need for open data. National Integrated ICT White Paper promotes informed, active citizenship by providing the framework to facilitate access to public data, and promotes efficiency and cost-effectiveness in the public sector by making it easier and less costly for government entities to access and re-use their own data and that of other public agencies.

The Draft Cloud and Data Policy (Electronic Communications Act 2005) from 2021 highlights a need for South Africa to develop an open data strategy/framework for the sharing of data, informed by 'Data for Good' principles, to enable access to relevant data for all South Africans, including NGOs, and enterprises large and small. The terms and conditions of such access to data will be defined in the open data strategy.

Are the national strategies binding documents (i.e. adopted in the form of laws or decrees) or are they just declaratory documents?
Strategies are binding documents.

Is there a specific policy for integration, inclusion of vulnerable groups (e.g. elderly, etc.) or accessibility for people with disabilities?
Among the six guiding principles for e-government services are the inclusion of indigenous languages in ICT applications and digital inclusion. According to the national e-government strategy, "The use of ICTs in government must ensure that all citizens have equal access. In a fair and rational society, all individuals have equal opportunity to participate in, or benefit from, the use of ICT resources by virtue of their citizenship, regardless of race, gender, religion, age, disability, language, or any other such factors."

Are the national strategies guided or are they involved in cooperation agreements, best practices, programs, associations of organisations such as UN Agenda 2030 SDGs, OECD, World Bank?
National e-government strategy contains a section on international benchmarking, where it acknowledges that "Governments have to pursue e-government as a crucial means to make its government more competitive, by leveraging the world's best information and communications technology (ICT) to deliver services to its citizens."

The United Nations (UN) developed a four-stage maturity model, which is used for ranking the UN member states' levels of sophistication of a state's online presence.

The four stages of the model are defined as follows:

1. The first stage is "emerging presence": In this stage, e-government websites provide static information.
2. The second stage is "enhanced presence": In this stage, the government provides greater sources of current and archived information, such as policies, laws and regulations, reports, newsletters, and downloadable databases. The presence is enhanced with one-way or simple two-way communication.
3. The third stage is "transactional presence": In this stage, a two-way interaction with citizens is possible. Citizens are able to pay for relevant public services.
4. The fourth stage is "connected presence": In this stage, websites are proactive in requesting citizens' feedback, encouraging participatory decision-making. Government agencies are citizen-centric, and services are customer-centric.

A benchmarking exercise of South African e-government activities against this resulted in a classification of level 2 (enhanced presence). The vision of digital transformation is to ultimately achieve level 4 (connected presence).

Are there any existing policies to zero-rate certain e-government services? Are there such policies for specific public sectors?

The COVID-19 crisis led to new policies regarding zero rating. South Africa declared a 'National State of Disaster' on March 15, 2020. The crisis highlighted the existing digital divide and the need for Internet access. The Minister of Communications and Digital Technologies issued the Electronic Communications, Postal and Broadcasting Directions (DTPS, 2020) on March 26. Subsequently, ICASA—the telecom regulator—issued the ICT COVID-19 National Disaster Regulations (ICASA, 2020) on April 06. Both these regulatory instruments have been used to maintain and improve Internet connectivity by temporarily allocating emergency spectrum, imposing obligations on telecom infrastructure and service providers to ensure continued service during the National State of Disaster, and by requiring MNOs to provide zero-rated access to certain government and local educational websites.

Directions were issued on zero rating of content and websites for health and education: basically, all COVID-19 websites identified by the Department of Health, as well as "local education content-related websites" (Department of Communications and Digital Technologies [DCDT], 2020). Any website wishing to be zero-rated has to fill up an application form (Government Gazette No. 43413 2020) and submit it to either the Department of Health, the Department of Basic Education, or the Department of Higher Education and Training.

Some of the over 1000 websites (crowdsourced list available) approved for zero-rated access include the COVID-19 South African Resource Portal; the Department of Basic Education (including its cloud and curriculum content resources); Department of Higher Education and Training (including its intranet and career services portal); various public technical and vocational education and training colleges, universities, and high schools.

How does the country rank on global digital adoption indices, such as the World Bank's Digital Adoption Index, the Digital Society Index, IMD World Digital Competitiveness Ranking, Global Open Data Index, etc.?

World Bank Digital Adoption Index (2022) is the simple average of three sub-indices: increasing productivity and accelerating broad-based growth for business, expanding opportunities and improving welfare for people, and increasing the efficiency and accountability of service delivery for the government. Last index from 2016, South Africa's average is 0.638083577 (business sub-index: 0.690170109; people sub-index: 0.497349918; and government sub-index: 0.726730764), meaning the country ranks 54th/183 overall and 34th/183 in terms of government digital adoption.

According to the IMD World Digital Competitiveness Ranking (2022), out of 63 economies that were analysed, South Africa's position in 2020 was 60 overall (rank 60 in knowledge, rank 55 in technology, rank 57 in future readiness).

The Global Open Data Index (Open Knowledge Foundation, n.d.) places South Africa 43rd out of 94 analysed countries.

The Department of Economic and Social Affairs of the United Nations launched the 11th edition of the UN E-Government Survey in 2020, providing a global assessment of the e-government development status of the 193 UN Member States. The Survey tracks the progress of e-government development via the e-Government Development Index (EGDI), which is a composite index based on the weighted average of three normalised indices: telecommunications infrastructure index, human capital index and online service index. South Africa ranks 78th out of 193 countries, with the EGDI 0.6891 (compared to 0.6618 in 2018). South Africa's telecommunications infrastructure index (TII) is at 0.5832, the human capital index (HCI) at 0.7371, and the online service index (OSI) at 0.7471. The survey also groups countries according to their E-Participation Index (EPI) level, where South Africa belongs to the very high EPI level (0.75 to 1.00) group. With an EPI value of 0.75, South Africa is the only African country in this group. The Open Government Data Index (OGDI) is 0.8969 and therefore classified as 'very high'.

2 Regulations

Is there any general regulation (e.g. law, decree, standards) to organise the digitalisation of public services, other than specific regulations that might apply to the key sectors identified below?
There are a few legislations that are (directly or indirectly) related to the provision, management or implementation of e-government. These are:

- The Public Service Act of 1994 and its subsequent amendments. This Act provides for, amongst others, the establishment of norms and standards relating to e-government and information management in the public service.
- The Electronic Communication and Transaction (ECT) Act of 2002 aims to provide for the facilitation and regulation of e-government services and electronic communications and transactions with public and private bodies, institutions and citizens.
- The State Information Technology Agency Act, 1998 (Act No. 88 of 1998) as amended in 2002, provides for the establishment of a company referred to as the State IT Agency (SITA). SITA is mandated to provide IT services to, or on behalf of, participating departments. Section 7(6) of the SITA Act requires the Agency to set standards for the interoperability of information systems and standards for a comprehensive information systems security environment for departments.
- The Public Service Regulations of 2016 (Department of Public Service and Administration, 2016) set out regulations for information management and e-government in Chapter 6.
- Minimum Information Security Standards (MISS). All persons working with public service information resources will be required to comply with the MISS.

- Minimum Interoperability Standards (MIOS) and Policy on Free and Open Source Software (FOSS).
- The Protection of Personal Information (POPI) Act of 2013, which aims at promoting the protection of personal information processed by public and private bodies and to introduce certain conditions so as to establish minimum requirements for the processing of personal information.
- The Protection of State Information Bill (2010) regulates the manner in which State information should be protected; promotes transparency and accountability in governance while recognising that State information may be protected from disclosure to safeguard the national interest of the Republic.

Is there any regulation mandating transparency audits for technologies (e.g. platforms, algorithms, cloud services, etc.) utilised by public administrations?
The South African Constitution states that national, provincial, and municipal budgets and budgetary processes must promote transparency, accountability, and the effective financial management of the economy, debt and public sector.

The Auditor-General of South Africa (2022) has a constitutional mandate to audit and report on the financial management in the public sector, and annually produces audit reports on all government departments, public entities, municipalities and public institutions.

AGSA gained autonomy in 1993 when it was set apart from the public sector, so it is legally, financially and operationally independent, and governed by the Public Audit Act, No. 25 of 2004. To generate income, government institutions are charged for the audits. AGSA reports directly to Parliament.

The Public Audit Act does not specify procedures for technologies utilised by public administrations.

Is there any specific regulation mandating requirements for public procurements and public tenders regarding digital public services?
The National Treasury (Department of National Treasury of the Republic of South Africa, n.d.) is responsible for managing South Africa's national government finances. The Government Technical Advisory Centre (2021) is a government component in the National Treasury reporting to the Minister of Finance. It is an agency of the National Treasury, established to support public finance management through professional advisory services, programme and project management and transaction support, which often includes the use and efficiency of technology across government. Financial management of public entities is in line with the Public Finance Management Act and Treasury Regulations.

SITA is responsible for the procurement of government IT services, and launched the g-commerce platform (State Information Technology Agency [SITA], 2017) to modernise and automate procurement functions within government departments and other state organs. It also released guidelines (SITA, 2018) for suppliers.

SITA's 2020–2024 strategic plan (SITA, 2020) states that "the introduction of automated systems and other platforms to improve turnaround times, eliminate subjectivity, promote fairness and limit corrupt tendencies in the supply chain management environment, whilst simultaneously releasing more resources (i.e. time &

money) for reinvestment in service delivery improvement" is critical to the procurement reform.

In line with the national e-government strategy, all government tender procedures must seek to enforce the policy of interoperability of systems.

Are digital public services subject to general data protection regulations? If not, is there any data protection regulation for digital public services?
According to the POPI Act, Chapter 4, Public services may be exempted from general data protection regulations if it is in the public interest to process personal information. Public interest in this case includes national security, prevention, detection and prosecution of offences, important economic and financial interests of a public body, historical, statistical or research activity, or the special importance of the interest in freedom of expression.

POPI Act (2019), Chapter 4:

Section 36:

Processing of personal information is not in breach of a condition for the processing of such information if:

(a) Regulator grants an exemption in terms of section 37; or
(b) processing is in accordance with section 38.

Section 37:

1. The Regulator may, by notice in the Gazette, grant an exemption to a responsible party to process personal information, even if that processing is in breach of a condition for the processing of such information, or any measure that gives effect to such condition, if the Regulator is satisfied that, in the circumstances of the case:

(a) the public interest in the processing outweighs, to a substantial degree, any interference with the privacy of the data subject that could result from such processing; or,
(b) the processing involves a clear benefit to the data subject or a third party that outweighs, to a substantial degree, any interference with the privacy of the data subject or third party that could result from such processing.

2. The public interest referred to in subsection (1) includes:

(a) the interests of national security;
(b) the prevention, detection and prosecution of offences;
(c) important economic and financial interests of a public body;
(d) fostering compliance with legal provisions established in the interests referred to under paragraphs (b) and (c);
(e) historical, statistical or research activity; or,
(f) the special importance of the interest in freedom of expression.

3. The Regulator may impose reasonable conditions in respect of any exemption granted under subsection (1).

Section 38:

1. Personal information processed for the purpose of discharging a relevant function is exempt from sections 11(3) and (4), 12, 15 and 18 in any case to the extent to which the application of those provisions to the personal information would be likely to prejudice the proper discharge of that function.
2. "Relevant function" for purposes of subsection (1), means any function—

(a) of a public body; or,
(b) conferred on any person in terms of the law, which is performed with the view to protecting members of the public against:
    (i) financial loss due to dishonesty, malpractice or other seriously improper conduct by, or the unfitness or incompetence of, persons concerned in the provision of banking, insurance, investment or other financial services or in the management of bodies corporate; or.
    (ii) dishonesty, malpractice or other seriously improper conduct by, or the unfitness or incompetence of, persons authorised to carry on any profession or other activity.

Are there any current or proposed regulations mandating the sharing of data with government agencies to enable better delivery of public services?
The Draft Cloud and Data Policy (Electronic Communications Act No. 36 of 2005) from 2021 defines "Data sharing" as sharing the same data resource with multiple applications or users. It suggests developing an open data strategy/framework for the sharing of data, informed by 'Data for Good' principles.

The National Integrated ICT White Paper promotes efficiency and cost-effectiveness in the public sector by making it easier and less costly for government entities to access and re-use their own data and that of other public agencies.

3 Institutions

Is there a specific body overseeing the digitalisation of the public sector?
The State IT Agency (2017) is responsible for all digital transformation in the public sector.

SITA was established in terms of the SITA Act, 1998 (Act 88 of 1998), as amended (SITA Amendment Act 2002), and its mandate is informed by, among others, the recommendations of the Presidential Review Commission of 1998. In executing its role, SITA is also guided by all public services legislation and regulations, including but not limited to:

(a) SITA Regulations of 2005;
(b) Public Finance Management Act, 1999 (Act 1 of 1999);
(c) Companies Act, 2008 (Act 71 of 2008);

(d) Public Service Act, 1994 (Act 103 of 1994), as amended by the Public Service Amendment Act, 2007 (Act 30 of 2007);
(e) Electronic Communication and Transactions Act, 2002 (Act 21 of 2002);
(f) National Key Points Act, 1980 (Act 102 of 1980), as amended by the National Key Points Amendment Act, 1985 (Act 47 of 1985);
(g) Government IT House of Values, as contained in the e-Government Policy;
(h) The Machinery of Government (May 2003);
(i) Minimum Interoperability Standards (MIOS);
(j) Minimum Information Security Standards (MISS);
(k) Preferential Public Procurement Framework Act (PPPFA);
(l) National Treasury Regulations;
(m) National e-Government Strategy; and.
(n) National Integrated ICT Policy White Paper.

SITA reports to the Department of Communications and Digital Technologies. In 2014, the Department of Communications split into two departments: the Department of Communications (DoC), which was responsible for broadcasting services and new media, and the Department of Telecommunications and Postal Services (DTPS), which dealt with the ICT sector, Internet access policies, and infrastructure. Under this arrangement, SITA started reporting to the DTPS starting in 2014 (when it was moved from the Department of Public Service Administration). Eventually, in 2019, the two departments (DoC and DTPS) merged again to operate as one central ministry leading the country's ICT agenda, under the name of the Department of Communications and Digital Technologies.

The Department of Communications and Digital Technologies can be seen as the overseeing body, although SITA itself is responsible for all digital transformation in the public sector.

If such a body exists, what is its status (e.g. an independent agency, a ministry, an inter-ministerial committee, an ad hoc body, etc.)?
SITA is listed as a Schedule 3A national public entity in terms of the Public Finance Management Act (PFMA). These entities are normally extensions of a public entity with the mandate to fulfil a specific economic or social responsibility of the government. They rely on government funding and public money, either by means of a transfer from the revenue fund or through statutory money.

Government is the sole shareholder of SITA, and the Minister of Communications and Digital Technologies exercises the custodian rights attached to the shareholder on behalf of the state.

The underlying operational principle of SITA is to be a self-funded and financially sustainable public entity. The SITA Act, however, makes provision for negotiation on this underlying principle, for the achievement of the overarching government goals.

If such a body exists, what are its prerogatives and powers?
The mandate of SITA is to improve public service delivery and promote the efficiency of government departments and public bodies through ICT.

SITA's mandatory services are:

- provision or maintenance of a private telecommunication network or a value-added network service (Act, Sec 7 (1)(b)(i)),
- provision or maintenance of transversal information systems (Act, Sec 7 (1)(b)(ii)),
- provision of transversal data-processing (Act, Sec 7 (1)(b)(iii)),
- procurement: every department must (subject to Act, Sec 7 (4)) procure all information technology goods or services through the Agency (Act, Sec 7 (3)),
- setting standards regarding interoperability and security (Act, Sec 7 (6)(a),(i),(ii)),
- certification against standards (Act, Sec 7 (6)(b)),
- provision of information system security (Act, Sec 6 (a)),
- development of information systems convergence strategy (Regulation, Sec 4.1.1 (a)),
- preparation of disaster recovery plan (Regulation, Sec 4.1.2),
- compilation and maintenance of information system inventory (Regulation, Sec 4.6).

SITA's non-mandatory services are:

- provision of ICT Training (Act, Sec 7 (1)(b)(i)),
- provision of application software development (Act, Sec (1)(b)(ii)),
- provision of ICT maintenance (Act, Sec (1)(b)(iii)),
- provision of Data Processing (Act, Sec 7 (1)(b)(iv)),
- provision of advisory services (Act, Sec 7 (1)(b)(v)),
- provision of ICT Management Services (Act, Sec 7 (1)(b)(vi)),
- provision of authentication products (Act, Sec 7 (6)(c)),
- ICT Research (Act, Sec 7 (6)(d)).

Is there an evaluation system or indicators to measure the progress of the development of digital government?

The national e-government strategy assigns the development of a Monitoring and Evaluation Strategy for e-Government implementation to the Department of Telecommunications and Postal Services (now DCDT—The Department of Communications and Digital Technologies was established in June 2019 by the merger of the Department of Communications and the Department of Telecommunications and Postal Services), with indicators agreed to by all relevant stakeholders. The model for monitoring and evaluation of e-government services projects will be developed and form part of this strategy, and will serve as a tool to assess the impact of the National e-Government Strategy. The model will also serve as a guiding framework for South Africa to improve its global rankings on advancing digital transformation of government services.

A review of the National e-Government Strategy and Roadmap will be conducted during every MTSF (Medium Term Strategic Framework) period to measure progress and impact of its implementation.

Is there a public company or any public–private partnerships working on the development of specific solutions for digitising the public sector? If the company exists, what is its function?
SITA is implementing an enterprise and supplier development (ESD) programme, providing a platform for emerging suppliers to become mainstream ICT suppliers for SITA and other public and private entities. The targeted enterprises are black-owned, youth, women, military veterans, rural, and people with disabilities. Preferential procurement provides a platform for SMMEs. The idea is to foster the establishment of new competitive companies in the ICT sector and use procurement to support skills development and job creation.

SITA and the National Treasury started forming industry partnerships and negotiating with various vendors. With the focus on licensing, the objectives were to:

(a) achieve efficiency across government through simplified ICT procurement,
(b) consolidate government contracts and purchasing power, and
(c) eliminate wasteful expenditure, resulting in cost savings across the board.

This resulted in framework agreements being entered into with the following vendors: Microsoft, ESRI, Software AG, CA Technologies, Cisco, IBM, SAP, Micro Focus, Dell/EMC, Huawei and HPE. These are applicable to all organs of state.

So far, SITA is a reseller of licences and products to all organs of state directly for the products of CISCO, Micro Focus, Huawei and HPE.

With cloud technology being identified as a priority and key investment, SITA launched the government private cloud ecosystem (GPCE). Leading the provision of cloud services to the government, SITA has partnered with the public and private sectors to migrate service delivery services to the cloud.

Specifically, SITA and Microsoft South Africa (Microsoft News Center, 2019) have announced the signing of a memorandum of understanding (MOU), which paves the way for government adoption of public cloud services.

The MOU, which was announced at the Govtech conference in Durban in October 2019, allows for government departments, through SITA, to move their services to Microsoft's Azure Cloud and endorses Microsoft as a key partner for the South African government to enable Digital Transformation.

What are the criteria aimed at guaranteeing the independence of the "third parties" auditing digital public service providers?
While the AuditorGeneral acts as the external auditor of all national and provincial state departments and municipalities, the oversight mechanism must annually appoint an independent external auditor to audit the accounts, financial statements, and financial management and performance information of the AuditorGeneral. The external auditors are engaged to express an independent opinion on the annual financial statements.

4 Key Sectors

4.1 Digital Identity

Is there a strategy to digitalise this sector or any areas of it?
The Department of Home Affairs (2022a) launched the Smart Identification Card System (Department of Home Affairs, 2022b) for citizens, which is widely rolled out, and the banking sector is assisting.

The Smart ID card securely stores the biometric information of the citizen, namely face and fingerprint. Security is achieved by using public key infrastructure (PKI) digital certificates. Additional features include safe storage of evidence of votes cast in local and national elections, as a means to eliminate election fraud. This verifiable digital identity of each citizen helps in the reduction of identity theft and marriage fraud, and allows service providers like banks to authenticate people using the biometric (face and fingerprint) details embedded securely in the card when they sign up new customers or transact with existing ones.

eHomeAffairs (Department of Home Affairs, n.d.) enables South African citizens by birth to submit ID and Passport applications online and make online payments for applications.

In December 2020, the Department of Home Affairs published a new Draft identity management policy (2020) for public comment. It defines digital identity as "a person's set of attributes that uniquely describes the person engaged in an online transaction under the identity ecosystem." According to DHA, identity management is an integral part of the 4IR era, the digital economy, e-identity, national security, and the use of technology by governments to improve the citizens' quality of life.

The new systems and operating model will be built around the new National Identity System (NIS), which will store the particulars of all persons, citizens and non-citizens who are within the territorial jurisdiction of the country, and replace the National Population Register (NPR). The NIS will be the backbone of identity management and linked to the systems for the civil registration of birth, nationality, citizenship, marriage and death. The modernisation programme consists of multiple short-, medium- and long-term projects. Smart ID card, fully digital ID and passport processes, online capture of biometrics at ports of entry and upgrades to the movement control and biometric systems are some of the elements that are being rolled out.

The policy elaborates the following principles:

- Universal coverage: provide legal identification to all residents—not just citizens—from birth to death, as set out in international law and conventions and their own legislative frameworks.
- Eliminating barriers to accessing and using an ID, including cost barriers and information disparities caused by the digital divide.
- Establishing an accurate and unique identity that is verifiable over the course of a person's life, from birth to death.

- Creating an interoperable and responsive platform, enabling different databases or registries to communicate with each other, exchange data, and efficiently facilitate identity queries.
- Using open standards to prevent vendor lock-in and ensure technology neutrality.
- Privacy by design.
- Financial and operational sustainability.
- Develop a comprehensive legal framework.
- Independent monitoring and oversight.

The phased-implementation approach envisions a policy and legal framework within a three-year horizon, a functional NIS within a five-year horizon and a fully replaced legacy model within a ten-year horizon.

Is the use of specific technologies for digital identity systems promoted or prioritised (e.g. AI, blockchain, open-source software)?
The Draft identity management policy (Department of Home Affairs, 2020) highlights the need for open standards and vendor neutrality, and privacy by design principles, meaning that no action should be required on the part of the individual to protect his or her personal data. To ensure prevention of leaks and loss or theft of data, the regulations should require physical, technical and administrative protection of data or information.

Is there a sectoral regulation in place (e.g. law, decree, standards) to organise the digitalisation of the sector?
The Identification Act, Act 68 of 1997, is somewhat outdated as it does not consider key local and global developments in managing official personal information.

The new draft identity management policy aims to address these and other issues, including identity theft. It suggests that the records are kept throughout people's lifespan. It also recommends that new legislation and the population register must make a provision that enables the establishment of a category that is neither male nor female, meaning that the sex and gender information in the population register must be able to be updated.

It also proposes that biometric information captured by surveillance cameras be linked to the population register and shared with police. While the DHA advances its plans to migrate the database to a biometric system, there is still no legislation regulating police use of facial recognition software (Cawthra, 2021).

One of the principles of the draft identity management policy is the development of a comprehensive legal framework to promote trust in the system, ensure data privacy and security, and ensure provider accountability. This would include not only laws and regulations for the identity system, but also regulations on data protection, digital or e-government, electronic transactions, civil registration, cybersecurity and cybercrime, and others. Basically, legislation establishing rules to govern accessing and processing the population register records must be in line with relevant policies and legislation such as the POPI Act, Cybercrimes Bill, and the Electronic Communications and Transactions Act.

Are there any policies promoting digital sovereignty for digital identity systems (e.g. data localisation, preference or obligation to utilise domestic providers, etc.)?

According to the Preferential Procurement Policy Framework Act (2000), preferential procurement regulations[1] (2017) apply to any organ of state (including a national or provincial department as defined in the Public Finance Management Act (1999), a municipality as contemplated in the Constitution, a constitutional institution as defined in the Public Finance Management Act, Parliament, and a provincial legislature) must advertise the invitation to tender with a specific condition that only locally produced goods or locally manufactured goods, meeting the stipulated minimum threshold for local production and content, will be considered.

A tenderer must submit proof of its B-BBEE status level of contributor. A tenderer failing to submit proof of B-BBEE status level of contributor is a non-compliant contributor to B-BBEE, may not be disqualified, but may only score fewer points in the final evaluation. Tenders are awarded based on a preference points system. Tenders valued at less than R50m are awarded on the 80/20 preference points system, whereby 80 points are allocated for price competitiveness and 20 points for a bidder's strength according to the B-BBEE scorecard. Tenders valued at more than R50m are awarded on the 90/10 system, whereby 90 points are allocated for price and 10 points for the B-BBEE scorecard.

B-BBEE means broad-based black economic empowerment as defined in section 1 of the Broad-Based Black Economic Empowerment Act (2004). Black Economic Empowerment is a programme launched by the South African government to redress the inequalities of Apartheid by giving non-white South African citizens economic privileges that are not available to White South Africans, in essence, wealth redistribution. It is a form of Affirmative action. Although race is the overriding factor, it includes measures such as Employment Preference, skills development, ownership, management, socio-economic development, and preferential procurement.

In terms of the ICT sector, BEE is implemented in a way that any company that wants to apply for a tender issued by the government, province, or city, to roll out services, has to comply with this requirement and have a certain number of black people in the management.

The draft identity management policy proposes that the government needs to own critical information infrastructure, and the technological sovereignty principle must be observed when designing the NIS (National Identity System), meaning ICT infrastructure needs to be aligned to the laws, needs and interests of the country.

Has the digitisation of the sector or any area of it been promoted because of the COVID-19 pandemic? If yes, then how so?

Not really. Even the e-services of DHA were closed during the COVID-19 lockdown. Instead, DHA was extending the expiry date until the end of October 2020, for all temporary identity certificates issued during the period of the national state of disaster (Mlambo, 2020).

[1] https://www.gov.za/sites/default/files/gcis_document/201701/40553rg10684gon32.pdf

Is there a specific body in charge of overseeing, coordinating or promoting the digitalisation of the sector?
The Department of Home Affairs is overseeing the digital identity efforts, while SITA is responsible for procurement.

B. Smart cities and digitised local administrations.

Is there a smart city strategy?
South Africa's 2012 National Development Plan does not specifically promote the concept of smart cities; however, it does identify ICT as a critical enabler of economic activity and envisages an increasingly important role of information infrastructure to connect public administration and active citizens.

Several policy documents relate to a shift to e-governance and efforts to improve digital access. National human settlement visions and objectives (which should be supported by all smart cities initiatives) are outlined in the National Development Plan (NDP) from 2012 (National Planning Commission, 2012), the Integrated Urban Development Framework (IUDF) (2023), and the Neighbourhood Planning and Design Guide (Red Book) (CSIR, 2019). Sector-specific strategies such as the ICT Roadmap (Department of Science and Technology & CSIR, 2013), the National Transport Master Plan (Department of Transport, 2016) and the South African Smart Grid Initiative see ICTs as catalytic to innovation and service efficiency (Söderström et al., 2021).

In his State of the Nation Address (SONA) in June 2019, President Cyril Ramaphosa expressed his dream of building a South African smart city, founded on the technologies of the Fourth Industrial Revolution. In the February 2020 SONA, this commitment was further elaborated.

The lack of a coherent smart city strategy at the national level is likely due to the constitutional framing, where city development is seen as a local government mandate. The South African constitution is very specific about the fact that local government drives local development and gives a lot of autonomy to local governments.

While not mandated by the national government, many smart city policies exist at the city level and are shaped by municipal governments. In fact, it can be seen as a form of reverse-scale policymaking where municipal initiatives push the transformation of national regulations rather than adapt them to local circumstances.

The South African Local Government Association (2018) developed a Local Government Smart Cities Framework. SALGA is a public entity established by the Organised Local Government Act (Act 52 of 1997) to assist in the comprehensive transformation of local government in South Africa.

Generally, one can say that the initial narrative around smart cities was about *digital cities*. It was around ICT infrastructure and the digital divide, and was shaped nationally. From there, with the emergence of the concept of datafication (globally), the trend moved towards smart (e.g. data-driven) initiatives, and these are being implemented locally.

Is the use of specific smart city technologies promoted or prioritised (e.g. AI, blockchain, open-source software)?

The PC4IR (Presidency of the Republic of South Africa, 2020) report suggests that smart cities initiatives will mostly make use of Artificial Intelligence (AI), the Internet of Things (IoT), blockchain and mixed reality (AR and VR). The report also states that "5G becomes the glue to everything smart, and it creates the super-fast highway in which all the other applications of a connectedness required in a smart city implementation is enabled." It acknowledges the role the telecommunication sector plays in 4IR initiatives.

In South Africa, the local governments drive their own smart cities agenda, so there is no specific prioritisation on a national level. While cities are taking very different approaches in their smart city implementation, in most cases, they involve the local government in partnership with a multinational technology company.

In most municipalities, the first step to digitalisation has been the provision of free Wi-Fi in public places and (in some cities) on public transport. Expansion of these aspirations includes e-service platforms for paying utilities, recording and reporting complaints, managing transport and logistics with AI technologies and smart CCTV for security purposes.

For example, the City of Cape Town's smart city initiatives make use of big data, machine learning and real-time communication and analytics for more efficient, usable networks.

Certain technologies, like AI and machine learning, are part of the focus of technological development in the context of the Fourth Industrial Revolution in South Africa. Their deployment has been mainly driven by the private sector, aiming to increase business efficiency, and to some extent by the public sector, with a focus on smart cities (Chair, 2020).

Is there a sectoral regulation in place (e.g. law, decree, standards) to organise the digitalisation of cities, and urban areas in general?

The legislative tool that has the biggest impact on how local government drives smart city strategies is the Municipal Systems Act (2000). It prescribes that each municipality has to prepare an integrated development plan. ICT strategies are often embedded in those.

Integrated development planning is a method to plan future development in municipalities. It was implemented after 1994 to overcome Apartheid's violent history. This new approach to local government has to be developmental and aims to overcome the poor planning of the past. Integrated development planning involves the entire municipality and its citizens in finding the best solutions to achieve good long-term development.

In the smart cities' context, this focuses on municipal indicator-based monitoring in municipal legislation suits the international trend towards data-driven urban management.

Are there any policies promoting digital sovereignty for smart cities (e.g. data localisation, preference or obligation to utilise domestic providers, etc.)?
According to the Preferential Procurement Policy Framework Act (2000), preferential procurement regulations apply to any organ of state (including a national or provincial department as defined in the Public Finance Management Act, 1999, a municipality as contemplated in the Constitution, a constitutional institution as defined in the Public Finance Management Act, Parliament, and a provincial legislature) must advertise the invitation to tender with a specific condition that only locally produced goods or locally manufactured goods, meeting the stipulated minimum threshold for local production and content, will be considered. A tenderer must submit proof of its B-BBEE status level of contributor. A tenderer failing to submit proof of B-BBEE status level of contributor is a non-compliant contributor to B-BBEE may not be disqualified, but may only score fewer points in the final evaluation. Tenders valued at less than R50m are awarded on the 80/20 preference points system, whereby 80 points are allocated for price competitiveness and 20 points for a bidder's strength according to the B-BBEE scorecard. Tenders valued at more than R50m are awarded on the 90/10 system, whereby 90 points are allocated for price and 10 points for the B-BBEE scorecard.

B-BBEE means broad-based black economic empowerment as defined in section 1 of the Broad-Based Black Economic Empowerment Act (2003). Black Economic Empowerment is a programme launched by the South African government to redress the inequalities of Apartheid by giving non-white South African citizens economic privileges that are not available to White South Africans, in essence, wealth redistribution. It is a form of Affirmative action. Although race is the overriding factor, it includes measures such as Employment Preference, skills development, ownership, management, socio-economic development, and preferential procurement.

In terms of the ICT sector, BEE is implemented in a way that any company that wants to apply for a tender issued by the government, province, or city, to roll out services, has to comply with this requirement and have a certain number of black people in the management.

Has the digitisation of the sector or any area of it been promoted because of the COVID-19 pandemic? If yes, then how so?
Not really. The pandemic has somewhat shifted the priorities of local governments. In fact, in certain areas where the government was being ineffective, there was a rise of self-organised initiatives by citizens. One of them is Cape Town Together (Human, 2020), a network of neighbourhood-level Community Action Networks (CANs) spread across the city. Neighbourhoods organise themselves into localised community action groups, usually starting with a few people on a WhatsApp or Telegram group and growing from there to support the specific needs of neighbours and community members through the pandemic.

Is there a specific strategy or regulation targeting the digitisation of land records or real estate records?
The Spatial Data Infrastructure Act, Act No. 54 of 2003, provides for the establishment of the South African spatial data infrastructure as the national technical,

institutional and policy framework to facilitate the capture, management, maintenance, integration, distribution and use of spatial information. It makes provision for an electronic metadata catalogue and for the determination of standards and prescriptions with regard to the facilitation of the sharing of spatial information. Survey of land in South Africa is regulated by the Land Survey Act, Act 8 of 1997.

The Chief Directorate: National Geo-spatial Information (Department of Agriculture, Land Reform & Rural Development, 2013) is the national mapping agency of South Africa. It is part of the Department of Rural Development and Land Reform. Together with the Chief Surveyor General and Surveyors-General, these agencies are essential for the South African spatial data infrastructure.

The NGI provides national digital aerial imagery coverage, establishes and maintains the national geodetic and control survey infrastructure, and provides national mapping, digital topographic and other geo-spatial Information.

The Chief Surveyor-General is in charge of such cadastral surveying and land information services. There are six Surveyor-General's offices in South Africa, each of which regulates cadastral surveys in the provinces for which it is responsible.

The Electronic Deeds Registration System Act (Act 19 of 2019) facilitates the development of an Electronic Deeds Registration System (e-DRS). The system is intended to take advantage of advances in ICT in the management of the security of property title.

Is there a specific body in charge of overseeing, coordinating or promoting the digitalisation of the sector?

Since smart city policies exist at the city level and are shaped by municipal governments, these are also the ones overseeing and promoting the sector. While the mechanisms for implementation of the smart cities initiative differ, in most cases, they involve the local government in partnership with a multinational technology company.

The South African Local Government Association (SALGA, 2019) developed a Local Government Smart Cities Framework (SALGA, 2019) in 2018 to provide municipalities with a digitisation blueprint, including an implementation roadmap to transform current municipal functions and operations into smart capabilities.

Is there any outstanding example of strategy or policy elaborated by a local administration?

The City of Cape Town's Digital City Programme[2] (City of Cape Town, 2017) focuses heavily on broadband expansion. As part of the Digital City Strategy, the City of Cape Town is focusing on four pillars (Boyle & Staines, 2019):

- Digital Infrastructure, by rolling out broadband infrastructure;
- Digital Economy, by creating a regional tech-hub;
- Digital Government, by making the processes "digital by default" and using digital tools to enhance the quality of the City's engagement with residents;

[2] https://resource.capetown.gov.za/documentcentre/Documents/City%20strategies,%20plans%20and%20frameworks/IDP%202,017-2022.pdf

- Digital Inclusion: contributing to closing the digital divide by promoting digital access and improving digital skills.

The city has also been quite progressive in the context of open data, making data available (City of Cape Town, 2022) that has been approved for use in terms of the Open Data Policy. The online open data portal provides free access to city information and helps to increase transparency, which empowers citizens to hold the city to account. It assists citizen engagement with the city and benefits the wider community and other stakeholders.

C. Digital money and payments.

Is there a strategy to digitalise this sector or any areas of it, such as a Central Bank Digital Currency program?

In May 2021, the South African Reserve Bank published a press release about the commencement of a study to investigate the feasibility, desirability and appropriateness of a central bank digital currency (CBDC) (South African Reserve Bank [SARB], 2021). This currency would be a general-purpose retail use currency, complementary to cash. The CBDC feasibility study is expected to be concluded in 2022.

Project Khokha, which focuses on the settlement of high-value transactions between commercial banks and other stakeholders at the wholesale level, was delivered by a collaborative team led by the SARB, consisting of seven South African settlement banks as well as technical and support partners.

Is the use of specific technologies for digital money/payments promoted or prioritised (e.g. AI, blockchain, open-source software)?

The SARB feasibility study will include practical experimentation across different emerging technology platforms. The study is expected to be concluded in 2022, and at the moment, there are no details about specific technologies.

In terms of Project Khokha, a proof-of-concept wholesale payment system for interbank settlement was built using distributed ledger technology.

The PC4IR report suggests that Artificial Intelligence (AI), virtual reality (VR), and blockchain will be embedded in the financial services industry and become mainstream. It is also becoming increasingly important to understand how to combat cybersecurity both from a legislative and from a consumer perspective.

Is there a sectoral regulation in place (e.g. law, decree, standards) to organise the digitalisation of the sector?

The South African Reserve Bank's (SARB) Fintech Unit was established to explore the implications of fintech innovation for the SARB and financial services in South Africa in a structured, organised and proactive manner. The main goal of the Fintech Unit is to respond to the rapidly changing environment by assessing fintech's impact on policies and regulations, and to assist in aligning policies and regulations with emerging innovation when required.

The Fintech Unit actively participates in international regulatory and standard-setting bodies through work undertaken by entities such as the Financial Stability Board and the Bank for International Settlements.

The Financial Sector Conduct Authority (FSCA) is responsible for market conduct regulation and supervision. The functions and purpose of the FSCA are defined in the Financial Sector Regulation Act, No. 9 of 2017 (FSRA).

Fintechs are subject to the same regulatory requirements as traditional service providers, as the financial sector legislation is often very broad and generic. Laws need to be updated to provide exemptions or specific requirements for new digital models. The Intergovernmental Fintech Working Group (IFWG, 2022) provides a set of recommendations to address these issues in the context of cryptocurrency, digital banks, and digital payments.

Are there any policies promoting digital sovereignty in digital money/payments (e.g. data localisation, preference or obligation to utilise domestic providers, etc.)?

According to the Preferential Procurement Policy Framework Act (2000), preferential procurement regulations apply to any organ of state (including a national or provincial department as defined in the Public Finance Management Act, 1999, a municipality as contemplated in the Constitution, a constitutional institution as defined in the Public Finance Management Act, Parliament, and a provincial legislature) must advertise the invitation to tender with a specific condition that only locally produced goods or locally manufactured goods, meeting the stipulated minimum threshold for local production and content, will be considered.

A tenderer must submit proof of its B-BBEE status level of contributor. A tenderer failing to submit proof of B-BBEE status level of contributor is a non-compliant contributor to B-BBEE may not be disqualified, but may only score fewer points in the final evaluation. Tenders valued at less than R50m are awarded on the 80/20 preference points system, whereby 80 points are allocated for price competitiveness and 20 points for a bidder's strength according to the B-BBEE scorecard. Tenders valued at more than R50m are awarded on the 90/10 system, whereby 90 points are allocated for price and 10 points for the B-BBEE scorecard.

B-BBEE means broad-based black economic empowerment as defined in section 1 of the Broad-Based Black Economic Empowerment Act (2003). Black Economic Empowerment is a programme launched by the South African government to redress the inequalities of Apartheid by giving non-white South African citizens economic privileges that are not available to White South Africans, in essence, wealth redistribution. It is a form of Affirmative action. Although race is the overriding factor, it includes measures such as Employment Preference, skills development, ownership, management, socioeconomic development, and preferential procurement.

In terms of the ICT sector, BEE is implemented in a way that any company that wants to apply for a tender issued by the government, province, or city, to roll out services, has to comply with this requirement and have a certain number of black people in the management.

Has the digitisation of the sector or any area of it been promoted because of the COVID-19 pandemic? If yes, then how so?

The fintech environment was affected by the pandemic, with consumers avoiding touching cash or point of sale devices, and e-commerce increasing significantly.

However, the significant uptake of digital services was due to sudden demand from the users, and not regulatory interventions or active promotion.

Is there a specific body in charge of overseeing, coordinating or promoting the digitalisation of the sector?
The Intergovernmental Fintech Working Group (IFWG, 2022) was established to coordinate, track and develop a common response to fintech regulation in South Africa. The founding members of the IFWG are the SARB, Financial Intelligence Centre, the Financial Sector Conduct Authority and National Treasury. IFWG membership has grown since its establishment and now includes the National Credit Regulator, the South African Revenue Service, the Prudential Authority and the Competition Commission.

In October 2022, the IFWG announced (SARB, 2020) the opening of another round of applications for its regulatory sandbox. The aim of the sandbox is a better understanding of the risks and benefits associated with new market solutions, and making more informed decisions.

D. Other relevant examples.

Is there any other sector (such as education, health, etc.) where a specific strategy or policy is in place to foster and organise digitalisation?
The South African Revenue Services (SARS, 2022) e-filing is one of the more sophisticated tax management systems globally, with good results on tax collection. SARS introduced its electronic filing initiative in 2001, in accordance with the government's broader e-Government strategy (the first DPSA strategy from 2001) in the public service. The main aim of an e-filing system is to facilitate the electronic submission of tax returns and payments by taxpayers and tax practitioners. Income taxpayers may, however, still submit their returns in the traditional way. Some of the tax services available electronically include Pay-As-You-Earn and Value Added Tax.

References

Auditor-General South Africa [AGSA]. (2022). *Home*. https://www.agsa.co.za/

Boyle, L., & Staines, I. (2019). Ureru Smart City Series Part 1: Overview and analysis of Cape Town's Digital City Strategy. *Urban Real Estate Research Unit and contributors*. University of Cape Town. http://www.ureru.uct.ac.za/sites/default/files/image_tool/images/383/Final%E2%80%93%20Overview%20and%20Analysis%20of%20Cape%20Town%27s%20Digital%20City%20Strategy.pdf

Broad-based Black Economic Empowerment Act 53 of 2003. *Government Gazette* (No. 25899). https://www.gov.za/sites/default/files/gcis_document/201409/a53-030.pdf

Cawthra, M. (2021, May). Big Brother South Africa will not only be watching you, he'll also share your biometric data with the cops. *Daily Maverick*. https://www.dailymaverick.co.za/article/2021-05-09-big-brother-south-africa-will-not-only-be-watching-you-hell-also-share-your-biometric-data-with-the-cops/

Chair, C. (2020). *My data rights: Feminist reading of the right to privacy and data protection in the age of AI.* https://mydatarights.africa/wp-content/uploads/2020/12/mydatarights_policy-paper-2020.pdf

City of Cape Town. (2017). *Five-year integrated development plan 2017–2022.* https://resource.capetown.gov.za/documentcentre/Documents/City%20strategies,%20plans%20and%20frameworks/IDP%202017-2022.pdf

City of Cape Town. (2022). *Open data portal.* https://odp-cctegis.opendata.arcgis.com/

Cooperative Governance Traditional Affairs. (2018, September). *Address by Deputy Minister Andries Nel at the Launch of GovChat.* https://www.cogta.gov.za/index.php/2018/09/25/address-by-deputy-minister-andries-nel-at-the-launch-of-govchat/

CSIR. (2019). *The neighbourhood planning and design guide (red book).* https://www.csir.co.za/neighbourhood-planning-and-design-guide-red-book

Department of Agriculture, Land Reform & Rural Development. (2013). *About NGI: National geo-spatial information.* https://ngi.dalrrd.gov.za/

Department of Communications and Digital Technologies No. 651. (2020, June). Directions on Zero-rating of websites for education and health issued under regulation 4(10) of the regulations made under the disaster management Act, 2002. *(ACT No. 57 of 2002). Government Gazette* (No. 43413). https://www.gov.za/sites/default/files/gcis_document/202006/43411gon651.pdf

Department of Telecommunications and Postal Services. (2017a, November). National e-Government Strategy and Roadmap. *Government Gazette* No. 41241. https://www.gov.za/sites/default/files/gcis_document/201711/41241gen886.pdf

Department of Telecommunications and Postal Services. (2017b, November). Digital Society South Africa: South Africa's National e-Strategy towards a thriving and inclusive digital future. *Government Gazette* No. 41242. https://www.gov.za/sites/default/files/gcis_document/201711/41242gen887.pdf

Department of Home Affairs of the Republic of South Africa. (2020, December). Draft Official Identity Management Policy. Public Consultation Version. *Government Gazette* (No. 44048). https://www.gov.za/sites/default/files/gcis_document/202101/44048gon1425.pdf

Department of Home Affairs of the Republic of South Africa. (2022a). *Home.* http://www.dha.gov.za/

Department of Home Affairs of the Republic of South Africa. (2022b). *Know your new Smart ID Card.* http://www.dha.gov.za/index.php/id-smart-card

Department of Home Affairs of the Republic of South Africa. (n.d.) *Welcome to eHomeAffairs.* Home Affairs. https://ehome.dha.gov.za/ehomeaffairsv3

Department of National Treasury of the Republic of South Africa. (n.d.). https://www.treasury.gov.za/

Department of Public Service and Administration of the Republic of South Africa. (2022). https://www.dpsa.gov.za/

Department of Public Service and Administration Republic of South Africa. (2001, February). *Electronic Government The Digital Future A Public Service IT Policy Framework.* https://www.westerncape.gov.za/text/2003/12/egovernmentpolicy.pdf

Department of Science and Technology & CSIR. (2013). *ICT RDI Roadmap.* https://www.dst.gov.za/images/ict_rdi_roadmap.pdf

Department of Telecommunications and Postal Services Notice 209 of 2019. (2019, April). *Government Gazette* (No. 42388). https://www.gov.za/sites/default/files/gcis_document/201904/42388gen209.pdf

Department of Telecommunications and postal services. (2020, March). Electronic Communications, Postal and Broadcasting Directions. *Government Gazette* (No. 43164). https://www.lexisnexis.co.za/__data/assets/pdf_file/0006/759507/Consolidated-Electronic-Communications,-Postal-and-Broadcasting-Directions-issued-under-Regulation-10-8-GN-417 of-2020-to-GN-451-of-2020.pdf

Department of Transport. (2016). *National Transport Master Plan (NATMAP) 2050 Synopsis Report.* https://www.transport.gov.za/natmap-2050

Department of Public Service and Administration. (2016, July). Public Service Regulations. *Government Gazette* (No. 40167). https://www.gov.za/sites/default/files/gcis_document/201607/40167rg10621gon877.pdf

Electronic Communications Act, 2005 (ACT No. 36 of 2005). *Invitation to submit written submissions on the proposed national data and cloud policy.* Department of Communications and Digital Technologies. Government Notices (No. 44389). (2021, April). https://www.gov.za/sites/default/files/gcis_document/202104/44389gon206.pdf

Electronic Deeds Registration Systems Act, No. 19 of 2019. (2019, September). *Government Gazette* (No. 42744). https://www.gov.za/sites/default/files/gcis_document/201910/42744gon1293.pdf

GovChat. (2021). *One Platform Connecting Citizens and Government.* https://www.govchat.org/

Open Knowledge Foundation. (n.d.). *Global Open Data Index: Table view.* https://index.okfn.org/place/

Government Technical Advisory Centre (GTAC). (2021). https://www.gtac.gov.za/

Human, L. (2020, March). *How a Cape Town group is helping neighbourhoods fight Covid-19.* Ground Up. https://www.groundup.org.za/article/how-cape-town-group-helping-neighbourhoods-fight-covid-19/

Independent Communication Authority of South Africa (ICASA). (2020, April). Information and Communication Technologies ICT COVID-19 National Disaster Regulations. *Government Gazette.* Vol. 658 (No. 43207). https://www.icasa.org.za/legislation-and-regulations/ict-covid-19-national-disaster-regulations

Itweb Business Technology Media Company. (2019, July). *Govt closed to open source.* https://www.itweb.co.za/content/WnpNgq2GPxwvVrGd

Microsoft News Center. (2019, October). *New agreement with Microsoft supports government to embrace public cloud.* News Center Middle East & Africa. https://news.microsoft.com/en-xm/2019/10/29/new-agreement-with-microsoft-supports-government-to-embrace-public-cloud/

Mlambo, S. (2020, August). Home Affairs e-services closed during Covid-19 lockdown – here's why. *IOL.* https://www.iol.co.za/news/south-africa/gauteng/home-affairs-e-services-closed-during-covid-19-lockdown-heres-why-bd3fa17c-b4bd-412f-a172-e2ada6fcdb75

Municipal Systems Act, 2000. https://www.gov.za/documents/local-government-municipal-systems-act

Söderström, O., Blake, E., & Odendaal, N. (2021). More-than-local, more-than-mobile: The smart city effect in South Africa. *Geoforum, 122*, 103–117. https://doi.org/10.1016/j.geoforum.2021.03.017

Plantinga, P., Adams, R., & Parker, S. (2019). AI technologies for responsive local government in South Africa. In *Global Information Society Watch. Artificial intelligence: human rights, social justice and development* (pp. 215–220). Association for Progressive Communications (APC). http://hdl.handle.net/20.500.11910/15173

Preferential Procurement Policy Framework Act, 2000: Preferential Procurement Regulations, 2017. (2017, January) *Government Gazette* (No. 40553) https://www.gov.za/sites/default/files/gcis_document/201701/40553rg10684gon32.pdf

Presidency of the Republic of South Africa. (2020). *Report Of The Presidential Commission On The Fourth Industrial Revolution.* https://cyberbrics.info/report-of-the-presidential-commission-on-the-fourth-industrial-revolution/

Protection of State Information Bill, 2010. https://www.gov.za/sites/default/files/gcis_document/201409/b6f-201015oct2013.pdf

State Information Technology Agency Act, 1998 (Act No. 88 of 1998). (2002). *Government Gazette.* Vol. 400 (No. 19371). https://www.gov.za/sites/default/files/gcis_document/201409/a88-98.pdf

State Information Technology Agency Act, 1998 (Act No. 88 of 1998). (2005). *Government Gazette.* Vol. 400 (No. 28021). https://www.gov.za/sites/default/files/gcis_document/201409/280210.pdf

State Information Technology Agency (SITA). (2017). *G-Commerce*. https://www.sita.co.za/content/g-commerce
State Information Technology Agency (SITA). (2018). *User Guide: Supplier Response Wizard*. https://www.sita.co.za/sites/default/files/Supplier_Response_Wizard_User_Guide_new_landing_page_distribution.pdf
State Information Technology Agency (SITA). (2020). *2020–2024 Strategic Plan*. https://www.sita.co.za/sites/default/files/Strategic%20Plan%202020-2024.pdf
South Africa E-Service Portal. (n.d.). https://www.eservices.gov.za/
South African Reserve Bank (SARB). (2020). https://www.resbank.co.za/
South Africa Local Government Association [SALGA]. (2019). *Annual Report 2018–2019*. https://www.salga.org.za/Documents/Documents%20and%20Publications/Annual%20Reports/SALGA%20AR2019_final.pdf
South African Government. (2022, November). *Minister Khumbudzo Ntshavheni launches Artificial Intelligence Institute of South Africa and AI hubs, 30 Nov.* Republic of South Africa. https://www.gov.za/speeches/minister-khumbudzo-ntshavheni-launches-launch-artificial-intelligence-institute-south
South African Reserve Bank (SARB). (May, 2021). *SARB commences feasibility study for a general-purpose retail central bank digital currency*. https://www.resbank.co.za/content/dam/sarb/publications/media-releases/2021/cbdc-/Feasibility%20study%20for%20a%20general-purpose%20retail%20central%20bank%20digital%20currency.pdf
South African Revenue Service (SARS). (2022). https://www.sars.gov.za/
The Intergovernmental Fintech Working Group (IFWG). (2022, October). *IFWG regulatory sandbox opening and inaugural feedback report*. https://www.resbank.co.za/content/dam/sarb/publications/media-releases/2022/fintech-iwfg-sandbox-report/Media%20Release%20on%20the%20IFWGs%20first%20Regulatory%20Sandbox%20Report.pdf
World Bank. (2022). *Digital Adoption Index (DAI)*. https://www.worldbank.org/en/publication/wdr2016/Digital-Adoption-Index

Senka Hadzic is a Senior Associate at Research ICT Africa, where she primarily researches alternative spectrum policies to enable small-scale operators and community networks. She was a postdoctoral fellow at the ICT for Development Centre at the University of Cape Town from 2016–2018. Her expertise is in low-cost connectivity solutions in the Global South, and she has consulted for a variety of organizations, including the International Telecommunication Union and Engineering for Change. Dr Hadzic completed her PhD in Electronics and Telecommunications Engineering at the University of Aveiro (Portugal) in early 2014, and since then, she has been working at the intersection of technology, design, and policy. She is a CyberBRICS Fellow.

Convergence and Divergence in BRICS Digital Transformations: In Pursuit of Sustainability and Sovereignty

Luca Belli and Larissa Galdino de Magalhães Santos

Abstract This concluding chapter draws conclusions from the analyses of this volume, with regard to the different policies, regulations, and initiatives adopted by Brazil, Russia, India, China, and South Africa (BRICS) to promote their digital transformation. The chapter emphasises the heterogeneity of policy and political structures that characterise the bloc's "competitive multilateralism," while also stressing the different strategic approaches of the countries to the governance and regulation of technology. Importantly, such approaches denote an increasing attention of the bloc members to the development of digital public goods, digital public infrastructures as an essential element of their digital sovereignty, as their capacity to understand, develop, and regulate digital technologies. To conclude this volume, this final chapter highlights what are the main elements adopted by the BRICS to shape their digital transformations. We contend that BRICS approaches denote their success or failure to connect key dimensions of digital transformation, such as governance, regulation, organization of financial resources, capacity to develop emerging technologies and provide digital public infrastructures, in order to leverage them to build their digital sovereignty and long-term sustainability.

1 Introduction

This volume explored policies, regulations, and digitisation initiatives adopted by Brazil, Russia, India, China, and South Africa (BRICS), with the ambitious goal of providing a complete picture of digital transformation strategies in the BRICS.

L. Belli (✉)
Center for Technology & Society, FGV Rio Law School, Rio de Janeiro, Brazil
e-mail: luca.belli@fgv.br

L. Galdino de Magalhães Santos
Electronic Governance Unit (UNU-EGOV), United Nations University, Guimarães, Portugal
e-mail: larissagms@yahoo.com.br

L. Belli, L. Galdino de Magalhães Santos (eds.), *SmartBRICS*,
https://doi.org/10.1007/978-3-031-98204-0_17

Our analyses of the BRICS strategies reinforce evidence of the heterogeneity of policy and political structures that characterise the bloc's "competitive multilateralism" (Stuenkel, 2020), while also stressing the different strategic approaches of the countries to the governance and regulation of technology. Importantly, such approaches denote an increasing attention of the bloc members to the development of digital public goods, digital public infrastructures as an essential element of digital sovereignty (Belli, 2021; Belli & Magalhães, 2023; Jiang & Belli, 2024; Belli & Gaspar, 2025), perceived as the capacity to understand, develop, and regulate digital technologies and data.

Furthermore, as we have stressed in the introductory chapter of this volume as well as in other CyberBRICS studies, it can be argued that BRICS countries have adopted successive strategies to leverage digital technology as a vector of "digital sovereignty."[1] In this publication, we have decided to adopt the definition of digital sovereignty as "the capacity to understand, develop and effectively regulate digital technologies, to retain agency, self-determination, and control over digital infrastructure, data, services, and protocols"[2] and we have analysed some of the key elements of digital transformation processes that play a fundamental role in constructing digital sovereignty.[3]

The study of convergences and divergences in the BRICS digital transformation agendas represents an opportunity to explore relevant issues for the future of the global governance of digital technologies, affecting virtually all countries, well beyond these five leading emerging economies. Our research also allows us to understand the role that strategic thinking regarding digital public infrastructures and digital public goods plays in advancing the considerably underexplored dimensions of digital sustainability and digital sovereignty in the context of digital transformation, as well as the importance of a coherent and well-structured implementation of such strategic visions to achieve successful digital transformation. Particularly, the development of and even exportation of digital public infrastructures is emerging as an alternative approach to establishing and consolidating digital sovereignty.

By way of conclusions and future research paths, we dedicate this book's final chapter to highlighting the main strategic elements adopted by the BRICS to shape their digital transformations. We believe that the diversity of the countries' approaches in key issues such as governance and regulation, financial resources, the capacity to provide digital public services, developing emerging technologies, and contributing to international development is key to identifying alternative paths to mainstream models of digital transformation. Indeed, usual models typically rely on

[1] See e.g. M. Jiang and L. Belli (Eds), (2024); L. Belli et al. (2023); L. Belli in L. Belli (Ed) (first edn, Springer 2021). L. Belli G20's Think20 (T20), (June 2023); L. Belli L in Belli, L. and Gaspar, W.B. (Eds.) (2023).

[2] This definition is provided in the works cited in the previous note.

[3] For a complementary set of analyses, see also Belli, L. and Magalhães, L. (Eds) (2024). Digital Transformation in the BRICS Countries. Special issue of the Computer Law & Security Review. https://www.sciencedirect.com/special-issue/10VRL9GGMQG

the achievements of some of the most developed countries but may not be fit for the specificities of most emerging economies of the Global South.

Paraphrasing the landmark report of The South Commission (1990), chaired by former Indian prime minister Manmohan Singh, famously stating that "the new locomotive forces have to be found within the South itself," we argue that BRICS countries have a considerable role to play as new "digital locomotive forces" (Belli, 2022a, 2022b) of the Global South, providing useful examples of how the developing world can cope with the specific digitisation challenges.

1.1 Digital Governance and Regulations

BRICS countries have promoted numerous digital transformation policies, strategies, and projects since the mid-2000s. After two decades since the inception of these initiatives, the countries have considerably refined their strategic thinking regarding digital technologies, updating several times their policy frameworks regarding digital partnerships, promoting digital public services, and experimenting with digital public infrastructures.

As this volume discusses, Brazil has instituted a robust e-government program, supported by the Law on Access to Information, a strong open data posture, and a new data protection framework, while also relying on the advice of a multistakeholder Internet Steering Committee (CGI.br), characterising the participatory Internet governance model of the tropical giant. Over the past decade, the Brazilian government launched the new Public Services Portal, Open Data Portal, and Digital Governance Strategy, organising its operations through the Brazilian Strategy for Digital Transformation. The creation of the General Data Protection Law, the National Data Protection Authority, the new Digital Government Strategy and Digital Government Law denote considerable normative and institutional advancements, reflecting the country's strong interest regarding the digital economy and digitisation of public sector organisations, while also revealing considerable contradictions.

The governance committees of the various governmental initiatives adopted over the past years have a considerably centralised configuration, frequently detached from stakeholder inputs and feedback (Magalhães, 2022), thus visibly clashing with the open and multistakeholder ideals professed by CGI.br. Furthermore, since the Temer administration, the digitalisation of Brazilian public services has increasingly been delegated to foreign tech giants, contradicting the previous posture based on the promotion of domestic and open software technology.

The Bolsonaro administration has also taken controversial measures regarding the sharing of data between government entities for public policy-making purposes. A general registry consolidating up to 50 databases, including enormous quantities of personal data, was created by the government. However, the lack of clarity of the governance committee and the suspicion of surveillance actions and data leakages led to the federal court's intervention, demanding that the government redefine its approach to data governance.

Over the past years, Russia has developed a considerable Electronic Russia Program to reform the public sector and build ICT capacity, gradually migrating all public services into a unified portal of state and municipal services. However, in recent years, Russia has adopted an increasing trend towards digital autarchy, a trend that has been intensifying since the invasion of Ukraine.

Like the other BRICS members, Russia has considered digital transformation as a strategic national goal to accelerate technology adoption, upgrading its economy and governance. A key goal, especially given the gargantuan size of the Russian territory, has been the establishment of a new broadband infrastructure able to transmit and process data at high speed, while also mandating the adoption of national software by governmental agencies. In this context, the Russian Digital Economy Program enabled the adoption of the Sovereign Internet Law in mid-2019, creating an autonomous segment of the Internet, dubbed the "Runet" and establishing strong data localisation regulation. Russia is therefore clearly leveraging digital transformation to achieve its own autarchic vision of digital sovereignty (Daucé & Musiani, 2021).

Although India shares the Russian and Chinese sensitivity, and even suspicion, regarding the Western, US-driven, digital development model, the Indian posture and governance structure for digital transformation suggests a much greater openness and willingness to capitalise on the strong IT capacities of the country, partnering with private sectors and technical community to build its "Digital India" vision. Since 2015, the Digital India programme has been centred on establishing new digital public infrastructures, capacity building, and services through a complex multilevel management structure, which became an instrumental element to build Indian digital sovereignty. The private sector, led by iSPIRT, created the India Stack, composed of various digital systems providing functions essential for public and private service delivery, such as APIs providing digital identity, enabling digital payments, and providing personal data consent management.

Regarding data governance, India has been developing a new legal and institutional framework for data protection, although this remains largely unfinished as it still lacks concrete implementation (Belli, 2022a, 2022b). Limited protections for personal data and specific sectors of the economy already exist; in addition, creating a committee for the discussion and governance of non-personal data has been acting in different digital transformation processes.

Over the past two decades, China created the State Council National Informatization Leading Group and the Central Cybersecurity and Informatization Leading Group, adopted an incredibly wide range of data and digital infrastructure-related policies and strategic investments, with a permanent double focus on digital transformation and cybersecurity. This culminated in the establishment of one of the most sophisticated examples of digital sovereignty, exercising undisputed control over the national digital ecosystem, and becoming one of the main digital powerhouses of the world in less than twenty years.

China led digital development and innovation initiatives through public–private partnerships, upgrading the public sector with the support and influence of Chinese tech giants. At the same time, Chinese has completely renewed its regulatory framework, introducing its famous Cybersecurity Law, a new Data Security Law and Personal Information Protection Law, and a host of new standards and regulations, whose implementation is supervised by the Cyberspace Administration of China, an extremely large authority consolidating competence as diverse as data protection, cybersecurity, AI, and content regulation.

Importantly, the main feature of the Chinese digital infrastructure and data governance regimes is the intimate connection with national security, which has been a constant concern of the Chinese government, making China one of the most advanced countries in terms of cybersecurity.

Lastly, South Africa has been an early mover, starting the debate on the national e-government strategy in 2002, but has subsequently advanced at a less accelerated pace, concretising its vision only a decade later. Indeed, it was only in 2012 that the strategy was developed. Subsequently, South Africa adopted the Electronic Transactions and Communications Act and the provincial e-government plans, followed by a new Promotion to Access of Information Act (PAIA) and Protection of Personal Information Act (POPIA). In 2019, the Presidential Commission for the Fourth Industrial Revolution began to develop a strategy based on the integration and promotion of emerging technologies. The Department of Communications and Digital Technologies is the central coordination point of the various departments involved in the implementation of the Fourth Industrial Revolution policy.

Despite the advancements regarding the South African governance framework for digital transformation, the complex scenario needs to be seen in light of some existing limitations in terms of broadband expansion and Internet affordability policies. The country released a new data and cloud policy in 2021 with some forward-looking recommendations, but the infrastructural shortcomings—including frequent power outages—and high demand for affordable access remain important challenges that need to be tackled to unleash the South African digital transformation program.

1.2 Financing Digital Transformation

Besides the need for strategic and long-term vision, the implementation of ambitious digital transformation plans requires careful financial strategy to be able to meet all strategic targets, investing public funds for transformative digital infrastructures.

The aforementioned consideration does not seem to have been uppermost in the Brazilian digital transformation strategies. Indeed, a recent OECD report (2020) on the matter has explicitly indicated the inconsistency of budget allocations, and the recent revision of E-Digital still lacks the definitions of budget specifications and instruments for measuring progress against targets. The Brazilian goals generally depend on transversal resources between different ministries, which are monitored by the General Coordination of Digital Transformation and consolidated by the Governance Committee.

As in the Brazilian case, the financing of the Chinese digital transformation strategy suffers a budgetary transparency deficit, especially as regards the public–private partnerships. To cope with this shortcoming, the Chinese government amended the Government Information Disclosure Regulations in 2019. However, subsequent plans to develop digital government and the Partnership Action Plan for Digital Transformation are based on the public–private partnership model, whose contract is exempt from oversight and a system of guarantees, thus generating risks for the public sector and reducing overall accountability.

The Russian Program for Digital Economy claims to have set aside around US$1.8 billion until 2025 to invest in regulation, personnel, education, research and technical skills training, infrastructure, and information security. Such important and welcome investment figures, however, need to be considered in light of the very special Russian context, which will likely lead to diverting public budget to war-related efforts.

As far as India is concerned, the government is the largest source of funding for digital transformation, despite partnerships with the private sector. A significant part of the ministerial budget is channelled toward the Digital India program. The Indian approach is particularly relevant for the particular focus on the development of Digital Public Infrastructures aimed at restructuring the functioning of public governance and economy, promoting transparency, and advancing productivity in many sectors, through its own India Stack.

In the case of South Africa, the strategy does not define a specific budget to finance the various actions, since the resources come from different government funds and agencies. Interestingly, the strategy proposes a review of the priority funds to support digital transformation with contributions from the licensing of telecommunications and broadcasting services. While the idea to encourage the development of digital infrastructure through public funding is laudable, South Africa still needs to find an efficient and effective public resource management model.

1.3 Expanding the Capacity of Digital Public Services

Regarding the capacity of digital public services, Brazil has made notable advancements with the digital transformation of the public sector through a unified portal of services and access to information. According to the Digital Government Strategy, 100% of services are expected to be digitised. Since the beginning of the COVID-19 pandemic crisis, the usage of digital public services has grown enormously and Brazil has adopted a more proactive and assertive posture, for instance introducing Pix, the public digital payment infrastructure, and enormous success story of digital transformation led by the public sector, now used to process payments daily by almost 70% of the Brazilian population.

However, the scenario at the state and local government level can be remarkably different. Only some Brazilian states have policies or plans to enable digital transformation linked to cybersecurity measures, systems integration, and e-service indicators, despite the recommendations of the Digital Government Law and the provision of digital public services as self-service and considerable advancement still needs to be done at the municipal level (Belli et al., 2024).

The Russian Federation has a national strategy for digitalisation of public services, which has been implemented for more than a decade and has been reflected in various state and federal programs, agendas, and laws. The Federal Government has formed developed the strategy in conjunction with the national program for the Digital Economy of the Russian Federation, which include the elaboration of new regulation, the establishment of capacity building initiatives, the promotion of research competencies and technical background, information infrastructure and information security The digital economy ecosystem results from a partnership of organisations that provide technology platforms, application services, analytical systems, and related services to public authorities, as determined by the Information Society Development Strategy.

The digitisation of public (and private) services in India has been promoted and developed through an overall strategy, Digital India, which is implemented through the India Stack. It is essential to highlight the relevance and unique character of this latter initiative, building digital public infrastructure that is deemed as an essential tussle of the Indian approach to digital transformation. The Indian approach is particularly noteworthy as it denotes a clear understanding of the regulatory value of technology, which can be used—and can be much more effective than traditional legal tools—to achieve desired policy aims, such as fostering openness, competition, and innovation or reaffirming sovereignty online.

The Indian case is also particularly interesting as it is the first large-scale experiment with the development of digital public infrastructure that is currently providing digital identity, instantaneous digital payments, and consent management tools to 1.5 billion individuals, amongst numerous other digital services built on top of them. Interestingly, these infrastructures can be managed through multistakeholder partnerships, such as the Unified Payments Interface, managed by a public–private venture, the National Payments Corporation of India.

In China, the Internet Plus project promoted an integrated approach to the digitalisation of public services, although many local governments had already started operating online portals autonomously before the initiative was launched. The institution of the National Platform for the Integration of Government Services in 2019 facilitated the sharing and exchange of data, establishing administrative authority over the collected data. Critically, the centralisation of digital services and data processing has enabled the government to promote its strategic vision of data, using it as a critical asset to enhance productivity and increase control. In this perspective, central, provincial, and municipal governments have all developed projects aimed at fostering the development of services, innovation, and commercial use of public data.

Since 2017, South Africa's National E-Government Strategy has aimed to modernise and transform the delivery of public services through the State Information Technology Agency. Partly due to a change of national government, the implementation of the strategy has not been coherent and homogenous, with an increasing focus on specific projects, especially amongst those put forward by the recommendations of the Presidential Commission on the Fourth Industrial Revolution. Starting in 2019, smart cities and digital financial services are increasingly mentioned as aspirational goals to be achieved, along with the promotion of emerging technologies, such as AI, IoT, and blockchain.

1.4 Using Emerging Technologies to Augment Transformation

While promoting the digitalisation of public services, BRICS countries have also considered the underlying need to expand the infrastructure upon which such services must be provided and accessed. In this perspective, all BRICS countries consider digital infrastructures and emerging technologies as essential levers of economic and social development, although in very different manners.

The Brazilian Strategy for Digital Transformation includes a relevant number of actions for the adoption of emerging technologies and the federal government has also launched sectoral strategies for Artificial Intelligence, smart cities, and the Internet of Things. Furthermore, the review of the Digital Strategy, E-Digital 2022–2026, reinforced digital inclusion actions and infrastructure implementation.

Concerning the provision of connectivity services, the General Telecommunications Law in Brazil was amended, resulting in the more flexible use of public infrastructure by concessionaires. However, problems related to low levels of investment in infrastructure in remote and rural areas, unaffordable access costs, and scarce digital literacy continue to persist. As regards emerging technologies, the past years have witnessed an intense—and largely unjustified—promotion of 5G technology, which is still largely inaccessible for most of the population, due to very embryonic deployment, typically limited to affluent areas in the largest cities.

China's digital infrastructure has remained under the perspective of national security and, consequently, digital sovereignty since 2013, when Internet regulation was debated. Recently, the government has enabled infrastructure reforms to foster emerging technologies involving 5G networks, data centres, AI, and others.

In a way, the "New Infrastructure" would be critical to China's political infrastructure, allowing the country to engage society and mobilise resources with the people's consent and obedience. At the same time, the investment-related initiative may be directly linked to the legal elements of "Critical Information Infrastructure," which resembles an institutional compromise between national security (particularly cybersecurity) and digital economic growth.

The private sector's digital transformation ecosystem does not welcome the government's legal measures and rules to protect "critical" information infrastructure due to the tendency of the State to restrict the business environment.

The data security law of 2021 exacerbated the threat of state intervention in the market, with the justification of a threat to national security. Legislative models are generally dubious and combine measures of regulatory power over data and safety classifications.

Russia has considerably increased investments in national broadband infrastructure, achieving high mobile penetration rates, and has prioritised the enhancement of cybersecurity capabilities, demonstrating a strong preoccupation for the establishment of secure digital infrastructures, probably also as a collateral effect of its increasingly tense international situation. In this perspective, Russia stands out for its Internet isolation plans, implemented since the 2013 Snowden Revelations and 2014 invasion of Crimea, and boosted by the adoption of the 2019 Sovereign Internet Law.

This mixture of security, control, and protectionist logics has also favoured the growth of domestic platforms aimed at developing domestic production and use of emerging technologies such as IoT, AI, and blockchain while diversifying the market for Russian products. However, the strong interventionist posture of Russian state, while having proved beneficial for the expansion of access infrastructure and investments in technology development, can be seen also as structural weaknesses, due to excessive state interference and frequent market constraints.

As mentioned above, India is a particularly interesting case study, having developed large hardware and software infrastructures, especially over the past decade, setting the bases for a strong digital transformation. Physical infrastructure has been expanded via the BharatNet project and the Common Services Centers creation has enabled significant connectivity improvements, including rural broadband, which has also been expanded by a thriving community network environment (Belur et al., 2021; Srivastava, 2021).

The physical infrastructure has been complemented by the India Stack's open APIs as well as other initiatives favouring multistakeholder collaboration between industry and state governments for strategic areas such as AI applications and IoT networks. Importantly, after having built its own vision for public digital infrastructures, India is increasingly considering exporting such a digital public good approach beyond its national borders, as clearly reflected in the Declaration resulting from the BRICS 2021 Summit,[4] organised under the chairmanship of India[l].

China's digital infrastructure has been considered a strategic lever of informatisation since 2013, and has been developed in constant synergy with cybersecurity enhancement, consequently strengthening Chinese digital sovereignty. In recent years, the government has promoted strong expansion and integration of digital infrastructure to foster the adoption of emerging technologies, such as 5G networks, data centres, and AI, among others. Furthermore, as India, China sees the expansion of digital infrastructure as instrumental to consolidate and expand their digital sovereignty, especially through the Digital Silk Road, part of China's enormous Belt

[4]BRICS. (2021). BRICS India 2021—XIII BRICS Summit—New Delhi Declaration. https://brics2021.gov.in/brics/public/uploads/docpdf/getdocu-51.pdf

and Road Initiative, currently considered as the biggest infrastructure undertaking in the world (Greene & Triolo, 2020).

In a way, the New Digital Infrastructure (Baark, 2022) developed by China over the past decade has become critical to China's political infrastructure, allowing the country to monitor society in a capillary fashion, while mobilising resources effectively. The investment-related posture aims at promoting "Critical Information Infrastructure," embedding the normative elements of national security (particularly cybersecurity) and the goals of digital economic growth. However, over the most recent period, the digital transformation ecosystem has had to cope with an increasingly heavy regulatory burden, having to comply with numerous regulations aimed at protecting critical information infrastructure. An example in this regard has been the introduction of data categorisation according to the associated risk, defined by the Data Security Law and subsequent regulations, leading to considerable restrictions in the type of processing allowed, especially regarding international data transfers.

Lastly, South Africa has been promoting ambitious plans set by the Presidential Commission on the Fourth Industrial Revolution—chiefly the establishment of 5G networks—while coping with pressing questions regarding basic connectivity infrastructure, especially considering still challenging levels of penetration among the poorest population. In this context, the Cloud and Data to Deliver policy project has become the government's investment priority with the launch of a government–private cloud ecosystem—MoU with Microsoft. Interestingly, the projects also recommend using open-source frameworks, standards, and open systems, thus enhancing the country's digital sovereignty by reducing reliance on foreign proprietary systems. At the same time, the initiative aims at tackling data governance, promoting a series of complementary principles on top of the binding rules set by the aforementioned PAIA and POPIA, including the principles of data for good, data localisation, data reuse, interoperability, and accessibility.

1.5 Conclusion: BRICS Lessons for Digital Transformation

The converging and diverging elements of digital transformation across BRICS countries provide evidence of how governments can adapt and innovate to increase their capacity to deliver services, design policies, manage businesses, and transform themselves. Although the current context may seem pessimistic, after the major impact of the COVID-19 pandemic, ongoing climate change, multiple international tensions, including war, and a digital cold war between the US and China, it is also worth stressing that this conjuncture creates opportunities for public sector reorganisations, catalysing innovation and stressing the need for sustainable digital transformation.

As governments, including the BRICS countries, try to find a new way of delivering to their nations, understanding, testing, and incorporating digital technologies, and processing growing data assets, there seems to be a common incentive to achieve sustainable transformation. Indeed, growing attention is paid to the development of new digital systems and digital public infrastructures, which facilitate essential state functions and the provision of (public) services.

In this perspective, this concluding section briefly resumes the BRICS approaches to (digital) governance and digital public infrastructure.

1.5.1 Multiple Approaches to (Digital) Governance

Public governance is the set of practices, laws, rules, procedures, and decisions that direct a particular government activity related to public goods and services, involving institutions, networks of actors, markets, and organisations (Belli, 2016; Filgueiras et al., 2023).

The analysis of divergences and convergences for the digital transformation of the BRICS highlights how different approaches to governance vary as governments shape policies and public services. Thus, strategies and experiences can diverge and converge regarding the patterns and processes by which "digital" politics, policy-making and policy implementation can take place. Filgueiras et al. (2023) emphasise that contingency and conflict impact the ways in which governance can diverge and converge as regards the evolving nature of interactions between stakeholders, whether (business) leaders, bureaucracies, hierarchies, markets, and networks.

Among the BRICS, digital transformation is triggering changes in the relationships between multiple actors who participate in several processes and institutions underpinning the national multistakeholder digital governance that shape approaches to digital policies, infrastructures, and services. In this perspective, digital governance, as a distinct type of governance, enables new ways of organising society, democracy and economy, creating, and redistributing value.

Although the authors do not intend to discuss theories of governance in the digital age in this chapter, it is important to note that the multiple approaches among the BRICS offer examples of institutional designs related to the new challenges that arise in this context, while providing alternative contributions to mainstem approaches to digital transformation.

Recognising the potential of the various BRICS governance models, we understand that multiple approaches are possible depending on the mechanisms of control, coordination, and the type of actors involved. Based on the framework offered by Hanisch et al. (2023), the analysis of the mechanisms and actors at stake allows us to categorise the national approaches to the establishment of digital policies and organisation of digital public services (Table 1).

Analog governance refers to centralised control structures, which depend on a vertical authority and focus on the institutional power to impose results and behaviours (Hanisch et al., 2023). As in the case of Brazil and South Africa, control and coordination mechanisms are mobilised to shape the interaction between bureaucracies and leaderships, which command the actions and define the projects assigned

Table 1 Digital governance approaches in the BRICS

Brazil	Analog and bilateral governance in the provision of services by the State as a platform
Russia	Analog and distributed governance through home platform ecosystems
China	Analog and distributed governance through platforms and a data marketplace based on public-private partnerships
India	Augmented and multilateral governance based on partnerships
South Africa	Analog and bilateral governance based on sectoral policies

Source: Elaborated by the authors

and executed by other parts of the government, public sector organisations, or via specific partnerships.

Augmented governance presupposes elements of distributed control and multilateral coordination. Actions are divided and attributed to different actors, sometimes of a non-governmental nature, who codify partial and complementary routines, as in an ecosystem (Hanisch et al., 2023). India's case is paradigmatic as its approach to digital governance and transformation presupposes facilitated multistakeholder involvement and coordination between private and public participants, which jointly design and implement the building block of governance and regulation.

On the other hand, China and Russia combine centralised coordination mechanisms to interact with bureaucracies, networks of private stakeholders, and distributed mechanisms to establish the interactions with the market, as an additional tool of implementation of state policies (Hanisch et al., 2023; Filgueiras et al., 2023).

It is important to recall that the purpose of digital governance is to foster and leverage multistakeholder consultation, cooperation, and coordination to deal as efficiently and effectively as possible with the challenges of digital technologies (Belli, 2016). Therefore, the emerging BRICS governance dynamics indicate that the successful management and regulation of "digital" affairs necessarily entail the presence of new actors, which are associated and integrated—with various degrees of impact—within the traditional structures of decision-making and development of digital public services and policies.

Public sector reform paradigms in the digital age among the BRICS countries corroborate the existence of multiple approaches to governance (Hammerschmid et al., 2023). Analog governance combines the paradigm of Traditional Public Administration and New Public Management, prioritising the internal and external collaboration of actors whose vertical coordination—that transmits rules in a hierarchical chain of command—is strained by the decentralisation of decision-making and by networks of actors. In other ways, expanded governance deals with aspects of New Public Management and Governance in a network, so that non-state actors are increasingly involved in formulating and implementing policies and providing public services. Therefore, non-governmental stakeholders become essential partners in a heterogeneous network.

A spectrum of combinations between analog and augmented governance allows decision-makers to manage governance mechanisms in a more flexible fashion, tailoring approaches according to each actor, type of relations—coordination, control, and achievement of governmental objectives—and desired trajectories (Hanisch et al., 2023; Hammerschmid et al., 2023). From this perspective, we observe multiple configurations of (digital) governance approaches related to digital governance, with a shared concern in the development of public digital infrastructures and the assertion of digital sovereignty.

1.5.2 Digital Public Infrastructures: A Shared Strategic Goal

In addition to governance mechanisms, BRICs are promoting Digital Public Infrastructures (DPI) as part of the ongoing goal to promote domestic innovation and "good digital sovereignty" (Belli, 2023), enhancing strategic autonomy and resilience. In this context, the continuous expansion of digital products and services through internal and external collaboration (private sector), leveraging the existing networks of stakeholders, is instrumental to the creation of digital public infrastructures able to support digital transformation and deliver digital (public) services and digital public goods.

Below, we offer a framework aimed at deciphering how stakeholders, political networks, institutions, and markets promote DPIs in the BRICS.

As illustrated by Table 2 above, BRICS have adopted different forms of public, private, and networked exchanges to develop the building blocks of their digital transformations. The DPI development in Brazil and South Africa still needs to fully integrate interoperability concerns, to ease information exchange between public and private sectors, which could considerably advance the creation of new solutions to shared problems while also fostering the use of open-source technologies. The DPI development in China, India, and Russia is stimulated by exchanges of knowledge, including in open source, between public and private actors, to enable the maintenance of digital public goods based on open innovation.

Importantly, the conditions related to the conception, construction and implementation of DPI must be considered carefully, so that digital (public) services are structured in a citizen-centric fashion, minimising risks, and positively contributing to the elaboration of data-based regulatory and legal frameworks, while also fostering access and inclusion.

From this point of view, DPI based on the perspective of digital sovereignty may have very different outcomes, depending on the perception of the concept. A more authoritarian or protectionist vision of digital sovereignty can undermine innovation, whether in the face of state regulation that applies surveillance and control measures in a digital environment or due to the lack of safeguards centred on full respect of fundamental rights, trust and involvement of the affected community.

Table 2 Digital public infrastructure in the BRICS

Brazil	DPI based on internal and external collaboration and partnership networks for specific sectors
Russia	Augmented and distributed DPI across an ecosystem of service platforms
China	Augmented and distributed DPI across platforms and the data marketplace
India	Augmented and multilateral DPI based on public-private partnerships
South Africa	DPI based on internal and external collaboration and partnership networks for specific sectors

Source: Elaborated by the authors

Conspicuously, digital access and digital literacy are critical drivers of DPI adoption. As countries navigate their DPI journey, measures related to governance and their digital transformation strategies must ensure that the digitisation of services does not deepen further existing socio-digital inequalities.

In this perspective, enhancing collaboration through open technologies and interoperable DPIs among BRICS countries would be particularly beneficial. The promotion of open technologies with easily accessible software, interface, and protocol for use and sharing is a sine qua non condition to promote digital public goods and to use collaboration and partnership networks to solve shared challenges to digital transformation.

DPIs and digital public goods are strategic assets for a digital transformation that can be both sustainable and sovereign, as they open opportunities to reshape cooperation patterns for developing the digital economy in a Global South-driven fashion. Therefore, promoting interoperable, accessible, and adaptable digital public goods allows countries to regain agency and control over technology and data, resulting in digital sovereignty.

The purpose of this volume has been to map the BRICS approaches to digital transformation and identify options between the multiple governance approaches that shape digital public policies and services. One of our main findings is that remarkably different governance paradigms can be adopted to nurture the development of digital public infrastructures toward sustainable digital transformation. The BRICS paradigms should be carefully analysed by emerging economies of Global South countries as they might offer more useful guidance than the classic digital transformation approaches, based on hardly replicable experiences of "Global North" countries.

References

Baark, E. (2022). China's new digital infrastructure. Expanding 5G mobile communications. *East Asian Policy, 14*(02), 124–136. ESSAYS. https://doi.org/10.1142/S1793930522000162

Belli, L. (2016). *De la gouvernance à la régulation de l'Internet*. Berger-Levrault.

Belli, L. (2021). BRICS countries to build digital sovereignty. In L. Belli (Ed.), *CyberBRICS: Cybersecurity regulations in BRICS countries* (pp. 271–280). Springer. Retrieved from https://link.springer.com/chapter/10.1007/978-3-030-56405-6_7

Belli, L. (11 July 2022a). *BRICS: The new digital locomotives*. Beijing Review. https://www.bjreview.com/Opinion/Voice/202207/t20220711_800300500.html

Belli, L. (2022b). New data architectures in Brazil, China, and India: From copycats to innovators, towards a post-Western model of data governance. *Indian Journal of Law and Technology*. https://www.ijlt.in/

Belli, L. (June 2023). Building good digital sovereignty through digital public infrastructures and digital commons in India and Brazil. *G20's Think20* (T20). https://t20ind.org/research/building-good-digital-sovereignty-through-digital-public-infrastructures/

Belli, L., & Magalhães, L. (Eds.). (2023). *Governança de Dados no Setor Público: Abertura de Dados, Proteção de Dados Pessoais e Segurança da Informação para uma Transformação Digital Sustentável*. United Nations University Press.

Belli, L. and Gaspar, W.B. (Eds.) (2025). The Quest for AI Sovereignty, Transparency and Accountability. Official Outcome of the UN IGF Data and Artificial Intelligence Governance Coalition. Springer-Nature. https://link.springer.com/book/9783032027610

Belli et al. (2023). Cibersegurança: uma visão sistêmica rumo a uma proposta de Marco Regulatório para um Brasil digitalmente soberano. FGV Direito Rio. https://hdl.handle.net/10438/33784

Belur, S. B., Raj, A., & Srivastava, R. (2021). Gram Panchayat Development Plan (GPDP): An opportunity for funding rural internet connectivity in India. In L. Belli & S. Hadzic (Eds.), *Community networks: Towards sustainable funding models*. Official Outcome of the IGF Dynamic Coalition on Community Connectivity. https://www.intgovforum.org/en/filedepot_download/92/20438

Daucé, F., & Musiani, F. (2021). Infrastructure-embedded control, circumvention and sovereignty in the Russian Internet: An introduction. *First Monday, 26*(5) Retrieved from: https://firstmonday.org/ojs/index.php/fm/article/view/11685/10122

Filgueiras, F., Palotti, P., & Testa, G. G. (2023). Complexing governance styles: Connecting politics and policy in governance theories. *SAGE Open, 13*(1). https://doi.org/10.1177/21582440231158521

Greene, R., & Triolo, P. (2020). *Will China Control the Global Internet Via its Digital Silk Road?* Published by SupChina. Retrieved from https://carnegieendowment.org/posts/2020/05/will-china-control-the-global-internet-via-its-digital-silk-road?lang=en

Hammerschmid, G., Palaric, E., Rackwitz, M., & Wegrich, K. (2023). A shift in paradigm? Collaborative public administration in the context of national digitalization strategies. *Governance*, 1–20. https://doi.org/10.1111/gove.12778

Hanisch, M., Goldsby, C. M., & Fabian, N. E. (2023). Oehmichen conceptual framework and research agenda. *Journal of Business Research*, Jana. Digital Governance: A 162, 113777, ISSN 0148-2963. https://doi.org/10.1016/j.jbusres.2023.113777

Jiang, Min & Belli, Luca (Eds). (2024). Digital Sovereignty from the BRICS Countries: How the Global South and Emerging Power Alliances Are Reshaping Digital Governance. Cambridge University Press. https://doi.org/10.1017/9781009531085

Magalhães, L. (2022). Brazil's over-centralised governance of digital transformation. *The African Journal of Information and Communication (AJIC), 30*. https://doi.org/10.23962/ajic.i30.14843

OECD. (2020). *On the way to the digital age in Brazil*. OECD Publishing, Paris. https://doi.org/10.1787/45a84b29-pt

Srivastava, R. (2021). Fostering global and local community radio partnerships for community network development: A case-study from India. In L. Belli & S. Hadzic (Eds.), *Community networks: Towards sustainable funding models*. Official Outcome of the IGF Dynamic Coalition on Community Connectivity. https://www.intgovforum.org/en/filedepot_download/92/20438

Stuenkel, O. (2020). *The BRICS and the future of global order* (2nd ed.). Lexington Books.

The South Commission. (1990). *The challenge to the South: The report of the south commission*. Oxford University Press. https://www.southcentre.int/wpcontent/uploads/2013/02/The-Challenge-to-the-South_HRes_EN.pdf.

Luca Belli, Ph.D., is Professor of Digital Governance and Regulation at the Fundação Getulio Vargas (FGV) Law School, Rio de Janeiro, where he directs the Center for Technology and Society (CTS-FGV) and the CyberBRICS project. Luca is also the editor of the International Data Privacy Law (IDPL) Journal, published by Oxford University Press, and Director of the Computers Privacy and Data Protection conference Latin-America (CPDP LatAm). He is currently a member of the Brazilian Presidency's National Cybersecurity Committee, and sits in the Advisory Council of the Brazilian Interministerial Committee for Digital Transformation. He is also a board member of the Global Digital Inclusion Partnership, and a member of the Steering Committee of the Forum for Information & Democracy. He is the author of more than 80 publications on law and technology, exploring data governance, cybersecurity, AI regulation, Internet access, and digital transformation. He has been consulted by several intergovernmental organizations and national regulators, including the Council of Europe, the International Telecommunications Union, the French Telecoms Regulator, etc. and his works have been quoted by numerous media outlets, including The Economist, Financial Times, Forbes, Le Monde, BBC, China Today, The Beijing Review, The Hill, O Globo, and Folha de São Paulo.

Larissa Galdino de Magalhães Santos is a Yufe4Postdoc, Marie Sklodowska-Curie at the Universität Bremen. Before, she was an associate researcher at the United Nations University, Electronic Governance Unit (UNU-EGOV). Larissa is also a Researcher at the Center for Technology and Society at FGV and CyberBRICS, Law School at Fundação Getúlio Vargas. Her research is located between government technology and innovation, with a special focus on open data, smart cities, and digital transformation strategies. Co-chair of the Open Data Charter Implementation Group, she is also a Professional Fellow at Fundação Getúlio Vargas for Europe and a Ph.D. in Political Science from the State University of Campinas.